Letters of
WILLIAM SHENSTONE

William Shenstone
From the portrait by Edward Alcock in the National Portrait Gallery, London

Letters of
WILLIAM SHENSTONE

Edited with an Introduction by
DUNCAN MALLAM

THE UNIVERSITY OF MINNESOTA PRESS, Minneapolis
LONDON · HUMPHREY MILFORD · OXFORD UNIVERSITY PRESS

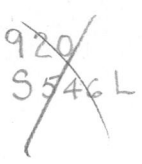

Copyright 1939 by the
UNIVERSITY OF MINNESOTA

ALL RIGHTS RESERVED. NO PART OF THIS BOOK MAY BE REPRODUCED IN ANY FORM WITHOUT THE WRITTEN PERMISSION OF THE PUBLISHER. PERMISSION IS HEREBY GRANTED TO REVIEWERS TO QUOTE BRIEF PASSAGES IN A REVIEW TO BE PRINTED IN A MAGAZINE OR NEWSPAPER.

Printed at the Lund Press, Inc., Minneapolis

To
CECIL A. MOORE

Preface

WHETHER Charles Lamb was right in thinking that Shenstone had captured "the true rustic style" in his pastoral poems admits of doubt, but generations of readers have confirmed Lamb's judgment that *The School-Mistress* is "the prettiest of poems." In all, there are a good dozen of Shenstone's poetical pieces which, besides maintaining their place in anthologies, are still read with genuine pleasure. But even enthusiastic admiration cannot stretch a small poet into a giant. A modest man, very shy indeed, he rated himself a minor singer and perhaps made a more accurate forecast of his fame than poets usually do. It must be admitted that the extensive space allotted to his verse in our histories of English literature is due not wholly to its intrinsic merit, but partly to its accidental importance as a poetical weather vane. It reflects, as perhaps no other verse of the time does, the conflict of theory destined in the course of the eighteenth century to undermine an old order and establish a new one. Although he himself contributed to the change in taste, he never ventured beyond a timid and disappointing compromise. In his poetry, in his landscaping also, he succeeded only in achieving a mastery of the "artificial-natural." If he had had the strength of conviction to free himself from the proscriptions of the old creed, his poetry might have come down to us a much more satisfying expression of a rich and fascinating personality than it actually is. Of this deficiency he himself was not unaware; the better we know the master of the Leasowes, the easier it is to suspect that he was haunted by his own indecision and at times oppressed with a sense of frustration.

As some others of his generation did, Shenstone sought in prose a freedom of self-expression not to be ventured upon in verse. This he obtained and enjoyed in some degree as the author of *Essays on Men and Manners,* work that occupied much of his latter life and was left in manuscript, to be published soon after his death. It was only, however, in his private letters — letters addressed to intimate friends and composed, most of them, with fastidious care, but apparently with no thought of publication — that he wholly shook off his inhibitions and dared to speak his mind freely. Almost inevitably much of his prose is concerned with critical problems, many of them related directly or indirectly to his own special interests as poet and landscape gardener. From his retreat on his *ferme ornée* he beheld a surprisingly large part of the national drama, and, in spite of his admitted indolence and fits of melancholy and ill health, he managed to record his reflections upon a great variety of topics, so many indeed that his prose taken entire affords an almost complete index of the intellectual and artistic interests of his time. The objection is sometimes made that his poetry is never better than pretty, partly because it lacks intellectual as well as emotional vigor. If this is a just criticism, abundant evidence is to be found in his critical pronouncements that he did not lack either strength or subtlety of mind. Moreover, some of his shrewd observations are as valid and as provocative now as they were when he set them down.

The private letters as well as the essays are rich in material of this kind and are therefore to be treasured as a source of information. To some readers they are more valuable for the revelation they afford of the man himself, a record of intimate personal traits, of amiable eccentricities, which are occasionally suggested in his poetry but with tantalizing vagueness. There is nothing pedantic in Shenstone's letters. He is not always preoccupied with the eternal verities. He often chronicles small beer, and does it well; he had a human weakness for gossip; and he liked especially to confide his most personal affairs, chiefly his ailments, both of body and mind. Though not the most brilliant letter writer in a century which produced Lady Mary, Horace Walpole, and Lord Chesterfield, he has this to recommend him above his superiors, that he is a more agreeable person to know. His style is freer and easier than theirs because he did not have his eye on Prince Posterity as well as his correspondent. If his effects are never so electrifying as the best of theirs, his quiet wit and humor have the charm of naturalness. If he lacks their excruciating cleverness, he lacks also their cynicism and cruelty.

The first to recognize the value of these letters was the poet's publisher and friend Robert Dodsley, an author in a way himself and a remarkably shrewd judge of popular taste. The volume of letters he published was, however, a mere selection, and although other letters have since found their way into print, only recently has any attempt been made to collect and arrange all the available correspondence. The present edition comes at an opportune moment, for various new studies of Shenstone denote a growing interest in phases of the poet's life and philosophy which can be fully satisfied only by a more careful study of his prose than it has yet received. Mr. Mallam is to be congratulated upon his discovery of several manuscript letters that would have eluded any but a most systematic search. Perhaps the most troublesome part of his task was the determination of the chronological sequence, for many of the letters bear no date, and the problem had been aggravated by erroneous conclusions of previous editors. Of the annotations it need be said only that they are an indispensable help even to readers familiar with the period and could have been provided only by a competent and conscientious scholar. Both the editor and the publishers of this book have earned the gratitude of many special students, and it is to be hoped that they may have contributed also to making William Shenstone known to many who have never before made his acquaintance or have known him only superficially.

CECIL A. MOORE

University of Minnesota
November, 1938

Editor's Note

THE one hundred and eleven letters composing the third volume of Shenstone's *Works* (1769), entitled *Letters to Particular Friends,* edited by Robert Dodsley and by him added to the two original volumes of 1764 containing the poems and the essays, form the nucleus of the present collection. All letters are individually identified in the notes. The Dodsley letters have presented many problems in the dating and arranging, most of which Professors J. E. Wells and J. F. Fullington have solved, but a few of which must, for the present at least, rest in conjecture.

Forty-seven of Shenstone's letters appear in Thomas Hull's *Select Letters,* published in two volumes by James Dodsley in 1778, a work now rare and difficult of access. From our present point of view, Hull was a most unsatisfactory editor: he was careless about dates; and he felt obliged to delete the names, printing only the initials, of persons then living, and to omit passages, and even whole letters, that he considered unfit for public scrutiny. Wherever possible I have had recourse to manuscripts for the sake of accuracy and completeness; and wherever I could with reasonable certainty, I have restored the names. The letters are otherwise as found in Hull.

Wherever duplicate letters have appeared, I have compared the texts and have tried to select the better; I have seldom given variant readings. Professor Fullington has advanced the interesting theory, in need perhaps of some further substantiation, that these duplicates often represent Shenstone's revisions and illustrate his habits of prose composition (*Modern Philology,* 29:323–34).

The twenty-six letters from Shenstone to Thomas Percy, which Professor Hans Hecht published in *Quellen und Forschungen* in 1909, appear in the present edition as collated with B. M. Add. MSS 28221. For reasons of his own, Professor Hecht did not always print the letters in their entirety but summarized portions of some of them. Percy himself valued these communications highly; in a note near the beginning of the manuscript (fol. 4) he says, "Of my Correspondence with Mr. Shenstone I have here preserved almost all his Letters and Billets, however inconsiderable: But of my *Own* (tho' all were returned to me after his Death) I have kept only a few, chiefly such as tended to explain his Letters, or were someway or other referred to in them." As a matter of fact, the correspondence is fairly complete.

A number of Shenstone's letters, singly or a few together, have appeared from time to time in various books and periodicals. In addition, nearly one hundred are, I believe, here published as wholes for the first time, from transcripts or from photostatic copies of holographs in various collections.[1]

It is clear from the many allusions Shenstone and others make to unpreserved letters, and from obvious gaps in even those parts of his correspondence generally regarded as most complete, that any edition can offer only a fraction of the total number he wrote. The present collection cannot make any pretense of even approaching the definitive. It does contain all the letters, and even fragments, to which I have been able to gain access, either in print or in manuscript. Other letters are bound to turn up from time to time, though it is hard to believe they will be of sufficient number or importance to change our estimate or greatly increase our understanding of the man who wrote them.

My purpose has been to provide, in recognition of the steady interest in Shenstone manifested in recent years, a documented collection of his letters, for the use of students and other enthusiasts, in the additional hope that the more casual reader may find it no less acceptable than it would be were it "happily destitute" of footnotes, those encumbrances from which even the best-natured and most patient readers are sometimes inclined to shy away. The notes are, I hope, sufficient to clarify most of the obscure allusions, whether to persons, places, literary works, or events. The texts of the letters I have not attempted to normalize in spelling, punctuation, or other conventional respects. I have reproduced them as found in the best available sources, retaining for their historical as well as personal interest Shenstone's idiosyncrasies,[2] his abbreviations, and even (when manuscripts could be consulted) his errors, which, however typographical they appear, must in fairness be attributed to him who made them and not to the most painstaking of proofreaders. Emendations have been made only where they seemed essential to intelligibility.

My debts for help in the preparation of this work are large and many. The researches of the scholars whose efforts have made much of what I have had to do comparatively easy, I have gratefully acknowledged in the proper places. My deepest debt of gratitude is owing to Professor C. A. Moore of the University of Minnesota, who first interested me in

[1] We learn as we go to press, of a forthcoming edition of the letters of Shenstone by Miss Marjorie Williams, a work of which we had long since reluctantly despaired and which we now welcome with renewed interest.

[2] Shenstone's manuscripts show that he commonly wrote the definite article y^e and that he used a great many abbreviations, such as y^t for that, y^n for than, wch for which, w^t for what, w^d for would, etc.

this undertaking and who has given me every kind of help and encouragement at every stage. My special thanks are also due to Professor M. B. Ruud of the University of Minnesota for editorial advice; to President G. S. Ford and to the Graduate School of the University of Minnesota for financial assistance; to Mr. H. G. Russell, Reference Librarian, and other members of the staff of the Library of the University of Minnesota for help in obtaining needed books and other materials; to Miss Myra M. Ward of Minneapolis for the gift of pictures and other valuable matter; to Professor J. F. Fullington of the Ohio State University and to the library of that university for the use of Mr. Fullington's unpublished doctoral dissertation; to Mr. Arthur Westwood, Assay Master at Birmingham, England, for supplying photostats of the letters to Matthew Boulton in the Assay Office Library; to the director and staff of the British Museum for supplying photostatic copies of many important items; to the director of the Bodleian Library for furnishing copies of manuscripts there; to the National Library of Scotland, and especially to Mr. W. Park, for the letters from the Watson collection; to the Huntington Library, San Marino, California, for a copy of the letter in its collection; to Lord Cobham, and to Miss Marjorie Deacon, Secretary, for the letter in the Hagley collection; to Miss N. Peacock of London for securing needed transcripts; to the Library of Harvard University, and to Mr. K. D. Metcalf, Director, for a copy of the letter in the manuscript collection of Harvard College Library; to the New York Public Library for a copy of the photostat in its possession; to the Public Library of the City of Boston, and to Director Milton Edward Lord, for the fragment in its manuscript collection; to the Library of Yale University for a copy of a letter needed for collation; to the National Portrait Gallery for the pictures of Shenstone, Robert Dodsley, and Richard Graves; to the staff of the University of Minnesota Press for their expert advice and editorial assistance; to Helen Mallam for the most extensive and valuable help in the preparation of the work for the press; and to a great many others, friends and colleagues, who have furnished me with materials and suggestions and have assisted me in ways innumerable.

D. M.

University of Minnesota
November, 1938

Introduction

THOUGH permeated with a gentle and mild melancholy and filled with complaints, sometimes petty, of poverty, discontent, and irritation often rising out of mere caprice, the letters of William Shenstone reveal the attractive personality of a man of good nature, fine taste, great sensitivity, a generous, engaging, and even noble character, wide interests, and a critical and philosophical cast of mind.

Interest in the writer of them, though perhaps never intense, has been persistent; and it has become increasingly personal. His *School-Mistress* and *Pastoral Ballad,* to say nothing of his meritorious elegies and shorter pieces, have long since won him a just position as a precursor of romanticism among the minor poets of the eighteenth century. His adornment of his *ferme ornée,* the Leasowes,[1] and his assistance to his friends in the ornamentation of their grounds, elevated his reputation as a landscape gardener to a high point during his lifetime; and his eminence of this kind has been adequately recognized and appreciated through the years. His *Essays on Men, Manners and Things* and his letters as hitherto known have established him as an exponent of "taste" and as a prose stylist in an age of good prose; Mr. Havelock Ellis[2] has called attention to his art as a *pensée* writer somewhat in the manner of La Rochefoucauld, and though perhaps Mr. Ellis has excerpted the best of the wit from the *Essays,* the reader finds them as a whole constantly entertaining, and interesting to compare with the letters, which often express more discursively the same critical and philosophical opinions there set forth. Shenstone's excellence as a writer of prose has yet to be stressed as emphatically as in justice to him it well might be.

Interest in the man himself, in the life and fairly typical activities of this eighteenth-century country gentleman of literary inclinations, in the outlook of one so situated as he, constitutes the principal justification for the publication of his letters to his friends and acquaintances.

He has not, I feel, been particularly fortunate in his biographers. The first, Robert Dodsley,[3] dealt with him extravagantly and rhapsodically rather than objectively; his strong bias in his friend's favor precluded

[1] See map, p. 267.
[2] *The Dial,* May, 1927; also introduction to *Men and Manners,* by William Shenstone.
[3] *Gentleman's Magazine,* April, 1764; introduction to Shenstone's *Works,* I (1764), i–viii.

any other treatment. Treadway Russell Nash[4] provides merely a short factual summary, probably contributed by John Scott Hylton,[5] in his *Collections for the History of Worcestershire.* Dr. Johnson's account of Shenstone in the *Lives of the English Poets,* though perhaps in part austerely just, is in the main adversely prejudiced and cruelly unsympathetic. It was partly to answer Johnson that Richard Graves wrote his *Recollection of Some Particulars in the Life of the Late William Shenstone,* which, in spite of the inaccuracies due to Graves's writing without memoranda after an interval of twenty-five years, is the best account of Shenstone ever written or likely to be written. In counteracting further the effect of Johnson's almost fatal injustice, Robert Anderson did Shenstone good service in a life (*Poets of Great Britain,* Vol. IX) that followed Johnson and Graves but drew upon some new materials as well. But the nineteenth-century essays, of which that of the Rev. George Gilfillan[6] is fairly representative, are sketchy, inaccurate, and unkind. Even the appreciation of Dean W. H. Hutton,[7] for all its urbanity, adds nothing to our knowledge of Shenstone; and the more recently published studies of any length[8] are too short, are not properly documented, nor at every point accurate, and though adding a good deal to our information, still in their superficiality leave much to be desired. Perhaps the final biography of Shenstone is yet to be written. His letters have by no means been fully exploited as a biographical source; it is to be hoped they will be.

The letters mention the place of his birth as the Leasowes; the later error stating it to be Wickstone or Wigstone, Miss Ward has with finality corrected.[9] But beginning, as we have them preserved, in 1736, they tell little else of his life prior to that year. The main facts may, therefore, for the convenience of present readers, be briefly reviewed. His father was Thomas Shenstone, gentleman farmer, of Halesowen, Shropshire; his mother was Ann Penn, of Harborough, in the parish of Hagley.[10] Wil-

[4] Not Thomas Nash, as Miss Williams mistakenly records in *William Shenstone,* Index, p. 150.
[5] F. and K. M. Somers, *Halas, Hales, Hales Owen* (Halesowen, Worcestershire: H. Parker, 1932), pp. 60–61.
[6] *Poetical Works of William Shenstone,* with life, critical dissertation, and explanatory notes, by the Rev. George Gilfillan (New York: Appleton, 1854).
[7] "A Forgotten Poet," *Burford Papers* (London, 1905), pp. 176–90. Originally in *Cornhill Magazine,* January, 1902, pp. 111–22.
[8] E. Monro Purkis, *William Shenstone, Poet and Landscape Gardener* (Wolverhampton: Whitehead Brothers, 1931); and Marjorie Williams, *William Shenstone* (Birmingham: Cornish, 1935).
[9] Myra M. Ward, "Shenstone's Birthplace," *Modern Language Notes,* November, 1936, p. 440.
[10] The early history of the Shenstone and Penn families has been worked out in detail by Miss Myra M. Ward in her "Studies in Shenstone."

liam Shenstone was born November 18, 1714.[11] His only brother, Joseph (1722–51),[12] of whom he was very fond, was according to Nash "bred an attorney at Bridgenorth, but never practiced." He died at the Leasowes. Shenstone's grief upon this occasion is expressed in letters to Jago, Wren, and Lady Luxborough.

William first went to school to Sarah Lloyd (the "school-mistress") and later to Mr. Crumpton of Solihull, Warwickshire, where he met Richard Jago; finally, on May 24, 1732, he was admitted as a commoner to Pembroke College, Oxford. Here he associated, to a greater or less degree, with a number of interesting personages, including Richard Graves, Anthony Whistler, George Whitefield, the Rev. Robert Binnel, and others, to whom he addresses letters or to whom he refers, and with Jago, of University College, through whom he probably had already been made acquainted with the much older William Somervile of Edstone, for a time chief poet of the "Warwickshire coterie." The "dangerous triumvirate" of Shenstone, Graves, and Whistler was broken only by the death of the last; and few others, besides Jago, were so intimate with Shenstone during his whole life. He was bashful and did not readily make friends, and it was his ideal to have few intimates and a large acquaintance.

He took no honors at Pembroke, but as Graves says employed himself with the study of physic (though according to Dodsley he was originally intended for orders) and amused himself with the study of English poetry. His early love of reading is legendary; most of his biographers tell the story of how his mother, on a certain occasion, placed beneath his pillow a piece of wood wrapped to resemble the book that William invariably expected to have brought home to him from market or fair.

At Oxford Shenstone enjoyed himself, kept his individuality by wearing his own hair, was one of the "bucks of the first head," kept late hours, talked with many and drank with all "except the water-drinkers";[13] but though he continued his name upon the college rolls for ten years, he never took a degree.

His father having died in 1724 and his mother in 1732, Shenstone's estate seems in the interval to have been legally in the hands of a guardian, John Spencer, Steward of Foley's Hospital at Oldswinford,[14] and to have been managed[15] by his uncle, the Rev. Thomas Dolman of Broom.

---

[11] All published biographies of any reliability agree that the date was November 18, not November 13, as the *DNB* records.
[12] Not Thomas, as the *DNB* mistakenly records.
[13] Graves, *Recollection*, pp. 16–17.
[14] George W. Marshall, ed., *Genealogist* (London, 1878), I, 210–13.
[15] Treadway Russell Nash, *Collections for the History of Worcestershire*, I, 529.

When he came of age (1735), and not only the Leasowes but an income of three hundred pounds a year from his mother's estate came into his possession, he was able to indulge his naturally somewhat indolent bent, though his "poverty," which confined him and was always a check upon his improvements to his beloved grounds, drew from him in the ensuing years many a cry of vexation, impatience, and frustration. In 1736, when his correspondence begins, he had, instead of living with his tenants at the Leasowes, who were also his cousins, begun to keep house at Harborough. Here he seems to have lived happily enough. Richard Graves spent a month with him there "in a very agreeable loiter."[16] Though he detested cards, disliked dancing, and much preferred conversation, he joined the gay and youthful society that gathered at Mickleton, where Morgan Graves (Richard's brother) and his sister dwelt; fell in love with Miss Graves; perhaps too with Miss Utrecia Smith; and displayed for female society a predilection that was fickle and characteristically fastidious. Considerably later (1743) he became enamored of Miss Carter at Cheltenham; later still he developed an affection for Lady Luxborough that was possibly not altogether platonic; frequently he paid tribute to the beauty and charm of women he met; never was he indifferent, though the contention is somewhat unconvincing that he sometimes made love to his maid.[17] He never married.

Only the first three letters belong to the Harborough period, and so important are they generally as sources of information that it is small wonder his biographers have little to say about years in which letters are few or entirely wanting. We have no epistolary record of the years 1737 and 1738. In 1739 he was apparently at the Leasowes, his permanent and final abode, from which for some years he made fairly numerous excursions to London, Bath, Worcester, Birmingham, and elsewhere, and to visit his friends, but where he tended with the passage of time to remain more and more closely confined, though by no means in seclusion.

When he first took up his residence at the Leasowes, Shenstone merely lodged with his tenants and relatives; not until about six years later (1745) did he take his estate wholly into his own hands. He improved the beauty if not the produce of his farm; he worked, health and spirits permitting, at his writing; he visited his friends, and received visits from them even when he was not well; he gave a great deal of time and attention to his correspondence, formulating and expounding his opinions, giving his advice freely, and when required, at length and in exact detail.

[16] Graves, *Recollection*, p. 36.
[17] J. F. Fullington, "Mr. William Shenstone," p. 170.

He was sometimes dilatory, but his life was much too busy and full for downright sloth to have had any important place in it; and his habit of postponing almost any project — a visit, the writing of a letter, the sending of a poem to his publisher — was a manifestation, when not of ill-health, of the meticulous fastidiousness ingrained in his nature. Most of his friends, and particularly Robert Dodsley, understood and generously allowed for this fundamental trait of his character. He spent his days and years less indolently than his letters sometimes lead us to imagine. But ambition waned as indolence increased (1740–44); after *Hercules, The School-Mistress,* and the *Pastoral Ballad,* the tempo of his literary activity appreciably slowed, though it never halted; he contributed to Dodsley's miscellanies (1748, 1755, 1758), and toward the end of his life (1761) planned to publish by subscription an edition of his poems, to include the elegies, never published during his lifetime; but this came to nothing. His health became worse and worse; he lost some of the relatives and friends he best loved — his brother Joseph in 1751, Maria Dolman and Anthony Whistler in 1754, Lady Luxborough in 1756; he was vexed by a protracted lawsuit; and the latter part of his life was distinctly less happy than the earlier. But of the details of the years from 1736 to 1763, the year of his death, I prefer that his annotated letters should here be the principal record.

For the analysis, criticism, or other discussion of his poetry and landscape gardening and for the treatment of other special subjects, I must refer the reader to the many biographical and special studies, a few of which are listed in the Bibliography, pages xxiv–xxvi. His letters describe the creation and constant embellishment of his *ferme ornée* and give interesting though sketchy accounts of many of his poetical pieces from inception to completion, as well as of plans never consummated. The first poem he willingly acknowledged was *The Judgment of Hercules,* published anonymously in 1741. His first small miscellany, *Poems upon Various Occasions* (Oxford, 1737), he had been at great pains to suppress, considering it unworthy. But it contained the first version, in twelve stanzas, of his most famous poem, *The School-Mistress,* published more confidently, but still anonymously, in 1742, in an expanded version of twenty-eight stanzas; reprinted in the first edition of Dodsley's *Collection* (Vol. I, January, 1748); and published again, in practically its final form of thirty-five stanzas, in Dodsley's second edition (December, 1748). For a bibliography of Shenstone's first editions, including all his contributions to Dodsley's miscellanies, the reader is referred to the work of Mr. I. A. Williams.

His letters must henceforth be my main concern here. Those early published and commonly known have been variously valued. Dr. Johnson honored, Horace Walpole scorned them; and other opinions have ranged from extravagant praise to indifference and from indifference to disparagement. The present reader will do well to evaluate them for himself. In any event he will discover that they represent a wide variety of moods and subjects, treated in a style appropriately varied yet always lucid, harmonious in sound and rhythm (Shenstone's ear was exquisitely tuned), and except in a few very informal letters, polished and exact. Professor Fullington is convinced that Shenstone took extraordinary pains to perfect the style of his letters, that he often wrote them several times over, and that the existing versions of approximate duplicates are rough and more finished drafts.[18] Though largely conjectural, this theory finds confirmation in Shenstone's habits of work and in his general character.

His earliest letters are effusions of youthful and light-hearted gaiety. They are witty and self-conscious, humorously introspective; he aims (only half seriously) at making them "as odd and fantastical as possible." He unfeignedly enjoys his "refined state of Indolence and Inactivity." As we continue to read, we become increasingly acquainted with his enthusiasms, his antipathies, his vagaries, as well as with the persons and events, the pleasures and perplexities, that fill his life and belie his occasional protestations of ennui. The letters of the middle period show a maturity characterized by nervous irritation, philosophical anxiety, introspective dissatisfaction, even self-reproach, but at the same time by a degree of resignation, and by an unflagging interest not only in the things he always held most dear — friends, literature, the Leasowes — but in local affairs, and in the life of the outer world, from which he sometimes vainly wished he had not so irrevocably withdrawn. His complaints are never a whine; he was better reconciled than many to the plight of being alive; he seldom railed at providence, but realized that his lot, which a stronger character might have improved, was happier than most, and that its disadvantages were mitigated by the happy circumstances of friendship, competence, and small successes, for which he could claim a modest share of credit.

The everyday philosophy he tried to live by was the utilitarian one which recognizes and accepts the necessary and regular alternations of pleasure and pain, the contrast of which appealed to his artistic sense and

---

[18] J. F. Fullington, "Some Early Versions of William Shenstone's Letters," *Modern Philology*, February, 1932, pp. 323–34.

harmonized with the moral-aesthetic conception of taste he derived from Shaftesbury. He was therefore seldom, despite a prevailing pessimism, utterly depressed; and his highest moments of exaltation were qualified by the philosophical certainty that worse moments must presently follow. To his romantic spirit, a *little* melancholy was "the most refin'd pleasure we know"; and he would not have escaped it if he could.

Perhaps this view, along with indifferent health and insufficient funds, contributed to his disinclination to stir far from home, and to an outlook predominantly passive. Though invited and even urged, he never visited the Continent or left England, except to step over the Welsh border, and toward the end of his life his excursions were ever fewer, of shorter duration, and to less distant places. From London in 1741, 1742, and 1744, he writes to his friends in the country, complaining of the expense of the town but obviously enjoying the coffee-house conversations, the political and literary gossip, and above all the drama, which he seems to have attended at every opportunity and upon which his observations are entertaining and discriminating. But at home again, he is, despite his complaints of solitude, happiest of all, creating his own amusements in the ease and relaxation of familiar and congenial surroundings.

The passing years mark the continuing development of friendships, sometimes of long standing, sometimes new,[19] though the fragmentary nature of the correspondence warns us not to rely too implicitly upon the preserved letters for data of this or any other kind. His known correspondents number more than a score; his close friends hardly exceed half that number. Best represented, aside from the ubiquitous Jago and Graves, is Lady Luxborough, most of whose letters to Shenstone were published in 1775.

At least as early as 1738[20] he was acquainted with this charming woman, his senior by about fourteen years. Mrs. Henrietta Knight, later Lady Luxborough, was the half-sister of Bolingbroke. After her separation from her husband in 1736,[21] she lived by agreement on her estate at Barrels, about fifteen miles from the Leasowes. Possibly Jago made her and Shenstone acquainted. In 1740 he reports having visited her, but the close friendship between them, always stronger on her side, appears from their correspondence not to have developed fully before 1747, and to have declined, on his part at least,[22] some time before her death in 1756. Pen-

[19] Marjorie Williams, "William Shenstone and His Friends" (Pamphlet No. 84, English Association, Oxford, 1933).
[20] The first allusion to her is his poem, *To a Lady of Quality, Fitting up Her Library, 1738*, in *Works*, I (1764), 133-34.
[21] Walter Sichel, "Memoir of Henrietta St. John," *Bolingbroke and His Times*, II, 469.
[22] Fullington recognizes this in his thesis, "Mr. William Shenstone," p. 36.

sive regret rather than grief is expressed in his letter to Parson Holyoake upon that occasion, and Shenstone hardly mentions her again.

Our letters from Shenstone to his other friends are regrettably few, in some instances as few as one or two, in others entirely lacking, though allusions show them to have existed in considerable numbers. "Jackie Reynalds," Lady Luxborough's friend as well as Shenstone's, appears in 1740 and except for references drops from sight after 1742. To Sherrington Davenport of Worfield, whom Shenstone knew at Pembroke, only three letters, widely spaced, are to be positively identified. Most of the letters to Anthony Whistler (one, of 1743, is extant) were destroyed by John Whistler at the time of his brother's death in 1754. Five letters to Christopher Wren between 1750 and 1754, nine to Matthew Boulton confined to the years 1758 and 1761, a dozen or so to John Scott Hylton between 1753 and 1759, a half dozen to Robert Dodsley between about 1755 and 1762, twenty-six to Thomas Percy between 1758 and 1763, five to Thomas Hull written in 1761 — these and a few more, with the fairly numerous and well-distributed letters to Graves and Jago, constitute the bulk of Shenstone's part in what must have been a fairly large correspondence, the other side of which, published and unpublished, is widely scattered and to some extent has been neglected, even by Shenstone's biographers.[23]

The letters record personal relationships in the main continuous, untroubled, and affectionate. Only with Whistler does friction appear, and that was minor and quickly forgotten. Throughout his life Shenstone seems to have cherished his friendships above all things. In his comparative isolation he depended heavily upon the letters of his friends not only for diversion but for spiritual sustenance. He reproaches his intimates for silence, not always quite justly; he shows constant interest in their affairs and fortunes; he plans to visit or meet them and repeatedly urges, even begs, them to visit him. When one dies, or loses a wife or father, he writes with a tenderness of feeling unmarred by sentimentality, in a vein consoling and philosophical without being either platitudinous or pretentious.

After friendship, Shenstone appears from the letters to have valued literature. He buys, borrows, and reads a goodly number and variety of the publications of many years, including books, pamphlets, and periodicals, and criticizes and discusses many of them with taste and acumen. He reads plays and verse, novels and travels, history, memoirs, letters, books of criticism, books of science, medical, political, and philosophical

---

[23] I refer of course only to the published biographies.

tracts and treatises, and his mention of them, casual or critical or merely whimsical, reminds us of how well he kept himself informed concerning the contemporary output, journalistic as well as literary. Nothing delights him more than the arrival of a packet of reading, unless it is the proofs of something he has written himself. His own writings he often discusses, as I have said, and he gives much literary advice to his friends. His assistance rendered Percy in connection with the *Reliques,* and Dodsley in connection with *Cleone,* the *Fables,* and other works, and his encouragement, often very concrete, of young unknown writers such as Woodhouse, are but a few examples among many.

A little below literature in his affections Shenstone places his landscaping, which he reports fully, a little vainly, and to one indifferent, a little tediously. He advises his friends, particularly Lady Luxborough, on improving their houses and parks, happy at the thought of emulation and never seriously resentful of rivalry, even at Hagley, where the comparatively rich Lyttelton, his neighbors and pleasant acquaintances, landscaped upon a scale calculated, in the opinion of some, to display the Leasowes to a disadvantage. He is satisfied that he can render his the most curiously beautiful place in the neighborhood, worth coming far to see, and his pride in his "visitants," many though by no means all of whom rode over from Hagley, is a foible as easily forgiven as understood. Especially in letters of the later years, the muster roll of the friendly curious is impressive, and it is meant to be.

I cannot hope to review, even in summary, the many aspects of Shenstone's life and character that the letters reveal; I can but mention a few more and then leave the reader to follow the rest in the texts themselves, and, if he chooses, in the notes. For full acquaintance he must go further, and reread the essays and poems.

Politics engaged Shenstone's attention mildly and desultorily. He was glad to help a friend gain votes, as he did on at least two occasions, but his motives, I feel, were quite as much those of personal loyalty as of political conviction; he may at times have entertained some slight hope of self-aggrandizement. While discussing politics rather often and at length, seldom very seriously, and never with heat, he professed no party, but only moderation, to the end of his life. Public life generally seems to have interested but never strongly to have attracted him. His public spirit was not wanting, but it was confined to such things as collecting money for some new bells for the parish chimes, or writing a petition, at the request of some neighbors, for a new turnpike. Toward the law he displayed an attitude of sophistication: he had seen enough of litigation in his suit with young Dolman over the Harborough property; and when a thief stole the fishes from his pond, Shenstone not only declined to prosecute but excused and even helped the fellow, incurring thereby the sharp censure of unnamed persons acquainted with the case.

The humanitarianism of his social views; the catholicity of his tastes and interests, which extended beyond literature and landscaping to music, painting, architecture, and other comparatively minor enthusiasms; these and a great many other interesting and significant phases of his thought, some of them more formally discussed in the *Essays*, are variously reflected in these less formal compositions, which the writer himself highly valued. "Could I be supposed to have the smallest pretensions to propriety of style or sentiment I should imagine it must appear in my letters" he wrote to Graves at the time of Anthony Whistler's death; the occasion of the remark was the destruction by John Whistler of Shenstone's letters to Anthony, the loss of which Shenstone deeply regretted, for they were, as he said, some of his chef-d'œuvres, and the history of his mind for many years.

His letters, indeed, best supplement our rather scanty knowledge of the life of this eighteenth-century gentleman of lovable, various, and complex nature. When death took him (February 11, 1763) in his forty-ninth year, his work was done and only his correspondence was interrupted; he had had his share of sorrow, though little adversity; and he had experienced as much happiness as one of his temperament could hope for. He has begun to be appreciated in just measure, and the recurrent interest in him, popular as well as scholarly, is evidence that he is unlikely to be either forgotten or ignored, and that increased understanding and sympathy will win and keep for him a gentle regard in human memory.

Selected Bibliography

The following bibliographical list contains the titles of only such books and articles as I have found especially useful for the study of Shenstone's correspondence and the biographical questions to which it gives rise.

CHURCHILL, IRVING L. "William Shenstone's Share in the Preparation of Percy's Reliques," *PMLA,* December, 1936, pp. 960–74.

COLVILE, FREDERICK LEIGH. *The Worthies of Warwickshire Who Lived between 1500 and 1800.* Warwick: Henry T. Cooke and Son. London: J. R. Smith, Soho Square, [1870].

ELLIS, HAVELOCK, ed. *Men and Manners,* by William Shenstone, selected and introduced by Ellis. Berkshire: Golden Cockerel Press, 1927.

——— "William Shenstone," *Dial,* May, 1927, pp. 381–96.

FULLINGTON, J. F. "Mr. William Shenstone," unpublished doctoral dissertation, Ohio State University, Columbus, Ohio, 1930.

——— "The Dating of Shenstone's Letters," *PMLA,* December, 1931, pp. 1128–36.

——— "Some Early Versions of William Shenstone's Letters," *Modern Philology,* February, 1932, pp. 323–34.

GRAVES, RICHARD. *Recollection of Some Particulars in the Life of the Late William Shenstone, Esq. In a series of letters from an intimate friend of his to ——— ———, Esq., F. R. S.* London: J. Dodsley, 1788. The letters are addressed to William Seward (1747–99).

GRAY, W. FORBES. "An Unpublished Literary Correspondence," *Cornhill Magazine,* July, 1926, pp. 77–93.

HAZELTINE, ALICE I. *A Study of William Shenstone and His Critics.* Menasha, Wisconsin: Collegiate Press, 1918.

HECHT, HANS. *Thomas Percy und William Shenstone, ein Briefwechsel aus der Entstehungszeit der Reliques of Ancient English Poetry,* in *Quellen und Forschungen zur Sprach- und Culturgeschichte der Germanischen Völker.* Strassburg: Karl Trübner, 1909.

HUGHES, HELEN SARD. "Shenstone and the Countess of Hertford," *PMLA,* December, 1931, pp. 1113–27.

HULL, THOMAS. *Select Letters between the Late Duchess of Somerset, Lady Luxborough, Mr. Whistler, Miss Dolman, Mr. R. Dodsley, William Shenstone, Esq., and Others.* 2 vols. London: J. Dodsley, 1778.

HUMPHREYS, A. R. *William Shenstone, An Eighteenth Century Portrait.* Cambridge: University Press, 1937.

HUTTON, W. H. *Burford Papers.* London: Archibald Constable, 1905.

KENWARD, JAMES. *Harborne and Its Surroundings.* 2d ed. Birmingham: Cornish, 1885.

Letters Written by the Late Right Honourable Lady Luxborough to William Shenstone, Esq. London: J. Dodsley, 1775.

NASH, TREADWAY RUSSELL. *Collections for the History of Worcestershire.* 2 vols. London: J. Nichols, 1781–82.

NICHOLS, JOHN. *Illustrations of the Literary History of the Eighteenth Century.* 8 vols. Printed for the author, London, 1817–58.

SHENSTONE, WILLIAM. *The Works in Verse and Prose of William Shenstone, Esq.* Vol. I, *Poems;* Vol. II, *Essays on Men, Manners, and Things.* London:

J. Dodsley, 1764. The third volume, *Letters to Particular Friends,* was added in 1769.

SICHEL, WALTER. *Bolingbroke and His Times.* 2 vols. London: J. Nisbet, 1901–02.

STRAUS, RALPH. *Robert Dodsley, Poet, Publisher, and Playwright.* London: John Lane, 1910.

WARD, MYRA M. "Studies in Shenstone," unpublished master's thesis, University of Minnesota, Minneapolis, Minnesota, 1935.

——— "Shenstone's Birthplace," *Modern Language Notes,* November, 1936, p. 440.

WELLS, J. E. "Pamela and Shenstone's Letters," *Nation,* August 10, 1911, p. 120.

——— "The Dating of Shenstone's Letters," *Anglia,* 35:429–52 (1911–12).

WILLIAMS, IOLA A. *Seven XVIIIth Century Bibliographies,* London: Dulau, 1924.

WILLIAMS, MARJORIE. *William Shenstone.* Birmingham: Cornish, 1935.

——— "William Shenstone, Letter Writer," *Review of English Studies,* July, 1933, pp. 291–305.

WYNDHAM, MAUD. *Chronicles of the Eighteenth Century: Founded on the Correspondence of Sir Thomas Lyttelton and His Family.* 2 vols. London: Hodder and Stoughton, 1924.

Table of Contents

Preface, by Cecil A. Moore... vii
Editor's Note... xi
Introduction... xv
Selected Bibliography.. xxiv

1736

1. Sherrington Davenport. October 19............................. 3
2. Miss Graves. October 30....................................... 4
3. Miss Lowe. Undated.. 6

1739

4. Richard Jago... 7

1740

5. Mr. Reynolds. August.. 8
6. A Friend. After September 24 or 29............................ 10
7. Mr. Reynolds. Probably autumn................................. 13

1741

8. Mr. Reynolds. January 16 or 17................................ 14
9. Richard Jago. January 21...................................... 15
10. Richard Jago. February 6..................................... 16
11. Richard Graves. After February 13............................ 18
12. Richard Jago. April 30....................................... 19
13. Richard Graves. June 8....................................... 21
14. Richard Jago. June 17.. 22
15. Richard Jago. July 22.. 24
16. Richard Jago. August 28...................................... 25
17. Richard Graves. September 23................................. 26
18. A Friend... 27
19. Richard Jago. November 25.................................... 29
20. Richard Graves. December 24.................................. 29

1742

21. Richard Graves. January 19 31
22. Richard Graves. February 33
23. Mr. Reynolds. March 9 34
24. Richard Jago. After March 35
25. Richard Jago. Before May 15 36
26. Richard Graves. May 17 or 18 38
27. Mrs. Henrietta Knight. May 39
28. A Friend. June 40
29. Richard Graves. June 41
30. Richard Jago. About July 19 42
31. Richard Graves. About August 44
32. Richard Graves. November 45

1743

33. Richard Graves. February 16 47
34. Mrs. Henrietta Knight. Probably winter 49
35. Richard Jago. Late 1743 or 1744 50
36. Richard Graves. July 3 52
37. Richard Jago. July 9 53
38. Richard Graves. Probably July 55
39. Richard Jago. After July 9 57
40. Anthony Whistler. Late summer 59
41. Mrs. Aubrey. Late summer 61
42. Miss Carter. Late summer 62
43. Richard Graves. November 9 64
44. Richard Graves. December 23 65
45. Richard Graves 67

1744

46. Thomas Smith. Undated 68
47. Thomas Smith. Undated 69
48. Richard Jago. March 1 69
49. Richard Jago. May 30 (?) 71
50. Richard Graves. Late 1744 or 1745 72

1745

51. Richard Graves. November 22 73
52. Miss Winny Fletcher. November 28 75

1746

53. Richard Graves. April 6 77
54. Richard Graves. May 11 79
55. Richard Graves. After August 18 80

1747

56. Lady Luxborough. August 10 82
57. Richard Jago. September 17 83
58. Richard Graves. September 21 84
59. Lady Luxborough. October 18 86
60. Lady Luxborough. December 26 87
61. Richard Jago. Late 1747 or early 1748 88

1748

62. Lady Luxborough. Fast Day 90
63. Richard Jago. February 14 92
64. Richard Jago. March 23 95
65. A Friend. After March 24 97
66. Lady Luxborough. Lady Day 98
67. Lady Luxborough. April 18 100
68. Lady Luxborough. May 5 102
69. Lady Luxborough. June 1 106
70. Lady Luxborough. June 16 108
71. Richard Graves. June 110
72. Richard Graves. June 30 111
73. Lady Luxborough. July 25 113
74. Lady Luxborough. August 15 115
75. Richard Graves. August 21 116
76. Lady Luxborough. August 24 118
77. Richard Jago. September 3 119
78. Lady Luxborough. Between September 5 and 11 121
79. Lady Luxborough. September 11 122
80. Richard Jago. September 11 124

81. Lady Luxborough. September 25 126
82. Lady Luxborough. November 9 128
83. Richard Jago. November 13 131
84. Lady Luxborough. December 18 132
85. Lady Luxborough. December 30 135

1749

86. Lady Luxborough. March 22 138
87. Lady Luxborough. April 7 139
88. Lady Luxborough. Between April 7 and 16 142
89. Lady Luxborough. April 23 143
90. Lady Luxborough. May 14 145
91. Lady Luxborough. June 3 147
92. Richard Jago. About June 1 149
93. A Friend. June 25 or 26 151
94. Richard Jago. July 9 152
95. Lady Luxborough. July 30 154
96. Lady Luxborough. August 9 155
97. Lady Luxborough. August 13 157
98. Lady Luxborough. August 20 158
99. Lady Luxborough. August 30 159
100. Lady Luxborough. September 10 161
101. Lady Luxborough. September 12 161
102. Lady Luxborough. Between September 20 and October 10 162
103. Lady Luxborough. October 18 165
104. Lady Luxborough. November 3 167
105. Lady Luxborough. Between November 3 and 8 169
106. Lady Luxborough. November 13 171
107. Lady Luxborough. November 26 176
108. Lady Luxborough. December 5 180
109. Lady Luxborough. December 7 183
110. Lady Luxborough. December 20 185

1750

111. Lady Luxborough. January 28 187
112. Lady Luxborough. February 4 189
113. Lady Luxborough. March 6 191

114.	Richard Jago. March 15	194
115.	Lady Luxborough. March 22	196
116.	Lady Luxborough. March 23	198
117.	Lady Luxborough. May 6	200
118.	Lady Luxborough. June 4	203
119.	Richard Jago. June 11	206
120.	Lady Luxborough. July 15	208
121.	Lady Luxborough. August 8	210
122.	Christopher Wren. September 9	212
123.	Christopher Wren. November 2	213

1751

124.	Richard Graves. February 16	215
125.	Lady Luxborough. March 10	218
126.	Richard Jago. March 28	220
127.	Lady Luxborough. April 24	222
128.	Lady Luxborough. May 24	224
129.	Lady Luxborough. June 14	226
130.	Lady Luxborough. August 8	229
131.	Richard Graves. September 17	230
132.	Lady Luxborough. Between September 14 and November 30	232

1752

133.	Lady Luxborough. January 1	234
134.	Lady Luxborough. January 25	236
135.	Richard Graves. February 14	238
136.	Christopher Wren. February 22	240
137.	Lady Luxborough. March 14	241
138.	Lady Luxborough. June 6	242
139.	Christopher Wren. July 22	244
140.	Richard Graves	245
141.	Lady Luxborough. September 30	247
142.	Richard Graves. October 3	248
143.	Richard Jago. November 15	250

1753

144.	Mr. ———. January	252
145.	Richard Jago. January 29	253

146. Richard Jago. February 27 254
147. Richard Graves. March 28 257
148. Lady Luxborough. April 2 259
149. Lady Luxborough. May 13 261
150. Lady Luxborough. June 22 263
151. Duchess of Somerset. June 23 264
152. Richard Graves. July 15 265
153. Lady Luxborough. July 19 269
154. Lady Luxborough. August 26 271
155. Lady Luxborough. September 18 273
156. Lady Luxborough. After September 27 275
157. Richard Graves. October 24 276
158. John Scott Hylton. October 25 277
159. Lady Luxborough. November 11 279
160. Duchess of Somerset. December 6 282
161. Lady Luxborough. December 12 284

1754

162. Richard Jago. January 29 286
163. John Scott Hylton. March 29 289
164. Richard Graves. April 19 289
165. Richard Graves. June 7 291
166. Richard Jago. June 16 292
167. Christopher Wren. July 6 295
168. Richard Graves. July 15 296
169. Lady Luxborough. July 17 298
170. Lady Luxborough. September 29 300
171. Lady Luxborough. October 13 301
172. Richard Graves. October 23 302
173. Sherrington Davenport. November 13 304
174. Lady Luxborough. December 8 305
175. Lady Luxborough. December 12 307

1755

176. Lady Luxborough. January 10 309
177. Richard Jago. January 22 310
178. Richard Jago, February 22 313

179. Lady Luxborough. February 27 315
180. Robert Dodsley. March 4 316
181. Richard Graves. March 21 317
182. A Friend. Undated 319
183. Robert Dodsley. March 23 320
184. Lady Luxborough. March 29 321
185. John Scott Hylton. April 1 323
186. Richard Jago. April 3 324
187. Richard Graves. April 4 325
188. Lady Luxborough. April 17 327
189. John Scott Hylton. May 3 328
190. Lady Luxborough. May 14 328
191. Mr. B——. October 330

1756

192. William Holyoake. April 21 331
193. Richard Graves. July 27 332
194. Tom Saunders. August 24 333
195. William Lyttelton. November 13 334
196. Richard Jago. December 14 335

1757

197. John Scott Hylton. January 1 336
198. John Scott Hylton. January 19 337
199. Richard Graves. March 7 338
200. Richard Graves. April 8 340
201. John Scott Hylton. May 21 341
202. John Scott Hylton. August 11 342
203. John Scott Hylton. August 18 342
204. John Scott Hylton. October 31 343
205. Robert Dodsley. December 21 343

1758

206. Thomas Percy. January 4 345
207. Richard Graves. Between January 5 and March 23 347
208. Richard Graves. May 30 349
209. Matthew Boulton. July 19 351

210. Richard Graves. July 22 352
211. Matthew Boulton. August 14 353
212. Matthew Boulton. August 17 353
213. Matthew Boulton. August 23 353
214. Matthew Boulton. September 18 354
215. Matthew Boulton. September 25 354
216. Matthew Boulton, September 27 355
217. Matthew Boulton. September 30 355
218. Richard Graves. November 25 355
219. John Scott Hylton. November 26 358
220. Thomas Percy. December 1 359
221. Richard Graves. December 25 361

1759

222. Richard Jago. January 6 361
223. John Scott Hylton. March 2 363
224. John Scott Hylton. March 11 363
225. Robert Dodsley. March 31 364
226. Richard Graves. April 18 366
227. John Scott Hylton. April 24 368
228. Thomas Percy. June 6 368
229. Thomas Percy. October 3 371
230. Richard Graves. October 3 373
231. Richard Graves. October 26 376
232. John Scott Hylton. November 13 379
233. Thomas Percy. November 23 380
234. Richard Graves. November 24 382
235. John Scott Hylton. November 30 383
236. John Scott Hylton. December 7 384
237. John Scott Hylton. December 9 385

1760

238. Thomas Percy. January 7 386
239. Richard Graves. January 8 387
240. Thomas Percy. February 5 389
241. Richard Graves. February 9 389
242. Thomas Percy. February 15 393

243. Richard Graves. July 7 395
244. Thomas Percy. August 11 397
245. Thomas Percy. October 1 399
246. Thomas Percy. November 10 401

1761

247. Thomas Hull. January 7 402
248. Robert Dodsley. February 11 404
249. Richard Graves. March 1 406
250. Thomas Percy. Undated 408
251. Thomas Percy. April 409
252. Thomas Percy. April 24 409
253. Richard Graves. May 2 410
254. Thomas Percy. June 11 412
255. Thomas Percy. July 5 412
256. Thomas Hull. August 29 415
257. Richard Graves. September 14 416
258. Thomas Percy. September 17 419
259. John MacGowan. September 24 422
260. Thomas Percy. October 425
261. Thomas Hull. October 18 430
262. Thomas Hull. November 26 432
263. Miss M———. December 8 433
264. Thomas Hull. December 24 435
265. Matthew Boulton. December 25 437

1762

266. Thomas Percy. January 437
267. Thomas Percy. February 3 439
268. Thomas Percy. March 3 440
269. John Livie. March 31 441
270. Thomas Percy. Undated 441
271. Thomas Percy. May 16 442
272. Richard Graves. May 20 445
273. John Livie. June 15 447
274. John Livie. July 7 448
275. Thomas Percy. August 10 448

276. Thomas Smith. August 27 449
277. Thomas Percy. November 14 449
278. Robert Dodsley. November 20 451
279. Richard Graves. November 20 454
280. Richard Jago. December 18 458

1763

281. Sherrington Davenport, January 4 459
282. Richard Jago. January 4 461
283. Richard Jago. January 11 462
284. Thomas Percy. January 16 463

Index 465

List of Illustrations

Portrait of William Shenstone .... *frontispiece*
Facsimile of a Letter from William Shenstone to Matthew Boulton   11
Henrietta Knight, Lady Luxborough 86
The Priory and the Priory Pool at the Leasowes 154
The Dwelling House and the Stables at the Leasowes 202
Map of the Leasowes 267
Robert Dodsley 316
Richard Graves 416

Letters of
WILLIAM SHENSTONE

Letters of William Shenstone

1. To SHERRINGTON DAVENPORT[1]

[Harborough,] Oct. 19, 1736

I am sorry to put you to an Expence for a trifling Letter at this Distance. It seems, too, to give you leave to expect something extraordinary, or uncommon. Whatever is so in my Letters, I am sure, must be on the bad Side. I may however have the greater Power to convince you, that Distance is incapable to separate you from my Thoughts.

I am, at present, in a very refined State of Indolence and Inactivity. Indeed I make little more Use of a Country Life, than to live over again the Pleasures of *Oxford* and your Company. You might convey me a Letter full, would you be so exceedingly good as your Promise. I am vastly self-interested, for I write only in order to beg a Letter from you, with very small Hopes of your receiving much Pleasure from mine.

I should here give you an Account of the Pleasures we have had at M[ickleton],[2] but my Paper won't contain it. There was one only wanting, *pour le comble* — you'll be the last to find it out — your Company. I aim at rendering my Letters as odd and fantastical as possible; but when I write to a Person of your elegant character, my Compliments degenerate into downright Truths, just (I was going to say) as the Sun turns bad Wine to Vinegar; but downright Truths are sometimes valuable, though a Person of your Taste might reasonably expect more refined — at least less obvious ones. Sometimes, however, Vinegar has also its Use, though to treat a Gentleman with it entirely may well create a *Nausea*. I fancy my poignant Simile grows stale by this Time. I write to an Intimate, and a Man of Sense, whose Good-nature will forgive what his Judgment may find fault with.

I hope your Ring gives you all imaginable Happiness, however fatal it may prove to female Ken. I suspect to hear of you as the finest Performer on the Spinnet in the World. Were I a Poet, I should be highly pleased to celebrate the admirable Conduct of your little Finger — "*Tui*

---

[1] Hull, *Select Letters,* Vol. I, No. I, where the addressee is indicated simply as Mr. D——. This is clearly Shenstone's Pembroke friend and neighbor, Sherrington Davenport of Worfield. See Fullington, "Mr. William Shenstone," p. 24.

[2] Mickleton, in Gloucestershire, where at the time lived Morgan Graves (Richard's elder brother) and his sister, was "the rendezvous of most of the young people of both sexes, in the neighbourhood." See Graves, *Recollection,* p. 40.

Pollicis Ictum," says *Horace;* vile Pedant that I am! who shall deliver me from the Influence of Formality?

I heard at *Oxford* of the Addition of the Side-Diamonds; I guessed, lest the Splendour should be extinguished by a greater, *où vous scavez.* I want to see you exceedingly; you are, I assure you, a vast Part of my Pleasure at Oxford, as Pope is in the Country; indeed, you might share that Effect with Mr. Pope, would you write. It is a Favour, for which I must grow importunate; notwithstanding which, the Favours I have already received, would make me uneasy, were I not conscious who bestows them.

Of all the moral Virtues, Gratitude is sure the most beautiful; so far from betraying any Thing mean or ignoble in her behaviour, she has an Air which naturally discovers her Quality. — I can't stay to describe her now — It is sufficient that I pay some sort of Tribute to her, when I call myself Mr. D[avenport]'s

Obedient, humble Servant,
W. S.

My humble Service to your Parents. — Direct to *Harborough*.[3]

2. To MISS GRAVES [1]

Sent [from Harborough] *Oct.* 30, 1736

I have sent the Patterns, though with far less Expedition than you might expect from one so entirely yours. The truth is, I was sensible how insupportable the Transition must be from your Company to none at all, so contrived to pay several Visits immediately after I had left M[ickleton]. You'll guess how sufficient a Mortification I found even thus. To pass from yours to the Company of dull Aunts and Cousins must needs prove tedious, as the Reverse would be agreeable.

As to the Draughts, I am satisfied in what a ridiculous Light they must appear; it was a Task I was very much unused to, and solicited rather out of an officious Fondness to be employed for you, than any Skill I was conscious of in myself. I must beg Mr. G's Pardon for engaging in a Work, wherein he is far my Superior. Such as they are, I beg you would

---

[3] Harborough, in the parish of Hagley, was the old family home of Shenstone's mother's family, the Penns. Here Shenstone kept house for a time after leaving Oxford and before taking up his permanent residence at the Leasowes. See Graves, *Recollection*, p. 32.

[1] Hull, *Select Letters,* Vol. I, No. II, where the addressee is indicated merely as Miss G———. Miss Graves, sister of Richard and Morgan, was for some years the object of Shenstone's affections. She is said to have inspired the earliest version of the *Pastoral Ballad.* See Graves, *Recollection*, pp. 47, 103.

believe they are the best I am capable of. I would rather have my Judgment than Care censured, in any Thing I am employed in for you. You'll be surprized to find them joined with a Paper scrawl'd over with dull Poetry: however, I must confess, as I wrote it to please myself, I sent it, not without Hopes that it might, in an inferior Manner, please you. One may sometimes amuse one's-self with what one can't entirely approve. As I can't flatter myself, your Judgment can excuse, so I can't apprehend your Good-nature will expose me. To vindicate my Character to you, as a Poet, I shall only join these alleviating Circumstances; First, that nothing makes so aukward a Figure in Verse (as well as in some other Respects) as Sincerity. Secondly, that these Lines were wrote when I had no great Flow of Spirits, namely, when I had just left M[ickleton], and you; but I shall want your Patience elsewhere, so will say no more about 'em — only this — that I should not have mentioned Miss L——, were I not persuaded that, as you are entirely free from the other Faults of your Sex, so you are from that of not bearing to hear another commended. (It is a Sign of a great Want of Accomplishments, when a Person is continually suspicious of being rivalled; and, for that Part, you may give every One many more than their Due, without the least Danger of being so.)

I could not help envying Whistler's[2] Happiness, when I came away; I fancy your Lives have been a constant Round of Delights; I don't know any Neighbourhood more likely to produce 'em. I could reconcile myself, however, pretty well to *Harborough's* melancholy Scenes, were I not conscious of such superior Pleasures, *où vous scavez*. You might convey me a Letter full of them, but you'll, perhaps, think it an impertinent Request. I could set what Value you please on the Favour, though the Pleasure I can't pretend to limit.

I must now break off my Letter in as aukward a Manner as I take my Leave, which is likewise usually most aukward, where I have most Respect. I'll e'en lay aside further Ceremony in this, as in the other Case, and say no more than that I am,

Madam, Your humble Servant
(In the most obsolete Sense)

W. S.

[2] Anthony Whistler (d. 1754) of Whitchurch, Oxfordshire, was, despite their minor disagreements, an intimate friend of Shenstone's from their college days until Whistler's death, at which time his letters to Shenstone were destroyed (much to Shenstone's regret) by John Whistler, Anthony's brother. Of Whistler's letters to Shenstone a number appear in Hull's *Select Letters,* Vols. I and II. But only one of Shenstone's to Whistler seems to have been preserved (Letter 40 below). Whistler was the author of a mock-heroic poem, *The Shuttlecock,* printed at Oxford in 1736, and was also a contributor to Robert Dodsley's *Collection.*

3. To MISS LOWE[1]

[Harborough, about 1736]

MADM,

I fancy I've been condemn'd a thousand times on account of not sending the tunes. One of 'em was Lent out, & I had not an Opportunity of Fetching it till last week. I don't know whether this Reason will prove sufficient but I assure you 'twas ye Real one. I tore 'em out of my Book & on y^t Account you have some others with them. I was willing you shoud have 'em in ye best shape possible, & dare say, you'll Improve as much upon 'em, as I have degenerated from 'em.

I want exceedingly to hear from you, but you'll scarce think it consistent with a rural reputation to write your self. 'Tis indeed scarce worth while to hazard it, to give me ever so great a Pleasure but I cou'd wish you'd here remember y^r Character of a Town-Lady. Lord! How does Miss Uty?[2] I didn't wonder you shou'd mutually envy each other since you are both so great objects of Envy. More Particularly as Modesty has taught you to think y^r own Merit small in Comparison with y^t of others. Voilá la seule source de toute envie! — I'm surely vastly Impertinent for I'm not Positive you understand French. But I guess'd y^t a Lady, so Accomplish'd in all other Particulars might. I fancy you've enjoy'd a vast deal of Agreeable gayety since I left you, whilst I have been wandring about Harborough's gloomy walks & Pools like a Shepherd "Despairing beside a clear stream." Oh I want to know whether or no for ye common good, of our Society in particular, as of our Country in general it is & may be Lawfull to admit without ye usual Number of Members being Present at ye Solemnity. For I judge it better to lay aside some Part of ye Ceremony yⁿ y^t any one shou'd Dye un-initiated, Whether or no as in Baptism — I was truly going too Far. I am safe enough. Let me go w^t lengths I will in subscribing myself

The humblest of y^r Humble Serv^{ts},

W. Shenstone

[1] This undated letter (Hull, *Select Letters*, Vol. II, No. XVIII), found in Bodleian Montague MSS 25448, fol. 98, was evidently written from Harborough about 1736 or shortly after.

[2] Utrecia Smith, the accomplished daughter of the Rev. William Smith, curate at Mickleton and tutor to Richard Graves, inspired Shenstone's Elegy IV, *Ophelia's Urn. To Mr. G——*. She died young; Graves's inscription to her is dated 1744. Shenstone also addressed an impromptu to her, "on her not dancing." See Graves, *Recollection*, pp. 115–17, 44.

4. To RICHARD JAGO [1]

1739

DEAR SIR,

As my head is considerably more confused than usual, by reason of a bad cold, I shall aim no higher in this letter than at bare *recitative,* reserving all my *airs* for a season when my mind is more in *tune.* Such, I hope, will be the time which you set apart to attend the *chief musician,* at Birmingham. I thoroughly design to lend an *ear* to *his* performance, on condition he will not refuse one to a proposal I intend to make, of having, one day or other, a merry strain at The Leasowes. But if you have any *penchant* to see the face of your humble servant at Birmingham, your most effectual way will be to inform him when these solemn nuptials betwixt Tweedle-dum and Tweedle-dee are to be consummated. I will, *certes,* not be absent at the throwing of the stocking, any more than Parson Evans in Shakespear would be "absence at the grace."[2] I have sent a song, not that I am sure I have not sent it before; but that, if you can see any joke that it containeth, the forementioned gentleman may be asked to translate it into music. When I use this expression, you will, peradventure, look upon it as my opinion, that in musical compositions, sound ought as much to answer sense as one language does another, insomuch that such and such thoughts ought to bring into our heads such and such sounds, and *vice versa.* But in case there is no sense, and no thought, the more languages a sentence is translated into, the more 'tis exposed. And in case it be the misfortune of my little piece to have neither, I beg that Mr. Marriett may not inform anybody what it signifies in music. As a farther proof of the confused state of my intellects, you see almost at the end of my letter, my thanks for the packet, &c. which ought to have been

---

[1] Robert Dodsley (ed.), Shenstone's *Letters to Particular Friends* (*Works,* Vol. III), No. I. The first three letters were written from Harborough; this is the first we have from the Leasowes, where Shenstone lived with his tenants, distant relatives, until 1745, when he seems to have taken full possession.

The addressee, Richard Jago (1715–81), an intimate friend and correspondent, was Shenstone's schoolfellow at Mr. Crumpton's, Solihull, and at Oxford, where he took his B. A. in 1736 and his M. A. in 1739. In 1737 he was ordained to the curacy of Snitterfield, Warwickshire. In 1746 he was appointed to the small livings of Harbury and Chesterton, and in 1754 was nominated vicar of Snitterfield, where he continued to live. In 1743 he married Dorothea Susanna Fancourt, daughter of John Fancourt, rector of Kimcote, where Jago himself became rector in 1771. His wife died in 1751, having borne Jago seven children; in 1758 he married Margaret Underwood, who survived him. Jago published his *Blackbirds* in Hawkesworth's *Adventurer,* No. 37 (March 13, 1753); he also contributed to Dodsley's *Collection.* His best known poem, *Edge Hill,* a narrative and descriptive piece in blank verse, which Shenstone saw in manuscript and commented upon in Letters 279 and 280, was published in 1767. His poems, with some account of his life, were published in 1784 by John Scott Hylton.

[2] *The Merry Wives of Windsor,* I, i, 275–76.

placed in the very front of it, in order to express, in some degree, the sense I have of your favours. I long to see you; and am, dear Sir,

Your most obedient and faithful servant,

W. Shenstone

SONG[3]

When bright Ophelia treads the green
In all the pride of dress and mien;
Averse to freedom, mirth, and play,
The lofty rival of the day;
Methinks to my enchanted eye,
The lilies droop, the roses die.

But when, disdaining art, the fair
Assumes a soft, engaging air:
Mild as the opening morn of May,
And as the feather'd warblers gay:
The scene improves where'er she goes,
More sweetly smiles the pink and rose.

O lovely maid! propitious hear,
Nor think thy Damon insincere.
Pity my wild delusive flame:
For tho' the flowers are still the same,
To me they languish, or improve,
And plainly tell me that I love.

5. To MR. REYNOLDS[1]

Leasowes, Aug. 1740

DEAR SIR,

Wonderful were the dangers and difficulties through which I went, the night I left you at Barels:[2] which I looked upon as ordained by fate for the temporal punishment of obstinacy. It was very kind, and in character, for you to endeavour to deter me from the ways of darkness; but having a sort of *penchant* for needless difficulties, I have an undoubted right to indulge myself in them, so long as I do not insist upon any one's pity. It is true, these ought not to exceed a certain degree; they should be

---

[3] Song XIX, *Poetical Works* (1854). The name Ophelia may here, as elsewhere (Elegy IV), refer to Utrecia Smith.

[1] Dodsley, *Letters to Particular Friends*, No. VIII. Wells verifies the date, *Anglia*, 35: 435. Mr. Reynolds is pretty obviously the "Jackie Reynalds" often referred to, particularly in the *Letters* of Lady Luxborough (for which see the Bibliography). He was chaplain to Lord Somervile of Somervile's Aston. See M. Williams, *William Shenstone*, p. 18.

[2] Barrels, about fifteen miles from the Leasowes, was the estate of Mrs. Henrietta Knight, later (1746) Lady Luxborough, who lived there after separation from her husband in 1736.

lenia tormenta; and I must own the labours I underwent that night did not come within the bounds which my imagination had prescribed. I cannot forbear mentioning one imminent danger. I rode along a considerable piece of water, covered so close with trees, that it was as probable I might have pursued the channel, which was dangerous, as my way out of it. Or, to put my case in a more poetical light, having by night intruded upon an amour betwixt a Wood-nymph and a River-god, I owed my escape to Fortune, who conveyed me from the vengeance which they might have taken. I put up finally at a little alehouse about ten o'clock, and lay all night awake, counting the cords which supported me, which I could more safely swear to than to either bed or blanket. For farther particulars see my epistle to the Pastor Fido of Lapworth. — Mr. Graves says, he should be glad to shew you any civilities in his power, upon his own acquaintance; and will serve you as far as his vote goes, upon my recommendation; but is afraid, without the concurrence of some more considerable friends, your chance will be but small *this* year, &c. If the former part of this news gives you any pleasure, I can assure you it gives me no less to communicate it; and this pleasure proceeds from a principle which would induce me to serve you myself if it should ever be in my power. — I saw Mr. Lyttelton last week; he is a candidate for the county of Worcester,[3] together with Lord Deerhurst; I hope Mr. Somervile[4] will do him the honour to appear as his friend, which he must at least think second to that of succeeding.

I hear you are commenced Chaplain since I saw you. I wish you joy of it. The Chaplain's title is infinitely more agreeable than his office; and I hope the scarf, which is expressive of it, will be no diminutive thing, no four-penny-halfpenny piece of ribboning; but that it will

> High o'er the neck its rustling folds display,
> Disdain all usual bounds, extend its sway,
> Usurp the head, and push the wig away.

I hope it will prove ominous, that my first letter is a congratulatory one; and if I were to have opportunities of sending all such, it would entirely quadrate with the sincere wishes of

Your faithful humble servant,
W. Shenstone

I beg my compliments to Mr. Somervile, Mrs. Knight, and your family.

---

[3] Mr. George Lyttelton of Hagley, Shenstone's neighbor, stood for the county of Worcester in 1741, but lost.
[4] William Somervile (1675–1742) of Edstone, author of *The Chase* (1735) and *Field Sports* (1742), a particular friend of Lady Luxborough and probably through her, or through Jago, a friend of Shenstone.

6. To a FRIEND [1]

[After Sept. 24 or 29, 1740]

SIR,

I cannot avoid imagining the first part of your letter was mere raillery. I am sure it gave me a good deal of pleasure (for I can bear very well to hear my foibles exposed, though not my faults), and on that account must needs make grateful mention of it. I acknowledge the oddness of the letter which occasioned it, and could not expect that such an ill-formed application could have produced an answer so very oratorical. In the first place, you lay open the subject, or indeed, what you call the offices in which I am pleased to employ you. In the next, you alledge your own inability to enter upon matters of such great concernment. That this is rhetorical, nay, pure rhetoric, I gather from the exordiums of all the declamations that I ever heard in my life. 'Tis, moreover, not uncommon with declaimers to give some reasons why they should not absolutely decline the subject, though they are sensible of their insufficiency (otherwise they might be expected to sit down, and hold their tongues). And this is what you have done, by saying that you are unwilling to dissent from the world in regard to the subjects you are engaged in; that you, therefore, chose to steer a middle course, by that means avoiding the imputation of presumption on the one hand, and indifference on the other. When this is done, you enter gravely upon the subject, and, to give it greater perspicuity, divide it into two parts. The first part happens to be "concerning the purchase of *an* horse." On this occasion, you inform me, that I am in a good country for horses; and secondly, that I have a number of acquaintance round about me, who are very well skilled in the nature of them. Now each of these informations seems, at first sight, to mean no more than what I have better opportunities of knowing than the person who informs me, and, on this account, to err in point of superfluity. But, upon second thoughts, they have *this force* (to speak like a grammarian); namely, that I am entirely negligent of my own affairs; and, secondly, that I care not whom I give trouble to, if I can but avoid it myself; so that the sentences have really a beauty, when one searches beneath their superficies. After you have said this and more, which includes all that can be said upon the subject, you descend to the second division, in relation to which I am too grateful to be otherwise than *serious* in my acknowledgements.

---

[1] Dodsley, *Letters to Particular Friends,* No. III, dated 1739. Wells corrects the date, *Anglia,* 35:430–31. I lack sufficient data to determine independently the identity of the "friend" to whom this letter is addressed. It might be Graves. According to Dodsley, this letter and Letter 11 (to Graves) are addressed to the same person.

Dear Sir,

I am employ'd by my Friend Mr. Hylton to request that you would procure for him an electrical apparatus; and this, with all the expedition that shall be consis:tent with your own convenience. He wishes it to be such as may effectually exhibit all the common experiments in electricity; & This he leaves entirely to your Judgment who are so much better vers'd in it: At ye same time he wishes it plain, & not to partake of Any elegance that tends to brighten the expence — Thus much for my Friend Hylton; and now, as touching my :self, I confess I could find much Pleasure in Researches of this sort; but as I have other avocations, & Lapal is so near, I

Shenstone to Matthew Boulton, July 19, 1758

I had not expatiated thus far, but to shew that I am not insensible of a sneer; nor should I expatiate any farther, but to prove that I am equally sensible of a favour.

I desire you would believe, that I absolutely assent to your critique: That some of your sentiments were my own before I communicated the verses; and others, as soon as you had favoured me with the discovery of them: That I would, *per praesentes,* return my thanks for them; which you might justly have claimed, whether I had approved them or not. One exception to this approbation my modesty bids me mention, on account of your too great partiality in my favour. My gratitude you are entitled to without exception or limitation.

It will, perhaps, gratify your curiosity to know, that Mr. G. has a copy of verses in the last magazine, entitled, "The little Cur."[2] There are several strokes that are picturesque and humourous; I believe it was done in haste. The motto is exquisite, and much more properly applied by Mr. G. than the Emperor Adrian, in my opinion, notwithstanding all that Pope says. Tell me your judgment of Mr. L[yttelto]n's in the same paper. The epigram "To one who refused to walk in the Park, &c." is a good one.

I have waved sending the verses to Mr. Somervile at present, because I hope to see you soon either at The Leasowes or at Birmingham. I cannot tell whether I shall have time to enclose in this letter my ballad. If I do, consider it only as some words that I chuse to make use of to some notes of which I am more than ordinarily fond.[3] It is as much designed for my own singing (in private I mean) as ever was a bottle of cherry-brandy for an old woman's drinking. Now I think of it, I really believe that I every day approach nearer and nearer to the capacity, the way, the insignificancy, of an old woman. Mrs. Arnold[4] has certainly, by her *charms,* her incantations, and her conversations together, contributed a good deal to this transformation. Pray come over if you can, and try to reinstate me in my right mind, in proportion to the soundness of which I shall be more and more

Your friend and servant,

W. S.

[2] The *Gentleman's Magazine,* September, 1740, p. 460. Mr. G. is probably Graves, and Mr. L———n, George Lyttelton.

[3] The tune "Come and listen to my ditty, &c." The words founded upon a true history of Queen Elizabeth, who, looking from a castle wherein she was a prisoner, and seeing a country milk-maid singing, expressed great envy at the girl's condition, and great dissatisfaction with regard to her own [Dodsley]. See Shenstone's *Works,* I (1764), 120.

[4] Mrs. Arnold was Shenstone's housekeeper until about 1753, when she seems to have been succeeded by Mary Cutler, whom Shenstone remembered in his will with an annuity of

7. To MR. REYNOLDS[1]

1740

SIR,

Your last letter gave me a good deal of uneasiness in regard to Mr. Somervile's indisposition. I hope, if he is better, you will omit no opportunity of gratifying me with the news of it. I shall be glad to employ you and Mr. Jago in my little rivulet before winter comes, when one must bid adieu to rural beauties. Those charming scenes, which the poets, in order to render them more compleat, have furnished with ladies, must be stript of all their ornaments. Those incomparable nymphs, the Dryads and the Nereids, which have been my constant companions this short summer, will vanish to more pleasing climes; and I must be left to seek my assistance in real beauties instead of imaginary ones. In short, I am thinking to live part of this winter in Worcester, or some other town. I was at a concert there, a very full one, lately. I observed Dr. Mackenzie[2] talking to Mr. Lyttelton; and I hope, on that account, he is in his interest: otherwise Mr. Somervile would do Mr. Lyttelton great service by engaging him. — Mr. Lyttelton took occasion to mention to me the obligation he lay under to Mr. Somervile for his letter, as well as his other designs in his favour — that he had long received great pleasure from that gentleman's pen, and wished for the honour of his acquaintance. I told him, I believed the satisfaction would be mutual, or to that purpose. He added, that The Chace was an *extremely* beautiful poem, the best by far ever written on the subject. But now the fiddles squeaked, the harpsichord jingled, and the performers began to feel the divine enthusiasm. The god of music invaded them as he did the sibyl of old:

> Deus, ecce Deus! cui talia fanti
> Ante fores, subito non vultus, non color unus,
> Non comptae mansere comae; sed pectus anhelum.
> Et rabie fera corda tument, majorque videri,
> Nec mortale sonans.

I am, Sir, with all due compliments to Mr. Somervile,

Yours sincerely,

W. Shenstone

---

30 pounds. Fullington ("Mr. William Shenstone," p. 170) thinks Mary Cutler was Shenstone's mistress. The evidence for such a supposition is not, however, particularly strong.

[1] Dodsley, *Letters to Particular Friends,* No. XI. Wells confirms the date as the autumn of 1740 (*Anglia,* 35:437).

[2] Dr. James Mackenzie (1680?–1761), educated at Edinburgh, practiced medicine very successfully in Worcester for many years. He was the author of *The History of Health and the Art of Preserving It* (1758) and of other writings.

8. To MR. REYNOLDS[1]

*From Mr. Wintle's Perfumer, at the
King's Arms, by Temple-Bar, Fleet-Street
[Jan. 16 or 17, 1741]*

SIR,

I am heartily obliged to Mr. Somervile, that he will make use of any means to serve me; more especially that he will take the trouble of consulting which may be most effectual to that end; and I desire you would represent these sentiments to him in the most expressive manner.

I have, since I arrived here (which was last Saturday night[2]), heard Lowe[3] sing, and seen Cibber act.[4] The laureat spoke an epilogue, made *upon,* and, I suppose, *by* himself, in which he does not only make a bare confession, but an *ostentation* of all his follies.

> Of *such* (says he) whoe'er demands a bill of fare
> May look into my life — he'll find 'em there;

or some such lines, I cannot accurately recollect them. I do not wonder he pleased extremely; but to a considering man there is something strangely disagreeable, to hear a scandalous life recommended by one of his age, and as much satisfaction shewn in the review of it as if it had been a perfect galaxy of virtues. An Athenian audience would have shewn their different sentiments on this occasion. But I am acting the part of Jeremy Collier, and indeed in some degree of an hypocrite, for I confess I was highly pleased with him myself. I have nothing to add, but a fine close, if I had it; as I have not, you must be content with the vulgar one, that I am

Yours sincerely,
W. Shenstone

---

[1] Dodsley, *Letters to Particular Friends,* No. IX, dated 1740. Wells corrects the date and supplies the month and day (*Anglia,* 35:435–36).

[2] The "last Saturday night" of Shenstone's arrival in London for this, his first, visit, must have been January 10, 1741 (Wells).

[3] Thomas Lowe, vocalist and actor (d. 1783), sang Arne's songs in *Twelfth Night,* January 15, 1741.

[4] The acting of Cibber to which Shenstone alludes was one of his few appearances after his retirement. He acted Fondlewife in *The Old Bachelor* and spoke the "Epilogue upon Himself" on January 12, 13, and 14, 1741. The lines Shenstone could not accurately recall were apparently these:

> If for my Folly's largest List you call,
> My Life has lump'd 'em! There you'll read 'em all.

Wells discusses these matters in *Anglia,* 35:435–36.

9. To RICHARD JAGO[1]

[London,] Jan. 21, 1741

SIR,

You see I am *extremely expeditious* in answering your letter; the reason of which is a very powerful one, namely, the information which I received last night, that it would be agreeable to you I should do so. Please therefore to set aside the sum of eighteen pence, or thereabouts, for letters which you will receive whilst I am in London; and, to make it seem less profusely squandered, consider it amongst any other casual expences which you carelessly submit to, merely to gratify your curiosity.

I went the other night, with the greatest expectations, to see "The Merry Wives of Windsor" performed at Covent-Garden. It is impossible to express how much every thing fell below my ideas. But I have *considered since;* and I find that my expectations were really more unjust than their manner of acting. *Persons,* in order to act well, should have something of the author's fire, as well as a polite education. And what makes this the clearer to me is, that you hear ten plays well read by gentlemen in company, to one that you find well performed upon the stage. — Nothing can be more ignorant or affected than the scornful airs which some people give themselves at a country play; because, forsooth, they have seen plays in town. The truth is, the chief advantage of plays in town lies entirely in the scenery. You seldom observe a set of strollers without one or two actors who are quite equal to their parts; and I really know of no good one at either of the two Theatres Royal, except Cibber who rarely acts, and Mrs. Clive. I will add one more, in *compliance* with my *own* taste *merely;* and that is Mr. Neal, a fellow, who, by *playing the fool,* has gained my particular *esteem.*

After the play, we had an *entertainment;* falsely so called! It was that of Orpheus and Eurydice,[2] the most *un-musical* thing I ever heard, and which lasted, I believe, three hours, with some intermixtures of Harlequin; both so dull, and yet heard with patience, that I was amazed, astonished, confounded: but really a *man* of *sense* ought not to be so; because they were not calculated for *him.*

I want you here extremely: pray come up for a week. I suppose you will not, so I will not argue superfluously. However, write soon; and believe that your letters are the most agreeable things in the world to, Sir,

Yours most faithfully,

W. S.

---

[1] Dodsley, *Letters to Particular Friends,* No. XII. Wells confirms the date, *Anglia,* 35:436.
[2] The "Orpheus and Eurydice" was probably that of Henry Somers, first acted in 1740, according to *Biographica Dramatica* (1812), IV, 108.

10. To RICHARD JAGO[1]

From Mr. Wintle's, Perfumer,
near Temple-Bar, &c. 6th Feb. [1741]

DEAR SIR,

I am now with regard to the *town* pretty much in the same state in which I expect to be always with regard to the *world;* sometimes exclaiming and railing against it; sometimes giving it a good word, and even admiring it. A sun-shiny day, a tavern-supper after a play well acted, and now and then an invigorating breath of air in the Mall, never fail of producing a chearful effect. I don't know whether I gave you any account of Quin's acting Falstaff in my former letter: I really imagined that I saw you tittering on one side me, shaking your sides, and sometimes scarce containing yourself. You will pardon the attitude in which I placed you, since it was what seemed *natural* at that circumstance of time. — Comus I have once been at, for the sake of the songs, though I detest it in any *light:* but as a *dramatic* piece, the *taking* of it seems a *prodigy;* yet indeed *such-a-one,* as was pretty tolerably accounted for by a gentleman who sat by me in the *boxes.* This learned sage, being asked how he liked the play, made answer, "He could not tell — pretty well, he thought — or indeed as well as any other play — he always took it, that people only came there to see and to be seen — for as for what was said, he owned, he never understood any thing of the matter." I told him, I thought a great many of its admirers were in his case, if they would but own it.

On the other hand, it is amazing to consider to what an universality of learning people make pretensions here. There's not a drawer, a chair or hackney coachman, but is politician, poet, and judge of polite literature. Chimney-sweepers damn the Convention, and black-shoe-boys cry up the Genius of Shakespear. "The danger of writing Verse"[2] is a very good thing; if you have not read it, I would recommend it to you as poetical. But now I talk of Learning, I must not omit an interview which I accidentally had the other night in company with Lord D—— and one Mr. C——.[3] We were taken to sup at a private house, where I found a person whom I had never seen before. The man behaved exceeding modestly and well; till, growing a little merry over a bottle (and

---

[1] Dodsley, *Letters to Particular Friends*, No. V, dated 1740. Wells corrects the date, *Anglia*, 35:433. The "friend" is evidently Jago. See Fullington, "Mr. William Shenstone," pp. 47–48.

[2] *The Danger of Writing Verse*, by William Whitehead, was published January 22, 1741, by Dodsley.

[3] Lord D—— is probably Lord Dudley. Concerning Mr. C—— I have no conjecture. Sir T—— L—— is evidently Sir Thomas Lyttelton, and Mr. L——, George Lyttelton.

being a little countenanced by the subject we were upon), he pulls out of his pocket about half a dozen ballads, and distributes them amongst the company. I (not finding at first they were of his own composition) read one over, and, finding it a dull piece of stuff, contented myself with observing that it was exceedingly well *printed*. But to see the man's face on this occasion would make you pity the circumstance of an author as long as you live. His jollity ceased (as a flame would do, should you pour water upon it); and, I believe, for about five minutes, he spoke not a syllable. At length, recovering himself, he began to talk about his country-seat, about Houghton-Hall, and soon after desired a health, imagining (as I found afterwards) that Lord D—— would have given Sir Robert's. But he did not, naming Sir T—— L——: mine, which followed, was that of Mr. L. Now, who do you think this should be, but honest Ralph Freeman (at least the writer of the paper so subscribed), your father's old friend and intimate, Sir Robert's right-hand, a person that lives elegantly, drives six of the best horses in town, and plays on St. John's organ: (you know Mr. L—— is not only Sir Robert's greatest enemy, but the Gazetteer's proper antagonist.) We were invited to see him very civilly, and indeed the man behaved with the utmost good-humour, without arrogance, or any attempts at wit, which, probably, would not have been very successful.—Ask your father what he would say to me, if I should join in the cause with his old friend, and take a good annuity under Sir Robert, which, I believe, I might have; and little encouragement, God knows, have I met with on the other side of the question. I say, I believe I *might have,* because I know a certain person gives pensions of three pounds a-week to porters and the most illiterate stupid fellows you can imagine, to talk in his behalf at ale-houses: where they sit so long a time, and are as regularly relieved as one centry relieves another.— At least tell him that I expect in his answer to my letter (which I shall not allow him to assign to you), he write something to confirm me in my integrity, and to make me prefer him, and you, and honesty, to lace, brocade, and the smiles of the ladies,

Et Veneri, & cunis, & plumis Sardanapali.[4]

But I hope to keep my Hercules in view,[5] whether in print or manuscript; and though I am as fond of pleasure as most people, Yet I shall observe the rule,

[4] Sardanapalus was the last king of Assyria, who is reported never to have done a manly action, except in his death. His exceeding effeminacy caused his subjects to revolt, and take up arms against him. They overcame him in the conflict; whereon he raised a funeral pile, and sacrificed himself on it, with some of the richest of his possessions. [Dodsley]
[5] *Hercules* was published April 23, 1741, inscribed to George Lyttelton, Esq.

Positam sic tangere noli.

I desire I may hear from you next post: I have a line or two, which I intend for the *sons of utter darkness*[6] (as you call them) next magazine: I would send them to you, for your advice; but cannot readily find them. I like every thing in Mr. Somervile's, but the running of the last line. I think to insert them. Should be glad to have a line or two of *yours,* that one may make a bold attack. I look on it as *fun,* without the least emotion, I assure you.

I am, dear Sir,
Your faithful scribbling slave,
W. Shenstone

11. To RICHARD GRAVES[1]

[London, soon after Feb. 13, 1741]

DEAR SIR,

I return you my thanks, most heartily, for the poetical resentment which you have shewn against my censurers, the Riddle-masters. I have sent Mr. Somervile's verses and yours to Cave;[2] though I am ashamed to own I neglected it so long, that, I fear, he will have no room for them this month. If you can extirpate false wit in a manner, you will do no small service to the true: you do no small *honour* to it, whether you extirpate the other or not.

You have heard of the motion;[3] have heard, probably, all that I can tell you of it: That it was ill-concerted; that it has done the opposition great disservice; that the King is now confirmed in the opinion of Sir Robert's honesty; that the younger Mr. Pitt's speech was the most admired on the opposite side, and Sir R[ober]t's on the court side; that they did not leave the House till five in the morning; that Sir R[ober]t and P——y are so violent, that the Sp[eake]r is continually calling them to order; finally, that the affair has occasioned this print, which I address to your curiosity merely, though the lines upon the Bishop are humour-

---

[6] The "line or two" for "the sons of utter darkness" was probably a contribution to a little controversy over riddles carried on in the *Gentleman's Magazine* during late 1740 and early 1741. According to Wells, "Shenstone and his friends had the worse of the contest." See *Anglia,* 35:432.

[1] Dodsley, *Letters to Particular Friends,* No. IV, dated 1739. Wells corrects the date, *Anglia,* 35:431–33. This letter is addressed, according to Dodsley, to the same person as Letter 6 above. It is apparently Graves, with whom he contributed to a controversy over riddles in the *Gentleman's Magazine* in October, 1740, and February, 1741. See Graves, *Recollection,* pp. 98–102.

[2] Edward Cave (1691–1754), publisher of the *Gentleman's Magazine,* 1731–54.

[3] The motion of February 13, 1741, to address the king for the removal of Walpole from office. The print mentioned was one of many which the motion occasioned.

ous enough. — Now I mention curiosity; do you take notice of the many quaint contrivances made use of to catch peoples natural inquisitiveness in the pamphlets, viz. "Are these things so?" — "Yes, they are." — "What then?" — "The devil of a story." — "Hoy, boys." — "Up go we." — And a thousand others. — What do you think must be my expence, who love to pry into every thing of this kind? Why, truly, one shilling. My company goes to George's Coffee-house, where, for that small subscription, I read all pamphlets under a three-shilling dimensions; and, indeed, any larger ones would not be fit for coffee-house perusal. — Lord Dudley lent me two sermons, given him at the House of Lords, which I read last night. In the first, there are a great many deep animadversions delivered in a style that is tolerable; in the other, there is as great a want of common English as there is plenty of common observations. — Have you seen the sermons on the Martyrdom and on the Fast-day? If you read either send for the first. — You'll find me degenerate from a gentle bard into a snarling critic, if my poem[4] does not please (you'll say I am no very candid one at present): but let its fate be what it will, I shall lay no small stress upon the opinion of some that have approved it. As it is at present *in keeping,* it discovers no uncommon impudence, and runs no very great risque; but who can answer for it, when it has the gracelessness to *come upon the town? — Ora pro nobis* must soon be my motto. Its virtues and faults will then be incapable of addition or diminution, and the pious assistance of friends must — but I am no Roman Catholic. — The intrinsic merit of a book when it is printed, as well as the past life and conversation of a man that is departed, must damn, or give it immortality — I mean, to a certain degree. I scribble what comes uppermost, and desire you would do the same. —

Yours,
W. S.

12. To RICHARD JAGO[1]

From Mr. Wintle's [London]
April 30 [1741]

MY GOOD FRIEND!

I heartily thank you for the service your letter did me; and a considerable service, no doubt it *is,* to raise the spirits of a person so habitually dispirited as I have been for some time. For this, and all former favours,

---

[4] *The Judgment of Hercules,* published by Dodsley, April 23, 1741.
[1] Dodsley, *Letters to Particular Friends,* No. VI, dated 1740. Wells corrects the date, *Anglia,* 35:434–45.

as the sullen fellow says in Shakespear, "I thank you; I am not of many words, but I thank you."[2]

I beg you would cease to apologize for your letters: In the first place, it will lay *me* under a necessity of doing *so;* and, in the next place, you may be assured, that no friendly letter of yours will ever be otherwise than infinitely agreeable to me.

I sent a letter to Mr. Marriett at Bath to be left with you at your former place of residence; you will be so kind as to give it to him.

If I wish for a *large* fortune, it is rather for the sake of my friends than myself: or, to compromise the matter with those moralists who argue for the universality of *self-interest,* it is to gratify myself in the company, and in the gratifications, of my friends.

Dr. Ratcliff has sent me a letter, which gives me much *satisfaction* in respect of my poem;[3] notwithstanding, he cannot forbear adding, that he expects to hear, since my pen has so well adorned the fable, that my conduct will with equal propriety and elegance illustrate the moral. However, the simple approbation of a *sincere* man affects one more than Pliny's panegyric could do from a more courtly one.

There are several errors of the press, which neither sagacity nor vigilance itself, I now see, can prevent, and which I beg you to correct with your pen in a copy which I must get you to present to C—— L——[4] together with the inclosed letter. Please to be at the expence of having it stitched in purple paper, and gilt at the edges; and I will repay you.

I was loitering yesterday in the coffee-room, when two persons came in, well-dressed, and called for my poem; read a page or two, and commended the four lines upon Mr. L——[5] extremely, ("Lov'd by that Prince, &c") repeated them forty times, and in the end got them by heart, mentioned them to a *third* person, who said he knew of no virtue that the Prince *was* fired with, and then endeavoured to mimic the Prince's way of talking; but, says he, *I'll* shew *the four best lines in the poem,* and then proceeded to " 'Twas Youth's perplexing stage, &c." which are flat enough, God knows — but to my first heroes; one of them reads, "When great Alcides to a grove retir'd." *Ay, ay, you know Mr.* L[yttelton] *did retire, he was in the secession; read on: you'll find he mentions Delia anon. Don't you remember Mr.* L[yttelton] *wrote a song upon Delia? but proceed — you'll find he is going to give a description of two ladies of different characters, that were in love with Mr.* L[yttelton].

[2] *Much Ado about Nothing,* I, i, 155–56. The "sullen fellow" is Don John.
[3] The poem is evidently *Hercules,* just published.
[4] Probably Charles Lyttelton.
[5] George Lyttelton, Esq., to whom the poem is inscribed.

One was (here he named two names, which I have forgot.) *Upon my word, it is fine: I believe it is Pope's; but how comes Pope to praise himself there?* ("Lov'd by that Bard, &c.") *No doubt, however, it was written by Mr. Pope or Mr. D——.*[6]

My critics proceeded to the reading of the last simile *immediately, without* the lines preceding it, and, agreeing that it was a very good thing, called out for "The Oeconomy of Love."[7] So you see "Laudant *illa*, sed *ista* legunt," is the case. A person cannot be supposed vain from the approbation of such critics, or else I would not have inserted such a *commendatory* paragraph. I never enquire how my poem takes, and am *afraid* to do so. However, I find *some do* allow it to be *Mallet's* — I am impatient till I hear from you: I shall be here till this day fortnight; afterwards at The Leasowes — I must add this, "Ne, studio nostri, *pecces;*" but at the same time also

O defend,
Against your judgment, your most faithful friend.
W. S.

These *opposite* petitions delineate my state of mind: it is well for me that I have you at Bath.

13. To RICHARD GRAVES[1]

Leasowes, June 8, 1741

DEAR SIR,

I write to you out of the abundant inclination I have to hear from you; imagining that, as you gave me a direction, you might possibly expect to receive a previous letter from me. I want to be informed of the impressions you receive from your *new* circumstances. The chief aversion which some people have to orders is, what I fancy you will remove in such as you converse with. I take it to be owing partly to dress, and partly to the *avowed profession* of religion. A young clergyman, that has

---

[6] Identified by Graves as Robert Dodsley (*Recollection*, p. 93).
[7] *The Oeconomy of Love* by John Armstrong (1709–79) was first published in 1736.
[1] Dodsley, *Letters to Particular Friends*, No. XIV. This is the first of many letters unmistakably addressed to Richard Graves (1715–1804), probably the most intimate of Shenstone's particular friends, and his best biographer. They met at Pembroke; Graves took his bachelor's degree in 1736 and his master's in 1740, after which he was ordained and became chaplain at Tissington, Derbyshire. In 1744 he secured the curacy of Aldworth, near Reading, and in 1748 the rectory of Claverton, near Bath. He was the author of more than a score of works in verse and prose. His best work, which was in prose, is represented by *The Spiritual Quixote* (1773), *Columella* (1779), and *Recollection of Some Particulars in the Life of the Late William Shenstone Esq.* (1788). See Charles Jarvis Hill, "The Literary Career of Richard Graves," *Smith College Studies in Modern Languages*, 16:1–15. Mr. Hill appends a bibliography of Graves's first editions.

distinguished his genius by a composition or two of a polite nature, and is capable of dressing *himself,* and his *religion,* in a different manner from the generality of his profession, that is, without formality, is certainly a genteel character. I speak this not with any sly design to advise, but to intimate that I think you very capable of *shining* in a dark-coloured coat. — You must consider me yet as a man of the world, and endeavouring to elicit that pleasure from gaiety which my reason tells me I shall never find. — It is impossible to express how stupid I have been ever since I came home, insomuch that I cannot write a common letter without six repetitions. This is the third time I have begun yours, and you see what stuff it is made up of. I must e'en hasten to matter of fact, which is the comfortable resource of dull people, though, even as to that, I have nothing to *communicate.* But I would be glad to know, whether you are under a necessity of residing on week-days; and, if not, why I may not expect you a day or two at The Leasowes very soon. — Did you make any enquiry concerning the number of my poems[2] sold at Oxford? or did you hear any thing concerning it that concerns me to hear? — Will S—— (for that is his true name) is the excess of simplicity and good-nature. He seems to have all the industry imaginable to divert and amuse people, without any ambitious ends to serve, or almost any concern whether he has so much as a laugh allowed to his stories, any farther than as a laugh is an indication that people are delighted. This, joined with his turn of thought, renders him quite agreeable. I wish it were in my power to conciliate acquaintance with half his ease. — Pray do not delay writing to me. Adieu!   W. Shenstone

14. To RICHARD JAGO[1]

The Leasowes, June 17, 1741

DEAR SIR,

If a friend of yours who lived in the farthest part of China were to send you a pinch of snuff wrapt up in a sheet of writing-paper, I conceive the snuff would improve in value as it travelled, and gratify your curiosity extremely by the time it reached your fingers ends. — Very true — you will say: — why then, *that very consideration* was my inducement to write to you at this time; and that sort of progressional value is what you are to place upon my letter. For, be assured, I am not ignorant how much this my letter doth resemble a pinch of snuff in point of

---

[2] The poems referred to are evidently copies of *Hercules.*
[1] Dodsley, *Letters to Particular Friends,* No. XVIII. The addressee, though Dodsley does not name him, I am inclined to think is Jago. According to Dodsley, Letters 14, 19, 25, and 30 are to the same person. There is nothing in any of these four letters to fix the identity of the addressee beyond question.

significancy, and that both the one and the other are what you may as well do without. — My letter is as follows.

You must know, in rainy weather, I always soothe my melancholy with the remembrance of *distant* friends only; you cannot easily conceive the high value I place upon their good qualities at such a time; so that at this very instant I am *impatient* to see you. To-morrow, if the sun shines bright, I shall only *wish* for your company as for a *very great good*. If you are unemployed when you leave Bath, I should think, you might stay some time with me this summer. Refined sense is what one is apt to value one's self upon; but really, unless one has a refined soul or two to converse with, it is an inconvenience. I have ruined my happiness by conversing with you and a few more friends; as Falstaff says to Hal, "Company, *witty* company, has been the ruin of me!" Before I knew that pleasure, I was as contented as could be in my solitude; and *now*, the *absence* of *entertainment* is a *positive* pain to me. London has amused me awhile with diversions; but now they are past, and I have neither any one about me that *has* the least *delicatesse*, or that I can inspire with the *ambition of having any*. — W—— W—— comes in a *dirty shirt*, and an old coat, without a stock, to pay me a visit. He pulled out a pair of scissars, and, giving them an intricate turn over his two thumbs, said, that *he* could do that, and I could make a poem; some for *one* thing, some for another:

> Hic nigrae succus loliginis, haec est
> Aerugo mera.[2]

It was *splenetic* weather *too*. — The man is curst who writes verses, and lives in the country. — If his *celestial* part inspires him to converse with Juno, his *terrestrial* one necessitates him to stoop to his landlady; so that he is in as disagreeable a situation, as if one person were to pull him upwards by the *head*, and another downwards by the *tail*. — Do you never find any thing of this? — I mean, that your *pride* and your *social* qualities torture you with their *different* attractions? Indeed one would always give way to the last, but that few are familiarity-proof, few but whom it teaches to despise one. Albeit I am conscious of the bad influence of freedom myself; yet, whilst it tends to discover wit, humour, and sense, it only renders me more and more

Your most obedient friend and servant,
W. Shenstone

[2] This passage, if *literally* translated, would read thus: — This is the juice of a black fish, this is mere rust; but in the *metaphorical* meaning of Horace, the first is used as *Envy*, the latter as bitter or reproachful words. [Dodsley]

15. To RICHARD JAGO[1]

[July 22, 1741]

Well! and so I sat me down in my room, and was reading *Pamela* — one might furnish this book with several pretty decorations, thought I to myself; and then I began to design cuts for it, in particular places. For instance, one, where Pamela is forced to fall upon her knees in the arbour: a second, where she is in bed, and Mrs. Jewkes holds one hand, and Mr. B. the other: a third, where Pamela sits sewing in the summer-house, &c. So I just sketched them out, and sent my little hints, such as they were, to Mr. R[ichardso]n. As soon as I had sealed my letter, in comes Mrs. Arnold[2] — "Well, Mrs. Arnold, says I, this Mr. Jago never comes — what can one do? I'm as dull as a beetle for want of company." "Sir, says she, the hen — " "What makes you out of breath? says I, Mrs. Arnold; what's the matter?" "Why, Sir, says she, the hen that I set last-sabbath-day-was-three-weeks has just hatched, and has brought all her eggs to good." "That's brave, indeed, says I." "Ay, that it is, says she so be and 't please G—d an how that they liven, there'll be a glorious parcel of 'em. Shall I bring 'em up for you to see? says she." "No, thank ye, Mrs. Arnold, says I; but aren't ye in some apprehensions from the kite, Mrs. Arnold?" — "No, Sir, says she, I hope there's no danger; I *takes* pretty good care of 'em." "I don't question your care, says I; for you're seldom without a duck or a chicken about you." — "Poor pretty *creters!* says she; look here, Master, this has gotten a speck of black upon her tail." — "Ay, I thought you weren't without one about you, says I — I don't think, says I, Mrs. Arnold, but your soul was design'd for a hen originally." "Why, and if I *had* been a hen, says she, I believe I should have done as much for my chickens as yonder great black-and-white hen does, tho' I say't that shou'd not say't, said she." Aye, that you would, thought I. "Well, but now when Mr. Jago comes, have you got e'er a chicken that's *fit to kill?*" "No, says she, I doubt there is ne'er-a-one." "Well, says I, Mrs. Arnold, you and your chicken may go down; I am going to write a letter." So I sat down, and wrote thus far: scrattle, scrattle, goes the pen — why how now? says I — what's the matter with the pen? So I thought I would make an end of my letter, because my pen went scrattle, scrattle. Well, I warrant I shall have little pleasure when

---

[1] Dodsley, *Letters to Particular Friends*, No. II, dated 1739. Wells corrects the date, *Anglia*, 35:430. Richardson's *Pamela*, which this letter parodies, was published in November, 1740.

[2] His house-keeper, of whom very respectful mention is made in the course of this correspondence. [Dodsley]

Mr. Jago *comes;* for I never fixed my heart much upon anything in my life, but some misfortune happened to balance my pleasure. — After all, thought I, it must be some very ill accident that outweighs the pleasure I shall take in seeing him.

W. Shenstone

Leasowes, July 22

16. To RICHARD JAGO [1]

Leasowes, Aug. 28 [1741]

DEAR MR. JAGO,

I find some difficulty in writing to you on this melancholy occasion. No one can be more unfit to attempt to lessen your grief than myself, because no one has a deeper sense of the *cause* of your affliction. Though I would by no means be numbered by you amongst the common herd of your acquaintance that tell you they are sorry, yet it were impertinent in me to mention a mere friend's concern to a person interested by so many more tender regards. Besides, I should be glad to alleviate your sorrow, and such sort of condolence tends but little to promote that end. I do not chuse to flatter you; neither could I, more especially at this time; but though I could perhaps find enough to say to persons of less sense than you, I know of nothing but what your own reason must have suggested. Concern indeed may have suspended the power of that faculty; and upon that pretence, I have a few things that I would suggest to you. After all, it is time alone that *can* and *will* cure *all* afflictions but such as are the consequence of vice; and yours, I am sure, proceeds from a *contrary* principle.

I heard accidentally of this sorrowful event, and accompanied you to London with the utmost concern. I wished it was in my power to mitigate your griefs by sharing them, as I have often found it in yours to augment my pleasures by so doing.

All that I can recommend to you is, not to confine your eye to any single event in life, but to take in your whole circumstances before you repine.

When you reflect that you have lost one of the best of men in a father, you ought to comfort yourself that you had such a father: to whom I cannot forbear applying these lines from Milton:

---

[1] Dodsley, *Letters to Particular Friends,* No. VII, dated 1740. Wells corrects the date, *Anglia,* 35:435. Jago's father, rector of Beaudesert, Henley-in-Arden, died in 1741.

> Since to part!
> Go, heavenly guest, ethereal messenger!
> Sent by whose sovereign goodness we adore!
> Gentle to me and affable has been
> Thy condescension, and shall be honour'd ever
> With grateful'st memory —
> > End of Book VIII. PAR. LOST. [ll. 645–50]

I would have you by all means come over hither as soon as you can. I will endeavour to render the time you spend *here* as satisfactory as it is in my power; and I hope you will ever look upon me as your hearty friend, through all the vicissitudes of life.

Pray give my humble service to Mrs. Jago and your brother.

I am, with the utmost affection,
Yours sincerely,
W. Shenstone

17. To RICHARD GRAVES[1]

The Leasowes, Sept. 23, 1741

DEAR SIR,

I was very agreeably entertained by your last letter, as indeed I am by every one of yours. It were affectation to except a paragraph or two on account of partiality, where, to say the truth, the partiality itself pleases one. This I am very positive of, that to have a friend of your temper and taste will always give me pleasure, whether I please the world or no; but to please ever so much, without some such friendship, would in all probability signify but little. I shall, therefore, value any means that tend to confirm my opinion of your esteem for me, preferably to any that shew me I am merely deserving of it. After all, though a very limited number of *friends* may be sufficient, an idle person should have a large *acquaintance;* and I believe I have the least of any one that ever rambled about so much as I have done. I do not know how it is, but I absolutely despair of ever being introduced into the world. It may be objected by some (but you will not object it,) that I may be acquainted with a sufficient number of people that are my *equals,* if I *will*. They may be my *equals* and *superiors* whom they mean, for aught I care; but their conversation gives me no more pleasure than the *canking* of a goose, or the quacking of a duck, in affluent circumstances: rather *less* indeed of the two, because the idea of the fat goose flatters one's appetite; but the *human goose* is neither fit to be heard nor eaten. I wish indeed to be *shewn into* good company;

---
[1] Dodsley, *Letters to Particular Friends*, No. XV.

but, if I can at all distinguish the nature of my inclinations, it is more in hopes of meeting with a refined conversation, than any thing else. I do not at all insist that my genius is *better* than that of my vociferous neighbours; if it is *different,* it is a sufficient reason why I should seek such companions as suit it: and whether they are found in high or low life, is little to the purpose. But you will perhaps discern the operations of *vanity* in all my endeavours; I will not disagree with you, provided you will allow *amusement* an equal share in them. It is the vanity to be intimate with men of distinguished sense, not of distinguished fortune. And this is a vanity which you should not disapprove, because it will bind me a lasting friend to you and your family.

I have been over at Shiffnall, and, in order to make myself agreeable, rode a-hunting with Mr. Pitt.[2] I confess I was somewhat diverted; and my horse was so much an enthusiast, as to be very near running headlong into a deep water. I believe, if I were to turn sportsman, I should soon break my neck for fear the huntsman should despise me.

I will certainly endeavour to see you at Birmingham; but beg you would write me a long letter in the mean time; and contrive, if you can, to make it look like a packet as your last did, for the sight thereof is exceedingly comfortable.

Though my wishes will not suffer me to believe that your eyes are in the danger you represent; yet, supposing them to be only very weak, I would recommend some musical instrument that is most agreeable to you. I have often looked upon music as my dernier resort, if I should ever discard the world, and turn eremite entirely. Consider what other amusement can make an equal impression in old age.

I have filled my paper, not without difficulty, through the barrenness of my brain and situation: my heart ever flows with the most warm streams of gratitude and affection for you. Adieu!

W. S.

18. To a FRIEND [1]

1741

DEAR SIR,

I wonder I have not heard *from* you lately — *of* you indeed I have from Mr. W——. If you could come over, probably, I might go back

---

[2] Shenstone was acquainted with Pitt through the Lyttelton family of Hagley. The relations of the Lytteltons and Pitts are discussed at length by Maud Wyndham in her *Chronicles of the Eighteenth Century.*

[1] Dodsley, *Letters to Particular Friends,* No. XVI. The identity of the friend to whom this letter is addressed must, for the present at least, remain a matter of conjecture.

with you for a day or two; for my horse, I think, gets rather better, and may, with indulgence, perform such a journey. I want to advise with you about several matters: — to have your opinion about a *building* that I *have built,* and about a journey which I design to Bath; and about numberless things, which, as they are numberless, cannot be comprehended in this paper. I am,

Your most affectionate friend,
W. Shenstone

Now I am come home from a visit — every little uneasiness is sufficient to introduce my whole train of melancholy considerations, and to make me utterly dissatisfied with the life I now lead, and the life which I foresee I shall lead. I am angry, and envious, and dejected, and frantic, and disregard all present things, just as becomes a madman to do. I am infinitely pleased (though it is a gloomy joy) with the application of Dr. Swift's complaint, "that he is forced to die in a rage, like a poisoned rat in a hole." My soul is no more suited to the figure I make, than a cable rope to a cambric needle: — I cannot bear to see the advantages alienated, which I think I could deserve and relish so much more than those that have them. — Nothing can give me patience but the soothing sympathy of a friend, and *that* will only turn my rage into simple melancholy. — I believe soon I shall bear to see nobody. I *do* hate all hereabouts already, except one or two. I will have my *dinner* brought upon my table in my absence, and the plates fetched away in my absence; and nobody shall see me: for I can never bear to appear in the same stupid mediocrity for years together, and gain no ground. As Mr. G——[2] complained to me (and, I think, you too, both unjustly,) "I am no character." — I have in my temper some rakishness, but it is checked by want of spirits; some solidity, but it is softened by vanity; some esteem of learning, but it is broke in upon by laziness, imagination, and want of memory, &c. — I could reckon up twenty things throughout my whole circumstances wherein I am thus tantalized. Your fancy will present them. — Not that all I say here will signify to *you:* I am only under a fit of dissatisfaction, and to grumble does me good — only excuse me, that I cure myself at your expence. Adieu!

[2] Probably Richard Graves.

19. To RICHARD JAGO[1]

The Leasowes, Nov. 25, 1741

DEAR SIR,

The reason why I write to you so suddenly is, that I have a proposal to make to you. If you could contrive to be in London for about a month from the end of December, I imagine you would spend it agreeably enough along with me, Mr. Outing,[2] and Mr. Whistler. According to my calculations, we should be a very happy party at a play, coffee-house, or tavern. Do not let your supercilious friends come in upon you with their prudential maxims. Consider, you are now of the proper age for pleasure, and have not above four or five whimsical years left. You have not struck one bold stroke yet, that I know of. Saddle your mule, and let us be jogging to the great city. I will be answerable for amusement. — Let me have the pleasure of seeing you in the pit, in a laughter as cordial and singular as your friendship. Come — let us go forth into the opera-house; let us hear how the eunuch-folk sing. Turn your eye upon the lillies and roses, diamonds and rubies; the Belindas and the Sylvias of gay life! Think upon Mrs. Clive's inexpressible comicalness; not to mention Hippelsley's[3] joke-abounding physiognomy! Think, I say, *now;* for the time cometh when you shall say, "I have no pleasure in them."

I am conscious of much merit in bringing about the interview betwixt Mr. L—— and Mr. S——;[4] but merit, as Sir John Falstaff says, is not regarded in these coster-monger days.

Pray now do not write me word that your *business* will not allow you *ten minutes* in a fortnight to write to me; an excuse fit for none but a cobler, who has ten children dependent upon a waxen thread. Adieu!

W. S.

20. To RICHARD GRAVES[1]

The Leasowes,
the Day before Christmas [1741]

DEAR SIR,

Though your last letter seemed to put my correspondence upon an ostentatious footing, namely, an inclination to be witty, yet I assure you

---

[1] Dodsley, *Letters to Particular Friends*, No. XIX. The identity of the addressee is somewhat doubtful; it appears to be Jago.
[2] A friend of Lady Luxborough's, who seems at times to have acted as her secretary. See numerous allusions to him in her *Letters*.
[3] John Hippisley (d. 1748), actor and dramatist, noted mainly as a comedian.
[4] George Lyttelton and William Somervile, whom Shenstone wished to bring together for their mutual advantage. See Letter 7 above.
[1] Dodsley, *Letters to Particular Friends*, No. XXIII, dated 1742. Wells corrects the date, *Anglia*, 35:441.

it was not any punctilious consideration of that kind that has kept me so long silent. Indeed with some people one would stand upon the nicest punctilios; for though ceremony be altogether lighter than vanity itself, yet it surely weighs as much as the acquaintance of the undeserving. But this is trifling, because it can have no reference to a person for whom I have the greatest affection.

In regard to my Oxford affairs, you did all I could expect. I have wrote since to Mr. M——, who, either for your sake or mine, will, I dare say, settle them to my satisfaction.

I wish your journey and head-ach would have permitted you to have been a little more particular concerning the seat of the Muses; but I suppose nothing material distinguished your fortnight.

Mr. Whistler has relapsed at Whitchurch; but purposed, when I last heard from him, to go to London before this time. I do not entirely understand his schemes, but should have been sincerely glad of his company with me this winter; and, he says, he is not fond of London. — For my part, I designed to go thither the next month, but the fever (which is chiefly violent in towns) discourages me.

Some time ago, I read Spenser's Fairy Queen; and, when I had finished, thought it a proper time to make some additions and corrections in my trifling imitation of him, The School-mistress.[2] — His subject is certainly bad, and his action inexpressibly confused; but there are some particulars in him that charm one. Those which afford the greatest scope for a ludicrous imitation are his simplicity and obsolete phrase; and yet these are what give one a very singular pleasure in the perusal. The burlesque which they occasion is of a quite different kind to that of Philip's Shilling, Cotton's Travestie, Hudibras, or Swift's works; but I need not tell *you* this. I inclose a copy, for your amusement and opinion; which, if franks are plentiful, you may return, and save me the *tedious* trouble of writing it over again. The other paper was, *bona fide,* written to divert my thoughts from pain, for the same reason that I smoaked; actions equally reputable.

Mr. Somervile's poem upon hawking, called, "Field Sports,"[3] I sup-

---

[2] *The School-Mistress* first appeared as a poem of twelve stanzas in Shenstone's earliest volume, *Poems upon Various Occasions* (1737), which the author was at considerable pains to suppress. In 1742 he published through Dodsley a revised version in twenty-eight stanzas, which appeared again in the first volume of Dodsley's *Collection* January 15, 1748. In Dodsley's second edition, December, 1748, the poem reappeared, with numerous verbal changes, in practically its final form of thirty-five stanzas, and it so appears in Shenstone's *Works,* Vol. I (1764). A type-facsimile of the 1742 edition was issued by the Oxford University Press in 1924.

[3] Published January, 1742.

pose, is out by this time. It was sent to Mr. Lyttelton, to be read to the Prince, to whom it was inscribed. It seems, he is fond of hawking.

I have often thought those to be the most enviable people whom one least envies—I believe, married men are the happiest that are; but I cannot say I envy them, because they lose all their merit in the eyes of other ladies.

I beg sincerely that you would write in a week's time at furthest, that I may receive your letter *here* if I should go from home this winter. I will never use any thing by way of conclusion, but your old Roman
Farewel!
W. Shenstone

21. To RICHARD GRAVES [1]

The Leasowes, Jan. 19, 1741–2

DEAR MR. GRAVES,

I cannot forbear immediately writing to you: the pleasure your last letter gave me put it out of my power to restrain the overflowings of my benevolence. I can easily conceive that, upon some extraordinary instances of friendship, my heart might be *si fort attendri,* that I could not bear any restraint upon my ability to shew my gratitude. It is an observation I made upon reading to-day's paper, which contains an account of C. Khevenhuller's success in favour of the Queen of Hungary.[2] To think what sublime affection must influence that poor unfortunate Queen, should a faithful and zealous General revenge her upon her enemies, and restore her ruined affairs!

Had a person shewn an esteem and affection for *me,* joined with any elegance, or without any elegance, in the expression of it, I should have been in acute pain till I had given some sign of my willingness to serve him.—From *all* this, I conclude that I have more humanity than some others.

Probably enough I shall never meet with a larger share of happiness than I feel at present. If not, I am thoroughly convinced, my pain is greatly superior to my pleasure. That pleasure is not absolutely dependent on the mind, I know from this, that I have enjoyed happier scenes in the company of some friends than I can possibly at present; — but alas! all the time you and I shall enjoy together, abstracted from the rest of our lives, and lumped, will not perhaps amount to a solid year and a half. How small a proportion!

[1] Dodsley, *Letters to Particular Friends,* No. XXII. Wells confirms the date, *Anglia,* 35:441.
[2] See the *Gentleman's Magazine,* January, 1742, p. 54, and the *London Magazine,* same date, p. 51.

People will say to one that talks thus "Would you die?" To set the case upon a right footing, they must take away the hopes of greater happiness in *this* life, the fears of greater misery hereafter, together with the bodily *pain* of dying, and address me in a disposition betwixt mirth and melancholy; and I could easily resolve them.[3]

I do not know how I am launched out so far into this complaint: it is, perhaps, a strain of constitutional whining; the effect of the wind — did it come from the winds? to the winds will I deliver it:

> Tradam protervis in mare Creticum,
> Portare ventis —

I will be as happy as my fortune will permit, and make others so:

> Pone me pigris ubi *nulla campis*
> *Arbor* aestiva recreatur aura —

I will be so. — The joke is, that the description which you gave of that country was, that you had few trees about you; so that I should *trick* Fortune if she should grant my petition implicitly. But, in earnest, I intend to come and stay a day or two with you next summer.

Mr. Whistler is at Mr. Gosling's, bookseller, at the Mitre and Crown, in Fleet-street, and enquired much after you in his last letter to me. He writes to me; but I believe his affection for one weighs less with him while the town is in the other scale; though he is very obliging. I do not know whether I do right, when I say I believe we three, that is, in solitary circumstances, have an equal idea of, and affection for, each other. I say, supposing each to be alone, or in the country, which is nearly the same; for scenes alter minds as much as the air influences bodies. For instance, when Mr. Whistler is in town, I suppose we love him better than he does us; and when we are in town, I suppose the same may be said in regard to him.

The true burlesque of Spenser (whose characteristic is simplicity) seems to consist in a *simple* representation of such things as one laughs to *see* or to *observe* one's self, rather than in any *monstrous* contrast betwixt the thoughts and words. I cannot help thinking that my added stanzas[4] have more of his manner than what you saw before, which you are not a judge of till you have read him.

W. S.

[3] This passage is nearly identical with one in Shenstone's *Essays on Men and Manners* (1764), p. 249. It would seem that Shenstone sometimes transcribed passages from his letters to his notebooks, or from his notebooks to his letters.
[4] See above, Letter 20, n2.

22. To RICHARD GRAVES[1]

*From Mr. Shuckburgh's, Bookseller,
in Fleet-street, your Brother's Lodgings
[London, Feb., 1742]*

DEAR MR. GRAVES,

I have just been spending my evening at a coffee-house; and, notwithstanding the confused effect of liquor, am sitting down to write to a person of the clearest head I know. The *truth* is, I write to please *myself,* which I can do no other way so effectually; upon which account, you are not obliged to me for the *advances* I make in correspondence. Extraordinary things will be expected from my *situation;* but extraordinary things ought never to be expected from *me.* I keep no political company, nor *desire* any, as, I believe, you know. If you enquire after the stage, — I have not seen Garrick; but, more fortunately for *you,* your brother *has.* Me nothing has so much transported as young Cibber's *exhibition* of Parolles, in Shakespear's *"All's well that ends well."* The character is admirably written by the author; and, I fancy, I can discover a great number of hints which it has afforded to Congreve in his Bluff.[2] I am apt to think a person, after he is twelve years old, laughs annually less and less: less heartily, however; which is much the same. I think Cibber elicited from me as sincere a laugh as I can ever recollect. Nothing, sure, can be comparable to his representation of Parolles in his bully-character; except the figure he makes as a shabby gentleman. In his first dress he is tawdry, as you may imagine: in the last, he wears a rusty black coat, a black stock, a black wig with a Ramillie, a pair of black gloves; and a face! — which causes five minutes laughter. — Instead of politics, I have transcribed these epigrams from the Evening Post — though I hate transcribing:

THE CHOICE, TO SIR ROBERT [WALPOLE]

When opposition against power prevail'd;
When artful eloquence and bribery fail'd;
Timely you quit the ship you could not steer,
Disdain the commons, and ascend a peer:
Conscious that you deserve to *bleed* or *swing,*
You chuse the axe as nobler than the string.

---

[1] Dodsley, *Letters to Particular Friends,* No. XXVII, dated "about 1743." Wells corrects the date, *Anglia,* 35:442–43.
[2] *The Old Batchelor* (1693)

With huge Antaeus as Alcides strove,
The son of Neptune one, and one of Jove,
Oft as he threw the giant on the ground,
His strength redoubled by the fall he found.
Th' unwieldy monster, sprung of mother Earth,
From *her* had vigour, as from her he'd birth;
Enrag'd the hero a new method tries;
High lifts in air, and, as he mounts, he dies.

I think the last a good thought; the first not a bad one, and what I have had in my head a thousand times. I saw Mr. Fitzherbert at Nando's, but chose not to reconnoitre him there, though to ask after *you*. I propose waiting on him at his lodgings for the same end. Pray write soon to me. I wish I could say more to deserve it from you — I would fain deviate from the common road in every letter I send you; but am so very uniformly your friend, that I cannot vary my manner of expressing how *much* I am so, which is all my letters aim at. Adieu!

W. Shenstone

23. To MR. REYNOLDS[1]

[London, Mar. 9, 1742]

DEAR SIR,

I thank you for the favour of your last letter, particularly your readiness in transmitting to me any thing of Mr. Somervile's. It so fell out, that Mr. Outing delivered to me the verses, and I had the pleasure of reading them, about a moment before he gave me your epistle.

The town expected something of importance, namely, a motion for a committee of enquiry into late measures, would be moved for to-day. If any thing of this nature has been carrying on, I will add an account of it before I close my letter. In the mean time it is, I believe, very credible, that Lord Orford has a continued influence over the King; and that the Duke of Argyle is sufficiently disgusted, to have talked of the resignation of his posts again.

An odd story enough the following, and I believe true! Somebody, that had just learnt that H——e W——'s gentleman's name was Jackson, writes a letter to Mr. Floyer, Keeper of the Tower, intimating his master's desire to speak with him. Floyer dresses the next morning, and waits upon H——e, comes into his room — "Sir, says H——e, I really don't

---

[1] Dodsley, *Letters to Particular Friends,* No. X, dated 1740. Wells corrects the date, *Anglia,* 35:436–37.

know you—" "Sir, my name is Floyer—" "Ay, by G——d, that may be; but, by G——d, I don't know you for all that—" "Sir, says he, I am Keeper of the Tower—" "G——d d——n your blood, says H——e, produce your warrant; d——n you, produce your warrant; or, by G——d, I'll kick ye down stairs—"

Frighted at these threats, the gentleman retired; and in his way home had leisure to consider the joke that was put upon him, and more particularly turned upon the person to whom he was sent.

If you direct a line to Mr. Shuckburgh's, bookseller, in Fleet-street, it will arrive agreeable to

Your humble servant,
W. Shenstone

March,
Tuesday night
My compliments to your patron.[2]

24. To RICHARD JAGO [1]

[London, after March, 1742]

DEAR SIR,

As I have no sort of library in town, I find several minutes upon my hands, for which, if I employ them in scribbling to my friends, they are but *slenderly obliged* to me. I hope no friend of mine will ever be induced, by my *example,* to do any thing but avoid it; I believe no one breathing can say with more truth, "Video meliora, &c." It is not from a spirit of jealousy that I would advise my acquaintance to seek happiness in the regular path of a fixed life. But, though I very highly approve it, and envy it, my particular turn of mind would be as little satisfied with it as it is like to be in a *different* one. Yet, however I *complain,* I must own I have a good deal reconciled myself to this mixture of gratification and disappointment, which must be my lot till the last totally prevails.

Yet, after all, to tell you the truth, I am not pleased with being advised to retire. I was saying the other day to Mr. Outing, that I *had* been ambitious more than I was at present, and that I grew less so every day. Upon this he chimed in with me, and approved my despondency; saying, "that *he* also had been ambitious, but found it would not do." Do you think I liked him much for this? — no — I wheeled about, and said, "I did not think with him; for I should always find myself whetted by disappointments, and more violent in proportion to the intricacy of the

---

[2] Apparently Lord Somervile, whose chaplain Reynolds was.
[1] Dodsley, *Letters to Particular Friends,* No. XIII, dated 1741. Wells corrects the date, *Anglia,* 35:437–39.

game." I spent a night with him and Mr. Meredith, and with him and Mr. Dean: in the latter party he had laid his hand upon his sword six times, and *threatened to put a dozen men to death,* one of which was Broughton² the prize-fighter. — Mr. Whistler's company seldom *relieves* me on an evening; and I go to plays but *seldom,* because I intend no more to *give countenance* to the *pit.* — I have got a belt!!! which distinguishes me as much as a *garter* — it captivates the eyes of all beholders, and binds their understandings in golden bandage. — I heard a pedant punning upon the word βέλτιστος; and a wag whispering that I was related to *Beltishazzar.* In short I may say, from the Dragon of Wantley,³

> No girdle, nor belt, e'er excell'd it;
> It frightens the men in a minute:
> No maiden yet ever beheld it,
> But wish'd herself tied to me in it.

The Dunciad⁴ is, doubtless, Mr. Pope's dotage, τοῦ Διὸς ἐνύπνια; flat in the whole, and including, with several tolerable lines, a *number* of weak, obscure, and even punning ones. What is now read by the *whole world,* and the *whole world's wife,* is, Mr. Hervey's Letter to Sir T. Hanmer.⁵ I own my *taste* is gratified in it, as well as that *unluckiness* natural to every one; though people say (I think idly) he is mad. For this *long* letter I shall expect *two,* soon after you have received it. Adieu!

Did you see a poem, called "Woman in Miniature," written with spirit, but incorrect? The people that were carrying Lord Orford⁶ in effigy, to behead him on Tower-Hill, came into the box where he was, accidentally, at George's to beg money of him, amongst others.

25. To RICHARD JAGO¹

[London, 1742]

DEAR SIR,

I trust you do not pay double postage for my levity in inclosing these decorations. If I find you do, I will not send you the *thatch'd-house* and

---

² John Broughton (1705–89) established a theater for boxing in Hanway Street in 1742. He was beaten by Slack in 1750.
³ This ballad appeared in Percy's *Reliques.*
⁴ A new edition of *The Dunciad* was advertised in the *Gentleman's Magazine* for March, 1742, p. 168.
⁵ Thomas Hervey's *Letter to Sir Thomas Hanmer* was published as a pamphlet about April 1, 1742.
⁶ Walpole became Earl of Orford February 9, 1742.
¹ Dodsley, *Letters to Particular Friends,* No. XX, dated 1741. Wells corrects the date, *Anglia,* 35:440. The letter evidently was written just before the publication of *The School-Mistress,* May 15, 1742. The addressee, though unnamed, is apparently Jago.

the birch-tree, with the sun setting, and gilding the scene—I expect a cargo of franks; and then for the beautiful picture of Lady Gainsborough, and the deformed portrait of my old school-dame Sarah Lloyd! whose house is to be seen as thou travelest towards the native home of thy faithful servant—but she sleeps with her fathers and is buried with her fathers—and Thomas her son *reigneth* in her stead!—I have the first sheet to correct upon the table. I have laid aside the thoughts of fame a good deal in this *un-promising* scheme; and fix them upon the landskip which is engraving, the red letter which I purpose, and the fruit-piece which you see, being the most seemly ornaments of the first sixpenny pamphlet that was ever so highly honoured. I shall incur the same reflection with Ogilby, of having nothing good but my decorations.

I have been walking in the Mall to-night.—The *Duke* was there, and was highly delighted with two dogs; and stared at me more enormously than ever Duke did before. I do not know for what reason; unless for the same which made him admire the *other* puppy-dogs, because they were large ones.

I expect that in your neighbourhood, and in Warwickshire there should be about twenty of my poems sold. I print it myself.[2] I am not satisfied about mottoes. That printed is this, "O qua sol habitabiles illustrat oras, maxime principum!" It must be short, on account of the plate. I do not know but I may adhere to a very insignificant one:

> En erit ergo
> Ille dies, mihi cum liceat *tua* dicere facta!

I am pleased with Mynde's[3] engravings; and I can speak without affectation, that fame is not *equally* in my thoughts.—One caution I gave to Mr. G——,[4] and it is what I would give to all my friends with whom I wish my intimacy may continue so much as I wish it may with you. Though I could bear the *disregard* of the town, I could not bear to see my friends alter their opinion which they say they have of what I write, though millions contradict them. It is an obstinacy which *I* can boast of, and they that have more sense may surely insist on the liberty of judging for themselves. If *you* should faulter, I should say you did not deserve your *capacity* to judge for yourself. Write soon—you never are at a fault— "tantummodo *incepto* opus est, cætera res expediet." Adieu!

W. S.

---

[2] Dodsley merely acted as Shenstone's agent.
[3] James Mynde, the London engraver.
[4] Probably Graves.

26. To RICHARD GRAVES[1]

[London, May 17 or 18, 1742]

DEAR MR. GRAVES!

I depended a good deal on an immediate answer from you, and am greatly fearful you never received a packet of little things which I sent you at Oxford, inclosed in a frank; though, if it arrived at all, it must have arrived several days before you left it. I beseech you to send me a line upon the receipt of these, which will free me from much perplexity; though it is doubtful whether I can defer my schemes so as to make your criticisms of service. I would have you send them notwithstanding.

I cannot help considering myself as a sportsman (though God knows how poor a one in every sense!) and the company as my game. They *fly up* for a little time; and then *settle* again. My cue, is to discharge my *piece* when I observe a number together. This week, they are straggling round about their pasture, the town; the next, they will flock into it with violent appetites; and then I discharge my little piece amongst them. — I assure you, I shall be very easy about the acquisition of any fame by this thing; all I much wish is, to lose none: and indeed I have so little to lose, that this consideration scarcely affects me.

I dare say it must be very incorrect; for I have added eight or ten stanzas within this fortnight. But inaccuracy is more excusable in ludicrous poetry than in any other. If it strikes *any*, it must be merely people of *taste*; for people of *wit* without taste (which comprehends the larger part of the critical tribe) will unavoidably despise it. I have been at some pains to secure myself from A. Phillips's misfortune, of mere *childishness,* "Little charm of placid mien, &c." I have added a ludicrous index, purely to shew (fools) that I am in jest; and my motto, "O qua sol habitabiles illustrat oras, maxime principum," is calculated for the same purpose. You cannot conceive how large the number is of those that mistake burlesque for the very foolishness it exposes (which observation I made once at The Rehearsal, at Tom Thumb, at Chrononhotonthologos;[2] all which are pieces of elegant humour). I have some mind to pursue this caution further; and advertise it, "The School-mistress, &c." A very *childish* performance every body knows (*novorum more.*) But if a person seriously calls this, or rather burlesque, a childish or low species of poetry, he says wrong; for the most regular and formal poetry may be called trifling, folly, and weakness, in comparison of what is written with a more *manly*

---

[1] Dodsley, *Letters to Particular Friends,* No. XXV, not dated. Wells supplies the date, *Anglia,* 35:442.

[2] Buckingham's play (1671). Fielding's *Tom Thumb* (1730) was revised and renamed *The Tragedy of Tragedies* (1731). Henry Carey's burlesque appeared in 1734.

spirit in ridicule of it. — I have been plagued to death about the ill execution of my designs. — Nothing is certain in London, but expence, which I can ill bear. Believe me, *till death,*

Yours, sincerely and particularly,
W. Shenstone

27. To the HONOURABLE MRS. KNIGHT[1]

[London, May, 1742]

Madam,

A Lady whose conversation is ever discovering somewhat new & agreeable, may possibly find some Amusement in a Subject that is new, tho' with no other Recommendation. Tis upon this Account that I beg your Acceptance of this grotesque Poem.

I took great Pleasure in seeing ye Piping Faunus at Rackstrow's, because, as it is certainly a genteel Design, it must needs prove agreeable to Mrs. Knight. Connoiseurs wou'd chuse to have his musical Intention express'd as it is at present by the Posture merely; if the Pipe was added 'twou'd be more obviously agreeable. If I might presume to advise, it shou'd be to calculate it in some Degree for Tastes less refin'd y^n your own, because there are millions of the former Species to perhaps one or two of the latter, & I know you take a superiour Pleasure in ye Satisfaction of others.

Trifles light as Air, or as ye Poem I am sending, acquire a fresh weight with me, as often as they give me an occasion of assuring you that I am, Madam,

Your most oblig'd & obedient h^{ble} Servant,
W. Shenstone

Nando's Coffee-House near Temple-Bar. May

The Share I had of y^t con: in Town was very agreeble to me & fortunate in it's consequences, as it gives me some Pretence for ye freedom of presenting you wth this little poem, & of assuring you y^t I am[2]

---

[1] This letter to Mrs. Knight, later (1746) Lady Luxborough, appears in Hull's *Select Letters,* Vol. I, No. XIII. A manuscript differing from Hull's version in only a few minor details is in the Yale University Library. The postscript is in the manuscript but not in Hull. Although only the month is given, the year is pretty evidently 1742. Of Lady Luxborough's *Letters,* the third, dated May 29, 1742, is obviously the answer to this, and the "grotesque poem" referred to at the end of the first paragraph is plainly *The School-Mistress.*

[2] This little passage, written upside down at the top of the first page of the manuscript, may be a postscript (Shenstone often wrote postscripts so), or it may be further evidence in support of Mr. Fullington's theory concerning rough and finished drafts; other fragmen-

28. To a FRIEND[1]

[London, June, 1742]

DEAR SIR,

You must give me leave to complain of your last letter, three parts of which is filled with mere apology: I thought we had some time agreed, for our mutual emolument, to lay aside ceremonies of this species, till I was made Poet-laureat, and you Bishop of Winchester. — Why Bishop of Winchester, for God's sake? Why — because — he is Prelate of the Garter — an order, in all kinds of ceremony so greatly abounding. — Here am I still, trifling away my time, my money, and, I think, my health, which I fancy greatly inferior to what it would be in the country. Truth is, I do make shift to vary my days a little here; and, calling to mind the many irksome hours, the stupid identity, of which I have been so often sick in the country, I conclude that I am less *unhappy* than I shall find myself at home. — However, next month I hope to see The Leasowes with an appetite. — Walks in the Park are now delightfully pleasant: the company stays in the Mall till ten every night. — Mrs. Clive, Mrs. Woffington, Barbarini, and Mr. Garrick (happy man!) are gone over to Ireland, to act there for two months. — Mr. Outing, the last time I saw him, told me how Dr. Mackenzie cured him of ever fighting with scrubs, &c. "I was just going, says he, to kick a fellow down stairs, when the Doctor cries out, 'Mr. Outing! hear our Scotch proverb before you proceed any farther; — He that wrestles with a t——d, whether he get or lose the victory, is sure to be b——f——t.' I had great difficulty (continued he) to contain myself till he had finished his story, but I found it so pat that it saved the fellow's neck." I wish *I* could *cure* him as easily of these Quixotical narrations — I know no soul in town that *has* any taste, which occasions me the spleen frequently. I remember W—— and I were observing, that no creatures, though ever so loathsome (as toads, serpents, adders, &c.), would be half so hated as ourselves, if we were to give vent to our spleen, and censure affections so bluntly as some people do. I would not venture this hint, if I did not believe you experience the same. For my part, people contradict me in things I have *studied,* and am *certain* of; and I keep silence even from *good words* (*bon mots*), though it is pain and grief to me. I must give up my *knowledge* to *pretence,* or vent it with *diffidence* to fools; or there is no peace. *These, these* are *justifiable* motives

---

tary writing on the manuscript, in Shenstone's hand, would suggest that this is one of the rough drafts.

[1] Dodsley, *Letters to Particular Friends,* No. XVII, dated 1741. Wells corrects the date, *Anglia,* 35:439–40. The identity of the addressee, evidently an intimate, is in doubt. It might be Jago.

to wish for some degree of fame; that blind people may not bully a man that has his eyesight into their opinion that green is red, &c. Deference from fools is no *invidious* ambition: I dare own to you that I *have* this; and I will contend that I have no more *haughty* one.—This subject I could expatiate upon with pleasure; but I stop: a tasteless fellow has spoiled my Mall-walk to night, and occasioned you some trouble in these dull observations.—I am

Yours affectionately,
W. Shenstone

29. To RICHARD GRAVES [1]

[London,] June, 1742

DEAR MR. GRAVES!

I am glad the stay you make in Herefordshire amuses you, even though it puts you upon preferring the place you reside at to my own place of residence. I do not know whether it be from the prejudice of being born at the Leasowes,[2] or from any real beauty in the situation; but I would wish no other, would some one, by an addition of two hundred pounds a year, put it in my power to exhibit my own designs. It is what I can now do in no other method than on paper. I live in such an un-oeconomical manner, that I must not indulge myself in the plantation of a tree for the future. I have glutted myself with the extremity of solitude, and must adapt my expences more to the sociable life. It is on this account that it seems more prudent for me to buy a chair while I am in town, than to carry down twelve guineas for the model of the tomb of Virgil, an urn, and a scheme or two more of like nature. — I long to have my picture, *distantly* approaching to a profile (the best manner I can think of to express myself,) drawn by Davison. I have seen your sister's, and think the *face* well done in every respect; but am greatly indignant with other things of a less fixed nature. The cap, though a good cap enough, has a vile effect; the formality of stays, &c. not agreeable — I do not know if you saw the picture of a Scotch girl there at full length? Miss Graves has the advantage of her's, or any picture there, in her person; but certainly this girl's hair is inexpressibly charming! there is the genteelest negligence in it I ever saw in any picture: — what follows, but that I wish your sister would give orders to pull off her cap, and have hair after the manner of this picture? — To speak abruptly; as it *is,* I disap-

---
[1] Dodsley, *Letters to Particular Friends,* No. XXIV.
[2] Shenstone really was born at the Leasowes and not at Wigstone. See Ward, "Shenstone's Birthplace," *Modern Language Notes,* November, 1936, p. 440.

prove it: were it altered, I should like it beyond any I ever saw. I am glad you are reading Spenser: though his plan is detestable, and his *invention* less wonderful than most people imagine, who do not much consider the obviousness of allegory; yet, I think, a person of your disposition must take great delight in his *simplicity,* his good-nature, &c. Did you observe a stanza that begins a canto somewhere,

> Nought is there under heav'n's wide hollowness
> That breeds, &c.?[3]

When I bought him first, I read a page or two of the Fairy Queen, and cared not to proceed. After that, Pope's Alley made me consider him ludicrously; and in that light, I think, one may read him with pleasure. I am now (as Ch——mley with ——), from trifling and laughing at him, really in love with him. I think even the metre pretty (though I shall never use it in earnest); and that the last Alexandrine has an extreme majesty. Does not this line strike you? (I do not justly remember what canto it is in)

> Brave thoughts and noble deeds did *evermore* inspire.[4]

Perhaps it is my fancy only that is enchanted with the running of it. Adieu!

W. S.

30. To RICHARD JAGO[1]

[London, just after July 19, 1742]

MY GOOD FRIEND,

Our old friend Somervile is dead! I did not imagine I could have been so sorry as I find myself on this occasion — "Sublatum quaerimus." I can now excuse all his foibles; impute them to age, and to distress of circumstances: the last of these considerations wrings my very soul to think on. For a man of high spirit, conscious of having (at least in one production) generally pleased the world, to be plagued and threatened by wretches that are low in every sense; to be forced to drink himself into pains of the body in order to get rid of the pains of the mind; is a misery which I can well conceive, because I may, without vanity, esteem myself his equal in point of oeconomy, and consequently *ought* to have an eye on his mis-

---

[3] Spenser, *The Faerie Queene*, Bk. I, Canto iii, st. 1, l. 1.
[4] *The Faerie Queene*, Bk. IV, Canto x, st. 26, l. 9. The last word is "aspire."
[1] Dodsley, *Letters to Particular Friends*, No. XXI, dated 1741. Wells corrects the date, *Anglia*, 35:440–41. The addressee, though unnamed, is apparently Jago.

fortunes: (As you kindly hinted to me about twelve o'clock at the Feathers) I should retrench; — I will; but you shall not see me: — I will not let you know that I took your hint in good part. I will do it at solitary times; as I may; and yet there will be some difficulty in it; for whatever the *world* might esteem in poor Somervile, I really find, upon critical inquiry, that *I* loved him for nothing so much as his flocci-nauci-nihili-pili-fication of money.

Mr. A—— was honourably acquitted:[2] Lord A——, who was present, and behaved very insolently they say, was hissed out of court. They proved his application to the carpenter's son, to get him to swear against Mr. A——, though the boy was proved to have said in several companies (*before* he had been kept at Lord A——'s house) that he was sure the thing was accidental. Finally, it is believed he will recover the title of A——ea.

The apprehension of the whores, and the suffocation of four in the round-house by the *stupidity* of the keeper, engrosses the talk of the town. The said house is re-building every day (for the mob on Sunday night demolished it), and re-demolished every night. The Duke of M[arlborou]gh, J[ohn] S[pencer] his brother, Lord C—— G——,[3] were taken into the round-house, and confined from eleven at night till eleven next day: I am not positive of the Duke of M[arlborou]gh; the others are certain: and that a large number of people of the first fashion went from the round-house to De Veil's, to give in informations of their usage. The justice himself seems greatly scared; the prosecution will be carried on with violence, so as probably to hang the keeper, and there is an end.

Lord Bath's coachman got drunk and tumbled from his box, and he was forced to borrow Lord Orford's. Wits say, that it was but gratitude for my Lord Orford's *coachman* to drive my Lord Bath, as my Lord Bath *himself* had driven my Lord Orford. Thus they.

I have ten million things to tell you; though they all amount to no more than that I wish to please you, and that I am
                      Your sincere friend and humble servant.
I am pleased that I can say I knew Mr. Somervile, which I am to thank you for.

---

[2] Mr. A——, James Annesley, tried for murder July 15, 1742. Lord A——, the Earl of Anglesey (Anglesea). A——ea, Anglesea. See *DNB* and Wells, *Anglia*, 35:441.
[3] Perhaps Lord George Graham. See the *Letters of Horace Walpole* (ed. Toynbee, Oxford, 1903), I, 259, Letter 89, to Horace Mann.

31. To RICHARD GRAVES[1]

[London, 1742]

DEAR MR. GRAVES,

Dr. Swift would not have scrupled to print your parody, with his name to it. Why should you, *without* your name? I had a violent inclination to print it in a large folio, four leaves, price four-pence: but I dare not do it, for fear you should think it of evil importance with regard to the clergy. You excel me infinitely in a way in which I take most pleasure; odd picturesque description. Send me word whether I shall print it or no — and that right soon. — I have lingered in town till now, and did not receive your letter till this morning. — I do not know whether I shall send you with this letter a little thing which I wrote in an afternoon, and, with proper *demands* of being concealed as the author, sold for two guineas. Next time I am in town, I will get money like a haberdasher. I will amuse myself with finding out the people's weak side, and so furnish them with *suitable nonsense.* — I would have you do the same. — Make your wit bear your charges. — Indeed, as to the little parody you send, it would fix your reputation with men of sense as much as (greatly more than) the whole tedious character of Parson Adams.[2] I read it half a year ago; the week after I came to town: but made Mr. Shuckburgh take it again, imagining it altogether a very mean performance. — I liked a tenth part pretty well; but, as Dryden says of Horace (unjustly), he shews his teeth without laughing: the greater part is *unnatural* and *unhumourous.* It has some advocates; but I observe, those not such as I ever esteemed tasters. Finally, what makes *you endeavour* to like it?

My printer was preparing his bill for the School-mistress, when I stopped him short, with a hint to go to Dodsley, who has not yet reckoned with me for Hercules. Let *the dead* bury their *dead.* Dr. Young's Complaint[3] is the best thing that has come out this season (these *twenty years,* Pope says) except mine, for so *thinks* every author, who does not think proper to say so: poor Pope's history in Cibber's Letter,[4] and the print of him upon the Mount of Love (the *coarsest* is most *humorous*), must surely mortify him. Your sister does me great honour to think my hint any thing; but I am quite zealous in my approbation of that Scotch

---

[1] Dodsley, *Letters to Particular Friends,* No. XXIX, dated 1743. Wells (*Anglia,* 35:443–44) fixes the date as August, 1742, at the latest.

[2] *Joseph Andrews* was noticed in the *Gentleman's Magazine,* Register of Books, February, 1742; a new edition was noticed in August.

[3] *The Complaint, or Night Thoughts on Life, Death, and Immortality,* I–IV, 1742.

[4] The first of Cibber's two letters to Pope, dated July 7, 1742.

lady's hair. I will *ever* aim at *oddness* for the future; it is cheaper to follow taste than fashion, and whoever he be that devotes himself to *taste* will be *odd* of course. — You send me the verses on Lord Ilay: they were hacked about town three months ago, and I saw them. The town is certainly the scene for a man of curiosity. — I do not purpose to be long away; but I must think of retrenching. — I have ten thousand things to tell you, but I have not room. Such people as *we* should meet as regularly to compare notes as tradesmen do to settle accounts, but oftener; there is no good comes of long reckonings; — I shall forget half — I think it should be four days in a fortnight — it would not do; — it would make one *mindful* of, and consequently more uneasy on account of, absence. Every one gets posts, preferments, but myself. — Nothing but my ambition can set me on a footing with them, and make me easy. Come then, lordly pride; &c. The devil thought with me in Milton,

>   *All* is not lost, th' unconquerable will,
>   And study never to submit or yield.[5]

I have been in new companies; but I see no reason to contradict my assertion, that I find none I like *equally* with *you*. Adieu!

W. Shenstone

32. To RICHARD GRAVES[1]

The Leasowes, Nov. 1742

DEAR SIR,

Presuming you may be at Tissington by this time, I write to solicit a description of the several adventures, accidents, and phaenomena, that have amused you in your travels; and will *equally* affect me as they relate to you. Above all things, be particular in regard to your calculations respecting Mickleton. I would have certainly met you there, as you desired me: there is no company I am fonder of than yours and your sister's; and no place at which I have spent more agreeable hours than Mickleton. But your brother has lost one of his recommendations in my eye; that is, his *irregularity* of house-keeping. He has several left which are sufficient to preserve my utmost esteem; but that was a jewel indeed! I love to go where there is nothing much more in form than myself. I have no objection to visit *young, unsettled people,* with a mountebank's inconsistency

---

[5] All is not lost — the unconquerable will,
And study of revenge, immortal hate,
And courage never to submit or yield:
    Paradise Lost, I, 106–08.
[1] Dodsley, *Letters to Particular Friends,* No. XXVI.

in my equipage. But where a considerable family keeps up its forms (as marriage requires), I should not care to appear with an hired horse, and a *Sancho* for my valet. The case is, I *could* live in a way genteel enough, and uniformly so; but then I must forego megrims, whims, toys, and so forth. Now, though it gives me pain, *sometimes,* not to appear of a piece; yet that *infrequent* pain is not a balance for the substantial happiness which I find in an urn, a seal, a snuff-box, an engraving, or a bust. Ambition, too, as it puts me upon wishing to make a figure, makes me very indifferent as to making a common every-day-gentlemanly figure; and saves me from appearing solicitous about the "res *mediocriter* splendidae," by raising my imagination *higher.* I pour out my vanity to you in cataracts; but I hope you will rather consider it is a mark of my *confidence,* and, consequently, my sincere esteem and affection: for, I take it, the former seldom subsists without the latter. And as to what I said about my love of flattery, I hope, you will not construe it as any *hint;* neither, if I am right, would you be so ungenerous as to comply with me. I sincerely think that flattery amongst foes is absolutely desirable; amongst one's *common acquaintance,* a behavior *rather inclining* to it: but amongst *friends,* its consequences are of too dangerous a nature.

I am so unhappy in my wintery, unvisited state, that I can almost say with Dido, "taedet coeli convexa tueri." I am miserable, to think that I have not thought enough to amuse me. I walk a day together, and have no idea but what comes in at my eyes. I long for some subject about the size of Philips's Cyder,[2] to settle heartily about; something that I could enrich by episodes drawn from the English history: *Stonehenge* has some of the advantages I like; but seems a dead, lifeless title. If you chance to think of a subject which you do not choose to *adorn* yourself, send it me to *write upon.*

I shall be vastly desirous to see you here in spring; and am in hopes Whistler will stay a month with me. I have sent an imperious letter about his dilatory correspondence. — He mentioned you in his last letter; was going to Oxford; thence to London: where, if he stays till February, I may see him. I hope you will write the very next post: you cannot oblige me or please me more than by so doing; if you think I deserve to be pleased, or am worth obliging. Adieu!

W. S.

[2] The most ambitious poem of John Philips (1676–1709), an imitation of Virgil's *Georgics,* published in 1708.

33. To RICHARD GRAVES[1]

Feb. [16,] 1743

DEAR MR. GRAVES,

You say it is no way unpleasing to you to receive my letters; if you say the thing that is not, the fault, like others, produces its own punishment. — You are now my only correspondent. I do not know what reason Whistler has for not caring to write, unless he thinks that we ought not to trouble ourselves about one another; but bend our whole endeavours to mend our fortunes; though I do not *know* his imaginations. I was afraid, after what I had said concerning *sameness* in my last, that you would interpret it to your own disadvantage; but was too lazy to write my letter again, trusting that I could deny the extent of my complaint to any one besides myself in some future letter. There is as much variety in your genius, as fortune can introduce into your circumstances.

Some time next week, do I purpose to set out for London.[2] The reasons for my going at all do *barely* preponderate. I cannot, *conscientiously*, print any thing. I have two or three little matters in hand: none that I am greatly fond of, much less that are at all mature. One is, what you have seen, though in its mortal state, "Flattery, or the fatal Exotic;"[3] so very quotidian and copious a subject, that I dislike it entirely. Another, "Elegies in Hammond's Metre,"[4] but upon *real* and natural subjects: this I have objections to. A third, "An Essay on Reserve;"[5] the subject genteel, I think, but scarce ten lines finished. A fourth, "An Essay, in

---

[1] Dodsley, *Letters to Particular Friends*, No. XXVIII.

[2] But I can find no proof of Shenstone's having been in London in 1743; at least we have no epistolary account of such a visit, though Wells says he was there in February (*Anglia*, 35:442) and so does Miss Williams (*William Shenstone*, p. 27), who says he stayed at Nando's. The letter she quotes, however, is one of 1744. Fullington (*PMLA*, 46:1130) accepts that Wells has shown Shenstone to have been in London in February of 1742, 1743, and 1744; but Wells has not done so; he has indeed shown Shenstone to have been in London in February, 1742, but for 1743 merely takes his declaration of intention to set out for London "some time next week" as evidence of his actually having done so. As for 1744, Shenstone was there in May, not February; Wells contradicts himself in dealing with Letter 49 (Dodsley, No. XXX) when he first says (*Anglia*, 35:443) he will show No. XXX to have been written from London about February, 1744, and then proceeds (p. 444) to show it was written probably on the very day of Pope's death, May 30, 1744. As a matter of fact, then, Shenstone seems to have been in London in February, 1741 and 1742; not to have been there at all in 1743; and to have been there late in the spring of 1744.

[3] "Flattery, or the Fatal Exotick" (Bodleian MS), apparently never published, appears in facsimile between pages 27 and 28 in Williams, *William Shenstone*.

[4] James Hammond's elegies were published in 1742; of Shenstone's, which were inspired by Hammond's, most appear to have been written in 1743 and 1744. See his prefatory essay on elegy in *Works*, I (1764), 3, as well as the elegies themselves.

[5] The "Essay on Reserve" apparently was never finished or published. At the end of his prose fragment "On Reserve," in *Works*, II (1764), 49–57, appears the note: "These were no other than a collection of hints, when I proposed to write a poetical essay on Reserve."

47

blank Verse, on Oeconomy, with Advice to Poets on that Head, concluding with a ludicrous Description of a Poet's Apartment."[6] I think it were better to *annex* that poem thus, to prevent its clashing, like an earthen pot, against Philips's silver vase, though his humour lies chiefly in the language. My favourite scheme is a poem, in blank verse, upon Rural *Elegance*,[7] including cascades, temples, grottos, hermitages, greenhouses, which introduces my favourite episode of the Spanish lady (you will wonder *how,* but I think *well*) to close the first book. The next, running upon planting, &c. will end with a vista terminated by an old abbey, which introduces an episode concerning the effect of Romish power, interdicts, &c. in imitation of Lucretius's "Plague of Athens," taken from Thucydides, Virgil's Murrain, and Ovid's Pestilence, &c. The two episodes in great forwardness; — but, alas! I do not like formal didactic poetry, and shall never be able to finish aught *but* the episodes, I doubt: unless I allow myself to treat the rest in *my own* manner, transiently — as Camilla skimmed over the wheat-stubble.

I have altered this ballad, you see; I doubt, not to your mind: but send your criticisms, and I will be all obedience. From London I will send you mine on your more important poem; your critique will be important upon my silly affair; mine silly, I am afraid, upon your momentous one — but you do not think it momentous, as you ought. Direct to Nando's. I am
Your most sincere and affectionate friend and humble servant,

W. S.

I question whether I should be more unhappy in any mere *mechanical* employment, for instance, making nails (which seems to deal as much in *repetition* as any trade), than I am in great part of my time when my head is unfit for study. — My neighbour is gone to London, and has left me a legacy of franks; so I shall be able to return your poem, &c. at least by parcels. I strenuously purpose to be there (or to set out) next week; but, as I *am* here at present, I think you ought to pay some deference to the *vis inertiae,* at least to the centripetal force of matter, and direct to The Leasowes one more letter, with your opinion concerning the various readings in the trifle I inclose, writing the first post that you well can. Once more Adieu!

Feb. 16, 1743

[6] *Oeconomy, a Rhapsody, Addressed to Young Poets* appears among the *Moral Pieces,* in *Works,* Vol. I (1764).
[7] Not to be confused with the later ode on *Rural Elegance* dedicated to the Duchess of Somerset. The two episodes referred to are preserved as *The Ruin'd Abbey; or, the Effects of Superstition* and *Love and Honour,* in *Works,* I (1764), 308 and 321.

34. To the HONOURABLE MRS. KNIGHT[1]

The *Leasowes* [1743][2]

DEAR MADAM,

As it has hitherto seemed good to you to expatiate pretty largely on so diminutive a Subject as a Thimble, I flatter myself that you may read with Patience an Account of the Life and Conversation of your most trifling humble Servant. Otherwise, I should not have told you, that I am extremely unhappy in my present Situation; that, when you left the Country, I had recourse to another Kind of natural Beauties, namely, that which is to be found in "Groves, Meads, and murmuring Streams," and so long as Summer was pleased to continue his Favours, I looked upon your Departure as what only changed my Pleasure to Amusement. Now, indeed, Summer has forsaken me likewise; the Trees and Groves are stripped of their Covering, and I am left without any Fence against Spleen, Vapours, Megrim, Discontent, and a numerous Train of such Sort of Beings, which plague me to Death, whenever I offer to recollect your Absence; and how often that happens, I leave any one to guess but yourself, because any one else is better acquainted with the numerous Ways and Means you have of rendering your Company agreeable. I appeal also to the same Persons to guess how provoking you are, when you mention the Possibility there was that I might have seen you at the *Leasowes* some Time ago. What need you tell one of it, since it could not be effected? Why will you put me upon cursing Fortune upon more Accounts than I have already Occasion to do? Pray let me endeavour to conform myself to my real Circumstances, rather than give me a Glimpse of the Pleasure which you was about to do me, and yet had not the Goodness to go through with. I want no Inducements to come to *Worcester*, since I discovered that you lived there, and that being all that was necessary, tho' you have mentioned others that are attractive.

I beg you would make my Compliments agreeable to Mrs. Winsmore, which you are best capable of doing, for two Reasons; first, because you know the Sincerity of my Esteem, and, secondly, because I have no Idea

---

[1] Hull, *Select Letters,* Vol. I, No. XII.

[2] Hull is of little help in the dating or placing of undated or misplaced letters. This letter is placed here merely by my own conjecture. Obviously it was written from the Leasowes in either the autumn or winter season, and since it addresses "Mrs. Knight" and not "Lady Luxborough" it probably was written before 1746, though Shenstone is not always careful to address her by the proper title (see Letter 57). It appears to be an answer to a letter of hers which has not been preserved, or at least of which I have no knowledge. Since Shenstone says in his postscript, "I believe I shall go to L[ondo]n the End of next Week," the letter might belong to 1741 or 1742, when he actually was in London in winter, or to 1743, when he declared his intention of going but, so far as I can discover, never went. It seems plausible that this declaration of intention is the same as he made in the preceding letter, to Graves.

how any Thing you say can be disagreeable. The Consideration that she remembers me, and that she spoke of me in the same Breath with Mrs. Knight (as my Vanity interprets your Letter) makes me so vain, that I, with the utmost Assurance, take the Liberty of subscribing myself,

Madam,
Your most obedient, humble Servant,
W. Shenstone

P. S. I believe I shall go to L[ondo]n the End of next Week. If I were to receive a Letter from you, as I put my Foot into the Stirup, I should bid Mrs. Arnold take in her Bottle, for I had no Occasion for a Cordial. Your Affair (*où vous scavez*) diverts me highly.

35. To RICHARD JAGO [1]

[1743 or 1744]

DEAR SIR,

It is not much above two hours since I received your obliging letter, and am already set down to answer it. — To speak the truth, I had almost given you over: I imagined you had taken umbrage at some expression or circumstance in my epistle, and were determined to make me sensible you did so by your silence. I hope, this error of mine will serve to establish one rule on *both* sides. — It is what ought, I am sure, always to take place, where people wish a perpetuity of friendship. I mean, never, upon circumstances of disrespect, to admit of circumstantial evidence.

I am very grave, so you may depend on the sincerity of all I shall say. I saw several beauties in your former elegy; but, though it was "formosa," it did not appear to me "ipsa forma." I like this that you have now sent *very* much.[2] It has a simplicity which your last a little wanted, and has thought *enough*. I begin to be seldom pleased with the compositions of others, or my own; but I could be really *fond* of this, with a few alterations that I could propose: — but you must know, at the same time, that these are such as no one would approve beside myself. — I know it. — However, there are some seeming *faults* in it.

I have been greatly mortified in my correspondents of late. — I even said in my haste, All friends are faithless. — G[raves], after a month's expectation, which he had confirmed to me, of seeing him here, let me know about a fortnight since, that I had more leisure than him; and,

---

[1] Dodsley, *Letters to Particular Friends*, No. XLVI, dated 1747. Fullington (*PMLA*, 46: 1133) fixes the date between February, 1743, when Shenstone began writing his elegies, and 1744, when Graves left Tissington for Aldworth.

[2] The reference is probably to Jago's two elegies *The Goldfinches* and *The Blackbirds*, both printed in Dodsley's *Collection*, Vol. IV (1755).

since it did not suit his convenience to come, I ought to take the opportunity of visiting him, and seeing Derbyshire while he continues in it. — W[histler] has not wrote to me these six weeks. — Outing has been, moreover, dumb for the same space of time; and I purpose in my heart to behave with some distance towards both, for this neglect (see my rule of circumstantial evidence).

It is pity you cannot spare a day or two to come and see me. My wood grows excessively pleasant, and its pleasantness vexes me; because nobody will come that can taste it.

Your health, according to your description, is much the same with mine; but, from the gaiety of your style and *designs,* I collect that it is greatly better.

I have an alcove, six elegies, a seat, two epitaphs (one upon myself), three ballads, four songs, and a serpentine river, to shew you when you come. Will the compositions come safe to you, if I send my book, which contains the *only* copies of several things (which I could not remember if they were lost?) — but I will not send them. If my horse gets well, I may essay a visit for two days, and bring them with me, that I may make comments while you read them, as beseemeth a genuine author to do.

I am raising a green-house from the excrescences of Lord Dudley's; but I do not find that "vient l'appetit en mangeant," that I grow fonder of my collection proportionably as it increases.

I should think myself fortunate enough at present, if, like you, I could only find that I had been mentioned for a vacant post; but I have withdrawn all my views from court-preferment, and fixed them on finding a pot of money, which I determine to be the far more probable scheme.

I have little health and frequent mortification, so that no one need envy me; and yet, I believe, there *are* that do. Is any enviable but such as are unambitious? I never shall be able to reckon myself of that tribe, which have engrossed all *happiness* to themselves, and left the rest of the world nothing but hopes and possessions. Yet I do not much feel the pains of ambition while I am conversing with ingenious friends of my own level: but in *other* company it hurts me. Let me advise you, now I think of it, to dread the company of silly people, out-of-the-way people, and, in one word, what men of genius call the *vulgar*. You run ten times the risque of being mortified, voluntarily or unknowingly, amongst the latter of these, to what you do amongst men of sense and politeness, be they ever so malicious; — but my paper is filled.

Do write soon.

36. To RICHARD GRAVES[1]

July 3, 1743

DEAR MR. GRAVES,

I did not part from you without a *great deal* of melancholy. To think of the *short* duration of those interviews which are the objects of one's *continual* wishes, has been a reflection that has plagued me of old! I am sure I returned home with it then, more aggravated, as I foresaw myself returning to the same series of melancholy hours from which you had a while relieved me, and which I had *particularly* suffered under all this last spring! I wish to God, you might happen to be settled not far from me: a day's journey distance, however; I mean an *easy* one. But the odds are infinitely against me. I must only *rely* for my happiness on the hopes of a never-ceasing correspondence!

Soon after you were gone, I received my packet. The history of Worcestershire is mere stuff. T——[2] I am so fond of, that, I believe, I shall have his part of the collection bound over again, neatly and separately. But sure Hammond has no right to the least *inventive* merit, as the preface-writer[3] would insinuate. I do not think there is a single thought, of any eminence, that is not literally translated. I am astonished he could content himself with being so little an original.

Mr. Lyttelton and his lady are at Hagley. A malignant caterpillar has demolished the beauty of all our *large* oaks. Mine are secured by their littleness. But, I guess, the park suffers; a large wood near me being a mere winter-piece for nakedness.

At present, I give myself up to riding and thoughtlessness; being resolved to make trial of *their* efficacy towards a tolerable degree of health and spirits. I wish I had you for my director. I should proceed with great confidence of success; though I am brought very low by two or three fits of a fever since I saw you. Had I written to you in the midst of my dispirited condition, as I was going, you would have had a more tender and unaffected letter than I *can* write at another time: what I think, perhaps, at all times; but what sickness can alone elicit from a temper fearful of whining.

Surely the "nunc formosissimus annus" is to be limited to hay-harvest. I could give my reasons: but you will imagine them to be, the activity of

---

[1] Dodsley, *Letters to Particular Friends*, No. XXXIV. Wells confirms the date, *Anglia*, 35:445. Fullington likewise (*PMLA*, 46:1130–31) throws light on the order of this letter in relation to the three following.

[2] Probably Tibullus, whom Hammond followed rather than Ovid in the writing of his love elegies.

[3] The Earl of Chesterfield.

country people in a pleasing employment; the full verdure of the summer; the prime of pinks, woodbines, jassimines, &c. I am old; very old; for few things give me so much mechanical pleasure as lolling on a bank in the very heat of the sun,

>When the old come forth to play
>On a sun-shine holiday—

And yet it is as much as I can do to keep Mrs. Arnold from going to neighbouring houses in her smock, in despite of decency and my known disapprobation.

I find myself more of a patriot than I ever thought I was. Upon reading the account of the battle,[4] I found a very sensible pleasure, or, as the Methodists term it, perceived my heart *enlarged,* &c. The map you sent me is a pretty kind of *toy,* but does not enough particularize the scenes of the war, &c. which was the end I had in view when I sent for it.

"O dura messorum ilia!" About half the appetite, digestion, strength, spirits, &c. of a mower, would make me the happiest of mortals! I would be understood literally, and precisely.

Adieu!
W. S.

37. To RICHARD JAGO[1]

The Leasowes, Saturday,
July the 9th 1743

DEAR MR. JAGO,

It is not a contrived apology, or an excuse, which I am going to offer for the disappointments I have given you. I have actually been so much out of order ever since I wrote to you, nay, ever since I *formed* a *design* of a Sunday expedition to L——, that it never has been in my *power* to execute my intentions. My vertigo has not *yet* taken away my senses: God knows how soon it may do; but my nerves are in such a condition, that I can scarce get a wink of even *disordered* rest for whole nights together. May you never know the misery of such involuntary vigils! I ride every day almost to fatigue; which only tends to make my want of sleep more *sensible,* and not in the least to remove it. I have *spirits* all day, good ones, though my head is dizzy, and I never enterprize any study of greater subtlety than a news-paper. I cannot say the journey to L—— would be at all *formidable* to me; for I ride about fifteen miles, as I compute it, every day before dinner. But the nights from home would be

[4] Dettingen, June 27, 1743.
[1] Dodsley, *Letters to Particular Friends,* No. XXXIII.

insupportable to me. I have fatigued Mrs. Arnold's assiduity to the injury of her health; by occasioning her to sit in my room a'nights, light my candle, put it out again, make me perspiratory wheys, and slops; and am amused by the most silly animadversions she is capable of making. I never knew her usefulness till now; but I *now* prefer her to *all* of *her station*. If I get over this disorder, concerning which I have bad apprehensions, you may depend upon seeing me the first Sunday I dare venture forth. I hope *you* continue mending. The benefit of *riding* is not only universal, and would cure *me* too, could I but make one previous advance towards health. Have you tried cold-bathing? Perhaps it may not suit your case. I wish I had not dropt it. I take my fluctuation of nerves to be caused, as that of the sea is, by wind; which I am continually pumping up, and yet find it still renewed. When I am just sinking to sleep, a sudden twitch of my nerves calls me back again — to watchfulness and vexation! I consider myself as in the state of the philosopher, who held a bullet betwixt his finger and thumb, which, whenever he was about to nod, was ordered so as to fall into a large brass pan, and wake him — that he might pursue his lucubrations.

I will mention one circumstance regarding the weakness of my nerves; — and not my spirits, for I told you those were tolerable: — the least noise that is, even the falling of a fire-shovel upon the floor, if it happen unexpectedly, shocks my whole frame; and I actually believe that a gun fired behind my back, unawares, amidst the stillness of the night, would go near to kill me with its noise.

I am just going to bed; and dare not be any more attentive, as I hope to close my eyes for a minute. So fare you well!

It is now six o'clock in the morning, and I have had about five hours middling sleep; which encourages me greatly: so I will *hope* to be able to see you next Sunday sevennight.

What think you of the battle?[2] Are not you so much in love with our King that you could find in your heart to serve him in any profitable post he might assign you?

Capt. L[yttelton][3] is wounded in the thigh.

When I ride in my chair round my neighbourhood, I am as much stared and wondered at, as a giant would be that should walk through Pall-mall. My vehicle is at *least as* uncommon hereabouts as a blazing comet. My chief pleasure lies in finding out a thousand roads, and de-

---

[2] Evidently Dettingen, June 27, 1743.
[3] Captain Richard Lyttelton, while serving as aid-de-camp to Lord Stair, was slightly wounded in the thigh by a musket ball at Aschaffenberg. Wyndham, *Chronicles of the Eighteenth Century*, I, 123.

lightful little haunts near home, which I never dreamt of: egregious solitudes, and most incomparable bye-lanes; where I can as effectually lose myself within a mile of home, as if I were benighted in the desarts of Arabia. Adieu!

38. To RICHARD GRAVES [1]

The Leasowes
[Shortly after July 9 or 16, 1743]

DEAR MR. GRAVES,

To-morrow morning I set out for Cheltenham, to make trial of the waters there. I shall, perhaps, add to this letter at several stages, and conclude it at the place to which I am going; so that, like those springs, you may, perhaps, find it impregnated with the nature of all those places through which it passes; perhaps quite the contrary.

―――, if I mistake not the man, is an encourager of works of taste, &c. though I am going to instance this oddly: he was a hearty stickler for my poem upon Hercules at Bath, as D. Jago sent me word. Perhaps it was complaisance to Mr. Lyttelton, with whom, Charles, &c. he is intimate, if, as I said before, I do not mistake the person. I flatter myself, I do not; and I hope that we two shall ever find the same persons, or the same kind of persons, our friends, and also our enemies.

If I get over this ill habit of body, depend upon it, I *will* have a *reverend* care of my health, as Sir John Falstaff advises the Chief Justice. I solve all the tempests that disturb my constitution into *wind*: it plagues me, first, in the shape of a bad appetite, then indigestion, then lowness of spirits and a flux of pale water, and at night by watchings, restlessness, twitchings of my nerves, or a sleep more distracted than the most active state of watchfulness. But I think purging lessens all these symptoms, and I trust my scheme that I am entering upon is right.

I was on Monday at Hagley, to wait on Mr. Lyttelton, who was gone to Sir John Astley's, to see his grand edifice. — As to Mrs. Lyttelton, if her affability is not artificial, I mean, if it does not owe its original (as it *ought to do* its *management*) to art, I cannot conceive a person more amiable; — but *sense* and *elegance* cannot be feigned: to *exhibit* them, is to *have* them.

How is my song set?[2] Miss Carrington procured it that favour; but I have never seen a copy, nor knew of its being to be printed. Howard

―――――――
[1] Dodsley, *Letters to Particular Friends,* No. XXXII, undated. Wells supplies the date, *Anglia,* 35:445. Fullington fixes the date more exactly, *PMLA,* 46:1130.
[2] We cannot be certain which song this is. The second one alluded to is *The Scholar's Relapse* (*Works,* I, 1764, Song XIII). The manuscript of which Miss Hazeltine treats in her *William Shenstone and His Critics* has at the foot of the page on which this song

has set another of mine, which I received last post; but my harpsichord is out of order, and I have found no one yet to explain the hieroglyphics which convey it. You may probably find it in some future number of the British Orpheus. "By the side of a stream, &c."

I am in as good spirits this instant as ever I was in my life: only "Mens turbidum laetatur." My head is a little confused; but I often think seriously, that I ought to have the most ardent and *practical* gratitude (as the Methodists choose to express themselves) for the advantages that I have: which, though not eminently shining, are such, to speak the truth, as suit my particular humour, and consequently deserve all kind of acknowledgment. If a poet should address himself to God Almighty, with the most earnest thanks for his goodness in allotting him an estate that was over-run with shrubs, thickets, and coppices, variegated with barren rocks and precipices, or floated three parts in four with lakes and marshes, rather than such an equal and fertile spot as the "sons of men" delight in; to my apprehension, he would be guilty of no absurdity. — But of this I have composed a kind of prayer, and intend to write a little speculation on the subject; this kind of gratitude I assuredly ought to have, and have. For my health, if one reflects, a country-fellow's stock of it would be unfit for solitude; would dispose one rather to bodily feats, and, what Falstaff calls in Poins, *gambol* faculties, than mental contemplations; and would give one that kind of pain which springs from *impatience*. My constitution was given me originally good; and with regard to it now (as G. Barnwell says) "What am I? — What *I have made myself.*"[3] Or, to speak with Milton,

> Him after all disputes
> Forc'd I absolve; all my evasions vain,
> And reasonings, tho' thro' mazes, only lead
> But to my own conviction. First and last
> On me, me only, as the source and spring
> Of all corruption, all the blame lights due.
> [PARADISE LOST, X, 828ff]

Though this is but vulgarly expressed in Milton neither.

Jago has been here this last week, and I drove him to Dudley Castle, which I long to shew you: I never saw it (since I was the size of my pen) before: it has great romantic beauty, though perhaps Derbyshire may render it of small note in your eye.

---

appears, "Set by Howard and printed vilely in his *British Orpheus.*" Miss Hazeltine also speaks (page 2) of *The Rose-bud* (Song XIV), "set by Galliard," and of Arne's melody for the *Pastoral Ballad* in Dodsley's *Collection*, Vol. IV (1755).

[3] George Lillo, *The London Merchant, or The History of George Barnwell* (1731).

One is tempted to address the K[ing] as Harry the Eighth does his wife, *mutatis mutandis:*

> Go thy ways, George!
> Whoe'er he be that shall assert he has
> A *bolder* king, let him in nought be trusted
> For saying false in that—
> [HENRY VIII, II, iv, 131–34]

I have a mind to write an ode in praise of him, and in rivalship of Cibber.— Mine should be of the ballad style and familiarity, as expressing the sentiments of a person returning from a dislike to a thorough approbation of him, which seems, at present, the sense of the nation.— But herein I am not in earnest.—

My pen has run on a whole page at random. It amuses me to encourage it, and so I will try to get a frank.

I am this moment arrived at Cheltenham, after an expensive and fatiguing journey. I called yesterday at Mickleton; saw the portico, and snapped up a bit of mutton at your brother's; drank a dish of tea with Miss S——;[4] and, in opposition to the strongest remonstrances, persisted in an endeavour to reach Cheltenham after five o'clock. The consequence was, that, about ten, I found myself travelling back again towards Stowe; and had undoubtedly wandered all night in the dark, had I not been fortunately met by a waggoner's servant, who brought me back to the worst inn but one I ever lay at, being his master's.— Here I am: which is all I shall say in this letter. Adieu!   W. S.

39. To RICHARD JAGO[1]

[After July 9,] 1743

DEAR SIR,

I long heartily to talk over affairs with you *tête-à-tête;* but am an utter enemy to the fatigue of transcribing what might pass well enough in conversation.— I shall say nothing more concerning my departure from L——, than that it was necessary, and therefore excusable.— I have been since with a gentleman[2] upon the borders of Wales, Bishop's Castle, from whence I made a digression one day beyond Offa's Dyke: saw mountains which converted all that I *had* seen into mole-hills; and houses which changed The Leasowes into Hampton-Court: where they

---

[4] Evidently Miss Utrecia Smith (Fullington, "Mr. William Shenstone," p. 64).

[1] Dodsley, *Letters to Particular Friends,* No. XXXI. Wells discusses the date (*Anglia,* 35:444–45) and Fullington fixes the month more exactly (*PMLA,* 46:1130).

[2] His new acquaintance, Lyttelton Brown of Bishop's Castle, alluded to in Letters 40, 41, and 42.

talk of a glazed window as a piece of magnificence; and where their highest idea of his Majesty is, that he can ride in such a coach as 'Squire Jones or 'Squire Pryce's. The woman of the inn, at one place, said, "Glass (in windows) was very genteel, that it was; but she could not afford such finery."

You agree with the rest of the married world in a propensity to make proselytes. This inclination in some people gives one a kind of dread of the matter. They are ill-natured, and can only wish one in their own state because they are unhappy; like persons that have the plague, who, they say, are ever desirous to propagate the infection. I make a contrary conclusion when *you* commend marriage, as you seem to do, when you wish Miss ———[3] may reconcile me to more than the *name* of wife. I know not what you have heard of my amour: probably *more* than I can thoroughly confirm to you. And what if I should say to you, that marriage was not once the subject of our conversation?

Nec conjugis unquam
Praetendi taedas, aut haec in foedera veni.

Do not you think every thing in nature strangely improved since you were married, from the tea-table to the *warming-pan?*

I want to see Mrs. Jago's[4] hand-writing, that I may judge of her temper; but she must write something in my praise. Pray see you to it, in your next letter.

I could parodize my Lord Carteret's letter from Dettingen, if I had it by me. "Mrs. Arnold (thanks be praised!) has this day gained a very considerable victory. The scold lasted two hours. Mrs. S———e[5] was posted in the hall, and Mrs. Arnold upon the stair-case; which superiority of ground was of no small service to her in the engagement. The fire lasted the whole space, without intermission; at the close of which, the enemy was routed, and Mrs. Arnold kept the field."

Did you hear the song to the tune of "The Cuckow?"

The Baron stood behind a tree,
In woeful plight, for nought heard he
But Cannon, Cannon, &c.
O word of fear!
Unpleasing to a German ear.

---

[3] Miss Carter, of whom Shenstone became enamored at Cheltenham. See Letters 40, 41, and 42.

[4] This makes it clear that Jago was married in 1743, not 1744, as the *DNB* says. See Fullington, *PMLA,* 46:1131, n8.

[5] Possibly Mrs. Mary Shenstone, wife of John, Sr.; or possibly the wife of Thomas Shenstone. See Ward, "Studies in Shenstone," p. 90.

The notes that fall upon the word "Cannon," express the sound with its echo admirably.

I send you my pastoral elegy[6] (or ballad, if you think that name more proper), on condition that you return it with ample remarks in your next letter: I say "return it," because I have no other copy, and am too indolent to take one. Adieu!

W.S.

40. To ANTHONY WHISTLER [1]

[Late summer, 1743]

DEAR MR. WHISTLER,

This is the first evening I have had to myself since I left *Cheltenham;* and as one wants some very favourite Subject to engross one's Thoughts a little, after a long Dissipation, I could think of nothing more effectual than a Letter to one who has so large a Share in them; beside, they have given me your Letter from *Bradfield,* and I am in Pain till I have acknowledged so affectionate and polite a Present. People, whose very Foibles are so many Elegancies, can scarce write any Thing more agreeable than a plain, unaffected Account of them. I remember, I used to think this a Kind of Distinction between Mr. Graves and you; that the one had the knack of making his Virtues unenvied, and the other of rendering (what I perhaps unjustly termed) his Weaknesses enviable. I am almost afraid of inserting this, lest it should seem to injure the superlative Esteem I have of you: but I must add, that I consider a Mixture of Weaknesses, and an ingenuous Confession of them, as the most engaging and sociable Part of any Character; if I did not, I could not allot them you, whose Manner is so distinguishedly amiable.

Since I left *Cheltenham,* I have been at Mr. B[rown]'s,[2] in *Bishop's-Castle.* I rode one Morning with him about three Miles, that I might say, I had been in *Wales,* and seen *Brecon, Caderidis,* and *Plinlimmon,* with an extensive Chain of other Mountains. I called at a small Alehouse, where the People lived all the Winter without any Glass in their Windows. I was wondering how they could live so, in a more cold Country than you have, perhaps, experienced. The Wife said, "True it was, she could like Glass very well." "Yes," says the Husband, "Glass is very

---

[6] The *Pastoral Ballad,* in four parts, written in 1743, *Works,* I (1764), 189–98, was published in Dodsley's *Collection,* Vol. IV (1755), where it was mistakenly attributed to Thomas Arne, who wrote some music for it.

[1] Hull, *Select Letters,* Vol. II, No. IV. The references to the Cheltenham visit fix the approximate date of this and the two following letters. They are undated in Hull.

[2] Lyttelton Brown. See note 2 to the preceding letter, and also allusions to him in the next two.

genteel, that it is." "Nay, says the Wife, not for the Genteelness neither, though it is very genteel, that's the Truth on't." This Circumstance struck me a good deal, that they should discover the genteelness of Glazing, and never once think of its *Expediency*. Mr. B[rown] is a Man you would like upon Acquaintance, though, as I remember, you had some Objection to the Superfluity of his Wit. We shall, in all Probability, have frequent Interviews with him at *Bath, London*, &c. He would fain have seduced me to have travelled into Portugal, &c. with himself, and one Mr. Moore, his neighbour; an agreeable, modest Man, and late Member for *Bishop's-Castle*. I declined it for two Reasons; first, on Account of the Expence, and secondly, that I could not think of spending two Years in this Part of my Life abroad; dead to one's own Country, and procuring, at best, very perishable, and useless Friendships in another. If I could have staid, I was to have gone with him to a *Welsh* Sessions, fraught with Irascibility. He is a Justice of Peace there.

As to good Acquaintance, though I much desire it, I have as literally a Genius for avoiding, as any one ever had for procuring it. I cannot approach within fifty Yards of Servility for fear of it.

I want sadly to talk to you about a thousand Things. I have some Notion of spending a Week at Mr. D——'s.[3] Act sublimely, and give me the Meeting then, notwithstanding.

Though I was enamoured with the Politeness of Mr. W——'s Conversation, I should not, perhaps, have been very forward to express my Sentiments, if you had not intimated, that he made favourable mention of me. I begin to grow a little pleased with Prudence, and I think it a Debt one owes her, to reserve one's Encomiums till one knows any one's mutual Sentiments; for certainly, he that happens to commend an Enemy, happens to condemn himself. I beg my Compliments.

I believe poor J. D——[4] is alive — Farther I cannot learn.

I did not think it possible, I could have been so much engaged by love as I have been of late. Poor Miss C[arter]![5]

It must necessarily be an Honour to a Girl, to have pleased a Man of Sense, (I know not but I am vain in supposing myself of that Number) let his Station be how low soever. Now it must be a Disgrace to captivate a Fool, however high it be; the former is the strongest Evidence of Merit, the latter of the Want of it.

Now I talk of Vanity, I beseech you never check yourself in your Let-

[3] Possibly Sherrington Davenport's, in Worfield.
[4] Evidently Jack Dolman, to whose death Shenstone refers in Letter 43.
[5] See Letter 39, n3 and Letter 42, n1.

ters—*I* don't purpose it; and I think it makes as pretty a Figure in the Letters of a Man of Taste, as it does in the Embroidery of a Beau. I am as much yours, as human Nature will admit of.

Adieu!
W. Shenstone

41. To MRS. AUBREY [1]

[Late summer, 1743]

Dear Madam,

I promised to give you some Account what became of *Cheltenham,* after Mr. A——[2] had pillaged it of all that was most valuable. Possibly before this Time, you may have forgot both my Promise and me, and it may not be extremely political to renew your Remembrance of a Person who has been so long seemingly neglectful. The Truth is, I can no more bear to be forgot by those I esteem, than I can be censured for Forgetfulness with Regard to them, and I know no Way but Writing, by which I can evade both.

Some sort of Apology I ought to make, that I did not write before; you will therefore please to observe, that I am but just arrived at Home, though I left *Cheltenham* the Day after you. I stayed, indeed, to hear Mr. B[rown][3] preach a Morning Sermon; for which I find Mrs. C—— has allotted him the Hat, preferably to Mr. C——. Perhaps you may not remember, nor did I hear till very lately, that there is a Hat given annually at *Cheltenham,* for the Use of the best foreign Preacher, of which the Disposal is assigned to Mrs. C——, to her and her Heirs for ever. I remember (tho' I knew nothing of this whilst I was upon the Place) I used to be a little misdeemful, that all who preached there had some such Premium in their Eye. This Hat, 'tis true, is not quite so valuable as that of a *Cardinal,* but while it is made a Retribution for Excellence in so (if properly considered) sublime a Function, it is an Object for a Preacher in any Degree. I am sorry, at the same Time, to say, that as a *common Hat,* merely for its *Uses,* it would be an Object to too many *Country Curates,* whose Situations and slender Incomes too often excite our Blushes, as well as Compassion. There should be no such Thing as a *Journeyman Parson;* it is beneath the Dignity of the Profession. If we had fewer *Pluralities* in the Church, this Indecorum might, in a great Measure, be abolished.

[1] Hull, *Select Letters,* Vol. II, No. XIX. The date, late summer, 1743, is established by the references to the Cheltenham visit.
[2] Evidently Mr. Aubrey.
[3] Lyttelton Brown of Bishop's Castle. See the Index.

Mr. N—— (*Squire* N——) I hear is fitting up his Castle at *L*—— for the Reception of the little Widow; and the Mercer at *Cheltenham* has completed his grand Arcade, for the better Disposition of his Crapes and Callimancos.

I am an ill Relater of Matters of Fact, and as I said before, did not continue above four and twenty Hours and some odd Minutes upon the Place longer than you that enquire after it: but I survived long enough to hear very frequent Mention of Mrs. A[ubrey], Miss Carter, &c. and such Mention, as has confirmed me in an Opinion, that Persons of real Merit, without any Expence of Airs, &c. will by Degrees engross the Admiration of any Place they come into. But this is a Kind of Language you would never indulge me in; you might very securely; for I should never be able to express half the sincere Esteem and Respect with which I am,

Madam,
Your most obedient, humble Servant,
W. Shenstone

42. To MISS CARTER [1]

[Late summer, 1743]

DEAR MISS CARTER,

Perhaps you may remember to have seen an odd Kind of Fellow when you were at *Cheltenham,* who threatened you with a Letter, and who is now endeavouring to be as *bad* as his Word; however he hopes for some little Partiality on his Behalf, having delayed the Execution of his Menaces for a considerable Time, and even now promising to say as few Things in your Favour as the real Sentiments of his Heart will admit of.

But Peace to Buffoonery.—After I parted from you, Mr. M——n, with great Simplicity, endeavoured to keep up my Spirits, by speaking in Praise of the Family we had left, as though that was not the ready Method to aggravate the Sense of one's Loss; and yet to aggravate it was utterly impossible in the Opinion of a Person already so sensible of it. But he mentioned one Article which was more successful, and that

---

[1] Hull, *Select Letters,* Vol. II, No. XX. The date is indicated by the references to the Cheltenham visit. Graves (*Recollection,* pp. 103–06) says Shenstone's *Pastoral Ballad,* first sketched out on his parting from Miss Graves, was enlarged and divided into four parts on his parting from Miss Carter at Cheltenham. Shenstone was infatuated, but as Graves says, his purpose probably never was marriage; and since Miss Carter's sister was the wife of a baronet of considerable fortune, the lady would doubtless never have condescended to Shenstone. She is the Delia of his elegies and songs (Fullington, "Mr. William Shenstone," pp. 64ff).

was a Proposal to accompany me to *Stoke,* and to let me know when it suited his Convenience.

When I came to *Cheltenham,* I was not unmindful of that solemn Vow that I had made, not to survive your Family there a single Hour: but I found it near five o'Clock, and my Conscience said, that as I had made it so late, by my Attendance upon you, though I did stay another Night, I hoped I might be excused. I have been, since leaving this Town, at Mr. Brown's, who lives upon the Borders of *Wales.* — Poor Man! He has been the most obliging Person in the World to the most stupid of Companions. 'Tis hardly possible to determine which was greater, the Zeal with which he shewed me his Fossils, Plants, Poetry, &c. or the stupid Inattention with which I observed them. He commends you and Mrs. Aubrey highly; so, indeed, do all I know, or I would soon forget that I had ever seen their Faces. He had found out a Method at last of seducing me to talk, by frequent Mention of your Merits, and it was a good While before I discovered his Artifice; and even when I had discovered it, I was ill able to elude the Force of it.

I am now just returned Home, which is my Apology for not writing to you about *Cheltenham* as I promised. I really scarce recollect any Circumstance belonging to it, except that you and Mrs. Aubrey were there the most favourable, agreeable, and praise-worthy.

What, does Mr. M—— boast of the glorious Absurdity he committed at parting, in mistaking my Horse for his? When I see him next, I will produce a Hundred I have been lately guilty of, to no one of which his is able to compare. His, you know, commenced in the very Moment of parting, and consequently was little wonderful, in Comparison of those I have since committed; besides, his Horse had a Spot or two of Brown on him, and was therefore easily mistaken at such a Time for one that was Sorrel all over.

After all, you are a very wicked Lady — you defrauded me of the Crosslet you promised me, putting me off with a single Bead; but it was yours, and that's enough. The most trivial Donation from a Person we esteem, has a large Value. I acknowledged to have a great *Penchant* for what the Vulgar call *Keepsakes.* The *French* are notably practised in these little Elegancies; we are not so much so, as, I think, a polished People ought to be.

I am, dear Miss Carter,
Your most sincere Admirer, and humble Servant,
W. Shenstone

Don't expose the Nonsense-Verses I gave you, I entreat you.

43. To RICHARD GRAVES[1]

[November 9,] 1743

DEAR SIR,

I am tempted to begin my letter as Memmius does his harangue. "Multa me dehortantur à vobis, ni studium virtutis vestrae omnia exsuperet." — You contrive interviews of about a minute's duration; and you make appointments in order to disappoint one; and yet, at the same time that your proceedings are thus vexatious, force one to bear testimony to the inestimable value of your friendship! I do insist upon it, that you ought to compound for the disappointment you have caused me, by a little letter every post you stay in town. I shall now scarce see you till next summer, or spring at soonest; and then I may probably take occasion to visit you, under pretence of seeing Derbyshire. Truth is, your prints have given me *some* curiosity to see the original places. I am grateful for your intentions with regard to giving me part of them, and impertinent in desiring you to convey them to me as soon as you can well spare them. Let me know if they are sold separately at the print-shops. I think to recommend them to my new acquaintance, Mr. Lyttelton Brown.[2] I like the humour of the ballad you mention, but am more obliged for your partial opinion of me. The notes that fall upon the word "Cannon, Cannon," are admirably expressive of the sound, I dare say: I mean, jointly with its echo; and so, I suppose, you will think, if you ever attended to the Tower-guns. I find I cannot afford to go to Bath previously to my London-journey;[3] though I look upon it as a proper method to make my residence in town more agreeable. I shall, probably, be there about the first of December; or before, if I can accelerate my friend Whistler's journey. The pen I write with is the most disagreeable of pens! But I have little else to say; only this — that our good friend Jack Dolman is dead at Aldridge, his father's benefice.

I beg, if you have leisure, you would inclose me in a frank the following songs, with the notes: "Stella and Flavia," "Gentle Jessy," "Sylvia, wilt thou waste thy prime?" and any other that is new. I should be glad of that number of the British Orpheus which has my song in it, if it does not cost above six-pence. Make my compliments to your brother and sister; and believe me, in the common forms, but in no common degree,

---

[1] Dodsley, *Letters to Particular Friends*, No. XXXV. Wells's discussion (*Anglia*, 35:445) and Fullington's (*PMLA*, 46:1131) tend to confirm the date.

[2] Of Bishop's Castle; referred to in the four preceding letters.

[3] But we have no letter of Shenstone's from London until the last of May, 1744. See above, Letter 33, n2.

Dear Mr. Graves's
Most affectionate friend and servant,
W. Shenstone

The Leasowes, Nov. 9th, 1743

Do write out the whole ballad of "The Baron stood behind a tree."

44. To RICHARD GRAVES [1]

The Leasowes, Dec. 23, 1743

DEAR SIR,

You may reasonably have expected a letter before now, either as an acknowledgement for your genteel present, or at least by way of information that I had received it. The prints have given me a pleasure, which, however considerable, would soon have languished, if I had bought them at a shop; but which is now built upon the esteem I have for the giver, and cannot have a more durable foundation.—As for the rest, I am most pleased with the view of Matlock, and shall have no peace of mind till I have seen the original. I have been gilding the frames, and wishing all the while for your company.

I will alter the ballad according to your advice; dividing it into three parts, and adding a stanza or two to the shortest, some time or other. I have had no opportunity of trying the tunes. "Arno's vale" has pretty words, and recommends itself to one's imagination by the probability that it was written on a real occasion—the similitude of rhimes in the close is inexcusable. For all that has been the subject of my letter hitherto, as the country people say, I can but thank you, and I do very sincerely; though as to the songs I will re-pay you.

I have your poem by me, which I have read often with the greatest pleasure. I have many observations to make; and only defer the communication till I know whether you have a copy at Tissington to turn to. I think the most *polite* and *suitable* title to it would run thus: "The Villa, a Poem, containing a Sketch of the present Taste in Rural Embellishments, written in 1740." Your preface has a pretty thought towards the close; otherwise is on no account to be admitted. Pardon my freedom; but, I think, there is no manner of occasion for a preface; and those strokes, which I *know* to be real modesty in *you,* the world will undoubtedly impute to affectation.—If you give me encouragement, I will be very minute in my criticisms, allowing you to reject ten to one that you admit of.

[1] Dodsley, *Letters to Particular Friends,* No. XXXVI. Wells confirms the date, *Anglia,* 35:445.

Whistler is gone to Bristol, and has bilked me.—I said, he is gone; but, I believe, he is only upon going—I linger at home, in hopes of gleaning up a little health, and through a dread of being ill in a place where I can be less attended on.—I can continually *find out* something in my preceding diet that, I *think, disorders* me; so that I am constantly in hopes of growing well:—but, perhaps, I never shall:

> Optima quaeque dies miseris mortalibus aevi
> *Prima* fugit, subeunt morbi—

When I was a school-boy, I never knew there *was any such thing* as perspiration; and now, half my time is taken up in considering the immediate connexion betwixt that and health, and endeavouring to promote it.

Mr. Lyttelton has built a kind of alcove in his park, inscribed, "Sedes Contemplationis," near his hermitage. Under the aforesaid inscription is "Omnia Vanitas:"—the sides ornamented with sheeps-bones, jaws, sculls, &c. festoon-wise. In a niche over it, an owl.

As to schemes, I have none with regard to the world, women, or books. And I hate, and have deferred writing to you (for some days) for that reason. I am sick of exhibiting so much sameness:—I am constantly poring over some Classic, which I consider as one of Idleness's better shapes. But I am impatient to be doing something that may tend to better my situation in some respect or other. It is *encouragement* can alone inspire one.

> Multa & præclare minantem
> Vivere nec *recte,* nec *suaviter*—

expresses the whole of me. Thus my epistles persevere in the plaintive style; and I question whether the sight of them does not, ere now, give you the vapours. I have had an old aunt that visits me sometimes, whose conversation is the perfect counterpart of them. She shall fetch a long-winded sigh with Dr. Young for a wager; though I see *his* Suspiria are not yet finished. He has *relapsed* into "Night the Fifth."[2] I take his case to be wind in a great measure, and would advise him to take rhubarb in powder, with a little nutmeg grated amongst it, as I do.

Dear Mr. Graves! write down to me; and believe me to be, invariably,
Your most sincere and obliged friend, &c.
W. Shenstone

[2] Noticed in the Register of Books of the *Gentleman's Magazine*, December, 1743.

45. To RICHARD GRAVES[1]

1743

DEAR SIR,

You must know, my last letter to you was written before I received yours from Tissington;[2] and I should take shame upon myself for not answering it, were I not furnished with this excuse—that I waited for a frank for you.—There are but few things I have to say to you, and such as are not worth transcribing; yet, as our distance from one another requires it, I will scrawl them over as negligently as I can, to let you see I lay no stress upon them. A good excuse for laziness! you will say: and lazy enough I am, God knows!—I believe, any one who knows me thoroughly will think, that there never was so great an inconsistence as there is betwixt my words (in my poem) and my actions.—This is what the world calls hypocrisy, and is determined to look upon with *peculiar* aversion. But, I think, the hypocrite is a *half*-good character. A man certainly, considering the force of precedent, deserves some praise who keeps up appearances; and is, no doubt, as much to be commended for talking better than he acts, as he is to be blamed for acting worse than he talks. So much for casuistry. I would seem, you must know, to have some meritorious views in talking *virtuously;* but who does not know that every one who writes poetry looks directly with his face towards praise, and whatever else his eye takes in is viewed obliquely? Praise, as I said to foible-confessing W——, is the desired, the noted, and the adequate reward of poetry; in which sort he that rewards me, Heaven reward him, as Sir John Falstaff says. There is something very vain in repeating my own sayings; but I could not conscientiously use a joke to you which I had used in another letter without owning it.—In short, it is necessary to have some *earthly* aim in view; the next world, whether it be in reality near or far off, is always *seen* at a distance. All that the generality of young people can do is, to act *consistently with* their expectations there. Now, though fame, &c. be obviously enough in the eye of reason dissatisfactory; yet it is proper enough to suffer one's self to be deluded with the hopes of it, that is, it is proper to cherish some worldly hopes, that one may avoid impatience, spleen, and one sort of *despair:* I mean that of having no *hopes* here, because one sees nothing here that deserves them. If I were in your case, I would make all the efforts I was able towards being a Bishop. That should be my earthly

---

[1] Dodsley, *Letters to Particular Friends,* No. XXXVII.
[2] Graves was chaplain at Tissington Hall, Derbyshire, for three years following his ordination in 1740.

aim: not but I would act with so much indifference as to bear all disappointment unconcernedly — as, I dare say, you will. — There is but one passion that I put upon an equally sprightly footing with ambition, and that is love; which, as it *regularly tends* to matrimony, requires certain favours from fortune and circumstance to render it proper to indulge in. — By this time you think me crazed — as it often happens to me to doubt, *seriously,* whether I am not: but if it be the "mentis gratissimus error," I do not mind. You are very obliging to endeavour to continue my madness and vanity. — I should be as glad to see Mr. Graves your brother as any one I know: I live in a manner wherein he would find many things to exercise his good-nature.

Pamela would have made one good volume; and I wonder the author, who has some *nice* natural strokes, should not have sense enough to see that — I beg you will collect all the hints, &c. of your own, or others, that you think may tend to the improvement of my poem, against winter; that you would mention any flat lines, &c. Write me word some time ere you come over; but write to me immediately. I am

Yours faithfully,
W. Shenstone

46. To THOMAS SMITH [1]

To
    Mr. Smith of Tennal
SIR,
    I have sent to demand the Hare which was cours'd in my Brother's Grounds, Kill'd by my Dogs, and taken from my Servants. I little expected this usage from the Persons that were concern'd in it.

I am, your Servt
Will. Shenstone

[1] This letter is reproduced from James Kenward's *Harborne and Its Surroundings* (2d ed., Birmingham, 1885), p. 39. The book is rare; I do not know of any copy except that in the British Museum. Of the three letters of Shenstone's that it contains Kenward says, "Mr. Thomas Sargeant kindly showed me in 1877, several original letters from Shenstone to Smith. I give three of these letters which are of interest." The letters and Kenward's remarks concerning them are found on pages 39 and 40 of his book. The present letter is not dated, and almost the only clue to the date is Shenstone's reference to his brother as though he were still alive. Joseph Shenstone died November 30, 1751. The chronological position of the letter is thus conjectural. According to Kenward, Thomas Smith was an attorney-at-law who inhabited Tennal Hall, Halesowen, between 1734 and 1747, and probably earlier and later. The reference in the following letter to "Cous. Shenstone" suggests the period of Shenstone's earliest residence at the Leasowes, between 1740 and 1745, before he took the management of the estate wholly into his own hands. He was then lodging with his tenants and kinsmen.

47. To THOMAS SMITH[1]

SIR,

I was inform'd and I believe with truth, that your Dogs had cours'd the Hare previously, but *lost* her, that the Hare coming accidentally into a Field where *my* Dogs were, the Noise generally made upon those occasions introduc'd *yours* a second Time, whilst *mine* were in the Pursuit, that She was kill'd in my Br^s grounds by my Dogs, and torn from them not without some Violence. I leave you to consider the Nature of this Behaviour which I can only be induc'd to over-look by your Promise to send me one of y^r next Hares you kill.

I am, y^r hum: Servt
Will. Shenstone

As ye Hare was design'd for Cous. Shenstone if you give *him* y^r next Hare 'twill be consider'd in ye same light.

48. To RICHARD JAGO[1]

The Leasowes, March 1, 1743–4

DEAR SIR,

You are upon very *good* terms with me, and *have* been all along. I guessed the causes of your silence, and have been sincerely sorry for them; not however that I did not believe you were more happy than any one in the world who is neither a lover nor a poet, though not able to turn himself for money-bags.—I am really going to London; and am about the purchase of an elegant pair of pistols from Birmingham. I indulge myself in this expence, because they shall serve in two capacities; one while to garnish my chair, another while my horse. And some time next week you will probably see your old friend on horse-back, armed *at all points,* and as very a knight to all *appearance* as any body.

> *Well! they say the Owl was a Quaker's Daughter*—*one knows what one* is, *but one does not know what one* shall be.[2]
> Ophelia in HAMLET

But I digress. If I just call to see you, God forbid that I should be burthensome to you. I will send my horses to H——, and lodge there,

---

[1] Reproduced from James Kenward's *Harborne and Its Surroundings* (2d ed., Birmingham, 1885). This letter is not dated but obviously follows the foregoing.

[1] Dodsley, *Letters to Particular Friends,* No. XXXVIII. Fullington's discussion (*PMLA,* 46:1131) tends to confirm the date.

[2] *Hamlet,* IV, v, 42–44: "Well, God 'ild you! They say the owl was a baker's daughter. Lord! We know what we are, but know not what we may be."

or somewhere. But I am perfectly impatient to unbosom my soul to you, and to see Mrs. Jago, whom I should have mentioned first. Wednesday or Tuesday indeed seems the most likely day. — Though I am not sure; nor do you confine yourself.

Poor Marriett! *I* too am emaciated; but I hope, by means of some warm weather, to acquire *plus d'embonpoint.* I design to call upon him, and keep him in countenance.

My ballad, in the midst of your hurry, must appear as ridiculous as Cinna the poet does, when he swears nothing but death shall restrain him from addressing Brutus and Cassius (and that the night before the battle) with two doggrel verses — and those the worst I have ever read; and that makes the simile the more just. It is now a good deal metamorphosed. Your parody is prodigiously droll, the first line delights me! I think I could furnish Mrs. K[night] with as good mottoes, and as cheap, though I say it, as any-body; but, alas! — Did I send you the following parody or no, before? I believe not. *Le voila!*

>   When first, Philander, first I came
>   Where Avon rolls his winding stream,
>   The nymphs — how brisk! the swains — how gay!
>   To see *Asteria,*[3] Queen of May! —
>   The parsons round, her praises sung!
>   The steeples, with her praises rung! —
>   I thought — no sight, that e'er was seen,
>   Could match the sight of Barel's green! —
>   But *now* since old *Eugenio*[3] dy'd —
>   The chief of poets, and the pride —
>   Now, meaner bards in vain aspire
>   To raise their voice, to tune their lyre!
>   Their lovely season, now, is o'er!
>   Thy notes, Florelio, please no more! —
>   No more Asteria's smiles are seen! —
>   Adieu! — the sweets of Barel's green! —

It is a kind of extempore, so excuse it. — You have seen the song of Arno's Vale.

I am taking part of my farm upon my hands, to see if I can succeed as a farmer; — but I am afraid I am under the sentence, "And behold, whatsoever he taketh in hand, it shall *not* prosper."

[3] Asteria is Mrs. Knight, and old Eugenio, William Somervile, who died in 1742. Shenstone's intimacy with the former had not yet developed to its greatest extent.

My good friend, I sincerely confide, that, however we may be separated, no time shall extenuate our mutual friendship. I am
>Your zealous, unserviceable friend,
>>W. Shenstone

49. To RICHARD JAGO [1]

[London, May 30(?), 1744]

DEAR FRIEND,

I shall send you but a very few lines, being so much indisposed with a cold, that I can scarce tell how to connect a sentence. I am just got into lodgings at a goldsmith's — a dangerous situation, you will say, for *me;* "Actum est, ilicet, periisti!" Not so; — for of late I have not so violent a taste for toys as I have had; and I can look even on snuff-boxes "oculo irretorto."

London is really dangerous at this time; the pick-pockets, formerly content with mere *filching,* make no scruple to knock people down with bludgeons in *Fleet-street* and the *Strand,* and that at no later hour than eight o'clock at night: but in the Piazzas, Covent-garden, they come in large bodies, armed with couteaus, and attack whole parties, so that the danger of coming out of the play-houses is of some weight in the opposite scale, when I am disposed to go to them oftener than I ought. — There is a poem of this season, called, "The Pleasures of Imagination," worth your reading; but it is an expensive quarto; if it comes out in a less size, I will bring it home with me. Mr. Pope (as Mr. Outing, who has been with Lord Bolingbroke, informs me) is at the point of death. — My Lord Carteret said yesterday in the house, "That the French and Spaniards had actually *said,* they would attempt a second invasion." — There is a new play acted at Drury-Lane, "Mahomet," translated from the French of Voltaire;[2] but I have no great opinion of the subject, or the original author as a poet; and my diffidence is rather improved by the testimony of those who have seen it. I lodge between the two coffee-houses, George's and Nando's, so that I partake of the expensiveness of both, as heretofore. I have no acquaintance in town, and but slender inducement to stay; and yet, probably, I shall loiter here for a month.

T—— H——[3] was knighted against his will, and had a demand made upon him for an hundred pounds before he could get out of St. James's;

---

[1] Dodsley, *Letters to Particular Friends,* No. XXX, dated 1743. Wells corrects the date, *Anglia,* 35:444. Akenside's *Pleasures of Imagination* was published January 16, 1744; the second edition came out May 20. Pope died May 30 of that year.

[2] The adaptation of the Rev. James Miller, acted at Drury Lane on April 25, 1744.

[3] Williams believes T—— H—— to be Thomas Head. *Times Literary Supplement,* September 1, 1927, p. 592.

so soon are felt the inconveniences of grandeur!—He came out of the court in a violent rage, "G—d! Jack, what dost think?—I am knighted!—the devil of a knight, e'faith!" I believe he was sincere in his disgust; for there had been two barge-masters knighted in his neighbourhood some time before.

I saw, coming up, Lady Fane's grotto, which, they say, cost her five thousand pounds; about three times as much as her *house* is worth. It is a very beautiful disposition of the finest collection of shells I ever saw—Mr. Powis's woods, which are finer.—Mean time, if I had three hundred pounds to lay out about The Leasowes, I could bring my ambition to peaceable terms. I am, dear Sir, with all affection, yours and Mrs. Jago's.

W. Shenstone

Write soon. It is this moment reported that Pope is dead.

50. To RICHARD GRAVES [1]

[Late 1744 or 1745]

DEAR MR. GRAVES,

There is not a syllable you tell me concerning yourself in your last letter, but what applied to *me* is most literally true. I am sensible of the daily progress I make towards insignificancy, and it will not be many years before you see me arrived at the *ne plus ultra*. I believe it is absolutely impossible for me to acquire a considerable degree of knowledge, though I can understand things well enough at the time I read them. I remember a preacher at St. Mary's (I think it was Mr. E——) made a notable distinction betwixt *apprehension* and *comprehension*. If there be a real difference, probably it may find a place in the explication of my genius. I envy you a good *general* insight into the writings of the learned. I must aim at nothing higher than a well-concealed ignorance.—I was thinking, upon reading your letter, *when* it was that you and Mr. Whistler and I went out of the road of happiness. It certainly was where we first deviated from the turnpike-road of life. Wives, children, alliances, visits, &c. are necessary objects of our social passions; and whether or no we can, through particular circumstances, be happy *with,* I think it plain enough that it is not possible to be happy *without* them. All attachments to inanimate beauties, to curiosities, and ornaments, satiate us presently.—The fanciful tribe has the disadvantage to be naturally prone to err in the choice of *lasting* pleasures: and when our passions have habitually wandered, it is too difficult to reduce them into their proper chan-

---

[1] Dodsley, *Letters to Particular Friends,* No. XXXIX, dated "about 1745." Fullington (*PMLA,* 46:1131–32) shows that the letter was written probably late in 1744 or in 1745.

nels. When this is the case, nothing but the change or variety of amusements stands any chance to make us easy, and it is not long ere the whole species is exhausted. I agree with you entirely in the necessity of a *sociable* life in order to be happy: I do not think it much a paradox, that any company is better than *none*. I think it obvious enough as to the present hour; and as to any future influence, solitude has exceeding savage effects on our dispositions.—I have wrote out my elegy: I lay no manner of stress but upon the piety of it.—Would it not be a good kind of motto, applied to a person you know, that might be taken from what is said of *Ophelia* in *Hamlet,*

>I tell thee, faithless priest!
>A ministring angel shall Ophelia be
>When thou art howling.[2]

I have amused myself often with this species of writing since you saw me; partly to divert my present *impatience,* and partly as it will be a picture of most that passes in my mind; a portrait which *friends* may value.—I should be glad of your profile: if you have objections, I drop my request.—I should be heartily glad if you would come and live with me, for any space of time that you could find convenient. But I will depend on your coming over with Mr. Whistler in the spring. I may possibly take a jaunt towards you ere long: the road would furnish me out some visits; and, by the time I reached you, perhaps, afford me a kind of climax of happiness. If I do not, I shall perhaps be a little time at Bath. I do not speak of this last as a scheme from which I entertain great expectations of pleasure. It is long since I have considered myself as *undone*. The *world* will not perhaps consider me in that light entirely, till I have married my maid. Adieu!

51. To RICHARD GRAVES[1]

The Leasowes, Nov. 22, 1745

DEAR MR. GRAVES,

My life, for aught I see, will pass away just as it *has* done, without introducing sufficient improvement into my circumstances to give a chearful cast to my correspondence. In *one* respect, in regard to my in-

---

[2] I tell thee, churlish priest,
A ministering angel shall my sister be,
When thou liest howling.
   Hamlet, V, i, 262–64.

[1] Dodsley, *Letters to Particular Friends,* No. XL. Wells confirms the date (*Anglia,* 35:446) and Fullington confirms Wells (*PMLA,* 46:1132).

violable friendship for *you,* I hope you will hear with some satisfaction that I continue still the same. And this kind of *identity,* I think, I could promise you, though every circumstance in my fortune, every particle of my body, were changed; and others, ever so heterogeneous, substituted in their place. After this, it would be no compliment to say, that the *pretended* heir to these kingdoms could not alter it, were he to subvert the British constitution; which must, out of all doubt, be the consequence of his success. The rebellion, you may guess, is the subject of all conversation. Every individual nailer here takes in a news-paper (a more *pregnant* one by far than any of the London ones), and talks as familiarly of *kings* and *princes* as ever Master Shallow did of John of Gaunt.[2] Indeed it is no bad thing that they do so; for I cannot conceive that the people want so much to be convinced by *sermons* of the absurdities of *popery,* as they do by *news-papers* that it may *possibly* prevail. The reasons and arguments too in favour of the present Government are so *strong* and *obvious,* that even I, and every country 'squire, and every country clerk, and Sam Shaw the taylor, seem to be as much masters of them as the Bishops themselves. I must not say we could express them so politely. — I like Secker's the best of any sermon on this occasion. He gives his audience a view of such evil consequences from a *change,* as no man of sense can possibly doubt of, when fairly stated: and, I own, I cannot see one single *good* it could produce, in compensation for its inevitable and abundant *mischiefs.* — I have read Dr. Sherlock's sermon on this occasion: and I have read Mr. Warburton's; and, at your request, I will read his Legation.

I have often thoughts of a jaunt as far as your country this winter. Some kind of pilgrimage I must make, to avoid a lethargy. — Public places I want to visit a little, to peep at and renew my idea of the *world's* vanity; but either Bath or London would steep me so far in poverty, that I should not probably emerge before the middle of next summer. I have spent this last summer agreeably enough with some of my young relations, Mr. Dolman's children. — They have an excellent taste for their years. — I have been upon several jaunts with the son to Litchfield, Worcester, Mr. Fletcher's, &c. amusing him, what I could, under the loss of his father. Miss W[inny] F[letcher] asked very earnestly after you. Two of the sisters have been with me at The Leasowes, and upon several parties of pleasure in my chair. — Broom is disposed of — I do not understand upon what inducement.[3] — After all, I am miserable; —

---

[2] 2 *Henry IV,* III, ii, 348.
[3] Apparently Shenstone wished to procure the living of Broom for Graves, but it was otherwise disposed of (Fullington).

conscious to myself that I am too little selfish; that I ought now or never to aim at some addition to my fortune; and that I make large advances towards the common catastrophe of *better* poets, poverty.—I never can attend enough to some twelve penny matter, on which a great deal depends. My amour, so far as I indulge it, gives me some pleasure, and no pain in the world.—I have read Spenser once again: and I have added full as much more to my *School-mistress*,[4] in regard to *number of lines; something* in point of *matter* (or *manner* rather) *which* does not displease me. I would be glad if Mr.——— were, upon your request, to give his opinion of particulars, for two reasons; as you say he has some taste for this kind of writing, and as he is my enemy, and would, therefore, find out its deficiencies.

I have a reason, of a most whimsical kind, why I would wish you to preserve this letter. Pray write soon, and believe me most affectionately
Your friend and humble servant
W. Shenstone

52. To MISS WINNY FLETCHER[1]

The Leasows, Novr 28—1745

DEAR MISS WINNY,

On a Time, as tis reported, the Mountains were in Labour; when after a long course of Pains & Inquietudes they made a Shift to produce that puny Animal a Mouse. Now that very individual Mouse, according to the mysterious & Figurative Import of Types & Shadows was the perfect Image & Representative of this mine Epistle. A groveling, starvling insignificant Production, conceiv'd wth much difficulty, & transmitted to you wth Confusion of Face. In short, you may look upon it as ye noble Booty you have taken, by baiting your Trap so artfully with Praise & Compliment about two or three Months ago— True it is, that considering ye Politeness & Complaisance of your obliging Letter, my Behaviour since must appear the most *unknightly* of all Proceedings. But your Packet did not arrive till three weeks after it was sent—So you will Excuse my Silence 'till the Day after I received it, & whatever was *more* than that, I freely acknowledge, came of Sin. However you will, upon Confession, pardon me, as you expect Pardon from your Confessor shou'd ye Benedictines & Friars get a Footing in this Island—which I find, your Brother is endeavouring to prevent.

[4] It will be recalled that *The School-Mistress* grew, between 1742 and 1748, from a poem of twenty-eight to one of thirty-five stanzas.

[1] Bodleian MS 25448, fol. 92ff. A version of this letter appears in Hull, *Select Letters*, Vol. I, No. V. Several letters from Miss Fletcher to Shenstone are also to be found in Hull.

I can be no longer ludicrous on this last Article. I am too seriously concern'd for his safety. Yet I don't fear that the Rebels will be defeated, & maybe, all Danger over in Less than a Fortnight. But General Wade's Behaviour, loitering so long at Newcastle, astonishes me. I was at Birm: on Tuesday morning from whence I saw ye Remains of Ligonier's Horse march with vast spirits & Alacrity. They wish to have what they *call,* the *Refusal* of the Highlanders. They are men of experienc'd Bravery, & fought like Furies at ye Battle of Fontenoy. May they do so now, & with better Success!

Binnel[2] told me your Brother wou'd borrow my Pistols. At that Time supposing him in Jest, I sent no very *serious* Answer. I now think it incumbent on me to say that I wou'd lend them him with all my Heart, but that one of them is broke in ye Stock, & cannot be fir'd with safety 'till it is stock'd afresh. Perhaps he might recollect it was so, when I was at Acleton.

We have been best Part of a Week at Lichfield, where we liv'd like Chickens in a Pen, confin'd & cramm'd, & where we serv'd God After the Manner of Popes & Cardinals — I only allude to Cathedral-Service. M^r & Mrs Dolman seem'd quite disposd to entertain us agreeably. The Son & Daughter, to say the least, appeard much more indifferent in that Particular. These, as Shakespear says, are *certainly* better X^{tians} or else worse than we.

You have escap'd me at Birmingham by concealing ye Time of y^r Visit. Surely you will come over to Broom e'er it be long & give me my Revenge.

Tell Mrs Anne my Ears make great Shoots, & such as may tempt her Hand egregiously. But if *I am* metamorphisd into an Ass entirely, I will come & serenade her in a Morning when she has been up late ye Night before.

I beg my Compliments to all Friends. I must not make my Letter much longer — The Mouse will grow to ye Size of a Rat — I beg you to accept this Idle Billet in Part of an Answer to y^r Elegant Letter, & in Lieu of a Thousand Professions of the Friendship and Esteem wth wch I am Dear Miss Winney

      Your most obedient & faithfull H^{ble} Servt
          W. Shenstone

[2] The Rev. Robert Binnel (d. 1763), rector of Newport, Shropshire, was one of Shenstone's Pembroke friends. Nash, *History of Worcestershire,* I, 530.

53. To RICHARD GRAVES[1]

[April 6, 1746]

DEAR MR. GRAVES,

I have lately received a letter from Mr. Whistler, which conveys your compliments to me, and, by so doing, prompts me to acknowledge the receipt of your last kind letter. I observe you adhere strictly to the apostolical precept of being "swift to *hear,* slow to *speak;*" the latter part of which, I would fain conclude, you understand too literally.

Your neighbour, I see, is not a little embarrassed with his mills at Whitchurch. I have long had an eye upon his advertisement in the London Evening Post, and been not a little scandalized thereat. What has the name of a poet to do with the publication of lands and tenements? or the idea of harmony with the noise of a water-mill? yet has he extracted music from the subject, and mirth from his misfortunes; having sent me a ballad upon the miller, written with much ease and some drollery.

As to the light in which you place your present fortunes, I can only say, that you have not that situation I could wish you for your *own sake:* for so far as I am concerned in your elevation, I can assure you very faithfully, that no circumstances in the world could more endear you to my affection, or recommend you to my respect, than the present. My *affection* you will easily observe, from the very *nature* of affection in general, would stand no chance to be increased by your promotion; and as for respect, if I knew the degree you desired, I would acquit myself of it to your satisfaction *now;* and were you settled at *Lambeth,* I should expect that you would require no *more* from me upon that account; at least in private: so that, so far as either *deference* or *friendship* is concerned, you are an Archbishop to *me* to all intents and purposes.—As to figure in the world, it depends much, I know, upon advancement; and yet even here you will be ever *sure* of that kind of weight which ingenuity gives; discernible to the *smaller* indeed, but undoubtedly the more *valuable* part of the world;—but this is improper, as it is *philosophy,* and as it is *advice;* neither of which is it suitable for me to suggest to you—"Alcinoo Poma, &c." As to the long series of *my* lamentations, I will not now enter upon the reasonableness of them. It is a subject, to tell you the truth, on which you cannot reply without some danger of hurting me.—As for politics[2] (you will blame this letter for dwelling so much

---

[1] Dodsley, *Letters to Particular Friends,* No. XLII. Fullington confirms the date, *PMLA,* 46:1132.

[2] Though mildly interested in politics, Shenstone always professed and, I believe, practiced moderation. He never became really heated in a political dispute; and his partici-

upon the subject of yours;) but as for politics, I think *poets* are *tories* by nature, supposing them to be by nature poets.—The love of an individual person or family, that has worn a crown for many successions, is an inclination greatly adapted to the fanciful tribe. On the other hand, mathematicians, abstract-reasoners, of no manner of attachment to persons, at least to the *visible* part of them, but prodigiously devoted to the ideas of virtue, liberty, interest, and so forth, are generally *whigs*. It happens agreeably enough to this maxim, that the whigs are friends to that wise, plodding, un-poetical people the Dutch — the tories, on the other hand, are taken mightily with that shewy, ostentatious nation the French. Fox hunters, that reside amongst the beauties of nature, and bid defiance to art, in short, that have intellects of a poetical *turn,* are frequently tories — citizens, merchants, &c. that scarce see what nature is, and consequently have no pretensions to a poetical taste, are, I think, generally argumentative and whiggish; — but perhaps I carry this too far. — Something there is in it, however, you will see: not that I would apply what I here say to particular revolutions; &c. I would only advance something general and speculative. Nor would I approve or condemn by this any one set of people now existing. Nor would I have you pretend to fish out my party from any thing I have said; for I am of none. — The letter I sent you last was *occasional,* and when I see you I will tell you the occasion. I absolutely agree with you in every tittle of your political observations — I am glad I do; for I know the poisonous nature of party: and though we are *neither* violent, yet I should fear it. My schemes are *doubtful* at present, but my face is set towards Bath — I am confident of the service those waters would do me. — I hope you will exhilarate me with a letter soon. — I would fain have furnished out a letter to amuse you after so long a silence, but I find myself unable; even *as* unable as I am to express the regard with which I am

Yours,
W. Shenstone

The Leasowes, April 6, 1746

pation in elections, as when he supported George Lyttelton, who stood for Worcester in 1741, or when he solicited the aid of Lady Luxborough in rounding up the votes in Oldbarrow for Lord Coventry in 1753, seems to have been motived as much by personal as by political considerations.

54. To RICHARD GRAVES[1]

The Leasowes, May 11, 1746

DEAR MR. GRAVES,

Though I feel an irresistible propensity to write to you this very post, yet I cannot say that I am able to advance anything tending either to your own or my satisfaction. — What is worst of all is, I cannot fix the time of seeing you with so much precision as I would always endeavour where my pleasure is so much concerned. — I will tell you the whole affair. — I have for a long season purposed to drink the Bath waters this spring; and *did* think of setting out in a week's time, when I received your letter purposing to stay there a month; and from thence take a circuit which should indulge me in a sight of you, Mr. Whistler, and some few others, in my way home. The latter part of this scheme (though far the more agreeable to me) was rather doubtful and precarious; depending (as you express it) on the state of my finances after a month's continuance at Bath; which I considered, and *do* consider, as a very probable means of bettering my constitution. Now I covet to see you so much, that I would bring nothing but health in competition. — What I wish *is*, that you could, with convenience, either *hasten* or *delay* your journey, that you might find me before mine, or after my return, though I should infinitely, and for many reasons, prefer the former. I long to talk with you particularly now. I have much to say in regard to our friend's amour, to which you alluded in your last.[2] I request it as a favour of you, that you would conjure him, by the friendship I have ever borne him, and by any esteem which he has ever professed for me, that he would do nothing very *material* in the affair till I have talked it over, and given him my faithful sentiments, "quod censet amiculus."

I am not willing the balance should turn entirely on the whig side: I would give it a greater equilibrium, if the following suggestion might effect it. Tories, I said, have great, and sometimes partial affections for the *person* of a king. — We will suppose the kings are alternately good and bad: their loyalty to the good one is commendable; their partiality to the bad one not to be vindicated. Whigs have *no* passion, *no* gratitude, towards the good prince: there they are wrong. They are severe upon the bad one, in which they are justifiable. I wish I had not begun these wholesale distinctions, this miserable specimen of my politics. I protest

---

[1] Dodsley, *Letters to Perticular Friends*, No. XLIII. Fullington confirms the date, *PMLA*, 46:1132.

[2] Fullington conjectures that this passage, possibly containing some editorial changes by Dodsley, refers to Graves's own love affair with Lucy Bartholomew, which culminated in marriage in 1748. See his article in *PMLA*, 46:1132.

against all epistolary disputes. I am now embarrassed in one, on much such another score, which fills up all my letter; for I love the last word, like a scold or a child. — I thank you for your little anecdotes from time to time: you may depend upon it, that I have never heard any thing *before;* for I never *do* hear any thing. — I am one very thankful letter in debt to your neighbour Whistler. I have at present nothing but the *propensity* of a good correspondent; but I will write soon. In the mean time, if you see him, ask him if he goes to Bath or Bristol this season. — I beg you would write to me directly *when* you can come, and how I may regulate my motions so as to be best assured of seeing you. — Pray do not neglect a post. I am

Yours most entirely,
W. S.

55. To RICHARD GRAVES[1]

1746, ineunte anno

DEAR MR. GRAVES,

I believe it is impossible for me to disagree with you on any other score, than the scanty pittances you allot me of your company; and, if I have disclosed any symptoms of resentment on that account, you will, perhaps, overlook them, out of regard to the motive from which they proceeded. — I thank you for your perusal of that trivial poem. If I were going to print it, I should give way to your remarks *implicitly,* and would not *dare* to do otherwise. But so long as I keep it in manuscript, you will pardon my silly prejudices, if I chuse to read and shew it with the addition of most of my new stanzas.[2] I own, I have a fondness for several, imagining them to be *more* in Spenser's way, yet more independent on the antique phrase, than any part of the poem; and, on that account, I cannot yet prevail on myself to banish *them* entirely; but were I to print, I should (with *some* reluctance) give way to your sentiments (which I know are just), namely, that they render the work too diffuse and flimsy, and seem rather excrescences than essential parts of it.

But of these things I say no more now. I purpose staying a month with Mr. Whistler, in December, if it suits him; and then I hope I shall have a great deal of your company. Let me hear something in your next of your *domestic affairs.* I beg you would not make any grand decision, without giving me some previous information. I esteem this as due to

---

[1] Dodsley, *Letters to Particular Friends,* No. XLI. Written after August 18, 1746, the date of execution of Lords Kilmarnock and Balmerino (Wells, *Anglia,* 35:446).

[2] See note on *The School-Mistress* above, Letter 20, n2.

the friendship I have so long professed for you, and from the friendship you have so long professed for me.

I look upon the death of the two Lords as equally decent upon their respective principles. Lord Kilmarnock, I suppose, joined the rebels through a view of bettering his circumstances, conscious to himself that he was guilty of a crime the moment he did so. This is agreeable to his speech before the Lords, and to that melancholy which he discovered upon the scaffold. Death, aggravated by guilt, would sit heavier upon him than upon the other, even supposing him to have had the same resolution. Balmerino's life was quite *unie,* and his death equal to the character he aimed at.[3] We are to observe, that he meant to suffer as a Friend to the Stewarts, a Soldier, and a Scotsman. The first he manifested when he came out of the Tower, by his reply of "God save King J[ame]s;" the second, by his dress, and numberless ostentations of intrepidity; the last, by his plaid night-cap. Did you hear the story of his sending a message to Lord Kilmarnock? "That he had been practicing how to lie upon the block; and had found out, the easiest way of receiving the blow was, to bite his tongue hard: or even if he bit it off, it was no matter, they should have no further use for it." His behaviour seems to have wanted coolness, or else to equal that of Adrian, Cato, Sir T. More, &c. or any of those heroes who had spirit enough to make an ostentation of their unconcern. I had, from the printed accounts of their behaviour, an idea of their persons, exactly conformable to the description I read afterwards in your paper; — but enough — you send me sterling matters of fact, and I return you tinsel observations. — I thank you for accenting Crŏmĕrtie and Balmĕrĭno; I learnt Cullōden from you *before.*

I have had little company since I saw you. — One day indeed I was surprized by a visit from Mr. Thomson, Author of the Seasons.[4] — Mr. Lyttelton introduced him. — I have not room to tell you all that passed. — They praised my place extravagantly; — proposed alterations, &c. Thomson was very facetious, and very complaisant; invited me to his house at Richmond. There were many things said worth *telling,* but not *writing* to you. — This has been a summer that I have spent more *socially* than any one these three years. I expect a good deal more company this week, the next, and the week after. — Lady Luxborough talks of coming, and I

---

[3] Shenstone further discusses the case of Balmerino in his essay *On Politicks,* in *Works,* II (1764), 152–53.

[4] Shenstone was a strong admirer of Thomson, whose death in 1748 prevented what might have developed into a close friendship.

believe *will*. — The visit would bring my little walks into repute. — When will the time come, that I shall enjoy your company here a month uninterrupted?
Dear Sir,
Yours most faithfully,
W. Shenstone

56. To LADY LUXBOROUGH [1]

Aug. 10, 1747

MADAM,

I am quite asham'd that it has not been in my Power to make a speedier Enquiry into the Event of your Ladyship's Journey. It wou'd give me the utmost uneasiness to find you underwent any Inconvenience from a visit which was calculated to give me so much Pleasure, and yourself so little.

I am somewhat apprehensive that one ought to guard not only against *Ambition* but even too much *Admiration,* if one wou'd prepare to live as it beseems a pious *Hermit* to do. Your Ladyship will observe therefore, how dangerous a visitant you are, & how much you must have retarded my Progress tow'rds an eremetical Temper of Mind; having diffus'd an Air of Dignity thro' my solitary Paths which will not fail to present itself as oft as I resume them. Perhaps Politeness Elegance and Taste may be some of those amiable Accomplishments which it may be allowable for an *Hermit* to admire under certain Limitations; If not, I can only say that I must remain a very *imperfect one,* so long as I remember ye Honour you have done me; And if I am not likely to succeed *that Way,* may as well indulge my Ambition to the full, which I never fail to do as oft as I am permitted to subscribe myself

Your Ladyship's most oblig'd & most
obedient humble servant
W. Shenstone

I hope to have an opportunity of waiting on your Ladyship at Barels very soon. In the mean Time, I wou'd beg leave to borrow Mr. Whitehead's & Mr. Mallet's Poems.[2]

Miss Dolman desires her Duty to your Ladyship. I am now at her Brother's at Broom, August the 10th, 1747.

---

[1] B. M. Add. MSS 28958, fol. 1ff. An undated version of this letter, with many minor and a few major differences, appears in Hull's *Select Letters,* Vol. I, No. XVII.

[2] Mallet's *Amyntor and Theodora* appeared in 1747.

57. To RICHARD JAGO[1]

The Leasowes, Sept. 17, 1747

DEAR MR. JAGO,

I think I have out-corresponded all my Correspondents; whether you are the last that is to be subdued, I cannot say; but the Rest are so fatigued, that they are not able to achieve a Line. Apprized of this, and being by Nature disposed to have Mercy on the Vanquished,

> Parcere subjectis, & debellare superbos,

I seldom write a Syllable more than is requisite to further some Scheme, or ascertain some Interview; the latter being the Purpose of this mine Epistle. I am in great Hopes I shall be at Liberty to see you, ere many Weeks be past, and would beg of you to let me know by a Line, when I am most likely, or when very unlikely, to meet with you at Home. The Reason why I can fix no week, at present, is, that I am in daily Expectations of Mr. Lyttelton, and the Hagley Family. I dined there, some Time since, with Mr. Pitt, Mr. Bouhours, Mr. Campion, and all the World. Mr. Thomson, that right friendly Bard, was expected, and I fancy may be there now. Mr. Lyttelton offered me the Visit, and I own I am pleased with the Prospect of shewing him something at the Leasowes beyond his Expectations. I have made a great Improvement in Virgil's Grove, since you were here, and have finished a new Path from it to the House, after the Manner you approved. They are going to build a Rotund to terminate the Visto at *Hagley;* I think there is a little Hill joining the Park, that would suit one better, tho' it will be very pretty where it is.

If I come to your House, I won't go to Mr. M[ille]r's.[2] He has been, twice, as near me as the Grange, with Charles Lyttelton, but never deemed my Situation worth seeing. I doubt you are a little too modest in praising it, wherever you go. Why don't you applaud it with both Hands? —

> *Parcentes ego Dexteras odi —*
> *Sparge Rosas —*

I am so very much enamoured, that is, so very partial to my native Place, that it seems a Miracle to me, how it comes not to be famous. But to be

---

[1] Both Dodsley (*Letters to Particular Friends*, No. XLVII) and Hull print versions of this letter; Hull's (*Select Letters*, Vol. I, No. XI), which seems the better, is here reproduced.

[2] Sanderson Miller of Radway, whose enthusiasm for Gothic architecture Shenstone deplored. He later visited Radway, however, and wrote a somewhat censorious description of the place (see Letter III).

serious — How my Lord Dudley³ is tumbled about the World! He was overturned in going to Town, and now again in coming back. Is not this falling up Stairs and down Stairs? — Nevertheless, he is safe and sound, and able to sit up with you and me till twelve or one at Night, as I know by last *Monday's* Experience.

I have somewhere about a thousand Things to say to you — not now tho' — Mrs. Knight's Visit I reserve till I see you. A Coach with a Coronet is a pretty Kind of Phaenomenon at my Door; — few Things prettier — except the Face of such a Friend as you; for I do not want the Grace to prefer a spirituous and generous Friendship to all the Gewgaws that Ambition can contrive.

I have wrote out my Elegies, and heartily wish you had them to look over, before I come, but I know not how to send them. I shall bring and leave much Poetry with you — *"Thus & Odores!"* — or rather a Covering *Thuri & Odoribus* —

      Yet, I pray you,
  If you shall e'er my foolish Lines repeat,
  Speak of me, as I am — nothing extenuate,
  Nor set down aught in Malice — then
        Must you speak
Of one who —
 Is, Sir,
  Your most affectionate and faithful Servant,
          W. Shenstone

58. To RICHARD GRAVES¹

The Leasowes, Sept. 21, 1747

DEAR MR. GRAVES,

I am under some apprehension that you dread the sight of a letter from me, as it seems to lay claim to the compliment of an answer. I will therefore write you one that shall wave its privilege, at least till such time as your leisure encourages, or your present dissipation does not forbid, you to send one. — I dare now no longer expatiate upon the affair you have in hand; it is enough for me if you will excuse the freedom I *have* taken. I have often known *delay* produce good effects in some cases which even sagacity itself could not surmount; and, if I thought I did

---

³ Ferdinando Dudley Lea, Lord Dudley (d. 1757), of Halesowen Grange, was a distant connection and close friend of Shenstone. See H. Sidney Grazebrook, *The Family of Shenstone the Poet* (1890).

¹ Dodsley, *Letters to Particular Friends*, No. XLV. Wells (*Anglia*, 35:446–47) confirms the date by reference to Bergen, taken September 16, 1747.

not go too far, would presume to recommend it now. You know I have very little of the temper of an alderman. I almost hate the *idea* of wealthiness as much as the *word*. It seems to me to carry a notion of fulness, stagnation, and insignificancy. It is this disposition of mine that can *alone* give any weight to the advice I send you, as it proves me not to give it through any partiality to fortune. As to what remains, you are, I hope, assured of the value I must ever have for you in *any* circumstances, and the regard I shall always shew for any that belongs to you. I cannot like you *less* or *more*. — I now drop into other matters. Bergen, I see, is taken at last; pray what are the sentiments of your political companions? I dined some time ago with Mr. Lyttelton and Mr. Pitt, who both agreed it was worth twenty thousand men to the French; which is a light in which I never used to consider it. Any little intimation that you please to *confer* upon me, enables me to seem *wise* in this country for a month; particularly if I take care to adjust my face accordingly. — As I was returning last Sunday from church, whom should I meet in my way, but that *sweet-souled* bard Mr. James Thomson, in a chaise drawn by two horses length-ways. — I welcomed him into the country, and asked him to accompany Mr. Lyttelton to The Leasowes (who had offered me a visit,) which he promised to do. So I am in daily expectations of them and all the world this week. I fancy they will lavish all their praises upon *nature,* reserving none for poor *art* and *me.* But if I ever live, and am able to perfect my schemes, I shall not despair of pleasing the few I first began with, *the few friends prejudiced in my favour;*[2] and then "Fico por los malignatores." Censures will not affect me; for I am armed so strong in *vanity,* that they will pass by me as the idle wind which I regard not. — I think it pretty near equal, in a country place, whether you gain the small number of tasters, or the *large crowd* of the vulgar. The latter are more frequently met with, and *gape, stupent,* and *stare* much more. But one would chuse to please a few *friends* of taste before mob or gentry, the great vulgar or the small; because therein one gratifies both one's social passions and one's pride, that is, one's *self-love*. Above all things, I would wish to please *you;* and if I have a wish that projects or is prominent beyond the rest, it is to see you placed to your satisfaction near me; but Fortune must vary from her usual treatment before she favours me so far. — And yet there *was* a time, when one might probably have prevailed on her. I know not what to do. — The affair was so intricately circumstanced — your surprizing silence after the hint I gave. — Mr.

[2] An allusion to his first published verses (Oxford, 1737), where this phrase appears in substance as part of the title.

D——³ offering to serve any friend of mine; nay, pressing me to use the opportunity. — His other relations, his guardians, teizing him with sure symptoms of a rupture in case of a refusal on *their* side. — Mr. P—— soliciting me if the place were *sold,* which it could not legally be. Friendship, propriety, impartiality, self-interest (which I *little* regarded), endeavouring to distract me; I think I never spent so disagreeable an half-year since I was born. To close the whole, I could not *foresee* the event, which is almost foretold in your last letter, and I knew I could not serve you; but I must render it a *necessary* one. In short, when I can tell you the whole affair at leisure, you will own it to be of such a nature, that I must be ever in suspence concerning my behaviour, and of course shall never reflect on it with pleasure. Believe me, with the truest affection,

                Yours,
                W. Shenstone

59. To LADY LUXBOROUGH¹

[Oct. 18, 1747(?)]

MADAM,

I was much concerned to hear by Mr. Williams's Account, last *Thursday,* that your Ladyship has been greatly indisposed. The Particulars of your Disorder he does not mention, but tells me, he was desired to give it as a Reason that I did not hear from you before. It is as natural for me to make Enquiry concerning the Recovery of your Health, as it is for me to wish it, which I very earnestly do; I have, therefore, sent an honest Neighbour of mine upon this Errand, who will be glad of an Opportunity of seeing *Barrels.* Poor Tom, my trusty Servant, has, ever since I came from *Barrels,* been in a very dangerous Way; and whether he ever may regain the small Share of Health he has been used to, is a great Question, else I had sent something sooner. But I must request your Ladyship not to write, if you find it the least troublesome. A verbal Message will be very sufficient, till such Time as you can write me a full Account of your Recovery.

I have no Particulars that can tempt me to enlarge this Letter, and, indeed, I hardly wish for any, lest I should accidentally let fall any Thing, that might tempt you, at this Time, to write an Answer; which, tho' so highly agreeable to me at a more favourable Season, can afford me little Satisfaction, when I conjecture that you write in Pain.

---

³ Evidently Mr. Dolman. Fullington (*PMLA,* 46:1132) believes this passage to refer to an unsuccessful attempt of Shenstone's to procure for his friend Graves the recently vacated living of Broom.
¹ Hull, *Select Letters,* Vol. I, No. XIV. The year is uncertain, and the letter is placed in its present position by conjecture merely.

Henrietta Knight, Lady Luxborough
Reproduced from Sichel, *Bolingbroke and His Times*, Vol. II

I hope Mr. Hall is recovered by this Time. As my rural Scenery could not attract him hither in Summer, I have little Hopes that my Conversation can have that Effect in Winter. Few Persons care to ride twelve dirty Miles in Winter, be their Charity ever so great,

>To see the dullest of the Sons of Men,

for such am I, without any Affectation, during the Winter-Season; altogether absorbed in what I think they call *Swiss-Meditation,* that is, *thinking upon Nothing.* A very unjoyous Circumstance this, for such of my Friends as vouchsafe to read my Letters. — But I digress — I pray for your Ladyship's Health and Happiness, hoping my Messenger may bring me an Account of both, agreeable to the Wishes of

>Your Ladyship's most obliged and obedient Servant,
>W. Shenstone

'Tis now Oct. 18th — but this Letter was wrote, in order to have been sent last Week. I sate up late with Lord Dudley one Night this Week. He often proposes your Ladyship's Health, and drinks it very respectfully.

The Inhabitants of our Parish have presented our Parson at the Visitation; on which Occasion, I have given myself the generous Air of observing a strict Neutrality — in other Words, I am a Person unconcerned.

60. To LADY LUXBOROUGH [1]

Decr 26 1747

MY LADY,

I have heard from several of my Friends, who are glad to gratify me upon any *good Foundation,* how favourably you are pleas'd to speak both with regard to the Leasows & myself. A *Reflection* so interesting as this, is what I never can esteem a meagre Diet. It is a *Dissert* indeed, but such as my Ambition can very well subsist on; as it had done for a considerable Time when *it* receiv'd a fresh supply in the Paragraph with which you lately honour'd me.

I have been long confin'd at Home by many *real* Impediments, & if there were any imaginery ones, your Ladyships Postscript was sufficient to remove them. Amidst a thousand of ye brightest Qualifications your Ladyship may consider yourself as no small Heroine; for you have at

---

[1] B. M. Add. MSS 28958, fol. 5. The letters exchanged between Shenstone and Lady Luxborough that have been preserved obviously represent only a fraction of the number written. In the letters of both, references to those we lack are frequent. She replies to this, however, in her No. LXXVI (*Letters,* p. 292), dated Sunday, December 27, but with the year wanting. Her letter is, of course, out of order; it should follow her No. V.

one stroke demolish'd ye most furious Lion upon Earth. You will be a little surpriz'd at the Atchievement I assign you, but all I mean is that *visionary Lion* which *Indolence* had station'd in ye way to Barels, as she does in ye way to all that is aimiable. I assure your Ladyship this Lion was delineated by her in ye most lively Manner, and yet perhaps not half so naturally as the Stag which Mr Outing, by your direction, sent me. *She* express'd not only the Teeth, the Paws, & the Voice of y^t terrible Animal, but whisper'd likewise at the same Time ye great Probability that I shou'd find your Ladyship to be in *Cheshire,* even supposing I cou'd 'scape his Fury. I approve of *her Artifice* in *one* Respect, as well as her *Justice:* She never durst presume to depreciate that infinite Pleasure I shou'd receive from your Ladyship's conversation, provided I *cou'd* surmount all Difficulties, & find you at Barrels. Had she proceeded *so* far, I shou'd have seen thro' her Delusions at once, as I now do. Perhaps she was desirous to revenge that little Abuse I bestow'd on her, long ago, in a printed Madrigal, tho a Revenge of this kind (had her Plot succeeded) cou'd not fail to appear very cruel and inadequate. Your Ladyship has dissolv'd the charm in a moment; & I am now amaz'd, (considering how far ye Hearths of Barrels exceed ye scenery of Stowe, whenever y^r Ladyship *draws near* 'em) y^t I have not *already* embrac'd the Pleasure I design to do myself *some day next Week.* I will then return your Pamphlets, tho I have only to say in regard to my Opinion of them, what is indeed it's highest Panegyrick, that it is entirely similar to your own. I am
          Your Ladyship's most oblig'd & most obedient Servt
                                    Will: Shenstone
The Leasows Decr 26
1747

61. To RICHARD JAGO [1]

1747

DEAR SIR,

    Being just returned from a small excursion, it was with the utmost pleasure that I read over your letter; and, though it abounds both in wit and waggery, I sit down incontinently to answer it with *none.*

    The agreeableness of your letters is now heightened by the surprize they give me. I must own, I have thought you in a manner lost to the amusements in which you once delighted, correspondences, works of taste and fancy, &c. If you think the opinion worth removing, you need

---

[1] Dodsley, *Letters to Particular Friends,* No. XLVIII. Wells (*Anglia,* 35:447) believes this letter should be dated late in 1747. Apparently it might be dated early in 1748.

only favour me with such a letter now and then, and I will place you (in my imagination) where you shall see all the favourites of fortune cringing at your feet.

I think I could add about half a dozen hints to your observations on electricity, which might at *least* disguise the facts; and then why will you not put it into some news-paper, or monthly pamphlet? you might discover yourself to whom you have a mind. It would give more than ordinary pleasure at this time. — Some other will take the hint. — Pity your piece should not have the advantage of novelty as well as of wit!

I dined and stayed a night with Dr. E——; he was extremely obliging, and I am glad of such a friend to visit at B. He asked much after you. — He shewed me his Ovid — I advised him to finish some one epistle *highly,* that he might shew it. — The whole will *not take,* though it goes against me to tell him so. I should be glad he could succeed at B.; and could I serve him, it would be with a safe conscience; for I take him to excel the rest of B. physicians far in point of speculation and diligence, &c.

I send you the song you asked for, and request of you to write me out your new edition of the election verses; and, at your *leisure,* a copy of the poem which we altered.

THE LARK[2]

Go, tuneful bird, that gladd'st the skies,
    To Daphne's window speed thy way,
And there on quiv'ring pinions rise,
    And there thy vocal art display.

And if she deign thy notes to hear,
    And if she praise thy matin song;
Tell her, the sounds that soothe her ear,
    To simple British birds belong.

Tell her, in livelier plumes array'd,
    The bird from Indian groves may shine:
But ask the lovely, partial maid,
    What are his notes compar'd to thine?

Then bid her treat that witless beau
    And all his motley race with scorn;
And heal deserving Damon's woe,
    Who sings her praise, and sings forlorn.

I am, Sir, Your most faithful friend and servant,
W. Shenstone

[2] Song IV, *Works,* I (1764), 152.

Have you read Watson, Martyn, and Freke, on electricity?[3] I accidentally met with the two former, by which my head is rendered almost giddy—electrics, non-electrics, electrics *per se,* and bodies that are only conductors of electricity, have a plaguy bad effect on so vortical a brain as mine.

I will infallibly spend a week with you, perhaps about February, if it suits you: though I think too it must be later.

I have been painting in water-colours, during a visit I made, flowers. I would recommend the amusement to you, if you can allow it the time that is expedient.

I trust you will give me one entire week in the spring, when my late alterations may exhibit themselves to advantage.

62. To LADY LUXBOROUGH [1]

1747–8 Fast Day

MADAM,

I am asham'd to think that I have suffer'd your Ladyship to make any Apology for my Reception at Barrels, when I ought immediately, upon my arrival at Home, to have obviated every thing of that kind by an Acknowledgment y^t I was never in my Life more agreeably entertain'd. I am ambitious enough to be pleas'd with ye Honour of your Ladyship's Company, tho' I had no Taste; & I have Taste enough, to be pleas'd with the Politeness of it, tho' I had no Ambition. If I found any uneasiness, it was to reflect how little I cou'd contribute towards your Amusement in return, & in that Respect only was my Ambition disappointed.

I was in Hopes your Ladyship wou'd have weigh'd those trifling verses[2] rather in the scale of *Sincerity* than that of *Poetry.* I meant them as a real expression of the satisfaction I found by your Fireside, & as an Intimation of my Thanks; which, (if I had attempted to return them

---

[3] Sir William Watson (1715–87), F. R. S., contributed to the *Philosophical Transactions* more than fifty-eight papers on natural history, electricity, and medicine; he was famous for his electrical experiments. In 1746 he published his "Experiments . . . on the Nature . . . of Electricity," and a sequel to it in the same year. His next paper on electricity was read January 21, 1748. The *Gentleman's Magazine*, Register of Books, announces in November, 1748, "An Account of some experiments made by some gentlemen of the Royal Society for discovering the force of electricity at a distance. By W. Watson, F. R. S." I am uncertain of the identity of Martyn. John Freke (1688–1756), F. R. S., was a surgeon who made experiments in electricity and published in 1748 "An Essay to Show the Cause of Electricity."

[1] B. M. Add MSS 28958, fol. 3. This plainly answers and confirms the date of No. VI of her *Letters,* written February 2, 1747–48.

[2] Apparently the verses *Upon a Visit to the Same* [i. e., a Lady of Quality] *in Winter, 1748,* in *Works,* I (1764), 135–36.

by word of mouth) I might have express'd with all the awkard Hesitation of a *Clown in earnest;* & yet if my Tongue had hesitated upon *that occasion,* I am sure it must have prov'd very unfaithful to my Sentiments.

Your Ladyship's Notion of solitude & of Company is extremely just. A polite & friendly Neighbourhood *in ye Country,* or, (in Lieu of that) agreeable visitants from *any* Distance, give a Person all ye Society he can extract from a Crowd; & then he has the *rural Scenery,* which is all *clear Gains.* For I fancy no one will prefer ye Beauty of a *street* to ye Beauty of a Lawn or Grove; & indeed the Poets wou'd have form'd no very tempting an *Elysium,* had they made a *Town* of it.

Your Ladyship also mentions ye checker'd scenes of Life. I believe I am as void of superstition as any person in the world, & yet I have accustom'd myself *so much* to consider Life in the same Light, that I find almost every Pleasure lessen'd by that very Consideration. I expect a Pain to ballance it. May Fate prevent my receiving any Pain to ballance the Pleasure which your Letter gave me! I'm sure it must be excessive. But as I had been plagu'd with a very dispiriting Affair before, I hope I am quit; & that your obliging Letter was to make me amends, as it did sufficiently. However this *Habit* of mind in *general* gives me some Evenness of temper; as my *uneasiness* is thus mitigated by *Hope,* & my Pleasure checqu'd by Fear — But not to trouble y^r Ladyship wth my Pains or Pleasures of *mind,* I will tell you my *bodily* sufferings, for ridiculing *formerly* the black Button & buttonhole on a Parson's great Coat. Surely no one may laugh at ye most *extrinsick* Circumstance of Orthodoxy, but a Punishment attends him. I mention this because Mr Hall's mistake must needs be owing to the want of this necessary distinction, & having sent *his* very regularly back to Birmingham, I was almost starv'd to Death before I cou'd compleat the Exchange.

I am very much oblig'd to your Ladyship for y^r Receipt to make sealing wax. I cou'd very conscientiously sign & seal my Respect for your Ladyship under every colour'd wax that you can direct me to make. I have not yet had an opportunity of experimenting on any of the colours. I think I shou'd be most pleas'd with a beautifull *yellow;* but I might perhaps be thought to discover a *Party*-spirit on y^e *outside* of my Letters, which I shall never do *within.*

Lady Hartford's Character[3] I have the greatest veneration for; pursuant to those Features of it, which your Ladyship describ'd to me, &

---

[3] Frances Thynne, Countess of Hertford, and later Duchess of Somerset, was one of Lady Luxborough's most intimate friends. To her Shenstone dedicated his ode on *Rural Elegance.* For his supposed attempts through Lady Luxborough to secure her as patroness, see Hughes, "Shenstone and the Countess of Hertford," *PMLA,* 46:1113–27.

also to a Letter of hers which you shew'd me concerning Ld Beauchamp's Death.[4] If she shou'd happen to speak of my Place to Mr Thomson, he *seem'd* here to be enough pleas'd with it, to countenance your Ladyships kind Partiality.

    I *did think* to have accompany'd this Letter with some little Pieces of Poetry that might amuse your Ladyship for the Space of ten Minutes; but it grows very late, & my Spirits have been dissipated all this day; so I beg leave to perform my Promise a short time hence, which I will not fail to do. Nevertheless I send a trifle, that was written *last* winter; a winter, that was not exhilarated by any visit at Barels. I send your Ladyship *Winter-songs,* little considering y^t your own (for Miss Nanny Knight) puts all mine out of Countenance, & has all ye advantages of Simplicity and Imagery. I will positively write no more of that kind. I have now tir'd your Ladyship with my Impertinence & ought to hasten towards a Conclusion. If you please sometime to honour me with a line, it will be a Favour I can no way deserve, but by the *Value* I shall *place* on it: But if that sort of Merit be admitted, I will no more allow any one a superiority in *it,* than in that Respect & deference with which I am, Mad^m
                 Your Ladyship's most oblig'd & most faithfull Servant
                                  Will: Shenstone

The Leasows. Fast-day, 1747–8

I will one day beg ye Favour of y^r Ladyship to lend me those Designs of Inigo Jones &c. I have a mind to have a small Hand-candlestick executed by y^r urn at ye beginning which I will draw out upon Paper, & return ye Book wth Care.

63. To RICHARD JAGO[1]

                                      Sunday, Feb. 14, 1747–8

DEAR MR. JAGO,

    I am tempted once more to apologize for the unseasonable visit I paid you, though I feel myself entirely innocent in that respect, even as much so as the post-boy was guilty; for had my previous letter arrived in due time, you had then been furnished with an opportunity of waving my company till a more convenient season. I was *only,* or at least, *chiefly* uneasy upon *your* account. I spent my time very agreeably, and only less

---

[4] In Hull, *Select Letters,* Vol. I, No. VIII.
[1] Dodsley, *Letters to Particular Friends,* No. XLIX. Wells confirms the date, *Anglia,* 35: 447. It is further confirmed by Shenstone's reference to mistaking Mr. Hall's coat for his own, also mentioned in Letter 62, of authentic date.

so than I might, had I not been conscious to myself that I was intruding upon domestic tendernesses.

I spent the Sunday night and the next day at Mr. Wren's;[2] and am now just returned from Mr. Dolman's, who has made me a genteel present of Spence's Polymetis.[3] I have not yet *read* many dialogues in it, but I have *dipped* in several; and have reason to be well enough satisfied with the simple and uninvidious manner in which he has introduced Mr. Lowth's poem.[4] I have long known of this intended *introduction* (which I accidentally found to have been settled betwixt them before I published *mine* on the same subject[5]), and a little dreaded the *form* of it. I have long ago made considerable improvements in mine, and have a mind one day to publish it once more; after which, let it sleep in peace. I have sometimes thought of printing my next title-page thus, viz. "Poems; consisting of Songs, Odes, and Elegies; with an improved edition of The Judgment of Hercules, and of The School-mistress." But I have but very few critical acquaintance, and I live at a great distance from those I have; stationed amongst the *makers* and the *wearers* of hobnails;

> Far from the joys that with my soul agree,
> From *wit,* from *learning* — very far from thee.
> PARNELL

I know I have thrown a great number of careless things into your hands. I know to *whom* I intrusted my follies; but I know *not* what they *are:* — I believe, in general, that they consist of mis-begotten embryos and abortive births, which it had been merely decent to have buried in — some part of my garden; — but I was morally assured that you would expose nothing of mine to my disadvantage. As to some that are *less imperfect,* you promised your observations, and I desire you would make them with the utmost freedom. I can bear any censure which you shall pass by way of letter, and I beg once more that you would not be sparing. It will be esteemed as great a favour as you can do me. When they have gone through your hands, and those of one or two more friends, I shall, perhaps, think of publishing them; though as to that, much depends upon the advice I receive, and previously on the opportunity I have of receiving it. I am in hopes that you will be pretty full in discovering to me, *which you dislike the least, what faults you find,* and *what improvements they are capable of.* I set you a tedious task; but I will return the favour as far

---

[2] Christopher Wren of Wroxall, the son of the great architect, was Shenstone's intimate friend. See the five letters to Wren.
[3] Published February 5, 1747.
[4] *The Choice of Hercules.*
[5] *The Judgment of Hercules.*

as I am able, either in *the same way* or any other. This brings me to say, that, if there be any compositions of yours that you would have me correct (and there are several of which I want a copy), I would beg you to send them. Your Blackbird excels any singing-bird I ever heard; and I beseech you to convey it to The Leasowes by the next opportunity, that he may acquire fame near other rills, and in other valleys, than those in which he was produced.

I have many compliments to make in your country; to Mr. H——,[6] Mrs. N——, Mrs. J——, Mr. F——, Mr. T——, and your brother. If I go over to Mr. W——'s, I will assuredly call and spend a night with you. — *That* is precarious. — But whether I do or not, I would willingly hope to see you this spring and summer more than once; as a *critic,* and as a *friend:* nor do I forget the promise of Mr. H—— and Mr. F——; — but of these things more when I send for the papers, which I purpose to do to-morrow fortnight, that is, the twenty-ninth of February.

I have suffered greatly by railing at the black button on a parson's great coat. Had Mr. Hall's been thus distinguished, he could not have mistaken mine for his own; which latter I sent in order to be commuted at Birmingham, and was almost starved to death before I could accomplish the exchange. There is no trifling with any *part* of orthodoxy with impunity. — That is the moral.

I have received a very obliging letter from Lady Luxborough,[7] wherein she tells me that Lady Hartford admires my place in her description. Mr. Thomson is intimate at Lady Hartford's; and I suppose Lady Hartford may have been informed by Lady L. that Mr. Thomson has been here; so I conclude, in mere vanity, that my farm is advancing in reputation.

What think you of Mr. Carte's History?[8] or what of his narrative concerning the Pretender's touching for the King's evil! I think one is not, however, to give up his book entirely; because with *all his superstition,* he may have several anecdotes that one would like to read.

I have had great expectations from the beautiful veins of a piece of oak of which I have had a table made; but, upon a thorough survey of it, it is so like nothing in the world as old B——'s callimanco night-gown.

I have nothing to add worth beginning upon another page; but I happened not to make a regular conclusion in my preceding one.

---

[6] I cannot with certainty supply the names here: Mr. H—— is probably Mr. Hardy; Mrs. J——, Mrs. Jago; Mr. F——, Mr. Fancourt; and Mr. W——, Mr. Wren.

[7] See her *Letters,* No. VI, dated February 2, 1747–48.

[8] The first volume of *A General History of England,* by Thomas Carte (1686–1754), was announced in the *Gentleman's Magazine,* January, 1748.

You must give me some time to colour you a collection of flowers (that octavo edition I shewed you here); and then I will make Mrs. Jago a present of it. I believe I can engage Mr. Dolman to assist me, who is much my superior in point of accuracy; and the inscription at the beginning is to run somehow thus:

>ELEGANTISSIMAE PUELLAE
>DOROTHEAE FANCOURT,
>QUAE PERDILECTI SUI CONDISCIPULI
>RICHARDI IAGO
>AMORES MERUIT,
>D. D.
>GULIELMUS SHENSTONE;
>DEBITAE NYMPHIS OPIFEX CORONAE.

That is, by trade a garland-maker; but this inscription I may alter, if I can think of any thing more expressive of the regard which I have ever borne and still bear you.

Lord Dudley is gone, and franks are no more. I have nothing to wish you but health and preferment: — "det vitam, det opes;" — with these you will easily compound that cordial *happiness,* having every other ingredient that is requisite at hand.

>I am, most affectionately,
>Your very faithful friend, &c.
>W. Shenstone

64. To RICHARD JAGO [1]

The Leasowes, Mar. 23, 1747–8

DEAR SIR,

I have sent Tom over for the papers which I left under your inspection; having nothing to add upon this head, but that the more *freely* and *particularly* you give me your opinion, the greater will be the obligation which I shall have to acknowledge.

I shall be very glad, if I happen to receive a good large bundle of your own compositions; in regard to which, I will observe any commands which you shall please to lay upon me.

I am favoured with a certain correspondence,[2] by way of letter, which I told you I should be glad to cultivate; and I find it very entertaining.

Pray did you receive my answer to your last letter, sent by way of

---

[1] Dodsley, *Letters to Particular Friends,* No. L. Fullington confirms the date, *PMLA,* 46:1133.
[2] Probably with Lady Luxborough.

London? I should be extremely sorry to be debarred the pleasure of writing to you by the post, as often as I feel a violent propensity to describe the notable incidents of my life; which amount to about as much as the tinsel of your little boy's hobby-horse.

I am on the point of purchasing a couple of busts for the niches in my hall; and believe me, my good friend, I never proceed one step in ornamenting my little farm, but I enjoy the hopes of rendering it more agreeable to you, and the small circle of acquaintance which sometimes favour me with their company.

I shall be extremely glad to see you and Mr. Fancourt when the trees are green; that is, in May; but I would not have you content yourself with a single visit this summer. If Mr. Hardy (to whom you will make my compliments) inclines to favour me so far, you must calculate so as to wait on him whenever he finds it convenient; though I have *better hopes* of making his reception here agreeable to him when my Lord Dudley comes down. — I wonder how he would like the scheme I am upon, of exchanging a large tankard for a silver standish.

I have had a couple of paintings given me since you were here. One of them is a Madona, valued, as it is said, at ten guineas in Italy, but which you would hardly purchase at the price of five shillings. However, I am endeavouring to make it out to be one of Carlo Maratt's, who was a first hand, and famous for Madonas; even so as to be nick-named "Cartuccio delle Madonne" by Salvator Rosa. Two letters of the cypher (CM) agree; what shall I do with regard to the third? It is a small piece, and badly blackened. It is about the size (though not quite the shape) of the Bacchus over the parlour-door, and has much such a frame.

A person may amuse himself almost as cheaply as he pleases. I find no small delight in rearing all sorts of poultry; geese, turkeys, pullets, ducks, &c. I am also somewhat smitten with a blackbird which I have purchased: a very fine one; brother by father, but not by mother, to the unfortunate bird you so beautifully describe,[3] a copy of which description you must not fail to send me; — but, as I said before, one may easily habituate one's self to cheap amusements; that is, *rural* ones (for all town amusements are horribly expensive); — I would have you cultivate your garden; plant flowers, have a bird or two in the hall (they will at *least* amuse your children); write now and then a song; buy now and then a book; write now and then a letter to
     Your most sincere friend, and affectionate servant,
                 W. Shenstone

[3] In his elegy *The Blackbirds*.

P. S. I hope you have exhausted all your spirit of criticism upon my verses, that you may have none left to cavil at this letter; for I am ashamed to think, that *you,* in particular, should receive the dullest I ever wrote in my life. Make my compliments to Mrs. Jago. — She can go a little abroad, you say. — Tell her, I should be proud to shew her the Leasowes. Adieu!

65. To a FRIEND [1]

[Soon after Mar. 24, 1748]

DEAR MR. ———,

With the utmost gratitude for the observations which you sent me, and with the highest opinion of their propriety in general, do I sit down to answer your obliging letter. You will not take it amiss, I know, if I scribble broken hints, and trace out little sketches of my mind, just as I should go near to explain it if I were upon the spot, as often as I think of you, which I beg leave to assure you happens many times in a day. They say, "A word to the wise is enough;" a word, therefore, to a friend of understanding may be supposed to be something more than enough, because it is probable he is acquainted with three parts of one's mind before. — The censure you have passed upon Milton's Lycidas, so far as it regards the metre which he has chosen, is unexceptionably just; and one would imagine, if that argument concerning the distance of the rhimes were pressed home in a public essay, it should be sufficient to extirpate that kind of verse for ever. As to my opinion concerning the choice of English metre, I dare not touch upon the subject; and I will give you my reason: I began upon it in a letter which I intended for you about a month ago; and I soon found that I had filled a sheet of paper with my dissertation, and left no room for other things which I had more mind to communicate. Beside, I found it so blotted that I did not chuse to send it; and as the subject is so extremely copious, I shall decline it entirely, till *talking* may prove as effectual as *writing.* — As to your advice with regard to my publications, I believe it to be just, and shall, in all probability, pursue it. — I am afraid, by your account, that Dodsley has published my name to "The School-mistress." I was a good deal displeased at his publishing that poem without my knowledge, when he had so many opportunities of giving me some previous information; but, as he would probably disregard my resentment, I chose to stifle it, and

---

[1] Dodsley, *Letters to Particular Friends,* No. LXII, dated 1750. Wells corrects the date, *Anglia,* 35:449-52. I have no satisfactory clue to the identity of the addressee.

wrote to him directly upon the receipt of yours, that I would be glad to furnish him with an improved copy of "The School-mistress," &c. for his second edition. He accepts it with some complaisance, desires it soon; and I am at a fault to have the opinion of my friends, what alterations or additions it will be proper to insert. I have scribbled a copy, which I send this day to Mr. Graves and Mr. Whistler; but I am greatly fearful I shall not receive their criticisms time enough, and I shall have the same longing for yours. A journey to Whitchurch, which I have long proposed, might unite all these advantages; and I heartily wish I may be able to effect it without inconvenience. If I go thither, I call on you.

I am, ever and entirely, yours,
W. Shenstone

66. To LADY LUXBOROUGH[1]

The Leasowes, Lady-day, 1748

MADAM,

After having own'd that the Fear your Ladyship has been under is in reality to be imputed to *me*, I am at a Loss for words to express my *concern*, or to alleviate my *Fault*. I will not in the least disallow, that the Book[2] came to Hand regularly, & much sooner than I cou'd reasonably expect it, or that the Letter inclos'd in it gave me uncommon Pleasure, as your Ladyship's never fail to do. I have nothing to say in my Behalf, but that I have never of late had such Health or Spirits as might encourage me to think I cou'd return ye Answer I *ought:* And even *to-night,* my Spirits are so bad, & my Head so confus'd, that I have no reason to hope these Lines can do any thing more than free you from your present uncertainty. But, if I am honour'd with a Line from your Ladyship hereafter, I will *immediately acknowledge* it as well as I am able, be my Capacity what it will. I do not know how far your Ladyship's Name may be distinguish'd by a Post-Woman's Ear; but *this* I know, that if I had been Mr. Holyoak, you shou'd have never known from *me,* that there was any Woman in the World who cou'd express herself concerning you with the Disrespect you mention. I am astonish'd no less at her *Forgetfulness.* There seems to me to be no surer method of conveyance to be found than this by the *Farmer;* by whom I sent my Letter to the Post-

---

[1] B. M. Add. MSS 28958, fol. 6. A version of this letter appears in Hull, *Select Letters,* Vol. I, No. XV, where it is dated March 15, 1748. No. VIII of Lady Luxborough's *Letters* is the reply to this.

[2] The book of Inigo Jones's designs. The letter inclosed is No. XXV of Lady Luxborough's *Letters,* dated Ash-Wednesday [1748]. See Wells, *Anglia,* 35:451–52. Shenstone's letter also answers her No. VII of March 22, 1748. Her No. XXV thus should precede her No. VII.

Office at Henley, & by whom, I suppose, your Ladyship convey'd your Parcell. An old-woman goes from my Neighbourhood three times a week to Birmingham, without a single exception, all the year round: Her Business is, to bring hither from the Post-Office everything that is directed to this Part of the Country. And, as she calls me her best Master, & knows how gladly I receive a Letter &c: she seizes what is directed to me with eagerness & rapidity. However, in obedience to your Ladyships Commands, I have sent this Letter to Master Holyoak[3] & shall have an additional Pressure on my Spirits 'till I hear you have been pleas'd to forgive my Neglect — I know extremely well that want of *Leisure,* and some *other* Excuses which are often made for not writing, can be of weight from *no* one but a Cobler that has ten or twelve Children dependent on a Tatching-end. But I know *as* well, that your Ladyship's is no ordinary correspondence, and that a Person ought to have his Head clear & his Imagination unembarrass'd when he sits down to answer any Letter of yours — For my Part I can hardly look upon this as any Letter at all, and will infallibly write *again* as soon as I can recover my natural state of Mind. I have as little Reason to consider ye Inclos'd as *Poetry.* But as they were *short* compositions, I had been writing them out yesterday with a design to send them to the Post-office to-morrow morning. (I mean yr Henley Post-Office.) I must own to your Ladyship, that they were written long ago. I am afraid I have tir'd you with madrigal & Roundelay. I hope when ye weather becomes finer, (with which my Spirits generally sympathize) to vary my Style for your Ladyship's Amusement — in the mean Time I have sent you a Poem written by a Gentleman of my Acquaintance,[4] and shewn up in *Print* for a College-Exercise. As it was never publish'd, you can scarce have seen it *before.* You will soon discover a *juvenile* want of Judgment in some Places; but, I believe the Elegance & variety of his Fancy, you will admire. He sometimes comes and stays a Month with me at the Leasowes in ye Summer; the next Time he does so, I will be oblig'd to your Ladyship for yr leave to introduce him at Barrels, where, if I am not mistaken, he will be pleas'd almost to a Degree of Enthusiasm.

As to *Dodsley's Collection*[5] I find it is approv'd on all Hands; tho' *I* shou'd have been much better pleas'd with him, if he had giv'n me previous notice ee'r he publish'd my School-mistress; that I might have

---

[3] She had instructed him to send his letter "to Master Franky Holyoake, at Mr. Bolton's, wholesale Toymaker, upon Snow-Hill, in Birmingham" (*Letters,* p. 10).

[4] Anthony Whistler's *Shuttlecock,* a mock-heroic poem composed in 1736. See Lady Luxborough's *Letters,* p. 13.

[5] The reference is, of course, to Volume I of the first edition, January 15, 1748. The second edition appeared in December, 1748. See the discussion by Wells, *Anglia,* 35:450.

spruc'd her up a little before she appear'd in so much Company. They tell me he purposes a *second* Edition, concerning wch I have wrote to him; &, with a view to which, I have declin'd ye Purchase of it in ye First: so that I have not seen it. Fitzosborne's Letters[6] I bought & read upon your Recommendation. I think they are written with Judgment, Elegance, & Fancy; but rather too much, with an *Eye to the Press*. They wou'd *read* much better with *real* Names; however I have been inform'd yt he abuses Dr. King under ye Character of Mezentius; that Dr. King was his wife's Father, & had spent her Fortune &c: Lord Bolingbroke's Tracts[7] I will buy and read, when I can *attend* & *think;* which is but very little during ye Winter-Season.

As to your Ladyship's Lameness, tho' it comes *last* in this irregular Letter, I assure you it gave me real concern to hear it was *bad,* and very sensible Pleasure to hear it was abated. I sincerely wish your Health & Happiness as you do yourself; and as I always experience this disposition of Mind, I will hope to be forgiven if I shou'd at any time fall short in my means of expressing it.

I am, Madam, your Ladyship's most oblig'd and
most obedient Servant,
W. Shenstone

I beg my Compliments to Mr. & Mrs. Holyoak.[8]

67. To LADY LUXBOROUGH[1]

The Leasows, April ye 18th 1748

MADAM,

Your Ladyship's obliging correspondence is the greatest Honour that was ever done me. I am sufficiently assur'd that a Profession of this sort cannot properly bear ye *Appearance* of a Compliment, for tho' I have a Few Intimates whose *Genius* & *Merit* I very greatly esteem, I was never very assiduous in cultivating The Friendships of my *Superiors,* & (whether thro *that Omission,* or any *other* Deficiency) certain it is, that

---

[6] Published by Dodsley October 3, 1747 (Wells, *Anglia,* 35:451). The first volume was first published in 1742. Both volumes were republished in 1747. The author was, of course, William Melmoth.

[7] *A Collection of Political Tracts by the Author of a Dissertation on Parties,* published in 1748.

[8] Mr. Holyoake, country clergyman and friend of Lady Luxborough, attended her at her death in 1756. See his exchange of letters with Shenstone on that occasion (Lady Luxborough's *Letters,* p. 189).

[1] B. M. Add. MSS 28958, fol. 8ff. This answers Lady Luxborough's letter of Easter Sunday, 1748 (*Letters,* No. VIII). It confirms the date both of this and of her answer, dated April 28, 1748 (No. IX).

I have acquir'd but Few of them. Be that as it will, I am never to be humbled by *Neglect,* whatever I might by *Favour* & *Prosperity.* In *this* latter Case, I believe, the *Contraste* betwixt my *good-Fortune* & my *Desert* might exhibit me to my own Eyes in a very mortifying Shape. I have some kind of reason to draw this Conclusion, because I am never more humble than at the Time I sit down to acknowledge, according to my small Abilities, the particular satisfaction I receive from your Letters. I am extremely glad to find that your *Gout* has entirely disappear'd from the Face of them. I hope it is also vanish'd in reality. And yet tho' I was really concern'd for your Pain, I was delighted wth y^e *Expressions* it drew from you concerning Riches, so exactly agreeable to *my Conduct.* But whether or no I am to be *"steep'd in Poverty to the very Lips"* (by which I suppose Othello means ye want of a Glass of Wine) I have ventur'd to write an Essay in verse entitled "The Œconomists," address'd to Poets.[2] Of this I will shortly beg your Opinion. My Friends seem to think it is wrote with some Spirit, but a Friendly *Ear* (tho' from a nobler *Motive*) is very near as partial as a Flatterer's *tongue.* However, welcome! ever welcome to *me* be an Error of this kind! I had rather be somewhat deluded by ye kind partiality of Friends, than acquire the greatest Fame, with no *genuine* Friendships at all. Your Ladyship will however observe, (what may be seen thro all my trifling Compositions) some Picture of *myself* in *this;* my Pleasures & Pains; wch circumstance may render it something more amusing; as This, tho' no very *agreeable* Portrait, is ye Resemblance of a person y^t has your Ladyship in ye highest veneration. I cannot transcribe this or any other Poem *now,* but I shall beg Leave to trouble you with it, upon ye Arrival of the first fair weather.

Your Ladyship's Sentiments concerning Mr Whistler's Genius are extremely interesting to *me,* & must give *him* ye most rational Pleasure. He does not indeed *want* to be inform'd of your Ladyship's Taste. If he *did,* the *Manner* in which you bestow your commendations, wou'd sufficiently prove ye Genius of ye Person that bestows them, & of consequence give them all the Weight he can desire.

Poor Dick Graves (of whom you may have chanc'd to hear me speak) has sent his Farmer's Daughter to a Boarding-School in London.[3] He says she was lately much admir'd at a Play, which she went to see for her Dancing Masters Benefit. He indited ye Sonnet I enclose upon leaving her there, and if Love *alone* can make a marriage happy, he can hardly fail of Happiness to the Degree I wish it him.

[2] *Works,* I (1764), 285.
[3] Lucy Bartholomew of Aldworth, Berkshire, whom Graves met there in 1744 and married in 1748.

My Lady Lyttelton was snatch'd away suddenly;[4] her illness, as far as I can find, being little else beside a common Cold; and as I ever experienc'd from her the most *Friendly* complaisance, I ought to mix a Tear with that stream which will not fail to be shed by all her poor neighbours.

When I began to write this Letter I did intend to have return'd, with Thanks, your Ladyship's Book of Inigo Jones's Designs; for I am afraid you want it; but As I have a mind to sketch out a Chimney-piece or two, I *will* hope to be forgiven if I keep it till next Thursday at which Time I will be sure to send it. I can not prevail on myself to send you the Size &c. of my Niches because I built them at random, whereas it will be expected from your Ladyship that you should build by ye rules of Art; which may be done altogether as cheaply. Besides, I have some Doubts whether ye middle Nich should not exceed ye others in Heigth & Breadth; & if your Ladyship will give me Leave, I will take a little Time to consider of ye most proper ornament I can contrive for y^t place to answer ye End you propose — As to ye Lady's *Achievements in Lead,* I have not ye highest Relish for any thing wch I esteem so *frail;* And if your Ladyship chuses to go to the expence of wood-carving, I shou'd think ye most proper ornaments on each side the stucco wou'd be "Lyres, Laurels, Fistulas, Pipes, Masks, &c: united by a kind of bandage falling easily down the Wainscott. These wou'd bear an obvious Relation either to the Busts or the Library. I am going to have something like ye Group I have enclos'd, engrav'd upon ye Lid of a standish, for wch I shall exchange some old Plate in London by Mr Outing's Assistance — I have but little Room to express y^t unlimited Respect with wch I wou'd Subscribe myself your Ladyships most dutifull & obedient Servant

Will Shenstone

68. To LADY LUXBOROUGH [1]

May 5th 1748

MADAM,

I have wasted half this Afternoon with a Tenant whom I've been endeavouring to seduce into an agreement to pay me half a year's rent; & ye Result of our conference, (little more agreeable to *me* than *him*) was, that he *wou'd* pay me half a years rent (at a Time that he owes me for *two* year's) but that he cou'd *not* fix any *time* because he was unwilling to

---

[4] Lady Christian Lyttelton, the wife of Sir Thomas, died in the summer of 1748. Wyndham, *Chronicles of the Eighteenth Century,* II, 1.

[1] B. M. Add. MSS 28958, fol. 10ff. This letter answers and confirms the date of Lady Luxborough's of April 28, 1748 (*Letters,* No. IX).

break his Promise. This Circumstance, together with that of rainy weather, render it a Point of self-*Interest* in me to engage in some Amusement which may engross my whole Attention; so that heavy *solemn* unvary'd Rains, & heavy illiterate worldly conversation may leave behind 'em no bad Impression. And all this Advantage I am in hopes to reap from an *Acknowledgment* of ye satisfaction your last Letter afforded me; Nor have I the least reason to doubt of success, if I can find but *half* as much relief in answering, as I did Pleasure in receiving it — Your Ladyship's verses to Mr Outing entirely convince me yt both your *Pow'r* & *Will* to confer Honour, where you do not entirely disapprove, are as great as I can desire. But in gratitude for the Honour you do *me* in that Epistle, I must be so free as to inform your Ladyship yt if you wou'd shun ye Character of a *Poetess* (wch as you well observe can make no addition to your Character) you must never write in Heroic verse with half the Elegance you *do*. The Consequence *will* be, that your *Logicians* & scholastick People will reasonably enough conclude yt you are at least a Poetess *potentially,* if not *actually;* & that it is entirely owing to your own perverseness, that you do not acquire a Reputation in *this,* as well as in every other sort of writing in which you have hitherto engag'd. For *my* part I am apt to agree wth ye Stoicks that a Person of an universal Genius is *ev'ry* Thing; a King, a Mathematician, a Poet, a Statesman &c: &c: for yt very Reason, because, wth proper contingencies, he has all these things in his Pow'r. So I give yr Ladyship warning, that you may look to it. Nevertheless, I wou'd not have you Endeavour to conceal your Skill in Poetry from those that you are pleas'd to honour with your *Acquaintance.* That were *now* too late; They know too well already yt you *only despise* those qualifications for which you are not admir'd, & for which they know you might be admir'd if you chose to be so — I like your Ladyships last sonnet extremely; & ye more, as I have ye same aversion with you to all affected Birds that quit their native notes. I purchas'd a charming Blackbird of one of my poor neighbours; which is now in my Hall, & has a variety of Notes that are both masculine & musical. If it were not for ye Faults wth wch I'm going to upbraid him, I wou'd compare his voice to your Lasp's Handwriting; which has all ye *Firmness* of a man's Hand, with all the the Delicacy of a Female's — But as poor People *admire* art, tho' they love Nature they have taught ye Bird by their foolish Pedantry to demean himself extremely: And when I've been admiring his Notes for ye Space of ten Minutes he sinks all of a sudden into calling out *Toby* & *whistling ye Horses.* Somewhat like ye Tinker in Shakespeare who forgetting his present Dignity is every now & then requesting a Pot of Beer. I like a Decoration in Spence, where there is an Ass in yᵉ Roman Toga instructing two harmless Pupils. I ought not here to mention yᵉ Jersey-man who taught me French; But tho' I can scarce *pronounce* it at all, I think I can understand it tolerably well, & I wou'd beg yᵉ Favour of your Ladyships Fr: Play for a Fortnight, if you please. I have suffer'd enough from the Character you describe, to relish yᵉ Pleasure of seeing it expos'd — your Lady'p made me laugh concerning My Friend Outing's Ear — May yᵉ Powʳ of Musick preserve *his* refind Taste for Operas & oratorios! But rather may Heav'n preserve his hearing, that he may not only hear what the *Multitude,* but what your *Ladyship says* & then I believe he need not *regret* so much as *despise* what yᵉ *Opera-Folk* sing — Now, I mention Mʳ Outing, I must say a word of yᵉ Amusements he has been so kind as to negotiate for me. The *Bust* arriv'd wᵗʰ your Ladyship's Letter. I fancy it to be a good Taste, in all stucco Rooms or wherever yᵉ Wainscott is painted like Stone, to have all carv'd work whether Busts, Festoons, Frames &c: of yᵉ same colour with yᵉ Room itself. Where that is not practicable, & where one has few visitants of yᵉ *most* refind Taste, I think *White* is unexceptionably yᵉ best Colour for most of yᵉ same Ornaments. I shou'd prefer yᵉ native colour of yᵉ Alabaster in a Bust to that *shining* which is given it by Paint; but as frequent Brushing wears away yᵉ Features Paint or varnish becomes *necessary*. I know very well yᵗ yᵉ antient statues, as Spence observes, were made to Shine so much as to dazle yᵉ eyes of yᵉ Spectators; but I think yᵉ Spectators eyes ought *not* to be dazled when they are to examine yᵉ Limbs & Features. On yᵉ whole, I approve Rackstrow's Marbling (which is only Varnish or white paint *varnished*) considering wᵗ I said before, & where this Room is not of Stone-colour — As for my Standish, I was in Hopes my old Plate of about 40 ozˢ wou'd have paid for it entirely; but yᵉ Man has risen in his Demands, proposing 40 oz for yᵉ Standish, & reckoning by the Ounce (8ˢ per ounce) which you will observe may induce him to add to its weight. I shou'd be glad to know yʳ Ladyship's Opinion of his Terms, tho I believe I must (If I pretend to *Œconomy*) at least *postpone* yᵉ Affair at present — Now I mention Œconomy I must acknowledge yᵗ yᵉ Notion yʳ Ladyship has of *mine* is as entirely just, as the Compliment you draw from it in regard to my Genius is properly to be imputed to your Ladyship's Kindness. I assure you I have had no more Œconomy than a Butterdish with a Spout at both ends, or yⁿ yᵉ Sluice of a Pond which lets out twice as much as comes in. But I have been taught some *speculative* Knowledge by a Reflection, how sufficient my Fortune might have been for all my *present* wishes, had I nurs'd it ever so little from the time I receiv'd it. My comfort is grounded upon a maxim y^t is most indisputably true, that a Person cannot *eat* his Cake & *have* it, & if the Cake *be* to be eaten he takes ye most seasonable Time who eats it when he's most a-hunger'd. Pray my Lady, don't examine this Doctrine too closely—I like Gay's *Motive* to Œconomy best; Independence; & yet I believe his Œconomy went no further than to superintend the Finances of his green-silk Purse. For *my* part, (&, I am *as* sure, for your *Ladyship's* part) I can no more than Brutus "wring from the Hard Hands of Peasants their vile Trash by any *Indirection*" or even by *all* the Methods that are strictly *legal;* & as for Expence I am chiefly faulty wth regard to little Sums. I have experience enough to know ye Danger of Pounds & tens of Pounds; but I never yet had a due veneration for Sixpence or a shilling, wch somebody says is a serious Affair. My whole *secret* is, when I've receiv'd a little Money, to *pay* away where I owe, without deliberating. You know Addison says tho' on another Occasion "The Person that *deliberates* is lost!" Company, Nay *superiour* Company, in Affliction, *lessens* one's grievances, & Mr Dennis *has* said that if Homer himself was not in Debt, it was—because nobody wou'd trust him. And thus much for Œconomy; till I have Leisure to send your Ladyship my *Aldermanly* Treatise on that important subject—It will be no bad digress[ion] here to speak a word of my Friend Graves's Proceedings.² Your Ladysp's Sentiment is very *ingenious;* but we will suppose that, however he prefer his Lucy to ye good Opinion of the wise world, yet he doesn't so *entirely* despise that Opinion as not to wish to *compromise* Matters (I must beg Leave to finish on the Cover) and to render his Conduct something *less* absurd, by rendering her Behaviour something less exceptionable. And who knows but as a *Lover,* he may hope to make them cry out as the old Trojans did upon seeing Helen on ye Walls, in the third Iliad. Graves looks upon London as a fiery Tryal. If he finds her false, he is at Liberty to decline; if true, as he *sincerely* wishes, She is all Gold thrice purify'd &c: &c: I wish to God there may be no Room to doubt of that Sincerity in *her* which I am pretty sure he cannot easily disbelieve.

² The allusion is evidently to Graves's marriage to Lucy Bartholomew (see the Index).

69. To LADY LUXBOROUGH[1]

The Leasows June ye 1st 1748
Almost-Night

MADAM,

I return my Lady Hartford's Letter[2] by the very first opportunity I meet with; & herein I but discharge my conscience; as I am in Duty bound to obey your Ladyship's Commands, & also, to be no way instrumental in delaying your Answer to a Letter which has afforded me the highest satisfaction.

As to the Choice or Preference of any Trifle of mine which may be thought most proper to send her Ladyship, it wou'd be most prudent in me to be guided by your own Opinion; as the Person best acquainted with Lady Hartford's Taste, & who, I am apt enough to flatter myself, wishes well to my Reputation.[3] The Esteem I share at Percy-Lodge is entirely of your own *creation;* & as you have almost literally *produc'd* it out of *nothing,* I dare say you *understand* & will *use* the most proper means to keep it alive. Otherwise, it were much better for *me* it had never existed, as a Fall from the greatest Happiness compleats our Idea of the most consummate Misery. Sure I am y^t for *my* Part, I am utterly unable to preserve my Lady Hartford's good Opinion, unless your Ladyship pleases to collogue with me so as to keep her in constant Hopes of something better than I have yet produc'd. I have written a pretty large collection of Elegies on almost every melancholy subject y^t I cou'd recollect; & I had some Thoughts of sending them to ye Press next winter, but I have now dropt y^t Design, as my Friends advise me to publish something else y^t may be of more *general* acceptation. I own they are in some Degree fav'rites with me, & if your Ladyship will please to read them in a Copy, which I have now no *Leisure* to transcribe, I will send them very soon. They are written rather wth ye Spirit of *Melancholy* yⁿ that of Poetry; if Melancholy may be said to be fraught wth any Spirit at all as I believe it *may;* for I believe a pretty *Spirit* may be distill'd from *Tears.* This last *conceit* is almost worthy Dr Yong; which brings it into my Head to say a word more concerning Hervey's Meditations.[4] I must own I do think it doubtfull whether y^r Ladyship will approve them; (tho' I read but *one* volume) & yet my Lady Hartford's opinion is most

---

[1] B. M. Add. MSS 28958, fol. 14ff. This letter answers and confirms the date of Lady Luxborough's of May 28, 1748 (*Letters*, No. X).
[2] In Hull, *Select Letters*, Vol. I, No. XIX. It is dated May 15, 1748.
[3] See Hughes, "Shenstone and the Countess of Hertford," *PMLA*, 46:1113–27.
[4] James Hervey (1714–58), *Meditations and Contemplations*, Vol. I, 1746; Vol. II, 1747.

literally just; they are undoubtedly *poetical* & *pious*, & so is Dr Yongs Collection of Night-thoughts; but surely as remote from true *Simplicity* as ye *arctic* is to the *antarctic* Pole.

The Essay upon Delicacy[5] recommends itself; since one is apt to imagine the author a Man of Taste from his choice of a subject. Mr Dolman sent for it upon sight of ye Advertisement, and as there is a mutual Intercourse betwixt his Library & mine, I shall in a few Days have an opportunity of giving your Ladyship my humble opinion of it's Merit.

Lady H. is a Patroness to *two* Mr Thomsons. Has your Ladysp seen A Poem upon Sickness?[6] in ye latter End of wch the Author introduces my Lord Beauchamp's Death, which is ye most poetical Part of ye Poem, so far as I have *read;* for I have only ye First Number. If you wou'd chuse to see it I will take care to send it — As to ye Castle of Indolence I find one Fault wth it already which is that it is printed in an odious *Quarto* & I never cou'd approve such un-*bindable* Editions. At least if it *may* be *bound,* it makes but an ordinary *Person of a Book.* I am always in Hopes yt whenever an Author is either a tall or even a middle-sized Man, he will never print a Book but in Folio, octavo, or duodecimo; & on the other Hand, when he is short & squat, I collect yt his partiality to a Figure of yt kind, will induce him, to my great discomfort, to publish in *Quarto.*[7] But Mr Thomson, who is certainly of ye *middle* Size, must be self-convicted. However I long to see his Book. My Schoolmistress, I suppose, is much more in Spenser's way than any one wou'd chuse to write in that writes quite *gravely;* in which Case The Dialect & stanza of Spenser is hardly preferable to modern Heroic. I look upon my Poem as somewhat more grave than Pope's Alley,[8] & a good deal less yn Mr Thomson's Castle &c: At least I meant it so, or rather I meant to skreen ye ridicule wch might fall on so *low* a subject (tho' perhaps a *picturesque* one) by *pretending* to *simper* all ye time I was writing. And now I am come to give an excuse, wch will, with yr Ladyship's *Candour,* apologize for this blotted Letter. I have "the Schoolmistress" to write over for Dodsley before I go to Bed to-night, consisting now of above 350 lines, in which I expect to make 350 blunders. His miscellanies are gone he says

---

[5] By Dr. Nathaniel Lancaster, the uncle of Thomas Hull. Published May 3, 1748. Reprinted in Dodsley's *Fugitive Pieces* (1761).

[6] William Thompson (1712?–1766?) published *Sickness*, a poem in three books, in 1745 and 1746. Dodsley was the publisher.

[7] Cf. *Men and Manners* (*Works*, Vol. II, 1764), p. 315.

[8] Pope's imitation of Spenser, *The Alley,* was published along with his other imitations of the English poets, in 1727; Pope himself said they were composed as early as the *Translations,* some when he was only fourteen or fifteen years old.

a 2d time to the Press, & I have reason to doubt whether my Improvements will even now come *time enough*. However I ought not to take a final Leave of you, 'till I have express'd the Pleasure I find in ye last Paragraph of Lady H's Letter; for I am by no means so selfish as to suffer ye satisfaction I take in what she says of my trivial Productions, to smother that I feel upon hearing of any News that must prove agreeable to your Ladyship. I am, very faithfully,

Your Ladyship's most oblig'd & most obedient Servant,

Will: Shenstone

I will undoubtedly wait upon yr Ladyship this Summer — I fancy I shall admire yr French Play — The Pantin made the Peace, no *doubt* —

70. To LADY LUXBOROUGH[1]

The Leasows, June ye 16th 1748

MADAM,

Since I wrote last to your Ladyship I have been unable to proceed in the Perusal of your Play, partly on Account of Company, & partly thro' a very dangerous Illness of my Brother's. Mr Hardy (a Son of ye Admiral's) did me the Favour to stay a week with me, but he is now gone & my Brother is recover'd; so having finish'd the Play[2] with Pleasure, I return it with Thanks. The Author, I suppose, must be a Man of Delicacy, if one may judge from ye Character he has chosen to expose; which, tho' too common in real life, is I think in a Manner new to the *Stage*. There is but little in it yt can raise a Laugh or even a Smile, but the Solidity of ye remarkable[3] Scene betwixt Ariste & Valere, and the fine Moral of the whole, has an admirable Tendency to *open ye Eyes,* & *reform* the *Hearts* of the Audience. Finally I conclude the Writer to be an honest Man; Otherwise he cou'd hardly have bore to have expos'd Dishonesty, wn connected with Genius; inasmuch as it must have been ye same as exposing himself.

To-morrow I expect some Company that will probably enough engage me for this Week. But the time will not be long now, before I change my native Haunts, for a Scene yt abounds with far superior Pleasures. The next time I have ye Honour to write to your Ladyship, I will take ye Freedom of fixing some Day when I would wait upon you at Barrels. I have often talk'd about it to Miss Dolman, and, if she happen

---

[1] B. M. Add. MSS 28958, fol. 16ff. Lady Luxborough's letter dated June 27, 1748 (*Letters*, No. XII) is the reply to this, which fact confirms its date.

[2] Called *Le Mechant,* now acting at Paris [Shenstone]. Gresset's comedy (1747).

[3] In the line above "remarkable" Shenstone has written "critical."

to be with her Brother at ye Time, We shall hope for Leave to pay our Respects, staying with yr Ladyship one whole Day, & part of ye two in which we travel.

Mr *Lyttelton* has near finish'd one Side of his Castle. It consists of one entire Tow'r, & three Stumps of Towers, with a ruin'd Wall betwixt them. Perhaps my Pen may better describe it thus.

There is no great Art or Variety in ye Ruin, but the Situation gives it a charming Effect: The chief tower is *allowedly* about 10 Feet too low. If your Ladyship shou'd ever have an Inclination to see ye Present Face of ye Park, Miss Dolman lives within two Miles of admirable Road, where you will find as good a Reception, & a far more friendly welcome yn from ye most self-interested Host. 'Tis also within a Mile of ye Bromsgrove Road.

I find this Moment ye Meditations of Mr Hervey on my Table, wch my Brother I see has purchas'd. I remember my Lord Shaftsbury, speaking of *many* that are vulgarly stil'd *good Books*, says, they *may be so* in ye *Main*, but he is sure the *Writers* of them are a sorry Race. Dr Wall's *Designs* are pious too, but (To speak in ye way of *Taste*) about two thirds as Good as the Worst of Quarles's Emblems. Nevertheless as *Designing* is not his Profession, I do not mean to reflect on his Ingenuity in ye least. I don't believe that a *twentieth* part of mankind can draw a human Figure that is a whit more like a *Man* than an *Elephant;* And I must say farther in Dr W.'s Behalf, yt he seems not have Justice done him by the Engraver — In ye First Volume, a huge tun-bellied Parson with a sleek simpering Face, & leaning very indolently against ye Pillar of a Church, is pointing to our Saviour wth a Crop. He is drest in his Canonicals, wch to be sure is inconsistent wth ye Roman Dress of the Person that stands by him. There is, I think, a further Impropriety in ye *Mottos,* but I will not enter on ye subject now.

Mr Smith ye Designer of ye Prints of Hagley-Park, Ld Tyrconnels &c: call'd here last week, & behav'd wth a Complaisance yt made us wish to serve him. He shew'd us one *Painting* of a scene at Hagley. He took a Draught of wt your Ladyship may remember *I* call *"Virgil's* Grove," *here.* This he purposes to insert in a smaller Collection; a Kind of Drawing-Book, wch, If judge aright, will please me much beyond his larger Prints. He wou'd insist on making me a Present of 5 Charming Ruins yt he has publish'd; &, if one is to believe all Persons of Business *interested* (wch nevertheless I am loth to do) He must needs imagine me to be a Person of greater Influence than I really am. Be that as it will, I am with the highest Respect

Your Ladyship's most obedient humble Servt
W. Shenstone

71. To RICHARD GRAVES [1]

The *Leasowes, June,* 1748

DEAR MR. GRAVES,

I find a very strong Impulse, prompting me to write to you this Evening. I don't know whether I ever let you into the Secret, that I receive an inward Satisfaction at the Time that I am sending you a Letter, and that this Action partakes of the Nature of all virtuous ones, in being its own Reward. However we are taught to hope for *other* and more *ample* Rewards attending Virtue, as I am inclined to expect a more considerable Pleasure, when I receive your Answer. My Soul now leans entirely on the Friendship of a few private Acquaintance, and if they drop me, I shall be a wretched Misanthrope. Is it a great Fatigue to you to sit down some vacant Half-Hour, and scribble me a few Lines, relating to the State of your Mind, and your Affairs? Dick Jago, who called accidentally at a Public-House, at *Mickleton,* told me, they heard ———;[2] mentioning, at the same Time, his thorough Conviction, that, *whatever* might prove the Event of this Affair, as *you* were a Principal, it would be as it *ought*. Mr. Smith, (the Designer) who knew you too, was here at the same Time, and many civil Things, very agreeable to me, were said in your Behalf; *"Immo, Omnes omnia bona dixere."* As to ———.[2]

I thank you for your little Strictures on the *School-Mistress*. I have sacrificed my Partiality to your unbiassed Judgment; *Multa gemens,* have I sacrificed it. The Truth Is, I am not quite convinced (tho' I have acted as if I were) that one should give up any Part, that appears droll in itself, and makes the Poem, on the whole, more agreeable, for the Sake of rendering it a more perfect Imitation of Spencer. But when you have more Leisure, and I collect my Pieces, I don't despair of furnishing a more compleat Edition yet.

Mr. Smith (whom I mentioned just now) has taken two Views of

---

[1] The date of this letter, which is printed in Hull's *Select Letters,* Vol. I, No. XX, is confirmed by the reference in it to Smith's draught of Virgil's Grove, the Leasowes, to which the same reference occurs in Letter 70, of authentic date. The two letters must have been written at about the same time.

[2] In his Preface (I, iv) Hull says he has "suppressed all entire letters, as well as distinct passages, which appeared to contain matter improper for public inspection . . ." He has also given only the initials of persons still alive at the time of his publication.

Hagley-Park, which, with two from other Places, compleat a Set; the Subscription-Price, half a Guinea; but he takes other little Views of the closer Scenes, and of Particular Beauties, which will form a Drawing-Book, and which I shall like beyond those I have subscribed for. Would you not be surprized to see a Draught of my Virgil's *Grove* inserted among the latter?—He took one, and promised to have it engraved, and inserted somewhere; but I had rather he should stay a Week, and take about four Views, and that you were here, and would give him some Instructions, and it should make a little Drawing-Book to sell for a Shilling. But, "Ah, me!—I fondly dream"—The Days of Fancy and dear Enthusiasm will never more return! Such as those that flew over our Heads when you were *here,* and at *Harborough,* on your first Visit;[3] when the *merum Rus* of the *Leasowes* could furnish you with pleasanter Ideas, than the noblest Scenes that ever Painter copied.

I am impatient to see you, and resolve to do so when *I can;* and I beg you will *project* some Means of coming to the *Leasowes* without Inconvenience to yourself.

I am,
Your truly affectionate,
W. Shenstone

I beg my Compliments to Mr. Whistler. I don't know whether I am more *ashamed* or *vexed,* that I cannot set out—to-morrow—for *Whitchurch;* but my Mind will not be easy till I have seen both him and you.

72. To RICHARD GRAVES[1]

The Leasowes, June the last [1748]

DEAR MR. GRAVES,

It is now, I believe, near half a year since I had the favour of a letter from you. When I wrote last, I discovered a more than ordinary solicitude for *one* immediate answer. It puzzles me to account for your unusual silence, otherwise than upon supposition of some offence you have taken: and it puzzles me as much to guess by what behaviour of mine I have been so unhappy as to give you that offence.

I am vain enough to imagine that the little merit I have, deserves somewhat more regard than I have met with from the world. Be that as it will, the disappointment I must undergo, by any *appearance* of

---

[3] Of this first visit Graves gives an account in his *Recollection,* pp. 36ff.
[1] Dodsley, *Letters to Particular Friends,* No. XLIV, dated 1747. Wells corrects the date, *Anglia,* 35:446.

neglect from the friends I value, would more effectually dispirit me than any other whatsoever.

I have published my design of visiting you, and Mr. Whistler in Oxfordshire, to all the world. A thousand incidents have hitherto interfered with it, which I will not now recount. But when I look back upon the regular succession of them, it looks as if Destiny had some hand in detaining me. The most *vigorous* of my *hopes* dwell upon seeing you next winter, though I am not a little indulgent to *those* that tell me I may see you long before.

I have brought my place here to greater perfection than it has ever yet appeared in; and, with the *mob,* it is in some vogue. Nevertheless, I do not know that I ever relished it less in my life than I have done this summer. Bad health, bad spirits, no company to my mind, and no correspondences, are enough to blast the sweetest shades, and to poison the purest fountains. Some of these misfortunes I can impute to my own misconduct, and it embitters them. The two last I can less account for, having at all times done all I was able to recommend myself to my *friends,* behaving at the same time with courtesty to the rest of the world. The fact is not true; otherwise I might resolve it into this, that I alone am idle, and all the world is *busy.*

I fancy you will imagine I lay too much stress upon Mr. Thomson's visit, when I mention the following inscription upon a seat in Virgil's grove:

CELEB 'MO POETÆ
IACOBO THOMSON, S.
PROPE FONTES ILLI NON FASTIDITOS
G. S.
SEDEM HANC ORNAVIT

Quae tibi, quae tali reddam pro carmine dona?
Nam neque me tantum *venientis sibilus* Austri,
Nec percussa juvant fluctu tam litora, nec quae
Saxosas inter decurrunt flumina valles.
V<small>IRG</small>.

I want your opinion of it, and whether it were not better thus,

——— THOMSON,
QUI CUM QUICQUID UBIQUE RURIS EST
AUT AMOENUM AUT VARIUM
MIRE DEFINXERAT,
HOS ETIAM FONTES NON FASTIDIVIT

But you will discover at first glance an impropriety in both.—Now I am upon inscriptions, I send you one from a coin dug up very near me a few weeks ago:

Round the head,
IMP.........V AUG GER DAC M
On the reverse,
SP QR OPTIMO PRINCIPI COS VI

Within which is an human figure sitting, with one hand reclined upon a wand; the other, as I take it, holding forth an olive.—I have given my opinion, it is one of Trajan's; and my virtuoso character will rest upon the truth of it. It is a silver coin, but very obscure. There appears a large mass of ruins, rough stone, very strongly cemented, where they found it—If you were here, it might amuse you.

Heaviness may endure for a night, but joy cometh in the morning. I have so settled a notion of the proportionate mixture of pleasure and pain in this life, that I expect one to succeed the other as naturally as day and night. I own, this is owing to the soul as much as to outward incidents. Sorrow prepares it for mirth, and *vice versa.*—The durations of both differ.—Last summer I spent agreeably; this quite otherwise.—To-day I have been quite melancholy; I expect happiness to-morrow, from either an aptitude of mind, or some incident sufficient to overcome its inaptitude.—Perhaps that incident may be a letter from you; I wish it may, and am most truly

Yours,
W.S.

I had a coin of Vespasian given me to-day, and I begin a collection; if you have any duplicates, you will please to oblige me.—I want to correct my elegies, by your assistance.—I will begin no more.

73. To LADY LUXBOROUGH[1]

The Leasowes, Sunday, July 25, 1748

MADAM,

When I received your Ladyship's Letter on *Friday,* I was just upon the Point of setting out for *Broom;* I therefore declined answering it, till I had spoke with Miss Dolman. It is now with the greatest Thankfulness for your obliging Invitation, and the most pleasing Idea of the Visit we propose, that I am to inform your Ladyship, we intend waiting

---

[1] The dates of this letter and of Lady Luxborough's of July 20, 1748 (*Letters*, No. XII), which it answers, confirm each other. Our only authority for this letter is Hull, *Select Letters*, Vol. I, No. XXI.

on you upon *Tuesday* or *Wednesday* sev'n-night. If you should have *much* Company at that Time, or the Visit should be otherwise unseasonable, your Ladyship will be so good as to let us know; if not, I will not fail to shew Miss Dolman the Way to the most agreeable Entertainment, and the most engaging Conversation, I have met with anywhere. Your Ladyship will not imagine that I understand *Entertainment* in the vulgar Sense; (tho' what I say is true enough in *that*) my chief Pleasures, I flatter myself, are Pleasures of the *Mind;* and I can say, with great Truth, that my Mind was never more *disposed* to be pleased any where *else,* or found equal Opportunities to gratify that Disposition.

Miss Dolman, tho' she has not seen much of the World, has done great Things, or, in other Words, has made good Use of the Opportunities she *has* had, if she can deserve any Part of that favourable Mention you make of her. All I know is, that she has Taste enough to put the Pleasure I have promised her at *Barrels* out of all Dispute.

I now proceed to other Things. I have sent your Ladyship the *first Number of Sickness,* a Poem, which is all I have. I *send* it as indeed I *offered* it, because it bears some Relation to Lady Hertford on Account of the Panegyrick of Lord Beauchamp, which I believe is just.

I have of late read the Life of Colonel Gardiner, being induced to do so by a Vision, which is described there, and which I hear Mr. Lyttelton countenances. I will give your Ladyship my Opinion of the Story, when I come to *Barrels.*

Pray don't buy the Books *I* talked of; you will hardly read them twice; and I can lend you Hervey's *Meditations,* the *Life of Colonel Gardiner,*[2] and, in a short Time, *Memoirs of Mrs. Pilkington,*[3] either of my own, or my Brother's. I beseech your Ladyship, that I may have leave to save you six Shillings, and three Shillings, and three Shillings; that is, according to the old Maxim, *(viz. a Penny sav'd, &c.)* put into the Power of my Gratitude, to be of about twelve Shillings significancy. By so doing, I shall not only talk, but proceed to one *ouvert Act* in the Cause of Oeconomy. — I wish it be not the only one.

In regard to Mr. Outing, I will only say, that I please myself with the full Assurance of meeting him at *Barrels.* It is out of my Power this Day to send you an *amusing* Letter, whether it be so at other Times or not. There is not a single Cloud or Dimness in the Sky, but has its exact Image or Counterpart in my Imagination; but one's Sincerity does not

[2] *Some Remarkable Passages in the Life of the Honourable Colonel James Gardiner* (1747), by Philip Doddridge (1702–51).
[3] Mrs. Pilkington's *Memoirs* were published in 1748.

suffer by Weather, tho' one's Vivacity may; and it is with the greatest Truth that I shall always remain,

Your Ladyship's
Most obliged, and most obedient Servant,
W. Shenstone

74. To LADY LUXBOROUGH[1]

[Aug. 15, 1748]

MADAM,

I'm sure I ought to neglect no opportunity of returning our Joint Acknowledgments for ye extreme Civility you shew'd us at Barrels. I am at ye same time to inform your Ladyship, that our *Delay* at Mr Loggin's was attended with no great Inconvenience in our Return Home: And this I ought more particularly to mention, as your Ladyship may accuse yourself of being instrumental in *it;* since we were tempted insensibly by the Pleasure of your Company to stay there somewhat longer than our Time wou'd well allow. We did indeed encounter certain Gate-posts in passing thro' some Neighbour's Grounds, but we arriv'd at Broom about Eleven of Clock at Night, entirely safe, & perfectly well-pleas'd. Miss Dolman & my Brother were extremely delighted with their Journey, & having seen little Company since have scarce talk'd of anything besides. Indeed the Ideas they must have receiv'd at Barels cannot be suppos'd to be easily eras'd, where the greatest Politeness was made use of to recommend ye greatest Variety of Amusements.

I long to hear what is become of Mr Outing; but 'till I *do*, I shall conclude he has marry'd ye rich Widow with the Farm in her own Hands, & yt he is busy in the Manufacture of Syllabubs for ye Regalement of his Friends. I mean this as Panegyrick, & yt I cannot conceive his Sphere so alter'd, but that his Benevolence will appear in some Shape or other.

To jumble some very different Spots of News together, after ye Manner of a Gazette, Mrs Lyttelton's Monument is arriv'd & put up at Hagley. A Locust has dropt at Birmingham which is shewn as a *Curiosity*, & 'tis to be wish'd it may continue so. The Clergyman who saw it told me it's head & wings resembled those of ye Dragon-Fly, & yt it look'd very formidable. I suppose ye common People will conclude from ye Death of ye Cattle & ye Arrival of this Insect, yt ye Plagues of Egypt are coming. If they cou'd convince my Friend Whistler yt the Frogs wou'd come next, he wou'd expire at ye Thought & never wait for ye Event.

[1] B. M. Add. MSS 28958, fol. 18ff. Lady Luxborough's answer of August 23, 1748 (*Letters*, No. XV) suggests that the "Monday morning" of this letter was August 15.

Your Ladyship's Camera obscura is at present wth Mr Dolman who purposes to try it upon his Machine, which he has near compleated. Some Means of excluding ye Light seems obviously requisite. A Coach *may* be darken'd & so it may be us'd upon ye Road; but I shou'd think not conveniently.

The Paper-Book[2] left in y^r Ladyship's Hands was what I intended to shew you, y^t I might not seem forgetfull of what I formerly propos'd. But your Ladyship is convinc'd by this Time how incompleat it is, & Will I dare say return me this Copy y^t I may do myself y^e *Justice* & y^e *Honour* of presenting you with an improv'd one. I purpos'd to insert some Things you have *not* seen, & to furnish you wth a something better Editⁿ of those you *have*.

I am going to procure a Convex Glass to see Landskips with, & to have it fitted up by a Joiner in my Neighbourhood. I fancy some of Smith's *designs* well colour'd will appear to great Advantage thro these Machines, but it wou'd be Pity to injure them by careless or unskilfull colouring.

If your Ladyship's Niches are Compleated you will give me ye satisfaction of telling me how you like them; & thus I finish my *Rhapsody;* which I think is not unlike a Beggar's Garment, consisting of mere Rags & Trumpery ill-tack'd together. *Albeit,* your Ladyship will see, thro' it, ye Real Poverty of my Imagination, & be induced to excuse it on y^t score & then I will pray as heartily for your Ladyship as any Beggar y^t subsists by your Bounty.

I am Madam your most oblig'd & most obed^t Servant

Will: Shenstone

The Leasows, Augst, Monday morning
1748

75. To RICHARD GRAVES[1]

This was written August 21, 1748,
but not sent till the 28th.

DEAR SIR,

How little soever I am inclined to write at this time, I cannot bear that you should censure me of unkindness in seeming to overlook the

---

[2] This is evidently the "green book" containing his poems, frequently referred to in their later correspondence. See Lady Luxborough's *Letters*, p. 45.

[1] Dodsley, *Letters to Particular Friends*, No. LI. The date, evidently supplied by Dodsley, is confirmed by Fullington in *PMLA*, 46:1133–34. Though Dodsley does not name the addressee, it is evidently Graves, and the occasion of the letter is his marriage to Lucy Bartholomew of Aldworth, Berkshire, with whose family Graves lodged while curate there.

late change in your situation. It will, I *hope,* be esteemed superfluous in *me* to send you my most cordial wishes that you may be happy; but it will, perhaps, be *something* more significant to say, that I believe you *will:* building my opinion on the knowledge I have long had of your own temper, and the account you give me of the person's whom you have made choice of, to whom I desire you to pay my sincere and most affectionate compliments.

I shall always be glad to find you *præsentibus æquum,* though I should always be pleased when I saw you *tentantem majora.* I think you should neglect no *opportunity* at this time of life to push your fortune so far as an *elegant* competency, that you be not embarrassed with those kind of solicitudes towards the evening of your day;

> Ne te semper inops agitet vexetque cupido,
> Ne pavor, & rerum *mediocriter utilium* spes!

I would have you acquire, if possible, what the world calls, with some *propriety,* an *easy* fortune; and what I interpret, such a fortune as allows of some inaccuracy and inattention, that one may not be continually in suspence about the laying out a *shilling;* — this kind of advice may seem extremely dogmatical in *me;* but, if it carries any haughty air, I will obviate it by owning that I never *acted* as I say. I have lost *my* road to happiness, I confess; and, instead of pursuing the way to the fine lawns and venerable oaks which distinguish the region of it, I am got into the pitiful parterre-garden of amusement, and view the nobler scenes at a *distance.* I think I can see the *road* too that *leads* the better way, and can shew it others; but I have many miles to measure back before I can get into it myself, and no kind of resolution to take a single step. My chief amusements at present are the same they have long been, and lie scattered about my farm. The French have what they call a *parque ornée;* I suppose, approaching about as near to a garden as the park at Hagley. I give my place the title of a *ferme ornée;* though, if I had money, I should hardly confine myself to such decorations as that name requires. I have made great improvements; and the *consequence* is, that I long to have you see them.

I have not heard whether Miss ——'s[2] match proceeded. — I suppose your objections were grounded on the person's *age* and *temper;* and that they had the less weight, as they supposed you acted indiscreetly yourself: I can say but little on the occasion. You know ——— better than I do. Only this I must add, that I have so great an esteem for your sister, that

[2] Evidently Graves's sister. See Fullington, "Mr. William Shenstone," p. 35.

it will be necessary to my *ease,* that whoever marries her she should be happy.

I have little hopes that I shall now see you often in this country; though it would be *you,* in all probability, as soon as *any,* that would take a journey of fifty miles,

To see the *poorest* of the sons of men.

The truth is, my affairs are miserably embroiled, by my own negligence, and the non-payment of tenants. I believe I shall be forced to seize on one next week for three years and a half's rent, due last Lady-day; an affair to which I am greatly averse, both through *indolence* and *compassion*. I hope, however, I shall be always able (as I am sure I shall be desirous) to entertain a friend of a *philosophical regimen,* such as you and Mr. Whistler; and that will be all I can do.

Hagley park is considerably improved since you were here, and they have built a castle by way of ruin on the highest part of it, which is *just* seen from my *wood;* but by the removal of a tree or two (growing in a wood that joins to the park, and which, fortunately enough, belongs to Mr. Dolman and me), I believe it may be rendered a considerable object here.

I purpose to write to Mr. Whistler either this post or the next. The fears you seemed in upon my account are very kind, but have no grounds. I am, dear Mr. [Graves], habitually and sincerely,

Your most affectionate
W. Shenstone

My humble service to your neighbours. —— Smith (whom you knew at Derby) will publish a print of my grove in a small collection.

76. To LADY LUXBOROUGH [1]

Broom, August ye 24th 1748

MADAM,

I date this from Broom,[2] where I happen to be upon an Affair alike disagreeable to my *Compassion* & my *Indolence;* & yet at ye same time extremely *necessary* & for y^t reason very *proper,* to apologise for ye short Answer I am oblig'd to give to your Ladyship's most agreeable Letter. The Affair I allude to is ye Distreining on a Tenant concerning which I was in deep consultation when I was told of your Servant's arrival. Pleasure & Pain continue to interfere! & I cou'd be well enough content

---

[1] B. M. Add. MSS 28958, fol. 20ff.
[2] Broom was the home of Shenstone's relatives, the Dolmans.

if they wou'd come separate: for I wou'd have my Pleasures untainted; & then when Pain was to arrive, wou'd prepare myself for it by giving myself up to no other Expectation. Sweet & Acid join'd together I believe recommend a *syllabub* of which Mr Outing (to my great grief) disallows himself a Manufacturer; but I think 'tis otherwise in *Life*, & y^t one wou'd wish to have them, *there,* by no means intermingled. In other Words, I wou'd be willing y^t *Pleasure* shou'd make Incroachments upon *Pain,* but *Pain* shou'd never revenge itself upon Pleasure. To put an End to this formal Casuistry, I do fully believe that when We see your Ladyship at Broom, we shall be *compleatly* happy, & I am extremely glad to hear y^t your Postilion gives a favourable verdict in Regard to the Roads. The Business I mention'd in ye first Part of my Letter took up ye Forenoon, & your Servant I fancy thinks it Time he shou'd be going. I must beg your Ladyship's Interest wth Mr Outing to obtain a Pardon for not answering his Letter, *now;* for I really am not able. I hope you will command him to believe y^t I was ever in Spirits when I met him, & that I shall be now as much as ever, *notwithstanding.*

      I am, Madam,
  Your Ladyship's most oblig'd & most obedient Servant
                Will: Shenstone

 There are now at Hagley Mr Lyttelton, Mr Pitt, Mr Miller ye Projector &c: &c:

 I beg your Ladyship wou'd excuse ye Blunders I have *committed,* & y^t Mr Outing wou'd forgive me ye Letter I have *omitted.* I wou'd have avoided *both* these Faults, but that I have compassion on your Footman who waits, & who has been so kind as to speak *smoothe* Things of ye Way y^t leads you hither.

 Mr Dolman desires his Compliments to Mr Outing & will be very glad to wait on him.

 My Brother desires his Compliments to your Ladyship.

77. To RICHARD JAGO [1]

           Sept. 3, Saturday night, 1748

DEAR MR. JAGO,

 I hardly know whether it will be prudent in me to own, that I wrote you a *long letter* upon the receipt of your last, which I now have upon my table. I condemn this habit in *myself* entirely, and should, I am

---

[1] Dodsley, *Letters to Particular Friends,* No. LII. Wells confirms the date, *Anglia,* 35:447–48.

sure, be very unhappy, if my friends, by my example, should be induced to contract the same. The truth is, I had not expressed myself in it to my mind, and it was full of blots, and blunders, and interlinings; yet, such as it was, it had wearied my attention, and given me a disinclination to begin it afresh. I am now impatient to remove any scruple you may have concerning my grateful sense of all your favours, and the invariable continuance of my affection and esteem. — I find by your last obliging letter, that my machinations and devices are not entirely private. — You knew of my draught of Hagley Castle about the bigness of a barley-corn; you knew of our intended visit to Lady Luxborough's; and I must add, Mr. Thomas Hall knew of my contrivance for the embellishment of Mr. Hardy's house. Nothing is there hid that shall not be revealed. — Our visit to Barrels is now over and past. — Lady Luxborough has seen Hagley Castle in the original: — and as to my desire that my draught might be shewn to no *Christian* soul, you surely did but ill comply with it when you shewed that *drawing* to a *Clergyman*. However, you may have acted up to my *real* meaning, if you have taken care not to shew it to any connoisseur. I meant chiefly to guard against any one that knows the rules, in whose eyes, I am sure, it could not turn to my credit. — Pray how do you like the festoons dangling over the oval windows? — It is the chief advantage in repairing an old house, that one may deviate from the rules without any extraordinary censure.

I will not trouble you *now* with many particulars. The intent of Tom's coming is to desire your company and Mrs. Jago's this week. — I should be extremely glad if your convenience would allow you to come on Monday or Tuesday; but if it is *entirely* impracticable, I would beseech you not to put off the visit longer than the Monday following, for the leaves of my groves begin to fall a great pace. — I beg once more, you would let no small inconvenience prevent your being here on Monday. — As to my visit at Icheneton, you may depend upon it soon after; and I hope you will not stand upon punctilio, when I mention my inclination that you may all take a walk through my coppices before their beauty is much impaired. Were I in a sprightly vein, I would aim at saying something genteel by way of *answer* to Mrs. Jago's compliment. — As it is, I can only thank her for the *substance,* and applaud the *politeness* of it. — I postpone all other matters till I see you. I am, habitually and sincerely,

Your most affectionate friend,
W. Shenstone

I beg my compliments to Mr. Hardy.

P. S. I am not accustomed, my dear friend, to send you a *blank* page; nor can I be content to do so now.

I thank you very *sensibly* for the verses with which you honour me. I think them good lines, and so do others that have seen them; but you will give me leave, when I see you, to propose some little alteration. As to an epistle, it would be excused with *difficulty,* and I would have it turn to your credit as well as my own. But you have certainly of late acquired an *ease* in writing; and I am tempted to think, that what you write henceforth will be universally good. Persons that have seen your elegies like "The Blackbirds" best, as it is most assuredly the most *correct;* but I, who pretend to great penetration, can foresee that "The Linnets" *will* be made to excel. — More of this when I see you. Poor Miss G[raves], J[ackie] R[eynolds] says,[2] is married; and poor Mr. Thomson, Mr. Pitt tells me, is *dead.*[3] — He was to have been at Hagley this week, and then I should probably have seen him here. — As it is, I will erect an urn in Virgil's Grove to his memory. — I was really as much shocked to hear of his death, as if I had known and loved him for a number of years: — God knows, I lean on a very few friends; and if they drop me, I become a wretched misanthrope.

78. To LADY LUXBOROUGH [1]

Septr 1748

MADAM,

I have not time to say anything more than that I am extremely sensible of ye Honour you intend me, & yt I shall be happy in waiting on yr Lassp, Mr Outing & Mr Hall. Were I to prolong ye Time by expressing myself more fully, I might justly risque the giving offence to your Servant; which it wou'd be as imprudent to do, as to irritate one's Jury. As it is, I have no Fault to find with him; He allows ye Road to be *practicable,* tho' not altogether so smoothe & easy as *my* Friend Johnson[2] represents it. I think Coal-carriers are transform'd into Angels of Light; at least *I* shall never esteem 'em to be Ministers of Darkness, whilst they give Representations so favourable to my Wishes — 'Tis very natural for me to fix on ye *former* of ye Days you propose, & accordingly I build upon ye Hopes of seeing your Ladyship on *Saturday:* But as I send to Broome

---

[2] See Fullington, "Mr. William Shenstone," p. 35.
[3] Thomson died August 27, 1748.
[1] B. M. Add. MSS 28958, fol. 22ff. This clearly answers Lady Luxborough's letter of September 5, 1748 (*Letters,* No. XVI) and confirms its date.
[2] Johnson, who lived at Northfield, supplied Lady Luxborough with coal (*Letters,* p. 48).

to-Night, I will presume upon your Ladyship's Goodness for Leave to *alter* that Day in Case I find any thing in Mr Dolman's Answer that requires it. If so, I will send my Servant to Barels on Thursday; otherwise I will by no means think of deferring my Happiness, for a moment longer y^n the time it is offer'd me. I am

> Your Ladyship's most oblig'd & most obed Servant
> Will. Shenstone

Miss Dolman talk'd of sending a Servant the Beginning of this week. I beg my Compliments to Mr Outing & Mr Hall.

79. To LADY LUXBOROUGH [1]

The Leasows, Septr 11th 1748

MADAM,

I cannot content myself even with the Pleasure I receiv'd from your Ladyship's Company, 'till I have had the additional satisfaction of hearing that you got safe Home. I hope you suffer to-day as little as *possible* from your Fatigue, by which *I* only was a Gainer. I was extremely sorry that I was not able to alleviate it by *suitable* Accomodations in Point of Lodging; I took care to state ye Case twice over to Mr Outing, & if your Ladyship had thought proper to accept of such a Bed as we cou'd furnish, it wou'd have been attended with no kind of Inconvenience to me, but on the contrary with the greatest Pleasure. Twas moreover a mortification to me to see you leave ye Company just as you had begun to brighten up the Conversation; when I knew what a Change wou'd be wrought by your Departure — I ought to inform your Ladyship y^t the Company, farther than Lord Dudley & his Sister, was accidental; only Parson Perry who din'd wth me on a paltry Dinner ye Day before, was told, y^t if he came y^e *following* Day, he wou'd partake of a better, as well as of your Ladyship's Company, which was far superior to any Dinner in the World. In Consequence of this He brought his Wife with Him — Mr. Sanders is an Apothecary of Stourbridge, eminent in his *Way;* a good-natur'd generous Man, that loves, (like me,) to have his Schemes & Machinations admir'd. He has distinguish'd himself by keeping Polypus's. I never saw him here before — Mr Corbett I never saw before. He is Son of Serjeant Corbett & is a young Barrister that has gone ye Circuit about twice; perhaps *not, hitherto,* very eminent in *his* Way. Things

---

[1] B. M. Add. MSS 28958, fol. 23ff. Lady Luxborough's letter of the same date (*Letters,* No. XVII) answers this, and the date of her letter is thus confirmed. They often exchanged letters by servant upon the same day, instead of using the post.

were in some Confusion when these People came, & I had not an opportunity of introducing Lord Dudley properly. Your Ladyship will not take amiss the Manner of his Address; He has no ill or sinister Meaning, & I think, at Table, endeavour'd more to please, than I have often seen Him. I'm sure I've great Reason to claim a like Indulgence, but I trust (as my Lord Stair said at ye End of his Declaration to ye States) y^t your Ladyship *on account of* y^e *sincerity of our Purpose,* & y^e *Uprightness* of our *Heart,* will *pardon all our Failings* — I do accuse myself however of some Rudeness in Regard to Parson Hall; & not the less so, for his good-Nature in seeming to disregard it; I have an extreme good opinion of Mr Hall, & I think there were some Freedoms taken w^{ch} (tho' trifling amongst *Friends*) as there were *strangers* by, were *wrong*. I hope your Ladyship also feels some Compunctions of this kind, wch may induce you the more readily to say something on my Behalf — After you went, the Company walk'd once more round my Walks, & gave them great Encomiums; which however made but faint Impression on me, after your Ladyship's Approbation — For want of proper Contingencies, how many Noble Schemes have prov'd abortive! My Lord Dudley shou'd have met your Ladyship in ye Morning & attended you thro my Walks with extraordinary *Complaisance* & *Sprightliness;* Your Ladyship shou'd have been *unfatigu'd* y^e *Moment* you got out of y^r Chaise; notwithstanding ye Length & Roughness of your Journey; & as you came to the Seat which commands ye Water in Virgil's Grove, I shou'd have come behind & dropt these Verses into your Lap, scribbled *extempore* no doubt with a blacklead-Pencil.

> Here Dudley deigns to spend a social Hour:
> Spring fast ye Greens! the favour'd Haunt embow'r!
> Here *Luxb'rough sate;* Ye Streams y^t gently glide,
> Whene'er you chance to meet a *richer* Tide,
> Ah! warn it not to slight your little Store;
> Say, Luxb'rough prais'd you, & you ask no more.

I believe I must beg y^t my Servant may stay till Morning at Barrels, as He will arrive late, & I can, on no other Terms expect a Line from your Ladyship.

 I am your Ladyship's most oblig'd & most obedient humble Servant
              Will: Shenstone

My Brother & Miss Dolman desire your Ladyship may accept of Their Compliments.

80. To RICHARD JAGO [1]

Sunday night, Sept. 11, 1748

DEAR MR. JAGO,

I take this opportunity of acknowledging the justice of your excuses. Mrs. Jago's present circumstances[2] render her visit quite impracticable, and yours I have the same kind of reason to dispense with; as I guess, that she could as soon take a journey *herself* at this time, as bear that *you* should. — But to say I was not greatly mortified, would be doing myself the greatest injustice. *Disappointed* I was, you may be sure, to hear excuses; even as much as Sir John Falstaff, when Mr. Dombledon put him in mind of *security,* instead of sending him *two* and *thirty yards* of sattin to make him a *short* cloak. And on the whole, I began to accuse you and Mrs. Jago of *colloguing* together, to fix your visit at a time when you were well assured you should have an *apology* to send me instead. Now, if I should press this accusation, pray how would you evade the force of it? — The next thing I am to speak to, is your verses. I have made you my acknowledgments *before;* and as you are so good as to accept them, I will not trouble you with additional professions, or repetitions of the past. I will depend upon your good-sense for an excuse, if I only add what I think proper as to any *alteration;* wherein I have a view to *your* credit, as well as my *own*. I confess it requires some nicety to inscribe such an elegy as "The Goldfinches" without the danger you foresaw. But I think it *may* be done (and *is* pretty nearly) in such a manner that no man of *taste* will be tempted to ridicule it; and as for the vulgar, of whatever *rank* they be, it is absolutely necessary many times to *give them up*. *Taste* and *tenderness* are absolutely connected; and you may very readily call to mind some charming things, that must excite the laughter of your men of *fire* and *banter,* but are by no means thought the worse of by men of *true genius*. I will only mention Andrew Marvel's *Fawn* in Dryden's Miscellanies. I inclose the elegy with some few proposed alterations, so I will not risque the *filling* my *letter* with criticism. I also inclose the other verses you sent me, which I think good ones, and to stand in need of little alteration, beside that of the inglorious name at the head of them; to which, notwithstanding, I will never submit. Pray who is the young gentleman that translates your elegy into Latin? — The new dress will give you some amusement; and, if these lines *be* the product of the genius of a boy of that age, he will in a year's time be able to extend the fame of your compositions. I shall then be glad to see "The

---

[1] Dodsley, *Letters to Particular Friends,* No. LIII. Wells confirms the date, *Anglia,* 35:448.
[2] The first Mrs. Jago had a baby every year for seven years and then died.

Goldfinches" under his hand; though I have no extraordinary fondness for the Latin poetry of a modern; at least, till your eldest son begins to translate our madrigals.

I have not yet seen Mr. Thomson's "Castle of Indolence." — I waited for a smaller edition; but am now too impatient not to send for it on Thursday next. — I am fully bent on raising a neat urn to him in my lower grove, if Mr. Lyttelton does not inscribe one at Hagley *before* me. But I should be extremely glad of your advice whereabouts to place it. — You speak of my dwelling in the Castle of Indolence, and I verily believe I *do*. There is something like enchantment in my present inactivity; for, without any kind of lett or impediment to the correction of my trifles, that I see, I am in no wise able to make the least advances. I think within myself I could proceed if you were here; and yet I have reason to believe if you *were* here, we should only ramble round the groves, and chat away the time; and perhaps *that,* upon the *whole,* is of full as much importance. — I do not know but I do myself some little injustice here, for I *have* wrote out my *levities* and my *sonnets,* good and bad, with many ornaments from the pencil; and the next thing I do will be to transcribe my elegies. The fault is, I take no pains to *improve* what I transcribe, and consequently am only able to exhibit my nonsense in a fairer dress. — You must give me leave, ere it be long, to insert two or three lines (I think in *verse*) before Mrs. Jago's flower-piece. — I am sure, I am obliged to her for a fruit I greatly love — it was not entirely ripe; but it was the only one I have tasted since I was last in London. — Yesterday dined here Lady Luxborough, Mr. Outing and Mr. Hall, Lord Dudley, Miss Lea, Counsellor Corbet and Mr. Saunders, Mr. Perry, Mrs. Perry and Miss Dolman, and half a dozen footmen beside my own servants and labourers; so you may guess we had no small fracas. I now sit down amid solitude and silence, and can hear little else beside the pendulum of my clock; — yet my spirits are no way sunk, but afford me just such a temperature of mind as inclines me to write to some familiar friend; albeit I have a thousand things to *talk* of to you, which I do not care to *write.* I hope to be able to spend a few days with Mr. Hardy, before his melons are all gone; and yet I would not have him keep one a *moment* longer upon *my* account. I desire he would accept of my compliments, as I trust he will. — Franks at present run low with me; but I send you *one,* which you cannot use so soon but I shall be able to send you others immediately. I wish I could send you any thing more than the means of obliging,

Sir, Your most affectionate friend, W. S.

81. To LADY LUXBOROUGH[1]

Sunday-night Sept 25, 1748

MADAM,

As your Ladyship *confers obligations* wth a Grace superiour to any one I know, so I cannot but observe that your *Menaces* afford me greater Pleasure than I cou'd receive from any Courtier's *Promises*—I hope to be doing some little erroneous Matter, ev'ry year, about my Farm, sufficient to call down upon me what you call the *Punishment* of a Visit, as often as your Ladyship is at Leisure to inflict it. I am going incontinently to raise an Urn to Mr Thomson in my *lower* Grove; & have this Ev'ning requested a very ingenious Builder from Birmingham to call upon me. So your Ladyship may *threaten* as much as you please, & I assure you I will provoke your Threat'nings as far as I am able. Now I mention Mr Thomson, I receiv'd yesterday y^e "Castle of Indolence."[2] I waited, I believe three Months, to buy it in a smaller Edition; & ye same Moment y^t I receiv'd y^e *large* one, I saw ye octavo *Edit:* advertis'd in ye Papers. It is I think a very pretty Poem, & also a good *Imitation* of *Spenser;* which latter Circumstance is ye more remarkable, as Mr Thomson's Diction was not reckon'd ye most *simple*. I own I read it wth partiality to y^e *Author,* as I had seen & lik'd y^e *Man;* as his Merit was but *inequally* recompenc'd; and as he is now *dead*. This last Article adds a *Tenderness,* tho' I must have read it wth ye Partiality of a Friend, had he been yet alive—There is a Compliment *again* to Mr Lyttelton. *That Gentleman* call'd on me last Saturday se'nnight, together with one Mr *Mitchell,* whom I know not; yet I think I have seen his *Name* somewhere in Print. They found me just as I had din'd, and as they were oblig'd to go back to Hagley to dinner, did little more than walk around ye House & approve my laying Things *open*. I remember'd my Disappointment *last* year, & being somewhat mortify'd at ye Shortness of the visit, I wish my Expostulations were not a little too *brusque*. However he gave me Hopes of seeing him again before he left ye Country, which nevertheless I do not much *expect*. Those Lines in ye Castle of Indolence are pretty,

> I care not, Fortune, what Thou canst deny;
> Thou canst not rob me of Free Nature's grace;
> Thou canst not Shut ye Windows of ye Sky,
> From whence *Aurora* shews her radiant Face.
> Thou canst not &cc—

---

[1] B. M. Add. MSS 28958, fol. 25ff. Lady Luxborough's letter of October 16, 1748 (*Letters,* No. XVIII) replies to this and its date is thus confirmed.

[2] *The Castle of Indolence* is noticed in the Register of Books, *Gentleman's Magazine,* May, 1748.

I know Mr Outing will be more delighted wth ye description of "A little, round, fat, oily Man of God" &c:³ which I own is very drole; & puts one in Mind of Dr Shaw — I hear my Lord Gower went to London *immediately* after ye Races at L'tchfield; extremely dissatisfy'd that ye Tories had *out-shone* Him. I have some Notion too, that he has not perform'd ye visit he promis'd at Hagley: There *was* a Report y^t he had been there, which prov'd a false one.

I heard too y^t Mr Lyttleton open'd a Letter at Hagley, & cry'd, "So! There's an End of ye Peace!" But of *No* Report will I assure ye Truth.

I scribbled yesterday a little *Autumn* Song,⁴ wch if your Ladyship desires, you shall see in my next.

I have not seen Lord Dudley since your Ladyship was here. We chose to drop our visit ye next Day, for particular Reasons — If Mr Sanders knew you call'd Him an *ingenious* Man, he wou'd ride precipitately to Barels with his Convex-Glass &c: behind him, & perhaps break it by the way. I have not yet receiv'd ye Glass he is to procure me, but I was thinking of a *small* Improvement of my own; which consists in pasting all ye Pictures on a long scroll of Canvas, like a welch Pedigree; & so having a Roller *behind* & *before,* turning on an Axis, by which means one may by turning round y^e *latter,* shew ye Pictures with all ye Ease imaginable — It was *not* thro' a *consciousness* of sneering that I desir'd some Apology to be made to Mr Hall; for I meant nothing like it; But Mr Perry happen'd to say y^t He thought I went too far; & I *now sincerely believe* y^t Perry was nettled *himself* at w^t I said about his Preaching for Mr Hall at Henley, & so took that method of endeavouring to mortify me. — September ye 28th. Thus far was written in order to have been sent last Monday, but ye Postwoman calling *prematurely,* I was oblig'd to wait for y^e *present* opportunity; and by that means am able to add a few Things which your Ladyship will please to accept upon ye Cover — For such do I design this to be — I have ventur'd to transcribe the Trifle I before mention'd as a mark of my *Simplicity,* tho' none of my Genius. I mean, that, as I wou'd be understood *literally* when I call what I write a *Trifle,* so it shews my confidence in y^e *Person's goodness,* to whomsoever that Trifle is communicated — *More* Interest for ye green Book — But why talk I of y^e *green*-Book? who am now writing out my lamentable Elegies in a Book as red as Blood — Your Ladyship knows that Red

---

³ An allusion to Mr. Hall. See Lady Luxborough's *Letters,* p. 58, where she so describes him.

⁴ A few lines are added after "approaching Pain" which spoil it for a song [Shenstone]. The poem alluded to is *Verses Written towards the Close of the Year 1748, to William Lyttelton, Esq.,* in *Works,* I (1764), 181–84.

is sometimes us'd for second-Mourning — & *Art* for ought I know may be fondest of *that* Colour, tho' *Nature* out of doubt deals far more frequently in Green — I saw my Builder this afternoon & we have fix'd upon the Model your Ladyship approv'd, without any Alteration. Twill be erected in about a Fortnight, as soon as He can compleat ye Pediment. I also gave Him a Model for an Urn to Mr Thomson, which I will sketch out for your Ladyship's opinion ye next Time I write. These two will be compleated, I believe, before Winter — And if I *live,* & can *content myself* wth *white-brick* for a building in ye Center of my upper Grove, I may, very possibly, execute that in ye Spring; And then I think my Place will not be so unpleasant yt any one need *studiously* avoid ye Sight of it — If your Ladyship have Dodsley's Miscellany, (tho' I do not remember to have seen it at Barrels) I shou'd be oblig'd if you wou'd lend it me — I have waited *long* for a second Edition wch Dodsley propos'd in great *Haste,* but I do not see it advertis'd *yet.* I desire my Compliments to Mr Outing & Mr Hall. I am
   Your Ladyship's most oblig'd & most obedient Servant
               Will Shenstone

If I do not see Mr Outing soon, I will take care to acknowledge ye Favour of his Last Letter. I am at present under ye Dominion of *Indolence,* & It is evry whit as certain yt my House is ye individual *Castle* wch Thomson describes, as yt ye Chapel of Loretto traveld from Jerusalem into Italy.

82. To LADY LUXBOROUGH [1]

           The Leasows Novr 9th 1748

MADAM,

 The Prospect I had of conveying your Ladyship a Letter by the Return of Mr Outing and Mr Hall has kept me silent till *now,* & will, I hope prove my Apology. But I shou'd be inexcusable if I defer'd a Moment longer to acknowledge ye repeated Pleasure & satisfaction I receive from your Ladyship's Letters: I may add, the Happiness I have enjoy'd, & may yet *hope,* from your conversation; & I think I ought not to *omit,* ye opportunity I have by means of your Acquaintance to shew ye trifles I write to a Person of so unexceptionable a Taste, as to render her Approbation very interesting; & at ye same Time of such a friendly Partiality, as not entirely to refuse that Approbation.

 I ask your Ladyship's Pardon for any Freedom's I have taken with

[1] B. M. Add. MSS 28958, fol. 29ff. This replies to Lady Luxborough's letter of November 2, 1748 (*Letters,* No. XIX), the date of which is thus confirmed.

your favourite season. It is not *Youth,* God knows, but a kind of premature Old-Age y^t makes me bid Autumn less welcome y^n I shou'd otherwise do. I am *afraid* now of what I have hitherto sought opportunities of indulging; I mean, that pleasing melancholy wch suits my Temper *too well.* This your Ladyship will discover by some very *solemn* Elegies wch I shall shortly put into your Hands. I cannot but consider Autumn as y^e *Follower* of Summer, & y^e *Harbinger* of a Season which your Ladyship yourself dislikes. And as it reminds one of past-Pleasure for y^t reason, & also of approaching Pain, It seems to centre in itself rather too *much* of ye douce Melancholie; a *little* whereof is ye most refin'd Pleasure we know — Your Ladyship will say, why do I raise an Urn to Thomson? The Pleasure *that* can afford must be of ye melancholy kind — Tis very true — But I can retire to Thomson's urn when I think *proper* (at least I cou'd if it was erected as at present it is *not.*) But Autumn obtrudes it's pensive Look in every nook & Corner. If it paints my Grove with ever so many colours, Those Colours are so many symptoms of *Decay:* For however *Nature* may carry on her *Scheme* alike in *all seasons,* The several *Parts* of her Dominion, the *Trees* & *vegetables* do no doubt flourish & decay by Turns. If It *strip* those Leaves & throw them into my Brook, tis all *right* & *natural,* but yet I had rather see my Brook uninterrupted, & running transparently over it's Pebbles — After all — I find myself wonderfully *inclin'd* to think wth your Ladyship. I read in your Ladyship's Letter all y^t cou'd possibly be said *for* Autumn: There was a fine Day or two succeeded, &, betwixt both, I was convinc'd y^t I ought to write a Recantation so far as concerns *Autumn at Barels,* & so far as concerns y^e *former Part* of it & with the Limitation, y^t I may give my Madrigal ye Title of "A *fine Day* in Autumn." But I laid aside ye Scheme in Hopes y^t your *Ladysp* whose *peculiar* favorite ye Season is, & who are capable of adorning ye subject in a better Manner y^n myself, wou'd please to throw into verse ye best things y^t can be said in it's Favour; And then even *Spring* shall give it Place.

I desire to subscribe to yours & Lady Hartford's Sentiment in regard to Thomson's Poem. It has several pretty Parts, & several pretty Paintings. I don't know how I came to express myself otherwise, for I did not entirely approve ye Plan at *first.* I think he shou'd by no means anticipate ye Diseases & Inconveniences of Indolence at ye End of his *first* Canto. You know there is a large Display of them in y^e *second,* where they wou'd have appear'd more strikingly had he not touch'd upon 'em before — I valu'd Mr Thomson as he was ye only Person of Figure y^t ever ye Hag-y-Family introduc'd me to; Tho' I once had hopes — but *they* are wither'd whether my Flowers (according to your Ladyship's Beautifull Quotation) are or no. In ye next Place he wou'd have prov'd a good Critick in regard to any little Thing I had intended to publish. & as he was in years, & his Reputation settled, cou'd have had none of those little Jealousies y^t often attend such kind of connections. Finally he wou'd have prov'd a very agreeable Friend & Acquaintance —but he is gone & his Death is of a Piece wth my Fortunes. However I will raise an Urn to him, & remember him wth Pleasure. Had he liv'd, he might have found *some* satisfaction here notwithstanding ye vicinity and ye Table of H——.

For an Acquiescence in seeing every Thing as he finds 'em, I know no one y^t I envy so much as my Lord Dudley. He does not only bring himself to *acquiesce* in what he *finds,* but it is a Reason with him y^t Things *shou'd* be so because they *have* been. And this even when Expence is not ye least concern'd. He will not remove some Pictures out of a Parlour where they are a kind of blemishes, to another Room where he knows they wou'd prove Beauties. He lets two giant yew-trees hide ye Pillars of his Gates, & spoil a good walk by ye side of them, at ye same time y^t he will very readily allow of their Impropriety. But this Insensibility *has* it's Convenience, for which, once more, I envy Him—

I own I took ye Hint of a Roller for y^t Shew glass from ye London Cries—I have had mine fitted up, (But shall not have ye Roller, till I have a better stock of Pictures. In ye mean time I have painted a couple of *Smith's Views,* & I believe that no Pictures in ye world can prove more striking. I send y^r Ladyship my Plan for ye Wood-work of these glasses, & therefore will say no more concerning them at present.

If y^r Ladyships *Eolian* Harp shall please me (and I intend to be within hearing of it soon) I promise to give up my Harpsichord immediately & suffer my right Hand to forget it's little share of Cunning, with all ye Content imaginable—moreover I will Have every Madrigal I writ to be sung to y^t Instrument only.

I have sent ye Shuttle-cock[2] for Mr Allen's Perusal, & have added a Translation from Horace wch I receiv'd sometime this Summer.

I can add no more at present; only I beg & entreat that this *random* Letter may be never brought to evidence against that invariable *Respect* wth which I am your Ladyships
     most oblig'd & most obedient Servant
            W. S.

[2] Whistler's poem; see above, Letter 66, n4.

83. To RICHARD JAGO[1]

Sunday, Nov. 13 [1748]

DEAR SIR,

I must fairly own, that I have not sat down till now to return my acknowledgments for your last most obliging favour; and yet I have been doing so in *imagination* almost every day since I received it. I have only to desire that you would not think me *stupid;* and then you must of course conclude me highly delighted, to find the verses which had so greatly pleased me, made so *particularly interesting* to me. In testimony hereof, I have caused these my letters to be made *patent,* &c. Furthermore, I am glad to see you dissent from some alterations I proposed; for which, generally speaking, I think I can see your reasons. As to any little matter which I have to mention farther, I choose to defer it till I wait on Mr. Hardy; which I purpose to do before this month is out. It may possibly *happen* the beginning of the next week; but I dare not lay such stress upon a future *event,* as to give you a commission to say so much to *him.* Instead thereof, please to make him my compliments, and tell him I talk of coming *very soon.*

I borrowed Dodsley's Miscellany of Lady Luxborough, in which are many good things. I long to be making a mark on the head of every copy (as I would do were the books my *own.*) Here a cypher: there an asterism of five points, and there one of eight. — If you, and Mr. W——, and Mr. G——,[2] and I, were together for a fortnight, to correct and revise, might not we make a miscellany of *originals* that would sell? — My fingers itch to be at it; — but I fear it cannot be. — Thomson's poem amused me greatly. — I think his plan has faults; particularly, that he should have said nothing of the diseases attending laziness in his *first* canto, but reserved them to strike us *more affectingly* in the last; but, on the whole, who would have thought that Thomson could have so well imitated a person remarkable for simplicity both of sentiment and phrase?

I study no connections in a letter; and so I proceed to tell you, that I have got a machine to exhibit landscapes, &c. to advantage. It costs about fourteen shillings, and I recommend one to you or Mr. Hardy. — Smith's Views (with a little colouring) appear ravishingly; — but if you are not content with *amusement,* and want *fame* (which differs about as much as *fox*-hunting from *hare*-hunting), you must *print.* However, if you can acquiesce in a *limited reputation,* to give you a proper weight at all your

---

[1] Dodsley, *Letters to Particular Friends,* No. LIV. Wells supplies the year, *Anglia,* 35: 448. Fullington confirms the month and day, *PMLA,* 46:1134.
[2] Pretty obviously Whistler and Graves.

visiting-places (which I think enough for all reasonable ends and purposes), take the following receipt.

A RECEIPT TO MAKE FAME

"Take a shoe-maker into your parlour (that is reputed a good workman), and bid him procure a piece of red or blue Morocco leather; let him shape this into the size of a quarter of a sheet of paper, or it may be something larger. Let him double it in such a manner as to leave some part to wrap over; then stitch it neatly at the ends, lining it either with silk or the best yellow leather he can meet with. Then must you bespeak a silver clasp, which you *may* have gilded; but be sure it be neatly *chased*, and properly annexed to the aforesaid Morocco leather. Make a present of this to the prettiest girl you know, but filled with half a dozen of your best compositions; take care that one be in praise of *her* ingenuity. For modesty's sake, desire her not to shew them to any living soul; but, at the same time, be careful that your clasp be splendid, and your letter-case made according to the foregoing directions."

Adieu! seriously yours,
W. S.

84. To LADY LUXBOROUGH[1]

The Leasows, December the 18th 1748

MADAM,

I have had such frequent Reason to be convinc'd of your Ladyship's great Penetration, that I have been assur'd for some Days past, you *must* impute my Silence to the real Cause. But upon the Receipt of y^r polite Reproof, my Crime begins to shew itself in very different Colours; & I am no sooner taught to think as I *shou'd* do, than I find it impossible for all the Sagacity in ye world to have known any thing of my Situation. 'Twere adding to my Offence to *despair* of your Forgiveness, wherefore I will presume to hope it may be punish'd rather according to the Light in which I *previously* consider'd it, than the Shape in which it *now* appears. At least I will flatter myself, that ye Sentence may be compromis'd, or adjusted by a Medium of *both;* inasmuch as Faults appear to us, I fancy, as much too excessive *after* they are committed, as they often, before-hand, appear too inconsiderable—Your Ladyship will please to remember, that at ye Time I had the Honour of your two last Letters,

---

[1] B. M. Add. MSS 28958, fol. 33ff. This answers Lady Luxborough's letters of November 13, November 20, and December 12, 1748 (*Letters,* Nos. XX, XXI, and XXII), particularly the last, and confirms the dates of all three. It also confirms the date of her letter of December 18, 1748 (No. XXIII), which answers this one. The interrelations of these letters are very plain when the letters are read together.

there remain'd but one entire Day before you set out for Somerville's-Aston.² That Day indeed (as my *only* Servant was extremely busy, & I knew your Journey was fix'd at all Events) I did, I own, neglect to make a proper use of; thoroughly resolving to wait upon your Ladyship either at *Aston;* or if that might not be, upon your Return, at *Barels*. In that Case I was in Hopes you wou'd have pardon'd my Neglect, & admitted of my Apology for declining a visit, which upon *all* Accounts must have been agreeable to my *Inclination*. The Truth is, I had some *secular* affairs to adjust with Mr Dolman (with whom I have a small Estate in Partnership) before I cou'd with Prudence move from Home; & in these I found myself engag'd till about Nine Days ago. *Since* that Time I have been setting out for Barrels Daily; and indeed from the *Beginning* have only defer'd writing, because I said within myself To-morrow or in a Few Days, I will make my Apology to my Lady in Person, & return the Books she was so good to lend me. *Many* Days the weather has discourag'd me, & I think this Last Week has not afforded a good one; so that finding myself detain'd within Doors, I employ'd a Mason and Carpenter to proceed in modeling my Parlour or rather converting a Kitchen into one. *When* they will finish, is beyond my Power of Conjecture; but untill they *do,* I am oblig'd to give *Directions*. The most that I shall gain, will be, a Room 17 Feet long, 12 F. & ½ Broad, and ten Feet two Inches high; the Walls plain stucco with a Cornish; a Leaden Pipe conveying water into a Bason at one End over a Slobb: At the other End a Door leading into a Room, that, (whenever I can afford to finish it) will be my Favourite. As you enter into this last, the *Point* of Clent-Hill appears visto-Fashion thro' ye Door & one of ye windows. (The same will be reflected in a Peer-glass at ye End of the former Room). This last Room I purpose to cover wth Stucco-Paper, to place my Niche-chimney Piece from my Summer house at one End of it, over that Mr Pope's Busto, &, on each side, my Books. The Windows open into my principal Prospect—I wish I was as certain you wou'd be *satisfy'd* with my Apology, as I am that you must be *fatigu'd*. And yet the mortifying Turn you gave to my late Silence (too severe if not meant in Raillery) requir'd this particularity. It grieves me to look Back how much of my Paper is already Employ'd, when I have more Acknowledgments to make to you, & to another Lady³ (by *your Means*) than ye whole extent of my Paper wou'd be able to convey. Were I not so much oblig'd to *you* on the *Dutchess's Account*

² Where Lady Luxborough was going to visit Mr. and Mrs. Reynolds. See her *Letters*, p. 63.
³ Lady Hertford. Her letter to Lady Luxborough, alluding to the death of her son, Lord Beauchamp, dated November 20, 1748, appears in Hull's *Select Letters*, Vol. I, No. XXIII. Lord Beauchamp died in Bologna in the autumn of 1744.

as I am, and cou'd therefore speak with Freedom, I shou'd be tempted to reproach your Ladyship bitterly for suffering her at any Time to complain of your Silence. Sure I am she writes with all the *symptoms* of Sincerity, & *Proofs* of Ingenuity; & that a Correspondence so polite as your Ladyship's must afford ye most sensible Pleasure to a Person of so good a Taste. I am afraid the Partiality she discovers for a muse so very humble as mine, must *appear* no small Objection to that Taste, as also to my Testimony; but I believe the *best* of Tastes may be prejudic'd by *Friendship*, & then it is a thorough vindication of her Grace, that she is influenc'd by *yours* — I am oblig'd by ye subscription to Mr Smiths views greatly. I hope your Ladyship will represent me in that Light, when you write to Percy-Lodge. It will be enough y^t I have Leave to transmit her Grace's Name to Mr Smith; The Prints will no doubt be punctually deliver'd, & I hope afford some Amusement. I guess by ye Letter you enclos'd, y^t you consulted Mr Smith's Interest further than a Subscription: These continu'd marks of your Regard to my Applications; deserve much more of me y^n mere verbal Expressions of my gratitude; and yet even those are more than I can deliver as I ought. I will not say (for the Heart of Man is deceitfull above all Things) how far Rank may find a Place in recommending ye Favours you confer, or the Genius you discover; But I shall hardly be persuaded y^t Persons so accomplish'd as your Ladyship or The Dutchess wou'd not excell all I know, as the Mathematicians say, in any *given* station.

I have not seen my Lord Dudley, I think, this Month, but intend to do so, soon. The last Time he was here he din'd upon a Turkey, with a quill *of which* I am this moment writing: And if there was one Grain of *Wit* in ye Letter I am sending, I shou'd think I had made a good use both of the Turkey, & his Quill — He generally goes to Town on the Back of Christmas, so that I am doubtfull whether you must expect him before next Summer.

As to Mr Allen, I desire my Compliments: As to Mr Outing, He and I must *compromise* ye Affair: As to Mr Reynalds, I will propose Terms of Accomodation & expect He will insist y^t I shou'd propose them a[t] Somerville's-Aston.

I have not so much as seen ye Peruvian Letters[4] advertis'd. I believe I shall send for Them, & will be carefull you shall see them as soon as they arrive.

I thank your Ladyship for ye Use of Dodsley's Miscell: They have afforded me much Pleasure. The Variety of Styles is an advantage to

---

[4] *Letters Wrote by a Peruvian Lady. From the French* is announced in the Register of Books, *Gentleman's Magazine,* May, 1748.

such Collections. I think, had he reduc'd them to *two* volumes, even tho' he had omitted *my* sublime Piece, the Garland had been more beautifull; But it is as good a Collection as one often meets with. Did your Ladyship ever see The *Flower*-piece. I bought it at Leak's in Bath by way of a temporary Amusement, many years ago. (There are *some* pretty Things, which do not occurr elsewhere, at least not often.

These Elegies I beg Leave to place in your Hands till I come to Barrels. The outside of ye Book seems to promise more Perfection than will be found within. I knew them to be very imperfect, several Things want to be accomodated to ye present Time, &c: Yet with a thorough Confidence that you will not *expose* them, I venture to send them for your Ladyship's Perusal.

    with all their Imperfections on their Head.

And I beg your Ladyship to make some kind of Mark on such as (with proper Alterations) you shou'd least dislike. The Seventh in ye order they now stand was partly design'd to commemorate my Lord Beauchamp; but I am convinc'd it wou'd be a cruel office to the Dutchess instead of a kind one.

I hope you will be pleas'd to acquaint me whether Mr and Mrs Reynalds come to Barrels this Xmas: I shou'd be glad to model my Journey so as to give them the Meeting. Mr and Miss Dolman desir'd their Compliments when I saw them last, presuming I shou'd see your Ladyship, in a Day or two's Time. Miss D. is now at Litchfield. To their Compliments I must add those of my Brother.

I suppose, Madam, you may by this time be abundantly weary of ye *longest* & *dullest* of Letters! Had I any gilt Paper I might have been properly *stinted,* but being forc'd to make use of this, I hope you will hereby discover yt I take a *Particular Pleasure* in writing to Barrels till such time as I meet with Lett or Impediment, thro' the scantiness of earthly Paper. As I now do, & must therefore subscribe myself your Ladyship's most oblig'd & most constant

          humble Servant
          Will Shenstone

85. To LADY LUXBOROUGH[1]

        Decem: 30th 1748, The Leasows

MADAM,

I think yt either Indolent or Irresolute People shou'd not ever delay

---

[1] B. M. Add. MSS 28958, fol. 37ff. This answers No. XXIII of Lady Luxborough's *Letters,* of which it further confirms the date. The date of her No. XXIV (January 4, 1749) is also confirmed by the fact that it is a reply to Shenstone's present one.

writing thro' an Intention of *coming:* For this Reason, tho' I design to wait upon your Ladyship in a very short Time, I look upon it as expedient to express my Thanks for your last Favour by some more early opportunity.

If I may give any Credit to w^t, I *think*, they call ye Doctrine of *Sympathy,* which has been enforc'd to me by my old Housekeeper for these many years past, I will give you my Sentiments concerning ye Application of *Quills*. In ye first Place however I must premise y^t Crows shall never be esteem'd inauspicious Birds by Me, since they convey me Intelligence of your Ladyship's Health & Welfare; & I think I may extend my Indulgence also to Ravens, with whose Quills, I presume, you wou'd be able to write more sprightly Things than any other Person with ye Quill of a *Mockaw*. As to ye Quills of Turkeys, (tho Indeed, I, who am no Hero made use of one) I think they are singularly proper for your Military Men; & that whether you regard ye Nature of y^e *Bird,* or ye Temper of his Feathers. The Bird you know is remarkable for empty Noise and ostentation, & then as to ye Quill it may suit a Person very well who has been accustom'd to write his meaning with ye Point of a Sword. I believe he will not find much *difference,* were he to try them both alternately upon Paper. To your Ladyship I wou'd recommend ye Quill of a Blackbird; a Bird that has both *spirit* & *Elegance* in his Notes; but as he seems to want *variety,* I must own I know no English Bird except ye Throstle that unites those three Qualities of all you write & say: And then a *Woodlark* or a *Nightingale* may be reckon'd to *excell* him, (whereas your Ladyship is *not* excell'd) & these last Birds (or perhaps ye former) have no *writeable* Feathers. I must therefore leave you to make use of whatever Quill you please; well knowing that you cou'd not write disagreeably even with the Quill of a *Bittern* — For *me* the Goose, ye Emblem of stupidity, will still retain a Feather; And, against ye Time I write in verse, I nourish a very fine Peacock whose harmonious Voice agrees to a tittle with my Versification; as I fear your Ladyship has too plainly experienc'd.

I think you, Madam, are a very good Judge of ye most learned Elegy I am capable of writing; But if you are fearfull of leading me into any Scrape by your Decision (which I own will have great weight with me) I must acknowledge myself very much *oblig'd* by your concern, tho' at ye same Time I endeavour to remove it, by owning y^t these Compositions will probably go thro many other Hands. I hope this will be an Inducement to your Ladyship to give me your Opinion which of ye Elegies are least to be dislik'd; The Preface will be either *partly* or entirely omitted.

If amidst ye many trifles which I trust (with entire Confidence) into your Hands, there be any Thing which you guess may be agreeable to the Dutchess, I shall be more & more oblig'd if you please to convey it. I can only say in general that the Hope of acquiring ye least share in her Grace's Esteem gives me ye greatest Pleasure, & I must leave your Ladyship to manage *for* me. I receiv'd yesterday from Mr Smith ye Letter I enclose. I send it amongst other Reasons yt I may not hereafter seem to have *conceal'd* any Self-*interest,* when you find that for ye Service I have done him, he obliges me wth a couple of Views taken from ye Leasows. I have said nothing in his Favour wch I do not think he deserves; & he was so kind to take a Draught without any kind of stipulation with me, or, for ought I cou'd see, *expectation.*

I know ye Want of gilt Paper is of little Moment to Persons who, like your Ladyship, can make their Letters shine by Dint of Genius merely; but 'tis otherwise with *Me.* I love to have my Scrip of Paper well ornamented *without,* for fear it shou'd have no Merit *within.* I love to have ye Impression of a Seal well taken off; & I am not entirely satisfy'd unless ye Sealing-wax itself be of a lively Orange-scarlet. — My Room wants now little else than stuccoing, & I am daily enquiring after a Person to do it — Since I wrote last, I have been carousing with ye Lord Mayor & Aldermen of Hales-owen; in other Terms, at ye Bailiff's Feast; from whence I escap'd without much Damage to my Constitution — I do not *much* recommend ye Flower-piece. There are some of ye best Things I have seen written by ye *ministerial* Writers in Lord Orford's *Ministry* — I am extremely glad to hear yt your Health is so much improv'd by a *Milk-diet:* It affords me a Prospect of your Longevity. I always approv'd it, but never had Resolution to make use of such other Regimen as was consistent with it — The Abele will imitate ye Noise of a Water-fall, very Luckily, near yr Ladyship's Hermitage — You judge extremely right with Regard to ye Urns. *That* your Ladysp approves, was fix'd on but ye top was not esteem'd unexceptionable. Perhaps at Barels I may find out a better — I beg pardon for *grouping* the particulars of this Page, but you will see my Paper oblig'd me — I am, Madam,

Your Ladyship's most oblig'd & most obedient Servt
W Shenstone

86. To LADY LUXBOROUGH[1]

The Leasows, March ye 22d 1748–9

MADAM,

At the Time I make my best Acknowledgments for ye very *elegant Reception* I met with at Barrels, I ought by no means to forget your Ladyship's kind *indulgence* to my *irregular* method of paying my visits: Nor indeed do I. The former I am to look upon as a Compliment to my *Taste* (in whatever Sense it be interpreted) as the latter was to my *Indolence*, which you will, I fancy, allow to have some small share in my complexion. Thus by one means or another your Ladyship engages all my Passions in your Favour, & my Reason here has no Pretence to check them—I return your two first volumes of Tom Jones which I have read with some Pleasure, tho' I see no Character yet yt is near so striking as Mr Abraham Adams. *That* was an *original*, I think; unattempted before, & yet so natural yt most people seem'd to know ye Man. As you have been so kind to give me ye reading of ye first volumes, I believe I must beg Leave to borrow ye remaining volumes before ye first Part of ye Story slips out of my Memory. When I came Home I found *Coriolanus*[2] & *Irene*[3] upon my Harpsichord, both which I have read, & ye latter of which I send your Ladyship. It has, I think, many Beauties in it, & ye Catastrophe affects one. And as to Coriolanus I have a much better Opinion of it yn I imagined I shou'd have. It is simple & natural both in Language Sentiment & Plot. The Fault of ye other is I think his too great uniformity in closing ye Sense at ye end of a Line or Couplet, & something in his Plot yt is not altogether pleasing. See Demetrius throwing down ye Poyson, & an Inconsistency in Abdalla's Character in *giving* ye Poyson. I beg Pardon for giving my opinion of Books yt your Ladyship has & will probably read; & of consequence form a better Judgment yn I am capable of doing. But on reading a new Play one has a natural Propensity to speak ones Thoughts, & ye concealment of them wou'd be *Affectation*—I remember I declin'd your Ladyship's offer of lending me some Book yt was marbled *red* for my Bookseller to bind by; I wou'd now be oblig'd to you if you wou'd lend me one, as I purpose to have my Pine's Horace bound in yt Manner & shall hardly be able to give my Bookseller a Right notion by any other means—I begin to suspect yt I

---
[1] Reproduced from the manuscript collection of Harvard College Library. Lady Luxborough's letter of March 23, 1748–49 (*Letters*, No. XXVI) is the reply to the present letter; the date of her letter is thus confirmed.

[2] James Thomson's tragedy appeared posthumously, it will be recalled, in 1749.

[3] Johnson's *Irene*, written in 1736 at Edial, was produced by Garrick in 1749 and published the same year.

shall be able to execute very few of those schemes out-of-doors, which I warm'd my Imagination with towards ye End of last Autumn. It will grieve me to exhibit so little Novelty in my situation, as I am afraid I must be content to do, when your Ladyship does me ye Honour of yr annual visit. But circumstances like mine admit of no variety. As you are acquainted with this Truth, I dare say you will out of pure kindness view ye *sameness* of ye Leasows with a favourable Eye — I have a Thought comes into my head which if you can at all avail yourself of, I shall be glad to have communicated. What if you were by means of about three yards of shrubbery on ye outside of your Lime-walk to render your Hermitage a Part of your Garden? Or ye walk may be contriv'd serpentine so as to join one of ye crooked walks in yr present Shrubbery, & so fill up with Shrubs ye gravel-walk which now ends in ye back Part of ye Summer house. I don't know whether I am not too free or whether if I were upon ye spot you might not give me Reasons to ye Contrary yt wou'd entirely convince me; But I hope you will excuse ye Liberty I take, as I can have no other motive yn ye Desire of adding a Trifle to ye Beauty of a Place where I have receiv'd ye greatest Pleasure. I shall be glad to hear when you put up your Pavilion at ye End of your Walk; & I cannot but think there shou'd be about two Trees of a side planted by way of Footing to ye Walk, & in a Line with ye two last Trees nearest your House — I beg my Compliments to Mr. Hall when he comes next to Barrels, & if [he] be extraordinarily hungry, I beg he may be regal'd with one Truffle upon some Cassavi-Bread — I will depend upon hearing by ye Return of ye Messenger how Mr. Allen does. I am sorry to send your Ladyship so dull a Letter; but in some Cases (as Mrs. Arnold well knows) ye *King* must lose his *Rights;* & there is another Right which you never *can* lose, I mean ye Respect with which I am your Ladyship's most obligd & most obed: Servt. W. Shenstone

I challenge yr Ladyship to make me an Impression on so bright a red; tho you must not endeavour at present, I know — yr wax is black.[4]

87. To LADY LUXBOROUGH [1]

The Leasows, April ye 7th 1749

MADAM,

I have sin'd in detaining your Ladyship's Books[2] so long, & am *sensible* enough of my offence to avoid ye like, I hope, on any future occasion.

---

[4] Written upside down at the top of the first page of the letter in MS.
[1] B. M. Add. MSS 28958, fol. 39ff. This answers Lady Luxborough's letter of March 23, 1749 (*Letters*, No. XXVI), of which it confirms the date.
[2] *Tom Jones* in six volumes (1749).

But Mr Dolman having read ye two former volumes, I was under a temptation of saving him ye Price of ye whole by lending him ye subsequent ones. My brother & I read them almost at y^e *same* Time; & *He* might in three more Days have done ye same; & *then* I cou'd something more reasonably have depended on your usual goodness for my Excuse. But when once one deviates from what is strictly right, one is often involv'd in such Degrees of wrong as we never dream'd of. Mr Dolman was interrupted in his Perusal of ye Books by Company, & ye consequence is that I have withheld your Books 'till now, tho' I was sensible your Ladysp had not read ye two last volumes — I think as you do y^t that ye Plan is by no means easy, but must own at the same time y^t several *Parts* have afforded me much Amusement. There is a good deal of wit dispers'd thro'out, or rather ty'd up in Bundles at ye beginning of every *Book*. You will conclude my Taste to be not extremely *delicate,* when I say I am cheifly pleas'd with ye striking Lines of Mr *Western's* Character. It is I fancy a natural Picture of thousands of his majesty's rural subjects; at least it has been *my* Fortune to see ye original pretty frequently. Tis perhaps a Likeness y^t is easily taken, & moreover he seems to apply it too indiscriminately to Country-gentlemen in general. But it is ye only Character y^t made me *laugh;* & y^t is a great Point gain'd, when one is in danger of losing *y^t Faculty* thro' Disuse. Tis moreover a Character better worth exposing than his Landlords & Landladys wth which he seems so delighted — his Serjeants & his Abigails &c: Your Book of Gardening is now at my Booksellers by way of Pattern: I will return it as soon as I've an opportunity — And the mention of this Book serves well enough to bring once more upon ye Carpet what I was saying about ye Alteration in your Garden. My Mistake lay in calling those Trees *Limes* which I find are *Service*-trees. In every other Respect you understand my Scheme, such as it it. I dont remember where abouts the Foot-path runs y^t leads to Henley. *That* may perhaps be an unanswerable objection; For I am afraid, to ye best of my Memory, it crosses your Service-walk. Otherwise The Advantage y^t wou'd follow from my Alteration would consist, in joining your Shrubbery to your grove by one continu'd walk of ye same kind; enlarging & greatly improving your Labyrinth of shrubbs which is I think rightly situated; avoiding both y^e *Tongue* & y^e *Ear* of ye scolding old-woman by filling up ye gravel walk in some measure with Shrubbs, & perhaps having a serpentine sand-walk return a little part of ye Way from your Gate; & having y^e *back Part* of y^r Summer-house conceal'd by Plantations of Trees in ye Corner that leads into your Pheasantry. When this was done wou'd there not be an opportunity of making some pretty open seat on a small mount at ye very lower end of y^r Grove just by ye Gate, which shou'd command (by lowering ye Hedgerow) the Walk of Trees on ye Hill ye Temple & ye country towrds Henley &c:? But all this may be liable to great Exceptions. As to your Ladyships Pavilion, I fear I should be as ill able as can be, to direct your Mason; Else would I gladly come over at any Time. My chief use wou'd be in laying out ye Ground, & here I think there is one Rule to be certainly observ'd, y^t your furthermost Trees shou'd not *seem* to join ye Front of ye Building by a Foot of a side at least, *when view'd from your Hall Door;* That being ye most distant Point from which it is meant to be seen. This may be effected by ye Distance at wch you place it from ye trees. As for any thing else, provided that Elm walk is to continue, The situation you chuse for it is I think unexceptionable — If Mr Hall persists in wishing me to assist him in ye Inscription he speaks of,[3] I will be of what service I am able. At the same Time I shou'd be oblig'd to your Ladyship if you wou'd convince him y^t tho' his Father's Character might be *better* & more *usefull* than many of theirs who are puffd away upon monuments, yet it will not well admit of Flourishes; & y^t it ought to be as plain as possible. This your Ladyship knows, & this he has too much sense to afford you any difficulty in demonstrating — My Lord Dudley has I find been tumbled out of his vehicle in his way to London, for y^e *third successive* Time. If he can but *over-turn* my Lord Ward there (with whom he has a suit in Chancery) It will make him some Amends. I have been busy in paving a small serpentine stream & planting Flowers by ye side, but I am afraid I shall find it impossible to preserve them. I would gladly enough compound ye matter wth ye Mob if they wou'd leave me about *Half,* particularly those you were so kind to give me. But I fear they wont, For tho' there are Primroses to be gather'd in ye Fields in Plenty yet if they can discover one that is apparently planted, they are sure to crop it. But tis chiefly done by children & such as can't read, were I to publish my *Placard* as they have done at Hagley-Park.

I take off my sealing wax by a Lamp instead of a Candle. I *do* not nor *will* I forget ye green Book.[4]

[3] For Mr. Hall's father, who had recently died.
[4] In it he had transcribed a number of his poems, particularly, apparently, his elegies, for her.

88. To LADY LUXBOROUGH[1]

[Between April 7 and 16, 1749]

I have sent your Ladyship a Book of Gardening,[2] which I borrowed, about five Years ago, of a Neighbour. If it will be of any Service to you, in modelling the crooked Walks in your Shrubbery, I shall be glad; and you may return it at your Leisure, as *I* do. It is written by a poor illiterate Fellow, notwithstanding its Dedication to His Majesty, *who is delighted with Enquiries into vegetable Nature.* You will see something of his Ignorance, perhaps, in every Page; more especially Page 204, first Part, where he talks of Minerva *and* Pallas for Statues, with many Blunders of like Nature.[3] It was written, seemingly, when the present *natural* Taste began to dawn, and which I wish, rather than hope, may last as long as Nature.

Mr. L[yttelto]n, you may perhaps hear, has been offered, and has refused the Place of Treasurer of the Navy, in Mr. D[oddingto]n's Room.[4] — What a Tide of Success!

May your Ladyship be as happy as Success ever made any Body! and that it is more in the Mind than Externals is to me a Demonstration. I'm sure I shall never be so happy, with all my Philosophy and *Success,* as an old Fellow who works for me: but I think your Ladyship has not only a right and philosophical Understanding, but good animal Spirits, which are half in half; so that you may be much happier than even *him,* which, I assure you, is to be greatly so.

I am now a little maudlin after Dinner, and if my Groups are inconsistent and queer, you must excuse me. I hope Mr. Allen is, by this Time, well. I have written a Line to Mr. Outing, at the Head of his Regiment. I am now to take my formal Leave, as I do after a long Visit; that is, with about half a Bow, and the Expression of about half I think; but I include as much as any Body, when I say,

I am
Your Ladyship's
Most obliged, and most devoted Servant,
W. Shenstone

If your Ladyship could spare me about three Eggs of your *Guinea* Fowl, I should be much obliged.

---

[1] The date of this letter (Hull, *Select Letters,* Vol. I, No. XVI) is established by No. LXIV of Lady Luxborough's *Letters,* the date of which, April 16, [1749], is established by its answering Shenstone's last (Letter 87) and being answered by his next (Letter 89).

[2] That of Batty Langley.

[3] Lady Luxborough alludes to the same errors in her *Letters,* p. 254.

[4] George Lyttelton's promotion and Doddington's resignation are recorded in the *Gentleman's Magazine* for March, 1749, p. 142.

89. To LADY LUXBOROUGH[1]

The Lea: Apr. 23 1749

MADAM,

I shou'd have prepar'd a Letter for last Thursday, but yt I did not receive yours before that Time & the present opportunity, upon one account or other is the First I have of obeying your Ladyship's commands — 'Tis nothing new to me to find you extract *Beauties* out of my *Blunders:* You are capable of doing ye same by those of Nature; at least if she may be suppos'd capable of making any such, which indeed she is not. *Blemishes* however she must have to ye eye of such *limited* Beings as can only comprehend a *Part* of her works; & those it is ye Province of *common* Tastes to render tolerable; & of such as *yours* to convert into Beauties. I cannot avoid pursuing this Thought a little farther. It is, I think, owing to ye limited Faculties of Men yt there is any *need* of Taste, to make alterations in our *Environs.* Suppose ye human Eye were capable of comprehending ye *Universe,* it wou'd be as absurd for him to design even such a garden as Lord Cobham's,[2] as it wou'd in his present circumstances, to make a Baby's Garden of half-an-Ell Square. If this be a true state of ye Case, then Taste in Gardens &c: has little more to do than to *collect* ye Beauties of Nature into a compass proper for it's own observation. But you'll say, whence then is ye necessity of making Alterations? Why in order to maintain a due Proportion betwixt ye objects you introduce; yt you may not have so much *Lawn,* as to have none of the Beauty of *Plantations;* so much *Wood* as to have no Flower-work, & so on. The necessity of smoothing or brushing ye Robe of Nature may proceed entirely from ye same Cause. Were one's Eye calculated to *take in* a *larger extent,* or, in other words, her whole Person, we shou'd not then discover ye *Dust* or ye *Rumples* — I beg Pardon for this long Digression. My purpose was to proceed immediately to speak of your Ladyship's Proposal of fitting up your Lime-walk with Shrubs, which I entirely approve; & of causing one of your Shrubbery-walks to wind across it into yr Abele Plantat{n} which I as much *admire*. I am in Hopes Mr. Langley's Book, (which I sent a week ago) may be of some little service; as He has a variety of Plans for Labyrinths; tho' I suppose it will not be proper to give into ye Tenth Part of ye Intricacy yt He does. The man is something illiterate, but his notions are not amiss in *many* Respects, I think. The query is, where-abouts yr continu'd serpentine shou'd

---

[1] B. M. Add. MSS 28958, fol. 41ff. This answers the misplaced No. LXIV of Lady Luxborough's *Letters,* and is answered by her No. XXVII of May Day, 1749, the date of which is thus confirmed.

[2] The famous garden at Stowe of Sir Richard Temple, Viscount Cobham (1669?–1749).

enter ye Coppice, which I must leave undetermin'd. Shou'd you think it agreeable to burst into light before you approach ye Hermitage, I fancy ye proper Place wou'd be opposite to y^r deep Precipice where you have planted some few *Quince*-trees. That Precipice to be ha-ha'd by a rough wall of about a yard at ye bottom, & ye rest to be thrown open to ye Field which I spoke of once before. If you think it more eligible to preserve y^e *retir'd Idea* 'till you enter ye Coppice, & not let ye Spectator know ye limits of ye wood-work on each Side him, then you will chuse to make it enter at some greater Distance; I mean somewhat nearer ye Corner of y^r Coppice. I cannot determine which I shou'd prefer myself. But your Ladyship, upon ye spot, will very easily determine justly. The Scheme of making y^r Serpentine walk thro' ye Abele will prove not only cheaper, but I think, more eligible. I suppose it will be proper to run it as much towr'ds y^e *Left* as you can, by which means you will very soon have it perfectly retir'd. And then I see no Reason why you shou'd not direct *another* crooked walk in your Shrubbery to end at ye Gate y^t opens to ye Service Trees, & let ye Gate continue. It will make a variety; The Bank and the Turf of y^e *Service* walk is charming. I woud then wish *that* entirely shut up at ye end next ye Hermitage, by which means your Shrubbery wou'd lead by different windings to two very distinct Beauties. I would have ye winding walks not too narrow, but I fancy those you have already made are of a proper Breadth. You will I suppose plant some kind of Shrubs amongst ye Abeles, by ye sides of y^r new walk. Thus I think I have said all y^t occurs to me concerning this propos'd alteration, which I greatly approve. I am glad to hear y^t you are putting up ye Pavilion, or at least doing something tow'rds it. What you *have* done is, I suppose, extremely *right*. I don't know whether I did not speak too *precisely* concerning y^e *Apparent* distance betwixt ye Building & ye Trees; But if you calculate, by putting up a couple of Poles (to represent ye Breadth of ye intended Buildings) & view them from y^r Hall-door, you will be able to adjust this distance to your mind. The Flooring of y^r Pavilion shou'd I think be black & white stone in Lozenges — I believe you will find ye Alteration you are making before your door a very great Improvement in Point of Beauty & Convenience. Quere, whether white lead, or a very deep lead-colour will least interfere with your view of ye Pavilion. I mean for your Palisades; Quere also, whether ye Dial placed in ye center of y^r Sweep will not also interfere with it? I dont know ye Propriety of Ld Archer's *Globe* in regard to his Obelisk, but his *Cross* I am *sure* can have none — I can by no means expect any Guinea-Fowl from y^r Ladyship, as your Flock is reduc'd so low; I am thankful for your obliging offer — I will examine ye Epitaph before I write again by your Ladyship's permission. I told Mr Hall at *first*, & have now Room to be convinc'd y^t if you wou'd vouchsafe to take ye Trouble upon you, you wou'd be by far ye more proper person. Sr Philip Sidney, I think, us'd to say y^t a Line of Chevy-chase affected him like ye sound of a Trumpet. I shou'd imagine y^e *Last* Trumpet cou'd hardly produce a more awefull Respect yⁿ ye first line of y^r Inscription is fitted to inspire. It introduces ye next part "Here lie" very elegantly no doubt; what Room there may be for y^r Ladyship's Exceptions to it I cannot easily determine. *Warmth* of *Sentiment* is ye most capable of being ridicul'd; but in my *present* way of thinking, I am for retaining it.

I have written your Ladyship a strange unceremonious letter: but you are kindly pleas'd to indulge me in this freedom, & I am aiming here *principally* to be of some little *Service*. I hope you will favour me with a Line as you proceed. I am ever with ye greatest internal Respect your Ladyship's most oblig'd & most

obedient Servt
Will: Shenstone

90. To LADY LUXBOROUGH [1]

The Leasows, May ye 14th 1749

MADAM,

Your Ladyship is extremely kind in giving me a Sketch of your Improvements; & I heartily wish you may find as much *Pleasure* in them, as I do, *Propriety*. The Removal of your Pillars was *necessary;* the joining of your Grass-Plots is *right;* & ye continuation you propose betwixt ye Shrubbery & ye Hermitage will, I fancy, add to ye Beauty of *both*. I am sensible how impertinent it is for me to propose Alterations, unless I were upon ye Spot; which I will contrive to *be* about ye Time you alter ye Shrubbery. I don't know what you will think of Mr Langley's Book; It afforded me some *Amusement,* as I had never seen any Book y^t treated of *modern Design* in gardening *before;* but ye Reason I sent it was merely y^t you might see his Plans for crooked walks; & if it furnish you with one *Nook* or *Angle* y^t you approve, I shall gain my Point. I have been embroidering my Grove with Flowers, till I almost begin to fear it looks too like a *garden;* If there arrive a Flowering-*shrub*, it is a Day of rejoicing with me; or (to use a term in *methodism* now so much in Fashion) a *Day of fat Things* (For you must know, I plant in all Sea-

---

[1] B. M. Add. MSS 28958, fol. 45ff. This answers Lady Luxborough's May Day letter (*Letters*, No. XXVII).

sons.) I began to complain of my Neighbours for pillaging ye Flowers, rather too soon. Since ye Publication of my *Edicts,* they have behav'd tolerably well. Half a dozen Flowers were cropt on May-morning, but the offenders have been detected, and brought to open Shame. And this, considering ye Numbers, y^t pay their Compliments to ye Place on Sunday-Ev'nings, is a *small* Infringement, scarce worth mentioning. I have bought Miller's book of gardening,[2] very elegantly bound; so you may expect me e'er long to talk like Solomon of all manner of Plants; from ye Cedars upon mount Lebanon, to the Hyssop y^t groweth against ye wall! But to speak seriously, I shall only dip into it, as your Ladyship does, *occasionally* — I hope ye Painting over ye Chimney-piece in your Library is alter'd for ye better. I forgot to mention one thing, wch is, y^t if any shades appear *at all,* now ye whole ground is darken'd, they shou'd be altogether on ye farther side from ye Window, y^t the Light coming in y^t *way* may seem to produce them from Bas-reliefs — I have attempted several Times to make *some* Corrections in Mr Halls Epitaph, but find myself so utterly unable to proceed, y^t It seems a Judgment on me for presuming to alter what you write. If I make any more *unsuccessfull* Attempts, I shall be quite convinc'd of it, & then I will only hint at a Line or two which I wou'd have your *Ladyship* alter, & ask your Pardon for detaining it so long. If I shou'd fancy myself to *succeed,* & communicate any alterations, I hope you will do Mr Hall so much *Justice* as to prefer your own Opinion to mine, wherever you happen to dissent from ye latter; assur'd y^t your opinion will infallibly *be* mine, ye very first opportunity y^t offers, to discourse about it — I think this kind of writing extremely difficult, less difficult perhaps in verse y^n Prose; tho' ye former c^d hardly be well executed in y^e *present* case; nor wou'd I attempt it upon any account whatever. Mr Dolman often talks of waiting on your Ladyship this Summer; If he continues able to perform ye Journey, I wou'd chuse it shou'd be some time while your Shrubs are in Blossom; which I think I haven't yet seen *with y^t advantage.* Indeed I ought, as ye Representative of my poor *Dryads,* to return your visit in ye season you visit *mine;* Instead of that you do Honour to *my* Place when it is in its perfection, & I see yours when at ye worst. 'Tis true I do it ye Justice to admire it *then,* & give it it's vernal Beauty as far as I can by Imagination; But my Imagination is not half so lively as your Shrubs are beautifull, & If your Ladyship permits, we wou'd do y^m ye Justice to take a view of them in all their glory — I return your Book with thanks. My Book-

---

[2] Miller's book of gardening may have been *The Gardener's and Florist's Dictionary* (1724) or the *Gardener's Kalendar* (1732) of Philip Miller (1691–1771).

seller has swerv'd entirely from his Pattern, yet at ye same Time has bound my Books so elegantly y^t I am hardly inclin'd to condemn his Deviation. He has brib'd me by an *old Fashion* reviv'd of marbling ye Edges of ye Paper which I think extreme pretty. Do not accuse this finical Taste of mine. Is it not happy y^t a Person of small Fortune can be pleas'd wth Trifles? And I assure y^r Ladyship at ye Same time I have as great a value for solid *Merit,* genius & generosity, as any one alive; consequently am as much as any one alive y^r Ladyships most devoted Servant

W. S.

91. To LADY LUXBOROUGH[1]

The *Leasowes, June* ye 3^d, 1749

MADAM,

Tho' I may seem to have been extremely lazy, I have really taken no small Pains in endeavouring to obey your Ladyship's commands. I wish when you peruse my Packet you may not rather think me to have been extremely officious. Tho' I shou'd imagine even *that* a Crime by no means equal to *Negligence,* in any Affair wherein you are pleas'd to employ me. How far I've err'd in *that* Respect, I am utterly unable to determine; as your Directions to me were not very explicit; and as I have not been favour'd with a single syllable from Mr Hall, to inform me whether, or how far, he approv'd of Alterations. But I will not call them *Alterations,* which I send; which are indeed only a small Cargo of different Expressions which you may reject or apply, entirely as you think proper. Nor shall it give me ye least Offence if you reject ye whole, so long as you will acquit me of Presumption in interfering. If I may speak my present Thoughts, I wou'd have the Epitaph be *short* & *general;* which is what I chiefly aim'd at in ye First & Second Numbers. In the third I have been more explicit; not with any view to have *ye whole inscrib'd* upon ye Monum^t, but y^t I may by that means happen to send *something,* in one Part or another, which you may chuse to appropriate. If Mr Hall approves of an *Epitaph* short & general, & which conveys a meaning pompous enough under a simplicity of expression, He may have a more particular Account of his Father taken off by Aris[2] upon a single sheet, & distribute half a score Copies amongst his Friends. This I think will be doing as much as ye greatest Filial Piety can desire. I am by no means

---

[1] B. M. Add. MSS 28958, fol. 47ff. A version of this letter appears in Hull's *Select Letters,* Vol. I, No. XXVI. Lady Luxborough's letter of June 4 (No. XXVIII) crossed his of June 3 on the road (as she says, *Letters,* p. 102). Hers of June 24, 1749 (No. XXIX) answers the present one, and the dates of her two letters are thus confirmed.

[2] Thomas A. Aris was a prominent Birmingham personage, printer, publisher, and from 1741, editor of the *Birmingham Gazette.* He died in 1761. (Hecht)

languid in my wishes to perpetuate his Father's Character. I believe he might deserve as *good* a one, as any Person in a publick station. But you remember those Lines of Mr Pope;[3]

> 'Tis from high *Life,* high Characters are drawn;
> A Saint in Crape is twice a Saint in Lawn.
> A Judge is just; a Chanc'lor juster still:
> A Gown-man learn'd; a Bishop what you will:
> Wise if a Minister; but if a King,
> More wise, more learn'd, more just, more evry-thing.

Where, by ye way, ye Second and Fourth Line dwell alike upon the Bishops. But ye whole Paragraph is extremely beautifull. What there is of *weight* in them, is, y^t the Character of a person in private Life must not be express'd too pompously. I am persuaded your Ladyship will manage it for the best, so I will now take leave of ye Subject. Is it to be executed soon, or may it be postpon'd till I have ye Honour of seeing you? I lead here ye unhappy Life of seeing nothing in ye Creation half so idle as *myself*. Mischievous People will think and act ten times as much in a Day, as I shou'd in a Century. I am however pretty frequently piddling in little Matters about my Farm. What do you think, Madam, of my publishing verses once a week upon my skreens or Garden-seats, for the Amusement of my good Friends ye Vulgar? The Verses for ye present week are publish'd in Virgil's Grove, Rue de Virgile, & run thus:

> Here in cool grott, & mossy Cell
> We Fauns & playfull Fairies dwell.
> Tho' rarely seen by mortal Eye,
> When ye pale Moon, ascended high,
> Darts thro' yon Limes her quiv'ring beam,
> We frisk it near this crystal stream.
> Then fear to spoil these sacred Bowers;
> Nor wound ye Shrubs, nor crop ye Flow'rs;
> So may y^r Path wth Sweets abound!
> So may y^r Couch wth Rest be crown'd!
> But ill-betide or Nymph or swain
> Who dares these hallow'd Haunts profane!
>   OBERON

NB. We have some People here y^t believe in Fairies; but then such People do not understand verses.

 My Method is a very cheap one. I paste some writing Paper on a strip

---

[3] *Moral Essays,* Epistle I, Pt. II, ll. 135-40.

of Deal, & so print with a Pen. This serves in Root-houses, & under Cover. Your Ladyship has been so unkind as not to let me know, since I wrote last, how your Pavilion proceeds; whether you are happy in Planning, or in beholding your Plans executed. May I hope to hear soon? Two hundred Pounds expended in a Rotund at Hagley, on Ionic Pillars! The Dome of Stone, with a thin Lead Cover under to keep out wet. Whilst I propose, or *fancy* I propose, to build a Piece of Gothic Architecture, at sight of which all the Pitts & the Miller's Castles in ye World shall bow their Heads abash'd: — like ye other Sheaves to Joseph's — I send you ye Plan. 'Tis for a Hermits Seat on a Bank above my Hermitage; which Hermitage I do not give up, notwithstanding ye Remonstrance of Mr L. himself. This said Hermit's Seat will amount, on a moderate Computation, to ye Sum of fifteen Shillings, & Six-pence three farthings. — Pray My Lady what is become of Mr Outing. Does he quit ye barbarous Trade of War, for ye Pleasures of repose this Summer? Or does your Ladyship expect him at Barrels? I have not weight enough wth him to obtain an answer to my Letter dated Feb — I long to see what it is my Ld Bolingbroke has publish'd,[4] & what he has atchiev'd to ye discomfort of all Grub street. I am, very constantly,

Your Ladyship's most oblig'd Servant
W. Shenstone

92. To RICHARD JAGO [1]

From The Leasowes, as it appears
on a rainy Evening, June 1749

DEAR SIR,

It would probably be so long before you can receive this letter by the post, that I cannot think of subjecting my *thanks for your last,* or my *hopes of seeing you soon,* to *such* an *uncertainty.* — I shall not now have it in my power to meet you at Mr. Wren's *immediately,* so would lose no time in requesting your company here *next week,* if you please. I hope Mrs. Jago also will accompany you, and that you will set out the first day of the week, even Monday; that you may not leave me in less than six days time under a pretence of necessity. As to the verses you were so kind to convey, I will take occasion when you come

To find out, like a friend,
Something to blame, and mickle to commend.

So I say no more at *present* on that head.

[4] See note 2 to the following letter.
[1] Dodsley, *Letters to Particular Friends,* No. LVI. Wells (*Anglia,* 35:449) confirms the date as after May, 1749, and Fullington (*PMLA,* 46:1134) establishes it as about June 1.

I love to *read* verses, but I *write* none. "Petti, nihil me ficut ante juvat scribere!" — I will not say *none;* for I wrote the following at breakfast yesterday, and they are all I have wrote since I saw you. They are now in one of the root-houses of Virgil's Grove, for the admonition of my good friends the vulgar; of whom I have multitudes every Sunday evening, and who very fortunately believe in fairies, and are no judges of poetry:

> Here in cool grot, and mossy cell,
> We tripping fawns and fairies dwell:
> Tho rarely seen by mortal eye,
> Oft as the moon, ascended high,
> Darts thro' yon limes her quiv'ring beam,
> We frisk it near this crystal stream.
> Then fear to spoil these sacred bow'rs;
> Nor wound the shrubs, nor crop the flow'rs;
> So may your path with sweets abound!
> So may your couch with rest be crown'd!
> But ill betide or nymph or swain,
> Who dares these hallow'd haunts profane.
>   OBERON

I suppose the rotund at Hagley is compleated, but I have not seen it hitherto; neither do I often journey or visit *any where,* except when a shrub or flower is upon the point of blossoming near my walks. — I forget one visit I lately made in my neighbourhood, to a young clergyman of taste and ingenuity. His name is Pixell; he plays *finely* upon the violin, and very well upon the harpsichord: has set many things to music, some in the *soft way,* with which I was much delighted. He is young, and has time to improve himself. He gave me an opportunity of being acquainted with him by frequently visiting, and introducing company to, my walks. — I met him one morning with an Italian in my grove, and our acquaintance has been growing ever since. — He has a share in an estate that is near me, and lives there at present; but I doubt will not do so long; — when you come, I will send for him. — Have you read my Lord Bolingbroke's Essays on Patriotism, &c.?[2] and have you read Merope?[3] and do you take in the *Magazin des Londres?* and pray how does your garden flourish? I warrant, you do not yet know the difference betwixt a ranunculus and an anemone. — God help ye! — Come to me, and be informed of the nature of all plants, "from the cedar on Mount Lebanon

[2] Bolingbroke's letters, the first *On the Spirit of Patriotism,* appeared, according to the Register of Books of the *Gentleman's Magazine,* in May, 1749.
[3] Aaron Hill's adaptation of Voltaire's *Merope* (1745) appeared in 1749.

to the hyssop that springeth out of the wall." — Pray do not fail to decorate your new garden, whence you may transplant all kinds of flowers into your verses. If by chance you make a visit at I[cheneton] fifty years hence, from some distant part of England, shall you forget this little angle where you used to muse and sing? "En unquam, &c. Post aliquot, tua regna videns mirabere, aristas."

I expect by the return of Tom to receive a trifle that will amuse you. It is a small gold seal of Vida's head, given by Vertue to a relation of mine, who published Vida, and introduced Vertue into business. — Perhaps you remember Mr. Tristram of Hampton, and the day we spent there from school; it was his.

I am, very cordially,
Yours,
W. Shenstone

93. To a FRIEND [1]

June [25 or 26,] 1749

Fie on Mr. N——! he has disappointed me of the most seasonable visit that heart could wish or desire. — My flowers in blossom, my walks newly cleaned, my neighbours invited, and I languishing for lack of your company! Mean time you are going to dance attendance on a courtier. — Would to God! he may disappoint *you,* according to the usual practice of those gentlemen; — I mean, by giving you a far better living than you ever expected.

I have no sooner *made* than I am ready to *recall* that wish, in order to substitute another in its place; which is, that you may rather squat yourself down upon a fat-goose living in Warwickshire, or one in Staffordshire, or perhaps Worcestershire, of the *same denomination.* I do not mention Shropshire, because I think I am more remote from the main body of that county than I am from either of the others. But, nevertheless, by all means wait on Mr. N——; shew him all respect, yet so as not to lay out any of the profits of your *contingent* living in a black velvet waistcoat and breeches to appear before him. True merit needeth nought of this. Besides, peradventure, you may not receive the first quarter's income of it this half year. He will probably do something for you one time or other; but you shall never go into Ireland, that is certain, for less than a deanry; not for less than the deanry of St. Patrick's, if you take my advice. Lower your hopes only to advance your surprize; "*grata*

---

[1] Dodsley, *Letters to Particular Friends,* No. LV. Wells (*Anglia,* 35:448–49) establishes the day of the month as June 25 or 26. The identity of the addressee, evidently a clergyman and an intimate friend, remains in doubt. It might be Jago.

supervenient quae non sperabimus." Come to me *as you may*. A week is elapsed since you *began* to be detained; you may surely come over in a fortnight now at farthest; — I will be at home. — However, write directly; you know our letters are long upon their journey; — I expected you the beginning of every week, till I received your last letter, *impatiently*.

For my part, I begin to wean myself from all hopes and expectations whatever. — I feed my wild-ducks, and I water my carnations! Happy enough, if I could extinguish my ambition *quite,* or *indulge* (what I hope I feel in an equal degree) the desire of being something more beneficial in my sphere. — Perhaps some few other circumstances would want also to be adjusted.

I have just read Lord Bolingbroke's three letters, which I like as much as most pieces of politics I ever read. I admire, especially, the spirit of the style. I as much admire *at* the editor's unpopular preface. — I know the family hitherto *seemed* to make it a point to conceal Pope's affair; and now, the editor, under Lord B's inspection, not only relates, but invites people to think the worst of it. — What *collateral* reasons my Lord may have for thinking ill of Mr. Pope, I cannot say; but surely it is not *political* to lessen a person's character that had done one so much honour.

I am, dear Sir,
Your affectionate
W. Shenstone

I have this moment received a long letter from Lady Luxborough;[2] and you are to look on all I said concerning both Lord Bolingbroke's affair and her resentment as premature. My Lady's daughter and son-in-law[3] visit her next week.

94. To RICHARD JAGO [1]

[July 9,] 1749

DEAR SIR,

It is now Sunday evening, and I have been exhibiting myself in my walks to no less than a hundred and fifty people, and that with no less state and vanity than a Turk in his seraglio. — I have *some* hopes of seeing you *this* week; but if these should happen to be frustrated, I shall find them revive with double ardour and vivacity the next. Did not you tell me of a treatise that your Mr. Miller had, where the author en-

---

[2] Evidently hers of June 24.
[3] Mr. and Mrs. Weymondesold. For other references see the Index.
[1] Dodsley, *Letters to Particular Friends,* No. LVII. Fullington confirms the date, *PMLA,* 46:1134.

deavours to vindicate and establish Gothic architecture? and does not the same man explain it also by draughts on copperplates? That very book, or rather the title and the author's name, I want. — I shall never, I believe, be entirely partial to Goths or Vandals either; but I think, by the assistance of some such treatise, I could sketch out some charming Gothic temples and Gothic benches for garden-seats. — I do also esteem it extremely ridiculous to permit another person to design *for* you, when by sketching out your own plans you *appropriate* the merit of all you build, and feel a double pleasure from any praises which it receives. — I had here last Wednesday Dean Lyttelton, Mr. William Lyttelton, Commodore West, Miss Lyttelton, and Miss West. They drank tea, and went round my walks, where they seemed astonished they had been so long ignorant of the beauties of the place; said, in general, every thing that was *complaisant* or *friendly;* and left me highly delighted with *their* visit, and with room to hope for many more. Mean time, why do not *you* come? I *do* say, you are not Pylades. — What! you think, because you have an agreeable wife, and five fine children, that you must employ all your time in caressing them at home, or laying schemes for their emolument abroad? Is this public spirit? is this virtue? or, if it be virtue, dost thou think, because thou are *vartuous,* there must be no cakes and ale? is it not your duty to partake of them with a *friend* sometimes; eating and relieving him under what Boileau calls,

  Le penible fardeau de n'avoir rien a faire;

And what Pope *(stealing* from the former) denominates,

  The pains and penalties of idleness?

Pray come the first day of the week, and let Mr. Fancourt accompany you. — I have not much to add by way of news. The Duke of Somerset is going to lay out thirty thousand pounds upon Northumberland-house; nine houses to be purchased and pulled down on the other side the Strand for stables; the Strand there to be widened: I cannot tell you half; but one thing more I will, which is, that there will be a chapel on one side of the quadrangle, with a gothic wainscot and ceiling, and painted glass; and ☞ in it a Dutch stove, contrived so as to look like a tomb with an urn upon it.

What need I *write* all this? am not I to see you in a few days? — Not a word more positively; saving what may serve to assure you that I am, dear Sir,

       Inviolably yours,

The Leasowes, July 9, 1749   W. Shenstone

95. To LADY LUXBOROUGH[1]

July ye 30th 1749
The Leasows

MADAM,

I will not interrupt your Ladyship's Amusement with a long Epistle at present: You are, as I have some Reason to suppose, far more agreeably employ'd. Your Improvements around Barrels are at this time giving a double satisfaction to a Person of your generous Sentiments, by pleasing *Those* whom you wou'd most desire they shou'd. Mr Williams, who is a benevolent Man, & (as ye Scripture phrases it) *bringeth good Tidings,* made very honourable mention of your Appearance at Birmingham, with Mr and Mrs Wymondsold. What Pity it is, you did not surprize me then with a Coach & Six, fluster me for about two Hours, exhibit my little Ferme ornee & return? I do not mean by way of discharging ye visit which you are so kind to honour me with Periodically, about this time of ye year; but merely en passant & as a visit *par dessus* — My Gothick Building is now compleated; at least exhibits its full effect; The Ground about it is turf'd, but wants Rain; a new Path is made to it, I think, much for ye better; by ye Side of this Path is a little well with a tree, yt I think is picturesque. The Floor of it is pav'd Carpet-Fashion, with black and white Pebbles; &, considering how hastily I collected & dispos'd them, has a pretty good Effect. Pray, Madam, is ye Duchess's Carpet-Pavement famous? I mention it, because, having had a second Visit from ye Hagley-Family (Mrs Pitt, Mrs Granville, Miss Lytt: Comdore West, Mr Lyttelton &c.) at this very Place they us'd the words *"it is a perfect Somerset."* Now Miss Lyttelton had just before had a violent Fall; & I want sadly to know whether they alluded to yt Fall or to ye Floor. I rather imagine it was ye Fall, for it happen'd to be a pretty extraordinary one. I shall now I fancy have many visits from yt Family to *see* or to *shew* my little Improvements. if I behave orderly & well. But I do not forget that it was your Ladyship commended *first,* & gave very liberal *Encomiums* to my humble Territories, when as yet they had none given them. — I am but just recover'd from a most violent Fit of ye Cholick; which was not tolerably subdu'd under many Days. It grew at last into an Inflammation, & I am even now taking Drops & Draughts in order to reduce the remaining Fever. But I now consider myself as *well;* & I now am impatient to see Barrels. Mr & Miss Dolman tell me they are ready, & ask me to go with them.

[1] B. M. Add. MSS 28958, fol. 51ff. No. XIII of Lady Luxborough's *Letters,* not dated, which clearly answers this, should be dated before August 7, 1749, and should follow her No. XXIX.

A Distant View of the "Ruinated" Priory at the Leasowes
From a recent photograph by Myra M. Ward

The Priory Pool at the Leasowes
From a recent photograph by Myra M. Ward

> Accurs'd be he, Earl Douglas said,
> By whom this is deny'd —
> CHEVY CHACE

Tom comes now merely to mention this and to enquire when it will be suitable to your Ladyship to receive us. The moment it is, we all set out, for about a couple of Days. I believe my Brother too intends it; so y^t if y^r Conflux of visitants be not yet over I *hope* & *beg* y^r Ladyship will make so free as to mention it. I said I wou'd not interrupt you by a long Letter, but I fear I have. I am therefore, in very *few*, but *sincere* Words, your Ladyship's most oblig'd

& most obedient humble Servant

Will Shenstone

Pray, my Lady, who is y^t *Warwickshire clergyman*[2] that supplants me in my Province of *Elegy*, & addresses y^r Ladyship?

96. To LADY LUXBOROUGH [1]

August ye 9th 1749

MADAM,

I believe I shall write very *incoherently*, but I flatter myself it will be *some* satisfaction to your Ladyship to find I can write at *all;* especially after an Illness which was sufficient to confine me to my Bed when you was, amongst strangers, in my Dining Room. — My Disorder began on Sunday morning after green tea, & as it continu'd ye whole Day & longer I was advis'd towards Night to put off ye visit by sending Tom on Monday morning early; but having momentary Hopes of it's *ceasing*, & imagining I cou'd not have Mr Meredyth's Company upon any *other* Day, I chose to *take my Chance* of being tolerably well ye *next*. Those Hopes, as it happen'd, were not well grounded; but I have too much *conviction* of your Ladyship's good-sense, to imagine you will require an *Apology* for Events y^t I cou'd not foresee; & for whatever might happen amiss in y^r Reception, that might be imputed *to such Events* by a Person of Candour. I will then save myself & your Ladyship ye trouble of *making* and of *reading one:* But I will by no means forget to assure your Ladyship y^t I enjoy ye *Honour* of y^r Visit, notwithstanding what happen'd; & as to the *Pleasure & satisfaction,* I find your Conversation, *that* I shall always partake of with gratitude, whenever it is *allotted* me;

[2] Lady Luxborough identifies the clergyman as Mr. Perks of Coughton. See her *Letters*, p. 40.
[1] B. M. Add. MSS 28958, fol. 53ff.

but must also submit to be depriv'd of, sometimes, as well as to other misfortunes. — I am concern'd to hear of what you suffer'd at Birmingham nor did I ever once dream of ye water's being ris'n. You had great good Fortune y^t you did not take Cold; & indeed so had *I;* for it wou'd have given me uneasiness, (tho' I were not faulty) in being accessary to a Journey, the Pleasure of which to you wou'd have been so ill able to ballance such an Inconvenience — I am greatly oblig'd to your Ladyship for ye Verses you design'd me. I am unable at present to tell you my Sense of them in Poetry, but if I may entertain your Ladyship with Honesty & Prose, y^e *unleaven'd Bread of Sincerity & Truth,* I can conscienciously say, that I think them *good Lines;* & whether I am not like to be greatly affected by y^e *Compliment,* I leave your Ladyship to guess — Mr Dolman came here yesterday; *Miss* Dolman was confin'd by her Servant-Maid's having ye Cholick; but will both of them wait upon you soon — And now let me speak to this Point — Immediately after you were gone my Disorder turn'd to ye Jaundice, which I find *they* make light of; but which I most earnestly long to see remov'd; being conscious y^t, upon it's removal, I shou'd be perfectly well — But I fear it will not be so easily effected — However I feed myself with Hopes y^t we may all come to Barrels next week; I wou'd not have them go *without* me, for more Reasons y^n one; as I wou'd not lose the Pleasure of pointing out w^t I think Beauties there, & as I think they wou'd be apt alone to be too much upon ye Reserve. But I will write to your Ladyship again on Saturday — Your Ladyship did not see, it seems, my little Serpentine Stream, that is pebbled — No great Beauty perhaps, but what introduces a *variety* into ye Walks — I shall, perhaps, if I get well & wait on you at Barrels, be tempted to beg ye Favour of a visit to repair my Loss of y^r Last — I long to know ye Particulars of y^r Introduction of ye Shrine for Venus into y^r Pavilion — Is it a Semicircle in ye Middle of ye Back-walk. — I beg my Compliments to Mr Hall; I hope he mentiond to y^r Ladyship y^t I press'd your stay as much as I thought consistent wth y^r *Freedom* of *Choice;* for it requires a particular Temper to be quite easy in a Sick House & if you cou'd not wave ye Fear of giving Trouble at y^t Time (as you in justice might) I knew you wou'd not be easy — I can by no means think ye Living worth Mr Hall's Acceptance[2] — My Brother & Mr Dolman desire their Compliments — They are just going to drink tea at Ld Dudley's. I am your Ladyships most entirely obligd

W. S.

[2] Mr. Hall was attempting to secure the living of Harborough (Lady Luxborough's *Letters,* p. 37). He later secured it.

97. To LADY LUXBOROUGH[1]

The Leasowes, August ye 13th 1749

MADAM

I defer'd writing 'till today, hopeing I might by this means be able to fix some time for our Visit on a less *precarious Footing,* than I cou'd *before.* But I cannot acquaint your Ladyship that my Health is yet confirm'd. Far from it. It is indeed tolerable, & *has* been since I wrote last; but there is not a Day passes in which I do not experience three or Four Returns of my former Complaint; short ones indeed, & not extremely painfull; but such as I cou'd not undergo without much *Regret* while I shou'd be enjoying your Company & your Improvements at Barrels. *This* I will promise your Ladyship that I will endeavour the more sollicitously to be well soon, that I may perform this Journey; but in ye mean Time having made that Resolution, it will be prudent for me not to think too much upon ye Subject; For yt would render my intermediate confinement extremely tedious. . . . I have taken some walks about my Farm and am not at all conscious yt I have taken any Cold, but ye Disorder has not been yet thoroughly remov'd by Med'cines. If this proves a good week with me, I tell Mr & Miss Dolman we will all set out to-morrow, that is, Monday-Sennight. In ye mean time if it prove less suitable to your Ladyship yt we shou'd come then, we will depend upon your waving ye Visit with all Freedom.

I have had many messages to inquire after my Health; *Theirs,* who, I guess'd, might really wish it, (amongst which I am convinc'd I may reckon your Ladyships) I took extreme kindly. Poor Ambrose seem'd to be concern'd *himself,* & deliver'd his message in a manner that became him. . . . Lord Dudley I believe wishes me very well, & has sent often. Sr Tho: Lyttelton sent his Gardener to-day on ye same Errand. Your Ladyship knows ye Fellow; My Brother has been taking him round my Walks, & ye poor Lout is extremely afflicted that he had not had ye disposal or laying out of every individual Place. He cou'd have done it to so much greater Advantage! Is not this provoking? To have Lady Luxborough commend in *general,* to have her write very elegant Lines upon my Contrivances, and then to have them all aspers'd by a mere *watering-*Pan? mangled by a mere Pruning-knife! Does not this exceed all Patience? Surely I shou'd think I did that Gardener Honour, if I suffer'd him to mark out ye Figure of a sallad-Bed. But ever since he has been able to raise Orange-Gourds, fit to be tipt with silver & to make Punch-Ladles, he has been so vain there is no endureing him. Yet a *Wind* may come &

---
[1] B. M. Add. MSS 28958, fol. 55ff.

destroy his Gourd, as it did ye Prophet Jonah's very suddenly, & then wherewithall shall he pride himself? — This is mere Raillery, for I do not hate, I only laugh at him — He talks of getting Leave to come over to Barrels soon —

I will now take my leave, & write again to your Ladyship on Thursday next or Saturday.

I am your Ladyships most obligd & most obedient Servant

W. Shenstone

I fancy ye new Mrs Lyttelton[2] plays finely on ye Harpsichord; They borrow mine in order to be ready for her, as soon as she comes down.

98. To LADY LUXBOROUGH[1]

The Leasows, Aug: 20th 1749

MADAM,

I can say with a safe conscience that No one was ever more impatient to make a visit, than I am to wait upon your Ladyship at Barrels: At this time particularly, as I long to make my Acknowledgements for your *last* obliging condescension, to see yr various Improvements, & to shew Mr Dolman the several Beauties & curiosities of ye Place. But I am in ye Condition of a *Spring* yt is push'd back, & ye more it is so, presses forward with ye greater Energy. I am this moment risen from my Bed, where I have lain down to remove a Fit of my Cholick, with ye Assistance of White-wine Whey & Blanketts. And this is ye means I've been forc'd to have recourse to every Day this week. For, if I escape a Fit all *other* times of ye Day, I'm sure to be troubled with it about half an hour after Dinner. And yet ye Disorder is pretty soon over, & ye Pain not extremely violent. But what can I do? I dare not risque having a Return upon ye *Road,* where I cannot apply to my usual Remedies — I must beg Leave to put off our Visit for a week longer, hoping I may by extraordinary Care be able to master my Complaint before that Time. And as this is ye real state of ye Case I will submit my Apology to your Ladyship upon this Issue.

I am at this instant as free from Pain as I hope *you* are; & if I had any Circumstances yt I cou'd foresee wou'd amuse your Ladyship in a Letter, I cou'd write them down with Pleasure.

[2] The first wife of George Lyttelton, Lucy Fortescue, had died January 19, 1747; the new Mrs. Lyttelton was Elizabeth Rich, daughter of Sir Robert Rich, at one time governor of Gibraltar. Wyndham, *Chronicles of the Eighteenth Century,* I, 207, 241.

[1] B. M. Add. MSS 28958, fol. 57ff. Lady Luxborough's letter of the same date (*Letters,* No. XXX) is a reply to this; its date is thus confirmed.

I am upon ye Search for a Motto to my Gothick Building, which I wou'd have consist of a Stanza or two of old English Verse; & which I wou'd cause to be inscrib'd in old English Letters. I've been looking over Spenser, but cannot yet fix upon one to my Mind. Perhaps your Ladyship may chance to find one. I begin to prefer English Mottoes in general. There is scarce one Gentleman or Clergyman in Fifty y^t remembers any thing of Classick Authors. But above all things, I long to have ye fine Compliment you pay me written by yourself upon one of my Skreens; You know it must be written by no *other* Hand; & if it might be, I'm sure I shou'd not chuse it shou'd.

I will not conclude without inculcating this necessary Assertion; That we all desire y^r Ladyship will not defer ye Reception of any Company you may expect, on our Accounts; I doubt our Propos'd visit may have caus'd you to decline some Company already. I beg it may do so no more. We will come on any Day you fix when my Disorder leaves me. My Cholick has been very capricious, but *I* am, Madam,

Your Ladyship's most constant & most oblig'd
W: Shenstone

I hope you will please to excuse ye Liberty I take in permitting Tom to stay all Night at Barrels; I c^d not send him earlier *to-day;* & *to-morrow* he will be employ'd in Harvest-work — My Service to Mr Hall.

99. To LADY LUXBOROUGH [1]

August ye 30th 1749

MADAM,

Tho' I am always extremely delighted with an opportunity of hearing from Barrels, yet *now,* at ye Sight of your Ladyship's servant my Conscience flew in my Face, and reminded me of a neglect in writing which I know not how to excuse — you were pleas'd in your last Letter to allow me some Time for ye Payment of my visit, 'till my Health shou'd be better confirm'd. This I thought a Liberty which in my present situation I ought not to disregard, & accordingly determin'd, with what Patience I well cou'd to defer my Journey to another week. I shou'd have certainly inform'd you of this *to-morrow,* but have very little to say for not doing so on Monday *last.* I have been now, many Days, without any considerable Pain. What I feel is generally about half an hour after dinner; some slight symptoms, which rather alarm than hurt me; and I believe I might

---

[1] B. M. Add. MSS 28958, fol. 59ff. This letter answers and confirms the date of Lady Luxborough's of August 29, 1749 (*Letters,* No. XXXI); it also confirms the date of her No. XXXII of September 8, which replies to the present one.

next week be able to travel to Persia, with a provisionary Box of Pills, & with Liberty to eat & drink what I've a Mind; That is, I might eat *Rice,* I fancy, very safely, but I must beg to be excus'd as to drinking *Sherbett*—When I said "Liberty to eat what I've a Mind," I shou'd rather have said "Liberty to eat what I've *not* a Mind." I must give up Sauces & every thing that relishes; excepting only your Ladyship's Conversation, which being a Pleasure of ye Mind only, I may enjoy without Regret or Measure. And indeed as for eating, the Breast of a Partridge or a Barn-door Fowl are very *pleasant* Food, & neither of *these* is in ye least degree formidable—So that, on the whole, I cou'd with great Alacrity set forward on Monday for my *own* Part, but Mr Dolman it seems goes then to Lichfield Races; & his Servant is now in the House in order to borrow my Horse. He has waited for me this Month, & wou'd hardly forgive me if I went to Barrels without him. The Delay however cannot be of long continuance, when Persons propose themselves so much Pleasure as we do from this Journey.

I take little Rides almost every Day & visit my next Neighbours. Yesterday I din'd with Lord Dudley by Invitation at a third Person's House; & the afternoon *before* I was at ye Grange. My Lord ask'd very kindly after your Health, & *wonder'd* you did not take a Bed at his House; upon which I took Care to deliver your Compliments.

I am oblig'd to your Ladyship for ye Eggs you sent me. I wou'd not eat one for the World; as I fancy I have some little Chance of raising a Breed from them. They shall be put under a Hen directly; who is to exert her Influence upon them, under ye Protection & *Auspices* of ye fortunate Mrs Arnold.

I am glad to hear of every contrivance near y^r Hermitage that seems likely to tend to ye Hermitess's *Repose*—I had just fix'd up ye Lines I enclose in my Gothick Building, when who shou'd arrive but Mr Lyttelton, Mr Pitt, & Mr Miller. Twas impossible for me to conceal them, as I was oblig'd to accompany my Visitants all round my Walks. They happen'd to be much commended; all, except ye two first Lines of ye last Stanza; which I knew were flimzy, but which as I thought the auntient Guise might possibly excuse. The Building itself escap'd full as well as I cou'd reasonably expect; indeed *better*. Many Parts of my Farm were extravagantly commended, but the Grove especially. The poor Summer-House was, as it were ye Scape-Goat, which suffer'd for all the Blunders I had committed else-where. I believe y^r Ladyship is my witness that I thought it bad, & talk'd of pulling it down long ago—but many things may be said in behalf of *me* tho' not of *it*. I built it merely as a *Study,* without regarding it as an *object;* & at ye Time I built it had no Thoughts of laying out my Environs; that's *one* thing. Another is, that I built it upon my *own* Land, & did not foresee a kind of Exchange (since made) by means of wch I might have situated it better. The Road *now* coming behind it, renders it intolerable — They spend an afternoon here with Mr Miller & whom besides I know not; perhaps to morrow. But I will detain yr Ladyship no longer now; I will write again on Saturday. I have kept your Servant long, & must conclude. I am whether in Haste or at Leisure, invariably

your Ladyship's most oblig'd hum: Servt
W.S.

100. To LADY LUXBOROUGH [1]

Sunday,
The Leasows, Septem: ye 10th, 1749

MADAM,

Being very uncertain whether this Letter will arrive before it become superfluous, I will say nothing more than that Mr Dolman &c: are just gone from hence in their Return from Lichfield Races; will Employ monday & tuesday in preparing their Linnen; & will, with me, wait upon your Ladyship on Wednesday next, some-time in ye After-noon. I beg my Compliments to any Friend to whom you have an *easy* opportunity of delivering them; and am with sincere Respect your Ladyship's

most oblig'd humble Servant
Will: Shenstone

101. To LADY LUXBOROUGH [1]

The Leasows, Septr ye 12th 1749

MADAM,

If my Letter had been sent yesterday by Mr Williams, as I hop'd it wou'd, I shou'd not have had altogether so much Reason to accuse myself of Neglect, as I seem to have at present. *That* Letter your Servant has now in his Pocket, & I chuse he shou'd take it, if peradventure it may prove any kind of Justification — Mr Dolmans *Continuance* at Lichfield is to be plac'd to ye account of some near Relations which he has there, & not of the Races only. But I hasten to repeat my Promise that if there be no *violent* Rain we will be at Barrels to-morrow in the Afternoon. I was by *Agreement* to be at Broom to-night, and to set out from thence with them in ye morning, but I believe now I shall perform

[1] B. M. Add. MSS 28958, fol. 61.
[1] B. M. Add. MSS 28958, fol. 63ff.

it all in one Day—I will not trouble y^r Servant with Instructions concerning the Turf-Seat—If you have Roots enough, & will give Tom leave when he comes with me to build himself such a *trophy* or two at Barrels, he will do it with great *inward* Satisfaction. He is my only Architect for this kind of Work, & I think as *good* & *safe* a one as I can discover else-where—Pray if you please, detain Mr Outing—but now I remember he doesn't propose going 'till Thursday next—Since I wrote last I have din'd one day at Hagley where I found Mr Lyt. Mr Pitt & Mr Miller flown; The first of these being call'd up to London on Business. Mrs Lyttelton I saw—Sr Thomas ask'd whether you had seen ye Park this year, &, I conceiv'd they wish you *had*. Since that I took a Ride thither with a neighb'ring Clergyman to see some things wch I never *had* seen before: The Cottage for one. But chiefly an Adjacent Wood of theirs call'd Wichbury, which as much exceeds ye Park for Views, as Hare-court Pump does the Streams of Aganippe—We were out for about Seven hours, dinnerless; & I came Home and eat too much—Doesn't y^r Ladyship remember that my summer-house *is* render'd of a Stone-colour & ye roof like Slates? It *is*. I am your Ladyship's

most oblig'd & obedient Servant
Will: Shenstone

102. To LADY LUXBOROUGH[1]

[After Sept. 20 and before Oct. 10, 1749]

MADAM,

A Person y^t has so little *claim* to Ceremony as myself, may well be suppos'd willing to lay but little Stress upon it; And yet if it was any way instrumental in procuring me a more speedy Letter from your Ladyship, I cannot say but it is an Article to which I am greatly oblig'd. I convey'd ye Message you were so good to send to Miss Dolman yesterday, & will make use of ye first opportunity she gives me to return her Acknowledgments. We arriv'd safe at the Leasows something after eight o'clock; having call'd to refresh our selves at Shirley-street, and also deviated from our Road in order to take a view of my Ld Archer's obelisk. As to ye Deficiency of *Balls* I believe I must give it up, *there;* because they cou'd not have been distinguish'd from his Salon, in Case he had chose them. Yet ye Obelisk continues to appear small to me, & I shou'd think must do

---

[1] B. M. Add. MSS 28958, fol. 180ff. Though undated in the manuscript, this letter answers Lady Luxborough's of September 20, 1749 (*Letters*, No. XXXIV) and is answered by her No. XXXV of October 10 (the year of which, though wanting, is obviously 1749). Her No. XXXV, begun October 10 but continued under the dates "Monday, 16th," "Wed. Oct. 25," and "Friday, 27th," also in part replies to his letter of October 18, 1749 (No. 103 below).

so, at ye Place from which it shou'd be seen. It has a good effect from some Lanes adjoining to ye Park, and it is no doubt capable of being made good use of, from ye Woods on each side his House. The Park itself seems as improveable as any Place I ever saw, & yields to Sr Tho's Lyttelton's only in regard to ye Country round it for I scarce remember any where such a Length of *even* Country as there is from Henley to my House. My Lord has a delightfull Valley, y^t runs crosswise, betwixt his House & his obelisk with Water enough to be thrown into what Shape he pleases — After observing thus much we proceeded forward, as I mean my Letter shall do. While I was enjoying your Ladyships Improvements, I find my own were undermin'd at Home. I was oblig'd, you must know, to a Neighbour for a Path which led thro' another Coppice to mine. This I have often been within a guinea or two of agreeing to purchase, & as often promis'd y^t no Step shou'd be taken in regard to it without my knowledge. But ye Proprietor happening to live servant wth y^e *Parson of our Parish,* was advis'd in my *Absence,* to stock up every Inch of it, & his Commands were obey'd so precisely when I came home, y^t ye Path was cover'd wth Roots & ye communication entirely obstructed. I believe I shall acquire a Path upon my own ground as good as that *was,* but nothing equal to what that might have been made at ye least expence imaginable. Had I been here when ye Fellow began, I cou'd have manifested it to be, and indeed have *made* it his Interest, to let ye Underwood remain. As it is, the Parson has renew'd his quarrel wth me which will probably last for Life; I am meditating Revenge on ye Persons y^t are engag'd in it; I have lost ye finest Opportunity of Improvement y^t ever Person had; & I shall never walk y^t way without ye disagreeable sense of Indignation — You must not think I wou'd hereby intimate y^t I repent my Journey, for it was every way agreeable — & this had been done I suppose ye very first time I was absent. — Mr Outing let me into ye Secret concerning your intended Urn & I approve y^r Design extremely. The chief difficulty will be where to place it. The Shape of ye Pedestal must be according to one of ye orders. Those must be chosen by ye Size of your Urn, & ye Size of your Urn adjusted by ye Place from whence it shou'd be view'd. I wou'd not have it calculated to be seen from your Summerhouse, & I wish you may not hereafter imagine y^t Arbor too close a situation. I rais'd two Pedestals for urns in my wood in much such Places, but I afterwards dislik'd, & remov'd them. I will think about it, & your Ladyship who thinks *better,* will consider of a situation in ye mean Time — I *knew* y^t lowering your *walk* to ye Pavilion w^d have ye Effect propos'd; but I wou'd willingly have produc'd the same by a more sudden slope at yᵉ End yᵗ you might not seem to *descend,* so far as yʳ Walk continu'd; but as yʳ Ladyship says yᵉ farther End is *higher,* you have acted rightly. I wou'd have yᵉ Instructions to yʳ Joiner to be, yᵗ he shou'd make yᵉ Pediment as low as they ever *are* made in other terms, not different from what is practis'd. Quere as to yᵉ use of three neat urns in wood upon yʳ Pediment. I have no particular fondness for them, but they wou'd heighten; & please *most* Eyes. The Alteration at this End of yʳ Shrubbery can be no otherwise than Right. If you have a Mind to have a small Passage there into your Garden you may crooken a Path thro yᵉ Shrubs & so hide yᵉ Gate. I shou'd be oblig'd to yʳ Ladyship if you cou'd learn what Books are usefull for young Beginners in Architecture. I have receiv'd Gibbs, which consists entirely of Plans, & supposes some previous knowledge — I met my Lord Dudley yesterday going round my Walks with his upper Servants, en famille, & I deliver'd him your Compliments. He enquir'd, and was glad to hear of your Health, wou'd be glad of an opportunity to wait on you, but could fix no Time. — I enclose to your Ladyship yᵉ Product of one Morning, & which may be rather call'd yᵉ Sketch or Plan of an ode yⁿ an Ode itself. But if it expresses about a tenth Part of what I think, & has any thing you do not disapprove in yᵉ *Design* or *Manner,* I give it up as to Brilliancies; & may correct it another Time. But till it *be* corrected you must give no Copy. I hope as I know it will give you Pleasure, yᵗ Mʳˢ Meredyth is arriv'd. Miss Meredyth will find out some large Oak, in some retir'd Corner where your Urn shou'd be Plac'd. She will also sketch out upon Paper yᵉ Effect it will produce. But I wou'd caution your Ladyship to take Particular care yᵗ it be not done so agreeably as to make you like upon Paper what you should not approve in yᵉ Execution. You may jogg her Hand (but dont say that I advis'd you) as she is drawing, & by that means stand a better Chance of not being impos'd upon by yᵉ Delicacy of her Pencil — This Letter is already a mere Rhapsody, and I can hardly render it less coherent let me write how I will, & therefore what if you were to plant here & there a Yew-tree in your Shrubbery to look wild & to continue about yᵉ Size of your other Shrubs. Moreover as you continue yᵉ Terras on yᵉ Side of yʳ Shrubbery Wou'd not here & there such a wild yew tree all along yᵉ Side have a good effect from yʳ Bowling-green &c: One thing I believe you will allow, that there shou'd be particular care taken to vary yᵉ Shrubs on yᵗ side so as to produce as strong a contraste as you can betwixt them; (Have you any Birch?) & I think yᵉ Shrubbery in general shou'd be permitted to grow thicker — You have this advantage from yᵉ Futility of my proposals yᵗ you may entirely neglect them, & I not be displeas'd which your Ladyship knows is a greater Priviledge y^n *my* Criticks are likely to allow me—We were all extremely pleas'd & oblig'd by our Reception at Barrels, & Miss Dolmans Scrawl appears to me too little to contain a quarter of what she feels on y^t occasion—But my own Letter is at least as much too long, especially as it has expatiated on other subjects to ye neglect of that on which it shou'd be most particular; I mean the sincerity with which I am your Ladyships most oblig'd

& most obedient Servant
W. Shenstone

I am upon revisal asham'd to send this stupid Letter; but to write another, I must have waited 'till Saturday. I beg my Compliments to Mr Hall.

103. To LADY LUXBOROUGH [1]

The Leasows, October ye 18th 1749

MADAM,

Your Ladyship cant imagine how I scold at old Emme[2] for permitting Mr Williams to say he has no Letter for me: And on Saturday Morning last, in case she did not succeed, I gave her positive orders to set fire to the Town of Birmingham. At last I *did* condescend to moderate my Injunctions, & consented that she shou'd only pull down *new*-street, the Square, & part of Temple-Row. As far as I can discover, she has not hitherto done it; so that it is in your Ladyship's Power to make ye Town appear worth saveing, if you will but throw half a Dozen Lines into it, of your own Hand-writing. It is not, I think, ye first Time that Cities have been spar'd, for the sake of some valuable manuscripts they contain'd. I forget the particular Instances, but I am sure there are *some;* especially when mighty Heroes, like me, have been concern'd. And why shou'd not I set as great a value upon what you write, which without a Compliment affords me more *interesting* Pleasure than the Works of Homer or of Aristotle.

Now tho' I'm well enough convinc'd that *one* single Letter of your Ladyship's outweighs more than fifty of mine, yet I cannot avoid requesting, that if ever hereafter you find me in ye least dilatory you wou'd admit, as Evidence in my Favour, this my present work of supereroga-

---

[1] B. M. Add. MSS 28958, fol. 64ff. Lady Luxborough's letter of November 1, 1749 (*Letters*, No. XXXVI) answers this and apparently encloses her No. XXXV. The date of No. XXXVI is thus confirmed. It begins "Pray read the inclosed letter first." The reference is evidently to her No. XXXV, which she began in answer to Letter 102 above, but kept by her and added to (see note 1 to Letter 102).

[2] Post-woman [Shenstone]. See the Index.

tion. And yet what shall it avail me, to have my *negligence* at one time contrasted with my *over-officiousness* at another. The truth is, I can neither *deserve* ye Favour of your Letters by *writing* or by *silence;* so, I am to impute it altogether to ye *activity* of your Benevolence. But as Sir John Falstaff says, "he is not only witty in *himself,* but the Cause that wit is in *other Men,*" so your Ladyship is not only thus obliging *yourself,* but instrumental in causing your Friends & ye Persons I esteem, to make favourable mention of me. I here think of Mrs Weymondsold; I must not forget Mrs Davis: Tis too obvious to mention the Duchess, & I am indebted to you lately for an Instance of civility from my Lord Archer. I can not repay you but in Proportion to a very limited Sphere, & so far as that extends, I shall never be wanting.

I hope your Ladyship is now planting furiously; I do not mean *rashly* & indiscreetly, but diligently & judiciously. I applaud myself for ye little Hint I gave for ye Encrease of your Shrubbery, & The Sweep for ye Coach. I can see no Reason to doubt of it's Propriety, or that it will afford you satisfaction, both which indeed are synonimous Expressions. I am sure you will acquaint me when your Urn & Pediment are compleated. Shall you have a glimpse of either while there is a yellow ling'ring Leaf upon ye Trees? For *my* Part, I cannot yet place Autumn upon a Footing with Spring; & I think ye Duchess of Somerset betray'd the cause she seem'd to defend by numbering the melancholy objects that season introduces. At least fifty Persons to one wou'd reckon *that* a disadvantage. And yet certain it is, that Melancholy has & ever had its Charms for Persons of ye *finest* Taste. Shakespear observes it. I wish you don't say that *I* too, by this last Sentence, have betray'd the cause I was seemingly defending; Be that as it will, I believe I shall venture to print my Madrigal on that occasion in some future Magazine of *this year;* least by appearing *afterwards* it shou'd grow *many* degrees inferiour to a last year's Almanack.

I enclose a Letter from Mr Whistler,[3] ye only one I've receiv'd from him for above this half year. I began indeed to grow a little jealous, that his Affection was going to sicken & decay but I find I have no Reason, if I may judge by his Letter; wherein he treats me with abundant partiality according to Custom. Your Ladyship I hope will excuse my communication of it.

I am, as often as my servants have Leisure, employ'd in extending my Path, so that it will now in a short time lead round my whole Farm, &,

---

[3] This is apparently Whistler's letter to Shenstone dated October 7, 1749, published in Hull's *Select Letters,* Vol. I, No. XXVIII.

if I be not mistaken, furnish out a *variety* of scene in Proportion to its Length.

I think ye Welchmen us'd to drink Sir Watkin's Health for *ever and two Dey;* I wish your Ladyship's as long, and am with like Attachment
Your Ladyship's most oblig'd, & most obedient Servant,
Will Shenstone

Is it contrary to ye Rules, pray to desire my Compliments to Mrs & Miss Meredyths, if they are with you? If so, I submit.

104. To LADY LUXBOROUGH [1]

Friday Morning 5 o'clock. [Nov. 3, 1749]

MADAM

Yesterday prov'd so extremely fortunate on Account of Amusements sent me, Compliments paid me, Friendship shewn me, & Honours done me, yt I think I ought to give it a red Letter in ye *Calendar* of my *Life*. Your Ladyships Packet wanted nothing to compleat my Happiness, when presently arrives old Emme with a Cargo of new Books & Pamphletts; sufficient of *themselves* to support my Spirits many Days. In short I was so *glad,* & so eager to write, that I cou'd not write *at all*. Accordingly I order'd some *Tinder* & *Matches* to my Bedside & resolv'd to wake early & write this Morning, And this is what I am now doing. Your Ladyships obliging Letter, which shews yt you have remember'd me at so many distinct Periods, has made me ample Amends for ye Doubts I have undergone by reason of yr Silence. At last indeed comparing all circumstances, I began to take Heart, & by ye Assistance of a strong Belief persuaded myself you were gone into Cheshire. This I had no sooner done yn Emme confirm'd me in the Opinion, by saying Mr W. did not know whether you were yet come Home. And now what Mischiefs may arise from a dilatory Conveyance of Letters! Miss Meredyths *first* agreeable Sketch did not arrive 'till last Night, When it ought to have done so on *Saturday*. On Saturday Emme had issu'd forth tow'rds Birmingham, full Fraught with Tinder-box, Matches, & Indignation! Desperate indeed had been ye Case of yt poor devoted Town, had not Mr Williams by his mild Demeanour & affable Deportment first cheated her of Resentment, & then of her Combustibles! Telling her an idle Story as how her *Eyes* wou'd be *sufficient* in case she kept her Resolution; But

---

[1] B. M. Add. MSS 28958, fol. 175ff. In the manuscript this letter is dated merely "Friday Morning, 5 o'clock." But it clearly answers Lady Luxborough's letter of verified date, November 1, 1749 (*Letters,* No. XXXVI) and the one enclosed (No. XXXV), which he received by messenger from Barrels and not by post. He answers at once; his letter is dated accordingly November 3, 1749.

alas! she had no more *Inclination,* than her Eyes had *Power,* to destroy a Town where her Friend Williams resided; whom she calls ye pleasantest spoken man in all the Wourld. So, in short, ye Town has held out, till now; and now seduc'd by y^r Ladyship & Miss Meredyth I have no more Inclination to fire it, y^n ye Person I employ. I shou'd express my Concern for y^r Ladyships late Illness but y^t I feel it so much more agreeable to forget it, in order to enjoy ye Pleasure of your Recovery — As to those trifling Verses you commend, I do not intend to alter above half a dozen words; For Instance *Rage* instead of *wrath* in ye last stanza, then *blame* instead of *Rage.* Bewail *for ever* instead of *incessant,* as giving a better flow & so forth; and then to *add* about 4 Lines in regard to this very Urn you are erecting — Mr Whistler is a sincere and generous Hearted Man — He will not come here till I've been at Whitchurch; but when He does, his greatest Pleasure will be to wait on your Ladyship — I am oblig'd to your Ladysp for ye Book of Architecture; shall pry a little into it, but shall be glad to hear of some modern Book or Book more generally us'd in ye same Way. — I hope to manage it so y^t you may not regret My Parson's Barbarity, especially as you never saw w^t that Coppice *might* have produc'd — I *never want* Inducements to come over to Barrels, I'm sure I see *Abundance* at *present;* If I have ye Happiness (as I am not without some Hopes I shall) to come while those Ladies are there, I must either give up my Dislike to Autumn, or you must allow me a Distinction betwixt Autumn at Barrels, & Autumn at ye Leasowes. This you very well may, & in Return I will proclaim *your Ladyship's* Autumn to be Finest of all Seasons. Indeed my Verdict is only *spacial* in regard to my *own* Country. I only say tis a *melancholy* season. There is Room for much *Debate* upon ye Pains or Pleasures of melancholy, *afterwards.* I remember y^t Sketch in Watteau. Tis no disadvantage to Miss Meredyths Copy y^t 'tisnt finish'd. Tis perfect in it's *Kind.* — I mean as a sketch. Tis what all must allow to be natural & affecting. I am highly oblig'd to ye Ladies for their Compliments, as these give me an opportunity of presenting Mine, & wishing them a Series of Fine Weather at Barrels — They will want nothing else — My Brother is from Home — I caus'd your Servant to see Ld Dudley's Green-house & to present y^r Compliments. He *saw* ye Pine-apples too, I suppose. Mr Hall's Sermon I will carefully return —

ADDENDA

I believe *sacred* Things are often us'd as a Cover for Profaneness; Mr Hall will excuse me, if, for once, I make mention of secular or *profane* Things, upon a Cover for *sacred.*

The Book you lent me treats of y*e* very Points I want to know; & *may* be very *accurate,* but y*e* Figures in y*e* Divisions are so small, & y*e* Style in some Places so obscure, y*t* I cannot help wishing for a better — Nevertheless w*th* y*r* Ladyship's Leave I will keep this something longer.

I am in y*r* Ladyships Mind concerning Gibb's.[2] One time or other I will *change* y*t* Book. I like but few Things in't. The Front of Prior's House is *one.* Colston's Monument *another;* an Urn or two, a Garden Building or two, & some Pedestals for Busts. that's all — An *Altar* had formd a *disproportionate* Pedestal. Otherwise y*r* Ladsp's Scheme of an altar to *Friendship,* w*th* M*r* Somerviles Urn upon it had been genteel.

105. To LADY LUXBOROUGH[1]

[After Nov. 3 and before Nov. 8, 1749]

MADAM,

Your Ladyship will please to observe y*t* y*e* remaining Part of my Letter will relate solely to y*e* Improvements you propose; & that if I seem to express my self *authoritatively,* I do it merely for y*e* Sake of *Brevity,* & not thro' any Presumption y*t* my Opinions are *conclusive* — Abruptly therefore, *Balls* will suit y*e* Simplicity of your Dorick Building better than *Urns,* & will come five times Cheaper — As to y*e* Urn you intend to M*r* Somerville, I have a great deal to say. The Shape of y*e* antique one you propose is not amiss, the *Antiquity* is certainly an Advantageous Circumstance; Nevertheless My Eye seems to require y*t* the lower Part of y*e* Urn shou'd be some thing *fuller.* However, I send your Ladsp (what they send *me* for) "Gibbs Book of Architecture"[2] where you may find a Number of Urns which may either tend to alter your Choice, or to confirm you in it. There are few pretty ones. The first of Page y*e* 140 seems to me as good as *any.* How can M*r* Hands dream of twenty Inches for y*e* Height of your Pedestal? 'Twill be a mere *Daading;* M*rs* Holyoak will not fail to call it a Child's *Play-gawd.* It must be at least as big as the Lesser ones at Hagley in y*e* *whole;* and as to proportioning y*e* Height of y*e* *Pedestal* you may have either y*e* taller *Corinthian* Pedestal, or y*e* lower *Ionick. That* will depend upon y*e* Place from whence tis to be

---

[2] "Gibb's book of architecture" might well have been that of James Gibbs (1682–1754), entitled *A Book of Architecture* (1728) or his *Rules for Drawing the Several Parts of Architecture* (1732).

[1] B. M. Add. MSS 28958, fol. 178ff. This letter, undated in the manuscript, is a supplement to the foregoing and is answered by Lady Luxborough's of November 8, 1749 (*Letters,* No. XXXVII), the date of which is thus confirmed. In the manuscript, Letter 104 is marked No. I and Letter 105 No. II; the two letters probably were sent together, as her No. XXXVII answers both.

[2] See note 2 above.

view'd. One thing I believe is certain, that to look *down* much upon Urn or Pedestal will produce a bad Effect — Wood is I find as dear as Stone; Stone in this Case is greatly preferable — I beg Leave to hesitate as to an *Altar*-Pedestal. Is it *proper,* considering ye *different* use of[3] Altars and Urns? Is it ever *done?* If you are satisfy'd in the *Affirmative,* yet undoubtedly Mr Williams's Notion is just, yt ye Altar shou'd be square; & that, for ye Reason he gives. *His* Altar is I think genteel — but it must have *Authority,* for if it be not a true *antient* Altar, it is *nothing;* As Altars are *particular* Kind of Things, & we have no *modern* Originals. As to his Management of ye Lyre and Wreath, I don't admire it; much less Mr Hands's Scheme, to have *Four* Lyres which wou'd introduce much *Formality* & *Sameness,* at as large an expence as might introduce *variety* — I wou'd by all means chuse to have two Festoons, join'd together by Flourish'd Knotts, surround ye Body of ye Urn. *From* these Knotts shou'd depend, on *one* side a Lyre, *obliquely;* & on ye *other,* the old Roman Reeds. I wou'd not have *more* instruments yn one in a Place. The Garland pendent betwixt these Knotts &c: will be ornament enough for ye two remaining Sides — I will venture to add my Thoughts here as to ye Inscription. There shou'd be one I think on *one* side ye Pedestal, expressive of his Character by a few Epithets; and as short as possible. After wch what if you were to put "HIS SALTEM!" which, I shou'd imagine, wou'd suggest *enough* to any *classical* Reader. On some *other* side of ye Pedestal I wou'd have a chosen Motto. Such as This —

      POSTQUAM TE FATA TULERUNT,
      IPSE PALES AGROS, ATQUE IPSE RELIQUIT APOLLO!

For I think it a *prime* good one, & what I wou'd use myself upon Occasion — And now am I come by slow Degrees to speak to ye Article of a *Place* for this Urn; of which I can say nothing, unless I were upon ye Spot. Tis ye nicest Thing in ye World to place an Urn judiciously, so yt it may have as solemn an Effect as possible; & be seen at a proper distance; & have just Scenery enough around it to make ye whole picturesque. And yet as difficult as it is, if your Ladyship will accept of my *implicit* approbation, I will very readily give it you in Favour of ye Place Miss Meredyth proposes; only ye Urn must *not* appear in a *direct Line* with ye Tree, if you please. I thought I was well acquainted with all your Environs but I am surprizingly at a Loss in regard to yr Sketch. I forget ye Steps, The Willows, the Tree &c: I believe I shall entirely approve of *Slopeing* ye Precipice — only leaving a small Part perpendicular at Bottom by way of Fence, & no where *visible* — I can say nothing more

[3] In the line above "use of" Shenstone has written "intent."

particular on this Occasion — only yt ye Place for yr Urn is certainly *thereabouts* — Let Mr Williams finish his Piece; give his Urn a little-bolder Relievo; try ye Effect of a Lyre & Festoons *as above;* bring a little Water before ye Urn from left to Right, which then may turn & lose itself amongst ye Trees. Then insert ye Inscription & Motto legibly — I fancy this wou'd render it no unaimiable Picture. I am your Ladyship's most oblig'd

W. Shenstone

106. To LADY LUXBOROUGH [1]

The Leasows, Novr ye 13th 1749

MADAM,

I can assure your Ladyship that Emme (Skudamore) receives *her* share of ye Pleasure you give by your Letters; All the Difference is, that she is never *more* happy, & I am never so *much* so as when she brings me a good Sizeable Packet from her Friend Mr Williams. This Pleasure of her's is not *vulgar;* since I pay her irregularly, and in the Lump; at what Intervals I think proper. Nor was it in ye least *her* Fault, that I did not receive your last Letter 'till late on Saturday; whereas your Ladyship expected I shou'd have *answer'd* it that very Day. What then remain'd for me but to fulfill your Commands as punctually as I cou'd, tho' not as I cou'd *wish*. In order thereto, I sent a Carpenter this Morning to take ye Dimensions of the Urns &c: at Hagley; and these you will find amongst the Draughts[2] I send (No II.) The lesser I suppose will be sufficient for your *Area,* and the *Distance* from whence you are to view ye Urn. I like ye *Ionick* best of any Pedestal; & shou'd do so, even if it were to [be] seen from *level* ground; but if you place your Pedestal *below* the Eye, I think it will be out of all *Doubt* that you shou'd chuse *no lower order*.

I have no other quere to make as to ye situation you propose, than *this;* viz whether you shall have Area enough round ye bottom of your Pedestal for ye *situation* to seem *natural* & *easy*. If so, I believe it will be a *good* one, tho' I hope to *see* it before your Urn is erected.

[1] B. M. Add. MSS 28958, fol. 66ff. This letter answers Lady Luxborough's of November 8, 1749 (*Letters,* No. XXXVII), the date of which is thus confirmed. Her No. XLI (wrongly placed in her *Letters*), dated simply "Tuesday," is a reply to Shenstone's present one of November 13, 1749, and is thus to be dated after November 13, 1749. Dodsley has placed it by a postscript dated "Tuesday Night, Dec. 12, 1749," which belongs not to this letter but to her No. XXXIX (see below Letter 108, n1). Her No. XL next intervenes before he writes to her again. It is dated merely "Wednesday" but refers both to matters mentioned in her No. XLI and to his letter, under present consideration, of November 13. The correct order of her *Letters* at this point is thus XXXVII, XLI, XL, and XXXVIII.

[2] Most of the sketches alluded to have not been preserved. All of the sketches that occur in the manuscript are reproduced.

Soon after I wrote last, I was endeavouring to make ye *Lyre* depend from ye Knott in a tolerable easy manner; but was not able to please *myself* in yt respect. Miss Meredyth I'm sure has candour enough to pardon me, when I own I am not entirely satisfy'd with ye Manner in which *She* has connected it. At the same Time, I am somewhat doubtfull, whether a *profest* Carver cou'd adjust this matter gracefully. At *best,* there is a Difficulty which your Ladyship mentions, & which I was in some measure aware of *before,* & this concerns the *projection* of the lower Part of the Lyre. All I can say is this, that if it *does* project, it must project so much (your Urn being small *downwards*) that it will injure ye Appearance of ye Urn from ye two remaining sides: And if it *bends with* the *Urn,* it will be strangely unnatural. Perhaps your Ladyship will ask the Carver's opinion here. This Consideration occasion'd me, (while the Man was measuring ye Urns at Hagley) to *try Fancies;* in order to discover whether you cou'd not introduce some of ye *Poetical Attributes* to advantage on the *Pedestal.* The Result of which, I send your Ladyship in these three or four Sketches. You will please to observe that the *Ionick* Proportion is not observ'd very accurately in any of ye Pedestals except Number V. And *even there,* not so in regard to ye *smaller members* of *Base* & *Capital.* And yet I believe the Plinth, ye Base, the Shaft, & the Capital are each of a proper Height, so yt you see the Figure of ye Ionick Pedestal in *general.* I will now speak a word concerning each Number.

No I I think the Oval wreath, manag'd in this manner, has a good effect within ye *oblong square;* and furnishes out an agreeable ornament for *one* side of your Pedestal. If you think so too, the Query then will be whether you like some such Festoon as this on ye same side of Urn, over it, or whether you wou'd not prefer ye antient Pipe & Fistula as being properly exhibited together or at ye same time with ye wreath below, & yet affording more variety yn ye Festoon here express'd.

No II If your Ladyship shou'd be inclin'd to give up the *surrounding Festoon* upon ye Urn (& take ye Pipe &c:) you will want some-thing by way of Ballance on ye opposite side, for wch Reason I have sketch'd out another sort of one upon ye Urn, & have shewn you the Effect of a Lyre upon the Pedestal. At ye same Time I own yt the Lyre on ye Pedestal *here* gives it too *considerable* an Air in proportion to the Urn; wch ought certainly to appear as principal.

No III. If the Lyre was too considerable *alone* on ye former Pedestal, you will have more just objections to this; so I say no more about it. As to the Festoons *round* the Urns, I speak *once for all,* that I prefer *natural Flowers* & did not mean any thing else, even in No I. tho I scrawl'd over those others for Quickness.

No IV. This may only serve to add to your Choice, and y^t but little truly.

No V. I believe you will like ye Proportion of this Pedestal; which, as I said before, may be right in *general,* (unless your Author deceives me.) The *Neck* or Part y^t comes betwixt y^e *Plinth* & the *Urn* is at *best,* I suppose, a *modernism,* and must not be allow'd you. I sketch'd it for variety. The Ornament upon ye Urn here I like a good deal, only it shou'd be somewhat *higher* on ye Body of it. Quere, whether this Ornament on ye Urn & a Lyre on ye Pedestal (of but low *Relieve*) wou'd not furnish out one handsome Side? And then ye Laurel wreath on ye Pedestal of No I, and the slight Festoon on ye Urn of No II, to decorate ye Pedestal and the Urn for another View. NB. This supposes your Views to be opposite.

As to what I call y^e *Necks* (for want of a better word) I can only wish you not to have them too *thick;* & I suppose both the *Urns* and *they* may be shap'd at Discretion. You lose some *relative* Beauty by receding occasionally from ye Antients, but you often gain some *absolute* Beauty by so doing.

Thus have I finish'd a tedious *Comment* on a very stupid *Performance;* enough to make you all wish me hanging by the string, on which I said the *Harp* shou'd Hang; but if your Ladyship can glean any thing from w^t I've been *saying* or *drawing,* I beg you wou'd apply it as you please. Compound, separate, transform the particular Parts & decorations as you think fit. I have no Fame in Building, at *present* to lose; And I wou'd give all I shall ever *acquire* to see this Urn both plan'd & situated so as to appear very *solemn* & venerable; infusing an agreeable Melancholy into all Bosoms y^t respected Mr Somerville.

I hope Tom will arrive before Mrs Meredyth's Departure from Barrels. I imagin'd their stay at Barrels had been longer, & then I propos'd to myself ye Pleasure of seeing them. I am not *contented* in this Disappointment; & yet I believe I *ought;* For I have an *Inklin* y^t your Ladyship has set me in a better Light, than my Conversation can ever answer. However if your Ladyship be so kind as to inform me when they come *next,* I will most eagerly risque any Disadvantage of *that* kind, to enjoy a Pleasure which will so amply ballance it. Methinks this last Sentence looks some how faint & languid, & to express but half my Sentiments. Your Ladyship however will witness for me, y^t I esteem no one but on account of *Taste* & *Generosity* of Temper, & will on y^t account vindicate my *Sincerity* when I desire my *best Respects* to M^rs & Miss Meredyths. I am to thank Miss Harriet for demolishing ye Precipice by ye Pitt Side, & converting it into a Slope, which, (as I *conceive* it), is ye very thing I've been labouring at ever since I knew Barrels. I am to thank Miss Patty for ye little Boy from *Watteau;* who, this Minute, peeps at me over my Chimney-Glass, and looks exceeding archly — Please, my Lady, to give my Service to Mr Outing if he comes, & tell him he neither visits me, nor gives me his Reasons — I'm oblig'd to your Ladyship for ye Sight of Mr Hall's Sermon: He applies many scripture Phrases very spirituously — Lord Dudley is gone this Day to London; call'd up I believe very suddenly; but on what Account, I cannot penetrate; tho' I sate up with him on Friday Night last to an Hour wn many Hearts are open — I conceive The Mechanick Part of Architecture to be a science easily acquir'd, & that a tolerable good *native* Taste is generally what gives ye Distinction — Old Pedley is hewing me two small Gothick Turrets for my building — He desires me to mention him to your Ladyship; says he has work'd you some Urns formerly & shou'd be glad to serve you hereafter. He is an honest man, will be *glad* to work *cheap,* & as to ye *manual operation,* I fancy works very well — I have made two little Islands in ye stream that runs thro Virgil's Grove; The *Stream* appears considerably larger, & ye *ground* is mended. I will not give my opinion of these Alterations *yet* — I have procur'd some charming Sans-pareille, with a Cargo of exquisite Havannah from London. As Cibber says *moderate matters* in ye Country serve for one's Amusement!

I have taken you too long from ye Conversation of your Visitants, when every Minute is valuable.

I desire to be always esteemd
    your Ladyship's most oblig'd & most obedient humble Servt
                    W. Shenstone

I sent a servant, because you desir'd to have ye Dimensions of ye Urns before Mrs Meredyth left Barrels.

Quere whether the Tibia &c: are ever carv'd wth out any *support;* but I believe they are — not to represent ye things themselves, but ye carving of an Urn.

Before I receiv'd your Ladyship's last Letter I had been scrawling upon Paper those small draughts that are mark'd No I. II. III.

No I. I have some little fondness for ye surrounding Wreath with 4 Knotts — but I think the Urn shou'd have *some* Decoration where ye Pedestal has any: And this wreath with 4 Knotts, instead of two, produces as little Irregularity as any thing — But after all, you like a plain Urn best; and a plain one no *doubt* will have ye best effect at a distance.

No II. A whim merely! And yet I think a French-Horn wreath'd with Laurel (in Allusion to ye Chace) wou'd be ye properest decoration in ye World for Mr Somerville. But As I cou'd not manage it so as to *look well* I dropt that, & give up *this*.

No III. I doubt this decoration upon ye Urn wou'd project so much as to be disagreeable on y^e *other* sides; even tho' you shou'd like it on *this*. I have also drawn it much too large.

After I receivd y^r Letter I drew No IV & No V.

No IV is I think a neat Urn, & I am much mistaken if you do not approve of that ornament on ye Pedestal. I added Flutes *here,* for a Reason before mention'd (viz) y^t ye Eye seems to require some ornament on ye Urn where there is some on ye Pedestal. And the Ornaments here will happen at proper distances.

No V. As I rather concluded from y^r Letter y^t you wou'd chuse this Very kind of Urn, I drew it with some w^t more Attention y^n ye rest. The Urn itself is I think well proportion'd, and ye Pedestal *pretty* exact according to y^r Friend Scammozi. Yet perhaps ye modern Practice may somewhat vary, & ye Pedestal may very safely, (& usually is) left to ye Workman. If Mr Hands supervises it, it will be right. His Calculation is so, & what makes ye difference at Hagley is ye Superior Height of a *Strawberry* to y^e *Ball* wch we propose: and tis better — y^r Ladyship must yourself determine whether you like y^e *double* Plinth above ye Pedestal wch raises y^r Urn about two inches & half. I us'd it on *mine,* & am glad I did; tho it is not so at Hagley.³ It must be considerd y^t my situation is extremely low, & y^rs will be upon ground y^t rises gradually — I believe I shall like it *there too,* but you may take Mr Hands's opinion when he comes — Most of y^e *Bodies* of ye Urns I draw are seven Parts at broadest an[d] *eight* Parts in Height. This (No V) for Instance is meant to be 21 Inches broad, & 24 high.

I am oblig'd to you for ye sight of y^r Urn, wch with ye Alteration of a proportionably thicker Foot & Cap will be pretty near alike to this (No V.) I fancy. I took ye Liberty to set a good joyner to copy it which he has done, very indifferently. Two of them make me top-ornaments for a triflingly small Cabinet wch you may remember in my Room. — I lead

³ Theirs are as Nº II & III. [Shenstone]

an Extreme dull Life this time of ye year, & am forc'd to indulge myself with continual Amusements from ye Bookseller. If I live to grow very old (wch I know I shant) I will have no other Bill. The Books I have *now* sent for are "The Life of Socrates,"⁴ & "The Theory of agreeable Sensations" lately publish'd; together with Langley's Book with ye quaint Title of "ye Builder's Jewell" — Has y^r Ladyship ever seen or do you care to see the genuine tryal of my Lord Lovat — In my opinion tis well worth reading. Poor old Lovat seems to represent Sr John Falstaff as well as Quin ever did. Tis a Pamphlett, but an half guinea one — & I can lend it you as well as not. — I desire my Compliments to Mr Allen & Mr Hall, hope to see y^r Ladyship at Barrels this Xmas, entreat y^t you would excuse this scrawl, & am once more, your Ladyships most oblig'd &c:

NB. a plain Inscription on ye Principal Side, only. Perhaps more in taste if without even Armigero Esq: Mottos on the other sides

107. To LADY LUXBOROUGH¹

The Leasows Novr 26 1749

MADAM,

I have been of late so conversant with *Lists* & *Astragals; Plinths* & *Cymatia;* y^t your Ladyship will have good Fortune if I entertain you with any thing besides. Yet of all ye Urns & Pedestals I have drawn within this Fortnight, I like none so well as ye sort you seem to prefer. The principal Debate I have with myself, is, how much or how little they shou'd be ornamented, & herein, (as different Tastes may be good in their kind) I think all persons y^t build, shou'd allow something to their own natural Relish.

I like y^e *situation* you propose for ye Urn extremely; at least I *remember* none so proper. The Idea of *y^t Place* has constantly occurr'd to me, as often as your urn was mention'd; and tho' I durst not be positive y^t your Ladyship and your *ingenious visitants* might not possibly discover some one scene y^t was preferable, yet I fancy most of my Letters of late must have glanc'd obliquely towards that very corner. I own I have some partiality for this double oak, as the First time I saw Mr Somerville at Barrels, I sate with him upon ye Bench y^t is at ye Foot of it. How far this

⁴ See Letter 114, n2.
¹ B. M. Add. MSS 28958, fol. 72ff. This answers Nos. XLI and XL of Lady Luxborough's *Letters* (see above, Letter 106, n1), and as she says in the beginning of her No. XXXIX of December 6, 10, and 12, crossed her No. XXXVIII of November 29 in Birmingham. The date of her No. XXXVIII is confirmed by this reference and by the fact that Shenstone's of December 5 answers it.

Partiality may depreciate my Decision, I must leave your Ladyship to determine. As to the management of this situation, ye secreteing ye Urn, ye distance it shou'd stand from ye Foot of ye Oak, & ye Breadth of ye Area that shou'd [be] left around it, I will offer my futile opinion when I wait upon you at Barrels, which I trust will be, sometime, before your Urn can be compleated. Mean-time, I can see no Reason why it shou'd not produce a good Effect from *several* Points of View. For Instance, "From ye Bottom of yr Service-walk & all along it, appearing hence in an open area slightly surrounded with a few trees & thickets: "From ye Coppice "From ye Place where your Chairs are and where you propose a Root-house: "From some Part of ye tall Elm-walk as one approaches ye House; And perhaps also, "from some Part of yr Shrubbery. All these, besides the near view, en passant, of ye Front which you intend to ornament. Of these, the View from ye Bottom of ye Service walk or Corner of your Garden, as far as I can recollect, will be by no means inferior to any of ye Rest. Perhaps your Ladyship may be well *acquainted* with all these advantages, but I chose to enumerate them, because if your Urn is to be calculated for all these Points, it ought out of doubt to have no *considerable* irregularity. I am of opinion your Ladyship need not fear ye *Laurel wreath* upon this Account; Unless the *Relieve* be very high indeed, it will hardly be discover'd from any Part but where you wish it *shou'd*. My Reason is, that you effectually lose sight of ye sides of a *square,* when you stand in Front of it; And tho a greater Projection may appear on them at some *considerable distance,* yet even *there,* such a *slight* projection will scarce be seen at all. (The Case is otherwise with a *Round* of which you see one half.) If your Ladyship think so too, you may carve this wreath on ye Pedestal very safely; If you think otherwise, you must either omit ye Laurel wreath, or add some slight Festoon to ballance it. Or something of this Nature

(Mantling, I think they call it) may serve, which I shou'd imagine must cost but a trifle. So much for ye Pedestal. Only I must add yt I blunder'd in respect of ye *Ionick* order. The *Shaft* of *that* is nearly square. Tis ye *Composit* you will find to answer your *Idea;* & if you direct ye Workman to let ye 60 *minutes* of his *model* stand for *Quarters-of-Inches,* it will produce you a Pedestal exactly similar to their smaller one at Hagley.

As to ye Inscriptions, if your Ladyship prefer an *English* one, and cou'd find a Motto in Mr Somerville's own Writings yt was both good in *itself* and *applicable* to this Purpose (as you know Shakespear's Pedestal is thus supply'd) it wou'd have a double Beauty. If otherwise, you make use of the *Latin* ones, The Inscription must also be in Latin *betwixt the Wreath;* the Motto "His saltem" on ye Plinth above it, and, (to avoid an improper Jumble,) that of Postquam &c: on y^t Side of ye Pedestal y^t Fronts ye Service Walk on ye upper part of the Shaft. It will also add something to ye Beauty of this side — And now for ye Urn itself properly so call'd. Since I wrote last I have discover'd a method of suspending ye Fistula which I believe your Ladyship will approve. And as you have no Fondness for ye surrounding wreath, you will probably think this itself to be ornament sufficient. Tis better *not* to add ye Lyre here because the Carving of these alone may be so much ye bolder; whereas if you adjoin ye Lyre, the multiplicity of Parts, in so small a compass, will occasion a confusion; & there will be no one Instrument distinguishable. If this single Trophy be not carv'd in very *high* Relieve (and I think it need not as you are to view this Front-side *near*) you will have no occasion for any more carving to ballance this in Profile, I believe. But if your Carver be of a different opinion he may add this kind of Festoon or this mantling on ye 3 remaining Sides —

This Ornament (something like a Strawberry) is upon ye top Of ye smaller Urn at Hagley.

If your Ladyship remember, I *said,* ye Foliage on ye Foot of ye Urn cou'd not be *allow'd* you, even tho you *had* a *Fondness* for it. I do now most explicitely & unconditionally give up the *Foliage,* not only *there,* but also on ye neck; and if you please, y^e . . .² also in . . . places; And if you shou'd insist n. . . ye Laurell . . . on ye foot of ye Pedestal. Your Urn will be in y^e *higher* taste, if you have no other carv'd work yⁿ the Tibia & Fistula suspended; but in this Case I cannot advise, because I cannot discover what I shou'd do myself.

Old Pedley is now at Work for me — The Devil take all Gothicism! I was told (& by an *experienc'd* Judge) that I might have two Pinnacles hewn in stone for my Gothick Building, for a *trifle.* They are now done, & have taken more stone than wou'd have built me an Urn; & cost me *within* a trifle as much as ye Building. I am as full of Cholers as Parson Hugh Evans was; but tis done! the Building *is* improv'd by them & I have gain'd *Experience.*

This last W**ee**k they have hewn me also an Urn, almost big enough for y^e *'Bacco*-stopper of an Inhabitant of *Brobdignag.* And yet, small as

² The manuscript is defective at this point.

it is, It has I think a charming Effect, from ye situation I have given it in Virgil's Grove. The Inscription I design for it has supply'd me with a Hint for a *Device* and *Motto* on a Seat. Tis I think a tolerably genteel one. This . . . The second is added by way of *Companion;* an Altar ornamented & highly blazing . . . with an Inscription to ye Goddess *Friendship*. But tis ye first y^t is y^e *galante* one, viz, An Urn upon it's Pedestal — the Motto "To *remember* you, than to *converse* with others." But this by way of deviation. To return to old Pedley. He desires his Duty to your Ladyship, & offers to undertake ye Urn, (at *Barrels*) & find Stone, (your own Teem drawing it Home,) for Four Pounds. He means, *exclusive* of Carving. At this Rate he will work it in *Cobberton* or *Commerton*-stone (some such Name) which he says is better y^n Warwick stone. But I fancy this is not material. He says ye Warwick-People *may* afford to do it cheaper (as He lives at a distance & must have some *previous* Trouble) but He questions whether they *will*. After all I *think* I can agree with him on terms more advantageous to your Ladyship. In ye mean time, you will please to learn what they will do it for, at *Warwick*. The *Terms* propos'd for one 21 Inches high, seem'd to me exorbitant; I hope they do not mean to *raise them* in proportion to this larger Size.

The Pamphletts & Books I receiv'd were, I thought, such as your Ladyship wou'd not regard. Of ye first Sorts were, a sale-work Performance entitled ye Life of Charles Duke of Somerset;[3] and a Letter from Dr Addington[4] of Reading on his refusing to consult wth a licens'd Physician — The *Books* were, Dr Grey's Edition of Hudibras,[5] Sandbys new Horace wth antiques, & a little History of England[6] wch I buy as a memorandum-Book.

Mr Wintle, of whom I buy my sans-pareille, is a Perfumer next Door to Temple-Bar. I think his sans-pareille is good — but his Havannah, & Lavender water are, I *know,* extremely in Vogue. He seems to me to have most things y^t he deals in good of their kind; and is a very obliging Man. I lodg'd there 3 Months one year, & have dealt with him for Lavender Water, Wash-Baths, & Havannah ever since.

I have been so tedious (as you must needs think me) in explaining my

[3] *The Memoirs of the Late Duke of Somerset* are noticed in the Register of Books of the *Gentleman's Magazine* for October, 1749.
[4] Dr. Anthony Addington (1713–90) was a physician of distinction; he attended Lord Chatham in 1767 and the Prince of Wales in 1788.
[5] Dr. Grey's *Hudibras*, with cuts by Hogarth, first appeared in 1744.
[6] *A Brief History of England; by Way of Question and Answer*, by J. Lindsay, is noticed in the Register of Books of the *Gentleman's Magazine* for October, 1749. This may be the one Shenstone bought.

insignificant opinions wth regard to ye Urn, that I have but little Paper left to make my proper Acknowledgments, for ye latter & very obliging Part of your Letter — No Entertainment can engage me more yⁿ what you give me a glimpse of in Miss Meredyths *Acting* Plays. I am particularly glad y^t She excells in ye charming Part of *Ophelia* — The Green Book *shall* be presented to you, with ye Addition of ye Ode your Ladyship mentions, and every other Improvement I am *capable* of makeing — My Summer-house must not come down as *yet*, for I cannot give up my good Friends y^e *Mob*, 'till my Place has a *larger* share of *polite* Admirers — I beg my Compliments to Mr Allen & Mr Hall, and am your Ladyship's most oblig'd and most obedient

Servt
Will: Shenstone

108. To LADY LUXBOROUGH [1]

The Leasows December ye 5th 1749

MADAM,

I remember, when I was of Oxford, the *Moderator* us'd to put an End to our Disputations-in-Form by ye Latin Word, "sufficit"; a word of altogether ye same Import with your Ladyship's "cela suffit." And indeed considering ye Futility of those Exercises in general, a very *slender* Portion of them might be said to be sufficient. But as every syllable of yours, is, without a *Compliment,* of greater Importance, you will never be able to produce ye Idea of Satiety, any more yⁿ you will to occasion an expression of it. Your Ladyship has indeed of late been mighty good; & I too, tho' not altogether so good, *did* write a Letter, and send a Packet, which you might *possibly* have receiv'd before you wrote your last. 'Twas an extreme dull Letter; all, as I remember upon ye subject of Urns; concerning which I must also introduce a Word or two in *this;* tho not just at present, least I scrawl my Paper over with nothing but *Circles* & Elipticks. I have interested myself in ye Westminster Election ever since ye Poll began, & shou'd be glad to find that Ld Trentham had exchang'd his seat in ye House of Commons for a Seat in ye French Play-house — as ye News-writer well expresses it. Is not y^t a droll application "Sr George he is for England &c:" I think wth your Ladyship entirely in

---

[1] B. M. Add. MSS 28958, fol. 76ff. This letter answers Lady Luxborough's of November 29, 1749 (*Letters,* No. XXXVIII). Her No. XXXIX of December 6, 10, and 12, 1749, replies to the present letter and to the one immediately following, which she meanwhile received. The date of her No. XXXIX is thus confirmed, including the misplaced postscript (see above, Letter 106, n1).

Regard to yᵉ Execution of Penter.² I admire, with you, the King's Speech to yᵉ Duke of New-castle; and think yᵉ Circumstance might be made good use of on Sʳ Watkyn's Monument. It might also have been a striking Part of Mʳ Cowley's Epitaph, yᵗ King Charles yᵉ second said "He had not left a better Man behind him in England." The Sayings of Princes will have an additional Weight; & this of his present Majesty, yᵉ *more* so, as it was spoken of a Person yᵗ he esteem'd his Enemy. Nevertheless there is a grand objection to my Scheme, which your Ladyship's Penetration has already discover'd, & which I need not therefore mention. You have sent me such a Deal of fashionable Intelligence, yᵗ I might *appear* polite at once, were I situated in a Country where my Politeness wou'd be *visible*. A Fashionable Word is certainly of equal Importance wᵗʰ a New fashion'd Sleeve or Skirt of ones Coat. I have sometimes known a poor Country Parson (when he has caught one at his Patron's Table) as glad of it as one yᵗ findeth great spoils; You tell me of yʳ *Epigrammatical* Turn of yᵉ very fashionable World. I can only say yᵗ I have remark'd *inexpressible* Folly in yᵗ Sphere ever since I can remember. Acrosticks! Riddles! Puns! Conundrums! Ideal Vomits! Selling of Bargains! &c: &c: What a Catalogue! As to Miss Hamilton's Ballad³ if I cou'd possibly tolerate *Puns* (on wᶜʰ yᵉ Whole depends) I shou'd call it a good one; For it is easy and genteel. As it is, it will be of great Use to me to shew about; since I have try'd it upon two or three common Capacities in my Neighbourhood, & it pleases them to yᵉ Life — Ought not one to envy yᵉ Gentleman his *Lady* much more yⁿ his Play;⁴ which I think as dull as most I have read, always excepting Dʳ Hoadleys⁵ — I remember there is a Dedication of Erasmus's Praise of Folly to Sʳ Thomas More, & in it a very far-fetch'd Pun upon his Name. Moros you must know is greek for a Fool. The Author tells him, that he was influenc'd in the Choice of his Patron by his Sur-name of *More* which was as nearly similar to yᵗ of his Subject (Moria or Folly) as he himself was distant from The Thing — The Planting in Lines *where you mention* is undoubtedly right; So are yᵉ Vistas you propose; & I wish your Ladyship better Luck

---

² See Lady Luxborough's *Letters*, p. 142. Fielding's pamphlet, *A True State of the Case of Bosavern Pen Lez*, is noticed on page 528 of the *Gentleman's Magazine* for November, 1749, and abstracted on page 512 of the same issue.

³ Lady Luxborough says (*Letters*, p. 144), "I will send you a good pretty innocent Ballad, wrote by a Miss Jenny Hamilton, a pretty girl about town, who is going to marry More, the author of the Foundling, and writes word of it herself in this manner to an intimate friend in the country. It consists, as you will find, of puns . . . upon his name . . ."

⁴ "*The Foundling. A Comedy.* by Mr. Moor, Author of the Fables for the female sex" is noticed in the Register of Books of the *Gentleman's Magazine* for February, 1748.

⁵ Dr. Hoadley's play was a comedy, *The Suspicious Husband* (1747).

among Ecclesiasticks⁶ yⁿ it has been my Lot to experience. I fear yᵉ Mischief *he* has begun in yᵗ Coppice will be of much greater Extent yⁿ I at first apprehended. I wish the King wou'd make him Bishop of Nova-Scotia, where he might display his Talent of extirpating Trees to yᵉ Benefit of yᵉ Country. *Here* his Advice has been prejudicial both to . . . ,⁷ and to yᵉ Owner — I have had a Mind to surprize your Ladyship next Spring with an Urn (not yᵗ before-mention'd) in a retir'd Part of my Farm wᶜʰ you have not seen; But I can contain yᵉ secret no longer — Old Pedley then and his Son have almost finish'd me a Plain Urn, wᶜʰ is to be set up on Friday next. I have gain'd some experience herein wᶜʰ may be of use to your Ladyship — First then yᵉ Stone itself will cost you about half a Guinea for yᵉ Urn & Pedestal, exclusive of Carriage. As far as I can gather, it is somewhat more yⁿ a Month's Work for *one* Man this Winter Time; & less in proportion for two. But herein I cannot be exact — As for yᵉ Stone it will cost you three-pence or three-pence half penny a Foot, & about 35 Foot will be sufficient on yᵉ Whole. I shou'd imagine a Plain Urn of this Size shou'd not exceed 3 Pounds, including stone and tho' you pay *full Wages,* wᶜʰ I own *I do not.* I took Advantage of old Pedley's Vacation, and *must* have done so, or dropt my Urn. I shall inscribe it on yᵉ Body of yᵉ Urn itself with only two Words & one Letter. I had a violent Hankering after yᵉ *surrounding Wreath* but found yᵗ yᵉ small *size* of yᵉ Urn (yᵉ same you propose) yᵉ *softness* of yᵉ *Stone,* & yᵉ *Dearness* of Carving, deterr'd me; the two former Circumstances I would have your Ladyship weigh deliberately. I *believe* Warwick stone is soft. I hope to hear from your Ladyship & am with all yᵉ Affection my Respect will permit me to express, Madᵐ

Your Ladyship's
W. S.

Don't, my Lady, speak of it; but Mʳ M[iller]⁸ tells it about yᵗ my Grove exceeds anything at Hagley of yᵉ kind; *but yᵗ yᵉ Buildings at Hagley are better!* Is not this drole?

⁶ Another reference to his quarrel with Parson Wilmot (see above, Letter 102).
⁷ The manuscript is defective at this point.
⁸ Mr. Miller, as Shenstone explains in Letter 110.

109. To LADY LUXBOROUGH[1]

Saturday-Night
The Leasows, December ye 7th 1749

MADAM,

I have Reason to think yt I am *now* trespassing upon your Ladyship's Patience; but my Motive for running some small Risque in this Respect, is as follows. Mr Pedley has, to-day, finish'd, & set-me-up a plain neat Urn & Pedestal; which, to say ye truth, I wou'd hardly exchange for either of their ornamental Urns at Hagley. He lives at some Distance Northward from hence, & will be now going Home, unless your Ladyship chuses to employ him. I told your Ladyship the Result of my Experience in my last Letter, as to ye Quantity of Stone, ye Time it takes up &c: I told you likewise that I took some Advantage of their Necessities in ye Price *I* gave them — but, as the 'Pothecary says in Shakespear,

My *Poverty* & not my *will* consented. —[2]

So, in Short, I now take ye Liberty of sending you the old Man's Son, with such *general* Proposals as they have this Moment made me "That they will either *agree* with your Ladyship by ye Day, or they will agree wth you by the *whole;* & find, or *not* find the Stone, as your Ladyship pleases: And in either of these Cases will finish your Urn *cheaper* yn you will procure it done at Warwick, leaving ye Determination to your Ladyship's own Breast. In other words they will compleat ye Urn & leave their Recompence to your Ladyship without farther Limitation; A Method wch I fancy you will hardly pursue —

I have nothing to *add* on this Head; I wou'd only do *them* ye *Justice* of *repeating,* that I think they have both *behav'd,* & *done their Work,* well. Pedley is an inoffensive old Man, & seems to discover, notwithstanding his Infirmities, yt He has seen a good deal of ye World — And if *ye World* be taken in a *Scripture*-Sense, he has seen too *much* of it. He has been a great Sufferer by Undertaking Birmingham new-Church; wch was, I think, a *Design* of ye late Groom-Porters. Certain it is, yt he has been a great Sufferer by the Groom-porter himself; concerning wch he relates a Story not much to ye Groom-porter's Honour. So yt if your

---

[1] B. M. Add. MSS 28958, fol. 78ff. Lady Luxborough's letter of December 6, 10, and 12 (*Letters,* No. XXXIX) answers both this and Shenstone's of December 5, as their interrelations clearly show. The date of her No. XXXIX is thus confirmed, as is likewise the position of the postscript, in her *Letters* mistakenly appended to her Letter XLI. Her undated fragment No. LXXXIV also seems to intervene here, as it contains the only allusion I have found to Shenstone's urn to Somervile, to which he refers in the present letter and that immediately following. Her No. LXXXIV might thus be dated between December 7 (or 20) and 28, 1749, and would follow her No. XXXIX.

[2] *Romeo and Juliet,* V, i, 75.

Ladyship happen to employ him, The Act of *Charity* with regard to *him,* will occasion a Satisfaction to a Bosom like yours, as well as yᵉ Act of *Piety* in Regard to Mʳ Somerville. Also, if you can supply them wᵗʰ Lodging wᵗʰout Inconvenience, it will be *some* Amusement to you to see how they proceed — Upon reviewing what I have wrote, I seem to *press* yᵉ Affair; which I do not *mean* to *do*. I wou'd have your Ladyship consult only your *own* Opinion. I am not in yᵉ least interested.

I mention'd, in a former Letter, your Ladyship's *returning* those Urns I sketch'd out; but I meant nothing more yⁿ what you might effect by committing them to the *Flames*. If you please to fix what Ornament you chuse, I can sketch it out as well as if you sent them — Perhaps tho' they may be of some Use to your Ladyship in explaining your meaning to a *Carver*. I am asham'd of yᵉ *Fluctuation* of my Opinion in regard to yᵉ Ornaments. I am now afraid the *Fistula* &c: will render yᵉ Side-Form of yʳ Urn vastly irregular. However yʳ Determination before this time is *deliberate,* & 'tis no wide conclusion, to add that it is *right* — NB. *Fluting* is now, in my Opinion, Abominable; Worst of all on yᵉ *Body* of an Urn; as it shews itself on yᵉ lesser urn at Hagley.

I have thoughts of inscribing *my* Urn to Mʳ Somerville; and if so, I hope your Ladyship will assist here in crowning it with an anniversary Chaplet, & makeing such Libations as I can afford of Port-wine — whilst we sit in a Circle round it — But this the Spring, yᵗ produces every thing thats agreeable must also produce. And I do hereby promise to be a very faithfull Pilgrim & Votary at yᵉ Urn your Ladyship shall erect. You know there were Devotions paid to our Lady of Walsingham &c: as well as to our Lady of Loretto; And tho' yours probably may be esteem'd Mʳ Somerville's primary & peculiar Urn, yet there may not be wanting those, who, in yᵉ Blindness of their Superstition, may to mine attribute equal Merit.

Poor Mʳ Somerville! What wou'd he say now — as a Separate Spirit — to see how we are employ'd? I leave it to yʳ Ladyship to pursue this Thought — I *turn'd* much of yᵉ Urn (properly so call'd) wᵗʰ my own Hands; wᶜʰ your Ladyship may also do & *add* to yᵉ Honour you do him, unless you think it too laborious. I hope to wait upon you e'er 'tis done, & am in yᵉ *mean* time, and shall be *then,* & at all times,
   your Ladyships most oblig'd & most obedient Servant
                Will: Shenstone

Mʳ Outing's Laziness first affected his *Riding;* next, his *Writing;* what can it influence next? — I am afraid when I meet him, I shall find him *dumb.*

110. To LADY LUXBOROUGH[1]

The Leasows, Decr ye 20th 1749

MADAM,

I am really concern'd for Mrs Davis's Loss, not only as it affects your Ladyship, but as she is a Person whom I thought extremely agreeable during the time I had an opportunity of seeing her at Barrels; & whom I have not ceas'd to esteem ever since — Now I mention *those Days,* I cannot avoid acknowledging that I never recollect them, but with a great *deal* of y^t melancholy satisfaction which Pleasures *past* afford one. Since that Time what a Number of Deaths, what a Number of Changes! And yet your Ladyship supports the Genius of the Place, & we find no kind of Deficiency while we converse with you at Barrels. Yet your *Ladyship* must suffer on these Accounts, & we are all *born* to suffer. It wou'd for ought I know bear some Dispute whether our Griefs (which are always heighten'd by a Delicacy of Imagination) are best reliev'd by downright *Philosophy,* or by y^e *Diversion* one may effect by means of *Amusement.* But I think it probable, y^t, wherever the Power of *Imagination* prevails, it will be most readily reliev'd by affording it a *Diversion*. And perhaps it may be *Philosophy* likewise so to do. I have my share of Misfortunes, & I feel them very sensibly; & if I were to fill my Letter with *these alone,* (as I cou'd *easily do*) what wou'd it avail? Evils there *are* in ye world which affect individuals, & also societies; but which are, no doubt, connected with ye good of the *Whole,* & must remain as long as that *Whole* continues. At least, if those *evils* are not connected with universal good, The *Principles* are *from* which they often flow. For Instance, moral Evil, (which wou'd be easily prov'd ye greatest) flows *from* ye Nature of Free-will itself. This occasions variety of Passions in ye world, & these, very often, malice and *mutual* Mischeif. I ask Pardon for this Pedantry, & will hurry out of it as fast as I can — Mr Outing is gone, I find, before this Time. He is a very sincere Friend, but a very indolent Acquaintance; a Fault of which it ill becomes me to complain — I am pleas'd with your Ladyship's Project concerning Pigeons; But we must not *practice* it. Old *Emme* wou'd inevitably fire her Musquet at them, tho' I believe at ye same time she hardly knows a *Gun* from a Beesom. There is a Person in this Parish, who, she thinks, will here after be her successor, & she hates him most inordinately. And I am sure y^e *innocence* of *Doves,* in this *Case,* wou'd not protect them — As to ye Designs for

---

[1] B. M. Add. MSS 28958, fol. 80ff. This answers No. XXXIX of Lady Luxborough's *Letters* and helps confirm its date. Shenstone's specific allusion to Lord Archer's inquiry establishes the position of her postscript, in her *Letters* mistakenly appended to Letter XLI. Her No. XLII of December 28, 1749, answers the present letter.

seals, (tho I laid ye chief stress on ye former) your Ladyship chose right. The Altar makes a better *Impression,* & ye Inscription is more in y^e *simple antique* taste. The former is ye more artfull & after ye manner of ye French — See what comes of Art and Disguise! The Person whose Name I wrote with a Dash was not Mr Meredyth, but Mr *Miller* — I wonder'd he shou'd speak of my Buildings as *any* thing; which are — *nothing.* My very Root-houses have as much Pretence to Architecture, as any Building I have; unless I may except this last Urn. And now the subject of Urns is very fairly introduc'd. I think the Price they ask at Warwick is not unreasonable. I very much question whether Pedley (if one reckons his Board) wou'd have done it for ye same. Indeed he said (as I mention'd before) y^t ye Warwick-People *might* afford to do it cheaper y^n He. He told me, before he went from hence, y^t he durst by no means venture to undertake it at a Distance from Barels; because, he thought, there wou'd be ye utmost Danger of breaking ye mouldings in ye Carriage. My Charity tempted me to say more y^n I needed in his Behalf, but I own I shall be very well satisfy'd with your having it done at Warwick; provided there can be any method found of conveying it safe to Barrels — Your objection to y^e *season* of y^e *year* is a very good Reproof of my *Precipitancy.* But *my* Work does not depend upon *Mortar.* The distinct Parts of ye Pedestal &c: are of one entire stone; except ye lower Plinth, (which had better have been so too), but was in Parts on acc^t of Carriage. I wou'd then recommend it to y^r Ladyship, to have y^e *"lower-Plinth,"* the Base, "the Shaft, and y^e *Capital* of ye Pedestal" of one entire stone, a-piece; The *"Plinth* or *Plinths,"* the "Foot," the "Body," & y^e "Top of Urn," ye same. The Workman will not object to it, as it saves in Work, what it wastes in Stone, & *more* — I have sent your Ladyship a few more Draughts, of which I will speak a Word on a separate Paper. I am well assur'd your answer was for ye best, when my Lord Archer did me ye Favour to enquire after my Place. If I have ye further Honour of waiting on Ld Archer in ye Spring, I shall probably mention ye Leasows as an easy distance from Sr Harry Gough's if my Lord shou'd be inclin'd to take an Afternoon's Ride. The Honour he wou'd do me wou'd be very certain; the satisfaction he wou'd find here wou'd be more precarious. I am very zealously your Ladyship's most oblig'd

W. Shenstone

111. To LADY LUXBOROUGH[1]

The Leasows, Janry ye 28th 1749–50

MADAM,

When I own that I have been return'd to the Leasows almost these nine days, you will scarce imagine me to have been so impatient, as I really *have,* to make my proper Acknowledgments for your obliging Reception at Barrels, & to enquire after ye Progress of ye Schemes you then took in Hand. But a kind of *tumultuary unsettled* Spirits after what *I* call a pretty *long excursion,* indispos'd me for writing; & I cou'd never write with any degree of satisfaction to myself, till now. *Now* indeed, I return to ye correspondence with which you are pleas'd to honour me, with my usual Pleasure; no Places I have seen, & no Conversations I have heard, being capable of extinguishing the Relish I have for your Ladyships Company & Barrels. My principal jaunt in ye way of curiosity was a Ride to Mr Miller's, of whom your Ladyship has formerly heard me speak.[2] He happen'd to be from home, but we saw his *Place,* and his Improvements round it. He lives at ye Bottom of a Hill wch communicates with Edge-hill. There is nothing beautifull in ye outside of his *house* but a couple of Bow-windows, built in ye Gothick Taste; which are really delightfull. His Farm lies betwixt his House & ye Hill. He has therefore, rightly enough, taken ye advantage of some *double* Hedges which surround his Farm to make a shady Path betwixt yt conveys you to his Hill. This Path very *fortunately* begins as soon as you come out of his Library or Parlour, an advantage, (I mean this of getting immediately into Shade), which *I* can never obtain for *my* situation. In this Path you have some Views over yt flat Country, *something* variegated, but not *much;* Before I go further, let me mention that his Trees are detestable, viz: old *Ashes* stunted & crop'd & newly sprouting out again: such as ought by all means to be destroy'd for ye sake of Trees of a more agreeable *Form;* more early *vegetation,* & more lasting *verdure.* Before we ascend the wood we are taken to an artificial Piece of ground & water-work. Tis a detach'd thing; utterly unlike, & I think inconsistent with ye genius of his Land in general. At ye Top of this is a Reservoir (which as Lord Bolingbroke well observes may spurt forth a little frothy water on some wdy Day, & be dry ye rest of ye year (alluding to our modern orators in Parliament). It falls over 3 rustick arches, runs down, thro broken stone work, to a Bason in ye midst of wch is a Jetteau; and on each side tumuls

---

[1] B. M. Add. MSS 28958, fol. 82ff. Apparently this and Lady Luxborough's letter of January 31, 1750 (*Letters,* No. XLIII) crossed in the mail.

[2] See the Index.

or little mounds of Earth artificially cast up. But this is a juvenile Performance, & only retain'd because it *is* there & has cost him money. After this we view'd an artificial Terrass y^t gives a view of ye Plain where ye Battle was fought,³ & of ye country round. This view pleases by dint of mere *extent,* for ye Country is not well variegated. From this you pass into his Wood, a slopeing Coppice like mine, but *larger.* He has here no building worth mentioning, & you pass by a winding ascent till you have a view of a hanging Lawn enclos'd on all sides with Wood-work. It has a wild & *Forest-like* appearance, and is terminated at ye End by a kind of *Eyetrap,* namely, ye End of a stable finish'd in ye way of a Door & Pediment, but slightly & in Plaister-work. I lik'd this Scene ye best of any, & I had ye Comfort to hear y^t Mr Lyttelton had done so before me. Hence you still ascend to a very large antique, octagonal Tower. The upper Room is highly finished in ye Gothick Taste; antique Shields blazon'd on ye Ceiling; Painted Glass in ye Windows, Gothick Niches, & Gothick Cornice. But on ye whole I am not pleas'd wth it. First, ye Stair-case breaks into ye Floor and is horrible; next, ye Height is so excessive y^t I cou'd not endure to look out of ye Windows; next, ye arch of ye Ceiling does not please me; & lastly, ye wretched Laboriousness & inconvenience of ye Ascent makes it not desireable to compleat a Room so expensively at that *Height.* Now as to ye Tower & Ruins he has added (for he has added a *Turret,* which is in *reality* some Poor body's Chimney & a magnificent stone Arch, which is ye Gate way to their House) they are to be consider'd from a different Point of view, namely his own House. Here I dont approve of them. First, because the Tow'r (of an extraordinary Height) attracts ye Eye too strongly, & takes from ye variety of which his Scene was capable. Next because the Ruins (tho a good deal of y^e *shatter'd* order when you are *near* 'em) at a *distance* seem too much a solid Lump, the Breaches & indeed ye Ruins themselves not being enough considerable. In ye last Place ye Top of ye Tower is detestable, & this he knows. I think I've nothing to add about his Place, but y^t he has taken advantage of a kind of separate Chappel in his Parish Church to make himself one of ye most magnificent & handsomest Pews I ever saw. Tis elevated almost equally with ye Pulpit & he has made a neat arch thro' which he enters it from without doors. Tis really stucco'd, has a Cornish, & a Cove-ceiling; & is large & Square; on one side of which is a plain marble monument to his Father — There is in his Churchyard ye Remains of a Monument to Captain Kingsmill, one of 4 Brothers y^t

---

³ At Edgehill the forces of Charles I and those of the Earl of Essex fought an inconclusive battle October 23, 1642.

were slain at Edgehill Fight. Tis entirely in Ruins; little more yn ye *cumbent* statue of *him,* remaining; but this perhaps not a bad one. Is it not astonishing yt Mr Miller does not remove this (since the Family takes no kind of notice of it) to some solemn Area in his wood before mention'd. Wou'd it not produce a striking effect there? as the story is both recent & real? Or, as ye Field of yt battle lies full in view & but just beneath his House, is it not strange yt he has not one Motto, Urn, or Obelisk, that might impress yt interesting Idea, & give a deep solemnity to his Recesses? I don't mean yt he shou'd bring *Party* into ye Case (tho this also wd suit *him,* or be at least consistent) but yt he might give an Urn or so to some worthy man yt was kill'd there, & add some Motto yt was *moral* yet *general*—Again, instead of concentrating ye View, & *forceing* ye Eye to his Castle, were it not better to have had *several* objects in his Wood, properly subordinate to one principal Building—But his *Scenes* are yet imperfect; & excepting his Castle, he has done infinitely less yn I expected. His Place may be greatly improved & no doubt it will; but he has a Dearth of Water, worse yn they at Hagley & which will subdue in me all envious Sensation when I view his Castle. I am tedious, & must have done. I send your Ladyship one more Draught of a Wreath interwoven wth ye French Horn. I am quite convinc'd yt it shou'd be wreathed somehow after this Manner. The twining wreath was *drawn* ye worst in those draughts I gave you, & that deceiv'd you; but whether or no, this be any better, pray, my Lady, give particular orders to ye Carver to twine ye Laurel round ye French Horn. I shall be glad to hear yr present Sentiments concerning ye Inscription. I am your Ladyships most oblig'd & most obedient faithfull Servant

Will Shenstone

I think on a revisal I am too censorious in regard to Mr Miller's Place—but I saw it at ye very worst time of ye year, & may give a more favourable Acct hereafter.

112. To LADY LUXBOROUGH[1]

The Leasows, Febr: ye 4th 1749–50

MADAM,

The Number of Lines I have wrote this day, and the unfitness of my Brain to dictate a single sentence, is past my Power of Expression. Yet

---

[1] B. M. Add. MSS 28958, fol. 86ff. This letter answers Lady Luxborough's of January 31, 1750 (*Letters,* No. XLIII), and confirms its date. The date is further confirmed by reference to a letter from the Duchess of Somerset (see note 2 below). Her No. XLIV answers the present letter.

am I oblig'd both by Interest and Gratitude to return the Letter[2] you so kindly communicated. And to return it without my sincere Acknowledgment were an injury to my real Sentiments; Therefore I must accompany it with a few Lines, & promise to add *more* & *better* hereafter — I would not give up ye smallest Part of the Duchess's Esteem to be inaugurated King of *Corsica* to-morrow; & shou'd I neglect your Commands in respect of her Letter, I might justly risque the Danger of never seeing any more of them. In *that* Case, what wou'd it avail, tho' She shou'd preserve some little Regard for me? Yet am I not so vain as to be ignorant y^t without your Ladyship's Interposition, there cou'd be no Hopes of it's Continuance — I think when I go to London, however, I shall have Effrontery enough, to get acquainted with that same Chaplain;[3] Some how or other, I know not how. I like him more for approveing y^n *simple* Performance y^n if he had applauded all I have wrote beside. Mr Outing's Letter arriv'd at the same Time with your Ladyship's. He says little more than to this purpose that he shall be glad to execute my Commands in Town; that he is a sincere *Friend,* tho' a dilatory *Correspondent.* I know him to be so, & therefore God bless him. Twill hardly ever be in *my Power* to do him any solid Service. I beseech your Ladyship to continue me in ye Remembrance of Mr Meredyth. He is *one* Man of ingenuity & Worth in a superiour station. Such an Acquaintance, as I wish; but find it difficult, to make — I wou'd willingly conclude here; but my vanity prompts me to tell your Ladyship, that the Earl of Stanford call'd on me with three other Gentlemen, this week, to see my Walks. Twou'd make you laugh to say that he was almost mir'd in them, but it was nearly the Case, in some particular Places. You know it is ye worst of *seasons;* & I may add it was ye worst of *Days* — However he was much struck with Virgils Grove, & particularly ye Cascade you were us'd to admire; gave it ye Preference to ye Rock Work &c: at Hagley, & said obliging Things. Had he indeed curs'd & calumniated every Part beside, I cou'd not have blam'd him, for we had Rain & Storm almost all ye Time we were walking. He gave me many friendly Invitations to Enfield, where he is building a Gothick Green-house; his visit does me Honour in my Neighbourhood, & so much for this Contingency.

I take it extreme kind of Mr Hall and am much oblig'd to your Ladyship for your Civility to Mr Pearsall, as *my Relation.* What his Book[4]

---

[2] The letter here referred to, from the Duchess of Somerset, dated January 21, 1749–50, is printed in Hull's *Select Letters,* Vol. I, No. XXIX.

[3] The Duchess of Somerset's chaplain, Mr. Lindsey, whom she describes as "betwixt sixty & seventy, very well bred, strictly pious, and . . . an admirable Scholar . . . a good judge of poetry . . ." praised Shenstone's *Ode to Autumn.* See Hull, I, 100–01, 110.

[4] I have not with any certainty been able to trace either Mr. Pearsall or his book.

will prove, I know not; and have taken it a little ill that I have not been made acquainted with it — My obligation to you is the same. I will write again soon, & beg you wou'd consider this scrawl as utterly inadequate to the Respect wth wch I have the Honour to be your Ladyship's most oblig'd & faithfull Servt.

W. Shenstone

113. To LADY LUXBOROUGH [1]

The Leasows, March ye 6th 1749–50

MADAM,

I ought indeed to have acknowledg'd the Favour of your Ladyships Letter, much *sooner,* but as a *true account* of my Delay will be it's best Apology, I beg Leave to offer it you as follows. Your Ladyship in your last Paragraph seem'd desirous yt I shou'd consider of something proper for a *Latin* Inscription to Mr Somervile; I thought this an affair yt requir'd some Deliberation, & accordingly indulg'd myself in ye Hopes yt I might be forgiven, if I allow'd myself some time to digest my Thoughts on ye occasion, having no Creature here to advise with, & having too often experienc'd ye Fluctuation of my own Opinions. The Result was yt I wrote down a Page or two by way of Specimens, from which I propos'd to select a few, for your Ladyships Choice. But as I remember'd yt you never own'd yourself acquainted with ye Pedantry of Latin Phrases, or ye antique turn of expressions in *that Language,* I did not care to send them to you, till I had consulted with some of my Friends.

Matters were in this State, when I was call'd away to assist at ye Fishing of a large Pool near Broom, which I have there jointly with Mr Dolman. There I spent all ye last week. Mr and Miss are both well, and at your Ladyship's Service. I return'd too late on Sunday Evening to be able to have my Letter ready for ye Postwoman ye next Day.

I was surpriz'd & concern'd at ye Duke of Somerset's Death; & considering how short a space he has had to enjoy his Honours & Estates; & to exhibit his many valuable Qualities with *advantage,* it cannot be thought strange that his Death shou'd appear *untimely.* Even many years hence it might have done ye same. Nothing now remains, but to pray for ye Duchess; that his Graces Death may not have too bad an Effect upon her Health and Spirits, as there is too much Reason to fear it will — Your Ladyship is *ingenious* in your generosity. I do not remem-

---

[1] B. M. Add. MSS 28958, fol. 88ff. This replies to Lady Luxborough's letters of Valentine's Day and of February 25, 1750 (*Letters,* Nos. XLIV and XLV) and confirms their dates.

ber y^t I *presum'd* to hope for ye Duchess's Acquaintance, when I mention'd my Intention of getting acquainted with her Chaplain. For I lik'd ye Man, exclusive of his *situation,* from y^t *kind* of Character ye Duchess gave of him, & perhaps not a little for his *Partiality* to *me* — At least If I had farther views, my Heart was not explicit, tho' your Ladyship, who knows my veneration for her Grace at all times, had sufficient Room to draw ye Conclusion. Sure I am that I am under ye utmost obligation for ye use you made of it.

 I am almost afraid to acquaint you, y^t I had wellnigh finish'd an Ode which I intended to desire your Las^p to present to her Grace.² As it is now neither to be *finish'd* nor *seen,* I will venture to give you this short account of it, that it was written in ye irregular way like y^t I had ye Honour to present to you; that it turn'd chiefly on ye Pleasures of Solitude & rural Amusement, & after excluding Several Classes of Men from any Pretensions to comprehend the Beauties of Nature, fix'd upon ye Person of true Taste as ye only adequate Spectator. Dont imagine I say this to excite y^r curiosity — The Account you gave me of Outing's Journey made me laugh heartily; Outing wou'd not desire to be Mr Addison's Angel, or to *ride in ye whirlwind* even tho' he cou'd *direct ye Storm.*³

 I am extremely glad to hear of any Accession of Happiness to Mr Meredyth's Family, as I am likewise to hear of large Fortunes being at any time in ye Possession of generous Spirits. Lord Stamford lives about Six Miles from hence ye direct Road (betwixt me & Stourbridge) is almost one continu'd Grotto, in other terms a *hollow*-way; practicable for an Horse, but for no wheel-carriage; I am not sure whether there be not some other y^t may be more so. Lady Stamford, I never saw, but she is esteem'd greatly amongst us for her Spirit Sense and Generosity — I heard this Story lately. She & Lord Stamford din'd at Lord Ward's, where ye latter was rallying my Lord Stamford for some event y^t happen'd while he was carrying ye Sword of State "What, my Lord, you had like to have kill'd your King!" To which my Lady Reply'd, If Lord Stamford *had* kill'd his king, it cou'd only have been imputed to accident; whereas if *you,* my Lord, had done ye same, it wou'd have been constru'd Rebellion Murder & High-treason. I am not intimate with my Lord having never been in his Company but one day y^t I din'd wth him & Lord Ward at Himley, except at Balls, & this many years ago. On ye whole these things consider'd I rather *wish* y^n *hope* for an *opportunity*

² *Rural Elegance.*
³ "Mr. Addison's Angel" is, of course, the Duke of Marlborough, and the reference is to Addison's *Campaign* (1705), l. 292.

on my *first visit* to procure myself yᵉ accumulative Honour of seeing them here jointly with yʳ Ladyship. And yet as I think to cultivate this Acquaintance (for they are easy of Access) I do *hope* as well as wish that I may hereafter find one.

I am oblig'd to you for yᵉ Pleasure you gave me in mentioning yᵗ I was remember'd by Sʳ Peter Soames, Mʳ Allen & Mʳ Hall. I hope Sʳ Peter has not quite left yᵉ Country.

And now am I to proceed to yᵉ Subject of Urns, in regard to which if I speak a little dogmatically, you must with your usual Candour attribute it to the fear I have yᵗ Ceremony wou'd make me tedious, & it is at best too heavy a vehicle for such futile Opinions as mine. In the first Place then I take it for granted yᵗ you prefer Latin Quotations — and therefore, a Latin Inscription, *I* say, of *Course*.

You will not have Room on yᵉ upper Part of yᵉ Front of yᵉ Pedestal to intimate more than yᵗ you Place it, out of Friendship, to yᵉ Memry of W. Som: Esq: Author of yᵉ Chase; & in my opinion tis all yᵗ you *shou'd* say there.

One Circumstance which made me acquiesce in an English Inscription was, that you cannot express *"Author of the Chase,"* in *Latin*, without a *Circumlocution*. (Perhaps,

  FACUNDI CARMINIS DE RE VENATICA
  AUCTORI CELEBERRIMO —

is as *short* as it can be express'd.) Well but supposing thus much express'd in Latin on yᵉ Front, then, I wou'd have *"Postquam Te &c:"* on ye Side next yᵉ Service Walk, & some other alluding to his *moral* Character on yᵉ opposite side. And thus your whole Aim is compleated.

You told Mʳ Allen my *only* objection to *"multis ille bonis"* when apply'd together with *Postquam Te Fata* &c: namely yᵉ different Persons of *Te* & *Ille*. Now if he Approves of yᵉ alteration of one Word in Virgils Line (tho it hurts yᵉ Line) Quem postquam Fata tulerunt, why then your Ladyship has two Mottos unexceptionably expressive of Mʳ S's different Characters; & then nothing to be done but to give you an Inscription. I cou'd acquiesce in this Proposal. But if Mʳ Allen will not allow of yᵗ Alteration (tho' tis often done) why then you are to desire him to think of some *other* expressive of the *same thing;* where there is yᵉ *second* Person us'd instead of the third; & I also will think yᵉ while as well as I can — Finally I *do* think you had better defer inscribing it for 3 weeks or a Month. I will readily come over for a Day, & see it done & a good Workman will do it in little more. For some very little addition in yᵉ expence (wᶜʰ you may adjust wᵗʰ the Builder *when he brings yᵉ Urn*) you may have a Person from Warwick at a Days warning; & it is a thing y^t ought to be thoroughly consider'd. Positively If I furnish ye Inscription, I must consult a little; but if you persist in requiring one immediately, I desire you will let me know as soon as you are at Leisure—and I will venture my Latinity in your Ladysp's Hands.

I am daily employ'd in finishing ye Scene where I have plac'd my Urn, makeing a Path to it; & have really found y^t Part of my Farm afford more Pictures y^n I cou'd possibly have imagin'd.

Now I talk of Pictures, has not Smith brought you his *"Select Beauties"?* He was here a fortnight ago & purpos'd to wait upon you wth them. Hagley is ye best, but seems to want something. Ld Tyrconnel's, next.

Your Ladyship says nothing concerning your Shell Urns—& I am afraid to enquire.

Aris furnishes me with my Paper, but I *bespeak* ye particular Sort. I never buy Pens, so can at present say nothing on y^t Head.

I am highly transported with this forward Season not only as it suits my Flowers, but as it *ripens* the Hopes that spring in my Imagination about this time of ye year; I mean ye agreeable expectation of waiting upon you at ye Leasows; where I shou'd be much more indifferent as to introducing new Improvements, if I thought they stood no Chance of entertaining *you*. I am your Ladyships most oblig'd

W:S

114. To RICHARD JAGO [1]

The Leasowes, Mar. 15, 1749-50

DEAR SIR,

Though I have not hitherto troubled you with a letter, I have not been void either of *inquiry* or *information,* concerning the state of your affairs, and of Mr. Hardy's health. Indeed it is now several weeks since I collected some particulars from your brother, and I am now impatient for further intelligence. As to the circumstances of our friendly reception at Wroxall, Mr. John Jago has probably enough acquainted you with them. He *would,* however, seduce me to give you a distinct account; being assured, as he says, that Mr. Wren's behaviour must afford a good subject for drollery. I do not know how far this would be proper; but I think, when I write again to my friend Wren, to give *him* a sketch of his own character, just as it appeared to us during the time of our visit.

[1] Dodsley, *Letters to Particular Friends,* No. LVIII. Wells confirms the date, *Anglia,* 35:449. An undated version of this letter also appears in Hull's *Select Letters,* Vol. II, No. III.

Perhaps it may avail a little. Amidst his violent passion for gardening, if he would but prune away some wild excrescences from one or two branches of his character, he might bring himself to bear good fruit. He should *weed* his *mind* a little; where there has sprung up a most luxuriant crop of puns, that threaten to choak all its wholesome productions — "Spinas animo fortius quam agro evellat." He has good sense and good-nature; pity he should disguise them! — not but that it is better to have the *substance* alone than the *forms alone,* and so I conclude. Since I came home, I have done little else than plant bushes, hazel, hawthorn, crabtree, elder, &c. together with some flowering shrubs that I have had given me, and some that I have purchased to the amount of twenty shillings. I think nothing remarkable has occurred; only, one miserable tempestuous day, I had my Lord Stamford, who called to see my walks. My Lord promised to come again in the summer, and invited me more than once to Enville. By the way, he is now building a Gothic green-house by Mr. Miller's direction, and intends to build castles, and God-knows-what. By all accounts, the place is well worth seeing when you come into the country, which I hope you will not fail to do this spring. Pray do not you embroil me with Mr. Miller, in regard to *any* observations I made in his walks. Remember there were a great many things with which I was highly delighted; and forget that there were a few also which I seemed less to admire. Indeed I thought it idle to regulate my expressions, amongst friends only, by the same rules which I ought to observe in mixed company. I say *ought,* for *he* has been exceedingly favourable to *me* in his representation of The Leasowes. — I hope to see Mr. Fancourt with you, when you come this spring; and why not your brother? he can spend half a week every now and then at Wroxall.

I have nothing to *insert* or *inclose* in this letter that can render it at all agreeable. — I cannot *write,* I cannot *think*. I can just muster up attention enough to give orders to my workmen; I saunter about my grounds, take snuff, and read Clarissa. This last part of my employment threatens to grow extremely *tedious:* not but the author is a man of *genius* and *nice observation;* but he might be less *prolix*. I will send you "The life of Socrates"[2] when I can get it home from Barrels. I wish both your circumstances and mine would allow of an utter *inattention* to them; and then, I believe, our natural indolence would be a kind of match for our ambition. I shall probably enlarge my acquaintance this year; but what *doth* it? the circle of my friends with whom I can be

[2] John Gilbert Cooper (1723–69) published his *Life of Socrates* in 1749. See Lady Luxborough's *Letters,* p. 183.

easy, and *amused* much, will continue small as ever. I could dwell a good deal upon this subject; but I have only room to desire you would give me your opinion how I should inscribe my urn to Mr. Somerville. "Author of The Chace" cannot be tolerably expressed in Latin without a circumlocution. I aim at brevity, and would therefore omit it. Pray read over the specimens I have thrown together, and *oblige* me with a speedy answer, if it extend to nothing else besides yours and Mrs. Jago's health, which I ought at this time more particularly to enquire after. I am
     Your most affectionate and faithful friend, W. Shenstone

115. To LADY LUXBOROUGH[1]

[Mar. 22, 1750]

MADAM,

I cannot with any satisfaction defer writing 'till Saturday, tho' I have a perverse Tooth that sollicits me continually to attend to nothing but the Pain it gives me — The weather of late has been a mere Coquette: Sunshine enough to tempt one out of Doors, Winds fraught with Tooth-Achs, Colds, & Disappointment! Yet to catch a glimpse of this *forward* Spring, do I ramble forth at least 20 times a Day;

Well-knowing Pleasure must be bought wth Pain! To-night however I can but think ye Price too *dear;* finding ye Pain more severe y^n usual, & being troubled also in *Mind* to think it shou'd interrupt me just at this time — You can't imagine how I fretted to hear y^t your Urn was damag'd. I cou'd not forbear saying, Why did they *send* it? Why did they *bring* it, till ye Cases were ready? And yet, for ought I know, ye Damage is all *imaginary:* I *do believe* they can *cement* it so y^t it will sooner break in any other Place; & when tis painted the Piecing will be hid for ever. If so what is an *accidental Fracture* worse y^n a *natural Joint?* Not a Jott — So I beg your Ladyship may be comforted, & accept of my Congratulation — You say 'tis seen from ye several Places we propos'd, Pray, Madam, does it appear as *considerable* as you would wish it? for as to it's being handsomely executed, I do not in ye least question it. And yet three Parts in four of it's Beauty must depend upon the verdure y^t Spring has in store for it — Your Ladyship was abundantly generous to Mr Smith. You don't know how to bestow with moderation: Otherwise, you had not sent me enough Jasmin-water to serve me a twelvemonth, when I litterally meant to beg no more y^n I describ'd. But no more of this, except my Thanks — I return to Mr Smith. I like ye Man, & I like *many* of his Landskips; these he has publish'd last, perhaps, as *little* as any.

---

[1] B. M. Add. MSS 28958, fol. 92ff. This letter replies to Lady Luxborough's of March 14, 1750 (*Letters*, No. XLVI), the date of which is thus confirmed.

His Roman & English Ruins, together wth his views of Derbyshire y^e *most* of any. I cou'd wish he cou'd make Vivares execute *all* his Engravings. What an immense difference! I will give up, if you please, ye Painting y^r Shrine of Venus after ye manner propos'd, but would likewise have your Ladyship *hesitate* a little before you make use of Moss Work &c. Is it not a Petitesse? — If not, I would however have y^e *whole back* cover'd as well as y^e *Niche,* to give ye Pillars in Front ye greater Advantage — I could wish Mr Smith (or myself) had never *acknowledg'd* y^t my Urn appear'd too little. I wish your Ladyship had not *heard* this previous Hint. For I am in Hopes ye Area will appear so much *contracted* when ye Trees y^t encircle it are thicken'd wth Leaves y^t it will not seem deficient in Size. If it *shou'd,* I will put a larger in the Place, & make use of this somewhere else. For I cannot agree to a Pyramid there, even if I c^d build one with rough Stone as cheap as an Urn — Mr Smith indeed propos'd it, but it really were so diminutive so pitifull an Imitation of those in Egypt (covering 11 Acres of ground) y^t to build one of 20 Feet, y^t one can't think of the latter without contemning ye former; & sure one cannot view ye Copy without recollecting ye original —. And yet a Pyramid has it's advantages — tis certainly a very solemn Ornament, & a very uncommon one. However you will see by this y^t we vary in our Ideas of proportion, as he thinks a Pyramid not too large, where I esteem an Urn insufficient. You planted *Abeles* for their *speedy Growth,* & I acquiesc'd; little dreaming then of ye superiour Excellence of *Sallows,* which grow as bushy as you please, & Eleven Feet high in a year, from little Pieces of a Foot long. Their Luxuriancy itself is delightfull. I planted several this day — The Picture of a Part of my grove will not *good,* nor *like;* yet I cou'd have been easy had it been engrav'd by Vivares. Indeed Vivares himself c^d not have made good Pictures of my Ld Gainsboroughs & Lord Byron's — One of them (wth his . . .[2] temple) has as much expos'd his Taste as ever did Lord Grimston[3] when he printed his "Love in a hollow tree." By ye Way is not Smith inexcusable for admitting ye Pot-boiling Cascades, & the Stables behind ye Hermitage (pretty in itself at my Ld Tyrconnels — Give me Leave, my Lady to speak to other Parts of y^r Letter (particularly ye obligation I am under to Mr Meredyth) in my next. I am most invariably y^r Ladyships   W. S.

My Tooth is easier — 'Tis, I think, March ye 22^d 1749-50
My Service to Mr Hall.

[2] The manuscript is defective at this point.
[3] William Luckyn, first Viscount Grimston (1683–1756) printed his play, *The Lawyer's Fortune, or Love in a Hollow Tree,* in 1705. It was ridiculed by Pope and Swift.

116. To LADY LUXBOROUGH[1]

The Leasows, March ye 23d 1749–50

MADAM,

I now sit down to add a word or two by way of supplement to my last; & this is but *right,* for I know not how it comes to pass, but your Ladyship most certainly says as much in *one* Letter as I can in *two.*

I don't remember what it was I said in Mr Meredyth's Favour which he seems so studiously to decline, & of which he makes such profuse Acknowledgment: But if it were any thing yt regarded Generosity of Sentiment, Delicacy in his observations, or an Ease & Politeness in his expressions, your Ladyship can bear me witness that I was struck with *them* on ye Sight of ye first Letter you shew'd me. Pray don't you recollect yt you confirm'd what I then said, and also intimated, that you had always thought the same? But I will not load Mr Meredith with any thing which he may *think* a Compliment; I will endeavour to meet him, ye first opportunity, & to deserve his Acquaintance by all means in my Power.

Your Ladyship is in some Haste to see your Urn inscrib'd, & tho' I have at least 30 different methods of doing it by me, I am quite clear in my Opinion, yt nothing more *can* be done in ye *space that is left* on ye Front, than to mention *his Name* & his being *Author of the Chace.* All I wou'd *wish* to add there, shou'd be an Intimation of the *Friendship,* to wch you pay this tribute; & *that* I suppose, when a Person erects an Urn, is generally taken for granted — Mottos are things that one *recollects* or *finds* accidentally; so that probably by a little Patience one might think of something better yn we now propose. I don't much *love* to alter a word in a Quotation, especially when ye verse is visibly impair'd — and as to ye Line Mr Allen proposes, to be sure the *Sense* is exactly what one would *wish* there, & it is a Line of Horace's, but does your Ladyship like ye Repetition of the S. S. Mult*is* ille bon*is* flexil*is* occidit. You'll say I'm too nice, & perhaps I am; nevertheless I think Mottos should be beautifull in themselves as well as pertinent; you will have them seen by *criticks;* & when they are once *cut* there will be no possibility of Alteration. I have inscrib'd mine to Mr Somervile in a kind of *general* way, but not *cut* ye Letters, yt I may alter them if I shou'd chuse it.

'Tis thus	Literally
GULIELMO SOMERVILE ARMIGO	TO WILLIAM SOMERVILE ESQ.
DE POESI BONIS A :LITERIS	WHO DESERVD VERY HIGHLY OF POETRY

[1] B. M. Add. MSS 28958, fol. 94ff.

PRÆCLARE MERITO	AND POLITE LEARNING
HANC SALTEM PONI VOLUIT	THIS AT LEAST WAS PLACD HERE
AMICITIA	BY THE DIRECTION OF
MDCCL	FRIENDSHIP

I don't much like it; If I *did,* I cou'd not offer it to your Ladyship, because you must needs have the Chace expressly alluded to. You'll say I have a very *glaring* Taste, when I mention, that when mine is *cut* I think to have ye Letters *gilded*. But I imagine to myself extraordinary Beauty in a gold Letter upon a simple stone colour. Another thing is, y^t it is sometimes done, & that by Persons of Taste; & lastly I will maintain, that it will not be half so *shewy* as if they were done in *black*. But I will drop this Subject (of wch you must be tir'd) to resume it once more when I have heard from you — As to ye Service walk I think you shoud make no scruple of Planting such Flowers as will grow *thro' ye Grass,* of which I fancy there are several. But what I want most of any thing is to have some kind of Fence on ye ouside y^t walk, y^t there may be no occasion for a Gate at ye End of ye Shrubbery. Perhaps it may be difficult to form such a Fence as you will like. I own I shou'd like to have ye Shruberry continu'd there & a Ha Ha behind, & then your Ha-Ha at ye Urn will be superfluous too — but there is no haste of this — twill be extreme beautifull in it's present state. The Ode I mention'd will I believe never be finish'd — The Merit of y^e *best* stanzas is not, I fear, sufficient to deserve y^t ye rest shou'd be *wrote afresh,* as must be ye Case if I revis'd it — Beside by shewing it you *now,* I must very evidently seem to have laid a trap for your curiosity; which I cannot bear to think of — The green Book will soon be finish'd as to ye transcribing Part, but if I am to illuminate it & so discover my Inability to paint as well as to *write,* I doubt I cannot promise it at present — Ld Lovat's Tryal was lent out when I mention'd it, but If it comes home to night, it shall accompany this Letter. I suppose the Bishop of London treats this Earthquake[2] as a Judgment, & inscribes it to Sr Piety Candle-cup & Dame Magdalene his wife: And yet, in the last Birmingham Paper, there are I think very cogent Reasons to suppose it was an Air-quake rather, & beneficial in it's Consequences—I have at last begun Clarissa, of which I have read two Volumes. I think ye Author a Person of refind understanding, but that he has Needlessly spun out his Book to an extravagant Prolixity — & which he would scarce have done, had he not been a *Printer* too as well as an *Author*. Nothing but *Fact* could authorize so much particularity,

---

[2] For an account of the earthquake, see the *Gentleman's Magazine* for March, 1750, p. 137.

and indeed not *that;* but in a Court of Justice — I met one Mr Chambers a week ago at Mr Clare's (a Gentleman in our neighbourhood) who is an Acquaintance, I find of your Ladyship's — The Bishop of Cambray had certainly no Invention — As for the rest, I suppose his Language is ye Language of most french Novels a mixture both of verse & Prose; & 'tis an unhappiness, I fancy, for a writer to have a genius partaking *equally* of both. I am highly honour'd by every Instance of your Ladyship's goodness, and

am your Ladyships most oblig'd hum: Servt
W: Shenstone

117. To LADY LUXBOROUGH [1]

[May 6, 1750]

M<small>ADAM</small>,

 I did indeed imagine that your Ladyship was gone to London upon Lady Bolingbroke's Death,[2] otherwise I shou'd have been uneasy under ye Suspicion that I had lost that Place in your Memory which It will ever be my Ambition to retain. You are exceeding kind in condescending to make an Apology for your Silence. I do very readily allow ye weight of it, & I shou'd have consider'd the *Condescension* itself as sufficient, whether y^e *Apology* had Weight or no. They tell me the Trees in Warwickshire are much more forward than ours; If so, I hope you enjoy the full Effect of ye Urn you have erected, wch I hope you find satisfactory. As to ye Method you propose of inscribing it, it has my entire Approbation; That you may believe me sincere in this, I cannot forbear mentioning that I had sent this very Motto "Debita &c:" together with twenty different kinds of Inscription, in a Letter to a young Clergyman of my Acquaintance,[3] for his Opinion; And this Collection was just return'd me when your Letter arriv'd. I think it superfluous to send it you; for I don't think you can find out any better there, or even so good as that you fix upon. However I will propose a Quere or two, which you will very easily solve yourself. First then Will it be possible to inscribe this Motto upon y^e *Plinth*, in Letters of any *tolerable Size?* & if it be, will it not together with the Inscription, and ye carv'd work below, give

---

[1] B. M. Add. MSS 28958, fol. 98ff and 96ff. This letter answers and confirms the date of Lady Luxborough's of April 25 (*Letters*, No. XLVII). Her No. XLVIII, dated "Sunday, 13th, 1750," replies to the present letter; its date is thus confirmed and the month is established as May.

[2] The second Lady Bolingbroke died March 18, 1750. Sichel's "1751" (*Bolingbroke and His Times*, II, 396) must be simply a misprint.

[3] Evidently Jago (see end of Letter 114).

a crowded Appearance to one Side of y^r Fabrick? You know who laughs at *Forty-five Mottos on forty five Plinths*. If so, will it not be better to make use of ye Side next ye Service-Walk (which is also a principal one) for ye Purpose abovemention'd. What think you of having it modeld in this manner, & inscrib'd on ye Upper Part of ye Die on this Side. As thus

> GULIELMO SOMERVILE ARM^O
> H. L. POSUIT MDCCL
> DEBITA SPARGENS LACRYMA FAVILLAM
> VATIS AMICI

Or else, wou'd you dislike to have y^e *Inscription alone* on ye Side of ye Service walk? as follows,

> GULIELMO SOMERVILE ARM^O
> H. L.
> SACRAM ESSE VOLUIT
> MDCCL

— Then on y^e *opposite* side (for I suppose there is some Area round it)

> DEBITA SPARGES &c:

You will here observe some difference betwixt sparg*ens* & sparg*es;* as the first will apply ye concern to yourself, the latter to any one y^t passes by — You will also observe a difference of another kind, if I am not mistaken; which is, that the Letters will *here* be an *embellishment* to ye Pedestal, but I am fearfull in ye other Place they will seem an Encumbrance. If you don't like y^e *Application* to y^r *Self,* I mean of shedding a tear over ye Ashes of your Poetical Friend (tho' I dont see *why* you shou'd disapprove it) you may use ye word sparg*es,* even in ye Method first-propos'd.

As to what you add about ye year, had you added ye foregoing Epithet *calentem* Debita &c, it wou'd have had weight, but as it is, I cannot think it of Importance. However you may use wch year you please. — I dont know how I came so precipitately to give my Opinion concerning French Novels. I dont remember y^t I ever read one; & perhaps imagin'd, too generally, that *Poetical Prose must* be like Cambrays. I am oblig'd to your Ladyship for ye Perusal of ye French Comedy.[4] I own I do not extremely admire it. I think ye Faux Savant, as he is drawn, is much to coarse to deserve the Satyr. Another of my objections, is, that in some Places he seems to think himself a man of Ability & Learning see Pag:65

[4] Lady Luxborough had previously written Shenstone, "A new comedy is acted at Paris, which I send you to read, as it is not in verse, and as it ridicules justly an Ignorant Pedant; . . ." (Lady Luxborough's *Letters*, No. XLVII, p. 202).

Scene ye 9th, whereas his Ignorance is so gross, y^t he must needs be *conscious* of the Contrary — The People must be kept out of the Service Walk at all adventures. I would render ye Attempt to pass that way so difficult, that their Feet shou'd insensibly lead them some other. But this *will* be done when you exchange ye Rails on ye side your Service Walk for a different Sort of Fence. As to the Seals, you do me great Honour in thinking any Hint of Mine deserves to be executed — For ye Rest, I must not praise ye Device because it was my own, but I may decently enough commend the Cutting which I think to be good — Will you be so kind as send me another Impression of each on *red* Wax, melted wth Spirits. That you sent me of y^e *Urn* was spoild by the Packthread on which ye Impression was taken. — My Wood-work is at present far from Perfection in Point of Verdure: I have also a good deal of ground fresh-leveld that is not yet green, tho' in a fair way to be so — I must acquaint your Ladyship (tho' my Schemes are *necessarily* limited) you will find here many little Matters that will be entirely new to you. I finish my Environ-Employments this Week, & the next shall begin to make some Alterations in my House.

I have read Clarissa with a great deal of *Pleasure;* will make no Remarks at present but y^t it wants to be abridg'd by almost one Half. You will guess by this that there are *some* very affecting scenes in it, or I must have read it with *disgust* on account of ye Superfluities. — The Author, in my Opinion, was guilty of ye same Fault in Pamela. The Style, (for Epistles) is almost universally good.

Poor Mr Hardy (whom I us'd to visit beyond Warwick) is gone! His Sale is next Tuesday se'nnight. I do not know of anything you wou'd chuse to buy there tho' I gave a Commission to bid for some one of his better Sort of Pictures — There is ye Model of a Ship to be A Gift of ye King of Denmark, as Mr Hardy us'd to say, to Sr Thomas Hardy his Father; cost 500ll; will sell, they say, for 50ll; but for which I would not give — Five Farthings. He was no extraordinary good Character: humor*ous* and humour*some:* no generosity in the World! And yet was not I altogether unconcern'd at his Death, as his Manner was singular, droll, & sprightly; seem'd to have no kind of Relation to, or Connection with Death, & Death-beds. I believe there are generally as many disgusted as pleas'd wth Falstaffs Death & his Misfortunes preceding it — His whole Behaviour ye same to ye last — at least mixing serious and ludicrous Things together so as to make a most grotesque Caracature of his final Scene — And yet it offends one to find y^t he had not one Friend or relation, not even his own Sister, y^t was concern'd at his Death — Nay what is more singular, (yet very accountable) not a single Servant Male or

The Dwelling House at the Leasowes as It Appears Today
From a photograph by Myra M. Ward

The Stable at the Leasowes as It Appears Today
From a photograph by Myra M. Ward

Female but *wish'd* for his Death, & rejoic'd *apparently* to see their Wishes Accomplish'd — Jack Reynalds was with me this last Week — What an Affair that of Miss Prett's! I hope your Ladyship will accept of this hasty Letter from a Person who has (at present as he may say) both Masons, Stone-cutters, & Carpenters about him, but who is with more respect y^n he can now express

    Your Ladyships most oblig'd & most obedient Servant

                  W. Shenstone

Sunday. May ye 6th 1750

 Since I clos'd my Letter, I have determin'd to send you ye Inscriptions I had been meditating & advising with my Friend upon, that you may know I have not been idle in this Respect, & for *no other purpose* whatsoever — For I do most earnestly desire you wou'd adhere to ye Inscription & Motto you propose — I can't say I calculated them *merely* for y^r Ladyship's Use — for I had my own also in View; resolving nevertheless to give you your Choice & take up with one of ye Remainder — I receiv'd them back with ye Asterisks you see, which by an agreement betwixt me & ye Person I consulted are intended to mark ye different degrees of Approbation, in proportion to ye Number he prefixes. Mr Allen or Mr Hall (to w^m my Compliments) will give you ye English of them if you have any *Curiosity* to know — for as I said before, you cannot do better than adhere to your own. The first, & last-but-one are added since I had them Home. I hope for ye Favour of a Speedy Letter from your Ladyship; My Correspondents are exceeding few; & in truth I dont much regret it, provided I cou'd be more often favour'd with a Line or two from Barrels.

 Please to return me these Inscriptions; I have not yet quite fix'd in regard to what I shall use myself.

118. To LADY LUXBOROUGH [1]

              The Leasows, June ye 4th 1750

MADAM,

 I should hold myself inexcusable in not sending a servant over to enquire after your Ladyship's Health, had I not been in constant Hopes of waiting upon you at Barrels before this time. Those Hopes have been hitherto frustrated; & as your Ladyship gave me a good account of your

---

[1] B. M. Add. MSS 28958, fol. 100ff and 49ff. The manuscript arrangement makes the postscript (dated simply Thursday, June 6) appear to belong to the letter of June 3, 1749 (Letter 91), but the context, especially the references to the pictures recently purchased, plainly shows the connection with the present letter, to which I am convinced the postscript belongs.

Recovery, & my Servant, my *only* Servant, is at this time extreme busy, I must beg you wou'd please to accept of this Letter by a more lingering conveyance. The Case is, I have been *amus'd* (shall I say, or *fatigu'd* rather) for these Six weeks with a considerable Crowd of Work men. I believe I told your Ladyship in my last, y^t having compleated my schemes for this year out of Doors, I was then beginning upon my House. I have not been a Day since y^t time without two Masons & their Attendants, two Carpenters & some times three, a Painter Plummer, glazier & the Lord knows who beside. My House is a bottomless Pit, as Swift said formerly of the Law: Or rather it is a *whirlpool,* which sucks in all my money & that so *deep* that there is not ye least glimpse of it appears thro' ye water. Accordingly, were your Ladyship to come over (which I hope will be the Case very soon) you will hardly discover what these Workmen have been doing. Why, nothing *ornamental;* but many things of a *convenient* kind, & which my Servants will more sensibly reap ye Benefit of, than either my *visitants* or *myself.* However I must acquaint you that *one* of my Alterations has been ye Enlargement of a Drawing-Room or Library (for I know not which I shall determine to make of it) And this will be but about 19 Feet by 12; yet when finish'd will be one of ye Pleasantest Rooms I shall have. It is as yet neither floor'd nor Plaister'd, & I'm greatly afraid will not be so this Summer.

 I bought two Pictures at Mr Hardy's sale, and, considering the cheapness of *these,* am sorry I had not more. One is an admirable Portrait by Wissing; the other a Flower-piece with some heterogeneous objects intermix'd; good only so far as relates to ye Flowers.

 You advise me to make use of those English Lines upon Mr Somervile's Urn, *myself;* I have some doubts concerning ye Propriety of *my* Dryads being said to have heard Mr Somervile's Harmony, as he was never here. I wrote them in pursuance of a Plan which your Ladyship once had of having *one* motto to express his *poetical* Character, & *another* to intimate his Virtue & his Friendship. This Plan you have much better executed by y^t expressive Line which you chose from Horace.

 I am oblig'd to you for sending y^e *Engraver's* Impression of ye Seals; but your Ladyship woud surely chuse to keep these *yourself;* & I wanted only such as you could very readily take off, to keep in my drawer amongst a number of others.

 I had here last Week Mr Clare, a gentleman of Fortune in our Neighbourhood; & Mr Smart a Clergyman remarkable as a Man of taste, & particularly so for drawing in Miniature — They offerd to take me in a Party (of wch Admiral Smith was to be one), to see Mr Anson's wth

whom Mr Clare is acquainted. I think your Ladyship express'd y^r Self much in Favour of that Place.

Not one single Jaunt have I had since I was at Barrels. I resolve *against* Indolence, but find it making continual advances. The Fault is not in my *mind;* I want better *animal Spirits.*

Poor Mrs Pitt (whom y^r Laship met in Hagley Park) died yesterday morning of a Lethargy; extremely lamented by her poor neighbours, & her inferiour Friends. She had great affability, of y^e *genuine Sort;* I mean, it was ye effect of her Benevolence.

I will still hope to wait upon you shortly at Barrels for a day, y^t I may see your Shrubbery in Bloom; & present my Petition y^t you woud condescend to take a view of mine.

Thursday, June ye 6th

I did think to have sent ye former sheet this morning; which having neglected to do, I will endeavour to make some Amends for my Delay by adding another; as an Author now & then throws you in a dull appendix *gratis* in order to attone for his dilatory Publication of a duller Piece.

What an immense deal must it have cost to fit up an House in ye manner you have done Barrels. Surely ye Inside expences of a House shou'd be always reckon'd at as much as the Shell. In regard to my *own* Habitation who *aim* at nothing y^t is extraordinary *there,* I am frighted at ye expence of common *Decencies;* nay almost, *necessaries.* I never walk beneath my Roof, but one Room cries out, "Pray why am not I paper'd"? On which another takes ye Alarm directly, & answers, "Why am not I stucco'd"? a Third, "Why have not I a Chimney Piece?" a Fourth, "Why not I, a new Floor?" to which two of them rejoin at once "And pray why have not we any Floor at *all?*" These are not a quarter of the Complaints; My Beds grown old and decrepit desire to resign their office in favour of others more alert & able. My Chairs suggest that they want *Companions;* that being divided one in a Room they are not able to perform ye Ceremonies of it. Nay ye very Pictures I lately purchas'd have caught ye Infection — *They* also are malecontents; calling out upon the Windows to afford them more Light, to which ye testy old Windows reply with a Sarcasm "Plague not us with your continual teizings: We transmit Light enough for all *ordinary* occasions; & peradventure, if [we] transmit *more,* it will be only to discover ye Cracks & the Imperfections y^t are in y^e". Midst all this Hellish uproar, I walk contemplative; seldom uttering a syllable beside these "Have *Patience* good People! Peradventure were I to satisfy all your Demands at *once,* I might ill afford to satisfy the Demands of Nature. Let your betters be serv'd first; *you* also in your turn shall find in me your most obsequious humble Servant & vassal."

Amidst all y^t has pass'd betwixt y^r Lasp and myself concerning *Urns,* I think you have never told me in direct terms y^t you like y^e *Execution* & y^e *situation* of y^{rs}. I wou'd fain seduce you to say thus much.

I want also to be resolv'd whether it is your Opinion y^t I may appear at Barrels with an unembarass'd Countenance, without ye green Book. What a deal of trouble has my foolish Vanity occasion'd you? For whether you esteem it a Piece of charitable complaisance to an idle writer to sollicit his performances; or whether you really *wish* to see them, in either Case my Proposal has occasion'd you more trouble than the trifles are worth. But my Promise I suppose I must perform; for shou'd *Complaisance* be your only motive in asking for them, I doubt I shall hardly persuade you to own so much. As for ye rest, I have almost *wrote* ye Book thro', but have neither Pencil, Colours nor Leisure, just at present, to add the little Sketches. When I say I have not Leisure, you will please to consider, I make it a point to be an Eye-witness of ev'ry alteration y^t is going forwards; & tho' it wou'd be more *agreeable* to me to be labouring for your Ladyships Amusement, I must attend my workmen whilst I have them; & I must have them if I wou'd be soon shut of them. I have said too much upon such a trifling matter. I fear you think so.

Most sincerely do I lament ye Loss of ev'ry Flower that perishes unseen by you. I have two or three Peonies in my grove, y^t I have planted amongst Fern and brambles in a gloomy Place by ye water's side. You will not easily conceive how good an Effect they produce, & how great a stress I lay upon them. I wou'd advise your Ladyship to plant many of them about *your* Grove, where, if I am not deceiv'd they wou'd appear surprizingly beautifull—Thus has my Pen run on 'till It has cover'd another Sheet; too carelessly, I must own, for the Respect with which I shall ever remain your Ladyship's most

oblig'd & faithfull Servant
W: Shenstone

119. To RICHARD JAGO[1]

June 11, 1750

DEAR SIR,

I acknowledge myself obliged to you for procuring me the pictures.[2] I received them both very safe, as I have a pretty strong assurance I *shall*

---

[1] Dodsley, *Letters to Particular Friends,* No. LIX. Fullington confirms the date, *PMLA,* 46:1135.

[2] Evidently Jago bought them for Shenstone at Mr. Hardy's sale. See Letter 117.

do most articles of which my servant Tom has the care. — He has punctuality and management, to *atone* for his *imperfections*. He brought me those paper-sculled busts from Wroxall entirely unhurt, contrary to the expectation of all that saw them; after which, he might undertake for almost any thing. — The portrait is undoubtedly a good one. I shewed it to Mr. Smart (who is a painter himself, though a clergyman), and he allowed as much; added also, that it had something of Sir Godfrey Kneller, as well as of Sir Peter Lely. — The flowerpiece is very good, so far as relates to the flowers; the dog and parrot abominable, and the grapes very exceptionable. I never considered the two flowerpieces at Icheneton with attention enough to cause a preference; having never any thoughts that *either* would fall to my share. I shall add nothing with regard to your choice; but that I sincerely *hope* yours is the better piece. I never heard of Casteels,[3] I own; nor can I find his name in any of my accounts of the painters, though they take in pretty modern ones: but I can say this for your comfort, that if he excelled in any thing, it was probably in flowers: for I see his name at the bottom of those flower-pieces that I have in water-colours, as the designer of them; and I think the designs are good. Though I could wish neither the Cupid nor the fruit-piece had escaped us, yet is there no blame to be laid at your door; at least supposing that you are endowed with nothing more than rational conjecture, and that you are not gifted with prophecy.

And now, having spoken, I think, to *most* parts of your letter, I proceed to say a word or two in the way of appendix. First then, after five or six weeks work of masons and carpenters, I plainly discover that my house is an unfinishable thing; — and yet, I persuade myself, there will never be wanting a room in it, where you may spend an agreeable day with your undoubted friend. — Did I ever tell you how *unseasonably* the three fiddles struck up in my grove about an hour after you left me; and how a set of ten bells was heard from my wood the evening after? It might have passed for the harmony of some aerial spirit, who was a well-wisher to us poor mortals; but that I think, had it been so, it would have been addressed to the *better sort,* and of consequence have been heard whilst *you* were *here*. This by way of introduction to what I am going to tell you. Mr. Pixell has made an agreement with his club at Birmingham, to give me a day's music in some part of my walks. The time is not yet fixed; but, if you were an idle man, and could be brought over at a day or two's notice, I would give it you, and be in hopes I could entertain you very agreeably.

[3] Peter Casteels (1684–1749), born at Antwerp, came to England in 1703.

You cannot think how much you gratified my vanity when you were here, by saying, that if this place were yours, you thought you should be less able to keep within the bounds of *œconomy* than myself. — God knows, it is pain and grief to me to observe her rules at *all;* and *rigidly* I never can. — How is it possible to possess improveable scenes, and not wish to improve them? and how is it possible, with oeconomy, to be at the expence of improving them upon my fortune? To be continually in fear of excess in perfecting every trifling design, how irksome! to be restrained from attempting *any,* how vexatious! so that I never can enjoy my situation — that is certain. — Oeconomy, that invidious old matron! on occasion of every frivolous expence, makes such a hellish squalling, that the murmur of a cascade is utterly lost to me. — Often do I cry out with Cowley,

> O rivers! brooks! when, when in *you,* shall I
> Myself, eas'd of *un-peaceful* thoughts, espy!
> O woods and groves! when, when shall I be made
> The happy tenant of your shade!

Paper fails; abruptly therefore, but sincerely and affectionately,

I am, dear Sir,
Yours,
W. Shenstone

120. To LADY LUXBOROUGH [1]

Sunday, July ye 15 1750

MADAM

With the utmost Thankfullness for ye agreeable Hopes you give me of waiting upon your Ladyship at the Leasows about ye 17th of this Month, I am oblig'd to sit down in order to defer my own Happiness for about a week longer. My Hay-harvest is but now compleated, & My Servants have been so universally employ'd in . . .[2]

I shall be utterly unable to put my walks in order in less time than a week. But I shall with ye utmost pleasure wait upon your Ladyship ye beginning of ye week after, I mean on Monday or Tuesday se'nnight, as I shall make use of the mean time to render my Environs less unworthy of your Notice. There will be a Bed for yr Ladyship, another for Mr Hall, a third for Mrs Ann & one & an half for your Servants of ye other Sex. There are many *Improvements* I wou'd wish compleated before you

---

[1] B. M. Add. MSS 28958, fol. 102ff. This letter answers and confirms the date of Lady Luxborough's of June 30, 1750 (*Letters*, No. L). Her misplaced and only partly dated Letter LXXI of "Sunday Night, St. Swithins, my Birth-day," which plainly answers the present letter, should be dated July 15, 1750, and follow her No. L.

[2] The manuscript is defective at this point.

came, but should I give ye least way to Views of that kind, the Lord knows when I shou'd have a Chance of seeing you. Let it suffice my Ambition, for ye Present, y^t if your Ladyship & I live, I may *hereafter* have an opportunity of accomodating you in less vulgar manner yⁿ I *now* can possibly do. I beg you would please to make my Compliments to Mr Hall, & acquaint him how much I desire to see him. I hope he did not *mistake* me when I ask'd why he would not take a ride some *afternoon*. I alluded only to ye Shortness of ye Way, & not to the Space of time I wou'd wish to share his Company.

I had yesterday a morning's Visit from Dean Lyttelton wth Mr Meadowcourt of Worcester. He says he lays no great stress on ye old Abby, wonders I should be afraid of *him,* & will promote my Application all that lies in his Power — Were your Ladyship to know ye whole extent of my Petition,[3] you wou'd not imagine it ye most unreasonable that ever was — Yet am I in some doubt whether I shall succeed.

As you are pleas'd to observe, there is Pleasure enough in forming a Plan & seeing it's progress, if we speak with relation to Projects of mere *amusement;* but in Projects y^t are altogether of y^e *convenient* or *necessary* kind (such as many I have lately engag'd in) One wishes to have them dispatch'd with as much expedition as possible. I must do but little more by way of *ornament* 'till next Winter; but in order to get a *habitable* Room below stairs, much must I *undergo* before winter arrives. With this Prospect before me I cannot avoid crying out with Aeneas "O Fortunati &c:"

Thrice happy You, whose walls *already rise!*

And yet I love, as does your Ladyship, to see Workmen about me, but my Finances will not let me see them, with out connecting an Idea of ye expences they occasion.

What does your Ladyship think of a small Excursion to my Lord Stamford's? The Family is now at Lord Wallingfords & will continue there till the End of August. I am apt to think we may *get thither* if the Roads *continue* good; For they tell me Hagley-Lanes have nothing disagreeable in them, except *Dust* — a thing extremely uncommon. And I dont know y^t we shall find it above 8 Miles thither, half ye way over level Downs & Commons. His Chinese house, Rotonde, Gothick Greenhouse &c will be new to your Laship as well as to myself. But of this more hereafter.

Many Thanks to your Ladyship for y^r rural Presents: rural indeed,

---

[3] His petition was probably to take stone from the old Abbey of Hales, in Shenstone's time used as a quarry by the people of the neighborhood. See Ward, "Studies in Shenstone," p. 41.

but having an Air of Elegance, as everything must y^t comes from Barrels. As to ye Sp: Geese Don Pedro⁴ has all ye stateliness of a Swan: Donna Elvira, his faithfull Consort, fill'd all my Vallies with Complaint for three long Summer's Days. Nor was there any Dervise here to interpret her Language, save ye learned Mrs Arnold; who told us she was expostulating about ye Loss of some young, y^t she had left behind her, & endeavouring to let them know ye Present Place of her Abode — If this was *not* ye Case, she was lamenting her Removal from Plenty & Splendour to Poverty and Obscurity. But she now seems contented under both.

I hear no more of ye small Figure y^t was talkd of. Sure I am that in their *Park* it is a mere *Concetti,* whereas it wou'd be proportionate & adapted to many Places in my Grove.

They do now entirely discard their Shell Urn, whatever is the Reason.

Why don't your Ladyship throw all y^r Hay-stacks into ye Form of Pyramids, & chuse out places where they May look agreeably? Tis no inconvenient Form for a Hay-stack, & they are made wth as much ease, as any. I have executed one so — but alas! *mine* — is little bigger y^n an Hen-pen.

Tho the Beginning of this Letter bespeaks some Delay, I am truly *impatient* to wait upon your Ladyship, & hope you will not add to y^t Delay, by defering my Pleasure any longer y^n ye Beginning of next Week. I am, Madam,

     Your oblig'd & most obedient Servt
         W: Shenstone

Lord Dudley not yet come down; but the Bells here rang about two Days ago for the Termination of his Law-suit wth my Ld Ward.

121. To LADY LUXBOROUGH¹

         Tis now August ye 8th 1750

MADAM,

The Return of Mr Moore affords me an opportunity of acknowledging ye Receipt of your last Letter, by which I am allow'd to expect ye Pleasure of waiting upon you soon. Indeed I grow a little *impatient* upon that Head; as the *weeds,* which I had been carefull to subdue in my Walks, begin again to rebell, at ye Instigation of these late Rains. But you promise to make Amends for your Delay by ye Addition of Mrs Wymondsold & Mrs Davis's Company. I should be a little sollicitous

---

⁴ See Lady Luxborough's *Letters*, No. LXXI, p. 281.

¹ B. M. Add. MSS 28958, fol. 106ff. This letter answers and confirms the date of Lady Luxborough's of August 2, 1750 (*Letters*, No. LI). Her No. LII of August 13, 1750, answers the present letter.

concerning ye Amusement wch so mean a cottage as mine can afford them, but that I am assur'd their *good-nature* must receive some satisfaction from the Pleasure they will occasion *me* — I depend upon your Ladyship's giveing me a Day or two's Notice — There is no Joke in surprizing such a mortal as me; whom you might find, very probably find sitting down to a single Pigeon; & throw me into *Confusion* by ye same means thro' which you *famish'd* yourselves. I should be heartily glad to see Mr Outing; to whom I beg my Compliments.

I am quite sorry I cannot employ Mr Moore, both on account of your Ladyship's recommendation, & of his own Appearance; which to *me* promises better things than that of Crosbie, who has been here twice on ye same Occasion; & to whom I gave a Promise that, when my Room was done, *he* should be ye Person employ'd. I do not know much of Crosbie's Merits: I know he workd for Ld Ward: but I then thought to have only plain walls & a plain Cornice: whereas I am now thinking to indulge myself in two or three slight Festoons — but all this must be *defer'd*.

Your Ladyship determines very justly; It will much improve my Lord Bolingbroke's Bust to have it painted in ye same manner wth mine of Mr Pope. Besides it will appear doubly better in a *Stucco-Room*.

You will no doubt make ye wash for your Summer House of a Stone-colour. You may try ye colour first on an hot Brick on which it will dry immediately. You have a good Sand near you. It should be done twice at *least*.

Your Ladyship has had much agreeable Company; I will not say more than your *Share*, because I think you deserve every thing y^t can contribute to your Happiness; & I am persuaded the Company of your Friends bids fairest so to do — Is it improbable Sr Peter Soame shou'd ever travel thro' my Neighbourhood?

My Lord Dudley came Home last Saturday, as I am well assur'd by Intelligence from ye Steeple & other concurrent Intimations; for I have not yet seen him.

That very religious Tyrant our Parson[2] (who destroy'd my neighbouring Coppice) attack'd last Sunday a most Noble & renowned Captain, in ye midst of his Sermon; taxing him wth snorting & sneezing to ye great scandal of him & his Congregation; comparing him to a Beast y^t perisheth; even to a Hog. And this was nothing more it seems yⁿ either a natural Imperfection, or a Habit wch the Man had got. Does it not put your Ladyship in Mind of The Montague's And the Capulet's Servant

---

[2] For a further account of Shenstone's quarrel with his parson, the Rev. Pynson Wilmot, see above, Letter 102.

in Shakespear? "Do you bite your Thumb at *me* Sir" "No, Sir! but I bite my *Thumb,* Sir."

At other times he has condescended to attack his neighbour Parson's Children of about four years old & under, telling them they were damn'd for being seen out of Doors on a Sunday & not reading the Bible.

Nay, at other times he hath stoop'd so low as to *pun* from his Pulpit; making Hales-owen and Hell's own to be in his opinion synonimous terms.

But I tire your Ladyship wth what regards you no otherwise yⁿ as it fell from a Person who has impaird ye Pleasure you us'd to take in my Scenery. I am your Ladyship's most oblig'd & faithfull Servant

Will: Shenstone

122. To CHRISTOPHER WREN [1]

The Leasowes, Sept. 9, 1750

DEAR SIR,

Pray, is laziness an excuse for not writing? Tell me.—However, if it be so, I am afraid I shall want an excuse for laziness: like the philosopher, who, supposing the world might rest upon a tortoise's back, found himself no less embarrassed for a pedestal to support his tortoise. I have, indeed, been pretty busy at home in raising a pool-dam, and have interchanged a few visits with such of my acquaintance as live within three miles.—What then?—I abominate all excuses that are grounded upon the business or amusements of an idle man—as if such a person's time was so wholly filled up, that he could not find half an hour to write a line to his friend. It is best to acknowledge laziness at first, and that there are particular intervals, when one is much less disposed to write even a few lines than at others; and then, as to laziness, one has nothing to do but to plead human frailty; which, if a person has not too many frailties besides, may perhaps be indulged him. However, "Veniam petimusque, damusque," will not fail to weigh with every good-natured man. The chief dealing I have with Harris the Jew is, for the intelligence which he brings me concerning you and Mrs. W[ren]; but it seldom amounts to much more than that you are well, and in your garden.

He is an Ebrew Jew, or he would tell me you had purchased a couple of genteel horses, or a chaise and pair, and were coming over to The Leasowes to spend a week with me.

---

[1] Dodsley, *Letters to Particular Friends,* No. LX. Fullington confirms the date, *PMLA,* 46:1135. Fullington has identified the C—— W—— to whom five letters in Volume III of Shenstone's *Works* are addressed, as Christopher Wren, the son of the famous architect ("Mr. William Shenstone," p. 156).

Nevertheless, I hope to see you soon; but *en passant* I assure you, I shall go in about a month to Mr. Jago's, and from thence to Mr. Miller's; who, I believe I told you, was here, with Mr. Lyttelton, Lady Aylesbury, Colonel Conway, &c. I think I never answered your query concerning Colonel Lyttelton. — He is the same person that you remember, and your prophecy concerning him has been literally accomplished. He is a man of courage, genius, generosity, and politeness; has been fortunate in the world; was made a Colonel at about six and twenty; distinguished himself in several campaigns; married the Duchess of Bridgewater; and had the other day about sixteen thousand pounds left him by Colonel Jefferies, a very distant relation. He has a seat, and speaks, in the House of Commons; has bought a town and country-house, the latter of which he is ornamenting in the modern way. His Duchess the most unceremonious even-tempered woman that lives. — So enjoy the spirit of prophecy, and exert it again. — It needs little more than good sense. Which of the historians is it, that foretold in his history a very remarkable series of events, by dint of this alone, and which were all accomplished? Let me know what you are doing now. Have you repaired the farm-house you talked of? — and have you remembered to make the man a couple of good large niches in his chimney-corner, where he and his family may spend a more comfortable evening than was ever spent by any first minister in Christendom — perhaps also converse more to the purpose? You tell me nothing of your Mr. Jago, Seignior Benedict, the new-married man.[2] — Tell him to leave his wife and family for a day or two, saddle his mule, and come over to The Leasowes. — Tell him, all pleasures are heightened by a little discontinuance. — Tell him, did I say? — how can you for shame advise him so contrarily to your own practice?

Believe me, dear Sir,
Very faithfully yours,
W. Shenstone

123. To CHRISTOPHER WREN [1]

The Leasowes, Nov. 2, 1750

DEAR SIR,

It never can be that I owe you for three letters; as to two, I will agree with you; one that I received together with my books, and the other soon after; but that I am indebted for more than these —

---

[2] Not, of course, Richard Jago, who was married in 1743, whose wife died in 1751, and who remarried in 1758. Possibly his brother John.
[1] Dodsley, *Letters to Particular Friends,* No. LXI.

>Credat Judaeus Apella,
>Non ego.[2]

Even that same "Judaeus Apella" who affords me this very opportunity of sending my compliments to you and Mrs. W[ren], and of assuring you, that if I had not purposed to have seen you, I had wrote to you long ago.

Master Harris talks very respectfully of your garden; and we have no dispute, save only in one point — he says, that you labour very hard in your vocation; whereas I am not willing to allow that all the work you ever did, or will do in it, is worth a single bunch of radishes. However, I dare not contradict him too much, because he waits for my letter.

How happy are you, that can hold up your spade, and cry, "Avaunt, Satan!" when a toyman offers you his deceitful vanties! Do not you rejoice inwardly, and pride yourself greatly in your own philosophy?

>'Twas thus —
>The wise Athenian cross'd a glitt'ring fair:
>Unmov'd by tongues and sights he walk'd the place,
>Thro' tape, tags, tinsel, gimp, perfume, and lace;
>Then bends from Mars's Hill his awful eyes,
>And, "What a world I never want!" he cries.[3]
>
>>PARNELL

Mean time, do not despise others that can find any needful amusement in what, I think, Bunyan very aptly calls *Vanity Fair;* I have been at it many times this season, and have bought many kinds of merchandize there. It is a part of philosophy, to adapt one's passions to one's way of life; and the solitary unsocial sphere in which I move makes me think it happy that I can retain a relish for such trifles as I can draw into it. Mean time, I dare not reason too much upon this head. Reason, like the famous concave mirrour at Paris, would, in two minutes, vitrify all the Jew's pack: I mean, that it would immediately destroy all the form, colour, and beauty, of every thing that is not merely useful. — But I ramble too far, and you do not want such speculations. My intent, when I sat down, was to tell you, that I shall probably see you very soon, and certainly remain in the mean time, and at all times, Sir,

>Your obliged and very faithful servant,
>>W. Shenstone

---

[2] "The Jew Apella may believe it — I cannot." This is the literal meaning of the passage; but Horace uses it after the manner of our familiar expression; "Let who will believe it, I will not." [Dodsley]

[3] *An Elegy. To an Old Beauty* (1722), ll. 59–64.

124. To RICHARD GRAVES[1]

The Leasowes, Feb. 16, 1750–1

DEAR MR. GRAVES,

Since I received your letter, I have been a week at W[hitchurch][2] I believe I may have told you, that I never was fond of that place. There is too much trivial elegance, too much punctilio for me; and perhaps, as you express it, too much *speculation*. But I was fearful I might entirely lose Mr. Whistler's acquaintance, if I did not make an effort once in five years to return his visit. Besides, I should have had no hopes of seeing him at the Leasowes hereafter; and I am extremely desirous of seeing both *him* and *you* here, having made many alterations which I do not undertake but with an eye to the approbation of my more ingenious friends; but he seems, to my great surprize, to renounce the thing called *taste* in buildings, gardens, &c. is grown weary of his own little embellishments at W[hitchurch], and longs to settle in London for the greater part of his time. This, I believe, he would put in execution immediately, but that he thinks it might give some uneasiness to his mother, if he should quit the house that she with so much difficulty obtained for him. I too am sick of the word *taste;* but I think the *thing* itself the only proper *ambition*, and the *specific pleasure* of all who have any share in the faculty of imagination. I need not mention my reasons; you will soon conceive them. And, however the case be, there is one branch of it which so totally engrosses the persons with whom I principally converse, that I was astonished to hear him speak even with indifference concerning the reigning taste for rural decorations. I could ill forbear telling Mr. Whistler, that he was not *literally* a beau in a bandbox; but the freedom might have given more offence than the joke was worth. He has improved the place extremely; but I do not like his colonnades. You know, nothing of that kind is tolerable, unless regularly executed in stone: that is one thing. Another is, that colonnades are ornaments which will not *bear* to be very *diminutive*. Mr. ——— (whose house only I saw) has been at the expence of a large cornice round it, in most elaborate brick-work; but with regard to his stucco-work *within* doors, he is quite *extravagant*. — I mention these things upon a supposition that you may like to hear *any* thing that regards the place; but indeed they are so mighty trifling, that I ought to doubt my supposition. I supped with Mr. P———'s family once

---

[1] Dodsley, *Letters to Particular Friends*, No. LXIV. Wells (*Anglia*, 35:452) confirms the dates of all the remaining letters (LXIII–CXI) in Dodsley's edition of Shenstone's *Works*, Vol. III.

[2] Where Shenstone visited Whistler. Graves discusses this visit, and the resulting temporary coolness between Shenstone and Whistler, in his *Recollection*, pp. 146ff.

at Mr. W——'s, and once at Mr. W——'s, and all was mighty well; only I happen to have a violent aversion to card-playing, and at W[hitchurch] I think they do nothing else: so that, on account of my ignorance at quadrille, or any creditable game, I was forced to lose my money, and two evenings out of my seven, at Pope Joan with Mr. P——'s children. Mr. W——, to make me amends, invited me to breakfast, and shewed me your verses. I assure you, you have no occasion for a better advocate than Mr. W——; whether with regard to his *judgment,* or his zeal in behalf of the subject, the verses, or the poet. I would fain have obtained a copy; but he did not care to give one without your commission. I hope *you* will oblige me so far. I like them very much; the subject is genteel, and the verses easy and elegant. We agreed upon one or two different readings; and one stanza that concerns cards should, I think, be corrected. Not that I would have you less severe upon cards neither; I was even glad to find, that you gave them so little quarter. I sometimes thought that Mr. W——'s seeming fondness for them was a kind of *contre-coeur.* Be that as it will, his objection to the stanza, as well as mine, was solely founded on the versification, not the sentiment. I liked his Latin verses; but they do not interfere with yours. Send me a copy, and confine my use of it by what limitations you please. My reigning toy at present is a pocket-book; and I glory as much in furnishing it with the verses of my acquaintance, as others would with bank-bills. I did not know when I went to W[hitchurch], but I might have heard Mrs. G[raves] *accused of certain questions touching their law* (I mean of forms and ceremonies;) but I did *not.* On the contrary, I had the satisfaction of hearing her person, her temper, and her understanding, much commended; but this I did not want: the delicacy of your taste is equal with me to a thousand commendations. Mrs. W—— is really so much altered by her indisposition, that I did not know her. She talks of going to Bath this season; — I talked of it too, and wish it of all earthly things. You must know, I could not have come to Claverton *instead* of going to W[hitchurch], as I did not determine on the expedition at home; but at a friend's house, where I was betwixt twenty and thirty miles on my way thither. Besides, I would allow myself more time when I turn my face towards Bath, than I could this winter. Your invitation, as it is very obliging, so it has many concurring circumstances to recommend it at this time. I want to recover my health, which must be recovered by Bath, or *nothing;* I want to have you read some trifles of mine, which must be ratified by you, or *no one;* but principally, and above all, do I long to see you, my old friend, and Mrs. G[raves], whom I expect you should render my new one. — I am obliged for your charitable endeavours to support my spirits. Your company would do it effectually, but scarce any thing less, in *winter*. Solitary life, limited circumstances, a phlegmatic habit, and disagreeable events, have given me a melancholy turn, that is hardly dissipated by the most serene sky; but in a north-east wind is quite intolerable. After a long state of this kind, upon every access of amusement, one is apt to think it is not *right* to be happy; that it is one of Wollaston's implicit lyes; a treating things contrary to what they *deserve*. — Your situation at Claverton is admired by most people; and, if you could connect some little matter in the neighbourhood, would be as surely envied.

It is now high time to release you. — This is not a letter, but an olio. I desire my compliments to Mrs. G[raves], and am affectionately and invariably

Yours,

W. Shenstone

As I must now use a frank, I will send you a few inscriptions: your imagination will supply the scenery, on which what merit they may have depends. There *were* different readings in the first copy, of which I beg your opinion.

STANZA THE FIRST
At least this calm sequester'd shade
Ambition never dares invade
No, &c.
But shuns, &c.

STANZA THE SECOND
Hither the plaintive *halcyon hies,*
Avoiding all the race that flies.

My design was only to convey some pleasing ideas of things, which, though proper to the place, a person might not chance to see there once in twenty times. Mr. Lyttelton and Lady Aylesbury *necessitated* me to give them copies, though they probably did it out of complaisance only: I gave them in the manner I send them you. I hope *you* have not entirely dropt your love for rural scenes, of which you were once so fond. I will allow your taste for medals to preponderate. — I beg, dear Sir, you would neglect no *opportunity* of calling on me. — I will come to Claverton when I can.

125. To LADY LUXBOROUGH[1]

The Leasows, March ye 10th 1750–1

MADAM,

I can very faithfully assure your Ladyship, yt the Pleasure I receiv'd from your French Letter was altogether equal to what I expected: & as I can hardly form an expression yt implies my Approbation more fully, I ought perhaps to add nothing more upon this Head. However I can ill avoid being more explicit; for besides that your Choice of words gives me an agreeable Idea of ye French Language, there is I don't know what kind of Pleasure arises upon seeing common or domestick Affairs treated of in a Language foreign to one's own. Perhaps it may however be all resolv'd into one's vanity, as it seems to give them an Air of greater Importance. I wish it may not be one Day my Lot to hazard a few French Lines to your Ladyship; tho' I fear I have in a great Measure forgot ye terminations of my moods and Tenses; and should of course make a thousand blunders in regard to ye peculiar Idiom. But if I *should*, I trust your Ladyship would be prevail'd upon to burn what I wrote *immediately*. You, Madam, have not only the Idiom, but seem even to *think* in French; if I may guess by the excessive complaisance you are pleas'd to discover. And surely it is oweing to the Delicacy of your Choice, or ye French have great Numbers of words more expressive than our own. For instance "Trop bonne pour avoir besoin de cet *Assaisonnement;*" I know not of any English word yt would be proper here besides *"Recommendation"*, which is greatly inferiour. I have observ'd ye same of many others: But I confine my partiality to their Prose; & I dare say your Ladyship who knows so well all ye *Beauties* of their Language, is also not unacquainted with ye *Imperfections* of it; by which means you find yourself so well enabled to disguise ye latter, at ye same time yt you are displaying ye former to so great an advantage — Notwithstanding ye suppos'd Qualifications of the Glums and the Gawries excites one's curiosity, The Book does not I think deserve a Place in your Ladyship's Library. It makes two vols in 12ves, Price Six Shillings. It came into my way, so I read it, giving it just attention enough to let it amuse me; And this is all I have allotted to any Book yt I have read for some months past. As to what I said of the *Scribleriad*,[2] you will observe I had read nothing but a few Quotations; & am now to request your Ladyship's

---

[1] B. M. Add. MSS 28958, fol. 109ff. Also published in Hull's *Select Letters,* Vol. I, No. XXXI. This letter answers and confirms the date of Lady Luxborough's of February 26, 1751 (*Letters,* No. LX), which is partly in French. Her No. LXI, dated "Equinox, past Midnight, 1751," answers the present letter.

[2] *The Scribleriad* (1751) of Richard Owen Cambridge (1717–1802), "an heroic poem in six books," was a satire on the bad taste of the times.

Opinion who have receiv'd y^e *Book* — Believe me, my good Lady, I am not *happy* in my subjection to *Indolence*. I long for nothing so much as to subdue the *Old Wizard,* who keeps me close confin'd; &, tho' he allows me ye use of Pen Ink & Paper, stupifies me to such a Degree y^t I can use them to no sort of Purpose. I long for ye nearer approach of Spring, to send him packing after his old Father Winter; y^t I may be able to acquit myself of *my* share of ye correspondence, & to deserve ye vivacity of *yours* somewhat better y^n I do. But when I shall be able to exchange ye Cypress grove, in which I am wandering at present, for ye more agreeable verdure of ye Myrtle & the Laurel, is a Question I cannot pretend to solve. Very pedantick truly this! but to proceed — I wrote many ludicrous things at College, & in ye former part of my Life; & one or two of these I am thinking to enclose to you, now & then, during this insipid season. Perhaps, taking, like Wood-cocks, ye Advantage of a Fog, they may hope for something better Quarter; but in truth they are much too *silly,* & your Judgment too *penetrating* to give any kind of Room for such an expectation. As to Printing, I will not say y^t I *never* intend it, but I must first be able to spend a few weeks with a college Acquaintance,[3] who is a Person of great Delicacy, and whose Friendship to me may perhaps induce him to examine my trifles with more attention y^n they deserve. No very agreeable task, to him or any one else! Mean time ye Complaint you make of y^r present want of Amusement affords me an occasion to pour in Floods of my written Impertinence — "The Progress of Taste" I mean't to have shewn you long ago — "The Snuff-box" (which by interweaving another Poem is now grown I see, a mere piece of Patch-Work, appears before you for no other Reason but y^t it happen'd to be transcrib'd in y^e *same Book* wth ye former) is interested in my desiring you not to read a Line of it. I send also ye ode I mention'd to the Dutchess,[4] & would ask your Ladyship in the first Place whether it deserve correction. If you happen to think it may be render'd tolerable, will you be so kind as to mark (in this Copy) any Improprieties, or propose any Hints of Improvement, which may occur to your Ladyship upon reading it. And this *can* be no difficult Task, if you will care to engage in it; whether in regard to ye Incorrectness of ye present Draught, ye brightness of your Genius, or ye Knowledge you have of her Grace's situation. I calculated y^e *subject* as well as I cou'd; but, I fear, I have made it produce nothing but common-place Thoughts. I think my Verses in general smell too much of King-cups & Daffodils; & considering how I pass my time they can scarce do otherwise. I would desire your Ladyship

---

[3] Probably Graves. See the preceding letter.
[4] Of Somerset. The ode, of course, is *Rural Elegance.*

not to shew anything I send in this Packet, at least to any critick; & shou'd be glad to have them return'd in about nine days or a Fortnight — A Word or two now in regard to ye propos'd alteration in your *Room*. If your Ladyship doesn't chuse to go to the expence of a *Carv'd*-frame, what think you of a white oval Frame to your glass in y^e *Middle,* and a Festoon on each side? This with ye Stucco need amount to no more y^n about Four Guineas. But the Room is mighty well, even now; & you are yourself ye Judge whether ye propos'd Alteration would afford you an answerable Amusement. I am greatly pleas'd with what your Ladyship mentions of coming to The Leasows; for tho' you will see but little *new* this year, yet by allowing yourself some *time* you will see the *same* with much greater Ease y^n you could before: If I shou'd add "Pleasure," I hope you wou'd indulge it to my Fondness for a Place y^t has engross'd my Care so long. You complain, Madam, of ye Want of *fresh Ideas,* (which I never yet observ'd in your Conversation or Letters, at any time or tide) what then must be my case? who see nothing Day after Day, but

> Bleak Mountains & wild staring Rocks!
> The wretched result of my Pains!
> The swains greater Brutes y^n their Flocks!
> And the Nymphs — as polite as ye Swains.
> vid: Answer to Collin's COMPLAINT.

I once thought to have inscrib'd these on a seat, but now I think my very Spleen forsakes me — I sent Tom with this packet because [it] might not otherwise have arriv'd the Lord knows when. Mr Williams *can* seldom send but on a Thursday, & sometimes you do not receive anything, till long after — I am your Ladyship's most oblig'd & most faithfull H. S.

W. Shenstone

My Brother,[5] who is here at present, desires his complim^{ts}.

126. To RICHARD JAGO[1]

The Leasowes, Mar. 28, 1751

DEAR SIR,

What a stupid fool was I, to shew you those letters of my friend Graves, wherein he declares himself so freely against a regular corre-

---

[5] Joseph Shenstone (1722–51), of whom the poet was very fond (see his letters to Lady Luxborough, to Graves, and to Wren on the occasion of Joseph's death). Of the younger brother Nash says, he "was bred an attorney at Bridgenorth but never practised" (*Worcestershire,* I, 528ff).

[1] Dodsley, *Letters to Particular Friends,* No. LXIII. Though not positively identified, the addressee seems to be Jago.

spondence! See the effects of it! You have taken immediate advantage of his example, and I must never more expect an answer to any letter that I send you, in less than half a century. I wrote to you after I came home, to thank you for all your kindness at I[cheneton], &c.; but not a syllable have I been able to receive from you, or a word that I could hear concerning you. I could, however, very easily convince you, that Mr. Graves (your precedent) is not altogether so hardened an offender as you may imagine. His last letter is a very affectionate recantation. I inclose that part of it which regards Mr. F[ancourt].²

What a number of schemes are irreparably broken by the sudden death of the prince of Wales! Yours, my good friend, which seems to be destroyed amongst the rest, has, I think, of late given you no solicitude. Your interest in Mr. N—— will remain the same, I suppose; and if he would but serve you nearer *home,* I will have no sort of quarrel with him that he did not transplant you into Cornwall.—It is at least some gratification to a person's self-love, when one finds the more *ambitious* hopes of more *aspiring* people as liable to be suddenly extinguished as one's own. However, the death of the Prince gave me a good deal of concern, though it no way affected my *particular* interest, as he had all the humane, affable, and generous qualities, which could recommend him to one's *affection.*

Mr. Graves has sent me two copies of verses: One on Medals, to Mr. Walker; and the other, on the late Memoirs of the London Heroines, Lady V[ane], Mrs. Pilkington, and Mrs. Phillips. Both good in their way, which you shall see when you come over.

Have you seen the first books of "The Scribleriad," by Mr. Cambridge?³ — The "Verses written in a Country Church-yard?"⁴ — Mr. W. Whitehead's "Ode to the Nymph of Bristol Spring?"⁵ — or, what *have* you seen? — You live infinitely more in the world than I do; who hear nothing, see nothing, do nothing, and *am* nothing. Remedy this unhappiness, by sending me somewhat that may rouse my attention. — I must except what I hear from my Lady Luxborough, who indulges me now and then with a letter in French.

If you should think this letter more than usually *dull,* you must know, that, since I saw you, I have been *generally* dispirited; till about a fortnight ago I found some nervous disorders that I greatly disliked, and

---

² Probably Mr. Fancourt, Jago's father-in-law.
³ See note 2 to the preceding letter.
⁴ Gray's *Elegy,* though begun as early as 1745, did not appear in an authorized edition until 1751.
⁵ Whitehead's *Ode to the Nymph of Bristol Spring* first appeared in 1751.

upon examination was told I had a nervous fever. For this I have been taking saline draughts and boluses, and *hope* I am something better; though I am far from well. I would not indeed have written to you at this time, but I chose not to defer sending the inclosed postscript. — You who have shared many of my *happiest* hours, will excuse the produce of a more than ordinarily dull one.

Mrs. Arnold comes up to enquire after my health, and wishes I may get better, that I may stir out and see the *pretty creatures in the barn*. It seems, she has a cow or two that have calved since I kept my room.

Why should I prolong a letter that has no kind of chance to afford you any amusement? Make my compliments to Mrs. [Jago],⁶ and believe me to be ever most affectionately

Yours,
W. Shenstone

I have just taken and signed a lease for life of the terrace beyond my wood, for which I am to pay annually the sum of one shilling. — Am not I a man of great worldly importance, to purchase ground and and take leases thus? — What matters it whether the articles that *secure* the premises to me would also *cover* them or not?

My service to Mr. F[ancour]t; — why will he not come and spend a week with me? — I think you cannot both be absent at a time.

127. To LADY LUXBOROUGH¹

[April 24, 1751]

MADAM,

I have only Leisure to give your Ladyship a very *short* Account of what has *befell* me since I had last yᵉ Pleasure of writing to Barrels.

I believe I complain'd, more yⁿ once, to you, of an unusual Depression of Spirits, in my Letters. Soon after this, I found some disagreeable Symptoms in my Nerves, wᶜʰ alarm'd me; & my Disorder was hereupon term'd a nervous Fever; for which I took a multitude of Draughts & Bolus's, tho' I am now convinc'd, a Blister had been yᵉ properest Application. I had no Physician, & indeed was not so much apprehensive of *Danger* as to substitute *that* in Place of less disagreeable Means. *Somewhat* better I have been since; However, if it really *were* a Fever upon yᵉ nerves, I think, in some Degree I am but rarely free from it.

---

⁶ Apparently Mrs. Jago, who died, however, this year.
¹ B. M. Add. MSS 28958, fol. 111ff. Lady Luxborough replies with her letter of April 29–May 1, 1751 (*Letters*, No. LXV), the date of which is thus confirmed.

After this my Brother was seiz'd here with a very dangerous Inflammation upon his Lungs: This Dr Hervey calls a true Peripneumony. 'Twas attended, at Intervals, with such inexpressible difficulty of Respiration, y^t I thought it impossible he shou'd survive many Hours. Dr Wilks was sent for at 12 o Clock at Night, in Hopes he might be brought to join Dr Hervey (whom we kept with us) ye next Day: but he refus'd this, & even a *second* Application, tho' we us'd the Interest of a Neighbour for whom he pretends a Personal Friendship. Had not my Brother's Disorder remitted, I purpos'd to send for Dr Wall from Worster. I can't here be *explicit* upon any Event. My Brother, we think now, is in a fair way of being Recover'd by Dr Hervey; & tho' he is in a very languid Condition, we hope for great Advantages from a Vomit, so soon as the Physician can assure us, y^t it may be safely administred.

These are melancholy Scenes, compar'd wth the Pleasures of your Ladyships Correspondence, which has been so long intermitted! — My Spirits have of late been so low, so much injur'd by watching, & so much varyd by sudden Hopes & Fears, y^t I believe any more *violent* Shock superadded, wou'd have gone near to have kill'd me. The Effects of the *Mind* upon weak & sensible Nerves, are as much unknown to one half of ye World, as ye violent Shocks of Electrical Experiments were to our Ancestors a thousand years ago.

But I now own y^t my Hopes preponderate; & y^t I shall with ye utmost gratitude receive a Line from your Ladyship, when you find it Convenient — I expected your Servant *before* . . .² I wou'd have made Shift to have acquainted you in a few scrawling Lines with our late Situation; persuant to ye Freedom in which you indulge me, & ye Friendship wth which I have ye Honour to be your Ladyship's

most oblig'd & faithfull Servant
Will: Shenstone

April ye 24. 1751
The Leasows:

My Brother desires his Compliments to your Ladyship — We desire to be rememberd to Mr Hall — Upon my Brother's dangerous Illness, I apply'd [to] a gentlewoman in my neighbourhood, a good motherly sort of woman, y^t puts me in mind of y^r Mrs Holyoak; she is now in my Room, and will continue sometime.

² The manuscript is defective at this point, but no words seem blotted or lost.

128. To LADY LUXBOROUGH[1]

The Leasows, May ye 24, 1751

DEAR MADAM,

I hasten to acquaint your Ladyship, in my first Paragraph, y^t my Brother is now greatly better; and, as we all Hope, in a very fair way of Recovery.

What small Hopes I have entertain'd for most part of ye time since I wrote last to Barrels, have been rather owing to a kind of Self-*flattery* & an unwillingness to *despair,* yⁿ any proper Foundation. But these three last days, his Disorder is so much abated that they seem to receive some Sanction from Reason. Not that I am *entirely* free from Apprehensions. The Asthmatical Complaint is fallen down into his Legs, where it continues at present. But what by means of Ass's Milk, (wch agrees with him,) the Advantage of a few fair days in which he has been carried, Sedan-fashion, about my Grounds, & ye most scrupulous Care in regard to what we suffer him to eat or drink, his Spirits, Pulse, Complexion, strength, & stomach are wonderfully restor'd.

I will not detain your Ladyship any longer on this Head, yⁿ to acquaint you that I have thought *about* writing to Barrels every day since your Servant was here; but finding, all along, such frequent Changes in ye Disorder, & being utterly unable to give your Ladyship any *satisfactory* account, I had not y^e *Spirit* to set Pen to Paper.

This has been to me the most disagreeable Season, for a continuance, I ever pass'd in my Life. Betwixt sleepless Nights, sudden Alarms, constant Sollicitude, the Return of my nervous Disorder, Confinement, & an entire Alteration in my way of Living, I found my own situation not a little endanger'd. I might add to these the uncertainty of Physicians the difficulty of obtaining satisfactory Advice, & ye no less difficulty of prevailing on my Brother to follow even a *small Part* of it. Such Persons as He ought always to be *well;* I mean to *guard more* than others against Diseases, as they have so little Patience in Reserve to submit to the Means of Cure — But to lead your Ladyship from ye sick Room into the open Air, a little. I am now beginning for ye first time to brush up my walks. The Trees & Shrubs are in full bloom, all of a sudden. I mean so far as concerns their green Leaves, for the *latter* have not yet flower'd. The Servants are now busy in cleaning my Grove &c: whither I now stray once or twice a day with great Complacency. And yet I now begin to

---

[1] B. M. Add. MSS 28958, fol. 119ff. A version of this letter is printed in Hull's *Select Letters,* Vol. I, No. XXXII. Lady Luxborough's letter of May 27 (*Letters,* No. LXVII) replies to this.

feel (more than I *could* before) for the misfortunes of my Friends. I doubt ye Death of poor Mr Hall's Brother,² will occasion him much worldly perplexity, as well as concern, at present. I would otherwise press him to spend a week with us at the Leasows, as some kind of Relief to *him,* & a great Pleasure to *us*. I think a Change of Place after such an Affliction is very often of no small Service. That Book of Mr Pearsall's which your Ladyship subscrib'd to, is come out, I *hear;* but I have had no Copies sent me hitherto. Your Ladyship, I know intended to oblige *me* by your subscription. That Point you can never fail to obtain; But I am sorry you shou'd *suffer* by these Marks of your generosity. More I am not at Liberty to say. You will please to mention this Publication to Mr Hall. I sent *his* Name, tho' I am not sure yt He subscrib'd, knowing he would be ye readiest of Men to serve an old Schoolfellow. I hear no more of Mr Smith & *his* Devices. I begin to be asham'd for him.

Would your Ladyship be so kind as lend me Pompey the little?³ I have read, as I said before, little beside Physick-books for this two-month & I want now to be indulg'd with something more amusing. I wont pretend to your Ladyship that I am a very great Physician, but I consider myself as qualify'd to make ye best *Nurse* of any in the three Kingdoms— I said *little besides Physick-books,* but I have seen Whitehead's Ode to the Bristol-Spring, which I dont much like; & the Verses in ye Country Church-yard wch (as ye Hagley gardiner said of my Grove) I like *too well*. Pray whose are they? If your Ladyship have any thing new besides, I would return it in a week. I hope your Ladyship will now speak about a time when I may have the long-wish'd for happiness of waiting on you at the Leasows. In ye mean time I am to return my Brothers Thanks, with my own, for every obliging Instance of your Regard, & to subscribe myself inviolably your Ladyship's most dutifull

and most obedient Servant

Will: Shenstone

May ye 25

I should have sent ye foregoing *Account* yesterday, but I find nothing in my Brother's Situation that need tend to discolour it. I *yet* hope, Madam that there is some good in Reserve for us, which may in some measure compensate for ye gloomy season we have past. I know not from what Quarter, but I still confide — I hope your Ladyship does.

I did not propose many alterations about my House this year, & I now

---

² Alluded to in Lady Luxborough's *Letters,* No. LXVI, May 6, 1751, p. 261.
³ *The History of Pompey the Little* (1751) by Francis Coventry (d. 1759?) is a prose satire in the form of a picaresque narrative of the vicissitudes a lap dog suffers in passing from master to master of very unequal stations.

shall effect *nothing*. But I know your Ladyship will feel some Pleasure upon finding me tolerably chearfull & content that Matters are not worse—I hope with this good weather your Ladyship's wonted Spirits will return, & that I too shall be able to correspond with, or to *see* you with greater Alacrity yⁿ I fear'd of late It would be in my Power to do. Miss Dolman desir'd her Compliments to your Ladyship, when she went from hence—I see I cannot yet write with any sort of Spirit, so I will relieve your Ladyship at once from so many insipid nothings, as I shoud probably add, if I proceeded.

—26th

We all continue on ye mending Hand—Tom was to have taken this *to-day,* but cannot possibly be spar'd, as my Brother is yet assisted in moving from Room to Room—He shall positively go to-morrow morning.

—27

I have nothing to add that is material. Mr Pixell has undertaken to copy Mr Somervile's Picture, but has not yet done it—There has been a Blight in my Grove which has injurd the Shade—but yet your Ladyship will own it is still pleasant.

129. To LADY LUXBOROUGH [1]

The Leasows, June ye 14th 1751

DEAR MADAM,

I had just been writing two Pages of a Letter in order to send it in ye Morning to Mr Williams, when, stepping out o'Doors to take a Peep at my Masons, I saw your Ladyship's servant arrive—Now I mention *Masons,* I will just add here, that I am doing a small matter to my Windows, wch I expected would give something of a better Air to my Front; but I now believe I shan't like it when 'tis done. When one has an old House to manage so irregular in all respects as mine, tis seldom y^t Embellishments give us any Pleasure. It seems only *maturing* & *perfecting* an *Error.* And to *correct* it, I am not able.

Joe[2] tells me he is in great Haste, wch puts me upon hurrying on, faster yⁿ my usual Speed, so y^t I shall be sure to *stumble.* When I *do,* your Ladyship will excuse it, knowing it is not any Fault of *mine* y^t I am not a Race-horse.

[1] B. M. Add. MSS 28958, fol. 113ff. This answers and confirms the date of No. LXVIII of Lady Luxborough's *Letters* of the same date as the present letter. It likewise replies in some detail to her No. LXVII of May 27, 1751.

[2] Lady Luxborough's servant.

My Lord Bolingbroke's Misfortune³ is a very severe one, & I am truly concern'd for it. I hope, if he finds not y^t Redress from ye French Parliament, which I wish him, he will however find a good deal from his own Philosophy — of wch no one seems to have more — I will keep secret, tho' I am exceedingly glad to hear of, the Probability there is y^t you may see him at Barrels. I think ye Visit cannot fail of proving very agreeable to *Him,* as I am sure it will, to your Ladyship. You will please to observe y^t I cannot speak above a Word in answer to anything you have so kindly communicated. I believe Joe thinks I am even now sealing up my Letter — whereas I fully purpose to write a Page or two more —

A great many Thanks to your Ladyship for y^r Eau de Mille-fleurs. If Mrs Weymondsold be so very good as to remember me when she sends for Perfumes &c: I wish I could with any Propriety suggest to her, y^t, as I use them chiefly in *Snuff;* I shou'd be mighty thankfull if she would procure me ever so small a Bottle of the Chymical *Oil* of Jasamin, rather yⁿ the *Water:* wch last when I drop't into Snuff very soon evaporates. I beg my Compliments, there.

I beg my Compliments also to Mr Hall & will *Recommend* it to him to *spend* a little time at the Leasows, after ye Fatigue of his Accounts &c: is over — I speak *interestedly* tho' for we shall be extremely glad to see him.

The King seems *unfeignedly* Fond of the Princess & her Children — & it is a very aimiable Feature in his Character — He shew'd Something of ye same tenderness upon ye Death of ye late Queen.

I think wth y^r Ladyship in regard to Miss Green's Behaviour;⁴ & did so upon first reading ye Paragraph in ye News-papers — One is too apt to think one's own Afflictions greatest — What can exceed ye Anguish wch this Event must occasion to old Mr Dalton? Or perhaps, Miss Green?

I approve of ye Paper-ornaments for any Ceiling at Barrels, where Fretwork may be proper —

I detest Lord Hallifax's making use of those Bristol-stone Pillars *within* his *House.* These Stones will serve to embellish some little grott

---

³ The adverse decision handed down by the French courts in the lawsuit carried on against Bolingbroke by the Montmorins, kinsmen of his wife, who contested her will on the grounds that her marriage had been invalid. See Sichel, *Bolingbroke and His Times,* II, 397.

⁴ Lady Luxborough comments (*Letters,* pp. 272–73), "I think I could never forgive myself if I had been the cause (though the Papers call it innocent) of Mr. Dalton's death; as Miss G[ree]n was, by her foolish action in giving the snuff-box *he had given her* to Mr. Paul." She goes on to describe young Dalton as a man of "great learning, great good nature, great honour and sobriety, and a most genteel behaviour." It was with Dalton that Lady Luxborough is supposed to have committed the indiscretion which occasioned her separation from her husband (Sichel, *Bolingbroke and His Times,* II, 469–70).

or Cell in your Coppice with great Propriety. I cannot invent any Form to please myself, unless I were upon ye Spot — Your Ladyship can, very readily, in my Absence.

The Apology you are so condescending as to make for delaying your Journey to ye Leasows is fraught with very important Articles indeed! I can say no more y^n this, y^n when I have hopes given me of waiting upon y^r Ladyship, I always think ye sooner ye better — the dryer ye roads the better — the longer the Days the better & the more in order my Walks, & ye greener my Trees, so much ye better — As for the rest I think your Apology of undoubted Weight; & shall be very proud to wait upon your Ladyship when *Fortune* (for ye Crime now is her's alone) will permit.

I had yesterday afternoon Captn West & his Lady & Children, Miss Lyttelton & Miss West, who walk'd round the Walks & drank Tea with me in ye Grove. NB. The Grove I mention has receiv'd some little Improvement — Mrs West is a Woman of Taste.

Latter End of last Week I met a Party in my Walks, the Men well-dress'd, the Women in handsome lac'd Jackets, whom I took some Pains to escorte & entertain — & who were as I found afterwards, a couple of Actresses from Birmingham — an Actor &c:

Mr Pixell took this Copy of Mr Somervile which I alterd with my own Hand, 'till I thought it *something* like — tis not so good as your Original by a great deal, w^n Compar'd — He is doing what he *intends* shall be *better — This* was never quite finishd — but I send it as an Echantillo. I propos'd it one Day to Mr Dolman to take a Ride in his Chair to Barrels, for a Night, when he was over last, (viz) about a Fortnight ago, & the Scheme was only broken thro' by something y^t he found deficient in regard to his Dress; for wch I was angry at him.

It is probable I shall *some* day (within a short time) but as yet an unfix'd & uncertain Day, do myself ye Honour & Pleasure of walking with your Ladyship thro' ye Shrubbery, and ye Coppice; the Walks of wch are now, Tom tells me, extremely elegant.

My Brother continues on ye mending Hand — desires his best Respects to your Ladyship.

I shall be as glad to see Autumn triumph over Spring, this year, as your Ladyship. She never certainly had so fair an opportunity. For my Part I can fairly say that I have neither had a Pleasure budded in my Imagination, nor scarce a Flower blossomd on my *Shrubs,* all this Spring. Y^r Ladyship excells in ye Products of both. May y^r Ladyship live long to enjoy ye Pleasures of y^r Imagination, & the Beauties of your

Environs, & may I long enjoy ye satisfaction & Honour of Subscribing myself your Ladyships most oblig'd & most obedient humble Servant

Will Shenstone

I suppose I've made 50 Blunders, for I wrote full-stretch.

130. To LADY LUXBOROUGH [1]

The Leasows, August ye 8th 1751

I was extremely sorry, dear Madam, to discover by the whole Cast of your Letter yt Depression of Spirits of which you so seldom Complain. I too have had my Share, as your Ladyship can witness, for all the former Part of This Season. But there is nothing of *Importance* in this World, beside the *Life* or *Death* of Friends. The Misfortune is that we seldom esteem any Thing so *trivial* as we *ought*. However, very inexcuseable should I *be*, if I kept silence long together, when your Ladyship so *obligingly* intimates yt what I write may afford you some small Amusement— The Verses[2] & the Letter I enclose will serve to clear up ye Mystery of what I wrote before— You will not *admire*, but you will wonder —All I shall say is, that I think Colonel Lyttelton has a *Heart;* & as I hope, Friendship enough to deserve this from me— His Letter remov'd ye Anxiety I was under, by shewing me in some Sort yt my Compliment was not *ill receiv'd;* & as to any thing farther it is hard enough to say— Some other Persons here complimented have been civil— Your Ladyship has every Claim to my Respect. You will please, Madam, to observe that the *Subject* of these Verses, the known Regard I bear you, together with my real Inclination, all requir'd yt your Name should not be omitted on an Occasion like This. Why I did not ask your Leave in the *first* Place, & why I made use of a compliment wch you formerly accepted from me, were both owing to the same Reason: I mean *Precipitation*. Had I detain'd ye Verses longer I did not know but the Dutchess[3] &c: might be gone from Hagley; (tho' I think by reason of ye Colonel's Indisposition, she remains there still.) Another thing, Lord Stamford dineing that day at Hagley, I chose rather yt he should see ye Compt paid him, as it were *accidentally* & at a *third place,* than have a Copy giv'n him, or at least be told of it in a more *formal* Way.

[1] B. M. Add. MSS 28958, fol. 117ff. This letter answers and confirms the date of Lady Luxborough's of August 1, 1751 (*Letters,* No. LXXIII). Her No. LXXIV of August 21 is the reply to the present letter.
[2] Shenstone's *Pastoral Ode,* to Sir Richard (Colonel) Lyttelton, whose patronage he hoped to obtain but did not. See *Works,* I (1764), 174ff.
[3] The Duchess of Bridgewater, wife of Colonel Lyttelton.

All this put together occasion'd me to take the Lines in an awkard hurry out of my Pocket Book, & send them without a Cover by an absolute stranger, Mr Burgess; who was with me & at a distance in the walks When the Colonel went away. So y^t you have here My Reasons for y^t painfull Suspence I mention'd; for my not adviseing with your Ladyship; & for any Confusion you may observe in ye Combination of Ranks, Characters, & Things. I have been forc'd to write out this from Scraps no bigger y^n a Cheese-paring; & as I have no other Copy, must desire your Ladyship to return this: wch must undergo some Corrections. Pray likewise, write me word as soon as possible, y^t you excuse me — And if you wou'd please to send me any Hints for it's Improvement, it would add to ye Obligation. I write from my Bed-side, upon my right Elbow, & in a very awkward Posture; so y^t you must forgive me, if I drop my Pen, after it has faithfully assur'd you that I am your Ladyship's *most* affectionate & oblig'd hum: Servt Will: Shenstone

Masons & Carpenters! The Lord deliver me!

131. To RICHARD GRAVES [1]

The Leasowes, Sept. 17, 1751

DEAR MR. G[raves],

I am very sensibly obliged to you for the *diligence* and *expedition* which you have shewn in answering my late request: I cannot feel the very *tenderness* of friendship to be at all abated in me by our long separation; nor will it at any time be possible I should, so long as I receive such testimonies of your usual *kindness* and *ingenuity.* — I have no sort of exceptions to make against the province in which you were engaged at Cheltenham, nor the light in which you appeared. What you lost in any one's opinion of your independency, you would gain in their idea of your merit, genius, and learning; and then you had all those other advantages *par dessu*. As to the compliments that were paid to Mrs. G[raves], you have something of the same sort of reason to be pleased with them, that I have to be pleased with those that are given to my place; which I consider as naturally possessed of many beauties, each of them brought to light and perfected through my own discernment, care, and cultivation. And then your pleasure ought to be so much greater than mine, as you have a nobler subject to enjoy. — Mrs. G[raves] has too much sense to object against the freedom of this similitude.

[1] Dodsley, *Letters to Particular Friends,* No. LXV. The context of this letter plainly shows it to be addressed to Graves, though Dodsley gives only the initial G.

I cannot help adding a few strokes to your picture of Mrs. S——. I think her an extremely *superficial* female-pedant: for, after an interval of many years since I first conversed with her at Mr. ———'s, I found her conversation turn solely upon the same *topics, definitions,* and *quotations*. I believe, I could easily enough have recommended myself to a greater degree of her favour: but her vanity and affectations were beyond what I could bear.— Your account of ——— is very picturesque, and agreeable to the idea I always had of him: but I believe that idea was perfected by what observations I made when I had some of his company at London.— There was something accountable enough to me in their burlesquing Mr. L[yttelton]'s monody.[2] He is, you know, engaged in a party; and his peom (though an extraordinary fine composition) was too tender for the public ear. It should have been printed privately, and a number of copies dispersed only among their friends and acquaintance; — but even so it would have been republished; — and it was too good to suppress. I wish the burlesquers of such *ingenuous* profusions could be punished, consistently with English liberty. "Where were ye, Muses, &c." is imitated from Milton, and taken by Milton from Theocritus. I write Greek wretchedly; but you will remember the passage,

Πᾶ πόκ' ἄρ' ἦθ' ὅκα Δάφνις ἐτάκετο; πᾶ πόκα, Νύνφαι;

I heard, once before, it was burlesqued under the title of "An Elegy on the Death of a favourite Cat;"[2] but the burlesque will die, and the poem will survive.— You tell me, "The author of Peregrine Pickle says, if you will flatter Mr. Lyttelton well, he will at last make you a Middlesex Justice;" and it happened oddly that, whilst I was reading your letter, a neighbour told me I was put in the commission of the peace. I have never received a single line from Mr. Whistler, and I believe my journey to W[hitchurch] has given the final blow to our friendship. Pray was not Mr. Blandy some relation of theirs, or only their attorney? The affair is uncommonly shocking; and I fancy the *genuine* accounts that Mr. W—— sends you will be curious anecdotes at Bath.— I suppose you have painted your room with oil-colours, and made it *really* handsome.— I drew out a festoon and a medal some time ago, for a pannel over Mr. P——'s chimney; but they knew not what to make of the medal, and had only the festoon executed in stone colour, by a common painter; yours is better, and in character.— I am a degree more frugal than you;

[2] George Lyttelton's *Monody to the Memory of a Lady* (his wife) was published in 1747. Smollett parodied it. Gray's *On the Death of a Favourite Cat* appeared in Dodsley's *Collection*, Vol. II (1748).

for I only use quicklime, and either blue or yellow sand, to take away the objection which I have to whited walls.

I paid a visit to Mr. Lyttelton, the Dean, &c. since he came down; but had little of their company, for they thought Sir Thomas was dying: however, by unparalleled strength of constitution, he lingered in violent pain till last Saturday, when he died,[3] very much lamented. He had good natural parts, well improved by reading modern writers, and by the knowledge of the world: extremely prudent, considerate, humane, polite, and charitable. — I have jumbled his more obvious qualities together, that you may not think I am usurping the province of a news-man. Sir George will lose no time in building a new house, or doing what is more than *equivalent* to the old one.

I want no *temptation* to come immediately to C[laverton]. This is a melancholy *season* with me always; whether it be owing to the scenes I see, or to the effect of hazy skies upon an ill-perspiring skin. — I can say no more at *present,* than that I most ardently desire to see you, and desire my humble service to Mrs. G[raves]. I have a chalybeate spring in the middle of my grotto: what think you of this inscription.

FONS FERRUGINEUS
DIVARUM OPTUMAE
SALUTI SACER

Is it antique?

I am, dear Mr. G[raves],
Your most affectionate
W. Shenstone

132. To LADY LUXBOROUGH[1]

The *Leasowes*
[After Sept. 14 and before Nov. 30, 1751]

DEAR MADAM,

Tho' I think it is a Sort of Maxim, that a Person in *London* seldom *complains* he is forgotten by his Friends in the Country, yet I cannot, by any Means, prevail upon my Conscience to acquit me of a Sort of disrespectful Silence, since your Ladyship went to Town. It was not either the Politics or the Amusements of our great Metropolis, that could make the Letters of your Friends appear impertinent, or even indifferent to

---

[3] Sir Thomas Lyttelton died September 14, 1751.

[1] This undated letter, published in Hull's *Select Letters,* Vol. I, No. XVIII, does not appear in the manuscript collection of Shenstone's letters to Lady Luxborough (B. M. Add. MSS 28958). It was evidently written after the foregoing letter to Graves announcing the death of Sir Thomas Lyttelton and before the death, near the end of November, 1751, of Shenstone's brother Joseph. Shenstone addresses Lady Luxborough in London, whence she has told him (*Letters,* pp. 288, 291) she is going to be with Bolingbroke, ill with cancer.

you; and tho' the sublime Entertainment you must receive from the Conversation of so great a Man as Lord Bolingbroke, might bid the fairest to do so, yet was I not without Conviction, that your Ladyship would feel some sort of Complacency upon the Sight of a Scrip of Paper, which should acquaint you that I was alive.

Alive, indeed I am; at least, if it may be called so, to exist among a Set of People, whose Employments, Passions, and Sentiments, are entirely foreign to my own; and where I see, and hear, and do nothing, but what I think may as well be left unseen, unheard, and undone. What can your Ladyship expect from a Correspondent so situated, beside pure Respect and Friendship, and many artless Assurances of their Reality and Continuance?

Mr. O[uting] stayed pretty near a Week with me. He has, I think, strict Honour, Good-nature, and good Sense. What he wants, in my Eye, is a little genuine *Taste;* for tho' good Sense may, by Degrees, enable a Person to discover the Beauties of Nature or Art, yet it can never furnish him with any extraordinary Relish or Enjoyment of them, which is the Effect of innate Taste alone, and which differs as widely from the former, as the Palate differs from the Brain. Your Ladyship has, I dare say, frequently made the same observation.

You will hear Sir Thomas Lyttelton, notwithstanding he complained always of his *Head,* died of a *Polypus* in the great Artery; which, I do not find, was ever, in the least, suspected by his Physicians; but which, if it had been ever so apparent, they could not possibly have cured. You will imagine that his Death must have thrown a Sort of Gloom round the Villages in his Neighbourhood. A numerous and fashionable Family animates a Country-Place to an inconceivable Degree. The Family at *Hagley* will be immediately dispersed. Miss Lyttelton goes to Lady Litchfield's, to the *Colonel's,* to *London,* and does not think to settle. Miss West goes first to *Stow,* and then intends to reside with her Brother the *Commodore.* Sir George and his Lady set out for London to-morrow, and as they propose to build, next Spring, upon the *old Foundation,* it may be many Years ere they come to reside amongst us, even for a small Part of the Summer.

Lord Dudley and I dined together at *Hagley* last *Wednesday,* where we found Lord Anson's Brother, and some other Company. Mr. Miller unluckily asked me at Table, how I liked the new Situation of their Column; which threw me under the necessity of offending either against the Rules of Politeness, or (what is more sacred with me) the Laws of Sincerity. The Truth is, I do not like it upon many Accounts; and I am persuaded, before many Years are past, they will be of the same Mind.

But least of all, do I approve their Intentions of building three new Fronts, and altering every Room by a gothic Model, and that with an Eye to Frugality, at the same Time that they have not an Inch of Gothicism about the House, to warp their Imagination that Way. But this Subject never fails to lead me too far; nor can I explain myself to the full, unless I could shew your Ladyship their Plan. The fine Situation they have, within an hundred Yards, they neglect; — in short, as it appears to me, they are going to sacrifice an Opportunity of rendering their Place compleat, for the Sake of an imperfect, but expensive Specimen of gothic Architecture; which, not having its Foundation either in Truth or Proportion, will fall into Disgrace again in the Course of a few Years — Can one then forbear crying out, "The Graces droop" — "Am I in *Greece* or in *Gothland?*" But as their Resolution seems fixed, I mention this in Confidence, and must, for the Future, lay my Finger on my Mouth.

Mr. S——[2] has so mangled and disfigured my *Grove,* that I dare not send it to your Ladyship, till he has altered the Plate, so as to render it less intolerable. Fluellin, as I remember, in Shakespeare,[3] speaking of the near Resemblance betwixt *Macedon* and *Monmouth,* observes, "There is a River in Macedon, there is a River also in Monmouth — peradventure, there be Fish in both. — Would you desire better Similitude?" S[mith] being a modest Man, has seemed to content himself with some such Degree of Resemblance: but I wish him well, and will cause him, one Day, to do the Place Justice, for his own Sake as well as mine — for his own, as his Piece will be seen by many who know the Place, and for mine, as the Place is known to afford the best Scene I have.

I am, &c.
W. Shenstone

133. To LADY LUXBOROUGH [1]

The Leasows Jan: ye first 1752

Dear Madam,

I had wrote to your Ladyship long before this time, to acknowledge the Kindness of your Letter & Present; but I have a most deplorable Account to give of my Delay, & what so good a Friend as yourself will not read without a sigh. Alas! dear Madam! I have lost my only Brother!

---

[2] Evidently Mr. Smith, of whose views of neighboring estates frequent mention already has been made.

[3] *Henry V,* IV, vii, 28ff.

[1] B. M. Add. MSS 28958, fol. 123ff. A version of this letter also appears in Hull's *Select Letters,* Vol. I, No. XXXIV.

[2] Joseph Shenstone (1722-51).

A more sincere or *truly* affectionate one never bore the Name. I cannot now add more, tho' I should not want matter to expatiate upon his Merit, were I not at ye same time to revive & lament the loss of it. The Impetuosity of youth & Temper wch alone could in ye least obscure *it,* were beginning to subside apace — But it has been his Lot to go before me, in ye very *Prime* of his Days, & eer ye Force of his Understanding, or ye Benevolence of his Heart has been half *exerted* or *known.*

Future Letters, & other Conversations may afford me an opportunity to pour out all my soul. At present I am not enough master of myself. I find all my Views intercepted; all my schemes & measures (& I may add my Heart itself) to be well-nigh broke on this occasion! Every object round me, every Source of my former Amusement, revives a train of Ideas which I am not able to support. I have procur'd a set of low Friends to accompany me, & to draw of my Attention; but (to confess my weakness to a Friend) my principal Relief since ye fatal *close of November* has been drawn from mere Stupefaction.

Pardon me, my good Lady; I did not mean to make a display of my affliction: It insensibly steals into my Letter. "I cannot but remember such men were, And were most *dear* to me." Since this unhappy Catastrophe, it has been my Fortune to hear of another[3] which must nearly affect your Ladyship. Believe me, Madam, I am far from an *unconcerned* Observer of Events y^t must naturally afford you either Pleasure or Pain: But I am not in a Condition to *receive* Relief, & how can I pretend to give it? One thing however I will venture to suggest — I think Caesar acknowledg'd, (at an earlier Period of life y^n what my Lord Bolingbroke arriv'd at), that He had liv'd enough, either in regard to *Nature* or to *Glory.*

During ye Height of our Afflictions, we can scarce believe it possible they should ever wear off. In my Case, there are some Particulars wch render it most improbable they *should.* Yet *Time,* we find, alleviates the Sorrows of *others;* & it is fitting we should hope *implicitly* y^t it may somehow diminish *our own.*

I am altogether ignorant where this Letter will find you; but I hope you will be so kind as to *write* or to *dictate* a Letter to me, & I will not cease praying that it may be the *former.* Let your subject be what you please; assure me only of ye continuance of your Esteem, & it will be of greater Service to me y^n whole volumes of Philosophy. But this is doing you injustice, for I have found my Philosophy of *none.* And there is nothing so satisfactory upon ye Death of Friends, as to receive fresh testimonies of Kindness from the *Best* of those that survive.

[3] Bolingbroke died December 12, 1751.

I am, dear Madam,
(with all yᵉ Tenderness of my present situation)
Your most oblig'd, faithfull, & ever-affectionate Servant
Will Shenstone

This is yᵉ third time I have begun to write to you, but I hope I shall find less difficulty when I am to answer your next. Above all things do I long to see you; & please myself with yᵉ Thoughts of it, when I hear you are return'd to Barrels — At present I am taking Medicines within doors for a kind of nervous Fever. *Some* Assistance I may hope from them, & that, I think, is *little:* Tis taking *Drugs* from yᵉ Shops to cure Anxiety of *Mind.*

134. To LADY LUXBOROUGH[1]

The Leasows, Jan. yᵉ 25. 1752

DEAR MADAM,

Very truly did I rejoice at the sight of your trusty servant, who has deliver'd your Packet with great Care & Expedition. Your Ladyship honours me with your Friendship, revives me by your Letters, and amuses me by a succession of elegant Presents, for All which Favours I can do no more than *thank* you; & that in yᵉ *vulgar* & *customary* way, like a Person not half so sensible of the obligation, as I feel myself to be.

I am very glad to hear, & I *think* also, that the Bath-waters bid fair for your *Recovery.* I hope you will partake likewise of the *Pleasures* of the Place; which, as your Complaints are nervous, must have an undoubted tendency to further *it.* What you say with regard to *my* coming to Bath is very just; & the Manner in which you invite me extremely kind & obliging. There is nothing could attract me thither *so powerfully* as the satisfaction I shou'd find in conversing with you: And yet I have other Inducements at this time, & those no way inconsiderable; The Melancholy yᵗ I feel at *Home,* the *suitableness* of the Bath-waters, & an Invitation from Mʳ Graves to Clarton within two Miles of yᵉ Place; one of yᵉ most familiar Friends I have, and of the most ingenious Men, I know — But before I must *think* of this Expedition I have a scene of Business to pass thro', which is a task as necessary, as it will be painfull.

It is not more irksome for your Ladyship's *hand* to write, than it is for my *Head* to express a single Sentiment; for which reason I avoid writing at present to any Person in yᵉ World but you. Since I wrote last, I have

---

[1] B. M. Add. MSS 28958, fol. 125ff. This letter answers and confirms the date of Lady Luxborough's of January 20, 1752 (*Letters,* No. LXXVIII). Her No. LXXIX of February 29, 1752, is the reply to the present letter.

been *forc'd* to drop ye method of raising my Spirits by Liquor &c: and have had Recourse to Amusements; which are another kind of *Inebriation*. I have bought an old Romish Missal on Vellum, highly illuminated &c: which contains some Indulgences y^t are very remarkable. I have had Toys from Birmingham for this Purpose, Patterns of Paper for my Drawing Room (where I live *continually*) and my Servants were gone out on such Sort of Errands, when your Joe pass'd by my window — Thus when the Evil Day arrives a Child may often support himself as well as a Philosopher. But perhaps it may *be* Philosophy to avocate one's Thoughts by any trifles whatever. This may be true; but yet we cannot always do so, without a *Consciousness* y^t we are defrauding Sorrow of it's *lawfull Claim*.

My Lord Dudley desir'd his Compliments to your Ladyship. He & two of his Sisters spent five Days wth me this Week. He will be in London to-morrow from whence I am given to hope that he will send me his Picture. I shall value it, as he is a truly benevolent Man, & one who has shewn me many Instances of Civility.

Mr Mallet seems handsomely rewarded for his Attachment to Lord Bolingbroke.[2] I suppose He will publish Manuscripts wch must prove exceedingly advantageous.

I have found much Entertainment in ye Perusal of Lord Orrery's Narrative;[3] & was glad to find that he gives your Brothers Character with so much Justice, Elegance & Propriety.

I have since glanc'd upon Mr Warburton's Edition[4] of Pope's Works; which abounds in scurrilities thrown upon his *own* Enemies, & in perversions of his Author's Meaning.

I trespass upon Joe's Patience, if not upon your Ladyship's; but I must ask your Leave to mention one more particular. 'Tis probable you may want Servants upon your Return to Barrels, & I shou'd take it as a great Favour if you w^d please to make Tryal of my Servant's Sister. She has good Sense, good Temper & a good Person; & It is my Opinion she would please your Ladyship. I am sure she would be zealous to do so — But if after Experience she shou'd be so unfortunate as to be disapprov'd, I *promise* it shall give no offence.

I am, dear Madam, with ye truest sense of all y^r Favours, your most oblig'd & faithfull Servt

Will Shenstone

[2] Bolingbroke willed the exclusive right of publishing all his works to David Mallet.
[3] *Remarks on the Life and Writings of Dr. Jonathan Swift; in a Series of Letters from John, Earl of Orrery, to His Son the Hon. Hamilton Boyle.* Announced in the Register of Books of the *Gentleman's Magazine* for November, 1751.
[4] Warburton's edition of Pope came out in 1751.

135. To RICHARD GRAVES[1]

The Leasowes, Feb. 14, 1752

DEAR MR. GRAVES,

You will be amazed at my long silence; and it might reasonably excite some disgust, if my days had passed of late in the manner they used to do: but I am not the man I was; perhaps I never *shall* be. Alas! my dearest friend! I have lost my only brother! and, since the fatal close of November, I have had neither peace nor respite from agonizing thoughts!

You, I think, have *seen* my brother; but perhaps had no opportunity of distinguishing him from the groupe of others whom we call *good-natured* men. This part of his character was so visible in his countenance, that he was generally beloved at sight; I, who must be allowed to know him, do assure you, that his understanding was no way inferior to his benevolence. He had not only a sound judgment, but a lively wit and genuine humour. As these were many times eclipsed by his native bashfulness, so his benevolence only suffered by being shewn to an excess. I here mean his giving too indiscriminately into those jovial meetings of company, where the warmth of a social temper is discovered with least reserve; but the virtues of his head and heart would soon have shone without alloy. The foibles of his youth were wearing off; and his affection for me and regard to my advice, with his own good sense, would soon have rendered him all that I could have wished in a successor. I never in my life knew a person more sincere in the expression of his love or dislike. But it was the *former* that suited the propensity of his heart; the *latter* was as transient as the starts of passion that occasioned it. In short, with much true genius and real fortitude, he was, according to the *English* acceptation, "a truly honest man;" and I think I may also add, a truly English character: but "habeo, dixi? immo *habui* fratrem & amicum, Chreme!" All this have I *lost* in him. He is now in regard to *this* world no more than a mere idea; and this idea, therefore, though deeply tinged with melancholy, I must, and surely *ought* to, cherish and preserve.

I believe I wrote you some account of his illness last spring; from which to all appearance he was tolerably well recovered. He took the air, and visited about with me, during the warmer months of summer; but my pleasure was of short duration. "Haesit lateri lethalis arundo!" The peripneumony under which he laboured in the spring had terminated in an adhesion of the lungs to the pleura, so that he could never lie

[1] Dodsley, *Letters to Particular Friends*, No. LXVI.

but upon his right side; and this, as the weather grew colder, occasioned an obstruction that could never be surmounted.

Though my reason forewarned me of the event, I was not the more prepared for it. — Let me not dwell upon it. — It is altogether insupportable in *every respect:* and my imagination seems more assiduous in educing pain from this occasion, than I ever yet found it in administering to my pleasure. — This hurts me to no purpose — I know it; and yet, when I have avocated my thoughts, and fixed them for a while upon common amusements, I suffer the same sort of consciousness as if I were guilty of a crime. Believe me, this has been the most sensible affliction I ever felt in my life; and you, who know my anxiety when I had far less reason to complain, will more easily *conceive* it now, than I am able to describe it.

I cannot pretend to fill up my paper with my usual subjects — I should thank you for your remarks upon my poetry; but I despise poetry: and I might tell you of all my little rural improvements; but I hate them. — What can I now expect from my solitary rambles through them, but a series of melancholy reflections and irksome anticipations? — Even the pleasure I should take in shewing them to *you,* the greatest they can afford me, must be now greatly inferior to what it might formerly have been.

How have I prostituted my sorrow on occasions that little concerned me! I am ashamed to think of that idle "Elegy upon Autumn,"[2] when I have so much more important cause to hate and to condemn it *now;* but the glare and gaiety of the Spring is what I *principally* dread; when I shall find all things restored but my poor brother, and something like those lines of Milton will run forever in my thoughts:

> Thus, with the year,
> *Seasons* return; but not to *me* returns
> A brother's cordial smile, at eve or morn.[3]

I shall then seem to wake from amusements, company, every *sort* of inebriation with which I have been endeavouring to lull my grief asleep, as from a dream; and I shall feel as if I were, *that instant,* despoiled of all I have chiefly valued for thirty years together; of all my present happiness, and all my future prospects. The melody of birds, which he no more must hear; the chearful beams of the sun, of which he no more must partake; *every* wonted pleasure will produce that *sort* of pain to

---

[2] *Verses Written towards the Close of the Year 1748, to William Lyttelton, Esq.,* in *Works,* I (1764), 181–84.
[3] *Paradise Lost,* III, 40ff.

which my temper is most obnoxious. Do not consider this as poetry.—Poetry on such occasions is no more than literal truth. In the present case it is *less;* for half the tenderness I feel is altogether shapeless and inexpressible.

After all, the wisdom of the world may perhaps esteem me a gainer. Ill do they judge of this event, who think that any shadow of amends can be made for the death of a brother, and the disappointment of all my schemes, by the accession of some fortune, which I never can enjoy!

This is a mournful narrative: I will not, therefore, enlarge it.—Amongst all changes and chances, I often think of you; and pray there may be no suspicion or jealousy betwixt us during the rest of our lives.

I am, dear Sir, most affectionately yours,
W. Shenstone

136. To CHRISTOPHER WREN[1]

[Feb. 22, 1752]

Alas! dear Mr. W[ren]! the terrible event has happened! I have lost the best of brothers; and you are to pity, not to condemn, your unfortunate correspondent.

About the middle of November I had prepared a letter for you, which lies now amongst my papers. At that time, amidst all my apprehensions, I had some hopes to support me; but before I could send it, my situation was greatly altered, and the month did not wholly expire,[2] till it had effectually rendered me the most wretched of mankind.

Thus much it was necessary I should tell you; you will pardon me, if I do not descend any farther into an account of merit that is lost, and of sorrow which is too apt to revive of itself. Be assured, it is to me a loss which the whole world cannot compensate; and an affliction which the longest time I can live will not be able to erase.

You said, you would let Master W[ren][3] come and spend a few days with me.—I beseech you do.—It will be some relief to me; and, God knows, I have occasion enough for every assistance that can be drawn from correspondence, company, or amusement.

You, Sir, I presume, proceed in the innocent recreations of your garden, and those may at least prove a balance for any small disquiets that

---

[1] Dodsley, *Letters to Particular Friends,* No. LXVII. Dated at the end, "ix Kal. March, MDCCLII." The date according to the Gregorian calendar, which in England replaced the Julian officially in 1752, is thus February 22, 1752.

[2] Joseph Shenstone died November 30, 1751, according to the epitaph on the stone in the Halesowen churchyard.

[3] Wren's son was Shenstone's pupil and stayed with him at times, as Fullington observes in "Mr. William Shenstone," p. 156.

attend you. If greater ills befal you, you have persons near you to alleviate them — a wife, family, visitants male and female, friends in abundance, and a table sufficiently hospitable to attract even your enemies. With me the case is otherwise. What I have undergone this winter, may you never feel so much as in apprehension!

Believe me, my friend, affectionately and invariably yours,

W. Shenstone

ix Kal. March
MDCCLII

137. To LADY LUXBOROUGH [1]

[Mar. 14, 1752]

DEAR MADAM,

I am glad to observe that your Ladyship's Handwriting is greatly mended, from which I please myself with drawing many agreeable Conclusions — Such as, that the Bath-waters agree with you, that your Spirits also are better, that you will soon return to Barrels, & that I shall have more frequent Letters from you. The terrible Events that have pass'd, since I *wrote* to Barrels with so much tranquillity, & *receiv'd* Letters from thence with so much satisfaction, seem to have been attended likewise with many other Irregularities — And tho' my unparallel'd Misfortune can never be repair'd to me, yet I shall feel much easier to myself, when my remaining Friendships and Amusements return to their wonted Course. In other words, whatever has pleas'd me during my poor Brother's Life-time, seems now even more pleasing than it did at the Time; & I shall seem to regain some of those former Satisfactions, when you begin to date from Barrels, and to describe again your Employments there. Bath is, *must* be, to me, for the present, quite out of the Question. For besides all other Impediments, I know not but such sprightly Assemblies, when one's Health or Spirits are disorder'd, rather give Pain than Pleasure. 'Tis like the Glare of Sunshine to Eyes that have been lately couch'd — But I have done, & I hope that your *Ladyship's* Spirits are good, or that you find by *Experience* that my Observation is not *true*.

I have amus'd myself of late with the Choice of Paper for two Rooms; & having seen more than fifty Sorts, have at last fix'd upon two y^t are flock'd: The one, a green and Buff-colour; the other a Red & Buff-colour. I have seen a small Specimen of the chew'd Paper for Ceilings; 'Tis pretty, but I think them *unreasonably* dear in ye Price of it.

[1] B. M. Add. MSS 28958, fol. 127ff. This letter answers and confirms the date of Lady Luxborough's of February 29, 1752 (*Letters*, No. LXXIX).

Mr Allen's House I saw when ye Shell of it was almost finish'd; by wch you will collect yt it is long since I was at Bath. I remember I thought ye situation pleasing; & the View from his middle Room delightfull. He is, I think one, amongst many other Instances, that Persons of the truest *native* Genius, are also Persons of the sublimest Generosity.

I shall be glad to hear from your Ladyship, whenever you find it least painfull to write, & just so much as you can write with Ease. I hear from few besides, nor are there many besides from whom I would wish to hear. Family Losses are of too tender a nature to be touch'd upon by a dull Instrument or an unskillfull Hand: And I receiv'd yesterday morning a Compliment of Concoleance, the Shock of which I did not recover during the rest of the Day. Yet this was from a Man of Sense, and one that seem'd to wish me well.

I return your Ladyship many thanks for accepting the Servant I propos'd to you. I have not often interfer'd on such occasions, & I began to think myself as unlucky in recommending *others*, as *myself*. *For* the Day after I had written, the Girl was taken ill, & it was as much as they could do to recover her in due time. She sets out from hence with Mr Joseph to-day; & my own maid with her, to return to-morrow. This I hope you will excuse. If her Health continues, I do not question but after some little time she will merit your Approbation. Her Family are honest, orderly People; & she will, at worst, prove *Faithfull;* tho' your Ladyship shall not hire a Servant that will be *more* so, than, Dear Madam,

Your most oblig'd & most obedient Servant,
Will Shenstone

The Leasows, March ye 12th 1752

138. To LADY LUXBOROUGH [1]

The *Leasowes*, June 6, 1752

My Conversation, dear Lady Luxborough, is by no Means equal to the Reception I find at *Barels*, and if you return me Thanks upon *that* Score, you make me doubly sensible how unable I am to make a due Acknowledgement.

The Day after I left *Barrels*, I had a Morning Visit from Admiral Smith,[2] Captain Whood, Mrs. Stanley, and her two Daughters, who en-

---

[1] This letter, published in Hull's *Select Letters*, Vol. I, No. XXXVI, does not appear in B. M. Add. MSS 28958. Lady Luxborough replies on the same date (*Letters*, No. LXXXI); they rather often exchanged letters upon the same day, by messenger.

[2] Admiral Smith was the illegitimate son of Sir Thomas Lyttelton and a London milliner. Fullington, "Mr. William Shenstone," p. 151.

gaged me to dine with Sir G. Lyttelton. These are Ladies of Taste, I think; but Admiral Smith is the Delight of Mankind! I forgot to mention Mr. Miller, who seems to recommend my Walks with great Cordiality. I see they condescend to look upon *modern* Plans at *Hagley,* and if they build anew, I suppose it will be in that Style.

Since this I have seen a good deal of Company, more of whom arrive to see my *Walks* than *me;* yet I am not jealous or invidious: my Walks are truly more deserving of this Favour.

Yesterday, I had the Company of Miss Lea,[3] and Mr. Hylton,[4] a very modest and ingenious Man, who came with Lord Dudley from *London;* besides two other Parties of Visitants, who engrossed my whole Day.

And now I sit down by *Five* in the Morning to answer your Queries concerning the Papier-Machée. It is bought of Mr. Bromwich, at the *Golden Lion,* upon *Ludgate-Hill.* What you will want, will be an Ornament for the Middle, and four Spandrells for the Corners. I have taken down the Pine-Apple from the middle of my Cieling, and send it you to see, together with some other Ornaments which were never yet fixed up. They will cost (I mean a middle and four corner Ornaments) somewhere about eight Shillings. You may ornament it *more* or *less* tho' as you please. As to the Cracks of your Cieling, (which I don't remember) if they are not violently bad, they may be mended by a common Mason, and the *Colour* will disguise them. As for putting them up, I will send you over a very agreeable Neighbour of mine, who was once an eminent Upholsterer, but now lives upon his Fortune, who seems glad of the Opportunity it will give him to see *Barrels,* and the Honour it will afford him of being serviceable to your Ladyship. They should be painted with Flake White and thin Starch; but all this he will manage to your entire Satisfaction. He is a Person of Taste, has seen a good deal of Life; and tho' he has had his Share of Difficulties, always chearful. You must not offer him any Thing. Thus have I been as short as I can, in pointing out your quickest Method of embellishing your Cieling. The whole Cove (except the Moulding) should be washed with Oker; but this you may defer, if you please, till Mr. Pixell arrives.

I beg my Thanks to Mrs. Weymondesold,[5] for her kind Remembrance of me: am a little fearful her Visit will be too late in the Year; but 'tis in Mrs. Weymondesold's Power to make *all* Seasons pleasing.

---

[3] Lord Dudley's sister.
[4] John Scott Hylton, whose origin is rather obscure, edited the poems of Richard Jago (1784). Shenstone wrote him a number of letters, beginning in 1753 (see Letter 158 and the Index). He lived at Lapall House, Halesowen.
[5] Lady Luxborough's daughter.

My Lord Dudley will be extremely glad to wait on Mr. Outing: but he must come hither first, and we will adjust the Remainder.

I have taken the Liberty to send this by my Servant Girl, who is desirous to see her Sister and *Barrels;* and really my Man is so much Assistant in the Way of fitting up my Room (which engages me) that I could very ill spare him.

I hope Mr. Price is recovered, by the Mention you make of his going again to *London.* I did not merely ask, but wish to see him here. And now I must leave your Ladyship for the Company of my Carpenters; yet am ever *uniformly* your Ladyship's most obliged

W. Shenstone

139. To CHRISTOPHER WREN[1]

July 22, 1752

Dear Mr. W[ren],

I do not know why I made you a promise of a pretty long letter. What I now write will be but a moderate one, both in regard to length and stile; yet write I must, *par maniere d'acquit,* and you have brought fourpence expence upon yourself for a parcel of nonsense, and to no manner of purpose. This is not tautology, you must observe; for nonsense sometimes answers very considerable purposes. — In love, it is eloquence itself. — In friendship, therefore, by all the rules of sound logic, you must allow it to be something; what I cannot say, "nequeo monstrare, & sentio tantum." The principal part of a correspondence betwixt two idle men consists in two important enquiries — what we do, and how we do; but as all persons ought to give satisfaction before they expect to receive it, I am to tell you in the first place, that my own health is tolerably good, or rather what I must call good, being, I think, much better than it has been this last half-year. — Then as touching my occupation, alas! "Othello's occupation's gone!" I neither read nor write aught besides a few letters; and I give myself up entirely to scenes of dissipation! lounge at my Lord Dudley's for near a week together; make dinners; accept of invitations; sit up till three o'clock in the morning with young sprightly married women, over white port and *vin de paysans;* ramble over my fields; issue out orders to my hay-makers; foretel rain and fair weather; enjoy the fragrance of hay, the cocks, the wind-rows; admire that universal lawn which is produced by the scythe; sometimes inspect, and draw mouldings for my carpenters; sometimes paper my walls, and at

[1] Dodsley, *Letters to Particular Friends,* No. LXVIII.

other times my ceilings; do every social office that falls in my way, but never seek out for any.

"Sed vos quid tandem? quae circumvolitas agilis thyma? non tu corpus eras sine pectore. Non tibi parvum ingenium, non incultum est!" In short, what do you? and how do you do? — that is all.

Tell my young pupil, your son, he must by all manner of means send me a Latin letter: and if he have any billet in French for Miss Lea at The Grange, or even in Hebrew, Coptic, or Syriac, I will engage it shall be received very graciously. Thither am I going to dinner this day, and there "implebor veteris Bacchi, pinguisque ferinae."

All this looks like extreme jollity; but is this the true state of the case, or may I not more properly apply the

Spem vultu simulat, premit atrum corde dolorem?

Accept this scrawl in the place of a letter, and believe me
Ever most affectionately yours,
W. Shenstone

140. To RICHARD GRAVES[1]

[Late 1752(?)]

DEAR SIR,

I did indeed give you up for lost, as a correspondent, and find by your letter y^t I am to expect but very few future ones. I will endeavour all I can to avoid any suspicion of your Indifference for my own satisfaction. But I don't know for certain y^t I shall be able, unless you assist my Endeavours, like my good Genius, by a course of suitable Epistles at certain distances. I myself correspond but very little now, so you will meet with the more Indulgence. I don't find by your Letter y^t you have much more Philosophy y^n me. I can't tell indeed what ye situation of y^t House is. I own mine gives me offence on no other consideration y^n that it does not receive a sufficient Number of polite Friends, or y^t it is not fit to receive 'em, were they so dispos'd. I wou'd else cultivate an Acquaintance with about Three or Four in my Neighbourhood, y^t are of a Degree of Elegance, and station superior to ye common Run. But I make it a certain Rule *Arcere profanū vulgus*. Persons of vulgar minds, who will despise you for ye want of a good set of Chairs, or an uncouth Fire-shovel at

---

[1] Hutton quotes this undated letter in his *Burford Papers,* pp. 188–89, from a manuscript. Although he says it was hitherto unpublished, a version, also undated, appears in Hull's *Select Letters,* Vol. II, No. II. Its position here is conjectural. The approximate date can be ascertained by reference to Aris's *Birmingham Gazette,* from which Shenstone quotes. The reference to Graves's picture, acknowledged in Letter 142 dated October 3, 1752, also suggests the date.

yͤ same Time yᵗ they can't taste any Excellence in a mind that overlooks those things; or, (to make a conceit of this sentiment) with whom 'tis in vain that yʳ mind is furnish'd if yʳ walls are naked. Indeed one loses much of one's Acquisitions in virtue by an Hour's converse with such as Judge of merit by Money &c. Yet I am now and then impell'd by yͤ social Passion to sit half an Hour in my Kitchen. I was all along an Admirer of Sʳ Thomas Head's Humour and Wit, And I beg you wou'd represent me in yᵗ light if occasion happens. 'Tis not impossible yᵗ I may penetrate this winter as far as yʳ neighbourhood, connecting a set of visits which I have in my Eye. Tell Mʳ Whistler when you see him that if he must have *some* Distemper, I cannot but be pleas'd yᵗ it is one which is a Forerunner of Longevity. Don't tell him so neither, for yͤ compliment is trite. From yͤ "Birmingham Gazette": "We hear that on Thursday last was married at Halesowen, in Shropshire, Mʳ Jorden, an eminent Gunsmith of this Town, to a sister of yͤ Rᵗ Honᵇˡᵉ Ferdinando Lᵈ Dudley." I was yesterday at yͤ Grange, where his old Father (wᵗʰ a number of People) was celebrating yͤ Nuptials of his Son; when in the midst of his Feasting, high Jollity, and grand Alliance, the old Fellow bethought him of a Piece of Timber in yͤ neighbourhood yᵗ was convertible into good Gunsticks, and had some of it sent for into yͤ Room by the way of Specimen! *Animae nil magnae laudis egentis!* Pray, is yʳ Sister at Smethwick? For I have not heard. You said you wou'd give me yʳ Picture, which I long earnestly for. Cou'dn't you contrive to have it sent me directly? I am quite in yʳ debt with regard to downright goods and moveables, and what is yͤ proper subject of an Inventory — *neque tu pessima muneru ferres divite me scilicet artium quas aut Parrhasius protulit aut Scopas — sed non haec mihi vis!* I will, however, endeavour to be more upon a Par wᵗʰ you with regard to presents, tho' I never can with regard to yͤ Pleasures I have receiv'd from yʳ conversation. I make People wonder at my Exploits in pulling down walls, Hovels, cowhouses, &c.; and my Place is not yͤ same. I am, that is, with Regard to you a Faithfull Friend, and hᵇˡᵉ servᵗ,

W. S.

Mr. Whistler and you and I and Sʳ T. Head (who I should name first, speaking after yͤ manner of men) have just variety enough, and not too much, in our Charcᵗ to make an Interview, whenever it happens, Entertaining — I mean, tho' we were not old Friends and Acquaintance.

141. To LADY LUXBOROUGH[1]

The Leasows, Septr ye 30th 1752

DEAR MADAM,

Your Ladyship is extremely complaisant with regard to y^e *number* & the *Choice* of Epithets you bestow upon ye Entertainment I was capable of affording you at The Leasows. Sure I am, that whether your Ladyship *makes* Visits or *receives* them, the Persons with whom you *converse* must ever think themselves Very greatly honour'd, oblig'd, & entertain'd.

I sup'd with Ld Dudley at the Grange on Wednesday last, where I deliver'd y^r Compliments; & found my Lord very much at your Service, & very stedfast in his Resolution of waiting upon you soon. We did not fix a Day, but I guess it will be toward ye End of a Fortnight; before wch Time you shall hear from me again.

I have order'd the Farrier to bring his Bill to me, & to take Care he *charg'd* no otherwise than if it had been my own Affair; as whatever concerns *your* Interest may be truly said to be.

Your Breakfast Room I am sure must be extremely handsome; your Design for ye upper Part of ye Frame to Ld Rochester's Picture, ye best y^t can be imagin'd, if you chuse to have the Break Continu'd: And in regard to this, I can hardly pronounce, unless I were to *see* the whole Effect.

The Honour of serving y^r Ladyship, and meeting with y^r Approbation, has render'd my Friend Pixell so vain, y^t it will take about five or Six Week's Mortification to bring him down to the Standard of other vainglorious Men; during wch time, I must not allow him his way in any single Article. He told me, before he enter'd my Hall, that he had been forc'd to *undo* what I had been doing in y^r Room; & before he had talk'd much more, discover'd that he had added many Things, which *I* must insist upon seeing undone. Y^r Ladyship must by all means bestow a little Carv'd Work over y^r Windows & Doors, wch was all I mean't to suggest by my *Charcoal Operations;* of wch I find Master Pixell has made a quite serious Affair. But real *Festoons* will not do upon Paper, much less, my ridiculous extravagances — Consequently the Wainscot s^d remain. He has more over made something, he says, round ye Marble Chimney piece with a bit of Flock Paper, wch must needs be sometime Supply'd by a small Wood-moulding. The Room is really an handsome one, & need not owe anything at all to Whim or Concetti — After all Mr Pixell is extremely sensible of your Ladyship's civility, & comes this moment to my little door to desire his Duty to you —

[1] B. M. Add. MSS 28958, fol. 129ff. This answers and confirms the date of Lady Luxborough's letter of September 28, 1752 (*Letters*, No. LXXXV).

The Day I came Home from Barrels, I had Two Persons, it seems, of *Taste* & *Fashion* to see my Walks — from Hereford; who told my Servant there was a Gentleman to come hither from thence in a Coach to see the same, to Day. Who it is *I* do not know, but He has a Park of his *own,* with Urns, Statues, Vistas & so forth — & how he'll get hither from Stourbridge, (where he lay last Night) — The Lord knows.

I expect Sr George Lyttelton's Family next Week; who, I *fear'd,* had taken offence that I had not visited them yet at Hagley: But I find all is well there.

The Middle of my Drawing Room Ceiling was render'd like to y^r Ladyships ye Monday after I came Home.

I thank y^r Laship for my Love-Apples, & will beg ye Favour of some Seed at a proper time of year: I hope you will suffer your Gardener to come to the Leasows, to see ye Green-house in my Neighbourhood, & take in my Walks; & as it runs strongly in my Head y^t Mrs Lane has an *admirable Taste* & would find some Pleasure here, I hope y^r Lasp will, when opportunity offers, give her Leave to come over — Poor Mr Joseph[2] will be impatient; I must therefore hastily beg with my kind Services to Mrs Davies & Mr Outing, to be ever esteem'd y^r most oblig'd & most obedient Servt

W: Shenstone

Mrs Pearsall, whom I saw on Thursday, is very much your Ladyship's Servant; was Full of y^r Encomiums, & thought herself quite unfortunate y^t she had so little of y^r Company.

142. To RICHARD GRAVES[1]

The Leasowes, Oct. 3, 1752

Dear Mr. G[raves],

I am very unfeignedly ashamed to reflect how long is it since I received your present, and how much longer it is since I received your letter. I have been resolving to write to you almost daily ever since you left me; yet have foolishly enough permitted avocations (of infinitely less importance than your correspondence) to interfere with my gratitude, my interest, and my inclination. What apology I have to make, though no way adequate to my negligence, is in short as follows. After

---

[2] Lady Luxborough's servant.

[1] Dodsley, *Letters to Particular Friends,* No. LXIX. Though Dodsley designates the addressee by only the initial G, the context of the letter clearly indicates that it is Graves. The date is confirmed by the reference to the visit alluded to in Letter 141 of authentic date.

the receipt of your letter, I deferred writing till I could speak of the arrival of your picture.—This did not happen till about a month or five weeks ago, when I was embarrassed with masons, carvers, carpenters, and company, all at a time. And though it were idle enough to say, that I could not find *one* vacant hour for my purpose, yet in truth my head was so confused by these multifarious distractions, that I could have written nothing satisfactory either to *myself* or *you*: nothing worth a single *penny,* supposing the postage were to cost you no more. The workmen had not *finished my rooms* a minute, when Lady Luxborough, Mrs. Davies, and Mr. Outing arrived, with five servants and a *set* of horses, to stay with me for some time. After a nine days visit, I returned with them to Barrels, where I continued for a week; and whither (by the way) I go again with Lord Dudley in about a fortnight's time. Other company filled the interstices of my summer; and I hope my dear friend will accept of this apology for so long a chasm of silence, during which I have been uniformly at his service, and true to that inviolable friendship I shall ever bear him.

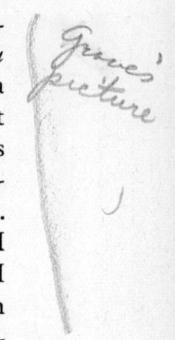

I proceed now to thank you for the *distinction* you shew me, in sending me your picture: I do it very sincerely. It is assuredly a strong likeness, as my Lady Luxborough with all her servants that have seen *you* pronounce, as well as I; consequently more valuable to a *friend* than a face he does not know, though it were one of Raphael's. The smile about the mouth is bad; as it agrees but ill with the gravity of the eyes, and as a smile ever so little *outré* has a bad effect in a picture where it is *constant,* though it may be ever so graceful in a person where it is *transitory*. However, this may be altered, when I can meet with a good painter. I have no *other* objection, but to the prominence of the belly. The hair, I think, is good; and the coat and band no way exceptionable. I have given it all the advantage I can: it has a good light, and makes part of an elegant chimney-piece in a genteel, though little breakfast-room, at the end of my house.

Mr. Whistler and I are now upon good terms, and two or three friendly letters have been interchanged betwixt us. He presses me to come to Whitchurch, and I *him* to come over to The Leasowes; but the winter cometh, when no man can visit.—The dispute is adjusted by *time,* whilst we are arguing it by *expostulation.*—No uncommon event in most sublunary projects!

Lady Luxborough said very extraordinary things in praise of Mrs. G[raves], after you left us at Barrels; yet I sincerely believe no more than she deserves. I took the liberty of shewing her your letter here, as it included a compliment to her which I thought particularly genteel. — She will always consider you as a person of genius, and her friend.

During most of this summer (wherein I have seen much company either here or at Lord Dudley's), I have been almost constantly engaged in one continued scene of *jollity*. I endeavoured to find *relief* from such sort of dissipation; and, when I had once given in to it, I was obliged to proceed; as, they say, is the case when persons disguise their faces with paint. *Mine* was a sort of *painting* applied to my temper — "Spem vultu simulare, premere atrum corde dolorem." And the moment I left it off, my Soul appeared again all haggard and forlorn. My company has now deserted me; the spleen-fogs begin to rise; and the *terrible* incidents of last winter revive apace in my memory. This is my state of mind, while I write you these few lines; yet, I thank God, my health is not much amiss.

I did not forget my promise of a box, &c. to Mrs. G[raves]. I had a dozen sent me, one or two of which I could have liked, had they been better *finished*. They were of a good oval, white enamel, with flowers, &c. but horribly gilt, and not accurately painted. I beg my best service to her, and will make a fresh essay. My dearest friend, accept this awkward letter for the present. — In a few posts, I will write again. — Believe me yours from the bottom of my soul.

W. Shenstone

I will send you a label for made-wine, after my own plan. It is enamel, with grapes, shepherd's pipe, &c. The motto "Vin De Paisan."

143. To RICHARD JAGO[1]

The Leasowes, Nov. 15, 1752

DEAR MR. JAGO,

Could I with convenience mount my horse, and ride to Harbury[2] this instant, I should much more willingly do so than begin this letter. Such terrible events have happened to us,[3] since we saw each other last, that, however irksome it may be to dwell upon them, it is in the same degree unnatural to substitute any subject in their place.

I do sincerely forgive your long silence, my good friend, indeed I do; though it gave me uneasiness, I hope you do the same by mine. I own, I could not readily account for the *former* period of yours, any otherwise than by supposing that I had said or done something, in the levity of my

---
[1] Dodsley, *Letters to Particular Friends*, No. LXX.
[2] Jago received the small living of Harbury in 1746.
[3] The first Mrs. Jago died in 1751.

heart, which had given you disgust; but being conscious to myself of the most sincere regard for you, and believing it could never be discredited for any *trivial* inadvertencies, I remember, I continued still in expectation of a letter, and did not dream of writing till such time as I had received one. I trusted you would write at last; and that, by all my *past* endeavours to demonstrate my *friendship,* you would believe the *tree* was rooted in my heart, whatever irregularity you might observe in the *branches*.

This way my situation before that dreadful aera which gave me such a shock as to banish my best friends for a time out of my memory. And when they recurred, as they did the first of any thing, I was made acquainted with that deplorable misfortune of yours! Believe me, I sympathised in *your* affliction, notwithstanding my own; but alas! what comfort could I administer, who had need of every possible assistance to support myself? I wrote indeed a few letters with *difficulty;* amongst the rest, one to my friend Graves; but it was to vent my complaint. — I will send you the letter, if you please, as it is by far my least painful method of conveying you some account of my situation. Let it convince you, that I could have written nothing at that time, which could have been of any service to you: let it afford you, at least, a faint sketch of my dearest brother's character; but let it not appear an ostentatious display of sorrow, of which I am by no means guilty. I know but too well that I discovered upon the occasion, what some would call, an unmanly tenderness; but I know also, that sorrow upon such subjects as these is very consistent with virtue, and with the most absolute resignation to the just decrees of Providence — "Hominis est enim affici dolore, *Sentire;* resistere tamen & solatia admittere, non solatiis non egere." Pliny. — I drank, purchased amusements, never suffered myself to be a minute without company, no matter what, so it was but continual. At length, by an attention to such conversation and such amusements as I could at other times despise, I forgot so far as to be chearful. — And after this, the summer through an almost constant succession of lively and agreeable visitants, proved even a scene of jollity. — It was inebriation all, though of a mingled nature; yet has it maintained a sort of truce with grief, till time can assist me more effectually, by throwing back the event to a distance. — Now, indeed, that my company has all forsaken me, and I am delivered up to winter, silence, and reflection, the incidents of the last year revive apace in my memory; and I am even astonished to think of the gaiety of my summer. The fatal anniversary, the "dies quem semper acerbum, &c." is beginning to approach, and every face of the sky suggests the ideas of last winter.—Yet I find myself chearful in *company;* nor would I recommend it to you to be much alone; you would lay the highest obligation upon me by coming over at this time.—I pressed your brother, whom I saw at Birmingham, to use his influence with you; but if you can by no means undertake the journey, I will take my speediest opportunity of seeing you at Harbury.—Mr. Miller invited me strenuously to meet Dr. Lyttelton at his house; but I believe my most convenient season will be, when my Lord Dudley goes to Barrels; for I can but ill bear the pensiveness of a long and lonely expedition. After all, if you *could* come hither first, it would afford me the most entire satisfaction.—I have been making alterations in my house that would amuse you; and have many matters to discourse with you, which it would be endless to mention upon paper.—Adieu! my dear friend! may your merits be known to some one who has greater *power* to serve you than myself; but be assured, at the same time, that no one loves you better, or esteems you more.

W. Shenstone

144. To MR. ———[1]

The *Leasowes, Jan.* 1753

DEAR SIR,

The Letter with which you favoured me deserves my earliest Acknowledgements, and will prove not a little serviceable, in regard to the Subscription we have in Hand. The whole Account of that Affair is as follows: I had been assured by Persons of Veracity, (amongst which I may safely name Lord Dudley, Mr. Pixell, and Tho. Cotterel) that you had generously made an Offer of twenty Guineas towards the Addition of two new Bells to our present Set; and that in Case the Parish would supply what was wanting, it would be a Pleasure to you, Sir, to have your Offer accepted. Upon this Encouragement, I determined to make Trial what a Subscription would produce, and accordingly drew up a Form for that Purpose; intending to write you an Account of the Undertaking, so soon as I could form a Conjecture of its Success. This I was upon the Point of doing, when I had the Pleasure of a Letter from you, which, nevertheless, was extremely seasonable, as it immediately removed a Doubt that began to spread, in regard to your Concurrence.

There is now subscribed, (exclusive of your Benefaction) the Sum of fifty Guineas; and I make no scruple of raising twenty more, by an

---

[1] I have no clue to the identity of the addressee of this letter. It appears in Hull's *Select Letters,* Vol. I, No. XXXIX. Allusions to the new bells in Letters 147 and 148 tend to confirm the date.

Application to such Persons as have not yet been solicited. Be our Progress what it will, I purpose in a few Weeks to give you a farther Account of it; in the mean Time, can assure you, that the Subscription will be pushed forward with all possible Diligence, that it may give us the earlier Chance for the Pleasure of your Company. I have only to add, that the Bells will never sound more agreeably, than when they ring for your Arrival; will be heard no where more advantageously than from some Parts of my Farm, and that you will find no one more desirous of making the Country agreeable to you than

Your most obedient humble Servant,
W. Shenstone

145. To RICHARD JAGO [1]

The Leasowes, Jan. 29, 1753

DEAR MR. JAGO,

Although I have many reasons to urge why I did not write to you before, or visit you from Barrels as I fully intended, I will venture to wave all particulars till I see you; and only assure you in the general, that I was never able to write any thing satisfactory, or to visit you, at that time, with any sort of convenience.

Believe me, my good friend, if *inclination* might have ruled, I had been with you at Harbury many weeks ago. Sure I am, they must be the *cares* of home, and not the *pleasures* of it, that *ever were* sufficient to detain me during the *winter season.* Nor do I think I have an enemy that wishes me more miserable than I have almost constantly found myself ever since the beginning of *it.*

I cannot even now fix a time when I can see you; and perhaps it may be deferred till Mr. Miller's place will have received some advantage from the spring; and in that case I would infallibly see my Lord Guilford's; but I leave this undetermined: and I hope, if you *can* wander from home with any kind of satisfaction, you will do me the justice to believe, that you have no friend alive who will more gladly receive you than myself.

I have papered some rooms this last year, and would willingly have you see them before their colours are vanished; which, I think, will unavoidably be the case of *one,* before a second summer be half concluded.

Thus is beauty as uncertain as either fortune or fame.

I suppose you have heard there is a citation from Doctors Commons, and a writ of "Ne exeat" out against Mr. W—— for an intrigue with ———. If you have not, be not *precipitate* in spreading the story.— They say, he has fled into France on the occasion.— What a shocking

---

[1] Dodsley, *Letters to Particular Friends,* No. LXXI.

affair is this! so early in life! so extensive, so lasting, so irremediable in its consequences! but,

> Sic visum Veneri! cui placet *impares*
> *Formas* atque *animos,* sub juga ahenea,
> *Saevo* mittere cum joco!

Your misfortunes and mine incline *us,* almost, to love *all* people that are miserable; but how will the daughters of the Philistines rejoice on the occasion; nay, almost countenance another's loss of virtue, by manifesting their own apparent want of humanity!

There is a most admirable piece of allegory on this head in the Female Fables,[2] by Brooks, if I mistake not; to whom the author in his preface acknowledges himself greatly indebted.

I am truly sorry to understand how much you are alone; I really imagined you were much happier in point of company than myself, as you live in a much politer neighbourhood; amongst persons of genius, learning, and humanity. And happier you *are;* for however I make a shift to scrape some company around me, they are such as can affect me with little else besides the spleen.

Do not dwell too much on subjects that make you thoughtful; superficial amusements are our point, till some time hence; I am an ill adviser; but I prescribe you the methods which I have found most effectual with myself.

I have not been forgetful of the task that you enjoined me, to give you my observations on the verses which you inclosed. — I will write my sentiments on a separate paper. Do not punish me with silence and suspence concerning you, but write. I can ardently desire what I but little deserve, being

> Your most affectionate friend,
> W. S.

146. To RICHARD JAGO[1]

> The Leasowes, Feb. 27, 1753

DEAR MR. JAGO,

I wrote you some account of myself, and inclosed some trivial criticisms, in a letter I sent you about a fortnight ago, which I hope you have

---

[2] "Fables for the Female Sex," by Mr. Edward Moore [1744]; a delicate and elegant collection. — The particular fable here alluded to seems to be "The Female Seducers," — *said* by some persons to be written by Mr. Brooks of Ireland; but no such acknowledgment is made in Moore's preface, who (by all accounts) was too liberal not to have confessed such an obligation if he had received it. Mr. Shenstone was indisputably misled by general report. [Dodsley]

[1] Dodsley, *Letters to Particular Friends,* No. LXXII.

received. — Tom comes now to enquire after your health, and to bring back my "Ode to Colonel Lyttelton;" in regard to which, I desire that you will not be sparing of your animadversions. I whispered my difficulties to Mr. Miller at Hagley, how delicate I found the subject, and how hard it was to satisfy either myself or others; in all which points he agreed with me. Nevertheless, having twice broken my *promise* of sending a corrected copy to Sir George, I was obliged to make my peace by a *fresh* one, which, I suppose, I must of necessity perform. — Give me your whole sentiments hereupon, I beseech you; in particular, and in general, as a critic and as a friend. — The bad state of spirits which I complained of in my last, for a long time together made me utterly irresolute: every thing occasioned me suspence; and I did nothing with appetite. — This was owing in a great measure to a slow nervous fever, as I have since discovered by many concurrent symptoms. It is now, I think, wearing off by degrees. I seem to anticipate a little of that "vernal delight" which Milton mentions, and thinks

>   able to chase
> All sadness, but despair,
> [PARADISE LOST, IV, 155-56]

At least, I begin to resume my silly clue of hopes and expectations; which I know, however, *will* not guide me to any thing more satisfactory than before. I have read scarce any new books this season. Voltaire's new Tragedy[2] was sent me from London; but what has given me the most amusement, *has* been the "Lettres de Madame de Maintenon."[3] You have probably read them already in English, and then I need not recommend them. The "Life of Lord Bolingbroke"[4] is entirely his *public* life, and the book three parts filled with political remarks.

As to *writing,* I have not attempted it this year, and more, nor do I know when I shall again. — However, I would be glad to correct that "Ode to the Duchess of Somerset,"[5] when once I can find in whose hands it is deposited. I was *shewn* a very elegant letter of hers, the other day; wherein she asks for it with great politeness: and as it includes nothing but a love of rural life, and such sort of amusements as she herself approves, I shall stand a good chance of having it received with partiality.

---

[2] Apparently *Catilina ou Rome Sauvee,* first acted in Paris February 24, 1752, and published that year. See G. Bengesco, *Voltaire, Bibliographie de ses Oeuvres* (1882), I, 51–52.

[3] Published in 1752.

[4] The *Memoirs of the Life and Ministerial Conduct &c. of the Late Lord Bolingbroke* were announced in the Register of Books of the *Gentleman's Magazine* for October, 1752.

[5] *Rural Elegance.* The letter mentioned in the next sentence is apparently that from the Duchess of Somerset to Lady Luxborough dated December 31, 1751, published in Hull's *Select Letters,* Vol. I, No. XLIII.

She lives the life of a *religieuse*. She has *written* my Lady Luxburough a very serious letter of condolence upon the misfortune in her family; and need enough has Lady Luxborough of so unchangeable a friend! for sure nothing could have happened to a person in her situation more *specifically* unfortunate.[6] — Mr. Reynolds has been at Barrels, I hear, and has brought her a machine that goes into a coat-pocket, yet answers the end of "a jack for boots, a reading-desk, a cribbage-board, a pair of snuffers, a ruler, an eighteen-inch-rule, three pair of nutcracks, a lemon-squeezer, two candlesticks, a piquet-board, and the Lord knows what beside." — Can you form an idea of it? if you can, do you not think it must give me pain to reflect, that I myself am useful for *no* sort of purpose, when a paltry bit of wood can answer so *many?* but, indeed, whilst it *pretends* to these exploits, it performs nothing *well;* and therein I agree with it. So true it is, with regard to me, what I told you long ago,

> Multa & praeclara minantem
> Vivere nec recte, nec suaviter!

We have a turnpike-bill upon the point of being brought into the House of Commons: it will convey you about half the way betwixt Birmingham and Hales, and from thence to Hagley; but, I trust, there will be a *left hand* attraction, which will always make you deviate from the strait line.

I should be ashamed to reflect how much I have dwelt upon *myself* in this letter, but that I seriously approve of egotism in letters; and were I *not* to do so, I should not have any other subject. I have not a single neighbour, that is either fraught with politeness, literature, or intelligence; much less have I a tide of spirits to set my invention afloat: but the less I am able to amuse *you,* the more desirous am I of your letters; which afford me the truest entertainment, even when my spirits are ever so much depressed.

That universal chearfulness which is the lot of some people, persons that you and I may *envy* at the same time that we *despise,* is worth all that either fortune or nature can bestow.

I am, with entire affection,
Yours,
W. Shenstone

---

[6] B. M. Add. MSS 23728, fol. 45, is an "extract of a letter &c.," which consists of the paragraph noted as far as the words "specifically unfortunate," quoted from the *Gentleman's Magazine,* 46:77. The following explanatory note is found at the bottom: "her ladyship's daughter Mrs. Wymondesold, had eloped with the Hon[ble] Josiah Child, brother to Earl Tylney, — in consequence of which, she was divorced from her former husband, and married her favourite."

147. To RICHARD GRAVES[1]

The Leasowes, Mar. 28, 1753

DEAR MR. GRAVES,

I am vexed to find you have no copy of those verses[2] — I must make a fresh enquiry; and should they happen to accompany this letter, as I fear they will *not,* be so good as to assist me all you can in the way of *hints* and *corrections* — corrections of what *is,* and hints of what *may be.* I do not reckon much upon these verses, or the patronage which you mention; though the Duchess is a woman of high reputation, and has as much benevolence as any woman upon earth.

I do *not* include the design of visiting Bath as a public place: I have long since given up such schemes of gaiety and expence. I visit *you* and *Mrs. Graves;* at the least, I mean to do so.

Inoculation is a point on which I never speak a syllable in the way of *pro* or *con:* I mean, not so as to influence particulars; for, in the general, I esteem it both right and salutary; and even *right* because we *find* it *salutary.*

I do not know whether I could not bear the *dishonour* of friends or relations better than their *death.* — It must afford one no small satisfaction to give them one's affection and assistance under every frailty to which human nature is exposed; at least, so long as they are true to friendship. It is Mr. Whistler's opinion, as well as mine. But Mr.——'s case is altogether different; and I make no question that he thinks as you do upon the occasion.

Poor Danvers's death affects me more than you would perhaps imagine. If you remember, I was at M—— when the scheme of his going abroad was in agitation. I think how this event must affect Mrs. T——, whose concern will not be *lessened* by her long separation from him. I dare say he reckoned upon his relations here as his *best estate,* whatever he might gain elsewhere: and, no doubt, the hope of retiring amongst them has been a constant spur to his diligence. — The event was always uncertain, and has proved at last unfortunate; yet, as Melmoth says very justly, "The course of human affairs requires that we should act with vigour upon very precarious contingencies." — I desire you would give me a sight of the Latin inscription.

I think it was the Gentleman's Magazine in which I was shewn your verses.

I have a particular and lively idea of your place; though I do not

[1] Dodsley, *Letters to Particular Friends,* No. LXXIII.
[2] *Rural Elegance,* which Lady Luxborough has urged him to finish and send. See her *Letters,* pp. 323, 325.

remember to have seen even such *parts* of a scene as I have united together in my imagination. I cannot think otherwise than that the front-door opens here, the garden-door there, the stream runs in this place, &c. &c.

Hac ibat Simois, haec est Sigeia tellus.

The sight of the place could not impress my imagination more deeply; though the impression I *am to* acquire will hardly leave one line of my present one remaining. *Cabbage-garden* ornée is very high burlesque, and affects the improvements of your friend too nearly.

Let me know in what manner Mrs. Graves and you are drawn. Be as particular as you please.

I could not be clear from your letter whether you had received the box or not. That, together with the tallies, lay on the table before me while I wrote to you last; and went with my letter to Birmingham. — Pray satisfy me directly whether you received them. — They are trifles indeed; but, as they acquit me of my promise, they are virtually of consequence.

Mr. Whistler has not answered a letter which I sent him above two months ago: nay, I think, a quarter of a year.

You are rich. — I have only to wish the continuance of your riches, with some diminution of your fatigue. And yet the most laborious man in the world is, I am fully assured, more happy than the *laziest*.

"The Rival Brothers" has some of Dr. Young's affectations; and I question if the moral be absolutely true — at least, Mr. Addison is in some measure against it: but, on the whole, I think it a noble Tragedy; abounding as much with refined sentiments and elevated expressions, as "The Gamester" and "The Earl of Essex" are deficient in *both*.[3]

My verses are not yet sent to Sir George Lyttelton; I start new difficulties, and cannot make them to my mind: yet have promised him a copy, and disappointed him thrice; and can hardly defer it much longer without great offence.

I have scarce been twenty yards from home this winter. Last night I visited one of my neighbours; and what with wine, sitting up late, a perfect flux of discourse, and a return home through the dark, found myself *vertiginous* before I was aware. Never did Prior's manly description, "I drank, I liked it not, &c." seem so natural to me as it does to-day. I am absolutely vile in my own sight, and I abhor myself in dust and

---

[3] Dr. Young's *The Brothers* ran eight nights at Drury Lane, beginning March 3, 1753. It was written many years earlier, but suppressed by the author when he took orders. *The Gamester* by Edward Moore (1712–57) and *The Earl of Essex* by Henry Jones (1721–70) appeared in 1753.

ashes. I was *never* so intoxicated as not to know what I said, or to talk mere nonsense; and yet how many things could I wish unsaid that I let fall last night!

We are going to add two new bells to our present set of six; to have a turnpike road from Hagley to Birmingham, through Hales; and to emerge a little from our obscurity. I am, dear Sir, with compliments to Mrs. Graves,

Ever most affectionately yours,

W. Shenstone

148. To LADY LUXBOROUGH[1]

The Leasowes, April ye 2^d 1753

DEAR MADAM,

Your Ladyship's Spirits appear no less perennial than your Genius; Mine alas! to say all in a few words, have been very little better than they were the last fatal winter! And tho' I was conscious w^t *apparent* cause I gave you to be angry with my silence, yet I could not bear the Thoughts of answering so polite a Letter as your last, with a Heart utterly depressed and a Head equally confus'd.—Les Morts n'ecrivent point, says Madame de Maintenon, & je me comptois de leur Nombre—I am here to thank you, Madam, for ye very strikeing Amusement I receiv'd from those Letters. I read them twice; and as I have sully'd the Copy you were so good as to lend me, I will send another wch I bespoke for myself, as soon as it arrives—The Memoirs of Ld Bolingbroke's Life abound too much with Politics for *me;* I believe The World also would be as well-pleas'd with ye more domestick Incidents relating to so great a Man. For this your Ladyship is in *all* Respects best qualify'd; & I could wish you to engage in something of this sort; if not for ye Publick, at least as an amusement to yourself & your Friends—or as a suitable Present to the now Ld Bolingbroke.

Since I have begun to mention Books,[2] Let me finish ye Subject. The Gamester I have read no more of than what I glean'd from the Quotations in ye Magazine. I never had any opinion of ye Genius of Mr Moore; and hardly think I shall change my sentiments on acc^t of this Performance. The Dedication I see is fantastical & affected—The Moral must on all Hands be allow'd to be truly *seasonable—*

The Earl of Essex I have read. The unfortunate Earl of Essex! whose story, whatever it may deserve, has never *yet* produc'd a good Line, &

---

[1] B.M. Add. MSS 28958, fol. 133ff. This letter also appears in Hull's *Select Letters*, Vol. I, No. XLI, where it is dated April 1, 1753. It replies to Lady Luxborough's of April 1, 1753 (*Letters*, No. XCIII), the date of which is thus confirmed.

[2] See note 3 to the preceding letter.

now scarce ever *will*. I am willing, with y^r Ladyship to make all Allowances for the writer.

The *Brothers* wch I have also read is I think noble Tragedy; full of refin'd & elevated sentiments, & generally speaking, of suitable expressions. I am not blind to many of it's Faults; Dr Young must be Dr Young; but I have read no Tragedy of late years that has affected me so much.

I don't remember to have heard you mention any thing of Voltaire's last Play.³ I therefore send it. These I think are all the new Pamphlets that I have seen this winter.

I am truly glad to hear y^t you had Mrs Davies so long at Barrels, to counter-plot the effects of this unjoyous season. For my own Part, I should have been glad to have join'd in that Contrivance, & to have been introduc'd to your Ladyship as regularly as y^r *Laurustinus*. But I have been little better in bodily health, than I have been in Mind. And *Home*, when one is not truly well, has more Attractions than Elysium. Pardon this unpolite Intimation, which seems to partake of selfishness. And yet it were *as* unpolite at least, to offer one's Company to another when one is not pleas'd with it one's self.⁴

The Jack was sent to Cotterel soon after it came hither: Tis possible your servant may find it ready to be taken home. I mean the Copy together with ye original.

I was two or three times in Company wth Captn Somervile, when he went to Westminster School. I would be glad to send my Compliments if there was a probability of his remembering me sufficient to render it proper.

I hear now and then of Mr Outing by means of Mr Hylton. Last week they were going upon a small expedition & he said, Outing blam'd him for not traveling, as he did, like an apostle viz with *one* Coat, *one* Shirt, *one* Pair of stockings &c: They were going to Charles Walker's Villa. Not his *Cabbage-garden orné,* as Mr Graves denominates his Place at Claverton & for wch I rebuk'd him. The Burlesque might spread too far.

I have promoted & accomplish'd ye addition of two new Bells to our present six; towards wch however I give only two Guineas.

I drew up a rough draught of a Petition to Sr G. Lyttelton in regard to our Turn-pike, meaning if it was approv'd, to correct & transcribe it — And Lo! the People of our Parish have sign'd & sent the Echantillon.

Pardon me if I stop here — I have many things to add if I had Leisure & Spirits; but y^r Servant waits, & I am but *now* to assert y^t I am dull.

³ See Letter 146, n2.
⁴ Hull's version here adds, "I deny that Penances can be done at Barrels. At the Leasowes, I have had many a Winter's Experience they may; and what adds to their Severity is, that they are no way meritorious."

I desire your Ladyship would make my Compliments to Mrs Davies. I am far from what I was when she saw me, but I am entirely at her service. I desire also to be remember'd to the rest of your Friends, & am Madam

Your Ladyship's most oblig'd & most obedient Servant

Will Shenstone

Mr Whistler has had ye Gout, ye most inconsistent of all disorders with ye Idea his Complexion . . .[5] Mr Graves & Mrs Graves have . . . just drawn by a second-hand, at Bath. He approves his own Picture, & says only y^t Mrs Graves's is as good as he *expected*.

149. To LADY LUXBOROUGH[1]

The Leasowes, May ye 13th 1753

DEAR MADAM,

I am *well aware* y^t my Pegasus is one of those dull Horses which will not bear to be *hurry'd*. Allow him but his *Time,* & he may jogg on *safely;* but urge him to move faster, & he is sure to break one's neck. Your Ladyship's, on the other Hand, is of a different strain; & is never known to stumble, 'tho' He have all ye Celerity of a Race-Horse. This Account being *literally* Fact, you must in justice excuse ye Defects of this Letter. Your Gardener is urgent to return this Evening; & I have defer'd rather too long to *begin* my notable epistle.

The first thing y^t occurrs to be consider'd is my Friend Pixell's affair.[2] I will not fail to *communicate* & to *press* Mr Reynolds's advice to him: As for y^e *Event* he must trust to Fortune, & has reason to acquit his Friends.

I am glad to hear y^t your Lasp's Health is mended; & y^t your Complaints, tho' grievous while they *last,* are such as do not threaten to continue: I too have had better Health & Spirits for these three last Days, a greater Quantity of both, could they be weigh'd, y^n I have been forc'd to *subsist* upon ever since I saw you at Barrels. I had reason to suspect some Inward Inflammation in ye winter: I liv'd maigre, & pursu'd a Regimen of warm dilutes within-Doors, 'till I found my nerves were totally relax'd, & my Skin not proof against an airing in my kitchen-garden. Hence Wind ye sure consequence of obstructed Perspiration, viscid Juices, & eternal Lassitude. Hence also the numberless effects of

---

[5] The manuscript is defective at this point.
[1] B. M. Add. MSS 28958, fol. 136ff. This letter answers and confirms the date of Lady Luxborough's of May 12, 1753 (*Letters,* No. XCIV).
[2] See Lady Luxborough's *Letters,* pp. 335-36.

wind upon the Nerves; Watching, when one should sleep; or sleep more anxious & less refreshing than wakefullness. I now begin to try the Bark in little Portions & by degrees; & my Spirits, to speak ye truth, are now not much amiss: Only my Head is *confus'd* as My Letter will testify.

I shall be extremely glad to meet Mrs Davies at Barrels, & I shall be extremely glad to meet Sr William Meredyth, at Barrels; & one or the other it shall go hard with me, but I *will* meet. In the mean time, let me *seriously* assert that your Ladyship's Menace is altogether too severe. Give my *Vanity* at least an opportunity of experimenting, whether I cannot make the Leasowes new to you, as long as we live.

I beg my Compliments & *Thanks* to Mrs Davies, when you see her. I am glad you like the few Lines to Sr William Meredyth: I know his *general* Accomplishments; I only wanted to consult your Ladyship about a *Propriety* of Compliment.

Mr Hylton *has* y^t disposition your Ladyship observ'd in him; & has also, (what you had not here any *time* to observe) no despicable share of Politeness Genius & Literature.

You might well laugh at ye Correspondence betwixt Lord Dudley & me. He is too diffident of his Abilities; & it would be no Discredit to his Character if he would write more frequent Letters.

Your Ladyship may be justly allow'd to laugh at my Apothecary's Apprehensions: But you cannot with so much Justice laugh at my contribution to ye Bells. I live but at ye Distance of *Half* a mile, upon an opposite Hill to that on wch the Church is built; a pine Valley betwixt, with a pretty large Piece of Water. Finally, there is no Place in the Parish where the Bells will sound more harmoniously y^n The Leasowes. And, by y^e *bye*, I knew from ye beginning.

I never hear from Mr Outing, & I never write to him. All I know is that

He is contented, so am *I!*

Yet I think him a truly honest Man, & wish him Prosperity. I agree with y^r Ladyship y^t Madame de Maintenon had much more worldly *Art* & *Design* y^n is suitable to a Person who so often uses the expression "pour faire mon salut" & "songez a votre salut," which are ever in her Mouth.

I have spoke to many Parts of your Ladyship's Letter — If your Gardener *must* go to-night, I ought to fill up ye rest of my Paper with my Thanks for ye offer of his Assistance, ye Love-Apple, & ye Brocoli-seeds. He has been shewn Ld Dudley's Green-house this Morning; & is now walk'd out to take a View of my Farm: But as the Day is rainy, & the Verdure of my groves, immature, I cannot give your Ladyship an Acquittance in Full for ye Promise you made y^t he should have a *sight of ye Leasowes*. I am ever

Your Ladyship's most oblig'd & most obedient Servt
Will: Shenstone

Mr Hume[3] is return'd, & seems highly delighted indeed! He has not seen ye Beau-monde of Hales here, on account of ye weather, but I hope he will however say enough to draw Mrs Lane hither whenever she is at Leisure.

150. To LADY LUXBOROUGH[1]

The Leasowes, June ye 22. 1753

DEAR MADAM,

It is now a great Length of time since I last had the Honour of a few Lines from your Ladyship; at least according to the *Chronology* of a Person who wishes to hear of your Health & Happiness so sincerely as myself. Mrs Davies did indeed inform me some weeks ago, that she had prevail'd upon you to take a View of ye Perfections of your Shrubbery &c: I hope to hear by ye Return of my servant that such walks as these have been frequently repeated; & y^t by enjoying them a little at first, you furnish yourself with strength & Spirits to enjoy them more & more. For my own Part, tho' I am greatly better yⁿ I was dureing the Winter, & have had a continuance of weather not at all unfavourable to the Views of the Country, yet I cannot yet fancy to myself y^t I have *begun* my *Season;* & am mighty willing to hope that I have much greater Happiness in *Reserve*.

Sir George Lyttelton has been at Hagley for a week or nine Days, & return'd yesterday to London. I did not see him all ye Time: Tho' I have thrice broke my Promise to him of sending him y^t Ode to his Brother; & tho' the rest of our Turn-pike-Commissioners all din'd with him on Wednesday last. Such is my *Impropriety* of Behaviour to *all* my Friends; & ye odd vicissitudes of my Health, (which I cannot easily *explain* to them) are ye real Cause: I hope y^t your Ladyship will not be my *severest* Accuser; tho' I have not paid my Respects to your Ladyship in ye manner my Inclination tells me I should have done.

I have after an unavoidable Delay, & some Difficulty, transcrib'd a Copy of this Ode To the Dutchess of Somerset.[2] I have indeed accom-

---

[3] Lady Luxborough's gardener.

[1] B.M. Add. MSS 28958, fol. 138ff. Lady Luxborough's letter of June 23-24, 1753 (*Letters,* No. XCV) replies to this. The date of her letter is thus confirmed.

[2] *Rural Elegance,* concerning which ode Shenstone had been extremely dilatory. For other references see the Index.

pany'd it with a few stiff Lines to her Grace;³ but I must absolutely depend upon your Ladyship to be presented properly: I mean with all that *Respect* & *Deference* of which you know me to be truly conscious for her Grace's exalted *Character,* & with all that profound *Humility* with wch I ought to inscribe so *superficial* a Poem.

The Bookseller made my Paper-Books too little; yet I could not endure to wait longer for others; However if your Ladyship thinks this Decorum may not be dispens'd with, I will once more transcribe this ode &c:

Ld Dudley is expected at The Grange next Tuesday. I long to see him for his *Honesty;* In such a scoundrell Parish as ours, it really *Shines*.

I have seen but little first-Rate Company this Season. *Some* I have, but strangers. One mighty agreeable young Lady whose Name was Ottley; Yorkshire. Two gentlemen, yesterday (wth Servts) one whose Name was Coom. They took a minute description of ye Place & every single Motto &c: I met them comeing up to the House; & had only a few Minutes' Conversation. As for Tradesmen & wt I am to call middlin sort of People, I have had more this year yn any of the Preceding.

Outing seems to me to be very frequently wth Lord Dudley in Town, & I should not be surpriz'd to see yt He *returns* with Him.

My amiable Friend, & your Ladyship's most faithfull Servant, Mr Hylton, will be down in a Fortnight. Either with Him, or young Pixell, do I then purpose to wait upon your Ladyship at Barrels — I hope Mrs Davies contributes often to your Amusement: I am sure she much wishes it. I beg my Compliments to all your Ladyship's Friends and am your Ladyship's most obligd

& most obedient hum: Servt

Will: Shenstone

I hope your Ladysp will renew to me the Promise of a visit this Summer — I answer'd Mrs Davies's Letter.

151. To the DUCHESS OF SOMERSET¹

June 23, 1753

MADAM,

I find myself at length enabled to obey your Grace's Commands, after a Delay, but ill expressive of the Pleasure with which I received them. By some Means or other, the Original of this Ode was mislaid, and it was

---

³ Letter 151.
¹ Hull, *Select Letters,* Vol. I, No. XLVI.

not immediately in my Power, from scattered Materials, to give it once more the Form, in which it now appears.

I fear it is no less requisite to make an Apology for the Freedom of inscribing it to your Grace from the Beginning. In this Respect, I have but little to offer, beside the flattering Imagination, that the *Subject* might recommend it. It would be no small Vanity in me to presume, that in Regard to the more elegant Amusements of a Country Life, I had the Honour to entertain the same Sentiments with your Grace; however, something of this Kind I must of Necessity confess, if I would give a genuine Account of the Liberty I have taken.

The additional Fragment was originally intended as an Episode to a much larger Poem on the Subject. It was thrown into its present Form soon after the Rebellion, and it is now transcribed, because I would not send a vacant Space in my Paper, wherein I had the most distant Chance of contributing to your Grace's Amusement.

Lady Luxborough, who does me the Honour of communicating these trifling Productions to your Grace,[2] will not fail to do me the *Justice* of declaring the singular Veneration I have for your Grace's Character. She will testify, with how much Diffidence I offer you such imperfect Compositions, written at a Distance from every judicious Friend, with too much Inaccuracy, by the Side of Meadows and Streams, from which little can be expected, but a Group of rural Allusions. Above all, she will be so obliging as to suggest, how little I am influenced by any other Ambition, compared with that of being esteemed,

Madam,
Your Grace's most devoted and most obedient Servant,
W. Shenstone

152. To RICHARD GRAVES[1]

The Leasowes, July 15, 1753

DEAR MR. GRAVES,

I send you my Ode, as I sent it to the Duchess some weeks ago. Why I pitched upon one reading sooner than another, I will not now explain: nor will I trouble you to make any fresh remarks upon it at present; only, when you happen to read it over at your leisure, if any thing occurs to you that would tend to perfect it, I would beg you occasionally to make some memorandums. I have not yet received an answer; but, as I ac-

---

[2] Shenstone's concern for the proper presentation of his ode to the Duchess is revealed in the foregoing letter to Lady Luxborough.

[1] Dodsley, *Letters to Particular Friends,* No. LXXIV.

companied the verses with a letter, I suppose I shall receive one in return. I also added, to fill a blank space in my paper book, a poem which I call "The Vista;" and which you may perhaps recollect; how properly I know not, for I had the benefit of no person's *judgment* or advice.

Lord Dudley made Mr. Dolman a present of a piece of plate, a large cup, in consideration of his sister's being at Broom about half a year. There was on it, one supporter awkwardly enough holding up the coronet in his paw, and from the coronet proceeded a label, with "Amoris ergo Dudley." I do not know who was the manager, or whence he had the inscription; but I think from Dr. H——. This is *elegant* and *enough*. Nevertheless, as there may be some convenience in dazzling the eyes of the people where I dwell, and as *such* eyes as theirs are not to be dazzled, and hardly *struck,* by *elegance* alone, I chose the method that was most *magnificent*. — I wish they are not invidious enough to say, that *his* arms are engraved there for want of some of my *own:* so I would not be long before I remove their notable suggestion. — I have truly so low an opinion of arms since they became purchaseable by money, and since the present unlimited use of them, that were I to find a coat to my name in the office which I did not like, I would not use it; but substitute what was more agreeable; yet some *sort* of *right* or *claim* is requisite to satisfy one's delicacy with an opinion of *property;* and indeed to fix one's *choice,* where one has the whole furniture of the universe for *its* object. — After all, the vulgar are more struck with arms than any thing; "stupet in titulis & imaginibus;" and, I believe, there were near two hundred people gathered round Lady Luxborough's landau at Birmingham, and declaring her arms to be very *noble,* or otherwise. — I do not, therefore, chuse to employ a vulgar *mind* about this matter. — Were you to go to London, I should gladly solicit *you;* or if you have any friend you could write to in town, to search the office; for really I have none that I like *for the purpose*. It will not cost above a couple of shillings. — I will send you a draught of the lid of my standish when it arrives — for I really do not know what Mr. Hylton will put upon it: I find, he consults with Dr. B——, my Lord's physician. — "De Dudley" would run most abominably, and "Baro Dudley" may be authorized by the frequent practice of Maittaire. — If it is inscribed "Dudley" *alone,* I can add the rest if I should hereafter think proper; and I wish it may be so.

My verses to the Colonel are not yet transcribed.

I think the Latin inscription to your brother very elegant; and I should not care to have any part of it omitted — I would, by all means, have this

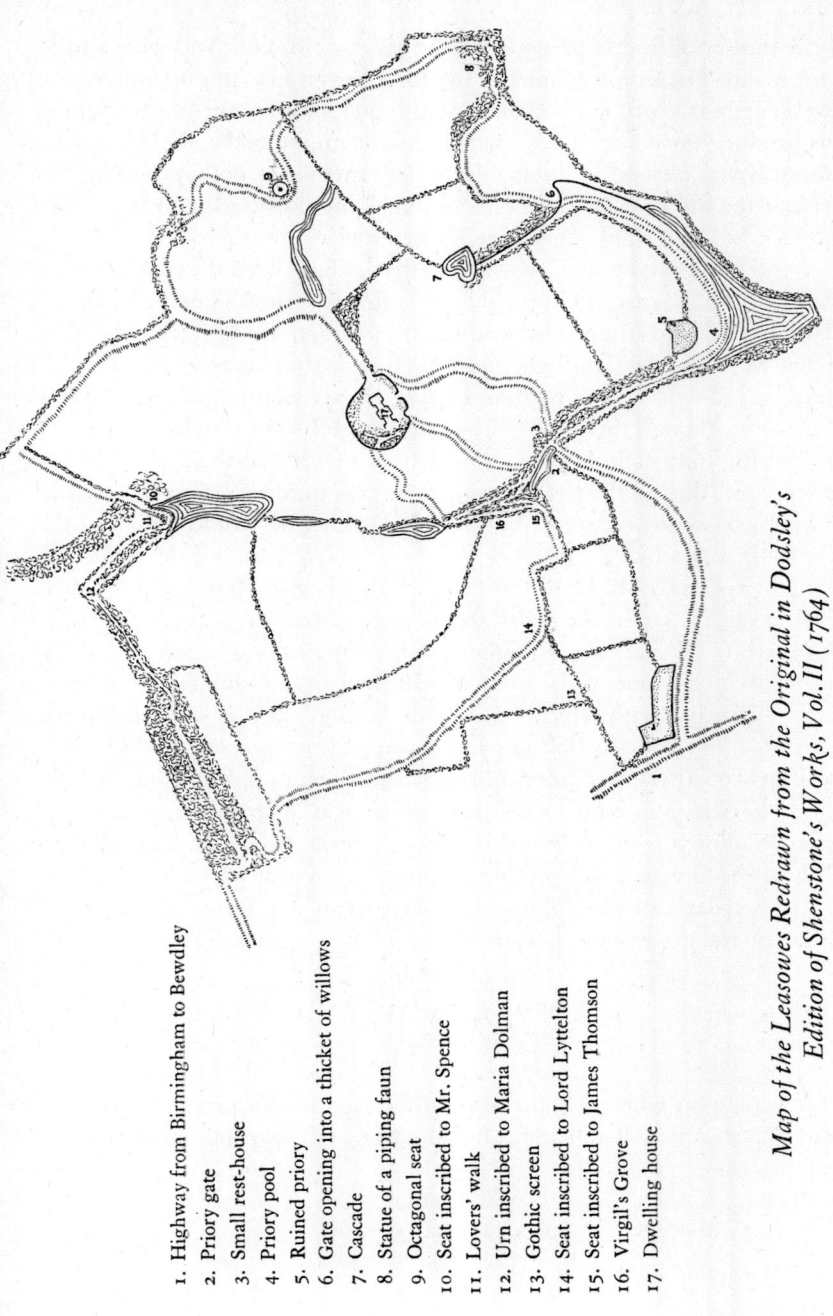

1. Highway from Birmingham to Bewdley
2. Priory gate
3. Small rest-house
4. Priory pool
5. Ruined priory
6. Gate opening into a thicket of willows
7. Cascade
8. Statue of a piping faun
9. Octagonal seat
10. Seat inscribed to Mr. Spence
11. Lovers' walk
12. Urn inscribed to Maria Dolman
13. Gothic screen
14. Seat inscribed to Lord Lyttelton
15. Seat inscribed to James Thomson
16. Virgil's Grove
17. Dwelling house

Map of the Leasowes Redrawn from the Original in Dodsley's Edition of Shenstone's Works, Vol. II (1764)

little history of his life perpetuated — "His saltem, &c." And were you to put it into English, it would be too long for an inscription; unless you were, by means of a printed elegy with notes, or any other such method, to produce the same effect; and then you might make the epitaph as short as you pleased. — After all, the *first* method is perhaps as eligible. When the affair is nearer a conclusion, I should be glad to be of any service. — I will think, and write again about it.

And now, having spoke to such matters as have been the subject of our late correspondence, I am at liberty to diversify my letter as I may. — I should be glad to know in your next, whether you have heard of late from Mr. Whistler; and whether he is confined at home as usual by his mother's state of health. I almost despair of ever seeing him again at The Leasowes, though there is hardly any pleasure I so much covet as that of surprising him with the *alterations* I have *made,* and the *articles* I have *purchased,* during the five years since he was in Shropshire: add to this, the several *acquaintances* I have formed which he would like, and the amusing visits I could pay hereabouts with freedom. — I do not know whether you saw Mr. Davenport and his family at Bath this spring. He is laying out his environs; and I am by appointment to go over the week after next. He has also a painter at this time taking views round his house, which is one of the most magnificent in our county; yet I never leave home but with reluctance. I really *love* no place so well; and it is a great favour in me to allot any one a week of my *summer*. Add to this, that my constitution requires nursing; and I am most *happy* where I am most *free*. It is in vain to say, they *allow* you all freedom, where you cannot allow it *yourself*. For this reason, I never more enjoy myself than I do at the Grange; and yet this to some may appear paradoxical.

I yesterday embellished my chalybeate spring. — The inscription that is *cut* on the stone is as follows, viz.

FONS FERRUGINEUS
DIVAE QUAE SECESSU ISTO
FRUI CONCEDIT
SALUTIS

Yet I question whether some of the following be not preferable; if they are, I beg you will tell me. One shilling and six-pence produces the alteration:

FONS FERRUGINEUS
DIVAE PER QUAM LICET
HOC SECESSU FRUI, &C.
SAL. &C.

or,
DIVAE PER QUAM LATEBRAE
QUAEVIS
OBLECTANT
&c.

or,
DIVAE LOCORUM OMNIUM
COMMENDATRICI, &c.

or
DIVAE NIMIRUM RUSTICAE
SALUTI SACER.

or,
DIVAE CUI DEBETUR
LOCORUM OMNIUM AMOENITAS,
&c.

or,
DIVAE PER QUAM LICET
INORNATO RURE LAETARI.

Believe me ever, with my best compliments to Mrs. Graves,
Your most obliged, and most affectionate, servant,
W. Shenstone

153. To LADY LUXBOROUGH [1]

The Leasowes, July, ye 19th 1753

DEAR LADY LUXBOROUGH,

Tho' I have not yet had the Opportunity, which I *soon expect,* of bringing one of my Friends to wait upon your Ladyship at Barrels, I am by no means void of Anxiety in regard to your Health: And the Last Account of it being so far short of what I could wish, I send Tom purely in Hopes of receiving a *better.* Should *that* be the Case, I would begin to flatter myself with the agreeable *Consequences* of your Recovery; amongst ye rest, the annual Visit you have hitherto been so good to make me. Tis owing to your Ladyship's Indulgence, yt the Prospect of this visit revives, with each returning year, as regularly in my Imagination, as the Leaves upon ye Trees, or the Flowers upon the Meadowes. May no unkindly Star contribute to robb me of ye Pleasure of your Company, or ye Beauty of a Season, so long as I live! At least may the Goddess Health be never averse to it, to whom I have of late been dedicating my *Chalybeate* Spring! The Inscription is as follows "FONS FERRUGINEUS &c:"

---

[1] B. M. Add. MSS 28958, fol. 140ff. This letter seems to reply to Lady Luxborough's of June 23–24, 1753 (*Letters*, No. XCV), the date of which is thus confirmed.

"The Chalybeate Fountain; sacred to the Goddess *Health*, by whose Favour alone we enjoy this Retirement" — There is a little *Art* appears in the stone-work round this Spring; & I think it not amiss; but I will not *anticipate* your Ladyship's opinion.

Ld Dudley has been arriv'd this Fortnight. He has made me a 4 Days visit since he came; proposes your Ladyship's Health to his company & will be extremely glad to wait upon you — I suppose when you come into this Country you will think it requisite to dine *there* the first Day; & I will afterwards beg ye Honour of conducting you to The Leasowes. My Lord *himself* does not regard the Ceremonial; but He has some *about* him, I know that *do* — your Intimation concerning Miss L. and Sally Rock was coincident with ye mention of it by some Company in my Drawing Room — & the first I heard of it. It seems Miss Lea has made a Conquest of Mr Warren a Buckinghamshire Gentleman, who is about Seventy; & poor man, violently afflicted wth the Gout; but will come to the Grange this Summer, if he be *able*. He offers a Landau & Four, unlimited Indulgence; & to put her Fortune in ye Stocks for ye Benefit of y^e *younger* Children — The Event I do not know: but it will, I *think*, be a Match.

But Miss L., all this while, has a Regard for Mr Hilton; Mr Hylton on ye other hand is enamour'd of Sally Rock (a secret) & how Fortune is to manage ye Catastrophe of this tragicomedy, is past my Comprehension to determine.

> The Maid for lovely Fore-head fam'd
> With Cyrus' beauties is enflam'd: } ill-translated
> While Pholoë, of haughty Charms,
> The panting Breast of Cyrus warms:
> So Venus wills! whose Power controuls
> The fond affections of our Souls!
> With sportive Cruelty, who binds
> Unequal Forms, unequal Minds!
>   Francis's HORACE vol 1. Page 121

Mr Hylton arriv'd at ye Grange & visited me yesterday; I hope very shortly to come with him to Barrels. He is zealously your Servant, &, if you will excuse ye familiarity of ye Sound, your *Friend* — I am going to dine with my Lord to-day upon Venison, where we shall wish it were as easy to *promote* your Ladyship's Health, as to *drink* it.

I am for my own part arriv'd at what I am to *call* Health; namely as good a state of it as I shall probably enjoy this Summer; perhaps, ever.

More of *Happiness* I shall partake when your Ladyship arrives.

Our Turnpikes take place — but will I fear produce but little Alteration this year.

I have nothing to add y^t can amuse you, so may as well conclude — Only Let me beg, if writing be troublesome to your Ladyship, y^t Mrs Lane may be permitted, now & then, to give me some Account of your Health — I am with ye most ardent wishes for it, Madam, your Ladyship's most oblig'd

& most invariable Servant,
Will: Shenstone

I never hear from Mrs Davies.

154. To LADY LUXBOROUGH [1]

The Leasowes, August the 26, 1753

DEAR LADY LUXBOROUGH,

I wrote a few Lines to Mrs Davies this afternoon, purposing to defer my Letter to your Ladys^p, 'till I could spare my Servant for a Day; by which means I might receive an *immediate* Answer in regard to your Ladyship's Health. But considering y^t I have but one only Servant about ye House, in Case any Company should arrive, I find it expedient to apply once more to my good Friend Mr Williams, who has always hitherto been punctual in furthering any Packet you were pleas'd to send me. I beg therefore, if your Ladyship does not care to write, that you would permit Mrs Lane to give me some Account of your Recovery, by ye very first opportunity that occurrs. There is no Friend you have y^t wishes your Health more sollicitously than myself; but as the sincerest Wishes of ye most faithfull Friends are mighty ineffectual Things, unless seconded by your own Endeavours, I really want to offer you something more significant y^n the mere Expression of my Wishes. *Advise* your Ladyship I cannot, without Presumption; but *Remind* you I *may;* for I am well assured you will not call *that* Presumption, which flows alone from Gratitude for many unmerited obligations. Without further Preamble I mean no more than this, that you would omit Nothing (for this & the two next Months y^t has been found so serviceable to your Health while Sr Peter Soame was at Barrels. I believe the principal of this Advice was Exercise & Regular Hours, & I add the two next Months, because one Part of this Prescription may not afterwards be so conveniently follow'd. Let me Add that I mention this for ye sake of yourself, who wish ye Happiness of your Acquaintance; for ye sake of your

[1] B. M. Add. MSS 28958, fol. 142ff. Lady Luxborough replies to this with her letter of September 12, 1753 (*Letters*, No. XCVI), the date of which is thus confirmed.

Friends who derive great Pleasure from your Conversation; & for ye sake of my own Sincerity, which ought ever to be held inviolable.

I mention'd to Mrs Davies in a Letter wch She will shew you, if at Barrels, what an Inundation of Company I have had since I came Home. I will not repeat the List, for this Reason. But I should act ungratefully if I should forget, on this Occasion, *who* it was that did me this Sort of Honour *primarily;* who it was y^t has never miss'd an opportunity of recommending either my Place or Me, And that with Spirit, & Ingenuity; And So long as I do not forget these Things, it is impossible y^t *Any* Visitants can erase the Memory of ye Obligations I have to Lady Luxborough. I need not say erase, for they tend naturally to revive it.

Lady Plymouth is a most aimiable Person, & I really think a very desireable Match for my Lord. I am to dine there some-time in a Fortnight.

Lady Gough seems a very friendly Sort of Woman; her Person but indifferent; She made much Enquiry after your Ladyships Villa, & I believe has a Longing to see your Shrubbery. I am to visit there also.

Miss Banks is a Person to fall in Love with; but, I am told, is too celebrated, & withall a Court-Lady.

Ld Temple was chiefly struck with ye View from my House, my Terras, & my Grove: Ask'd me to call on him & take a View of Stowe — To make your Ladyship laugh a little, if you please. Ld Dudley had stay'd a Night here, & Mrs Rock had been teizing him to dress, telling him she was sure some Company would drop in, and surprize him. He, in a kind of Pett, swore he would not stir a step let who the Devil *would* come; And that selfsame Instant enter'd Ld Temple & Miss Banks & caught him in his Night-Cap &c.

The Paragraph to Dean Lyttelton (in ye ode you know of) made Ld Temple laugh abundantly. That with the ode To the Dutchess of Somerset, & The Verses upon Autumn were read at Hagley-Table, & were all more extoll'd than they had any Pretence to deserve. Some Particulars, in regard to the Colonels ode, I would mention, but have neither Room nor Time. Nor indeed are they much material.

Mr Hylton is gone to dine with Ld Dudley to day: otherwise I should have many Compliments & Acknowledgm^{ts} to make on his Behalf. But He talks of conveying them in a Letter of his own.

If your Ladyship *should* have an opportunity of writing, I should be very highly delighted with a Line of your own. If not, I'm well assured you will suffer Mrs Lane to write to Me. I am,

Dear Lady Luxborough!
          Your most oblig'd and ever obedient hum: Servt
                          Will: Shenstone

155. To LADY LUXBOROUGH[1]

Septr ye 18th 1753

DEAR MADAM,

I hope your Ladyship will readily enough believe that an Account of your Recovery, from your own Hand, was the most agreeable Intelligence I could possibly receive. Somewhat heighten'd I may now confess, it was, by the *Surprize* it gave me: For tho' I really thought it in your *Power* to recover, When I saw you last; I was not a little fearfull that you would not use ye Means which to Me seem'd absolutely indispensable. Your Ladyship will see so many Instances of ye Joy it gives your Friends to find you on ye mending Hand, that I hope your natural Philanthropy will induce you to persist in such a Regimen as you have found to be of Service. And what if after a little time your strength should be so much advanc'd, that I should pronounce it not only possible, but expedient for you to make a Journey to the Leasowes, by way of Exercise? I doubt your Physician has too much Integrity to accept a Bribe, or I would infallibly take a Ride to Worster, & endeavour to make him of my Party.

I have had a perpetual succession of Company ever since I wrote to you. L^d & Lady Ward sent to have the Roads examin'd — & I was told by Captⁿ Whood that I was likely to see L^d & Lady Anson, with Mr Anson, this Week; when they were to be at Hagley. Sr George Lyttelton; Admiral Smith; & Mr Berkeley, Member for Glostershire, have been here; — But I will not fill this Letter with Names; I may perhaps, when the Season is over, make tryal how brilliant a List I can furnish, for y^r Amusement. Sir George made very friendly Inquiries after your Ladyship's Health, & seem'd truly concern'd at the Account I gave Him. Glad I am that it is now in my Power to give one more *agreeable*.

I have engag'd my Vote to Mr Coventry; & as it is entirely my Lord Foley's Resentment y^t prevents a Compromise, I could wish your Ladyship would support me in my Endeavours to Serve Ld Coventry. There are a Number of Votes, I think, in Old-barrow, for wch I, last Election, apply'd to Mr Somervile. If you want a List I will procure one: But in the mean time it will give me great Pleasure to find y^t I have ye Honour *to think wth your Ladyship,* when I am *forc'd* to turn my Thoughts towards a Subject on which I think so *little,* as Party. The Probability, & Danger of a Minority seems, as far as *I* can judge, to demand a Whig-Parliament.

I desire my Compliments to M^r & Mrs Holyoake & if I am not impertinent, would request their Assistance in ye same Cause. My Lord

---

[1] B. M. Add. MSS 28958, fol. 146ff. Lady Luxborough's reply is her letter of September 18, 1753 (*Letters,* No. XCVII), the date of which is thus confirmed.

Dudley will be excessively glad to return them his Thanks at The Grange. He din'd here yesterday, & is *zealously* at your Service.

I forget what I said of Miss Peggy Banks; but I could hardly say *too much*. She lives mostly wth Lord Temple, goes in Parties with the Pelhams, is as remarkable for her Taste & Reading as her Beauty & Behaviour. I most solemnly assure your Ladyship that I did not know when I wrote my last Letter, that she would be an 100,000ll Fortune.

I beg the Favour of your Ladyship to convince Mr Reynolds y^t I wish impatiently to see him, & will infallibly see him ye first opportunity that offers. He does not well, to be angry with a Person who so truly esteems him — I must defer my Letter to Mrs Davies for a day or two, & shall be in *Woefull Plight,* if *she* takes it amiss, I'm sure. But pray, my Lady, ask her one Question, Why Part of a select Company may not make an autumnal visit, & unite with ye rest to make another in the Spring? Winter is too dark a Medium for me to look thro; at least clearly.

I have Mr Hylton's Prints & Pictures here, wch I shew to my Company, & it adds to their Entertainment — It has been unlucky for me this year y^t so many of their Visitants at Hagley cannot *walk* — I believe I should else have had the *Duke of Beaufort* wth his Dutchess (Mr Berkeley's Sister) Sr *Richard Lyttelton* wth his new Ribband, & her Grace his Wife; & I am just now forc'd to hear y^t Ld Anson is a miserable Walker — But I shall have no Cause to complain; having far out-shone all my *Neighbours* in y^e *Splendour* & y^e *Number* of my Visitants. I was us'd to consider your Ladyship as a Star y^t was particularly friendly, to me, as well as distinguishedly bright. — Y^r Absence will be a terrible Drawback upon the Lustre of this Year; & I wou'd give fifty of my *Lesser* Stars for Your Appearance. But I fear it will not be — I must take Leave upon another Paper — I have now determin'd to send Tom with my Letter hopeing your Ladyship will please to dispatch him in the Morning, because I have Company that dines with Me to-morrow — It would be of great Importance to me, if your Ladyship would be so good as to send me a favourable Answer in regard to the Votes at Oldbarrow; at least such as I might repeat with Propriety to Sr George Lyttelton, whom I shall see again this Week. He either has more Insincerity than I *suspect* in him, or He is very respectfully y^r Ladyship's Friend —

If y^r Ladyship have Plenty of Melons, I am tempted to be so impertinent as to beg one by Tom's Return.

My Pen is in a rambling Humour — & if I *cou'd* detain Tom any longer, It would tell you a Multitude of Things — Nothing however more true or so important to me, as that I have the honour, to be, Mad^am y^r Ladyships most oblig'd   W. Shenstone

156. To LADY LUXBOROUGH[1]

Friday, Septr 1753

DEAR MADAM,

I write a *few* Lines to give your Ladyship my Reasons why I cannot write a *Many*. Your Servant found me at The Grange with Lord Dudley; who, by the way, desires his best Compliments & Thanks for your Endeavours to Serve Mr Coventry — But before I could well open your Letter, Mr Joseph told me that Captn Somerville & Mr John Reynolds were that Moment arriv'd at The Leasowes. *This* brought me home in an Instant; & This also is ye Reason y^t I cannot allot more y^n a few Moments of the few Hours they stay with me to express how much I think myself oblig'd by y^r Applications at Oldbarrow. They are now gone wth a Servant to see one *half* of the Walks *before Dinner*. The Paths I fear mighty slippery, & the Hedges wet — But the Sun I see shines out, & we may hope a fine Afternoon — I have scarce pass'd a single Day without a *Deal* of Company, ever Since I wrote to you last. Lady Lyttelton with Miss Lyttelton, Miss West, & two officers, here I think last Tuesday — Allow'd the Roads to be quite good, & had a favourable Day; was in Appearance greatly struck with my little Scenery, (having never seen our Parish before) & talks of coming again this Season.

I heard Since I wrote to y^r Ladyship that Miss Banks's Fortune is only 10,000ll. So that I cannot make out ye 100,000ll. any otherwise than by presuming She has 90,000 Pounds worth of extrinsick & intrinsick Merits.

My best Compliments to Mrs Bartlett & Mrs Davies. I *do* owe Mrs Davies a Letter wch I will Shortly fill with my Acknowledgments for ye laborious & unpleasing Task She undertakes at my Request.[2] I din'd on Wednesday at Sr Harry Gough's, & yesterday wth my Ld Dudley at Admiral Smiths; *He* was indeed from Home, but we found *an* Admiral Cotterel there, & three very agreeable young Sea-officers, Capt^{ns} Hamilton, Beecher, Whood. I shortly go wth Ld Dudley to visit Lord & Lady Plymouth — By the Way L^{dy} Plymouth had a *Triumph* at Sr John Packington's wch I want room & Time to display — Rejoice my good Lady at every Acquisition of acquaintance I make & be well assur'd that every Friend of Mine Shall be a Friend of yours if it be in my Power to make Him so. I am wth much unmannerly haste — but the utmost

Respect y^r most oblig'd
W. S.

---

[1] B. M. Add. MSS 28958, fol. 144ff. This letter answers and further confirms the date of Lady Luxborough's of September 18, 1753 (*Letters,* No. XCVII), which her No. XCVIII of September 27 supplements. From the context it is apparent that Shenstone wrote after receiving hers of the 27th.

[2] The transcribing of his poems from the "green book" he gave Lady Luxborough.

157. To RICHARD GRAVES [1]

The Leasowes, Oct. 24, 1753

DEAR MR. GRAVES,

After a Long Season of Vanity and universal Dissipation, I return with unfeigned Pleasure to a Correspondence with my dearest and most familiar Friends. So just is your Notion of the Permanency of my Affection; and so true it is, that much greater *Civilities,* than any *yet* shewn me by the Great, can never alter my Opinion of the Valuableness of your Friendship. Will you believe my simple Assertion, or shall I take Pains to prove it by the very Nature of Things? I cannot esteem it necessary.

Your Accounts of Mrs. Walker's[2] Death was new to me. I will write to Mr. Whistler shortly, and am in Hopes, I shall *now* prevail with him to give me some few Weeks of his Company. Amongst the Strangers who visited my Walks this Summer, there were three or more, as their Servants informed us, who had recourse to these Amusements, on the Death of their Relations. Perhaps the Sight of an old Friend is no less serviceable on such Occasions.

Your Stream, I find, is very considerable; I dare say Horace's was not larger, though mentioned as *"rivo dare nomen idoneus; ut nec* frigidior *Thracum nec* purior *ambiat Hebrum."* And you are mistaken in imagining that there is no *Notice* taken of it, for I assure you I have heard it commended here this Summer: I forget by whom. You shew excessive Delicacy in your Dislike of its running over Water-Cresses as Pot-Herbs. Pray what can at once have more Beauty and more Propriety, supposing your Stream to pass through the Kitchen-Garden? But I will not quarrel with you about the *Kind* of Aquatick, if you will allow me to think nothing more pleasing than *Greens beneath transparent Water.*

When I can fix upon a Painter, to draw me an Head of Lord Dudley, (for which he promises to sit at the *Leasowes*) I will endeavour to get your Picture altered; though Bond,[3] whose Painting I have heard much celebrated, made no Scruple to pronounce it an admirable Portrait.

I am glad enough to hear of your Encrease of Salary, and begin to think a Sort of Affluence a little more *essential* to Happiness than I have formerly done. Only remember you are *thin,* and do not injure your Constitution.

I enclose you a Copy of that Ode to the Duchess.[4] It would *admit* of

---

[1] Hull, *Select Letters,* Vol. I, No. XLIV.
[2] Whistler's mother, who had remarried.
[3] Mr. Bond, a painter in Birmingham, an artist of great taste and ability. The Editor of these letters is in possession of an admirable likeness of Mr. Shenstone painted by this gentleman for which he is proud to make this public acknowledgment. [Hull]
[4] *Rural Elegance,* of frequent earlier reference. See the Index.

many *Emendations,* if it does not want many *Corrections;* but I know not when it will receive either, and I chuse moreover to send it in the Dress it wore at *Hagley* Table. I would send you moreover the Ode to Sir Rich. Lyttelton,[5] but that it would be grievously irksome to transcribe it at this Time. The *Antiquary* Character given the [Dean] is not approved. I vindicated it as far as was decent for me; but I believe I must exchange it for a Compliment upon his *Humanity.*[6]

Sir George, the Dean, Mr. Lyttelton, &c. made me a Morning's Visit yesterday, and took me with them to Dinner at the *Grange.* Sir George goes next Week to *London,* and the Family will disperse.

Dodsley adds this Winter a fourth Volume[7] to his Miscellanies. He wrote to me last Week, to beg a few Copies of Verses; I shall send him the Autumn Verses,[8] and two Copies that are upon my Seats, *"Oh, let me haunt this, &c."* and *"Oh, you that bathe in courtlye Blysse, &c."* in old Characters. Give me your Opinion, what else of mine; and whether I shall send any Copy of yours: they will be read by the polite World. What do you think of getting your Verses upon Medals inserted? But he talks in his Letter as if they must be sent *immediately.*

I desire my Compliments to Mrs. Graves, and am satisfied that I can never be otherwise than what I am at present,
      Your most affectionate Friend, &c.
           W. Shenstone
Excuse this villainous Scrawl; I am not half in Spirits.

158. To JOHN SCOTT HYLTON[1]

The Leasowes, Oct. 25, 1753

Dear Mr. H[ylto]n,

This can prove no other than an heavy, stupid Letter, agreeable to the present Disposition of my Mind. The most it can pretend, is to acquaint you, in vulgar Terms, that you retain your usual Place in my Affection and Esteem; yet this may be no trivial Information, now you have accepted a Place at Court, and have left your Friends at Liberty to form conjectures about your future Conduct; to continue, or to dismiss you, as our Electors do their Representatives. Be this as it will, I confess

---

[5] The *Pastoral Ode to . . . Sir Richard Lyttelton,* of earlier reference. See the Index.
[6] The stanza remains, however, unaltered. See Shenstone's *Works,* I (1764), 179.
[7] The fourth volume actually was published in 1755.
[8] *Verses Written towards the Close of the Year 1748. To William Lyttelton, Esq.* The other verses mentioned appeared in Dodsley's volume; also the *Pastoral Ballad,* and a number of other pieces. See I. A. Williams, *Seven XVIIIth Century Bibliographies,* pp. 56–57.
[1] Hull, *Select Letters,* Vol. I, No. XLV.

that I rechuse you, and wish that every Court in *Europe* consisted of as honest Men.

You are in the right to decline taking M——s, if you find the Scheme too expensive; and as he could not have come into your Service, without purchasing his Time out from his Master, I believe it will now be his Point to continue with him till the Expiration of his Indentures.

I am now in some Sort of Doubt, concerning the Management of my Snuff-Box; whether to have it repaired in the cheapest Way, with a figured Tortoise-Shell on the Top, and a Plain Tortoise-Shell in the Bottom; or to exchange the Gold of it, and have a figured Tortoise-Shell Box with a gold Rim, *like yours with a gilt one,* only in the Shape of an oblong Square, a little rounded at the Corners. I should have no Thoughts of this, but that my own seems too little and unmanly. Give me your Opinion soon; though, if this latter Scheme includes much Expence, proceed with the former, if you please, immediately.

I desire my gold Clasp and Rim may be immediately exchanged; I shall have a new gold Clasp and Rim: perhaps, may enclose a Pattern for the former, before I seal this Letter. Quaere, therefore, whether the Man, who makes it, will now allow most in the Exchange.

I believe I shall defer the Purchase of my favourite Waistcoat till the Spring. My Visitants begin to fail me, (though Sir George Lyttelton, the Dean, and Mr. Lyttelton, were here yesterday) my Verdure abandons me, and I have little else to do, than go to sleep for the Winter.

Pray send me the Verses on Miss B——r, by the honourable Personage. As to mine, you may give Copies, if you please; but as they are not fully corrected, I hope whoever has those Copies, will take care they be not printed. I can say nothing polite at present, so must defer my Acknowledgements to the Ladies at *Woolston,* till I write to you again.

Your Letter to Lady Luxborough was promised, so I think you should by all Means write, though I confess it appears to have been rather too long deferred.

And now having spoke to the principal Parts of your Letter, let me consider what I have to add.

First, then, your Tenant, old Mr. P——s, of the Hill-Top, was carried in a Hearse, through my Grounds, to be buried yesterday. Mr. I—— has been two or three Days in this Country adjusting Matters with your Tenants. . . .[2]

C——y tells me, you may have your Place supplied at the Expence of five Pounds *per* Year. If so, is it not your Point to come down and live at

---

[2] Here Hull has, according to his common practice, deleted a sentence or more.

Lappal? I do not herein speak merely for my own Sake. Sir George told me yesterday, that he had secured me Bloomer's Cottage. I said, I was obliged to him, but did not ask, after what Manner. He promised to come and dine, and stay a Night with me next year. In the mean Time, I am beguiled of his dining with me, by *your* venerable D——; for having had an Offer from him, from Mr. Lyttelton and the Dean, to take a Dinner here this Week, the D——, through his great Address, conveyed all these Honours to the *Grange;* and to-morrow, it seems, Sir George dines with Mr. Pearsall. I remonstrated upon this to Mr. Lyttelton, at the *Grange,* in a Manner pretty forcible, and yet tolerably decent. He excused for himself and them in a Manner that made me quite satisfied with *him*. He is an excellent young Man.

Let these Things serve as Lessons to you, who are a Courtier, not to hope from Ambition to receive the "Plaisir sans Peine."

Adieu!

I am truly yours,
W. Shenstone

159. To LADY LUXBOROUGH[1]

The Leasowes, Novr 11th 1753

DEAR MADAM,

It is now so long since I had the Honour of hearing from you, that I begin to be not a little anxious about the Progress of your Recovery. I do beseech your Ladyship to believe me so much your Friend as to deserve at least some Intelligence concerning the State of your Health. Tho' I will not entertain a Doubt of my preserving some Place in your Esteem, I cannot avoid Some awkard Sensations on the Account of your unusual Silence. It appears, some how or other, as if you were in Some Degree estrang'd to me.

Since I wrote last to your Ladyship, I have had no great Share of Company; & it grows expedient for me to make Some *winter*-friends amongst my own *Parishioners*. I had the *offer* of a visit from the Captains Somerville, Mr Outing & Mr Reynalds, but could on no account receive them, thro' a Pre-engagement at Lord Plymouths. Thither I went with Lord Dudley & stay'd from Thursday 'till Saturday. I was receiv'd with so much Politeness by both Ld & Ldy Plimouth yt I am morally certain Some good Friend of mine had been prejudicing them in my Favour: & I am much inclin'd to suspect your Ladyship of this Sinisterity —

---

[1] B. M. Add. MSS 28958, fol. 150ff. Lady Luxborough's letter of November 12, 1753 (*Letters*, No. XCIX) replies to this.

Since this I have *made* three visits; to Admiral Smith, to Mr Pitt at Hagley, & to Mr Clare at Clent. The week following I had Sir George Lyttelton; who enquir'd after your Ladyship in a very friendly manner, & seem'd truly glad to hear the account I gave him of your Recovery. I did not fail to acquaint him of the Progress you had made amongst your voters. I *hope* the Opposition is over, but I am sure our separate obligations must continue — The Same week produc'd me a Visit from the very venerable The Dean of Exeter, with Durant their Parson. From Mr Lyttelton *twice,* who came the second time to dine with me; From Mr Miller twice, who came the *first* time to dine with me; From the Captains Hamilton & Whood, two of the Admiral's Domesticks. Mr Lyttelton at present stands higher in my Esteem than ever; The Dean something lower; Mr. Miller the Same.

Other Visitant of any Importance have I not seen; saving that this Morning Ld Plimouth wth some Company surpriz'd me about Breakfast time. I enquir'd whether his Lordship had heard of late from Barrels, & he told me, No; but intended to send over soon. They stay'd till after two, & then went to dine at Stourbridge. I look upon my Season as now entirely over; wch has been both *open'd* & *clos'd* very magnificently by Ld Plimouth.

Mr Hylton is now in Town; whither he has *hawl'd* a thousand guineas in order to buy his Place at Court; has disagreed with the Proprietor & lodg'd his money in the Funds; is twenty Pounds out of Pocket, he says, by the *trifling* of a bonny Scot, & vows to have no dealings with any of his nation more — For my Part I am no way concern'd for his Disappointment, as I never *greatly* approv'd his Bargain. He purposes to write to your Ladyship Soon, & to make his Acknowledgments for ye Civilities he receiv'd at Barrels; but he is not a little embarass'd about an Apology for his neglect of doing this before.

That ode of mine to The Dutchess is got into several Hands, & I am not a little suspicious y^t it may arrive at the Press in some way or other which I shall not approve. Dodsley, for the conveyance of whose loitering Epistle, I am truly oblig'd to your Ladyship, would be glad to print that Ode. He is now, at this very time, publishing an additional Vol. of his Miscellanies.[2] I have nothing in my Hands correct, nor have I time to get any thing corrected by reason of the Distance of my Friends; but I think this ode as correct as any thing I *have;* & if it would not be disagreeable to her Grace, I should be glad of her Permission to print it, at

---

[2] The fourth volume of the *Collection* did not appear until 1755, and *Rural Elegance* first appeared in Dodsley's fifth volume, published March, 1758.

this time. I look upon Dodsley's as a reputable Collection, that will be seen by ye best of Judges, yet so as that their Censure cannot fall wholly upon any *one Piece.* — But the late arrival of his Letter allows me no time for Application — What would your Ladyship advise me, in this Case? — I think to send him something of Mr Whistlers, & something of Mr Graves, to-morrow.

Mrs Davies, to whom I desire my *Thanks,* a better word than my *Compliments,* is at this very Instant accusing me of Ingratitude — I will write to her speedily, but to-day it is impossible.

I want to *tell* you forty things relating to our visit at Hewell-grange; but I cannot think of *writing* them. L^d & L^dy Plimouth are very highly in *my* good graces; I think I have some little share in *theirs.* I guess'd once that L^ds Plimouth & Dudley would become extravagantly intimate; you know that the virtues of benevolence, & uprightness of heart, are common to them both — Yet I never in my Life beheld so striking a Contraste! I shall, I believe, have some little share in ye disposition of Ld P.'s environnes, & I sincerely think I could do him some service. I only wish I had known his Lordship before he began that Piece of water. I told both him & L^dy P. my mind very emphatically & *ingenuously* y^t very Day I came, & they had both the good-sense to hear me, & to thank me for it. That Side ought apparently either to have been cover'd with water, at any given expence, for near an 100 yards lower; or it ought to have been thrown into a broad Serpentine River, the fens drein'd; & the ground slop'd down to it, from about the Present hahah. The stream is sufficient for any sort of purpose. The *Cascades* might have been *display'd,* or the *stoppages* where they *were,* conceal'd wth aquatick Plants, as had been thought most agreeable; & I think, by proper *management,* the expence of either of these Schemes might have been less than the Present. The Reasons I go upon will appear yet more striking when the opposite ground becomes a Part of their Park, wth garden Seats; from wch the House will make a very magnificent Figure — Enough of this. The Management of their Rooms has my thorough approbation. Hagley-House is to be fix'd at last in the very grounds where I always wish'd it; It affords me a triumph; in *my own breast;* For I never dar'd speak freely on ye Subject; nor is it *my* Opinion that has given the least turn to it — at least not that I know of.

I have been makeing a little Alteration in ye Room over my Hall; wch is now my Library upon a Somewhat a better Foot y^n it has hitherto been; yet I retain my Press bed in it for unexceptionable Reasons. My little Breakfast-Room has a glass, & is become my Dressing-room.

Mr Hylton makes enquiry how far our Freedom *over ye Bottle* & *upon* the Bottle at yr Ladyship's House, has disgruntled Mr Outing. I told him I could not say, for that I neither see nor hear from him.

Other Matter know I not, saving that Ld Dudley, who often drinks your Health, has much irritated his great toe by hitting it against the Beds-foot whilst he was stroling thro' the Dark in full Quest of the Chamber-pot. It is now on the mending Hand.

We met Mr Winnington & his Lady at Hewell, & I went with Ld P. & him, on the Friday, to Mr Vernon's of Harbury. There I saw Mr Coventry; Mr Payne; Mr Greatheed's brother, & a Room full of Company — My Expedition on the whole was greatly entertaining.

Your Ladyship must permit me to talk in this Manner upon Paper, as I should do in Company. I have neither a Head to contrive, a Correspondent to supply, or a Neighbourhood to produce any *amusing* materials — Yet I *wish* you Amusement, Health, & Happiness; every *Sort* of Happiness, wch I wish for myself. I beg you would write me as much as you can without Fatigue, & believe me ever most respectfully

Your Ladyship's most oblig'd & most obedient Servant

Will: Shenstone

My Service to Mr & Mrs & Miss Holyoake.

160. To the DUCHESS OF SOMERSET[1]

The Leasowes, near Birmingham,
December the 6th 1753

MADAM,

I receiv'd the honour of your grace's Letter, the beginning of last week; and as Lady Luxborough had before acquainted me how long my packet had been detain'd at Barrels, I consider'd myself as highly indebted to you, for the early intimation you were pleas'd to give of it's arrival. I should have been *as* early in returning your grace my best acknowledgements, but that my House has been since fill'd with such a sort of company as left me no opportunity. And though I *immediately* determin'd to perform your grace's commands,[2] I was not so readily

---

[1] This letter, which appears among the Percy Family Letters at Alnwick (No. 31, p. 251), is quoted by Helen Sard Hughes in her article on Shenstone and the Countess of Hertford in *PMLA*, 46:1113. The Duchess acknowledges this letter from Shenstone with one dated December 18, 1753 (Hull, *Select Letters*, Vol. I, No. L).

[2] In her letter to Shenstone of November 20, 1753 (Hull, *Select Letters*, Vol. I, No. XLVII) the Duchess requests that he substitute dashes or stars wherever her name or that of her dwelling, Percy Lodge, is mentioned in his ode, *Rural Elegance*. Ultimately, however, it appeared with the names in full.

satisfy'd after what manner I might best apologize for the surprize and Trouble this address has occasion'd you.

Neither of these did I, in reality, forsee: For when Lady Luxborough inform'd me of your permission to send that Poem, I took it for granted she had told you previously, to whom it stood inscrib'd. But as she has the most entire Respect for your grace, & at the same time is pleas'd to allow *me* also some share of her esteem, it is but *just* to acquit her Ladyship of any sinister Intention.

If I could suppose that, by this application, I had incurr'd your grace's displeasure; or that *Politeness* had too great a share in the Complaisance with which you treat me, I would here enumerate such particulars as might best excuse my presumption. Sure I am, that I could not acquiesce; under an apprehension so painfull to me. But I will not give it admission. I will believe your grace sincere in one part of your letter, as well as another; and as I am convinc'd that you do not chuse I should insert your name before this Poem, I will rest satisfy'd that you are no way offended by my *inclination* to do so. I will, for my own *Peace,* believe that you are not angry with me; I will, for my own *Happiness,* imagine that I retain some place in your esteem: My *Ambition* will find it's account in the Compliment you make these verses; & even my better Judgment seems to clear me of having mistaken your grace's Character. Pardon this, I humbly beg your grace: For have I not some room to suggest, that the Character I have drawn, in some measure, accounts for your Prohibition, as your Prohibition seems to vindicate the Character I have drawn?

I am truly sensible of the honour you do me, Madam, in offering to give my Friend Dodsley a copy of that Elegy.[3] It has of late been somewhat enlarg'd, and is inscrib'd to Mr. William Lyttelton, who was the Person that first brought poor Mr. Thomson to The Leasowes. It is now in Dodsley's hands; & will, I suppose, be printed, with some other of my trifles, in the volume he is going to publish.

It will afford me, Madam, all the satisfaction I can reasonably desire, if you will allow me the liberty of transmitting to you such compositions as I write occasionally, & as I judge least unworthy of your grace's perusal. There is an ode to Sir Richard Lyttelton,[4] written in 1748: and which compliments some persons that are of your acquaintance. What I write, I would not totally suppress; yet I would desire only to exhibit it to persons of candour & of delicacy. If your grace gives me this Permission, it will much oblige me; if the request be impertinent, your least

---

[3] It appeared in Dodsley's *Collection,* Vol. IV (1755).
[4] The *Pastoral Ode,* of earlier reference. *Works,* I (1764), 174–81.

Intimation shall restrain me; but it is not even in your *Grace's* power, to restrain that *inward* respect, & *silent* veneration, with which I am, Madam!

    your grace's most oblig'd & most obedient humble Servant

                  Will: Shenstone

161. To LADY LUXBOROUGH[1]

        The Leasowes, Decr ye 12, 1753

DEAR MADAM,

I am truly impatient to receive a few Lines from your Ladyship, & accordingly have sent Tom through roads not a little formidable, (with your permission) to stay all night. I hope you will not regulate your answer by the Lines I now am scribbling, but will also remember the size of the Packet I sent before.

There are no Incidents occurr to me, which will afford your Ladyship the least amusement. Ld Dudley with his sisters & domesticks spent some days with me here last week; but he was *ill,* & indispos'd for conversation, to a degree that he may *reasonably expect*. His Coal-mines will prove advantageous; but what are they to *me?* unless he will take such care of his health, as will give Hopes that he may long enjoy them; otherwise, they may only tend to animate *benumb'd serpents.* You remember the Fable.

If Mr Hylton have not acquitted himself of his Letter to your Ladyship, pray notifye, that I will wrap a large Flea in a piece of white paper, & will cause the Postboy to put it in his ear. It shall be one of ye more active Sort, nor shall He, without some difficulty, get shut of his troublesome *inmate* — The extract I gave you from his Letter was genuine; & if your Ladyship will permit him to send you the news of the town, there is no doubt y^t he has Leisure & opportunity.

The Scene is chang'd with me, from what I found it in the Summer. Instead of the daily arrival of truly fashionable company, I see nothing but Robin Red-breasts driv'n to visit me by stress of weather; or Tom-tits seeking out where they may secure themselves for ye winter: yet the Red-breasts give me their song, & it is infinitely better than *my own.*

Lonesom as I am, I see no objects of envy near me: for were all ye amusements of my neighbours group'd together & given me in a Dish or Punch-bowl they would not tend to render me one whit happier than

---

[1] B. M. Add. MSS 28958, fol. 154ff and 108. To this letter Lady Luxborough replies with one of December 15, 1753 (*Letters,* No. CII), the date of which is thus confirmed. Her No. CI, also dated December 12, 1753, went astray, and Shenstone did not get it before writing his, the postscript of which is dated December 14.

I am. I could venture to assert the same concerning the principal Amusements of our metropolis. And, I think, your Ladyship will be ready to join me.

Dodsley sent me his Agriculture;[2] & least *peradventure* you may not have seen it, I give it Tom for your perusal. How far the Town will relish it, I know not; but it is written with much *art,* & infinitely beyond what they cou'd reasonably *expect* from him. While your Ladyship reads Page ye 59, Canto the third, should you not be apt to imagine he had seen Virgil's grove? or, from some of ye preceeding Lines, should you not be apt to think he had seen Barrels? Had he appropriated these Lines to either of our Places, we should hardly envy the compliments he pays Chiswick, Esher, Worburne or Hagley — But of this enough; for I do not pretend to criticise — He is, at this instant of time, expecting a large cargo of my verses — but my cargo will not *yet* set forwards, & when it does, will not be large — Truth is, my mind is somewhat alter'd — I cannot bear to send him *stuff;* and as to my *better* compositions, my friends induce me to think I might print them in a more advantageous manner, both with regard to *Reputation* & *Profit.* For Instance, The Elegy on Autumn, Ballad on Princess Elizabeth, Ode to Memory, Inscriptions & a few things more might have made me a 1^s pamphlett y^t would have had some chance to have been acceptable — but proceeded unadvisedly, & must extricate myself as I can. My Friend Graves, & I have had a mighty *busy* correspondence. He has a talent for criticism, wherein *over-delicacy* at least when 'tis ballanc'd by my own excessive Indolence, is scarce a Fault — I receiv'd the Fable I enclose from him, which he offers to address to me. But, whatever Answer I return him, The Fable itself is humorous — you will laugh at his "doughty disputants" — & return me ye composition.

Sr Charles Grandison[3] is much admired — & if I cannot borrow, I will purchase it — but I should be glad to have ye concluding volume promisd us, at a time less *indefinite* — If y^r Ladyship have any new Pamphletts you will I know be so good to lend me some.

I could be glad, were it agreeable to y^r Ladyship, y^t our Servants might be a little harrass'd with alternate Journeys to Barrels & to The Leasowes. It would exhilarate this dull Season. At least it would have that effect wth me — My Letters would pretend to little more than a

---

[2] Robert Dodsley published in November, 1753, "a long and rather dreary poem in blank verse, called *Agriculture.*" *Public Virtue,* of which this was to be the first book, never was finished. See Straus, *Robert Dodsley,* p. 181.

[3] *Sir Charles Grandison* came out in 1753 and 1754. The *Gentleman's Magazine* noticed the first four volumes in November, 1753, the fifth and sixth in December, 1753, and the sixth and seventh in March, 1754.

repetition of good wishes & My Compliments to all Friends — To keep one's pen in motion when one has nothing to say, is like rapping at a Door when one has no Sort of business — It alarms, not gratifies the attention. Tis better pass by in Silence, especially as y^r Ladyship knows me for what I truly am, namely,

y^r most oblig'd & most obed^t
W Shenstone
Friday Decr the 14th

One Day has past, & it has been *impossible* for Tom to proceed so far as Barrels. I trust he will be able to set forward to morrow —

I had the Honour of answering the Duchess's Letter last Thursday se'nnight; but was too late for the Post; & she would not receive my Letter till *Tuesday* last. I promis'd to obey her commands most punctually, but I *said nothing* about my Intention of with-holding y^t Ode from Dodsley — If your Ladyship writes to her, I desire you would do *the same;* & only assure her grace of my entire respect, & implicit obedience to her commands, at all times — I think it would be *suitable* enough to *Dodsley,* agreeable to Mr Somervile's *friends,* & no injustice to his *memory,* if some few of his stragling Pieces were inserted in this collection. If your Ladyship thinks with me, I will transcribe for the Press any little Pieces you are pleasd to send me & will make no alteration but when the verse is *manifestly* deficient. But as, I hinted before, this must be done *soon,* or quite omitted — I told your Ladyship that I had, one night, added a stanza to ye enclos'd Verses. I therefore enclose a copy; & should be glad if you could be prevail'd on to give me your opinion of their merit, with ye same Frankness as tho' they were written upon any other person.

I have nothing to add — why cease I therefore to wrap these Papers in a Cover, after I have bid your Ladyship once more Adieu?

— I talk'd of sending Dodsleys Agriculture — but lo! it is lent out; & I am oblig'd to defer it 'till another opportunity.

162. To RICHARD JAGO [1]

The *Leasowes, Jan.* 29, 1754

DEAR MR. JAGO,

I am at a Loss how to begin this Letter. I will not, however, in the usual Way, give you a tedious List of Apologies in the Front of it. Some

---

[1] Hull, *Select Letters,* Vol. I, No. XLIX, and Dodsley, *Letters to Particular Friends,* No. LXXV. Hull's version seems the better and is here reproduced.

Account of my Silence you will find dispersed throughout the Letter, and as for what is deficient, I will depend upon your Friendship.

There has not been a Person here since you left me, of whom I could obtain the least Intelligence concerning you; and as an Enquiry by the Post was my only obvious Method, and as I both owed and promised you a Letter at Parting, I do acknowledge myself to blame, notwithstanding all the Excuses I can make.

Amidst all that Conflux of Visitants whom I received this last Season, I was hardly once *so* happy as I was in *your* Company: I was the happier in seeing you so, and if you remember, I took Notice at the Time, how little your Vivacity was impaired, in comparison of mine. If I was then but a sorry Companion, it was not Solitude and Winter that could make me a better *Correspondent.* That Gaiety and Humour, which you was once so partial as to discover in my Letters, will hardly appear again there, even to the Eyes of my most partial Friend; at least, they will not enliven any Letter that I write in Winter. Yet Friendship still remains; Friendship, like the Root of some perennial Flower, perhaps even then gathers Strength in Secret, that it may produce a better Display of its Colours in the Spring.

This I do not pretend to be an adequate Apology. I know, my dearest Friend, that you both like to see and to hear from me at all Times; but it proves that you have no *great* Loss, either of my Letters or my Company.

I am, as the Phrase is, deeply penetrated by the Civility of your Neighbour, Mr. Miller. He took a short Dinner with me once, dropping Sir George at Mr. Pearsall's; he could not have pleased me better: he afterwards breakfasted here, and in general seemed fond of every Opportunity of bringing good Company to my Hole, the *Leasowes.* Do you think that *Radway* or that *Harbury* have no Attractions for me? You know me too well to imagine it — But I truly am not well enough to dare to be from Home. Friends will say, "You may be as free at my House as at your own," and they will mean what they say. But what is this to the Purpose, if you cannot make yourself so?

I cannot pretend to give you a Detail of what passed since I saw you. Lord D——[2] with myself made one Visit to *Hewell.* I will not say, that his Lordship only, for I also was received in the politest Manner imaginable. We met Mr. and Mrs. Winnington. We took a Trip to Mr. Vernon's, where we met also Mr. Coventry, and a deal of other Company.

[2] Probably Lord Dudley.

All this would afford Subject for Conversation betwixt you and me, but I must not use so much of my Paper to this Purpose.

Lord P[lymouth]'s Piece of Water should have been only a large Serpentine Stream. I can give you many Reasons. I think him such a Sort of Character, as may *shine* in Company upon growing older; he is, and must be beloved already: he has been here once since, and talks of causing me to come and design for him in his Park. The Plan for the House is right, supposing it right to continue it. His Park may have many Beauties. I hope some Time to meet *you* there.

My Ode after long Delay has been sent to the Duchess of Somerset. It has produced me two genteel Letters from her Grace, and I am pleased with the Event, for some Reasons which I could mention.

Soon after this, Dodsley asked me to contribute to a fourth Volume of his Miscellanies. I meant at first to do so pretty largely; but I afterwards changed my Mind, and determined to send only little Pieces. I did send him several of my own, some of my Friends Whistler, and Graves, and some accidental Pieces of yours, which lay in my Drawer. I meant to send something of yours of my own Accord, if I was hurried, otherwise not without applying for Consent. He wrote me word, last Week, that his Publication must be deferred, upon Account of the Elections, so that we shall now have Time enough to meet or write upon the Subject. What I purposed was your *Linnets,* "I owe, &c." Dick G[rave]s sent me the inclosed little comical Fable; I made some few Alterations, and put it into Dodsley's Hands. Be so good as to return it, as I have now no other Copy.

Some Correspondence I have had this Winter with Mr. H[ylto]n, about Toys and Trinkets, which he gets done for me in *London*. He is by far a better Friend and Correspondent than a Poet. Should you take a Trip to Town, he would be quite *proud* to see you.

I am like the rest of the World, perusing *Sir Charles Grandison*. I don't know whether that World joins me in preferring the Author's *Clarissa*. He wants the Art of Abridgement in every Thing he has yet wrote.

My dear Friend, pardon this flegmatic Letter, and cherish and preserve your own Vivacity. If Occasion offers, do not neglect to call upon me, for my own Sake, and believe you have not alive a more lasting, or, more affectionate Friend, than

W. Shenstone

163. To JOHN SCOTT HYLTON[1]

March 29, 1754

DEAR MR. H[YLTON],

I write in the utmost Astonishment and Confusion of Spirit! — I wonder Mr. C—— did not give me some Intimation of Miss D[olman]'s Illness before.[2] However, all her Relations will think themselves lastingly indebted both to him and to all beside who have contributed their kind Endeavours to further her Recovery. We are under a terrible Anxiety concerning her. Satisfied as I am of the Abilities and Vigilance of Dr. B——, and convinced of the friendly Care of her Acquaintance who attend her, I shall dread to look into the Letter that I expect by to-morrow's Post. God grant it may be favourable! I have Hopes given me to-night; Mr. D[olman] sends me Word, that the Letter he received on *Thursday* (probably written after yours) acquainted him, that the Pustules began to turn; that she was then better, and that they hoped the worst was past.

Believe me uniformly your Friend, but do not expect me to dwell upon many Particulars to-night, nor suffer any Thing I have said to discourage you, in your Scheme of retiring into this Country. Will not the *Grange,* or the *Leasowes,* be endurable for one half Year, and that the *Summer* half Year, when they dress themselves afresh to please you?

Your Cabinet nor Oysters are neither *yet* brought me, whatever be the Reason. Leave my Compliments to dear Miss D[olman], and all that attend on her. Send me five Lines at least every Post next Week.

Adieu!

164. To RICHARD GRAVES[1]

The Leasowes, April 19, 1754

DEAR MR. GRAVES,

It is a long, long time, according to the computation of friendship, since I had the pleasure of a line from you; and I write chiefly to remind you of it, not with any hopes of affording you the amusement of a single minute. In truth, I have not spirits for it. The severity, the duration, the solitude, of this winter have well-nigh exhausted them. — The succession, the regular succession, of pain and pleasure becomes every day more clear to me. It begins to seem as ordinary as the course of day and night. Thus my last summer was the most amusing I ever saw; my

---

[1] Hull, *Select Letters,* Vol. I, No. LIII.

[2] Hull (Vol. I, No. LII) prints a letter from Hylton dated March 29, 1754, informing Shenstone of the death of his young relative, Maria Dolman, of whom he was particularly fond. She died in London, of the smallpox. Hylton wrote Shenstone again April 13, giving him a detailed account of Miss Dolman's death (Hull, Vol. I, No. LV).

[1] Dodsley, *Letters to Particular Friends,* No. LXXVI.

winter the most disagreeable — allow me to except one only; I mean, that ever-mournful winter which robbed me of my dearest relation.[2] Sometimes this pain and pleasure are contrasted within the compass of a day; sometimes in different weeks, &c. &c. However, do not think me superstitious; there is hardly a person that is *less* so. Yet I am firmly persuaded of the alternation, either in the mind, or in the events themselves. My summer, I said before, was highly entertaining; my winter rendered equally disagreeable, by a long-continued squabble among our principal parishioners, and by the death of my best-beloved and the most accomplished of my relations, M[aria] D[olman]. She risqued going to London for the sake of finding something *new;* was seized with the small-pox, and died in all her bloom. — The natural consequence which we should draw from observations of this sort is, equanimity; "aequam memento rebus, &c." and again, "sperat infestis, metuit secundis, &c." Enough of this, which I should not mention but that the fact itself strikes me continually more and more; and were I to mark the pleasing and unpleasing parts of my existence in an almanac, as the Romans did their *Fasti* and *Nefasti,* I know not if, at the year's end, the black and white marks would not nearly balance each other.

I have bought "Hogarth's Analysis:"[3] it is really entertaining; and has, in some measure, adjusted my notions with regard to beauty in general. For instance, were I to draw a shield, I could give you reasons from hence why the shape was pleasing or disagreeable. I would have you *borrow* and read it.

Grandison I cannot think equal to Clarissa; though, were merit in this age to be preferred, the author of it deserves a bishopric.

Jago has been fortunate for once; but the value of his livings must be exaggerated in the newspapers.

If Mr. Whistler would give me a visit in the height of my season this year, I should look upon it as one of the most pleasing events that could happen to the remainder of my life; and I would not presume to hope that fate would ever allow me a repetition of it.

My love of toys is not quite exhausted — I have purchased, or rather renovated, some that are both rich and beautiful, though short of what I meant them. I have amused myself with designing little ornaments this winter, some of which may turn to account under the management of some Birmingham mechanic. — To achieve *ease,* in that season, is the most that I can *hope;* and it is more than I often *obtain.*

[2] His brother Joseph, who died November 30, 1751.
[3] Hogarth's *Analysis of Beauty* was published in 1753.

Excuse this worthless letter; which *must* cost you money, as they tell me franks are useless. I could not avoid some uneasiness upon reflecting how long you have been silent. Present my best compliments to Mrs. Graves; and pay a tribute of one single half-sheet to that affection with which I am ever

Yours,
W. Shenstone

165. To RICHARD GRAVES[1]

The Leasowes, June 7, 1754

DEAR MR. GRAVES,

The melancholy account of our dear friend Whistler's death was conveyed to me, at the same instant, by yours and by his brother's letter.[2] I have written to his brother this post; though I am very ill able to write upon the subject, and would willingly have waved it longer, but for decency. The triumvirate, which was the greatest happiness and the greatest pride of my life, is broken! The fabric of an ingenuous and disinterested friendship has lost a noble column! yet it may, and *will*, I trust, endure till one of us be laid as low. In truth, one can so little satisfy one's self with what we say upon such sad occasions, that I made three or four essays before I could *endure* what I had written to his brother. — Be so good as excuse me to him as well as you can, and establish me in the good opinion of him and Mr. Walker.[3]

Poor Mr. Whistler! how do all our little strifes and bickerments appear to us at this time! yet we may with comfort reflect, that they were not of a *sort* that touched the *vitals* of our friendship; and I may say, that we fondly loved and esteemed each other, of necessity — "Tales animas *oportuit* esse concordes." Poor Mr. Whistler! not a single acquaintance have I made, not a single picture or curiosity have I purchased, not a single embellishment have I given to my place, since he was last here, but I have had his approbation and his amusement in my eye. I will assuredly inscribe my larger urn to his memory; nor shall I pass it without a pleasing melancholy during the remainder of my days. We have each of us received a pleasure from *his* conversation, which no other conversation can afford us at our present time of life.

Adieu! my dear friend! may our remembrance of the person we have lost be the strong and everlasting cement of our affection! Assure Mr.

---

[1] Dodsley, *Letters to Particular Friends*, No. LXXVII.
[2] The letter of John Whistler to Shenstone is in Hull's *Select Letters*, Vol. II, No. XXIV. It is dated May 26, but the year (1754) is wanting.
[3] Whistler's stepfather.

John Whistler of the regard I have for him, upon his *own* account, as well as his brother's. Write to me directly if you have opportunity. Whether you have or no, believe me to be ever most affectionately yours,

W. Shenstone

I beg my compliments to Mrs. Graves.

166. To RICHARD JAGO [1]

The Leasowes, June 16, 1754

Dear Mr. Jago,

Were I to pronounce my sentence upon the long suspension of our correspondence, I should impute the blame of it, in almost *equal* measure, to *yourself* and to *me*. To you, for an omission of the letter you *promised* me when last in town; to me, for waiting in expectation of it, and for neglecting to do *justice* to the sentiments of my heart on the occasion of your late preferment. Great were the hopes I had indeed conceived, that your increase of revenue had been accompanied with a place of residence which was more *to your mind* than that where you at present abide; but I do not find by any accounts that you propose to leave Harbury: for which, no doubt, you have reasons which I do not yet penetrate, but which may demand my assent the moment you discover them. I have but little to say of the life I have led since you received some account of me from Mr. Hylton in London. The Winter, or at least its *ministers,* continued to tyrannize during the *minority* of Spring; and the Spring has alike been slow in giving up the reins to Summer. Of consequence, I seem in a sort of middle state, betwixt a dull half-animated grub and an insignificant loco-motive fly. Neither in the *one* state or *other* am I of the least importance; but, from the advances which I have *already* made, you are *somewhat* the more likely to find me in your garden. About a fortnight ago I received a line or two from our intimate acquaintance and school-fellow Mr. Hall. It was brought me by Sir Edward Boughton's gardener; a fellow of good taste, to whom Mr. Hall desired I would cause The Leasowes to be shewn. I find you have delighted Mrs. Hall by some alterations which you propose for their environs, and which they thoroughly resolve to put in execution. When I come over into Warwickshire, as I hope to do soon, I shall be very glad to make them a visit in your company. My spirits, though far from good, are better in the main than they were in winter, and on some peculiar days are raised as high as to *alacrity; very* seldom higher, seldom so high.

---

[1] Dodsley, *Letters to Particular Friends,* No. LXXX.

You must (from hence at least) take matters in the order or rather *disorder* in which they occur: Mr. Miller, I saw on Wednesday last in Lady Lyttelton's coach, who stopped two minutes at my gate on her return from London. I enquired concerning you; but could gather no intelligence. — Mr. Hylton, who is now in Warwickshire (if he have not strolled to London), has been with me several months this summer. He is adding a room or two to his place, which lies very near me; and purposes to reside there as soon as it is finished. The situation is not void of beauties; but, if you will pardon the vanity, must veil its bonnet to mine. I have heard of planting hollies, pyracanthas, and other berry-bearing greens, to attract those Blackbirds which you have so effectually celebrated: it shall be *my* ambition to plant good neighbours; and, what with Lord Dudley and his exotics, Mr. Hylton with his fossils, and myself with my *ferme ornée,* is there not some room to expect that we may attract the tasters this way? but first we must take some care to *advertise* them where their treasures lie. — Another day is passed, and Mr. Miller, &c. has again been with me, and waked me out of a sound sleep to breakfast. — He mentions with what reluctance he *left* a surveyor at Radway, employed in taking plans of the field of battle near Edge-hill. This he purposes to enrich with a number of anecdotes, gleaned from his neighbourhood; which must probably render it extremely entertaining: and surely Edge-hill fight was never more unfortunate to the nation, than it was lucky for Mr. Miller! He prints, together with this plan, another sheet of Radway Castle. I approve his design. He will, by this means, turn every bank and hillock of his estate there, if not into *classical,* at least into *historical* ground.

I have done mighty little about my grounds since last winter. As indolence has on *many* occasions contributed to *impair* my finances, it is but just that it should sometimes contribute to *restore* them. Yet I am not quite destitute of something new for your amusement.

Of late I have neither *read* nor *written* a syllable. What pleased me last was "Hogarth's Analysis." I expect Dodsley down every week; and as he will spend a few days with me, I could wish you were to meet him. His genius is truly poetical, and his sentiments altogether liberal and ingenuous.

I am, at present, a surveyor of roads; employed in repairing my lane to the turnpike. How glad should I be to meet you, and to shew you its *beauties!* to shew you Mr. Hylton's new series of coins; — his *designs* as well as his *performances* at Lappal! — how glad should I be to see you! yea, I would hardly fail to return with you to Harbury; were you to add this one obligation. I left Mr. Miller in doubt whether he would not see me at Radway some time next week. Evil and capricious health (the particulars of which would make a detail of no importance) destroys all my punctuality, and bids me promise with *fear*. You, I trust, are mostly at home; and were you to be at Snitterfield, I would follow you without reluctance. So, with hopes to see you shortly either in Warwickshire or Shropshire, I relinquish the subject.

I have reserved a very melancholy subject for the last. May you, and Mr. Graves, and myself, stand firm to support the fabric of friendship, which has lost a very beautiful column in poor Mr. Whistler! he died of a sore-throat, which in a few days time turned to an inward mortification. — I will say no more on the occasion: very affecting has it been to me. — God preserve your life, your happiness, and your friendships! and may you ever be *assured* of *that* with which I am, dear Sir,

Your most affectionate humble servant,
W. Shenstone

Shall I beg a line from you, as soon as may be? — I do, most earnestly.

I am given to understand that I may expect a visit this summer from the Bishop of Worcester; from Lord Ward, Lord Coventry, and Lord Guernsey. — It may be so; but honours of *this sort,* which would formerly have affected me, perhaps *too* deeply, have now lost much of their wonted poignancy. Can *such* persons bear to see the scenes *riant,* and to find the *owner* gloomy? Let *them,* as they are *able,* make my circumstances more affluent; and they shall find the *reflexion* in *my* face and in *their* reception; but, as this will never be, it is no compliment to declare, that an hour or two's interview with you or Mr. Graves outweighs the arrival of the whole British Peerage.

Something else I have to say. Young Pixell last winter told me, that the organist of Worcester had set your Ode (The Blackbirds) to musick; that he *liked* the music; and that he would sing it next evening at the Birmingham concert. I have not heard him mention it *since,* and I *forgot* to enquire; but, if you happen to have the notes, I should be glad if you would inclose them for me.

I have been of late much bent upon the increase of *horns* in this neighbourhood. — Do not interpret me *perversely;* I mean French-horns only. My Lord Dudley has had a person to teach two of his servants — nothing — at my instigation; but your old acquaintance Maurice, *who lives at the corner of my coppice,* will exceed them in a week by means of a good ear. I have borrowed a horn for him. Adieu!

167. To CHRISTOPHER WREN[1]

DEAR MR. W[REN], July 6, 1754

You do me justice in believing, that I am truly sorry you have not been well. A degree or two of regularity more than what you have already will, I fancy, restore your health, and my satisfaction; and I beg you will afford me the earliest account of your recovery.

I considered Master W[ren]'s visit as an absolute engagement, and remained at home in constant expectation of him for a fortnight together, — I am, however, not sorry, for his own sake, that he is gone to Oxford, especially as you seem to have an assurance of its proving advantageous. Pray assure him of my earnest wishes for his happiness, and that The Leasowes will be always at his service, whenever, through the fickleness of human nature, he thinks proper to give up a Muse for a Waternymph.

I expect Mr. Hylton daily. — He was last week in London, and is now, I believe, at Coventry. — He will probably visit you before he comes into this country. — He talked of it when he left me. — I am obliged to be brief.

Post-Woman waits for me, "multa gemens." Dodsley is the man for your purpose — He has, with good genius, a liberal turn of mind. — I expect him to spend a few days here every week. — I will, if he returns through Warwickshire, occasion him to call upon you; but you know he is often lame with the gout, and will hardly be able to make any long digression.

Your case is exactly mine. — You say, you cannot bear wrongs with patience, but you can sleep and *forget* them. — So can I — so do I. — Did I never tell you (if not, I do so now) that indolence will, in a thousand instances, give one all the advantages of philosophy? and pray, if you call me lazy any more, take care that you do not use an expression by way of disparagement, which I consider as the highest honour. I am a fool, however, for discovering my secret. What a number of compliments might you have made me unwittingly!

> Tacitus pasci si posset corvus, haberet
> Plus dapis, & rixae minus invidiaeque.

Had I time, I could comfort you under your ill usage, by discovering to you the similitude of my own situation.

Excuse this scrawl; accept my compliments; carry them to Mrs. and Miss W[ren]; and believe me ever your obliged and most obedient humble servant, W. Shenstone

[1] Dodsley, *Letters to Particular Friends*, No. LXXXI.

168. To RICHARD GRAVES[1]

The Leasowes, July 15, 1754

DEAR MR. GRAVES,

The *particulars* relating to our poor friend's departure occasioned me much concern, and indeed some tears: yet as *those* particulars are what one covets to hear, and the melancholy which they produce is never unmixed with pleasure, I think myself much obliged to you for the care you took to convey them. It is possible, the letters I wrote to you and Mr. J. Whistler might appear too tender from a *mere* friend of the deceased; but there is a sympathy betwixt friends, which is not always found amongst relations; nor does *kindred* imply *friendship* a whit more than *friendship* does *kindred*. It is not many weeks ago, that I had a bill filed against me in Chancery by young D[olman], the only near relation I have by the mother's side, and the next in lineal succession to my share of the Penn's estate. — Do not let this surprize you — I believe the affair will be accommodated.[2] — He only wanted to procure a division of the Harborough estate at a large expence, which might be better adjusted without *any;* in other words, to run his head against a stone-wall, that he might have a chance of causing it to tumble upon *me*. Would you consent that I should suffer him to have the mansion-house at Harborough thrown into his lot? Were I so to do, I could make it advantageous to myself, and the dispute were at an end; but I have a kind of romantic veneration for that *place* and *family;* which, if you remember, I have expressed in one of my best elegies.[3]

Pray what will become of our letters to Mr. Whistler?[4] As I am not conscious of anything dishonorable in mine (and I am *sure* I may say the same of yours) methinks I could wish that they might not be destroyed. It is from a few letters of my own or others alone, accidentally preserved, that I am able to recollect what I have been doing since I was born.

I met, when I was last at Barrels, a surgeon of Bath, whose name, I think, was Cleland. He knew your name and place; but, I find, was not personally acquainted with you. — I am glad enough to hear that your place gets into vogue. It is, I think, what you should *chuse,* upon all accounts. Let the beauty of the place guide them to the merits of its *owner*. I have often thought, myself, that were a person to live at the Leasowes, of more merit than myself, and a few degrees more worldly prudence, he could scarce want opportunities to procure his own ad-

---

[1] Dodsley, *Letters to Particular Friends,* No. LXXVIII.
[2] This vexatious piece of litigation dragged on for years, however, and is often alluded to in following letters.
[3] Elegy XV. [Dodsley]
[4] They were destroyed by John Whistler. See below, Letter 172.

vancement. My rural embellishments are perhaps more considerable than yours; but then the vicinity of Bath might occasion you a greater conflux. — Your inexpensive illuminations please me highly. I have purposed these many years to purchase a set of tin-lamps, of about fourpence apiece, to stick against trees, and to use upon occasion in my coppice; or rather in my grove, where some of the water-falls would not fail to shew delightfully.

You asked me about Jago's preferment.[5] The living *last given* him by the Bishop of Worcester is, I believe, near an hundred pounds a year. With this, he has Harbury, of about fifty; and Chesterton, a sort of chapel of ease, about forty; in the *whole,* therefore, about a hundred and ninety: but then he is obliged to keep a curate; and what I think yet worse is, that he cannot make it *convenient* to *live* at his new situation, which is a pretty one.

I have had some visitants this season; indeed as many, and as considerable, as such a sort of season could afford me. A Scotch peer called upon me in his way through Birmingham; his title was D[elmany]. He seemed to have a very clear head, a very polite and easy manner, and all the refinement of true taste, *without* the warmth of appetite. — I could not help thinking him, on many accounts, characteristic of the Scottish nation.

Would to God I could see you and Mrs. Graves here this summer! I have the same wish it may be *my* lot to visit *you* next autumn. Be assured, I *purpose* it.

I expect Dodsley every week. He will, I am convinced, be for publishing his Miscellany next winter. Would Mr. W[histler], think you, agree, that you and I should be allowed to publish such of poor Mr. Whistler's papers there, as we judged were most likely to do credit to his memory?

Adieu! dear Mr. Graves. Let us reconcile our affections to the ordinary events of life; and let us adopt my friend Jago into our second triumvirate. I am, however, always, with *peculiar* attachment, yours,
W. Shenstone

My best compliments to Mrs. Graves.

P.S. Since I wrote the foregoing, I have had Mr. Davenport of Davenport-house, with all his family. — His brother, the clergyman, remembered you by your picture. — His wife is the finest *person,* &c. I have seen here, except Lady Aylesbury — ingenious, easy-behaved, and of an excellent temper. — They come to Bath in a fortnight.

Since that time, Sir George Lyttelton, Mr. Lyttelton, and Miss Lyttel-

---

[5] Jago was in 1754 nominated to the vicarage of Snitterfield.

ton.— Sir George thinks some alterations requisite in my verses, to which I cannot easily bring myself to conform — but must.

I look upon my scheme of embellishing my farm as the only lucky one I ever pursued in my life. — My place now brings the world home to me, when I have too much indolence to go forth in quest of it.

169. To LADY LUXBOROUGH [1]

The Leasowes, July the 17th 1754

Dear Madam,

They say the dullest ecclesiastick may *remind* the ablest scholar of matters wherein he is not capable to *instruct* him. Such is *my* Plea; who though I am not to inform your Ladyship what Pleasure your visits afford me, & how much it is your duty to communicate happiness, yet may, allowably I hope, *remind* you that ye year rolls on apace. Sorry am I to observe that it has carry'd off your noble Friend, the pious, the benevolent, and all-accomplish'd Dutchess of Somerset. It would be presumption in me to lament *my* share in the Loss of her. Notwithstanding ye veneration I had for her character, notwithstanding ye gratefull sense I entertain of her many civilities, it will perhaps much better become *me* to condole with your Ladyship for *yours*. . . . What an uncomfortable Summer is This! Scarce one single Day that ye sun is not obscur'd Either by rains or clouds, or it's efficacy destroy'd by raw unwholesome winds. I have seen but little company this year as yet; & my walks have been so much neglected in expectation of better weather, that I have hardly *wish'd* for any visitant yt should be drawn by mere *curiosity*. Twas in such a wretched condition yt they were seen, some weeks ago, by a Lord Delmany: A Scotch Peer, who made an excursion hither from his Road thro' Birmingham to Scotland. Pray, does your Ladyship remember any such title? for, hearing it only *whisper'd* to me, I am not sure that I spell or pronounce it right. He has an Estate pretty near Ld Somervile, & is, I think, related to Ld Primrose. Admiral Smith I see *often* here, who comes in a friendly way, & takes such a dinner as I can provide for him, extempore. I will not make my Letter a muster-roll of Names; only Lord Dudley I must add, who spent a few days with me last week; drank *deeply* to your Health, & wishes *cordially* to see you. Did you say nothing when I was at Barrels that connects July & Sir Peter Soames? Certain it is, that He & Barrels & July occurr together in my Imagination; & I cannot any other way, be able to account for it. Should it be preternatural

---

[1] B. M. Add. MSS 28958, fol. 156ff.

Inspiration & Truth, I beg you would offer him my most respectfull compliments & wishes for the Honour of shewing him The Leasowes.

I have done but little since your Ladyship was here; & yet, supposing I had done a great *deal,* can you think me so *unpolitical* as to lessen your surprise by *previous* Delineations. I know too well; & am too much interested in ye Impression I wish you to receive from ye Place itself. Thus much however Let me tell you, my little Pavilion in ye water is no more! I yesterday enjoy'd it in Ruins, but my Pleasure was mix'd with melancholy; as the case would be, were I to survey ye noblest Ruins upon earth.

Your Ladyship afforded me a Precedent when you pull'd down your Temple in ye Avenue. I appeal to you therefore whether it be not *fortunate* to raise such² sort of buildings whereof the raising and the destroying³ affords almost equal Pleasure. Every constituent part of the universe is changeable; & *beauty* itself is not more necessarily pleasing to ye Imagination, than *variety.* Let us keep the secret to our selves, my Lady; & not let ye silly *world* understand how idly they calculate, when they endeavour to produce objects of *perpetual* amusement.

Were it not for Fear of treason, I should almost presume to advise your Ladyship to demolish ye Pavilion at ye End of your Bowling-green, upon ye foremention'd principles. Sure I am yt, for a trifle of expence, your Ladyship might give that Place a new & I *think* more elegant appearance.

The Bricks to be us'd in building a strong wall at ye back of yr Pheasantry. A Slope & a gothick-skreen (wood) to be plac'd agst it. Shrubbery, continu'd to ye end of it, to hide any part of ye House wch you do not wish to appear. What ground is gain'd, to be added to the green: & this, I should think, *all* yt the *Place itself requires.* But I remember, this moment, yt you once propos'd a green-house there. I therefore drop my suggestion, with this only remark, that *refinement* is an *endless Thing;* & as the *value* of such amusements is in proportion to ye *appetite,* no person living should pretend to fix how far another should pursue it.⁴ This needs explanation. All I mean is that as your Ladsps Fortune has enabled you

---

² Neither very good, nor very bad. [Shenstone]
³ In the manuscript, "rise" is written directly above "raising," and "destruction" directly above "destroying."
⁴ The rest of the paragraph is inserted in the manuscript as an explanatory note above and between the lines.

to gratify your Taste for elegance, more than mine has done your *relish* may become *weaker,* tho more *distinguishing* than mine.

I remember I took a scanty Leave of every-body when I left Barrels. Mrs Reynalds did not visit me. Mrs Davies I must write to. Lady Luxborough will, I hope, let me hear from her soon, & believe me ever her most oblig'd

& most obedient Servant

Will Shenstone

My Comp. to yt Family at Oldbarrow

170. To LADY LUXBOROUGH[1]

The Leasowes, Sept: 29. 1754

Dear Madam,

After assuring your Ladyship of the great Pleasure I receiv'd during the Time I had the Honour of your company at The Leasowes, I am to hope for the additional satisfaction of hearing that you feel no Inconvenience from your Journey. . . . When I left your Chaise at ye End of Birmingham, I purpos'd only to beg a Draught of Perry at Mr Baskerville's Door; but was soon prevail'd on to alight, & spent an hour or two very agreeably. They both seem'd extremely sorry that your Ladyship had not time to call; which I assur'd them was the Case. I found them sitting in their Parlour with a Busto-maker hard at work in finishing the Bustos of Mr & Mrs Baskerville; "serving God with his Talent", as I think, was Sir Godfrey Kneller's Phrase, when he painted on a Sunday. The Bustos are greatly like, & if well manag'd in Point of Hair and Drapery, will, I think, be very genteel ones. His Price is two Guineas. But as He came thither from Stratford you may possibly have heard the maker's Character. I should make ye frightfullest of *Bustos,* or I do not know but I should employ him. . . . On Monday I was surpris'd by Lord Sandys & his Son, whom I accompany'd round the *greater Part* of my walks; but who shewd less *Appetite,* (if not less *Discernment*) for matters of this kind, than almost any Persons I have seen here. The Son however seems to have more Taste than the Father. On Tuesday I receiv'd the Northfield-Family, agreeable to ye message you saw: Ld Dudley met them here; & the greater Part of the Company, Mr Lloyd especially, had Taste & Politeness enough to make my Day very satisfactory. I will not however trouble your Ladyship with a Detail of my Visitants, more or fewer of which have arrivd every Day this week. Pray

---

[1] B. M. Add. MSS 28958, fol. 158ff. Lady Luxborough's letter of September 29, 1754 (*Letters,* No. CXII) replies to this and its date is thus confirmed.

does your Ladyship know a Mr Bingley or Dingley? He seem'd a Person of Fashion, & came hither with his wife & a large Party to see my new Cascade by moon-light on Friday. . . . Your Ladyship will please to observe from what has been said, that I could not with the least convenience send a servant to Barrels upon this Errand *before*. I hope, sincerely hope, that Mrs Davies has not yet left Barrels. I mean chiefly, that I wish her to be *long* or very *often* with your Ladyship; but at present I mean also that you should assure her of my *unfeigned* Thanks for her company, & her assistance in makeing the Leasowes once more agreeable to Lady Luxborough. I desire also my compliments & Thanks to good Mr Holyoak; hopeing, e'er long, that Mrs Holyoak will deserve my thanks on ye same occasion; and, in the mean while, will accept my Compliments.

I have an odd kind of Favour to beg of your Ladyship; but wch, if attended with the least Inconvenience, I *as* sincerely beg you would refuse me. I had a small Fruit-piece (a Painting) sent me of a Present last week, for which I want a Frame; & having heard, accidentally, that your Ladyship has many Frames you do not use, am tempted to enquire whether you could conveniently supply me with any that might be made to fit a Picture of two Feet two, by Seventeen Inches or rather better. I beg, if inconvenient, you would make no sort of scruple to refuse it. I suppose, so long as this weather continues, (and the Glass I see is high) my occupations will be much the same as you found them; at The Leasowes. But after the first Day's rain, the Face of things will be revers'd. I may then take the Cynick's Lanthorn, & creep about with my Friend Hylton in search of one conversible creature, by Day-light: But I rather believe we shall take a different method, & move directly to Barrels, where we shall be well assur'd of finding all that we can wish from Genius, Taste, Politeness, & hospitality. I am with veneration ever your

Will: Shenstone

171. To LADY LUXBOROUGH [1]

The Leasowes, October ye 13. 1754

DEAR MADAM,

After the perusal of your Letter, I wrote immediately to Lord Dudley upon the subject of it;[2] and thought proper that your Coach-man should accompany my servant to The Grange. Accordingly they both are gone,

---

[1] B. M. Add. MSS 28958, fol. 160ff.

[2] Mr. Belchier (see postscript) was a clergyman in financial difficulties whom Lady Luxborough sought to help by application through Shenstone to Lord Dudley, who was to secure Belchier some respite from pursuit by his creditors. See Lady Luxborough's *Letters*, pp. 376–77, 384, 387–88.

with orders to wait 'till they receive an Answer from Mrs Rock. What the Event will be, I do not know; but am willing to hope the best; & am well assur'd it must give no small Pain to his Lordship either to leave his Priviledge un-supported, or to refuse any Request that your Ladyship is pleas'd to make.

I am afraid my Letters henceforth will begin to savour much of Winter, of whose un-joyous approach we have had no trivial Specimens. Yet I *guess* that Autumn will oblige us with some Smiles at *Parting;* enough at least to render agreeable the small Excursion your Ladyship proposes. I also have a Journey, or two to perform, & that to Places which are ambitious of being seen in their proper Season. However, as to this next Week, I must devote it wholly to my *own;* and considering how much *Time* & *Labour* has been bestow'd upon it, this year, my Friends will not take it amiss if I seem attentive to the Produce of *Them*.

I expect Mr Hylton here to-day, or to-morrow: How long he means to stay, is unknown to *me;* perhaps also to *Himself,* but I hope it will be long enough to accompany me to Barrels.

I return your Ladyship my best Thanks for ye beautifull Frame you were so kind to send; but, on the other Hand, it gives me some Confusion to think that even the least capital of your Pictures should so suffer by my Impertinence.

The Servants are return'd, & my Lord desires *I* would write to Mr Crawley, an attorney in London, & his intimate Acquaintance. I suppose he means to *Sign* what I write; and as for the rest I purpose y^t ye Letter shall go by to-morrow's Post.

I beg my Compliments to all the good Friends, y^t were so kind as to send me *theirs*.

I can add nothing to amuse your Ladyship: I can only add a certain truth, that I am ever most respectfully your Ladyship's most oblig'd & most obedient Servant

Will: Shenstone

I will detain Mr Belchier's Letter, as it may assist me in the Letter I have to write.

172. To RICHARD GRAVES[1]

The Leasowes, Oct. 23, 1754

Dear Mr. Graves,

It is certainly some argument of a *peculiarity* in the esteem I bear you, that I feel a readiness to acquaint you with *more* of my foibles than I care

---

[1] Dodsley, *Letters to Particular Friends,* No. LXXIX.

to trust with any other person. I believe nothing shews us more plainly either the different *degrees* or *kinds* of regard that we entertain for our several friends (I may also add the *difference* of their *characters*), than the ordinary style and tenor of the letters we address to them.

I confess to *you,* that I am considerably mortified by Mr. John W[histler]'s conduct in regard to my letters to his brother; and, rather than they should have been so unnecessarily destroyed, would have given more money than it is allowable for me to mention with *decency.* I look upon my letters as some of *my* chef-d'oeuvres;[2] and, could I be supposed to have the least pretensions to propriety of style or sentiment, I should imagine it must appear, principally, in my letters to his brother, and one or two more friends. I considered them as the records of a *friendship* that will be always *dear* to me, and as the *history* of my *mind* for these twenty years last past. The amusement I should have found in the perusal of them would have been altogether innocent; and I would gladly have preserved them, if it were only to explain those which I shall preserve of his brother's. Why he should allow either *me* or *them* so very little weight as not to consult me with regard to them, I can by no means conceive. I suppose it is not *un-customary* to return them to the surviving friend. I had no answer to the letter which I wrote Mr. J. W. I received a ring from him; but as I thought it an inadequate memorial of the friendship which his brother had for me, I gave it to my servant the moment I received it; at the same time I have a neat standish, on which I caused the lines Mr. W[histler] left with it to be inscribed, and which appears to me a much more agreeable remembrancer.

I have read your new production with pleasure; and as this letter begins with a confession of foibles, I will own, that through mere laziness I have sent you back your copy, in which I have made some erasements, instead of giving you my reasons on which those erasements were founded. Truth is, it seems to me to want mighty few variations from what is now the present text; and that, upon one more perusal, you will be able to give it as much perfection as you mean it to have. And yet, did I suppose you would insert it in Dodsley's Collection, as I see no reason you have to the contrary, I would take any pains about it that you should desire me. I must beg another copy, at your leisure.

I should like the inscription you mention upon a real stone-urn, which you purchase very reasonable at Bath: but you must not risque it upon the vase you mention, on any account whatever.

Now I mention Bath, I must acquaint you, that I have received intelli-

---

[2] This passage is often quoted or alluded to as evidence of the value Shenstone placed upon his letters.

gence from the younger Dodsley,³ that his brother is now there, and that none of the papers I sent him are yet *sent to press;* that he expects his brother home about the fourth or fifth of November, when he proceeds with his publication. Possibly you may go to Bath whilst he is there, and, if so, may chuse to have an interview.

I shall send two or three little pieces of my own, in hopes that you will adjust the reading, and return them as soon as you conveniently can. All I can send to-night is this "Ode to Memory."⁴ I shall in the last place desire your opinion as to the manner of *placing* what is sent. The first pages of his Miscellany must be already fixed. I think to propose ours for the last; but as to the *order,* it will depend entirely upon you.

Adieu! in other words, God bless you! — I have company at the table all the time I am writing. Your ever most affectionate

W. Shenstone

173. To SHERRINGTON DAVENPORT¹

The *Leasowes, Nov.* 13, 1754

SIR,

The Arrival of your Servant gave me a retrospective View of my own intolerable Omissions, and oppressed me with somewhat like the Load of an evil Conscience. I must allow that Appearances make against me; and yet I must and will assert, that there is no one has a truer Respect for Mr. D[avenport], a deeper Sense of his Civilities, a greater Relish for his Company, or a more lively Desire to partake of those Beauties which he is daily distributing round his Situation. Of these last, Miss F—— F——² has sometimes favoured me with the greatest Encomiums: I am sure she knew how much I should enjoy them, and might also mean them as Inducements (which I never yet wanted) to hasten the Visit I intended you at W[orfield]. Alas! neither her Pleasure in giving me these Descriptions, nor mine in receiving them, were unmixed with Pain; as she was too often forced to adjoin but an indifferent Account of poor Miss D[avenport]'s Health. For this, and for the Affliction it occasions you and Mrs. D[avenport], I really feel a Concern that I am not satisfied to express in the ordinary Forms of Condolence.

I have passed this Summer in a Series of Dissipation; betwixt some Events disagreeable enough, and others that wear at least the Appearance of Pleasure. I have done (what *I* must call) a good deal round my Place.

³ The letter from James Dodsley referred to is preserved in B.M. Add. MSS 28959, fol. 14.
⁴ *Works,* I (1764), 117ff, dated 1748.
¹ Hull, *Select Letters,* Vol. I, No. LVI. Though Hull gives only the initial of the addressee, the context pretty plainly indicates Sherrington Davenport of Worfield.
² Possibly Miss Fanny Fletcher.

Company produced new Operations, and new Operations produced almost daily Company. The Line of my Path is now almost universally extended to the Sides of Hedges, and, together with some slighter Improvements, have been added two new Cascades: of the first of these, I believe you have heard some Account; it is really, if you'll pardon such an Expression from the Proprietor, a very *great* Thing for the *Size* of it.

My Servant has been *weekly* upon the Point of setting out for D[avenport] House, ever since the Time I first heard of your Return to it: but as he is here much less of the Footman or Groom, than the River-God, he has been almost continually called upon to unlock and conduct his Rivulets; for this Fortnight, indeed, or three Weeks last, he has been less importuned on that Score; but then, during that Space, arrived a Visitant, who is now with me in the House, and, till the Time of whose Departure was ascertained, I was unable to fix a Day when I could wait upon you and Mrs. D[avenport]: I hope to do so about the Middle of next Week; and will not fail to send Tom over upon *Monday* or *Tuesday*. If he can be of any possible Service, in Regard to the Cascades you proposed (and I think his Head a clear one) you are welcome to command him over as often as you please. I have detained your Servant much beyond the Time he purposed to return. I can therefore only desire my best Compliments to Mrs. D[avenport], and assure her, that my Muse is not less at her Service, and beg your Acceptance of this Ode to &c. and would, I am sure, esteem it greater Honour to embellish your Place than mine. I wish you do not find it obscure; however, if it discover but an ordinary Talent for Poetry, it will discover at least a warm Attachment to rural Improvement. With this I shall be quite contented, so long as I think it has the least Tendency to recommend me to Mr. D[avenport]'s good Opinion.

I am, dear Sir,
yours and Mrs. D[avenport]'s &c.[3]

174. To LADY LUXBOROUGH [1]

The Leasowes, Decr 8th 1754

DEAR MADAM;

I know not what to say. I wish it were in my power to draw up an apology in as dear and forcible a manner as you have brought my accusation. But to dispose and give weight to an hundred little excuses, (each

---

[3] The letter is unsigned.

[1] B. M. Add. MSS 28958, fol. 162ff. This letter answers and confirms the date of Lady Luxborough's of December 4, 1754 (*Letters,* No. CXIV). Her No. CXV of December 8 is the reply to the present letter.

of which, when taken separately, can pretend to small Importance) would be a task very difficult for *me;* & to your *Ladyship,* I think, extremely unamusive. Pardon me therefore, my good Lady, *implicitly;* & believe that in so doing you have escap'd a most tedious narrative. I have met with numerous avocations of a very different nature: Some regarding *business,* and utterly displeasing; others of a mixt kind, & neither pleasurable nor painfull; — very few, since I saw your Ladyship, which I have thoroughly enjoy'd.

When Mr Belchier's[2] Messenger arriv'd here, my Lord Dudley had been gone to London about a week. I therefore wrote that gentleman a short message, intimating my wishes for his Freedom Health and Happiness; acquainting him, that I had, at your Request, done all that lay in my power to serve him; and that All I could do, from that time, was to transmit his Letter to my Lord D. in London; which I would not fail to do by the following Thursday's Post. Indeed the Servant's own account of his master *here* gave me some cause to conclude that your Ladyship was deceiv'd in Him. I trust what you will further collect from ye Letters I have enclos'd may indeed occasion you to compassionate his distress, but will at the same time discover how improper it must have been for my Lord to appear in support of his written Protection.

Sir William Meredyth does me a great deal of Honour in his remembrance of me; & whatever I receive from him will of course be very acceptable. I heartily wish him all the Pleasure which his situation, his time of Life, & his numerous accomplishments so fairly promise him; & 'tis none of my least ardent wishes that I may one Day meet him at Barrels. Mean time, the little quotation he gives you from Horace Walpole's speech is truly humorous; & I am glad that Sir Williams Correspondence restores to your Ladyship some of that Amusement, of which London robbs the Country at this time of the year. I beg yt when you write, you would offer him my best Respects.

I am sorry to hear of poor Mr Bradley's Death; who appear'd to me to be a Person of great good-nature, & of a true natural *Taste* under the disadvantages of worldly Business. I beg my humble Service to Mrs Bradley.

My Lord Dudley & Miss Lea are now in London; where my Lord has purchas'd a new Coach & a Pair of Horses; which are expected to convey them to the Grange before Christmas.

Mr Hylton has been with me for these six or seven weeks past; & purposes to reside in this neighbourhood all the winter. Could I have remov'd the Panic apprehensions under which he labours as an *Horse-*

---

[2] See above, Letter 171, n2.

man, he would long ago have waited upon your Ladyship at Barrels. I trust however I shall be able to bring him with me, before the Close of this present December.

I am at this time embarass'd with a Promise which I made last year to Dodsley — I then offer'd to contribute some few Pieces towards his Miscellany; either of my own; or of my Friends, whose Permission I could procure. Accordingly I have taken some Pains in His behalf; and am willing enough to send him half a score of my smaller madrigals. But then it is a Point with me not to publish aught that may be altogether unreputable; or y^t may prejudice the Publick against any thing I may print hereafter. And, in this respect, I am irresolute what to send him. Will your Ladyship be so kind as to honour me with your Opinion, in regard to a Song or two which I enclose for your Perusal.

There is a Song or two written by your Ladyship,[3] y^t I think extremely elegant. "Hark to the Blackbird's &c:" and "The Sun his gladsome beams" &c: The latter of these equal to any song in the Language. I think it pity they should be suppress'd and should be heartily glad if you would permit him to print them with any Limitations you think proper for me to mention. I am clear & positive in my opinion of their *Merit*.

I beg y^t your Ladyship would wave all sort of Compliment in respect of the Pieces wch I send for your Perusal; *Severity* is ye most *friendly* when one is upon the Brink of the Press. I beg my Complim^{ts} to Mr Outing, who will not refuse me his assistance also. I trust that, before the Close of Christmas I shall see him in Warwickshire, if not in Shropshire. I desire always to be esteem'd

  Your Ladyship's most oblig'd & most obedient hum: Servt
              Will Shenstone

I shall probably write again before the Close of this week; as I have some other little Pieces wch I have thoughts of sending to Dodsley: at least if I find by your Ladyship's answer . . . the Trouble I give you is not . . .[4]

175. To LADY LUXBOROUGH[1]

The Leasowes Decr 12. 1754

DEAR MADAM,

It is my *misfortune*, not my *Fault*, to write to your Ladyship in the greatest *Hurry*. I am sure your goodness will therefore excuse me, if

---

[3] Lady Luxborough's songs here alluded to were published in Volume IV of Dodsley's *Collection:* the first entitled *The Bulfinch in Town*, "By a Lady of Quality"; the second, *Song. Written in Winter, 1745*, "By the Same."
[4] The manuscript is here defective.
[1] B. M. Add. MSS 28958, fol. 165ff. To this letter Lady Luxborough replies with one of December 12, 1754 (*Letters*, No. CXVI), the date of which is thus confirmed.

every thing I say in this Letter be expressive of it. I hope also that Mr Outing will accept my Thanks at present, & allow me to answer his Letter when I have a better opportunity.

Shall I tell your Ladyship a Secret? I was so thoroughly convinc'd of the Merit of your little Pieces, that I sent them to Dodsley very near a Month ago.² It is true, had I not obtain'd your Leave to print them (which I always meant to sollicit) I would, most assuredly, have stop'd the Publication: but far happier am *I* in the Liberty that you have given me.

I believe the Press waits for my Contributions at this very time: I purpose therefore to compleat what I mean to add of my own, by next Saturday's Post; & should think myself oblig'd, if you would please to return the Copies I now send, (together with what I sent before,) by the Servant. As to those I now Send, I need not give your Ladyship or Mr Outing much trouble. There seem not to be above two that have y^e *least* pretensions to appear in Print. The one "those Stanzas address'd to your Ladyship upon furnishing y^r Library": The other, "that Ode to Lucio." However I shall be very glad to receive an Opinion so just as yours, or His.—

I wrote to Mr Crawley on Monday last; &, in the Letter, took the Liberty of assuring Lord Dudley that your Ladyship would altogether acquiesce in his Conduct towards Mr Belchier.³ I also left him no Room to blame either your Ladyship or myself.

I dare detain Tom no longer. He will, as it *is,* arrive much later at Barrels than I wish Him. I beg however that your Ladyship, with Mr Outing, will afford me what assistance you can & at this Juncture; I will write again to Barrels by ye way of Birmingham, when I hope to signify a week when Mr Hylton & myself may have ye Pleasure of waiting on you. I am, Madam,

    Your Ladyship's most oblig'd & most obedient hum: Servt

                                Will Shenstone

² Lady Luxborough's contribution to Dodsley's fourth volume consisted of four pieces: *The Bulfinch in Town,* "By a Lady of Quality"; *Song. Written in Winter, 1745,* "By the Same"; *Written to a Near Neighbour in a Tempestuous Night, 1748,* "By the Same"; and *Written at Ferme Ornée, near Birmingham; August 7, 1749,* "By the Same."

³ It is interesting to learn (Lady Luxborough's *Letters,* pp. 404–05) that Mr. Belchier proved unworthy of her concern for him. See above, Letter 171, n2, and Letter 174.

176. To LADY LUXBOROUGH[1]

The Leasowes, Jan. 10. 1755

DEAR MADAM,

I do not wonder that your Ladyship esteems my silence *unaccountable*, as I have the strongest *Inducements* to write that either *Pleasure* or *Gratitude* can afford me. . . . And yet the total Reason why I did not write before, was oweing to the necessity I was under of attending to Dodsley's publication: & the state of my health and Spirits at this time of the year. It has been my wayward Fate to study the Refinements of Poetry, when my Head was hardly sufficient to indite a Piece of common Prose. Much indeed am I oblig'd to your Ladyship & Mr Outing for the Propriety of the Remarks you sent me; and yet in *one* Respect they gave me Pain, as they discover'd how much more *wisely* I had acted, had I come over to Barrels about a Month ago, brought my Madrigals in my Pocket, & *there* finish'd this affair with Dodsley agreeable to our joint Opinions.

Your Ladyship has so admirable a talent at Impromptus (I speak very *seriously*) that I cannot forbear asking the assistance you can lend me in an *hour or two's time*, this Evening. The Objections you made to the Canto on *Sollicitude*[2] I believe are entirely just. I have therefore omitted a considerable part of it, and endeavour'd to improve the rest; but with what *success*, I want greatly to be satisfy'd. Never was I puzzled more than in tricking out that pastoral Fop Sir Paridel; yet I think, that when my head is *clearest*, there is no kind of Humour in which I could more *easily* succeed. The Stanzas in particular, wherein he compliments his Mistress by the trite resemblance of Flowers, cost me no small Pains. Your Ladyship, if you cannot any way *approve* them, will I'm sure *assist* a poor bewilder'd Poet who applies to you as a *Genius*, a *Florist*, and a *Friend*.

That you may be more easily induc'd to make free with *my* said performance, I discover to your Ladyship ye Liberties which I have taken with *yours*. Amongst the Rest, that of sending it to Dodsley is what I beg you would forgive. I really thought it would appear well at the Close of your other pieces; & it shews a disdain of[3] an art in which you cou'd so easily excell.

I shall be glad if your Ladyship and Mr Outing approve this Copy of the Princess Elizabeth; as I shall not have time to make any important alteration. The Autumn Verses have been in Dodsley's hands this twelve-

---

[1] B. M. Add. MSS 28958, fol. 167ff. This letter answers and confirms the date of Lady Luxborough's of January 7, 1755 (*Letters*, No. CXVIII).
[2] *Pastoral Ballad*, Canto III.
[3] Above "disdain of" in the manuscript Shenstone has written "contempt for."

month; & I *hope* they do not *want* an amendment, which I'm *sure* they will not *have,* as matters are circumstanc'd.

I have not time to express my sense of Sir William Meredyths complaisance, but will take some other opportunity. Pray, what was Mr Pit's Embarasment?

Mr Belchier's is an handsome Letter; and I am glad for his *own* sake that he has not miss'd his voyage. I will the first convenient opportunity return his Protection to Lord Dudley.

You have *read* that Mr W. Lyttelton is appointed Governor of S. Carolina; but you may not have *heard* that Admiral Smith stands Candidate for Bewdley in his Room, & is oppos'd by Mr Winnington.

Mr Hylton desires his most respectfull compliments to your Ladyship; & returns you many thanks for ye honour of your Intelligence concerning a Horse that would suit him. *This* really *would* suit him; & he would be extremely safe in dealing with Mr Holyoak; but it seems he *now* does not purpose to buy *any,* amusing himself with the *Mere Possession* of a Kettel he dares not bestride.

Your Ladyship is extremely kind in *asking* my Company, at a time of year when neither my head, my spirits, nor my temper renders me worth any one's company, correspondence, or Notice. For this week or nine days past, I have indeed been more particularly heavy & dispirited. I will however wait upon your Ladyship soon; as soon as it becomes possible you should receive any Amusement from my Company. Mr Hylton intends to come with me; & in the mean time, I will *write.* Your Ladyship says nothing of *your* Health; I will therefore, for *my own* sake, believe that you are well. You would *always* be both well and happy, if health and happiness depended *less* upon externals, and more upon the inmost wishes of, Madam,

Your Ladyship's most oblig'd & most obedient hum: Ser^vt

Will Shenstone

177. To RICHARD JAGO [1]

The Leasowes, Jan. 22, 1755

Dear Mr. Jago,

I am sure you must be puzzled how to account for my silence, after the honour you have done me by your verses, and the request you made that I would *write.* — I am also as much at a loss how to give a proper weight to my apology. To say I have been ill, would perhaps imply too much; when I would only allude to that state of heaviness and dejection

---

[1] Dodsley, *Letters to Particular Friends,* No. LXXXII.

which is so frequently my lot at this time of the year; and which renders me both *averse* to writing and utterly dissatisfied with every thing that I *do* write.

If at any time my head grew a little less confused than ordinary, I was obliged to devote my attention to the affair in which I had so *foolishly* involved myself with Dodsley. You are unable to conceive what vexation it has given me: I could not endure to *disappoint* him: of consequence, it has been my lot to study the delicacies of *poetry* when my brain was not sufficient to indite a piece of common prose; but as the *mouse* (by which I mean my *own* performances) will so soon make its ridiculous appearance, it were totally impolitic in me to expatiate on the labours of the *mountain*. — The first letter I received from you left me greatly dissatisfied. I was then to send D[odsley] my *final* instructions in a post or two. — You took little notice of any query I made; and intimated a disapprobation, which agreed *too well* with my own internal sentiments. — I knew not but you were *angry* at the *liberties* I had taken; though I could have suppressed any single paper which I had then conveyed to London. — Little did I *then* imagine that it was in my power to have protracted the affair till *now*. Had that been the case, I should have troubled you with repeated embassies; for I abhor the tediousness of the post, and my servants do little at this time of the year that is of more importance than their master's poetry.

Your next letter convinced me that you had taken no offence; and so far I was happy: but then I wanted to have your Goldfinches as correct as your Blackbirds; there were *some* things I wished you to alter; and others in regard to which I was desirous to speak my *sentiments*. Add to this, my own *verses,* with which I was infinitely *more* dissatisfied. Why then did I not write? — The true reason was, that I was pressed by D[odsley] to send conclusions every post; and though I have had all this leisure (as it *happens*) since you wrote, I never could *depend* upon more than the space of a day or two. Besides, criticisms in the way of letter are extremely tedious and dissatisfactory; insomuch, that I am thoroughly determined never to print any thing for the future, unless I have the company of my friends when I send to the press. Hurried as I then was, I sent up your two copies, and what I propose for him of my own, with a kind of *discretionary* power to select the best readings. How you would approve of this measure I knew not; but I had this to plead in my behalf, that D[odsley] was a person of taste *himself;* that he had, as I imagined, many learned friends to assist him; that his *interest* was concerned in the perfection of his Miscellany; and that I submitted my own pieces to the same judgment.

After all, I am but indifferently satisfied with the present state of these contributions. D[odsley] writes just so much as he deems *necessary* in the way of business, and passes by a thousand points in my letters which deserve an answer. His last acquaints me, that he has spent a whole day in the arrangement of what I have sent him; and that he purposes to send me *proof-sheets* before the close of this week, desiring I would send them back by the return of the post. Whether they arrive on Saturday or on Monday, I can keep them till the Thursday following.

And this brings me, in the last place, to the main purpose of this letter. — It is a request on which I lay great stress; and which you must not refuse me upon almost any consideration. — I beg, in short, that you would promise me the favour of your company on Monday (or even Tuesday) next, if possible; and let us jointly fix the readings of *your* pieces, of my *own,* and those of our common *friends*. — You will immediately comprehend the *expediency* of this; now, in particular, that our names are to appear. *Some* alterations I think *necessary* in your Goldfinches,[2] and there are two or three stanzas which I think you might improve. — Nevertheless, I will not pretend that this journey is so *requisite* upon your *own* account as *mine;* and will recommend it upon no other footing than the pleasure you will receive by the obligation which you will confer.

I thought to have concluded here; but, as an envelope is now become altogether necessary, have a temptation to proceed which I did not see before.

It is now become Friday the twenty-fourth of January. The packets I send, and the request that I make upon so *little* warning will, at first, astonish you. — Unforeseen interruptions would not suffer me to dispatch my courier sooner. — What then remains, but that I endeavour to adjust this affair agreeably to its *present* circumstances?

You will readily conceive, from what you observe in my packets, how desireable your company is to me at this juncture. Supposing it then in your *power* to come over on Monday, Tuesday, or even Wednesday, I am inclined to believe you *will*. Supposing it *not* so, I can foresee you will not have leisure to satisfy my queries by the return of the bearer: and what I would *next* propose is, that you would either suffer me to send again to you betwixt this time and Thursday next; or that you would

---

[2] Both Jago's *Goldfinches* and his *Blackbirds* appeared in the fourth volume of Dodsley's *Collection* (1755), along with other of his verses.

yourself dispatch a purpose-messenger, and allow me to pay for his journey. — In either of these *latter* cases, I am sure you so well know the nature of my present irresolution, that you will endeavour to afford me all the assistance you are able.

Adieu! my dear friend! and depend upon my best services on every possible occasion.

I am ever your most affectionate and most obedient servant,

W. Shenstone

178. To RICHARD JAGO [1]

The Leasowes, Feb. 22, 1755

DEAR MR. JAGO,

I received a letter from Dodsley, dated the fifteenth of February; informing me that you were then in town, had been with him, and left your directions whither he might send you a set of Miscellanies.

February the twentieth, and not *before,* arrived young H―― with your letter; very obligingly intended to give me previous notice of your journey; but which, by the iniquity of chance, tended only to acquaint me with an opportunity which I had *lost*.

There is nothing could have been so fortunate as your journey to London, had Mr. H. thought proper to bring your letter in due time. — What excuse he made for his neglect, or whether he made any, I have really forgot. This I know, that the whole affair has been unlucky. There has been abundant time for consultation, and a perfect series of opportunities of which we have not been suffered to avail ourselves. It is now three weeks or a month since I corrected the proof-sheets; was so hurried in the doing of it that I scarce knew what I wrote; and yet, in spite of all this hurry, the book is hitherto unpublished. *Now,* indeed, it must be much too late for alterations, as D[odsley] has given me some room to expect a book this very day. — I know but little what he has done in consequence of that discretionary power with which I, through haste, was obliged to intrust him: but in what I have done *myself,* you may expect to find all the effects of *dulness precipitated.*

It is now the twenty-third of February, and I have received no fresh account of our friend Dodsley's proceedings; nor am I able to *trace* them, as I expected, in the news-papers.

As to your share of this Miscellany, you can have no cause to be dissatisfied. — After what manner he has thought proper to print Lady

[1] Dodsley, *Letters to Particular Friends,* No. LXXXIII.

L[uxborough]'s verses,[2] I am a good deal uncertain; but I apprehend he has not followed her own readings very precisely, and that the blame thereof is to be thrown upon me. — I am concerned for the memory of my poor friend Whistler, and regret that his *better* pieces did not fall into my hands. I think that Dodsley, however, would have done him greater justice, had he inserted his translation of "Horace and Lydia." It is true, the translations of that Ode are out of number; but *his*, if I mistake not, had many beauties of its own. — I do not know whether I ever hinted to you, that *his* genius and that of Ovid were apparently congenial. Had he cultivated his with equal care, perhaps the similitude had been as obvious as that of your twin-daughters. — Mr. Graves has one small well-polished gem in his collection; his verses upon Medals.[3] — His little conjugal Love-song is also natural and easy. — I *told* you what I least disliked of my *own* puerilities. — If the printing of my Rural Inscriptions be *invidious,* it was altogether owing to the instigation of Sir G[eorge] L[yttelton]. There are four or five little matters, which, if he have printed with my name, incorrect as they are, I shall be utterly disconsolate; at least, till I get sight of a succeeding impression. — For though I am not much solicitous about a poetical reputation (and indeed it is of little importance to so *domestic* an animal as myself), yet I could ill endure to pass for an affected, powerless *pretender.*

And now no more upon the subject. — I have nothing to add that can the least amuse you. — You, who have been conversant with all the busy and the splendid scenes of life, can want no materials to make a letter entertaining. — Indeed you never *did.* — I shall be glad, however, to receive a *long* one, upon what subjects you please.

I have passed a very dull and unamusive winter; my health indeed rather better than I experienced it last year; but my head *as* confused, and my spirits *as* low. I live in hopes of an opportunity of seeing you at Harbury; but I begin now to receive visits as an honest beggar does an alms, with my humblest thanks for the favour, and with a despair of making a return.

Perhaps my next letter may discover somewhat more *resolution:* inclination I never want; being at all times with singular affection yours,

W. Shenstone

[2] See above, Letter 174, n3 and Letter 175, n2.
[3] Graves's *The Cabinet, or Verses on Roman Medals. To Mr. W.* appeared in Dodsley's *Collection,* Vol. IV. There follow three other poems "By the Same": *Panacea; or the Grand Restorative; The Heroines, or Modern Memoirs;* and *The Parting. Written Some Years after Marriage.* The last is the "little conjugal Love-song" alluded to.

179. To LADY LUXBOROUGH[1]

The Leasowes, Feb: 27. 1755

DEAR MADAM,

I find it necessary to write to your Ladyship this week, not being able to endure that you should think hardly of me during the time that may elapse before I can possibly see you. When I have the honour of doing so, I trust that I can eraze any unfavourable impressions, & very fairly acquit myself of all voluntary neglect. Mean time let me only beg that you would suspend your accusation. I wish I could fix a time for the performance of this visit, but it is not in my Power. Such weather as the present does not only numb one's Limbs, but extend it's severity to our projects, hopes, & resolutions. Your Ladyship well knows how winter affects *me;* & have indeed yourself remark'd it in the very style of my Letters. I am dull enough to be unworthy of a conversation much inferior to yours; & if I add that I am a little peevish withal, I shall do myself no Injustice. Were it then possible to retain the same venomous or torpid Qualities when arriv'd upon the coast of Barrels, I ought in common Policy to confine myself at Home. But I have been and am confin'd upon a different score; a kind of Partition-Treaty with Master Dolman:[2] and when this is concluded or broken off, as I trust will soon be the Case, I shall not then draw excuses from the stupidity with which it is my Fate to be *visited* in Winter. I have indeed sometimes imagin'd that I brighten'd up in your company, when I had before esteem'd it as impossible as that you should polish a piece of Cynder or of spunge.

I have expected to see Dodsley's miscellany advertis'd these six weeks ago. Had he allow'd me but one half of this time to deliberate, I could have adjusted the share we have in it much more to my own satisfaction. I know but little what he has done in consequence of that discretionary power, with which, thro' mere Haste, I was oblig'd to intrust him; and this possibly at a time when his own Hurry was as great as mine. But this I know, y^t in all I did myself you may expect to trace the Finger of Stupidity precipitated.

Stupidity however is many an honest man's Lot: Presumption is less excusable; and it is with the utmost humility that I beg your Ladyship's Pardon for the Liberty I took in proposing what I thought might be for the Improvement of your verses. I have only this to plead, that you write these lively pieces almost extempore; that you lay no stress upon them,

---

[1] B. M. Add. MSS 24419, fol. 3. Also published in Hull's *Select Letters,* Vol. I, No. LVII. It seems to be a reply to Lady Luxborough's letter dated Valentine's Day, 1755 (*Letters,* No. CXIX).

[2] See above, Letter 168 and note 2 thereto.

and scarce ever revise them; that, on these accounts only, I thought it possible an expression not altogether exact might here and there escape you; that finding my proposals disapprov'd, I did all my *time* would *allow* to cause Dodsley to have recourse to your original readings: And if He have not done so *universally,* (as I apprehend may be the Case) those readings may be restor'd in any future Impression — I will resume the subject on some other occasion; at present let me only mention that Dodsley when he wrote to me last, desir'd my opinion whether or no he should be thought impertinent if he presented your Ladyship with a compleat Sett of his Miscellanies. It seems the three first volumes are out of Print at this time; but will be reprinted in about a Month. The fourth, he gives me reason to expect every day —

I am particularly glad to hear that your Health is tolerable during this rigorous weather, as it gives me Room to conceive the advantage you may derive from better. How do I long for the approach of Spring! Methinks I could travel Leagues to meet it, were it possible by so doing to bring it faster on it's way — And yet unless it should supply me with Health as well as with Company with spirits as well as spring-flowers, and in one word re-enliven both the Farmer and the Farm, what would it avail? The two Canary-birds that were given me about 3 weeks ago sing whilst I am writing; sing from morn to night & that wth all the vigour which the Spring itself could inspire — Yet I do not half enjoy them: my mind is not in tune: The Commencement of my Spring must receive it's date at Barrels — I am with constant attachment y^r Ladyships most obligd

W. Shens:

180. To ROBERT DODSLEY [1]

The Leasowes, March 4th 1755

Dear Sir,

I return you many thanks for the Compliment you make my Friends & Me in the offer of a sett of miscellanies & I dare say L^{dy} Luxborough will take it well to be included in it. My Expectation of seeing the last volume advertis'd, was the reason I have not made you this acknowledgment before.

---

[1] B. M. Add. MSS 28959, fol. 38. A note (fol. 2) preceding the letters from Dodsley to Shenstone reads, "Letters from my worthy friend Mr. Robert Dodsley; A very eminent Bookseller in London; Author of the Miller of *Mansfield,* (his native place) the Toyshop, the Oeconomy of Life; above all Cleone & Melpomene; with many other Pieces. A Person whose writings I esteem in common with the Publick; But of whose Simplicity, Benevolence, Humanity, & true Politeness, I have had repeated and particular experience. Will: Shenstone." Ralph Straus prints the present letter, without the postscript, in his *Robert Dodsley,* pp. 129–30.

Robert Dodsley
From the portrait by William Alcock in the
National Portrait Gallery, London

The Delay has given me some Pain; not thro' the least Impatience of seeing my Trifles made publick; for I am really fearfull of the appearance, & could wish a longer time to adjust the state of my contributions. But this very Wish makes me reflect upon the time that has elaps'd since I wrote to you; & of which, I trust, I could have avail'd myself to your satisfaction & my own. I suppose that the Impression must now be taken off; if otherwise, & that for any particular Reason you have chosen it should be deferd I should be glad that you would afford me ye earliest Intelligence.

       I am ever faithfully & affectionately yours,
                 Will: Shenstone

My Lord Dudley will accept my respectable Compliments & pardon my Freedom in requesting y^t he would frank me these few Covers. We are told here y^t my L^d has lately taken a House in Town, which seems to[2]

181. To RICHARD GRAVES [1]

         The Leasowes, March ye 21 1755

DEAR MR. GRAVES,

 Pardon the arrival of this one more Letter without a Frank: I have sent some covers to my Lord of Dudley who is in town, & shall probably enough receive them before I write again.

 There is nothing that I can less forgive the world than your want of Leisure. Do not misinterpret me or take amiss what I say. I know you to be infinitely more happy than my self who am cloy'd with it; but it would add something to my happiness, if not to your own, that you had more vacant spaces or Intervals of time to employ in those refin'd amusements for which you are so exquisitely qualify'd.

 I am in doubt whether I should add mottos to my seal, of which I have the least *distrust:* or not rather cause the circumference, which at present is rather of the largest, to be contracted. Should you have struck out any thing, since you wrote to me, you will be so good as let me know.

 As to Sun-dials, I never much affected the things themselves, nor indeed any mottos with which I have seen them inscrib'd. Perhaps this Indifference may arise from no very commendable sources: a reflection upon my own want of Proficiency of mathematicks, and an habitual consciousness of my own waste of time. However I have often had thoughts

---
[2] The manuscript abruptly ends here.
[1] B. M. Add. MSS 21508, fol. 38ff. A version of this letter also appears in Hull's *Select Letters,* Vol. I, No. LVIII.

of placing a slight one somewhere upon my premises, for ye sake of inscribing it with a couple of Lines from Virgil.

> Sed fugit interea fugit, irreparabile tempus
> Singula dum capti circumvectamur amore.

All the Lines of Virgil afford me that sort of pleasure which one receives from melancholy musick: and I believe I am often struck with the turn and Harmony of his expression, where a person less attach'd to these can discover no great beauty.

I told you how much I was vex'd that Dodsley did not suffer me to avail myself of the time that pass'd from the correction of the proof-sheets to the Publication of his book. He has at last sent me a Copy which I receiv'd last thursday se'nnight. I wish the last stanza of Whistler's verses upon Flowers[2] had remain'd as He himself wrote it: but being somewhat dissatisfy'd with the original reading, & having no time left to improve it myself, I left it to D—— who I think has made it worse. However in this respect and some others it may be proper to fix one's eye upon a subsequent impression; & Dodsley has acted as discreetly as it was possible for him to do, considering what Instructions were given Him, and how *much* was left to his discretion. Our contributions may be said to begin with Mr Somerville's address &c: Page 302. amongst wch he has inserted two odes,[3] (Page 305 & 307) to wch I am a stranger. The Song mark'd J. S. H. is my Neighbour Mr Hylton's; who has a pretty collection of Drawings, Petrefactions & Coins. The Lady of Quality, you know:[4] and as to all the Pieces y^t follow, you know ye authors of them as well as I do — I will not anticipate your own observations, but I cannot help remarking that Milton's Il penseroso has drove half our Poets crazy. It has however produc'd some admirable odes to Fancy, amongst which that of Warton (not in this vol.) I think deserves the preference: and after His, Merrick's Penshurst, & the ode on Solitude[5] are of the same tribe and are good. The Pleasures of melancholy and Mariotts ode to Fancy of ye same tribe, & indifferent[6] — There is nothing I am more pleas'd with than Father Francis's Prayer.[7] Mr Berkley repeated it to me

---

[2] Whistler's poem *Flowers* is followed in Dodsley's *Collection*, Vol. IV, by another, entitled *Song*.

[3] Dodsley identifies the author of the two odes as Mr. Parrat. See Letter 183, n2.

[4] Lady Luxborough.

[5] *Penshurst* appears on pages 50ff of Dodsley's *Collection*, Vol. IV (edition of 1770), where it is ascribed to "the late Mr. F. Coventry." The *Ode on Solitude* (pp. 229ff, same edition) is by Dr. Grainger.

[6] *The Pleasures of Melancholy. Written in the Year 1745*, by Thomas Warton, appears in Dodsley's *Collection*, Vol. IV (edition of 1770), pp. 210ff. The *Ode to Fancy* follows several other pieces by Marriott, pp. 287ff.

[7] *Father Francis's Prayer. Written in Lord Westmorland's Hermitage* appears in Dodsley's *Collection*, Vol. IV (edition of 1770), pp. 258–59.

in my Root-house this last summer, & I think said it was Mr Wests—
I could wish I had made you some compliment in this vol. for particular
reasons; & had resolutely done so had your own diffidence permitted me—

I have, now and then, some thoughts of printing that "ode to the
Dutchess," together with something sufficient to make a 12 or 18-penny
Pamphlett,[8] about ye time the Parliament rises — but not unless it sits
'till June as was reported, & not unless you will promise me the Favour
of your assistance.

Tis the Property of great delicacy to be often-times too diffident: Possibly then you may not long persevere in that manner of spelling your
name wch you seem at present to prefer. Yet is nothing so clear to me as
that yourself & your relations should spell their Name *Greaves* to the end
of the world. Nati natorum & qui nascentur ab illis —

Cowper's performance is all that you think it: but would you see both
his style & sentiments effectually demolish'd look into ye account of Books
in that gents. Magazine where it was first advertis'd.

You will guess that I shall want impatiently to hear from you; when
you have receiv'd y^r sett of Books, or perus'd them elsewhere.

I am ever most affectionately yours,[9]

182. To a FRIEND [1]

DEAR SIR,

When I promised you some Poetry for Mr. S——, I am afraid that,
through my Desire of recommending myself to his Family, my Tongue
out-run my Wit. If I laid any Sort of *Stress* upon what I was to send, I am
very sure it did so; and when you have read the Trifles enclosed, you will
be of the same Opinion.

It is probable, however, that I had an Eye to a larger Ode of mine,
upon the Subject of Rural Elegance, which I have not now Time either
to correct or to transcribe; but which I will not fail to communicate to
them upon some future Occasion.

Or if my Promise regarded a Translation of the Mottoes *here,* I shall
have the best Opportunity of performing it, when I take the Freedoms
you have allowed me, with your polite Description of my Farm.

---

[8] This project, several times alluded to, was never carried out.
[9] The letter is unsigned.
[1] Published in Hull, *Select Letters,* Vol. II, No. V. The addressee is not named, but the context suggests Robert Dodsley. The letter is not dated in Hull, but the reference to the ode on *Rural Elegance,* evidently still in manuscript, indicates a date before March 23, 1758, when the ode was published in Dodsley's *Collection,* Vol. V. Dodsley first visited the Leasowes late in August, 1754; possibly it is to his description of the farm that reference is made. Thomas Percy also wrote a description of the Leasowes in 1753. The chronological position of the letter is conjectural.

Am I wrong in detaining that Paper? — For positively, these last few days I have found myself a good deal feverish, and my Head has been so much confused, that I was almost tempted to omit this Message. In this Case, I think your Good-nature would have acquitted me of *Disrespect:* but I could not suffer you to leave the Country with so bad an Opinion of my Punctuality.

It remains, that I present my best Respects to Dr. Turton and his Lady, and that I wish you an agreeable Journey to *Oxford*. I purpose, in a few Weeks, that you shall be enabled to say something more particular, in Regard to M——'s Poetry; in the mean Time, I desire that he would accept my Compliments, and my Thanks for the Pleasure his Verses have afforded me. Above all things, assure Mr. Arnold of my most unfeigned Esteem; and if he discovers any Partiality for my Place or me, encourage it, that it may induce him, on a proper Occasion, to favour me once more with his Company. You see, I am availing myself of *your* Interest, to make all your Friends my own, and to attone for this Piece of Selfishness, it shall not be my Fault, if every Friend I have be not yours, at least, with some Share of that Regard with which I am,
dear Sir,
your most faithful, humble Servant,
W. Shenstone

183. To ROBERT DODSLEY [1]

The Leasowes, March the 23^d 1755

DEAR SIR

I had the pleasure of receiving the fourth volume of your miscellanies, which arriv'd as I remember last thursday was se'nnight. I am oblig'd to you for the care you took to forward it, when printed, as well as for all that Trouble I occasion'd you, *before*. Some Improvements may be made in a subsequent Impression; & whenever this is propos'd I dare say you will give me notice. In general, you have done all that I could expect from a Person of Genius and a Friend.

It remains for me to wish that the Book may fully recompense you, I will not only say, for the Pains you have taken, but for the Discernment you have shewn. It contains many excellent pieces, that are entirely new to me: & if others that are no less excellent have been printed before, it cannot reasonably be objected by such as consider your first Design.

Is it impertinent to ask the Names of those Persons who have not inserted them? If so, I drop my enquiry. The Pages, where their Lines

---

[1] B. M. Add. MSS 28959, fol. 39. Straus prints this letter, with omissions, in his *Robert Dodsley*, pp. 130–31.

occurr, are, 73. 114. 119. 170. 200. 202. 227. 228. 233. 250. 253. 265. 267. 305. 307.²

Should the Parliament sit till June, I have some thoughts of printing my ode upon Rural elegance; together with some such other Pieces as may make a 12 penny pamphlett.³ But if my Purpose continues you will hear from me again soon, & I shall send you up a copy, about half-correct, for your Opinion.

I hope Mʳ Baskerville meets in London with the encouragement he deserves.⁴ I long to hear from you upon all accounts, am, your most affectionate

& most obedient Servant

Will Shenstone

184. To LADY LUXBOROUGH¹

The Leasowes, March the 29. 1755

DEAR MADAM,

It was not before yesterday that I receiv'd this Parcell² from Dodsley; & it is with Pleasure I hasten to execute his commission. The several Setts he mentions were bound so much alike, that it was impossible for me to make your Ladyship any *particular* Compliment. The Sett which I have sent, is at least *as* handsome as any; and I cannot pretend to think it *handsomer,* till it has receiv'd your Arms at the Beginning. As to the Share we have in this volume, There is nothing I can well *add* to what I said in my last Letter: This however I would *repeat,* that whatever your Ladyship disapproves may be rectify'd in some future Impression; & that I beg you would in no sort condemn me, 'till you have heard the whole I have to say. The Volume has many good Pieces in it which are new to me; and if some others, perhaps as good, have been printed formerly in Pamphletts, it is allowable enough as it is consistent with Mʳ Dodsley's first Proposal. There is one little Piece which strikes my Fancy greatly. Tis Father Francis's Prayer, in Lord Westmorland's Hermitage. Mʳ Berkley repeated it to me in my Root-house last Summer, and, as I remember, told me it was written by Mʳ West — But I mean to see your

---

² Dodsley replies (B. M. Add. MSS 28959, fol. 42), "Those you enquire after are — Page 73 Soame Jennings Esqr. 114 Mr. Trap. 119 unknown. 170 Mr. Lovibond. 200 Unknown. 202 Unknown. 227 Mr. Dodington. 228 Unknown. 233 Dr. Grainger. 250 Unknown. 253 Mr. T. Warton. 265 Mr. West. 267 Mr. Moore. 305 and 307 Mr. Parrat."

³ See Letter 181, n8.

⁴ Of this project, probably the edition of Virgil published in 1757, Dodsley says, "Mr. Baskerville's Specimen is much approv'd, & he has met with great Encouragement at both the Universities" (B. M. Add. MSS 28959, fol. 42).

¹ B. M. Add. MSS 28958, fol. 169ff.

² Containing the fourth volume of Dodsley's *Collection.*

Ladyship soon; I should hope in a Fort-night's time; & shall then find much more Pleasure in discovering my Sentiments on this occasion. On Monday next, I think to write to Mr Dodsley; & am glad of the Liberty you allow me to oblige him with a sight of your Letter.

Thus having at last brought this affair to a conclusion, & being *willing* at least to hope that I have done my Friend some service, I no further concern myself about such Laurels as the World can *bestow* upon me, but fix my Thoughts on such as I can *purchase* at Coventry of Mr Whittingham. I mean that I am daily expecting a score or two from that Quarter, to shade the wretchedness of my Barns & out-houses. The mighty Caesar, whose Head was bald, you know, priz'd Laurels upon such another score; and was not more delighted with any Decree of Senate y^n that which allow'd him to wear a wreath perpetually.

I have receiv'd Mr Outing's Epistle with Pleasure; but as I have nothing to communicate beside what this Letter contains, & as he left it somewhat uncertain whether he should remain at Barrels 'till now, I have not indeed wrote, but am entirely at his Service. It is a prodigious long time since I heard any thing of Mrs Davis: I should be oblig'd if your Ladyship w^d give me some Intelligence concerning her. Governor Hylton, as Mr Outing styles him, has gott Possession of his Castle. But as a Sportsman *buys* Game and then pretends that he *shott* it, or as Pyrrhus *bought* Towns & then boasted that he *took* them, Even so — Plain enough does it appear to me that he has given his tenant a year's rent to which he had no sort of Pretensions; and that in the making of this *separate* Treaty he has had no regard to the satisfaction of me his Friend and *Ally* — He has of late given away his Kettel; but this upon such terms as to leave me quite uncertain, whether Mrs Stanton, when she *sold* Him the Horse, us'd him worse, than He has done his Landlady when he *made her* a *Present* of Him. Notwithstanding all this, He shall accompany me to Barrels; & is perhaps more likely to do so, now this *Shadow* of a Horse is remov'd.

Your Ladyship bids me scatter Flowers upon the road I have to pass. Do you not here, in other words, bid me be happy, & be well? I am sure at least you *wish* me so; but as there [are] Few in comparison, that equal you in Point of Genius, there are I think *almost* as Few y^t equal you in Point of Spirits. Let me add, that, Universal *Chearfullness* is the Gift of Nature only, and is worth every other advantage that she or Fortune can bestow. I am ever, Madam,

   Your Ladyship's most oblig'd & most obedient Servant,
                Will: Shenstone

I do not think it quite fair for me to take advantage of Dodsley's offer; but If I should cause Him to give any other sett away He should, I think, present one to Lord Grey.

Y^r Ladyship will please to return me Dodsley's Letter.

185. To JOHN SCOTT HYLTON[1]

April [1] 1755

I desire my Compliments to Mr Hylton; & am tolerably well: Have however taken a second Purge to-day, & intend to take another on Friday, by which means I hope to acquire at least a little more agility for ye ensuing Spring, y^n has been my Lot this Winter — Many thanks for ye Picture which (wth ye exception of one or two Faults) is in ye main a very laudable Performance. — You do right to keep Robin in constant employ — Priest brought 4 loads of Lime & I sent him positive orders to take you two of them to Lapell; which he as positively refus'd to do — I went to him in a sort of Pett; but upon his assuring me y^t he would take you some in a day or two, & upon hearing a very good Character of his Honesty, was induc'd to let him have his way — w^ch *possibly* too, I could not have *prevented*. You do right in planting Poplars, if you can find them suitable Places: I must myself put a Period to my Plantation for this Season; & endeavour to get my Walks in some sort of order to be exhibited — As far as I can find, their new Chancel at Hagley is a mere Mausoleeum; & contains such a *Display* of Pedigree &c: as one w^d think must prove invidious to ye last Degree — I will tell you more of it w^n I see you.[2] Mr Kendall brought some company here yesterday, from whom I gain'd my Intelligence — Adieu.

Young Lea call'd on me yesterday on his Way to London; where he is to be ordain'd on Sunday next, & after that go on board ye Ship that is appointed for him. He apologiz'd for not calling on you, & desired me to make his Compliments.

---

[1] B. M. Add. MSS 27548, fol. 24ff. The beginning of this letter may be wanting; the first page preserved is marked 2; the letter nevertheless seems complete, by context. The letter is dated April, 1755; April 1 is written at the right in another hand.

[2] As I understand, ye Dean & all ye living Part of the Family have their arms there, distinct; with their Names &c: beneath. [Shenstone]

186. To RICHARD JAGO[1]

The Leasowes, April 3, 1755

DEAR MR. JAGO,

I have so long expected the favour of a few lines from you, that I begin at last to question whether you received the letter I sent you. It was inclosed in one to Mr. M[iller], whom I requested to further it with all convenient expedition. I am neither able to recollect the whole contents of it; nor indeed, if I *were,* could I endure the thoughts of transcribing them. The chief intention of it, however, was to acquaint you of Mr. H——'s unhappy delay in the delivery of that letter with which you favoured me from Radway.

What confirms me in a suspicion that my last letter miscarried is, that Mr. Wren lately acquainted me of your being at Wroxall upon business, and of your making some slight mention of Mr. Dodsley's publication, without intimating that you discovered any design you had of writing to me. This is mere preamble and stuff: implying nothing more than the desire I have to *hear* from you, when it ought also to express how impatiently I long to *see* you. Worldly concerns and my winterly state of health have detained me at home for these many months past: worldly concerns may have confined you likewise; but as your health and spirits are universally better than mine, and as you have much less dislike to travelling than myself, I would hope that my absence from Harbury will never cause you to *neglect* any *opportunity* of coming hither. For my own part, I have been meditating upon a visit to you all this winter; and do, at this time, resolve most strenuously to perform it before June. But the many such schemes of pleasure in which I have been disappointed are a sort of check upon my expressions, and make me promise with *fear.* As to Dodsley's performance, which you must have received before this time, I will make no observations till I have the pleasure of seeing you: and yet there are many points I would discuss, and many accounts I want to give you. So many indeed, that they would furnish out perhaps a superficial drawling letter; but would serve infinitely better for conversation, with the book before us. The volume, I am told, is well received in town; though political intelligence must engross much of its present attention.

Mr. Hylton is in my neighbourhood, and upon the point of settling at his farm. Could you possibly spend a week with us, we would try to make it agreeable. At all events, I beg to hear from you; and that, not merely as it will afford me great pleasure, but as, at the same time, it will

[1] Dodsley, *Letters to Particular Friends,* No. LXXXIV.

ease me of some solicitude. I will not make this a long letter, though I wish to receive a long one in return; having a head very little qualified to add anything that may amuse you, though a heart very sincerely and affectionately at your service.

W. Shenstone

187. To RICHARD GRAVES [1]

The Leasowes, April 4, 1755

DEAR MR. GRAVES,

You will be harrassed with my letters till you condemn my excessive leisure as loudly as I have lamented that you should ever feel the *want* of it. Nor is it a point so easily decided *which* of us may be the greater *sufferer;* you through my *officiousness,* or I by your long *silence*. Yet the partiality which you have ever shewn me will, I think, dispose you to receive my letters more patiently than it is in my power to sustain the loss of *yours*. After all, I should not write at present, but that the Miscellanies with which Dodsley compliments us arrived last week at The Leasowes. I desire therefore you would acquaint me, whether the sett that he means for you should remain here till your arrival; or if you chuse that I should send it by the Birmingham-stage to Bath. Having made this enquiry, I was thinking to conclude; but cannot reconcile myself to the *novelty* of sending *you* three empty pages. The Parliament will rise too soon for the publication of my "Rural Elegance;" and having performed my promise to Dodsley, I think no more about such *laurels* as the *public* can bestow upon me, but am giving all my attention to such as I can purchase of my nursery-man. I wish, however, that the volume may recompense Dodsley for his trouble: I may also add, for his ingenuity, and for his politeness in giving each of us a compleat sett. They are elegantly bound, and all as much alike as possible.

The present crisis of state-affairs does not seem to favour his publication, as the attention of the public must lean greatly to that quarter. I saw a letter from Sir William M[eredyth] (who corresponds with Lady Luxborough), which placed the struggles of the ministry in a clearer light than they had yet appeared to me. It seems that persons of all denominations are for carrying on the war with vigour; and the King's application for a Vote of Credit was received with general approbation. The zeal of the Parliament was indeed so remarkable on this occasion, that, instead of the 600,000*l.* at first intended, it was thought proper to propose a million. But the services were ascertained, and the Chancellor of the Exchequer made accountable for the application of it. The aug-

---

[1] Dodsley, *Letters to Particular Friends,* No. LXXXVI.

mentation of the fleet with 20,000 seamen; the raising 5000 marines on a plan of dividing them into small companies, which will render them more useful both by sea and land; the completion and reinforcement of the Irish regiments; are the uses to which this million is to be appropriated. Mr. Fox and his land-war-party sat mute, whilst Mr. Legge with great openness and perspicuity explained the present schemes; as they were calculated to exert our whole strength at sea, and, if possible, no where else. Mr. Dodington, who, it seems, has not spoke of many years, charmed every body. His wit did not only entertain, but animate and affect his hearers. *"It were better,* he said, *than lose the dominion of the Ocean, that the Ocean should overwhelm us: for what Briton could wish to leave a posterity crawling upon this island, only to feel the tyranny, and swell the victories of France?"* It seems, F[ox], in his opposition to the Duke of Newcastle, is supported by the Duke of Cumberland, his army, and the Scotch: that the ministry (or the D. of N——'s party) seem not displeased with a prospect of uniting with the Tories, who now hold the balance; and it seems the Tories, by Sir William's letter, are as little displeased to unite with the ministry.

You will guess that good part of this political account is *transcribed;* and you will guess aright. I had some thoughts that it might amuse you, and had no occasion to use other expressions. — Let me now, once more, return to the futile objects of my *own* amusement. The impression upon this letter will be taken from my new seal. The motto that I have pitched upon is, SUPEREST MEMORIA: though I yet retain some hankering after the single word PRAETERITIS. Probably this, however, is not the last seal that I shall cause this man to cut in steel. The altar is not yet finished: ANTE OMNIA MUSAE; but it does not quite satisfy me. — I will inclose the two last letters I received from Mr. Dodsley; but you must not think I build too much upon any compliment which he there makes me. — It is true, I think him a very sincere man; but he cannot have been conversant so long with modern-writers, but he must conjecture, when their piece is published, that they a little hunger for applause. I am now uncertain whether you will receive a letter from him; as he has, unaccountably I think, sent your books *hither,* and not to Bath. I am, however, fully satisfied, that your first and last pieces, more *especially,* do credit to his collection, and must please all persons of taste.

I desire my best respects to Mrs. Graves, who will be pleased to see the affection that subsists betwixt you perpetuated. She will also feel some satisfaction in the professions of friendship that are made you by your most affectionate and faithful humble servant,

W. Shenstone

188. To LADY LUXBOROUGH[1]

The Leasowes, April 17th 1755

DEAR MADAM,

Tho' I have nothing to communicate which can prove the least entertaining, yet it is expedient that I should return Sir William Meredyth's Letter, lest I should any way appear ingratefull for the Pleasure it afforded me. The Disputes of Senators, the Division & subdivision of Parties are for the most part as little *known* to me, as what passes in the Star *Aldebaran*. I will not confess that I am as indifferent concerning them: my Ignorance not so properly arising from the want of publick spirit, as from a voluntary Inattention to matters I can no way influence. However a little first-rate Intelligence, at Intervals, affords me Pleasure; & Sir William's Letter, being entirely of that sort, has given me a *Competent* knowledge of what is doing at the Helm. I do entirely think with your Ladyship that the Ministry should take advantage of the national Ardor to make now a very vigorous effort at Sea. I have no Reasons to give but what are obvious to all the world; yet reasons of this kind are sometimes not the weakest — Since the arrival of your Letter I have had *other* fresh Intelligence, that the Ministry, if they can possibly avoid it, will make no war at *All*.

I have not heard from Mr Dodsley since I wrote to you last. Indeed I did not write to *Him* before last Monday, when I convey'd to him your Thanks & compliments in your Ladyship's own Hand-writing. I then wrote also to Mr Arne; whom I requested to *compleat* the musick to my Pastoral.[2] But as I offer'd him no *Money,* & have no hopes of prevailing but by Dint of *Complaisance,* it is possible, nay probable, that He may not comply.

Mr Giles, who cuts my seal, is a most exquisite Hand in *Steel*. I shall soon, I hope, be able to give you a better Impression; but am not myself yet master of the method by which he gives them upon Bark. Tis somehow done with the stroke of a Hammer, & of Consequence hardly practicable after the Seal has been Sett. 'Tis to be observ'd also that common Clay is a yet better material; as I can sufficiently demonstrate when occasion serves.

Did your Ladyship ever see the four Roman Ruins publish'd by Arthur Pond. They cost me twelve Shillings. I caus'd Aris to procure them for me, & have ask'd Mr Hylton to colour them. You cannot conceive the magnificence of their effect in a Camera.

[1] B. M. Add. MSS 28958, fol. 171ff. To this letter Lady Luxborough replies with one of April 27, 1755 (*Letters,* No. CXX), the date of which is thus confirmed.
[2] Arne had already written a page of music for Shenstone's *Pastoral Ballad;* it was published (as was the *Ballad*) in the fourth volume of Dodsley's *Collection.*

The weather is beginning to amend, & promises a pretty forward Spring. I hope your Ladyship will reap the Benefit both in Point of Health & Pleasure. I exhibited my Place to some Company yesterday, which is the first time I have done so ever since last November.

Lord Dudley remains in Town — I feel myself grow dull, & will therefore bring my Letter to a conclusion whilst I am *aware* of it. Your Ladyship will present my Compliments to Mr Holyoak & his Family, & believe me to be ever

Your most oblig'd & most obedient H. Servant

Will Shenstone

189. To JOHN SCOTT HYLTON[1]

3 May 1755

My Service to Mr. Hylton, & desire he would prescribe some such Medicine as He thinks proper for Tom[2] to take. His Costiveness, want of Spitting, & the Coldness of ye Weather do not suffer Him to mend, & yet any very strong evacuant would weaken him too much. He wishes for something to make him spit; but as this evacuation is more difficult to produce than others, even [whe]ther He should not principally take some thing modern laxative & Diuretick. His Liver seems to be affected full as much as his Lungs: His Cough shakes Him to Pieces; These Complaints he has long undergone, And yet with some Assistance from Medicine his abstemiousness has preserv'd, & I hope will preserve his Life.

have sent y^r Pharmacopeia.   W. S.

190. To LADY LUXBOROUGH[1]

The Leasowes, May the 14th 1755

DEAR MADAM,

Appearances are much against me; and if your Ladyship be inclin'd to *trust* them, I do not doubt but at this time I lye under your Displeasure — Yet were I to relate but one Half of my story, I could sure turn every part of your *Disgust* into *Compassion*. For were I to relate *Half,* your *Penetration* would guess the *rest,* & I am sure you are too much my Friend not to sympathize in my Distresses. What I allude to here is my vexatious Dispute with little Dolman.[2] For, what betwixt

---

[1] This letter came up for sale at Hodgson's, London, July 25, 1933, and was bought by Mr. Spenser of New Oxfordshire, who kindly permitted a transcript to be made.

[2] Shenstone's servant.

[1] B. M. Add. MSS 28958, fol. 173ff.

[2] See above, Letter 168 and note 2 thereto.

his own Perverseness & the Insidiousness of his Attorney, I ought to be —somewhat else than what I am, to cope with them. When I wrote to your Ladysp. last, a Negotiation was upon the Carpet, & proposals passing on each side. In the midst of this, & without ye least Notice, They abruptly caus'd my *answer* to be demanded in Chancery. The Consequences of *delaying* this may be disagreeable to the last degree; And I do not question but this little Fellow may have malignity enough to cut my throat. At least his Behaviour of late makes me think so, who in return for such Services as he could not easily requite, has offer'd me such Injuries as he cannot possibly compensate — This is Truth; & my Embarrassment must be my Excuse for the Present, & God knows how much longer. Mr Hylton when he writes, shall give your Ladyship concurrent evidence. He indeed is now become the perfect "Squire of Dames" & has been in constant Employment ever since my Lord's Family arriv'd.

The Letter I enclose is one of the politest I have yet receiv'd from Mr Dodsley; & I take it for granted y^t I do no wrong in shewing it. All His last Letters to me remain at present unanswer'd: So do many Overtures of Friendship from Persons I respect: Lord Stamford sent his Compliments as he *went up* to London, & I promis'd to wait on Him the Moment He came down. He return'd back to Enfield with his Family last Sunday, sent three Servants with a Request that a Sir Harry (Somebody) might see ye new Cascade — I am much in ye same situation with regard to Mr Davenport & Mr Dean — Do not imagine, I beg your Ladyship, that I speak this out of *Vanity* — I wish I was as guiltless of every sin, as I am of Vanity, *at this time* — But rather observe, y^t I am quite a stranger to every Pleasurable Hope or Purpose, &, for this reason only, defer the mention of ye visit I would make at Barrels — My Walks are indeed pleasant, for any One besides myself: I hope your Ladyship's afford *you* the same Pleasure they do to others.

Mr Clare, whom you have heard mention'd by Mr Chambers of Kidderminster, is made Deputy-Cofferer in ye Place of Mr W. Lyttelton — This affords me some surprise, not only ye offer, but ye Acceptance — Admiral Smith is yet in Town, & in case of war proclaim'd, which may not be the Case, will be sent, it is reported, with an honorable Command to the West-Indies. Sir George Lyttelton comes down in June, & his Chancel-window is compleated. Perhaps in some future Letter I may give a Description of this Chancel — But what talk I of future Letters, when if my Dispute should happen to be ended, I should immediately fly to wait on y^u in Person? M^r & Mrs Graves are to arrive here next saturday Se'n night — I could not bear to *decline* a visit which is offer'd me so very seldom, else am I greatly apprehensive that I shall be ill at Leisure to receive them.

I am moreover under a Promise to accompany them to Barrels — God grant yt Events may prove happier y{n} I foresee! 'Tis all I can say at present — I must needs see Guy-cliff.

I am with unvaried respect & gratitude
Your Ladyships most oblig'd
W. Shenstone

191. To MR. B———[1]

The Leasowes, Oct. 1755

DEAR MR. B———,

The affectionate Letter I received from you ought to have been answered by the next Post; it had been so, if I had pursued the Dictates of a Heart, I will not say, altogether happy in our Reconciliation, but more properly in the Manifestation of our ever-undivided Friendship. I have had a large Conflux of Visitants this Summer, and the Dissipation they have occasioned me, was for the most Part very agreeable. But it must not be by any Accession of *Pleasure,* that I attempt to excuse my unseasonable Neglect of writing; for Pleasure I have in writing to my Friends, when my Mind is free from Anxiety, and that Pleasure connected with a Duty I owe to Friendship, superior to what is claimable by any mere Visitant or Acquaintance; yet I cannot but confess the Change which a very few Years have wrought in me; for surely it is not long since I wearied you, and the rest of my Correspondents, with my *Assiduity;* where I now write *one* Letter, I then wrote *twenty:* mean while, the Warmth of my Heart is not diminished, with regard to Friendship; I know it from the Pleasure which the Receipt of your Letter gave me. Of this Kind are the only Pleasures which accompany us through Life; they encrease upon Repetition, and grow more lively from Indulgence. "Vient l'Appetit en mangeant," was, I think, an Answer made by a French Courtier to his Sovereign, when it was objected to him by the latter, that there was no End to his Importunities. But whatever odd Instances may be found of a perverted Appetite, the Maxim is only universal, in regard to social Pleasure. The Case is not the same, with regard to Pleasures of Sense; it is not so even with regard to Pleasures of Imagination. Accordingly, though I first embellished my Farm, with an Eye to the Satisfaction I should receive from its Beauty, I am now grown dependent upon the Friends it brings me, for the principal Enjoyment

---

[1] Hull, *Select Letters,* Vol. I, No. LIX. The identity of the addressee must for the present remain a matter for conjecture. It might be Robert Binnel.

it affords; I am pleased to find them pleased, and enjoy its Beauties by Reflection. And thus the durable Part of my Pleasure appears to be, at the last, of the social Kind.

With much Willingness would I have waited upon your Friend Colonel C—— this Year, but for the perplexing Law-Suit[2] in which I am involved with young D[olman]. It has made me rude to my Superiors, deaf to all inviting Offers, and neglectful, at once, to my old Friends and my new. Pray make my Compliments to him, and assure him how sensible I am of the Honour he has done me. Another Year, if I live, will, I hope, make me some Amends for this, by affording me an Opportunity of waiting upon him and you.

Pray also make my Compliments to Mr. and Mrs. P——, and Dr. C——, and my Peace with the *A——n* Family, or any other where you visit, that may mistake Necessity for Disrespect. Above all, recommend me to Mrs. B—— in the best Manner you are able, which, I take it, is by assuring her, that I ever have been, and am, and will be while I live,

Dear Mr. B——, your affectionate Friend,
W. Shenstone

192. To WILLIAM HOLYOAKE[1]

April 21, 1756

DEAR SIR,

It is not easy for me to express how much I think myself obliged to you for the particulars with which you favour'd me on this mournful occasion. I receiv'd only a few lines from Mr. Davies and Mr. Outing, excusing themselves on account of their melancholy situation, that on the loss of so intimate a Friend as Lady Luxborough, one is anxious to become acquainted with every little circumstance that attended it. For this I am indebted to you, Sir, and Mrs. Holyoake: so indeed is every one indebted who wish'd well to Lady Luxborough. For I know of nothing that was so much a ballance for the variety of her affections, as the advantage of two such compassionate and ever hospitable Neighbours. To you she had recourse upon many a severe and pressing occasion, and had great reason to be convinc'd how much preferable your Friendship was to that of the more gay and more capricious world. Even on the last and most important occasion, your best offices were not wanting: and if we consider her advantage merely, I know not whether her best

---

[2] See above, Letter 168 and note 2 thereto; also the preceding letter.
[1] Parson Holyoake wrote Shenstone on March 29, 1756, informing him of Lady Luxborough's death (see her *Letters*, pp. 414–16). Shenstone replied with the present letter, printed in Colvile's *Worthies of Warwickshire*, pp. 488–89, and quoted without the date by Miss Williams in *William Shenstone*, pp. 74–75.

Friends ought to wish her Life prolong'd. Her enjoyments of Life must have diminish'd yet farther, and it is not very improbable that her mortifications would have encreas'd. In regard indeed to ourselves the case is much otherwise; and whatever may be now expended upon embellishments at Barrels, it can hardly ever be, the agreeable object from your House that it has been. I do therefore sincerely condole with you upon the loss of your accomplish'd neighbour, and the loss of all those chearfull ev'nings which we might have expected to pass in her company. But as pleasures of this kind are to be no more our lot at Barrels, let me beg leave to put Mrs. Holyoake in mind of a promise she once made me: the acquittance for which will not be valid, unless deliver'd to her at the Leasowes. On the death of one's Friends, one ever finds a propensity to think on those that remain; let me therefore have ye comfort of considering your Family in that Light, and the pleasure of subscribing myself
    Dear Sir,
        Your ever affectionate, and obliged, humble servant,
                Will Shenstone

193. To RICHARD GRAVES[1]

From Mr. Baskerville's, Birmingham,
July 27, 1756

DEAR MR. GRAVES,

It were needless for me to recommend to you a person whom you so truly esteem as Mr. Dodsley; and from whom you will gladly receive a visit, not more upon *my* account, than upon *his* and your *own*. — All I beg is, that, considering the shortness of his time at Bath, you will be acquainted with him at first sight; which, I think, should ever be a maxim with persons of genius and humanity. — He has made a few days extremely agreeable to me at The Leasowes; has been shewing me his new Tragedy,[2] which I wished you also might peruse. If I be not unaccountably imposed upon by my friendship for the writer, the extraordinary merit of this performance is altogether unquestionable. — I will not inform you through what hands it has passed in town; because I would have you communicate your sentiments to him with entire freedom, being assured the delicacy of them may *yet* be of service, and that the openness with which you communicate them will be infinitely pleasing to Mr. Dodsley. He has done me the honour to ask me for an epilogue: — I *wish*, but *fear* to undertake it. — Should any lucky hint

---

[1] Dodsley, *Letters to Particular Friends*, No. LXXXVII.

[2] *Cleone* (1758). Shenstone and Graves collaborated on the epilogue, as future references in the letters clearly show (see the Index). It was, however, principally the work of Graves.

occur to *you,* I well know how much you are able to manage it to advantage. In that case, I would beg a line from you the first opportunity.— What talk I of a line from you, who am at this very time many letters and apologies in your debt! but I cannot add many syllables to the letter I am writing — I will write again in a few days. Mean time, my compliments to Mrs. Graves; and remember, that Mr. Dodsley and you become well acquainted at first sight.

I am ever, dear Mr. Graves,
Your most affectionate humble servant,
W. Shenstone

194. To TOM SAUNDERS [1]

The *Leasowes, Aug.* 24, 1756

DEAR S[AUNDERS],

I am truly glad to hear of your Reception with our worthy Admiral,[2] to whom I will take the first Occasion of conveying my Acknowledgements. It is not quite clear from your Letter, whether you are Mate or Midshipman; but whatever your Post may be, I hope, and make no Doubt, that you will endeavor to fill it as becomes you. Should you happen to be continued in the Admiral's own Ship, you will have the Honour to serve more immediately under the most generous Man alive; whose Penetration will not suffer any Degree of Merit to escape his Notice, and who will allow yours the more Consideration, on Account of his Regard for me. As the best means, therefore, of promoting your Interests, you will need to concern yourself little further, than to deserve well; and this by an uniform Course of Diligence and Sobriety, by the strictest Attention to Honour and your Duty, and by a Conduct entirely free from all Artifice and Disguise. You have an honest, open Countenance; I do not in the least question that you will verify it in your Behaviour; neither do I drop *any* of these Hints, as though I mistrusted your Conduct; I do unfeignedly believe them to be every one superfluous: however, it may prove a Satisfaction for you to reflect, that the Temper, which I trust is natural to you, is what I think most likely to recommend you to the Admiral. And be assured, that you shall acquire no Reputation in the Service, which shall not be seconded by all the Interest and good Offices of your affectionate Kinsman,

W. Shenstone

[1] Hull, *Select Letters,* Vol. I, No. LX. The identity of the addressee, whom Hull designates merely with the initial S, is a matter of conjecture. I believe him to be Tom Saunders, Shenstone's young relative, to whom he alludes in Letter 224.
[2] Probably Admiral Smith.

195. To WILLIAM LYTTELTON[1]

[Nov. 13, 1756]

SIR,

I cannot proceed to the subject upon which I am requested to write, without availing myself of the occasion it affords me to acknowledge the civilities I received from you in this country. The Book in particular you were so kind to leave me upon your Departure, was the more pleasing instance of your Regard, as it show'd you not wholly indifferent to a Place in my Memory; where you never can exist but amidst Ideas of the utmost Respect, and the most cordial good wishes for your Fortune, Fame and Happiness.

The Person whom I would willingly recommend to your Excellency is a native of the Parish where I live: an Excise-man; his Name Green; of about thirty years of age. Both Sir Thomas Lyttelton and the Dean of Exeter[2] have taken particular Notice of his Brothers, and done them repeated Services. But Sir George Lyttelton's application in the Behalf of *this* young man happened not to prove effectual; neither indeed that of the City of Bristol who had so high an Opinion of his Merit as to petition their Representatives in Parliament for his Advancement.

The Particulars of his past and present situation you will condescend to learn from his own account, on the Truth of which you may depend. He is allow'd by all that know him to be a very honest, sober, diligent and ingenious man; but so depress'd by the continual Inefficacy of the schemes concerted in his Favour, that he has at length chalk'd out one of his own; and, in short, feels a violent Propensity to take his Chance in a Country where Governor Lyttelton presides. What Opportunities you may find of serving him, I am in great measure ignorant; but have Hope y^t occasions are not wanting; at least of rendering his situation more agreeable to *Him* than it is at present. Should This be the case, I flatter myself that you will afford him all the encouragement he may deserve; as you will thereby pursue the dictates of a just and benevolent heart, not uninfluenced by the Share which *I* shall take in the obligation.

I believe you will receive a Letter on the same occasion from Mr Hollier; who is ardently your Well-wisher, and whom, I guess, you will not be unwilling to Oblige.

The situation of our publick affairs you will hear from abler Corre-

---

[1] This letter is reproduced by permission from the original, which is among the Hagley Papers at Hagley Hall, Stourbridge, Worcestershire. The addressee, William Henry Lyttelton, the youngest son of Sir Thomas, and the brother of George and Charles, was Governor of South Carolina from 1756 to 1759.

[2] Charles Lyttelton, then Dean of Exeter, was later Bishop of Carlisle.

spondents. As for me, I am employ'd, as usual, in the little embellishments of my Ferme ornée, from which, during the summer season, I derive much tranquil Amusement. But I cannot avoid wishing *You,* Sir, all the more animated Pleasures of active Life, and all those external Advantages that your just and disinterested Administration will deserve. At least the conscious Reflections that shall succeed it, will hereafter tend more than either Wood or Water-Nymphs to enliven your Retirement.

I am, Sir. with the most *willing* Respect,
Your Excellency's most obligd & most obedient Servt
Will: Shenstone

The Leasowes, Novr 13. 1756

196. To RICHARD JAGO [1]

The Leasowes, Dec. 14, 1756

DEAR MR. JAGO,

Though the silence that has prevailed for so long a time betwixt us be, I fear, to be placed to *my* account, yet do I by no means imagine that you will desire me to fill half this letter with apologies. Suffice it, that I owe all the world, at this time, either letters, visits, or money: yet that my *heart* is as well disposed in each of these respects, as that of any one person who is insolvent. The regard indeed that I owe to you has been a troublesome inmate within my bosom for some time past; making daily remonstrances against the injustice which I have done it; and urging me strenuously to take horse, and make my *personal* apologies at Harbury. — I return you many thanks for Mr. S——'s company, and for the sight of the manuscript which he shewed me. Alas! that I cannot spare money to drain and to improve my lands, or to put almost any part of his excellent rules in execution! and yet that Mr. Childe of Kinlett (hearing my place always termed a *farm*) should come expecting to find all things managed here according to the perfection of *husbandry!* As little *can* I pretend to improve Mr. S——'s treatise, as his treatise *will* my farm: no farther at *most,* than in what regards the *style,* or *plan* of his performance. Yet could I wish to see both *it* and *him* again before he prints it; wishing him all the success which his very *endeavour* deserves. Assuredly the present is not the *time* for his publication: more *immediate* remedies than can be derived from agriculture are become absolutely requisite to relieve the sufferings of this nation. — I should be extremely well-pleased to visit you at Harbury, but cannot even propose to myself

[1] Dodsley, *Letters to Particular Friends,* No. LXXXV.

that happiness at *present;* and were I even to *promise,* have but too much reason to know the *uncertainty* of my *performance.* Yet am I sensible enough we *ought to meet,* if we purpose that what we print should have the advantage of our mutual criticisms. Let me then *conjure* you to come over, at your convenience, for a few days, that we may agree at least upon some *general* points, and make no worse a figure in the future Miscellany than we have done in the foregoing.² — But I have really more things to *say* than I will pretend to *crawl* upon *paper;* nor can I endure to retail a few particulars, while I am impatient to communicate the whole.

Let me acquaint you while I remember, that there is at this time a Mr. Duncombe and his son, clergymen, that are publishing a new translation of Horace.³ Whatever you may think of their *success,* after *Francis,* I believe I may pronounce them men of real merit, and in no wise destitute of learning or genius. They have requested me to communicate any *version* or *imitation* that I can furnish, either of my own or of any friends; wherefore, if you *have* any thing of this sort, I should be glad if you would put it in my power to oblige them. The son has an "Ode to Health"⁴ in the fourth volume of Dodsley's Miscellany.

Under the head of intelligence, I have mighty little to convey. The house at Hagley is in a manner finished, so far as concerns the shell; and wants nothing besides a portico to be as compleat as most in England. — Pray remember me to Mr. Talbot, Mr. Miller, and Mr. Holbeach; should they call upon me next year, they will find my place better worth their notice.

I am and *have* been ever, cordially and most affectionately,

Your most obedient Servant,

W. Shenstone

197. To JOHN SCOTT HYLTON¹

[Jan. 1, 1757]

My Compliments to Mr. Hylton, Mr. Smith's Family, & Company: I drink each of their Health's in a glass of White-wine, & of red — Let them do, as they are done by — I want, (for a particular purpose) a sheet or two of Mr. Hylton's marble-Paper — If he has any, he will not fail to

² See the *Edinburgh Review,* No. 1. [Dodsley]
³ The Duncombes' translation of Horace is reviewed as *The Works of Horace &c.,* by William Duncombe, Esq. and John Duncombe, M. A., in the *Gentleman's Magazine* for June, 1759, p. 287. The second of the two volumes comprising the work was advertised in the magazine for May (Register of Books, p. 233).
⁴ John Duncombe's *Ode to Health* appears, as Shenstone says it does, in Dodsley's *Collection,* Vol. IV (pp. 268–70 in the edition of 1770).
¹ Boston Public Library, Ch. G. 13. 45. Only the fragment as given is preserved.

send it — Messieurs Green, (Amos)² Wood, . . .³ but I will promise they shen [*sic*] end in nothing but Good-will — I believe yt He & I, (as well as all other Sensible men) agree in our real Sentiments, & only differ in Expression — My Turkey? &c: goes to Mr. Dodsley's tomorrow afternoon — if Mr. Hylton have any Commands, I will obey them, in my Letter —

Jan: ye first — 1757   Will. Shenstone

198. To JOHN SCOTT HYLTON¹

[Jan. 19, 1757]

My Compliments to Mr Hylton; & desire to know in what manner he has pass'd his Day — Mr Hollier, notwithstanding weather & Roads, came to dine here — Mrs Southall here also — Old Master Wight, and a Tenant from Clent — My Head in much disorder, & my Spirits wholly unfit for ye Overtures of accommodation I am to make Mr D. tomorrow — To-morrow indeed I am to *send* 'em, but it is on *Friday* yt he dines with Mr Hollier — At ye same time I think it requisite to see Mr Millward,² *previously* — & this can only be to-morrow — So let me beg yr Prayers as for a Person troubled in Mind, Body, & Estate. — I will concur in any thing you think rational for ye Service of Haycock — I see I have forgotten my *third* Person, so may as well proceed in ye Second — I deem'd it no way improbable yt you would have thought it a proper thing to spend a Night with Dr Wall — His Conversation, at *least,* wd have rewarded you. — Mrs Southwell acquaints me yt Lord Dudley receives a weekly Paper, he knows not from whom; but wch Mrs Rock imagines to be sent by *Some* one, in mere Deference to my Lord's Dignity — Can you guess wt this Paper is, or may be — ? Assuredly, none other yn *the world* wch appertains to *me* — Oh that infernal old Hag, ye Post-woman! But let me *suspend* my Rage, 'till I am convinc'd, past all *Doubt* — Thus has my Pen run on, (like a Person yt out-rides

---

² Shenstone's punctuation is here slightly confusing. "Amos" pretty evidently goes with "Green" rather than with "Wood," and the reference is apparently to Amos Green, the Birmingham painter whom Shenstone knew and befriended (see the Index).

³ The manuscript is defective here.

¹ This letter is reproduced from a holograph (fol. 59ff) in the Watson Collection deposited in the National Library of Scotland, Edinburgh.

² An interesting though obscure instance of Shenstone's philanthropy, connected with the name of Mr. Milward, is found in the following note (B. M. Add. MSS 28959, fol. 55): "The Bearer M. Rice has a number of Children, & One whom I would recommend to Ld Foleys Hospital — I believe him in no way disqualify'd, to be a proper object of Charity & should be glad if he could be sent as one for the Choice of the Masters. If you or Mr Cor can be of any service in ye affair, I should be at all times ready to acknowledge my Share of ye Obligation."

his Horse,) and with much bustle produces nothing more yⁿ an assurance of ye Cordiality wth wch I am — Mr Hylton's most obedient

Write me a few Lines, if you are able —   W. S.
Jan: 19. 1757

199. To RICHARD GRAVES [1]
The Leasowes, Mar. 7, 1757

DEAR MR. GRAVES,

I have passed a very dull and unamusive winter here — the worse, for being neither *disposed* nor *qualified* to keep up a correspondence with my friends; with *you,* among the *chief;* and yet it is upon you that I must depend to make up my deficiences with Mr. Dodsley. — The poor man has been afflicted with the most *lasting* fit of the gout he ever underwent before. His patience, on these occasions, is inimitable. — His excursion to the *Regions of Terror and Pity*[2] is not the only instance of his ability to compose verses in the midst of pain. When he sent me a copy of it, he let me know, that he had transmitted another to you by the same post: I should be glad to receive your remarks upon it, ere I communicate my own. I have, for some weeks past, found my head so terribly confused, that it has been with difficulty I could *think* or *express* myself on the most superficial topic. I hope, in a little time, to be able to examine it more attentively than I can at present: yet, in the mean while, must acknowledge, that I think his subject capable of furnishing extraordinary beauties for an Ode: and *such,* I think, he should *call* it; dropping the narrative parts and the connexions as much as possible. I cannot wish him to print it without very *material* alterations, and what would occasion almost the same trouble as it would require to *new-write* it. I do not mean this as a condemnation of what he has already done, so much as a proof of my opinion how much he will be able to improve it. *After all,* it will scarce affect me half so much as his Tragedy. He is so *honest* a man, that the work he has to give the world is much better than the specimen: or, to borrow an idea from my *situation,* the grain that he has to deliver will prove much better than the sample. It is with shame I acknowledge I have not yet sent him his epilogue; and I feel the greater compunction of mind upon this score, as it is possible he may impute my neglect to Garrick's refusal of his play. This weighs nothing with you

---

[1] Dodsley, *Letters to Particular Friends,* No. LXXXVIII.

[2] Dodsley's ode *Melpomene, or the Regions of Terror and Pity,* which Shenstone saw in manuscript, was issued anonymously in November, 1757; the *Gentleman's Magazine* lists the ode in the Register of Books for November and December, 1757. See Straus, *Robert Dodsley,* pp. 212-17.

or me; a thousand motives may affect a Manager, that have little or nothing to do with the merit of the performance; yet he may so far thank Mr. Garrick, that whatever his refusal takes from the *reputation* of his Tragedy, it will, through Dodsley's industry, add apparently to its value. I have not yet been able to satisfy myself with every part of your epilogue, and must either omit sending it at present, or must send him an imperfect copy. If you write to him, let me beg you to give the most favourable account you *can* of me.

Somebody acquainted me (I think it was Mr. Talbot) that your old friend Ballard had bequeathed you his coins for a legacy. I was truly glad to hear it; but have wondered since, that you never once informed me of so considerable an acquisition.

I remember a poem of yours, called ——, upon the present taste in gardening; which you will not wonder if my late employments make me wish once more to see. Be so kind as to send me a copy of this, as well as of any other little pieces that you have in your bureau. Some of yours deserve a better place than what is assigned them in the Magazine. In particular, I remember that upon Enigmas, and Mopsy. Be assured, I will make no *use* of *any* without your previous consent. You know, I suppose, that Dodsley's other Miscellanies do not appear before next winter. — I received from him, together with his Ode, a few Elegies published by Mr. Whitehead.[3] They are, I think, worth your perusal; and designed by my worthy friend to excite my emulation. Alas! that I am so ill able to deserve the encouragements which I receive from him!

My neighbour Baskerville, at the close of this month, publishes his fine edition of Virgil.[4] It will, for *type* and *paper,* be a perfect curiosity. He follows the Cambridge edition.

What think you of their management in regard to Mr. Byng?[5] I cannot help thinking the King should *pardon* him. The Court-martial, by acquitting him of cowardice or disaffection, have left no *motive* for his *negligence,* beside an *error of his judgment:* for we *cannot* impute it to *supineness, indifference,* or *inattention*. And then to sentence a man for error, is to expect infallibility. That twelfth article of war is most undoubtedly ill expressed. — Pray do not forget my best respects to Mrs. Graves. Let me hear from you soon, and believe me ever yours,

W. Shenstone

[3] Whitehead's *Elegies: with an Ode to the Tiber* (published by Dodsley), noticed in the *Gentleman's Magazine,* Register of Books, April, 1757.
[4] John Baskerville (1706–75), the famous printer, published his first work, a quarto edition of Virgil, in 1757.
[5] The *Gentleman's Magazine* for April, 1757, pp. 173–76, carried a full account of the case of Admiral Byng, his alleged misconduct, his trial, sentence, and execution.

200. To RICHARD GRAVES[1]

The Leasowes, April 8, 1757

DEAR MR. GRAVES,

What remarks I had to make upon our friend Dodsley's Ode,[2] I sent him the last post. I would gladly have occasioned them to pass by Claverton; but, having delayed them so long, I was impatient to convince him that I had not *wholly* disregarded his request. They are indeed pretty copious: and yet I have reserved to myself the privilege of re-criticising when I see his altered copy. I recommended to him the addition which you proposed, and some others; and if he will but take the pains that I have chalked out for him, I doubt not that he will render it an excellent Ode, though he may not find it a very *popular* one. I have also sent him a copy of our epilogue,[3] not much different from what you saw; to these I added my little Ode on Lady Luxborough's furnishing her library,[4] and Perry's Verses upon the Malvern-waters. At the close of these last, there appears (with Perry's approbation), a short address to Dr. Wall of Worcester;[5] a very eminent physician, and the great patron of this mineral, who has promoted a subscription in the county towards *building,* near this well, for the accommodation of strangers.

I purpose also to give Dodsley the little Ode I inclose; and would beg the favour of you to advise me concerning the additional stanzas, to fix the readings in the rest, and to return me the copy.

I come now to analyze your remark on Ballard's legacy; which is indeed very ingenious, but will scarce bear examination; nor do I think that you rather wish to have *found* that set of medals, than to have them *given* you by a deceased friend. Assuredly, if we do not allow pleasure to be *predominant* in this kind of melancholy, we destroy the foundation of all tragic or elegiac writings; Melpomene has no place amongst the Muses; and the pains that we have taken with our friend Dodsley's pensive Ode have been employed to no purpose. But you want not these pedantic flourishes, and are wholly of my mind.

Martin's Magazine is, I believe, pretty obscure; and I wonder where you got a sight of it. It was, however, fortunate enough for *me* that you

---

[1] Dodsley, *Letters to Particular Friends*, No. LXXXIX.
[2] *Melpomene*, published anonymously in November, 1757. See the preceding letter and note 2 thereto.
[3] To Dodsley's tragedy *Cleone*, which Shenstone and Graves apparently did in collaboration.
[4] Dated 1738 in Shenstone's *Works*, I (1764), 133ff.
[5] Dr. John Wall (1708–76) practised medicine in Worcester between 1736 and the year of his death. Perry's verses are entitled *Malvern Spa* (1757). They are inscribed to Dr. Wall and found in Volume V of Dodsley's *Collection*.

gave no copy of "James Dawson."⁶ I never yet saw your verses *on that Grotto,* or from *Phaedrus,* and I want to see your W—— once more, concerning which you are silent. Your "Pepper-box" and "Mopsy" might, I think, appear in Dodsley's Miscellany, either *with* or *without* your name. I also want a copy of your verses upon Riddles; and whenever you have a leisure hour, should be glad if you would look them out and send them.

Go and think yourself an happy man; at least, if your children be recovered, as I am inclined to think they are: and give my service to Mrs. Graves, for the happiness that she occasions you; of which I cannot but partake, being, with constant and sincere affection, your most obliged humble servant,

W. Shenstone

201. To JOHN SCOTT HYLTON[1]

[May 21, 1757]

I desire my Compliments to Mr Hylton, & that he wou'd send me a Purge — I think, of Manna & Crem: of tartar.

Yesterday I had Mr James Pixell; & after him, Captⁿ Wight, who kept me up 'till about eleven — However in yᵉ afternoon I sent to enquire after Lᵈ Dudley's[2] health, & whether they expected Dr Wall to make a *second* visit at the Grange. The Latter I did, at Mrs Fieldhouse's request; but it seems they do not expect him, unless they send a purpose. Prehaps, My Lᵈ's Disorder was an apoplexy, which makes me think his Indisposition was *once before* of yᵉ same Sort — Could Mr Hylton contrive, or could I help him to contrive a second Visit from yᵉ Doctor — for yᵉ general Advantage, for unless Mr Hylton find himself better to-morrow, I woud wish *him* to take advice as well as Mrs Fieldhouse.

Cum omnia sint in incerto, fare Tibi

Will: Shenstone

21 May 1757

I have been greatly feverish, & out of order, all to-day; Mr Barker found me very unfit to receive him, but I gave him an Invitation to see the Leasowes at a better time. Since they went, I had James & Evers; on yᵉ Subject of yᵉ Captain's building; & thus betwixt one thing or another my spirits have been wholly dissipated. Adieu.

---

⁶ Shenstone's *Jemmy Dawson, a Ballad; Written about the Time of His Execution, in the Year 1745,* in *Works,* I (1764), 185–88.

[1] This letter is printed from a photostat in the manuscript collection of the New York Public Library. The original was the property of the Author's Club of New York City until sold at auction by the American Art Association, New York City, April 24, 1935.

[2] Lord Dudley died in 1757.

202. To JOHN SCOTT HYLTON[1]

11 Aug. 1757

Our Compliments to Mr Hylton — who will be so good as Let me know how far John Taylor has proceeded with Mr Dean's Case — (He seems extremely angry, y^t it is defer'd —) We want also to hear how the Bodies of the Darbies are to be dispos'd of — I *mean* principally, *where*.

Will Mr Hylton be so good as Look *himself,* or Lend *me Books* to Examine, how far ye word dicat or dat, dicat &c: may be us'd (wth Authority) without an accusative Case after it; to intimate ye thing inscrib'd — I am forc'd, thro hurry of servants to send Will back with this, & to desire he may return again when he shall be immediately dispatch'd to Birm. Mr Dodsley is writing for ye Post —

We met Mr Knight & a flashy West Indian (one Mr Marchant) at the Inn at Enville — went to Worfield in ye Evening, where we found Mr Davenp^t gone to Breden; lay there; din'd yesterday wth the same Gent^{men} at Hagley; saw ye House agⁿ & Park; & returnd home pretty late — I expect ye same Gent. wth others about 5 this afternoon; when we shall be glad of Mr H.'s Company. What a Metamorp: at ye Grange!

W.S.

Did Mr Hylton steal any of Mr Dodsley's Fables — He misses his Earthquake & Thunderstorm, & (as he thinks) some one besides.

203. To JOHN SCOTT HYLTON[1]

Augst 18th 1757

Our Compliments to Mr Hylton — We are inclin'd to think y^e *Time* He should pitch upon for his Eclogue should be y^t of Montezuma's Death or then-abouts. That the Speakers should deplore the revolution in their affairs & alternately, recollect ye prodigies &c: preceding ye appearance of ye Spaniards: should describe the Light in wch their artillery Shipping &c: appeard to them &c &c: and that in ye Course of the Dialogue should be interspers'd *continual* allusions to ye particularities of their Country; whether in regard to Dress — Fruits, Diet, Customs &c &c: In short Mr H. is to remember y^t the Beauty of his Eclogue must turn upon American Peculiarities —

W.S.

---

[1] B. M. Add. MSS 27548, fol. 26ff.
[1] B. M. Add. MSS 27548, fol. 28.

204. To JOHN SCOTT HYLTON[1]

[Oct. 31, 1757]

My Compliments to Mr Hylton — I have been a good deal indispos'd to-day — The Bells, it was affirm'd, rung for Harry Smiths Peerage (tho' in reality it was only for ye marriage of Miss Harley) — At noon Mrs Southwell came & din'd with me; soon after w^{ch}, arriv'd Mr Knight of Woverley, whom I attended round my Farm. In ye morning also I saw Mr Hollier, who scarce thinks my L^d's estate will pay Legacies & Interest of Money — I am now alone, very dull & dispirited, but am going to peruse Mrs Jones's[2] writings, whose *Prose* at least, is very lively & entertaining; some of her Verses also, very spirited — I rec^d ye enclos^d from Giles, & this Letter as I suppose from y^r Brother —

31 Oct:r 1757   Will: Shenstone

205. To ROBERT DODSLEY[1]

Tuesday, Decr 21, 1757

DEAR SIR,

I receiv'd your Letter this morning to my no small Confusion — Yet blame I *no* one beside myself; or rather that Incapacity I feel for *Criticism*, which alone can make me wish, in any sort, desire to delay your publication. When I sent my last Packet, I purpos'd by ye next post to explain the uses for which it was intended — I have *not* done so — have not been *able* to do so — & *now* am *surpriz'd* to find y^t another Sheet is gone to the Press for According to ye Construction I put upon y^r last Letter, I thought it might not be altogether too *late,* if I regulated ye whole by X^{tmas} I hope y^e *Elegy* is not yet begun in Sheet B.; & even thus, if it were not inconvenient to stop ye press a little, I would rather it were done, yⁿ otherwise. I think to write again, & have reserv'd my *only* Frank, for to-morrow — Mean time I give you my Thoughts in regard to ye Compositions *your Letter mentions*. In ye Ode to Health, I could propose no better word yⁿ *falling* instead of *mouldering;*[2] & if you happen to prefer y^e *Latter,* I will by no means disagree with you.

In regard to the Song "I told my nymph" I desire y^t you would follow *all* ye readings you propose. The same, as to ye Compliment 1743. As to ye Ode 1739, I am neither wholly satisfyd with y^r reading or my *own.* However; does not Aid in ye first Line *run* better yⁿ Charms? Love's

---

[1] This letter is reproduced from a holograph in the Watson Collection deposited in the National Library of Scotland, Edinburgh.
[2] This obscure person was perhaps the Mary Jones whose *Miscellanies in Verse and Prose* (1752) and *Poems* (1753) were published by Robert Dodsley. I have not seen her work.
[1] B. M. Add. MSS 28959, fol. 87ff.
[2] "Mouldering" was kept. See Dodsley's *Collection,* Vol. V.

imperial pow'r was known is flat, & Love *here* is a *Person,* tho' a *Passion* in yͤ 5ᵗʰ Line — But I leave you to *penetrate* my reasons, why I propose yͤ following alterations, for yʳ Choice.³

I

'Twas not by Beauty's aid alone
fancy'd
That Love usurpd his airy throne
fancy'd
His magic powr displayd
His tyrant sceptor swayd
improve
A mutual kindness must conspire⁴

II

'Twas not thro Beauty's aid alone
That Love's insidious pow'r was known
  Or ever breast, betrayd
A mutual kindness &c:

I think yͤ *second* preferable; as "insidious" suits better with *"betrayd"* in yͤ *next* Line, & not wᵗʰ "was known" in *this.* The *"betray'd"* used in yͤ next stanza may be exchangd for reveald, or some word of equal Import — I don't Know *why* I prefer "Lips at once & Eyes" &: so very probably you are in yͤ right — *Quick* Lightnings doesn't *run* so well as "the Lightnings &c:" but is perhaps preferable on *another* score — as to the rest, please to follow your own readings in regard to this Ode — The Plate will require but very trifling alterations, if any & may be sent at a Minutes warning.

   I have but a mean Opinion of two or three amongst yͤ songs; & was thinking, (with this last ode, Lysander & some few other Pieces in my Manuscript) yᵗ I could have supply'd their Place to advantage. Do you remember yͤ Verses on yͤ Kid? — but I will write again to-morrow, & speak more Explicitly on the Occasion —

   Do you think Mʳ H. Walpole wou'd Oblige me wᵗʰ a Copy of yͤ Travels he has lately printed?⁵ (Hentznerus, I think is yͤ Name —) I do not mean any otherwise than thro' *your* Mediation.

---

³ In Dodsley's *Collection,* Vol. V, the lines go as follows:

'Twas not by beauty's aid alone,	'Tis kindness that secures his aim,
That love usurp'd his airy throne,	'Tis hope that feeds the kindling flame,
His boasted power display'd:	Which beauty first convey'd.

⁴ There follow two lines which Shenstone has crossed out: "To fan yͤ languid sparks of young desire, which &c." "Of love" is written in the line above "of young desire."

⁵ Paul Hentzner (1558–1625), *A Journey into England in the Year 1599,* printed at Strawberry Hill in 1757.

You judge rightly of me in thinking how much it pains me to print precipitately — My *gratitude* suffers equally in subjecting you to Inconvenience. I am therefore truly under much anxiety — but wth abundance of good-will, Dear M[r] Dodsley

Y[rs] Very affectionately

W Shenstone

Pray write

206. To THOMAS PERCY [1]

The Leasowes, Jan: 4th 1758

DEAR SIR,

The beginning of your Letter puzzled me; being conscious that, a few weeks before, I had sent your Elegy & Song to M[r] Dodsley, *without* that regular examination which you desired me to bestow upon it; & which Nothing but a total want of Leisure could have caus'd me to decline. However, upon second Thoughts, I recollected that M[r] Dodsley & myself had formerly taken some Pains, (and, I believe, some *Liberties* too) with the Pieces to which you alluded. Be this as it will, you are most evidently in y[e] right for not adopting *implicitly* what was done in your absence; nor can M[r] Dodsley or myself wish to debarr you of a Privilege, which, on a similar occasion, we should be so ready to demand *Ourselves*.

Upon ballancing the account of our Pamphletts & so forth, there appears due to you certain Portions of *Apology* & *Acknowledgement*, which if you are so good as to accept, I need say no more upon the subject. I like the *Sentiments* in general which run thro' M[r] Cambridge's Epistles;[2] but, as to the *species of writing,* think it not very material whether we import *that,* or the French Gawses.

I have enclos'd the Ballad of Gill Morrice for your Perusal; at the same time that I very much question whether *Child* Morrice be not the juster title. You pique my Curiosity extremely by the mention of that antient Manuscript; as there is nothing gives me greater Pleasure than the *simplicity* of style & *sentiment* that is observable in old English ballads. If aught could add to that Pleasure, it would be, an opportunity of

[1] B. M. Add. MSS 28221, fol. 7ff. The Percy-Shenstone correspondence was published (1909) with an excellent introduction and copious notes by Professor Hans Hecht, in *Quellen und Forschungen,* to which the reader is referred for the letters of Percy. The principal interest of this correspondence lies, of course, in the exchange of ideas concerning the *Reliques.* See also Irving L. Churchill's article, "William Shenstone's Share in the Preparation of Percy's Reliques," *PMLA,* December, 1936, pp. 960–74.

[2] Not Cambridge's but John Gilbert Cooper's. See Percy's note, B. M. Add. MSS 28221, fol. 5b; also Hecht's note, pp. 95–96.

perusing them in your company at the Leasowes, & pray do not think of *publishing* them, untill you have *given* me that opportunity — And what, if at the same time, I should recommend the example to you, of my Neighbour [Hylton] who would esteem no one *Coin* or *Fossil* he possesses, of a Rush, if he knew the world, for the merest trifle, could obtain possession of a *duplicate?* But this you'll say is a kind of selfishness allowable only in a *Virtuoso* — suppose then you consider your MS. as an hoard of gold, somewhat defac'd by Time; from which however you may be able to draw supplies upon occasion, and with which you may enrich ye world hereafter under more *current* Impressions.

Do you hear that Mr Johnson's Shakespear[3] will be publish'd this Winter? I have a Prejudice (if *Prejudice* it may be call'd) in favour of all he undertakes; & wish ye world may recompence him for a Degree of Industry very seldom connected with so much real Genius. I am likewise impatient to see the new Tibullus[4] — or *should* be so, had I finish'd the Proof-sheets which I detain from Mr Dodsley.

I should be heartily glad if I could give you a better account of my *Punctuality* as a Correspondent; but your *Candor,* I trust, will make up ye deficiency, as you will never find me wanting in the sincerity of my Esteem. I am

Sir,
Your most affectionate humble Servt
Will: Shenstone

Let me beg ye Favor of a Line from you, when you are at Leisure.

GILL MORICE

In place of ye 14th stanza read ye three following: —

14

>Gill Morice sate in gude grene wood;
>He whistled & he sang:
>O what mean A' the folk coming?
>My Mother tarries lang.
>His hair was like the threeds of gold
>Shot frae ye burning Sun;
>His lips like roses drapping dew;
>His breath was a perfume.[5]

---

[3] The "Proposals" were published in 1756; the edition came out in 1765.

[4] Dr. James Grainger's translation, Smollett's unfavorable review of which gave rise to a sharp controversy between them (for later allusions see the Index).

[5] Above line 8 Shenstone has written as a variant, "When as his race (ye Sun's) was run." Between Stanzas 14 and 15 are the words, "I wish you w^d mend this Rhyme. 'tis Pity &c."

15

His brow was like ye mountain snae
Gilt by ye morning beam;
His Cheeks like living Rose's glow;
His een like azure stream.
The boy was clad in robes of green,
Sweet as ye infant spring;
And, like the Mavis in ye bush,
He gart ye vallies ring.

16

The baron came to ye grene wood,
Wi mickle dule & care;
And there he first spy'd Gill Morice
Kameing his yellow hair
That sweetly wav'd around his Face,
That Face beyond compare!
He sang sae sweet it might dispell
A' rage but fell despair.[6]

     Nae wonder &c.

207. To RICHARD GRAVES[1]

[Between Jan. 5 and Mar. 23, 1758]

DEAR MR. GRAVES,

Do you know my hand-writing? — It is really such a length of time since you had demands upon me for letters, that I am hardly able to enumerate the several causes of my neglect. *This* I know, that scarce a day has passed, during this interval of silence, in which I have not *remembered* you with the most affectionate esteem. — I *hope* you correspond with our friend Dodsley; and that it is not altogether disagreeable to you, to find he is printing some of your verses. He has many, alas! *too* many, of mine; which I suffered him to take away in summer, and which the state of my winter health and spirits renders me but ill able to revise. I believe, I am, even now, the principal cause that his two volumes remain yet unpublished; nor can I express the pain it gives me, to be thus detrimental to his interests, and to delay the publication of so much better pieces than my own. I am also dissatisfied upon *another score:* I mean,

---

[6] In the margin, written vertically, appear the words, "This, considering Addison's Note upon Milton's 'able to chase All sadness but despair,' [*Paradise Lost,* IV, 155–56] looks a little more modern yⁿ ye rest, but may not be so — "

[1] Dodsley, *Letters to Particular Friends,* No. XC, dated "about 1757." Fullington corrects the date, *PMLA,* 46: 1135–36.

that I have been wanting to myself, in not asking the benefit of your advice; which I have heretofore experienced to be at once so *comfortable* and so *advantageous;* but although the scheme was projected in summer, the business of correction was (by *me* at least) deferred till winter, and then I had neither spirits to *correct* or to *correspond.*

I am really as much obliged to you for the pains which you took on my behalf in London, as though the *subject* of your enquiry were a thing of more *importance* to me; but, indeed, you can hardly conceive how indifferent I am now grown, not only as to articles of *that sort,* but to aught that regards external splendor.

I really have not time to enter upon the merits of inoculation; but am very sure that Mrs. G[rave]'s danger was enough to influence your determination. I am heartily glad to hear of her recovery; and can but look upon the weeks which I purpose to pass some time hereafter with you at Claverton, as the most agreeable of any that belong to the remainder of my life. I am sensible, that if I *coveted* to *shine* in poetry, I should lose no time in visiting public places: but my wishes of that sort are most extremely limited, and I shall visit *you* on the account of *friendship;* that is (past all doubt) on a much *better principle.*

I have *long* meant to write to you, and have accordingly given *some* answer to most parts of your last letter. Nevertheless, the occasion of this present letter is quite of another kind. — A young painter[2] of my acquaintance is advised to go to Bath; has a recommendation to the Bishop of B——, who will introduce him to the Duke of N——. And though I cannot so easily bring him acquainted with nobles or prime-ministers, I can give him directions to my friend, who, in point of taste, is their superior. The person then, who, I suppose, will be the bearer of this letter, has, by dint of mere ingenuity, risen to a considerable eminence in fruit-pieces, &c.[2] He has been employed by Lord Lyttelton, and is much admired at Oxford: for my own part, I believe you will think he is in few respects inferior to, and has (if I am not mistaken) some advantages of, Stranover; but you will see his pieces. All I have to say further on the occasion is, that he is a native of our parish, and a particular friend of *mine;* and if it were in your power to promote his interest at Bath, you would not only highly gratify *me,* but at the same time do a service to one of the least assuming, most ingenious, and most amiable men I know. — I beg my best respects to your family, and am, dear Mr. Graves, most affectionately yours,

W. Shenstone

[2] Amos Green (1735–1807) of Halesowen. See the *Memoir of Amos Green Esq.*, "written by his late widow" (York, 1823).

208. To RICHARD GRAVES[1]

The Leasowes, May 30, 1758

DEAR MR. GRAVES,

I thank God, I have recovered a tolerable degree of health this spring; though by no means free from so much heaviness and lassitude, as renders me averse to all activity both of body and mind. In the course of my disorder, so long as I could bear to think of *any* sublunary enjoyment, I remembered my friends, and of course thought much of *you;* but its advances were so precipitate, when I sent for the physicians, that I soon received a *wrench* from every object of this world: and it was by slow degrees, even after my recovery, that my mind took so much root again as appears necessary for its immediate support. I suppose you have been informed that my fever was in great measure hypochondriacal; and left my nerves so extremely sensible, that even on no very interesting subject, I could readily think myself into a vertigo: I had almost said an epilepsy; for surely I was oftentimes near it. It became, therefore, expedient for my recovery, to amuse myself with a succession of the most trivial objects I could find; and this kind of carelessness I have indulged till it is grown into an habit. Even letters to my friends are hardly consistent with my rule of health; yet I could be no longer silent with regard to *you,* without feeling a sensation that would hurt me *more.* This may fairly enough be termed the first *letter* I have wrote since my recovery; wherein if I should tell you one half that I am inclined to do, relating to this dreadful illness, what room should I then leave to speak on any other subject? I must, therefore, tell these things by word of mouth, or write them some other time. The journies which my friends, and indeed physicians, propose for me, are what certainly bid fairest for the completion of my cure: yet there are many, many things, which, however unfit for the task, I must endeavour to adjust before I can leave home with any possibility of enjoyment. Need I mention any other than my cursed embarassment with D[olman], who, during my *danger,* was induced to stop proceedings; but is now beginning law afresh, and, by the removal of tenants from *his* share of the Harborough estate, has now wriggled himself into possession of almost one half of *mine?* However, I am not without hopes of seeing all terminated in a little time; nor entirely without a prospect of seeing you at Claverton this summer. That you may think this the more probable, I am pressed by two young gentlemen, whom I very much esteem, to accompany them on a visit to Mr. Bamfylde in Somersetshire. These two gentlemen are, Mr. Dean and Mr. Knight. Perhaps you may have heard of Mr. Bamfylde, who is very much at Bath; is there now with his

---

[1] Dodsley, *Letters to Particular Friends,* No. XCI.

lady, or has left the place but lately; and whose fortune, person, figure, and accomplishments, can hardly leave him long unnoticed in any place where he resides. Yet my visit to Estercomb must be of secondary consequence to me, whilst you live by the road-side. I am much obliged to you for your compliment on my Poematia in Dodsley's Miscellanies; which came very seasonably, considering how I had been mortified by the first sight of what was done. To speak the truth, there are many things appear there very contrary to my intentions; but which I am more desirous may be attributed to the unseasonableness of my fever, than to my friend D[odsley]'s precipitations. My purpose was to acknowledge as *mine,* none of the pieces which now follow the longer Ode to Lady Luxborough. Her name was actually erased; as also my own at the close of your Fable. The verses by Mrs. Bennet to Mr. Richardson were absolutely new to me; where my name occurs again. All this is against me; as a thing in itself invidious to have one's name recur so often, and as my *own lines contradict* the merit which my friends so liberally allow me. The verses of mine in the sixth volume (which was printed before the fifth) were printed without my knowledge; and when I sent up an improved copy, it arrived a good deal too late. As things happen, I am made to own several things of inferior merit to those which I *do not* own. All this is against me; but my thoughts are avocated from this edition, and wholly fixed upon a future; wherein, I hope, Dodsley will be prevailed upon to omit some things also from *other* hands which discredit his collection: and, to balance *all my discomforts* on this head, the world will know that I am esteemed by a person whom I esteem so much as you. I know not how it happens, but the taste for humorous poetry does not prevail at this time: yet I cannot agree with Mr. J. Warton, that it is no poetry *at all,* any more than that a good representation of Dutch boors is not a picture. — His brother, the Professor, is to be here with his pupil Lord Donnegal, &c. this summer. — Mr. Spence[2] and Mr. Dodsley will stay a day or two here this month in their way to Scotland; and Mr. Home, the author of Douglas, &c. called on me, and we spent an evening together at Admiral Smith's. Thus my *ferme ornée* procures me interviews with persons whom it might otherwise be my *wish* rather than my good-fortune to see. Would to God, it could attract *you,* whom I more long to see than any one! and let me tell you, there were considerable additions made to it last year: Dodsley's present of Faunus; a new Gothic-building, or rather a skreen, which cost ten pounds; and the ruins of a Priory, which, however, make a tenant's house, that pays me tolerable

[2] Joseph Spence (1699–1768), author of the *Anecdotes, etc.,* wrote Shenstone an interesting letter acknowledging this visit, published in Hull's *Select Letters,* Vol. I, No. LXI.

poundage. — I am growing a little into *your* taste: why should not you advance farther into *mine?* I mean, I have a love for medals, by means of some that have been given me: yet do not think that I shall ever rival *you* — my object is only *beauty,* and I love only those of exquisite workmanship; so that this is no more a rivalship than that of two persons who admire the sex, but love different individuals; a rivalship, which, I trust, is more likely to cement our friendship than disunite us; which it is my *conviction* and my *comfort* no *sort* of rivalship will ever do. I have hardly room to express my good wishes for long health and happiness to Mrs. Graves and your little family, and to subscribe myself, my dear friend,
Your ever affectionate humble servant,
W. Shenstone

[margin: beauty of medals]

209. To MATTHEW BOULTON [1]

[July 19, 1758]

DEAR SIR,

I am employ'd by my Friend Mr Hylton to request that you would procure for him an electrical apparatus; and this, with all the expedition that shall be consistent with your own convenience. He wishes it to be such as may effectually exhibit all the common experiments in electricity; & *This* he leaves entirely to your Judgment who are so much better vers'd in it: At ye same time he wishes it *plain,* & not to partake of *Any* elegance that tends to heighten the expence — Thus much for my Friend Hylton; and now, as touching myself, I confess I could find much Pleasure in Researches of this sort; but as I have other avocations, & Lapal is so near, I have agreed with my Neighbour for certain Portions of electrical Fire, for which I am to furnish him with Cascade-water as often as he finds occasion. To be more serious, there is *one* Advantage I chiefly hope from his Lucubrations, I mean, that they will draw you oftener into this Country, of whose Conversation I am at all times very desirous to partake. I return you many thanks for the Honor done me by Mr Franklyn, & hope, whenever you have opportunity, you will oblige me with Favors of the same kind. I am, dear Sir,
Your most oblig'd and very affectionate Friend,
Will. Shenstone

July ye 19th 1758

N. B. Mr Hylton thinks yt *Oak* may supply all ye purposes of Mahogany in ye Frame.

[1] This letter, as well as Letters 211–17 and 265, is reproduced from a manuscript deposited in the Assay Office Library, Birmingham, England. The addressee, Matthew Boulton (1728–1809), the famous Birmingham hardware manufacturer, was at this time making

210. To RICHARD GRAVES[1]

July 22, 1758

DEAR MR. GRAVES,

It gives me great anxiety when I reflect how long I have waited for the satisfaction of a line from you. I beg, if you are alive and well, you will let me know so by the next post.

Mr. Dodsley and Mr. Spence[2] have been here, and stayed a week with me. The former was in certain hopes of seeing you in town; but I do not find that he either saw or heard from you, which *adds* to my anxiety.

I have seen few whom I liked so much, upon so little acquaintance, as Mr. Spence; extremely polite, friendly, chearful, and master of an infinite fund of subjects for agreeable conversation. Had my affairs permitted me, they had certainly drawn me with them into Scotland; whither they are gone, for about a month, upon a journey of curiosity.

I believe it will give you pleasure to hear that my lawsuit with D[olman] is accommodated, by the generous interposition of my Lord Stamford; concerning whose benevolence and magnanimity it is impossible for me to speak in the terms which they deserve. It is ended, I hope, not very *disadvantageously* for me; apparently with *one* advantage, of being intirely exculpated in the opinion of all mankind. The common method (as M. Bruyere observes) is to condemn *both* on these occasions. This suits people's indolence, and favours their impartiality. And though the equitableness of my whole conduct in this affair was self-evident to all that were near me, yet I found many that were inclined to blame us *both*, and *some* that I could never convince till *now* that the fault was not *wholly* mine.

Your "Pepper-box and Salt-seller" are in one of the Chronicles.— They pillage Dodsley's two last volumes of all that is worth perusal. I surely have some friend amongst the writers of the Monthly Review; for I have not only escaped a flogging, but am treated with great civility.

I never know how to leave off when I begin writing to you, having always a great deal to say: I only purposed you a few lines, to desire you would write directly. Pray make my best compliments to Mrs. Graves, and believe me ever yours most invariably,

W. Shenstone

small metal wares in his factory upon Snow Hill. It was in 1762 that he moved to his great factory in Soho, two miles north of Birmingham. Boulton is perhaps best known as the associate of James Watt in the production of steam engines, a relationship that began around 1769 and became a partnership about 1775. Samuel Smiles in his *Lives of Boulton and Watt* (1865) makes no mention of Shenstone.

[1] Dodsley, *Letters to Particular Friends*, No. XCII.
[2] See Letter 208, n2.

211. To MATTHEW BOULTON[1]

The Leasowes Augst ye 14th 1758

My best respects to Mr Bolton; and if the Corner Ornaments for the Chaise are finish'd, I should be glad enough to receive them — as also to know, whether any step be taken in regard to my four Bells —

Mr Hylton, I presume, purposes to wait upon Mr Bolton this Week — I have burnt my Fingers with electricity already;[2] having told ye story of Mr Franklyn's bottling up ye Lightning, 'till I am thought as great a Lyar as a Popish Legendary.

I desire Mr Bolton would let me see him here, as *soon* and as *often* as is Consistent with his better Employments —

Will Shenstone

212. To MATTHEW BOULTON[1]

August ye 17. 1758

My best respects to Mr Bolton, with abundance of thanks for ye favor of his Letter — Mr Green[2] did not bring me ye Pattern before Monday last; when I found it expedient to change y^e *delicacy* of the Model, for somewhat y^t was better calculated to make a Figure at a distance — Mr Bolton will see my Intentions when Mr Green returns ye pattern; which I beg he would get executed as soon as possible. & gilt in ye Manner he proposes. The *best* and y^e *shortest* method has been taken in regard to the Bells. I am asham'd to give Mr Bolton all this trouble, but shall be glad on every occasion to testify ye Esteem with which I am his very affectionate Friend &c

Will: Shenstone

213. To MATTHEW BOULTON[1]

Aug: 23. 1758

I desire my best Respects to Mr Boulton; and if the P. chaise ornaments happen to be *cast,* should be oblig'd to Him for a sight of them, before he gives orders for ye gilding.

I am told, Mr Boulton has a Dove that is a *widower;* and in case he do not purpose to provide him a companion, should be almost tempted

---

[1] Reproduced from a manuscript in the Assay Office Library, Birmingham, England.
[2] For other evidence of Shenstone's interest in electricity see the Index.
[1] Reproduced from a manuscript in the Assay Office Library, Birmingham, England. Two versions of this letter, displaying only verbal differences, appear in the collection: the cruder, inferior one, not reproduced, is dated Wednesday, August 16, 1758.
[2] It will be recalled that Amos Green was in Matthew Boulton's employ.
[1] Reproduced from a manuscript in the Assay Office Library, Birmingham, England.

to request y^t he might cohabit with some of mine. Mr Boulton will please to observe y^t the request is quite *conditional*.

The enclos'd Impromptu may amuse Mr Boulton for a moment, but he must give me his word & honour y^t he will make no other use of it, before I see Him.

Will: Shenstone

214. To MATTHEW BOULTON [1]

[Sept. 18, 1758]

My Comp. to Mr Boulton, who will discover by ye enclos'd what I know of the affair — I could indeed wish, ye Copy I sent Mr Boulton were either *return'd* me or *burnt;* and any others destroy'd, if M^r B^n knows of any. I could also wish y^t M^r B^n would take no Notice of Giles's Letter; which I only send as the *laziest* method of explaining my present situation. Finally, I could wish, y^t Mr Baskerville would not be so extremely idle as to give a Construction to this Trifle, which cannot possibly be countenanc'd by any *one* Consideration.

Mr Boulton will be so good as acquaint me when I may expect the Chaise-Ornaments: Mr Knight, who is going to bespeak a Chaise at Birm. prefers this very Form to all others.

Will: Shenstone

Septr 18th 1758

215. To MATTHEW BOULTON [1]

Septr 25th 1758

I desire my Compliments to Mr Boulton; & if the Chaise Ornaments happen to be ready, should be glad enough to have them sent by ye bearer.

I hope y^t Mr Baskerville has by this time been induc'd to construe y^t idle ballad according to ye sense that was obviously intended; & y^t I shall have no farther occasion to say any thing on that subject. I have receiv'd ye 2 Copies I gave to M^r B^n and Mr Giles. Had I given Copies to Mr Baskervilles *enemies,* ye case had been very different.

Pray when is Mr Holton furnish'd wth his electrical Apparatus? and when is Amos Green expected.

Will: Shenstone

[1] Reproduced from a manuscript in the Assay Office Library, Birmingham, England.

216. To MATTHEW BOULTON[1]

Sept 27. 1758

My Compliments to Mr Boulton with many Thanks for his Care in ye execution of ye Pine-apples. They will do mighty well; nevertheless the *Leaves* or *lower part* of the Fruit would shew much better if it were a little *fuller* & more *plain*. I am to bespeak a sett for Mr Knight; &, if it be not much *trouble,* would propose this alteration; not otherwise. I am now dispos'd to give Mr Boulton some additional plague about ye *Bells*. See ye trouble he brings upon himself by his *known Inclination* to oblige; especially when it is once discover'd by a person of a scheming turn. What does Mr B. think of a scheme for enamel'd star's for Horse's fore-heads? Would to God, I could discover a Scheme by wch I could oblige Mr Boulton in return.

Will. Shenstone

217. To MATTHEW BOULTON[1]

[Sept. 30, 1758]

My Compliments to Mr Boulton, & I would beg ye Favor of Him to send me two or three pair of shoe & knee-buckles, for Choice —

I am sorry to clogg my offer of a Pair of Guinea-fowl, with any Stipulation: I cannot, *will* not stipulate; for I'm very sure if my Breed should fail, & Mr Boulton's prove prolific, he will very readily supply me with a pair of young ones, some time hereafter — If they are not rightly pair'd Mr B. will send me Word — It is a Species in wch ye distinction of sexes is not easily discernible —

Will: Shenstone

Septr 30, 1758

218. To RICHARD GRAVES[1]

The Leasowes, Nov. 25, 1758

DEAR MR. GRAVES,

I have had daily expectations of a line from you these two months: conscious, however, that I did not deserve any; and affording a manifest instance of the infatuations of self-love. The last letter that I received of yours is dated the close of July, since which time I have been chiefly engaged in my customary amusements; embellishing my farm, and receiving the company that came to see it. My principal *excursions* have been

---

[1] Reproduced from a manuscript in the Assay Office Library, Birmingham, England.
[1] Reproduced from a manuscript in the Assay Office Library, Birmingham, England.
[1] Dodsley, *Letters to Particular Friends,* No. XCIII.

to Enville, on Lord Grey's birth-day; to Lord Ward's, upon another invitation; and to the Worcester Music-meeting. I need not mention what an appearance there was of company at Worcester; dazzling enough, you may suppose, to a person who, like me, has not seen a public place these ten years. Yet I made a shift to enjoy the splendor, as well as the music that was prepared for us. I presume, nothing in the way of harmony can possibly go further than the Oratorio of "The Messiah." It seems the best composer's best composition. Yet I fancied I could observe *some parts* in it, wherein Handel's judgment failed him; where the music was not equal, or was even *opposite,* to what the words required. Very many of the noblesse, whom I had seen at the Leasowes, were as complaisant to me as possible; whereas it was my *former* fate, in public places, to be as little regarded as a journeyman shoe-maker. — There I first saw our present Bishop; also our late Bishop's monument, which is fine. — Lastly, there I first saw my Lady Coventry; to whom, I believe, one must allow all that the world allows in point of beauty. She is certainly the most *unexceptionable* figure of a woman I ever saw; and made most of the ladies there seem of almost another *species.* On the whole, I was not a little pleased that I had made this excursion; and returned with double relish to the *enjoyment* of my *farm.* It is now high time to take some notice of your obliging letter. I think I was not told the purport of the journey you made to London; so can only say, I am very sorry for the aggravating circumstances of your disappointment; and hope, long before this time, that Mrs. Graves is quite recovered. — Did I forget to make your excuses to Dodsley or no? — he was here (as I remember) soon after, with Mr. Spence, in their way to Scotland — Mr. Spence, the very man *you* would like, and who would like *you,* of all mankind. He took my Elegies into Scotland, and sent them back on his return, with a sheet or two of criticisms, and an handsome letter.[2] — How much am I interested in the preservation of his friendship! — and yet, such is my *destiny* (for I can give it no other name), I have never wrote to him *since.* This *impartiality* of my neglect, you must accept *yourself* as *some* apology. But to proceed; Mr. Spence chose himself an oak here for a seat, which I have inscribed to him,

(SPENCE'S OAK)
EXIMIO NOSTRO CRITONI
CUI DICARI VELLET
MUSARUM OMNIUM ET GRATIARUM CHORUS
DICAT AMICITIA

[2] Published in Hull's *Select Letters,* I, 238ff.

I absolutely *forgot* to talk to Dodsley about your ———,³ and I am vexed; because I could with a safe conscience have raised his idea of your abilities. However, it is not too late, even if you care to publish it this winter. — His play comes on (I fancy *this very night*)⁴ at Covent-garden. What he says in behalf of this step is, that there was no glimpse of probability, that Garrick would ever admit it at the other house.⁵ Mrs. Bellamy is his Cleone, and speaks the epilogue, of which more anon. I suppose he acts by Lord Chesterfield's opinion: for I know, when he was going to print it (since he came home) with a *proper* dedication to Mr. Garrick, my Lord then prevented him, telling him, it *would* be acted one day or other. — Did I ever send you a copy of the epilogue, with all the additions and alterations? Dodsley first liked, then disliked it, and lastly liked it again; only desiring me to soften the satire, shorten the whole (for it was upwards of sixty lines) and add a complimentary close to the *boxes*. — All this I have endeavoured, and sent it him last Monday. *You* would not care to own it; and he would fain have *me;* but I think neither of us should run the risque, where so little honour is to be acquired; yet Mr. Melmoth's name to the prologue is an inducement. — I was very near surprising you at Claverton this autumn, with my friend young Knight, in his way to Mr. Bamfylde's; but he goes *again* in spring, and I shall certainly accompany him; I have *bespoke,* but not yet *procured* any, horses for my chaise. It is a neat one, you will find; and I have made two or three excursions in it. — I saw Mr. Patchen's "Topographical Letters" soon after they were published. — If you continue to me the honour of a shield in your Gothic alcove, the field should be either "Or, three king-fishers proper," or, with the addition of a chief gules, three trefoils argent — no bar, cheveron bend, &c. — More of this when I write again. Motto, FLUMINA AMEM, SYLVASQUE INGLORIUS — RURA MIHI.

I cannot recollect my company of the season, to tell it you. Sir Francis Dashwood, Lord Litchfield, and Mr. Sheldon, were here together in the beginning of the autumn; and I have strong invitations to visit them. — I have a very genteel letter from Sir Francis, offering me gold-fishes; and I have a double inducement to visit Mr. Sheldon, as he lives near Mickleton, and is the most agreeable man alive. — Your acquaintance Lord W—— dined and spent good part of a day with me. Under a sort of

---

³ Graves's "comic romance," *The Spiritual Quixote* (1773). See C. J. Hill, "The Literary Career of Richard Graves," *Smith College Studies in Modern Languages,* 16:19 (1934–35).
⁴ Dodsley's *Cleone* was first acted at Covent Garden December 2, 1758. It ran sixteen nights. Much of its success was due to the acting of Mrs. Bellamy (Genest, IV, 559–60). Two thousand copies of the first edition were sold at once and five weeks later a fourth edition was in preparation. See Straus, *Robert Dodsley,* pp. 200ff.
⁵ He says, the players liked it, and seemed inclined to take pains with it. [Shenstone]

gloomy appearance, a man of admirable sense and some humour. I put him in mind of you, and the remarkable monument at Cambden. — Mr. Thomas Warton was also here with Lord Donnegal, and has since sent me his "Inscriptions", which are rather too simple, even for my taste. — Bishop of Worcester with his family and company — Lord Willoughby — Lord Foley — I mention Lord Foley the rather, because I shall call on your friend Dr. Charleton[6] (who was also here) to pass a day or two with me at Whitley. — I shall pass also a day or two at our Bishop's, whom I met since at Enville. These two (*propose* what I *will* besides) will probably be the principal, or only excursions that I shall make this winter. — God send it may no more affect my health than it has hitherto done! — I am at present tolerably well, and live more temperately than before. — Would to God you could come over; go with me to Dr. Charleton's, and Lord Foley's, and Lord Stamford's, and pass a week here! I would meet you with my chaise at Worcester, or even farther. I have finished a building opposite to the new stable, which I think you saw. — They together give my house a degree of splendor. Did you see my Priory? a tenant's house, one room whereof is to have Gothic shields round the cornice. — I am in some doubt whether to make it an House of Lords or House of Commons; if the former, my private friends will have shields round my Gothic bed-chamber. — The wretch is cursed that *begins* a letter with no better a pen than I *finish* one with. My dear friend, write directly a long letter. — Keep me alive in the memory of Mrs. Graves, and believe me ever yours most affectionately,

W. Shenstone

I have received a present of the Edinburgh Homer[7] (2 vols. folio) from the Solicitor General, Mr. Pringle;[8] and many other books from other gentlemen of Scotland.

219. To JOHN SCOTT HYLTON[1]

Novr 26, 1758

Dick is going to Birm^n and shall take ye Letters y^{t2} . . . been sent — I can't *account* for ye expensiveness of y^r . . . Journey to Coventry — surely he w^d need to lodge but one Ni[ght] there, & w^d have his Victuals

---

[6] See Letter 257, n2.

[7] Allan Ramsay's *Miscellany*. See the end of Letter 220.

[8] Andrew Pringle (d. 1776), afterward (1759) Lord Alemoor, the great lawyer and pleader, was Scottish solicitor-general.

[1] Reproduced from a holograph in the Huntington Library, San Marino, California.

[2] The corner of the manuscript is torn off.

at Mr Inge's — I know . . . few Instances of *Attorneys,* where both ye Gent^n & even ye M[*an*] are not swallow'd up in ye Lawyer — "He will make you a schedule *thereof;* & at ye bottom *thereof;* will remain a blank space for you to sign y^r Name *thereon*" — But let us comfort ourselves that it is much less eligible to *be* Lawyers, y^n to *suffer* by em —

Mr Hylton may write to Mr Percy when he pleases; but ought not to send any acc^t from ye Leasowes 'till I can enable Him; wch at present cannot be —

Will: Shenstone

220. To THOMAS PERCY [1]

[Recd. Dec. 1st 1758 — P]

DEAR SIR,

It is really a shame to acknowledge *now,* the Favour I receiv'd from you so very long *ago;* but it would be a much *greater,* not to acknowledge it at *all:* And indeed it were a very *preposterous* kind of Hypocrisy, to conceal the Pleasure I have received, on which I am to ground the Hopes I entertain of your Correspondence. I have perform'd about one *half* of ye request you were so *complaisant* to make, with regard to your Poetry. The rest, with your Leave, I must defer a little longer. I think y^r Elegy on Ld Sussex[2] extremely easy and genteel. Pardon ye Hints I have interlin'd, and only use what you approve of them. When you have so done, I should esteem it a Favour, if you would please to send me a fresh Copy. I have enclos'd a few Pieces for your *Amusement;* which I send with no other Limitation, y^n that you will keep them from the *Press.* Possibly I may be one day tempted to furnish out a small Miscellany; having a press in my own *Neighbourhood,* so very favorable to my *Indolence.* Y^r Friend D^r. Grainger, with a Mr Luard, pass'd a Day with me: And a very agreeable Day it *was,* not inferior to any one I have spent, since I had ye Pleasure of seeing you. The Doctor, on reading y^t urnal Inscription (POSTQUAM TE FATA TULERUNT IPSA PALES AGROS, ATQUE IPSE RELIQUIT APOLLO) made me a Compliment on ye Subject, as polite as it was extemporaneous:

> S—— with you I'd weep ye Dead;
> With you of Fate complain —
> But tho' Apollo's self be fled,
> And Pales — *you* remain.

---

[1] B. M. Add. MSS 28221, fol. 12ff. The date is in Percy's hand. See Hecht for an excellent and elaborate annotation of the entire Percy-Shenstone correspondence.
[2] Verses on the Improvements designed at Easton Maud^t 1758. [Percy]

They were going into Scotland: *both* Persons of Taste — The D^r a Person of much real Genius & Learning; & I cou'd wish to see them oft'ner.

I met Mr Wright at Erville, upon Ld Grey's Birth-day — Mr Baldwyn also & Colonel Cotes were here; & as I remember (or am *inclin'd* to remember) made honourable Mention of *you*.

Mr Spence and Mr Dodsley render'd a week here very agreeable to me. Mr Spence chose himself an Oak; on wch I put ye following Inscription —

SPENCE'S OAK

PERAMABILI NOSTRO CRITONI

CUI DICARI VELLET

MUSARUM OMNIUM & GRATIARUM

CHORUS

DICAT AMICITIA

Other additional Inscriptions — with some y^t are *intended,* I reserve for a future Letter — amongst which, you must not be angry, if you happen to trace y^r own Name.

Dodsley's Play³ has either *been* acted, or comes on, at ye new House, this Week. It is a point I have much at Heart to see this Play triumph over it's Antagonists. You will not want a *Foundation* to do it some Honour as you see occasion; but Let ye Author's merit & my request incline you to be rather luxuriant in it's Commendation.⁴

Baskerville's Milton, they tell me comes out in ye Xtmas holidays — I have company while I write, & must, *unwillingly,* take my Leave at present — Be so good as to return me ye printed Verses upon the Leasowes, and believe me ever & most affectionately yours.

Will: Shenstone

Mr Pitt of Shifnel (here wth Mr Slaney) says he gave you those old Ballads — The Pilgrim you sent me is mighty pretty, as ye Plan is different from what one has ever seen. I have had ye Edinburg Homer, A miscellany of Allan Ramsays — Scotch Proverbs — Scotch Ballads presented me from Caledonia — & am grown almost a Scotch-man. — Excuse this. —

³ Cleone, a Tragedy. [Percy]
⁴ I cou'd indeed wish, y^t you wou'd give him a copy of commendatory verses. [Shenstone]

221. To RICHARD GRAVES[1]

Christmas, 1758

DEAR MR. GRAVES,

There *can* be nothing more welcome to me than the intelligence which you give of your intended visit at The Leasowes — God knows how few of these interviews may for the future be allotted to us; and I should be glad at least to testify the joy which they afford me, by meeting you at Birmingham, or elsewhere within one day's journey for my chaise. — Pray be so good as to give me one more letter before you set out. — Very glad should I be to pay my respects to your brother at Mickleton, for whom I have the truest respect; but dare not give encouragement, for fear that aught should interfere. — I have ten thousand things to say to you; but will defer them, I think, *all*. I am positive your ———[2] may be made *advantageous* to you by means of Dodsley; and even *reputable,* if you so please. — Will not Mrs. G[raves] accompany you? pray convince her of my sincere regard.

I want to congratulate you on your escape from the small-pox, in a manner *different* from your ordinary acquaintance; yet am not able to express my sentiments — guess the rest; knowing, and sufficiently knowing, that I am, with constancy and ardour, your most affectionate friend,

W. Shenstone

222. To RICHARD JAGO[1]

The Leasowes, Jan. 6, 1759

DEAR MR. JAGO,

If you knew the maxims on which I conduct myself, you might call me perhaps *unpolite;* but, I think, by no means *unfriendly;* I mean with respect to the *ordinary congratulations* on your *marriage*.[2] Were you and I less intimate, less experienced, and less assured friends, it had been no venial omission to have neglected such a ceremony. Perhaps I should not have neglected it; but as I have the satisfaction of believing that you would rejoice in any success of mine, so I hope you would not distrust my sentiments upon any change of your condition which you yourself esteemed for the *better*. I do indeed, my worthy friend, wish you much joy, both *now* and at *all* times; and you will ever discern it in my face,

---

[1] Dodsley, *Letters to Particular Friends,* No. XCIV.
[2] Graves's *Spiritual Quixote* (1773). See C. J. Hill, "The Literary Career of Richard Graves," *Smith College Studies in Modern Languages,* 16:19.
[1] Dodsley, *Letters to Particular Friends,* No. XCV.
[2] The first Mrs. Jago (Dorothea Susanna Fancourt) had died in 1751. Jago married Margaret Underwood, who survived him, in 1758.

as often as fortune grants us an interview. Mr. S—— is a benevolent man, and I am sure would withhold no information that tended to *illustrate* our friendship on either side.

I have thoughts of proceeding on to Harbury, whenever I come to Mr. Wren's; as I have long enough made my friend a promise, and intend ere long to do. Many reasons occur why I cannot set forward tomorrow morning: are these reasons substantial, or no other than the sly and sophistical insinuations of indolence? — surely the former.

Dodsley, and indeed Mr. Spence, both expect me in town this February. — I fear it will not be; but if it *should,* how readily would I give notice, and become obliged to you for your company!

Though I should have *expected* you would select a partner whose society you could enjoy, yet I was not a little satisfied with the hint given me in your letter, as well as in one I had before received from Mr. S——. It is not for such ladies as you and I esteem, that Mrs. Bellamy's[3] extraordinary lecture was intended; and a *lecture* it would have been with a vengeance, had not D[odsley] omitted some thirty lines, and substituted about twelve or fourteen of his own. However, he is now going to print his fourth edition of it; in which the original epilogue will be restored, as well as considerable improvements introduced into his play. He sold two thousand of his first edition the very first day he published it.

I have so *much* to tell you, and of so *various* kinds, that I am afraid to expatiate upon *any* one article. Cannot you make a shift to call upon me, before *my public life* arrives? — I would send my chaise to meet you at any place you should appoint.

I have passed my winter hitherto pretty chearfully amongst my books, in what I *call* my library. It now better deserves that name, by the form I have given it, and the volumes I have added. Mr. S——would tell you something of my *other* occupations.

I could wish that you would favour me with a copy of your "Essay on Electricity,"[4] and with any new copy of verses of your own, or of your friends. — Be not apprehensive: there shall nothing appear in print of your composition any more, without your explicit consent. — And yet I have thoughts of amusing myself with the publication of a small Miscellany from neighbour Baskerville's press, if I can save myself harmless as to expence — I purpose it no larger than a "Lansdown's," a "Philips's," or a "Pomfret's Poems."

Have you read my friend Dr. Grainger's Tibullus?[5] It affords you an

---
[3] See epilogue to *Cleone* [Dodsley]. The epilogue was written by Shenstone and Graves.
[4] Never published.
[5] See the Index.

elegant edition of a good translation and of the text. He is engaged in a war with S[mollett], and has just sent me his pamphlet; which I could wish you to read, in order to form a judgment of S[mollett]'s character. — Spence, I see, has advertised his "Parallel betwixt Malliabecqui and his Taylor."[6] It is merely a charitable design: and such are now all Spence's views.

What remains of my paper must be employed not in *mere* ceremony, although in something that bears the form of it: in my best compliments to Mrs. Jago, and my offer, not indeed of a part of the friendship which I owe you, but rather of an equal quantity; in an assurance of the cordiality with which I shall rejoice to see both her and you; and in confirmation of that affection with which I have ever been, and am, my good friend, your most obedient servant,

W. Shenstone

223. To JOHN SCOTT HYLTON[1]

[March 2d 1759]

The Green is right — I wish I *could* get some Liquid Verdigrease; but have many times endeavoured to make it, without effect — you must not speak one word against taking this sett of Lettering types; as I myself take an octavo Sett, and ye opportunity of borrowing each other's, will be so wonderfully convenient — you will Learn to Letter in a days time; & may make *immediate* experimts on some of yt blue Paper; first rubbing it over wth glase of egg; then, slightly, wth sweet oil; then lay on L. gold — then apply ye Letter just so hot as not to burn — I will tell Mr Dodsley how ye small sett is dispos'd — they will be about 7s or thereabt Mr M'Leod says — It is impossible to find a *slip* to night — were I as low a Punster as Pixell, I wou'd say yr Boy may find *Many*.

224. To JOHN SCOTT HYLTON[1]

[Sunday 11th March 1759]

My Compliments — I return *Some* of Mr Hs Books, & will e'er long dismiss ye remainder — Fiddian may go with Dick, if he will be here by six o'Clock to morrow morning — otherwise, Miss Wight comes this afternoon to see what can be done by means of Mr Hs three-pence. At

---

[6] *A Parallel, in the Manner of Plutarch, between a Celebrated Man of Florence, and One Scarce Ever Heard of in England,* published by Dodsley, was advertised in the Register of Books of the *Gentleman's Magazine* for February, 1759.

[1] B. M. Add. MSS 27548, fol. 29. The date is in a hand other than Shenstone's.

[1] B. M. Add. MSS 27548, fol. 30. The date is in a hand other than Shenstone's.

present, it lies *wholly* upon *me* to fetch both news & Letters—I mean for a *certainty*—nor can I, even thus, answer by return of Post; without sending twice the same Day—'Twould be prodigiously convenient to have Letters &c arrive regularly, by 12 o Clock, on Post-days—Mrs Acton *has* some turn for *Elegance* (unless Miss Wight be *too much* attach'd to her)—and would have given Clem a better Turn both in point of *happiness* & *Figure*, might she have had her own way—Mr Hylton's review never came but I will give Aris a trimming, to-morrow. Mine I send; which will occasion me to buy a Book or two—Poor Grainger has *not quite Justice* done him[2]—

I had yesterday 2 Letters from Tom Saunders at Guadalope; which I directly sent to Admiral Smith; & now, to his sister Wilkinson—He is Lieutenant (now) in ye Bervick—Mr H. heard of our success there—I have got ye Admiral's Douglas &c: with a 2^d double entendre—Mr Dodsley (wth a short Letter) has sent me a pair of Swans from London, in a Cage as big as Mr Hylton's Shop—they come home to-morrow—The Cutts to Pamela are elegant, but not so *accurate* as I wish 'em; & must be returnd by Fiddial in ye morn: being M'acleod's. I will get Mr H. some Russia L. at Birm: if he will; but there are *two* sufficient reasons why he must not trust to this at John Taylors—Let ye Emerald go.

225. To ROBERT DODSLEY [1]

March 31, 1759

DEAR MR. DODSLEY,

I am afraid you think me negligent: know then that I sat down last *Thursday,* to write you a long Letter, about seven o'Clock at Night, when I discovered that the Post went out at that very Hour I sat down to write. I had immediate Recourse to such Consolation as the Case admitted; and supposed a Letter received on *Monday* Morning, might do near as well as one on *Saturday* Night, considering that *Sunday* intervened, which must be a leisure Day, *even* for Printers. But in good Earnest now, do you *think* me lazy? Or have not you, under your present *Dissipation,* an *heavier* Complaint against my *Diligence?* You and I shall hardly agree about the *Means* of *estimating* Letters; you, conscious of your own Genius, are desirous to value them by their Weight; while I, conscious of my late Industry, would fix their Value by the

[2] The allusion is probably to Grainger's feud with Smollett over Tibullus. See the Index.
[1] Hull, *Select Letters,* Vol. I, No. LXIV.

Number of *Words*. What Pretensions, pray, can you suggest, for so very *perverse* a Manner of Reckoning? Is not *Industry* a *moral Virtue?* And are not many written Words a *Proof* of Industry? But though your *Ingenuity* be even a Miracle, you will hardly prove it to be a *moral Virtue,* unless, indeed in the *Way you manage it;* and *so, all* your Faculties are moral Virtues: however, we less *artful,* or less *heroick* Personages, must magnify the Virtues that we *have;* of these, Industry is one, though perhaps *this* had been scarce *allowed* me, till within these three or four Months past. I say, that we, who are the *Animae nil magnae Laudis egentes;* we, the *Animae viles, inhumata infletaque turba:* In other Words, the *Numerus,* and the *"nati Fruges consumere;"* if *we* would appear considerable, pray what Method can we take? I know, indeed, but two; the one of disparaging *your* Abilities, which is not quite so feasible; the other, of taking all occasion to magnify our own good Qualities. If then, Industry be a Virtue, I am possessed of it very remarkably: Not a Moment of my Time passes, but I am employed, either in overseeing Labourers; reading Robinson's *History of Scotland;*[2] writing in my Paper Books,[3] ('tis not material *what,* but writing;) perplexing the *Birmingham* Artists with Sketches for Improvements in their Manufactures, which they *will* not understand; and lastly, and finally, feeding my Poultry, my Ducks, my Pigeons, and my Swans; which last give me as much Pleasure, as what I had before gave me Vexation. No inconsiderable Panegyrick, I'll assure you! And surely this is not only *Industry,* but an *Industry* of a *better Kind* than what employs the *Animae viles* of a Drawing Room. And now this *last Instance* of my great Industry puts me in Mind of asking you a Question:

Pray now, you that are a Mythologist, what an absurd Man you are, not to jump at an Invitation to come directly to the Leasowes? Here am I, (like your Friend Aesop, before Ogilby's *Fables;*[4] or like Adam, in our old *Bibles*) sitting once or twice a Day with every created Animal before me. Is not this the only Residence for a Person that is writing Fables?[5] 'Tis true, this very Person may contemplate better in a *Crowd,* than *another* in the Depth of Solitude: *you* may far surpass *me,* who thus *converse* with the Birds, while he describes a Sparrow from *Pall-Mall,* or a King-fisher from *Charing-Cross:* but *Imagination* is a prodigious *Heightener;* and unless he paints them from Life, may he not *attri-*

---

[2] William Robertson (1721–93) published his *History of Scotland* in 1759.
[3] This is almost the only allusion in Shenstone's letters to his writing in prose (*Men and Manners*).
[4] The translation of Aesop's *Fables* by John Ogilby (1600–76) was published in 1651. Part II appeared in 1665.
[5] Dodsley's *Select Fables,* with a "Moral Index" by Shenstone, were published in 1761.

bute to a *King-fisher* much finer Feathers than he in Truth possesses? Pray take the Opinion of Mr. Spence — how I blush, whilst I recollect that Name! And yet, were it not for my *own* Omissions, it must revive *only* my most *favourite* Ideas. Surely 'tis written in the Book of Fate, that I shall discharge my Debt within a Post or two; for Fate evidently enough interferes, or I could never have been so long silent. I am almost ashamed to desire my humble Respects to him, and yet it is impossible for me to suppress my Feelings.

I must now proceed to Business. Past six o'Clock once more; but the Post now goes out at ten. If you *can* procure me the quarto Cuts for Milton, it will be a very desirable Favour.

Mr. Bond has made some Alteration in your *Grove,* which I thought very pretty on its *Arrival;* yet, perhaps, he may be right enough, if Mr. Grignion can comprehend his Meaning. The Trees he means *on the wrong Side the Water,* are some of those opposite to the Letter *S,* which I have put upon the Back: but I am fearful of *spoiling;* and must beg Mr. Grignion would re-compare the Print with Mr. Bond's original Drawing, then retouch his Plate, and let me have a few more Proof-Sheets of both the Prints. Give me one or two Lines by *Return* of Post, if possible.

No Books ready? I want Mallet's Works, bound in *Russia* Leather, and lettered on Green. Pray excuse this last vile Page. I have wasted my Time, and now am utterly at a Fault for it.

W. Shenstone

226. To RICHARD GRAVES [1]

The Leasowes, April 18, 1759

DEAR MR. GRAVES,

You will think my silence long; and I should be sorry to *have* you quite regardless of it; although, I fear, it must be my fate to trespass frequently upon your kind solicitude. — I have no excuse to make, beside some frivolous avocations, and *much* of that heaviness and lassitude which disinclines one to write letters. — I passed the former part of my winter with more vivacity than I did the latter, or even the incipient spring; owing, possibly, to these cold winds, which will not permit me to use my wonted exercise. You will laugh at the word *vivacity,* when applied to so dull an animal; but I speak comparatively of that unmeaning drowsiness which is my lot at other times, and *was,* in some sort, while you were here.

Mr. Dodsley tells me, he received a letter from you, acquainting him

---

[1] Dodsley, *Letters to Particular Friends,* No. XCVI.

that Cleone would be played at Bath: I should be glad to receive from you any particulars of its success. He is publishing an elegant edition of it, which I expect by this very post. The new plate of my grove, which will appear at the end of his Melpomene, is perhaps liable to some exceptions, but by much the best that has yet appeared: do not forget to send me your objections to it. As to the Epilogue, I have totally banished, I think, every one of the lines which he *substituted*, have left to him the choice of two or three readings for the four last lines; and though none of them quite please me, yet the epilogue, on the whole, discovers more of genius, is more spirited, and less inaccurate. I shall be glad to find that you think the same with me.

In regard to your place, so far as I can form an idea of it, I would have you consult *self*-amusement; I mean, without too much regard to what *others* say or think. As to distinguishing your ingenuity (which I unfeignedly desire you may), the press affords you more *adequate* materials than either your fortune or perhaps your place. Do not imagine, however, that I shall not be much delighted with every stroke I trace of yours at Claverton. My faculties are very strongly intuitive in respect of every thing belonging to you; and I should be ashamed if any nook or angle that you had rounded, any wall that you had ruinated, any stream that you had diverted, or any single shrub that you had planted, should elude my discovery: yet you will shine *more* by means of the press; and if I said any thing concerning your ———[2] that did not *encourage* you to perfect it, I am sure I must use terms very inexpressive of my meaning. Without any more words, let me *intreat* you to proceed with it: give a *full scope* to your imagination; and if there should be aught one would wish *retrenched,* it is mighty *easily done.*

I have indeed *thoughts* (for I *never* use the word *resolutions*) of publishing my Elegies next winter — you will gainsay, when I tell you my intention of publishing also my very Farm; at least, about eight or ten scenes taken from it, by way of top and tailpieces for those Elegies. — The world will perhaps tax my vanity; but I do not in the least care. — The pleasure which that world gives me, I am very conscious, will not be too *high;* and I am determined that the pain it may seek to give shall bear proportion: yet should I be sorry to obtrude stuff upon it, either from the pencil or the pen; and my good friend Mr. Dodsley has sometimes pained me not a little.

I tell you, you *cannot* allow for winter. That very scene near Priory-

[2] Graves's *Spiritual Quixote* (1773). See C. J. Hill, "The Literary Career of Richard Graves," *Smith College Studies in Modern Languages,* 16:18.

gate shews not a bit of roac in *summer;* though the consciousness of a firm rail there would add to my tranquillity.—Mr. Knight has given me Strange's prints, which I hear are fine. Dodsley gives me swans: but for these two months past I have been a librarian, or rather a bookbinder; yet nothing more *unfeignedly,* than your, and Mrs. Graves's, most affectionate humble servant,

W. Shenstone

227. To JOHN SCOTT HYLTON [1]

24 Apr: 1759

This Picture will go near to please Miss Lea — As for *precision,* it is in vain to think of it, till I can procure some Impressions in blue, on a Paper yt is Less exceptionable. I cd wish ye Light had fallen on ye Birds back; which Amos Green wd not allow — Tis *there* ye blue is so very *lively,* as to make ye *whole bird* appear of yt colour.

Mr Hylton had better attempt no other, till we have fresh impressions, & ye body of a K. fisher. I go to-morrow to Mr Dean's, and from thence, *perhaps* to Mr Knight's where I am askd to meet Mr Palmers Family — I hear no News saving wt Mr Wight & Dr Altree tell me, yt Parson Wilmot, & Parson Lea had a sort of Brush in Hagley Lane — last week — Parson Lea sent me his Son's Letter to ye Admiral, with a circumstantial & even pompous acct of their Capture. The Adml says, 700 £ to 'em at *Least.*

The little girl said "four of them little ones were to visit Parson Boyce at Whitsuntide — but did not know how they sd get thither: told me Mrs Boyce said I was a mighty good-natured man & yt she didn't doubt I shoud very readily lend 'em my P. Chaise. Such are ye words of *pertness* mixt with *cunning* — wch I am never inclin'd to gratify — Dodsley's Play[2] is worse in one or two places, but better in an hundred & fifty — inexpressibly amended.

228. To THOMAS PERCY [1]

The Leasowes, June the 6th 1759

DEAR SIR,

It is perhaps no uncommon Case for ye magnitude of a Debt to *preclude,* or at least to *retard,* every step towards a Discharge. In truth, the

---

[1] B. M. Add. MSS 27548, fol. 3 . This letter is without formal beginning or close.
[2] The revised edition of his tragedy *Cleone.*
[1] B. M. Add. MSS 28221, fol. 17ff. A version of this letter also appears in Hull's *Select Letters,* Vol. I, No. LXV.

many Favors you have confer'd upon me by the Packets I have received from Easton-Mauduit, have made me quite asham'd of such a *partial* Payment, as my *Hea[l]th* & *Leisure* would have permitted me to make. When I complain of indifferent Health, I mean no other yn a kind of *Drowsihed* or *Lentor,* which has somewhat infested me all this Season. Perhaps it were better *express'd* by the disreputable name *stupidity.* Be that however as it may; It is by *this* alone I have been disqualify'd for those refin'd sorts of Amusement, in which your obliging Letters, & the Packets enclos'd in them, requir'd me to engage. — I have been expected to pass a week at Shifnall[2] ever since the beginning of May; where I was by *particular* appointment to meet our Friend Mr Binnel.[3] The Visit *is not* laid aside; but will not probably take Place till after a Fortnight or three weeks. One Pleasure I expect from it (beside what I shall receive from Mr Pitt & Mr Slaney's Company) turns upon the opportunity it will afford me of reading over with Binnel yt Translation of Ovid's Epistles: and it has been with *this* view, in some measure, that I have defer'd ye examination you desir'd me to bestow upon it. In *general,* I wou'd wish you to make it as just to the Author, and to yr own Sentiments, as you can; and *afterwards* employ *me* as a *mere* Musick-master, whom you would wish to tune yr Harpsichord: At *most,* to retrench any little Incroachments upon Simplicity, ease of Style, and Harmony.

I want to communicate *many* things; but must defer *most* of them 'till I *see* you. And pray, Let Mrs Percy know that I am one of your *peculiar* Friends; & then I hope she will not scruple to recompence me with an *irregular* Visit by way of *Distinction.* I brought my Friend Jago's new Bride to pay me that Compliment ye other Day.[4]

Mr Dodsley, in his last Letter, desir'd I would present you with his new Edition of Cleone; which is ye only one *you* should preserve. It is, according to my exactest calculation, *improv'd* in about an 100 Places, merely *alter'd* in about 6; & perhaps *injur'd* in about 4. I will either keep it till you come; or send it *directly,* if you will acquaint me *How.*

I had retouch'd and transcrib'd both Edom of Gordon & the Gentle Heardsman, long before ye arrival of yr Letter. The *former* I read to a *Scotchman,* who seem'd a good deal pleas'd with it. Your *supplemental* stanzas to ye g. Herdsman, must undoubtedly approach much nearer to what was ye *orig: reading.* than those which I have substituted; having not ye *final* words to direct me. — I will not send them you *now;* because

---

[2] With Mr. Humphrey Pitt, uncle to Mr. Binnel. [Percy]
[3] The Rev. Robert Binnel (d. 1763), rector of Newport, Shropshire. See Nash's *History of Worcestershire,* I, 530, and Hecht's note to this letter.
[4] See Letter 222, n2.

I would multiply your Inducements to pass a Day or two at the Leasows, at this best season of ye year.

You must by all means read Dr. Young's "Conjectures on original Composition";[5] even tho' it shou'd dissuade you, when you have compleated Ovid, from undertaking any more *translations*. I should not *murmur* at y^e *effect;* provided it stimulates you to write *Originals*. I have Likewise read y^e "Essay on the present state of Learning &c":[6] written by a Dr. Goldsmith, whom you know; & whom such as read it, will *desire* to know. I dissent from him however in his Partiality to Rhime (I mean in works of Length) but as to ye present pomp & Haughtiness of style *instead* of *sentiment*, am entirely of his Opinion. Caractacus[7] I've not yet seen. La Motte has lately afforded me not a Little entertainment: I read it on acc^t of *Dodsley*, who, you know is writing *Fables*, & ask'd my Thoughts upon the *subject*. Pray keep me well with Dr Grainger — I'm quite asham'd of my neglect — Had I known his Intention of *answering* Smollet,[8] I would have us'd my endeavours to dissuade him. The *properest* answer had been convey'd in a few short notes in ye next Edition of his Tibullus. Pray have you seen Smollet's reply? I suppose, sufficiently scurrilous — Y^r Friend Mr Johnson was so good as to send me a Little Poem call'd ye Parish Clerk (by Vernon)[9] including a Comp. on my Schoolmistress. I am surprizd at the *Language* & *Harmony* of Period — shall send for his Whole Book; & wish to do the Man some real Good.

Y^e 'Bacco-stopper[10] you gave to [Hylton] has been ye occasion of a Plot, at the *Denouement* of which, It will be worth y^r while to be at the Leasowes.

Suffice it, that I accompany'd y^r Favor[11] with a forgd Letter from Mr Moody; mentioning y^e *Disposition* of one Mr Fitzdottrel, Cabinet-Maker (of whom ye said Moody is feign'd to buy ye Stopper) before ye Mayor of Stratford, in regard to its *authenticity* — offering to join Mr [Hylton] in ye purchase of y^e *whole Tree* — M^r [Hylton]'s reply (*intercepted*) desires only a *part* of the Tree to make a *Cup*, whereon he

[5] Listed in the *Gentleman's Magazine*, Register of Books, May, 1759, and analyzed there in a long note (p. 230).
[6] Listed in the *Gentleman's Magazine*, Register of Books, May, 1759.
[7] A tragedy by William Mason (1725-97).
[8] For Grainger's controversy with Smollett see the Index (under Tibullus).
[9] A common soldier, originally bred a Buckle-maker at Wolverhampton. [Percy]
[10] Mr. Moody, who kept the great Toy-shop at Birmingham, had to sell a Parcel of Tobacco-Stoppers the Top of wch consisted of a Head of Shakespeare indifferently cut, made of Mulberry Wood, from a tree pretended to have been planted by Shakespeare. I bought one for a Shilling & sent it to Mr. [Hylton] who collected curiosities. [Percy]
[11] The Tobacco-Stopper had been left at Mr. Shenstone's in order to be conveyed to Mr. [Hylton]. [Percy]

purposes something carv'd in Basso Relievo. Moody is made to answer, y^t he has purchased the Tree, & sends H. one large *Arm* thereof wrapt up in brown-Paper — Moreover, (according to ye natural Propensity of Tradesmen) gets him the Cup *made* & *Carv'd* — In *one* Compartment, Fitzdotterel making Oath before ye Mayor of Stratford — In another, Shakespear, with a gardiners apron, planting ye very tree; & Moody, in the *Middle,* shewing it to M^r [Hylton] on the *right.* — The Cup is now in my Bureau — with ye Figures well-enough executed. Moody also is made to tell of a Man at Nottingham, y^t has a Large Collection *in His way;* which he thinks he would be glad to part with, having a Family of 10 Children to whom ye Money would do more good — Moody is then desir'd to procure *the List:* and *here* you must assist me. I have gott for Him, the Spoon wth which old Parr eat Buttermilk; and am promis'd a *real* King William's-Bib, for M^r [Hylton] to wear on ye Day of his Patron-saint — But with regard to these things at *present,* Lay y^r Finger upon y^r upper Lip.

I had ye enclos'd *King-fisher* engrav'd for me — purposing to assume it for Arms — but this the *profane* & *vulgar* must not know; on whom *Arms* strike no small Impression. (Qui stupet in titulis & imaginibus. Hor.) This *grove* you will have more agreeably at ye End of Dodsley's Cleone — My best respects to Mrs Percy —

I am with great Regard Y^r most obed^t

Pray write directly.   W. Shenstone

229. To THOMAS PERCY [1]

The Leasowes, Octr 3^d 1759

DEAR SIR,

May I wish you Joy of your Deliverance from the Crew of Workmen of which you complain'd, & of the Pleasure you receive from the Birth of an Infant,[2] come to divert you in their Room? Tis upon *your* account only, I can forgive him for the Interruption he gave to the visit you intended me; and yet forgive Him, I believe I must; provided he will not disturb you while you are engag'd in writing to me. I hope some time to wait upon you in Northamptonshire; but this year, it was impracticable. I certainly owe all the world either visits, Letters or Money. I began to *fancy* I had perform'd Feats this season; but now I sit down to reflect, I can trace nothing but neglected civilities & broken engagements

[1] B. M. Add. MSS 28221, fol. 27ff.
[2] I am congratulating you on ye birth of an imaginary child, yet am ignorant, whether you wish y^t your child shou'd be born so soon. [Shenstone]

in all the Counties round me. Neglected, I mean, & broken by myself. What a Temptation, to *Me,* is your old Folio of MS. ballads —! At present Let me thank you for the Spanish Ballad you were so kind to send me; which is indeed a good one, & admirably well translated. Edom of Gordon, of which you desire a Copy, must receive great alteration towards the Close, before I can *endure* that you should see it; and as to the Heardsman, I will indeed send you *my* additional readings if you still desire them; tho' they can only afford you ample Reason to be perfectly satisfy'd with your *own.* — If you do not receive your Cleone by this Post, I will take particular care that you shall receive it in a Post or two — I was going to color you a King-fisher &c: when Mr Hylton requested *He* might have the *merit* of coloring & conveying them to your hands. I can spare you a few more of each, if you have any Frd that would be oblig'd by them. — Mr Binnel I have not yet seen, and must needs be under disgrace in the neighbourhood of Shifnal: yet have I offer'd to return home with *him* from the Leasowes, come when he will. — There is one or two fine Odes in Caractacus. As for the Epigoniad,[3] if you will excuse me, I will wholly decline the reading of it. My head will bear but a limited application; & it must be Books from which I have greater expectations, to which for the future I allott a part of mine. Rhime seems *actually* to have lost much ground in all Poems of this Nature; & were Pope's Homer to make its first appearance now, he would be *greatly* blam'd for making use of it — I told Mr —— about the Etymologicon,[4] & presume he has acquainted you with its arrival. By the way, I made a visit to Mr Stratford at Merevale in Warwickshire, who was complaining yt (tho' a subscriber) he had never yet receiv'd Mr Lye's Book. I told him I would cause Mr Lye to be inform'd of it, and did not doubt but I could procure[5] the book. — I will occasion Pixell, when I see him next, to send ye Music-b: to my Lord Sussex. — The Plott is not unravell'd yt concerns [Hylton].[6] The Ldy, who acted as my Amanuensis, is but just return'd from Bath. Pixell gave me ye enclos'd List, which however is too ludicrous for anyone to swallow — your Coin & your Nemean Lion will be wonderfully to my purpose; as likewise your shell, ye definition of which made Dodsley and me laugh abundantly — As to any account of Inscriptions or Improvements at the Leasowes, I will defer it till I can

---

[3] *Caractacus,* a tragedy by William Mason (1725–97). *Epigoniad,* an epic poem of nine books in heroic couplets, by William Wilkie (1721–72). It was first published in 1757 and reissued in 1759. See Hecht's note, p. 105.

[4] The *Francisci Junii* . . . *Etymologicum Anglicanum* of Edward Lye (d. 1761), published in 1743. See Hecht's note, p. 106.

[5] Above the line are the words, "He said he subscrib'd to some Doctor."

[6] Concerning this hoax see the preceding letter.

send you a Little Plan of my Farm; which I have lately had survey'd, & reduc'd to a small scale. I shall there with a very few words, give you a full Idea of all that's done — And now, I think, I have taken notice of all ye topics in your Letter; except y^r request for a Motto to ye Beehive; which does not *yet* occurr to me. Is there, however, no stanza you could adapt to your purpose in ye First of Dr Akenside's Odes.[7] Ego apis matinae &c.

I have been reading, with some Pleasure, the Letters of Mme de Sevigné. The Translation, which fell in my way, is very inaccurate yet somewhat spirited; & seems the *hasty* production of some *French*-man, by no means void of *Genius*.

Mr Cambridge, Author of the Scribleriad[8] and many other pieces, calld & din'd with me about a fortnight ago. He seems to have genius; & the excrescence of genius somewhat of Caprice & Concetto. Dodsley who stay'd wth me about 5 weeks, went from Bi^rm^m to Bath; where he is now, I believe, with Spence & Whitehead, & in full expectation of seeing me. This is one of ye many broken engagements, which I alluded to before — I took Dodsley to Mr Davenport's, but, as it was a week later y^n we had appointed, had ye mortification to find the Family from Home. To *divert* vexation, on my Return back, I compos'd the Lines I send, for ye Venus in His Grotto — Tis, you know, ye Venus of Medici; which has a more bashful attitude y^n any other, & is almost hid there in a Recess. Give me y^r opinion of y^m, or propose any Improvement. There is no one knows of them but Dodsley. Excuse w^t I have scrawld in a paroxysm of dullness — as it is the dullness of your faithfull & very affectionate

W. S.

230. To RICHARD GRAVES[1]

The Leasowes, Oct. 3, 1759

DEAR MR. GRAVES,

Depend upon it, I shall see Claverton before winter. — The mischief is, that, with as violent a propensity as ever person felt, I shall not be able to reach your hemisphere while Mr. Spence, Mr. Dodsley, and Mr. Whitehead, give it such peculiar lustre in my eyes. This I did not despair of doing at the time Mr. Dodsley left me at Birmingham. It turned upon an event which I did not indeed explain to him, the accommodation of the affair with D[olman]; which concerns near one half of my little fortune, and which, if I have any luck on my side, must now be perfected

---

[7] Mark Akenside (1721–70) published his *Odes on Several Subjects* in 1745.
[8] See the Index.
[1] Dodsley, *Letters to Particular Friends*, No. XCVII.

within a fortnight. I was shewn the rough sketch of our *conveyance* last Saturday.—Once for all, my indolence is not in fault; my health and my worldly embarrassments *have* often been so, and at present *are*. "Pol me miserum, patrone, vocares, si verum, &c."

Dodsley, to give his book eclat, should allow himself time to *abridge* and *polish*. It is not enough, in my opinion, merely to surpass L'Estrange and Croxall.[2] The grand *exception* to Fables consists in giving *speech* to animals, &c. a greater *violation* of *truth* than appears in any other kind of writing! This objection is insurmountable. Their peculiar *advantage* is to remove the offensiveness of advice; in order to which, one should perhaps pursue a medium betwixt the superfluous garniture of La Fontaine, &c. and the naked simplicity and laconicism of Phaedrus. In respect of his own new-invented Fables, I wish him to devise uncommon subjects, and to inculcate refined morals. But pray send me *your* two directly, which will answer all that I expect in Fables.

Did Mr. Dodsley tell you of the seat of my shrubbery, which I had taken the freedom to inscribe to you? I could not *satisfy* myself in an inscription; and, from a kind of spleen and aversion to delay, made use of the shortest that I could devise. The seat and scroll are elegant. The inscription, only,

>AMICITIAE ET MERITIS
>RICHARDI GRAVES,
>IPSAE TE, TITYRE, PINUS, IPSI TE FONTES, &C.
>VOCABUNT.

I will not be so affected as to pretend that the much greater compliment you design *me* is more offensive to my modesty than it is pleasing to my friendship. I wish however it could be a little shortened. The "inter hortensis elegantiae studiosos" seems a little too verbose for inscription. Beside, I had *rather* the compliment were not thrown with so much *emphasis* upon any skill I have in gardening; but in some sort *divided* betwixt *that* and *poetry,* if you perceive no great objection; suppose,

>AMICATIAE G. S.
>QUI,
>NAIADAS PARITER AC MUSAS
>EXCOLENDO,
>SIMUL ET VILLAM EIUS ELEGANTISSIMAM
>NOMENQUE SUUM
>ILLUSTRAVIT.

[2] The *Fables* of Sir Roger L'Estrange (1616–1704) were published in 1692 and 1699; those of Samuel Croxall (d. 1752) in 1722.

or,
ET NOMINI SUO
NON EXIGUUM DECUS
ADDIDIT.

or,
AMICITIAE G. S.
QUI,
NAIDAS PARITER AC MUSAS
FELICITER EXCOLENDO,
SIMUL ET PATERNA RURA
NOMENQUE EIUS
ILLUSTRAVIT.

or,
AMICITIAE G. S.
QUI
BENIGNAS PARITER EXPERTUS EST
NAIADAS ET MUSAS.

or,
CUIUS VOTIS
FAVERUNT PARITER NAIADESQUE, &C.

A motto,
(FORTUNATUS ET ILLE DEOS QUI NOVIT AGRESTES)
PANAQUE, SILVANUMQUE, SENEM, NYMPHASQUE SORORES.
V IRG.

"Illustravit" seems an happy word here, if it do not savour too much of *nobility:* villa, I presume, implies no more than a country mansion-house.—But I leave the whole to your discretion.

Now you speak of *our* Arcadia's, pray did you ever see a print or drawing of Poussin's Arcadia? The *idea* of it is so very pleasing to me, that I had no peace till I had used the inscription on one side of Miss Dolman's urn, "Et in Arcadia Ego." Mr. Anson has the two shepherds with the monument and inscription in alto relievo at Shugborough. Mr. Dodsley will borrow me a drawing of it from Mr. Spence. See it described, vol. I. page 53. of the Abbe du Bos, "sur la poesie et la peinture."³

Tell Mr. Dodsley, if he be yet at Bath, that Mr. Cambridge called and dined with me; answering precisely to the idea which I had conceived of him from Mr. D[odsley]'s account. I wish to God he may have brought you acquainted with Mr. Spence; to whom you are, in my estimation, the most *like* of any one I know. Is Mr. Spence yet at Bath?

³ See note 3 to the following letter.

Mr. D[odsley] is gone, or going. Either he or the former told me that anecdote of Pope and the Prince of Wales long ago. Pray read Madame De Sevigne's Letters[4]—they have amused me much of late. I hope, within a post, to send you a neat plan of my farm, &c: the same to Mr. Spence by your means, if he be at Bath. Do you hear who is to be bishop of Worcester? Give me the earliest intelligence you can gather. The late Bishop visited me last year; and intended, I hear, to have done so this. I wish we may have another as obliging and polite as I always found his late Lordship.

 I want to inclose some little engravings, &c. to you, but must wait till I can get a frank. Write *directly*, for this once, I beg you, though you prove dilatory another time. Of all books whatever, read Burke (second edit.) "Of the Sublime and Beautiful;" and of all points whatever, believe that I am, with my best good wishes to Mrs. Graves, dear Sir, ever your most affectionate and invariable friend,

W. Shenstone

DI MEMORIA NUDRISSI PIUQUE DI SPEME.

How do you like this motto for an urn?

My best compliments to Mr. Spence and Mr. Dodsley, if at Bath. I will write soon to each of them.—Your garden is as pretty as you can make it.

231. To RICHARD GRAVES[1]

The Leasowes, Oct. 26, 1759

Dear Mr. Graves,

 I want no conviction of the pleasure which you will receive from the termination of my infernal law-suit. It must, if I have *any* luck, be finally adjusted in about nine days time; after having robbed me of my peace for six of the best years of my life. During the *former* part of life, I languished for an acquaintance somewhat more extensive: and when the company that flocked to see my place removed all grounds of *that* complaint, this accursed dispute arose, and mixed with every enjoyment that was offered me.—I have sometimes found entertainment in balancing the good and evil that has been allotted me in general; and have in the end imagined the good prevalent, and that I have great reason to be thankful for more happiness than I deserve. Yet are there many awkward circumstances that forbid the *scale* to fall *precipitately;* among the chief,

---

[4] The letters of Madame de Sévigné began to appear in 1725; in 1754 and again in 1756 they were published in eight volumes. In the foregoing letter, to Percy, Shenstone says he has been reading them in an inaccurate but spirited translation.

[1] Dodsley, *Letters to Particular Friends*, No. XCVIII.

I place the distance to which I see you and one or two others removed. This is indeed an heavy article, and, were it not for letters, would be insupportable.

As to Mr. Dodsley's collection of Fables, you are mistaken if you think that I perused the quarto book. I dipped into it here and there, and thought there wanted *much* alteration. There was a little book with a paper-cover, on which I bestowed no small pains; and when I had so done, crossed the Fables which I thought might well enough pass muster. Addison would have been the best writer of Fables of any author I know — the purity of style — the conciseness — the dry humour — and the familiar manner. As to Dodsley's publishing this winter, he may possibly do so without loss of credit; but when one considers that they are, or ought to be, the standard for years to come, one can hardly avoid wishing him to give them the polish of another summer.[2] 'Twas fortunate that you pitched upon "the Raven and Magpie" to transcribe for me; as Mr. Dodsley had sent me "The Sun-flower and the Tuberose" *before*. I think the last somewhat inferior, but will re-consider it before I write again. The Fable which I literally translated from Phaedrus was "The Wolf and the Crane," in order to give Dodsley an idea on *what* Rollin laid the stress in Fables.

As to the inscription, I will endeavour to adjust it to your mind — "Meritisque reconditoribus" may do, but is not explicit enough. I want fully to express a character that shines remarkably among select acquaintance, and yet (through extreme refinement) makes less figure in the public eye.

I had made the same objection to Burke's chapter upon *words* — and yet there seems to be something right in it. Du Bos (which I have only seen in *French,* but which I believe is also translated) consists of three volumes 12 mo.[3] His subjects are pleasing, and his knowledge may be entertaining; but his genius seems not very profound, from the little that I have consulted in him.

Dodsley is *precisely* what you say of him; an object of esteem and love, and in some *degree* of admiration. His *ear* does not wholly please me in writing, and yet he is intimately affected with music — Lord L[yttelton]'s ear is perhaps the reverse. I mean, he does not much regard music, yet writes harmoniously in verse and prose.

Robertson I think to buy — Butler also, though I shall not admire him — Lord Clarendon, when I am *rich* — Rasselas has a few refined

[2] Dodsley's *Select Fables* were published in 1761.
[3] Apparently the *Reflexions critiques sur la poesie et la peinture* of the Abbé Dubos (1670–1742), first published in 1719 in two volumes and often reprinted in three.

sentiments thinly scattered, but is upon the whole below Mr. J[ohnson]. Did I tell you I had a letter from Johnson, inclosing Vernon's Parish-clerk? Pray take Dodsley's advice in regard to your ———;[4] and heighten the ridiculousness of your *heroe*, which *his* kind of *lunacy* will countenance, yet admit him to say good things: but do not make *any* alteration in the narrative of your own story—at least, till I have again perused it.— Do not spurn this fifty pounds. It will procure you numerous conveniences, which you would perhaps otherwise deny yourself.

I have passed four or five days, betwixt this week and last, at my Lord Ward's at Henley. This has furnished me with franks, beside the consolation I derive from *having paid* a visit of *this kind*. It is "spinis e pluribus *una* saltem exempta." The *restraint* renders them *Spinae*. I hope I may say so without umbrage, or giving an appearance of disrespect; for Mr. W[ard] is an agreeable man, and my reception was very polite.

I have three or four more of these superb visits to make, and which I may not omit without giving real offence. To Lord Plymouth, next week; Lord Stamford's the week after; then to Lord Lyttelton, at our Admiral's; and then to Lord Foley, if your friend Dr. Charleton will accompany me; then, &c. alas! alas! "Quid me exempta juvat spina?" — I must conclude upon a separate paper. That your *expectation* may not *deceive* you in regard to the plan I promised, I inclose a survey of my farm, reduced to miniature by a neighbouring artist. Let me know if it bring the place to your memory. I think to have a plate (which may be done at Birmingham for six or eight shillings), that shall leave me no trouble but to tinge the impressions with colours, in order to give my friends. But do you advise me to engrave *this,* or another that is twice as large?

I have purchased "Gerard upon Taste,"[5] the author of which is a Professor at Edinburgh, and the book commended in the Review — you will say that the Reviewers are partial to Scotch-people — I know nothing of that, but the book is learned, and on a pleasing subject — I may perhaps add a very *important* one — for surely it is altogether unquestionable that taste *naturally* leads to virtue. I am however in some doubt whether it will give you that amusement which Burke's has done.[6] —

[4] Graves's *Spiritual Quixote* (1773). See C. J. Hill, "The Literary Career of Richard Graves," *Smith College Studies in Modern Languages,* 16:19.
[5] The *Gentleman's Magazine,* Register of Books, May, 1759, announces this work as "An Essay on Taste. By Alexander Gerard, M. A. professor of moral philosophy and logic at Aberdeen. With three dissertations on the same subject. From the French of M. de Voltaire, M. D'Alembert, F. R. S. and M. de Montesquieu."
[6] Burke's essay on the *Sublime and Beautiful* appeared in 1756; the second edition (1757) contained the *Discourse concerning Taste.*

I *must* now take my leave, having engagements of a different kind; but not till I have desired my hearty respects to Mrs. Graves, and her acceptance of this "Grove and King-fisher." I am, dear Mr. Graves, ever and most entirely, your very affectionate,

W. Shenstone

232. To JOHN SCOTT HYLTON [1]

13 Novem: 1759

My Compts — It is indeed impossible for me to help Mr Hylton (or Any one else) to Money before Dolman pays me: which however I expect, *weekly*. It was in full *assurance* of this Payment, that I incurr'd expences *Last* year, which have, during ye Course of *This,* both distress'd me & injur'd my creditors.

What I send, wth ye 2d part of Jortin, is all I recd from Heron — I did not subscribe so much by way of Amusement, as thro' mere compassion —

Thoughts of ye Author of ye "Essay on Spirit" (Bp of Clogher, I presume; *who* is He?) are written in a Masterly way.

Any good News from Coventry? It appears from ye Lines Mr H. wrote with Litmus, yt it keeps it's color *best* in ye *fullest strokes* — an argument perhaps yt it should be *thicker*.

I want my Polygraphici, as we have now some small-Beer Wort.

The Lines at ye End of ye impartial Review are good — & as, I conjecture, our Friend Percy's.[2]

Admiral Smith goes to Hawn daily, & *certainly* intends to carry off ye Widow.

Alcock shou'd, by *promise,* have come yesterday — but he regards neither promise, nor Politeness — What he does for *me,* I mean to be done *last*.

W Shenstone

Novr 13. 1759

I shall, when Alcock comes, borrow all kinds of Heads Mr Hylton has, to chuse an Attitude.

---

[1] B. M. Add. MSS 23239, fol. 51.
[2] *The Impartial Review: or, Literary Journal,* No. 1 (November 1, 1759). I have not had access to this.

233. To THOMAS PERCY[1]

The Leasowes, Novr 23^d 1759

DEAR SIR,

What an aversion I have to writing, unless to such a Friend as you, who will allow me to write with perfect Freedom! The rest is mere "tædet, it irketh; oportet, it behooveth." And perhaps, "tædet, it irketh," *because* "oportet, it behooveth". This I learnt from Lily's Grammar.[2] — Pray, No more of your *ideal* Brat, that you say is to be dropt at the Door of the Publick — I am a simple-minded Man; & have nothing to do with Metaphor, or any such *Vanties* — In truth, I meant no other y^n a mere corporeal Child; with down-right Legs & Arms; of an *original* Composition, & true *English* Constitution; the perfect Picture of his Father and Mother; &, in one word, ye joint Production of yourself and good Mrs Percy. Indeed, before I seald up my Letter, I began to entertain a Doubt whether I was not *premature* in my Congratulations.

I know nothing of ye Work you *now* discover yourself to have undertaken;[3] but am very sure I shall be right-glad to be favor'd with any Piece of your Publication.

I never see Smollett's reviews — But pray tell me, Did you write that Libel on Him, which appears at the End of a Review, lately publish'd, and styld the *Impartial?*[4] The verses are correct and Spirited; & I had good Reason to think them yours.

You have enjoin'd me a very difficult Task in regard to the Willow-tree; especially if you lay me under that restraint, which you have observ'd *yourself,* in regard to the Rhimes. I own, I am not quite satisfy'd with either of ye Versions. I return them; & if aught occur to me y^t tends to their Improvement, will communicate it. In ye mean time, by the Paper accompanying them, you will partly see what I *wish* effected.

The Verses on ye Venus Marina, I have shewn to my Friend Graves; & they will be so much *alter'd* in Consequence of a Hint he gives me, that I beg you w^d burn the present Copy. I could wish, moreover, that you may have said nothing concerning them; for as M^r D———t[5] is gone to *live* at Bath, I may perhaps like to make some other use of Them.

G. Herdsman, Boy & Mantle, & Edom of Gordon; when I have *time;* but why not rather, when I have the Pleasure of seeing you at the Leasowes? A Grove & King-fisher or two, I enclose.

[1] B. M. Add. MSS 28221, fol. 29ff.
[2] This is, of course, the famous Latin grammar of William Lily (1468–1522).
[3] Hau Kiou Choaan, a Chinese Novel, 4 vols. 12mo. [Percy]
[4] *The Impartial Review: or Literary Journal,* No. 1 (November 1, 1759).
[5] Possibly Sherrington Davenport.

I do not like y^r Bee-motto — as being neither *moral,* nor *affecting;* which, when Mottoes are *not,* they had certainly better be quite omitted — For what need of Intimation y^t a Bee makes Honey out of Flowers? I will transcribe Akenside's Ode for you, but it cannot come by the Present Post.

M^r [Hylton] is impatient for his *Curiosities;* tho He is at this time sitting for his Picture, which you will say, perdie, is *None.* He *shall* not be offended at the Receipt of aught you send Him. I swear by the Ventletrap itself — by the Icthyodontes cuspidatus — Nay even by King William's Bibb; & by the Porringer of old Parr.

Ovid is safe in my Bureau — and when you tell me y^t you wait on *my account,* I will be as expeditious as Crispinus. But I really propos'd myself a double Pleasure in ye examination of it with our Friend Binnel.

Positively, I never will *attempt* to translate that Epigram.[6] Do you know that I *hate* Epigrams? & more particularly such very quaint Ones, where it wou'd give No Pleasure to succeed. Pardon me for not complying with your Request; which w^d be indeed a *different* & *real* Pleasure.

Have you seen Gerard on Taste? Dr. Smith on Moral Sentiments? Hurd's Dialogues Moral & Political?[7] All of which I've bought, but not quite read — S^r Ed. Lyttelton says, Hurd's *first Dialogue* will be *omitted* in [the] next Edition — It sneers Dodsley, very causelessly; & is also infinitely *below* the Author —

Mr Duncomb[8] sent me his first Vol. of Horace, together with One of ye Satyrs *inscribed to Me* in MS. But Lo! on purchasing ye 2^d vol., he has chang'd my Name to *Dr Hawkesworth* — This I have *occasion'd* & indeed deservd, by not answering his obliging Letter — However; you see what I lose by writing to *you* instead [of] other persons; and ought surely to make it up to me, whenever occasion Serves — Pardon the *Freedom* of this Letter — I indulg'd ye Humour that was predominant, as every true born Poet should — I hope I've said nothing inconsistent with ye respect I bear to you & Mrs Percy. Adieu.

W. S——e

[6] An epigram sent to Mr. Shenstone at the request of Dr. Stonehouse of Northampton [Percy]. Dr. James Stonehouse (1716–95), physician and theologian [Hecht].

[7] The *Essay on Taste* of Alexander Gerard (1728–95) was published in 1759. The *Theory of Moral Sentiments* of Adam Smith (1723–90) appeared first in 1759. Richard Hurd (1720–1808) published his *Moral and Political Dialogues* in 1759; they were enlarged and republished in 1763. [Hecht].

[8] The first volume of the *Works of Horace in English Verse* by William Duncombe (1690–1769) appeared in 1757, the second in 1759 [Hecht]. John Duncombe collaborated with his father in this work (see the Index).

234. To RICHARD GRAVES[1]

The Leasowes, Nov. 24, 1759

DEAR MR. GRAVES,

Though I write to you again so soon, yet it really grieves me to hear the complaint which you so often make for want of time. I, who have time to *waste,* by lustres, cannot have patience with the world, that suffers *you* to want the leisure which you would employ to so much better purposes. Perhaps, however, you are as *happy* as more leisure could *make* you; the case is not so *clear* as to leave me satisfied of the contrary. And yet, as the pleasures of imagination have an undoubted claim to a real existence, they must surely afford very *lively* sensations to persons of your sensibility and refinement.—Be this as it may, I *will* always *murmur* that you can so ill spare time for literary amusement. Nevertheless, make *one* effort, and finish the task you have now before you. I must confess, you may naturally reply, that I am now become an interested person; but *this,* I am sure, will be no check to your activity.

Mr. William Duncombe sent (with the first volume of Horace) one of the satires in MS. *inscribed to me.* Upon purchasing, however, the second volume, I find *my* name is changed to "Hawkesworth."[2]—Who knows but I lost this compliment by writing to you, my friend, while I should have been writing to him?—If so, indeed, you ought to make it up to me; and I am sure I shall prize *your* compliment beyond that of which I have been deprived.

The view of B[elton], which you mention, I have indeed seen a long time ago; but surely the *water-fall* is quite detestable. There is something on each side, as I remember, that puts one in mind of a porridge-pot boiling over beneath the pot-lid. The appearance of the house and the back-ground is better; this was adjusted by the painter, the other (as I think Smith told me) by an old house-steward of Lord T[yrconnel]'s.

I have inclosed another copy of the lines to Venus, for your emendation.—Thank you for the stanza you introduced.—I meant, indeed, *before,* to allude to *natural* beauty more than *moral;* but did not fully enough express myself. There remains no transition now but from *animal* beauty to *inanimate;* which is easier.

You will observe, that I take great liberties with the Fables you ask me to revise.—Dodsley must think me *very* fantastical or *worse,* while I was correcting those he wrote at the Leasowes.—I find my *ear* much more apt to take offence than most other people's; and, as *his* is far less

---

[1] Dodsley, *Letters to Particular Friends,* No. XCIX.
[2] However, this inscription to Hawkesworth does not appear in Duncombe's second volume. [Hecht]

delicate than mine, he must of course believe, in many places, that I altered merely for alteration's sake. I cannot be easy without some certain proportion betwixt one sentence and another; betwixt one member of a sentence and another; without a melody at the close of a paragraph almost as agreeable as your "magnificent salon."

I have not written to Dodsley any decent letter since he arrived at his house in London.—I must now apply myself to write half a score Fables, and, if he chuses it, a translation of La Motte's Discourse upon the subject.—Your reply in regard to the delay of *my* publication cannot be answered; that is certain.

Whitefield's Journal, I *fear,* is purged of its *most* ridiculous passages.— Dodsley brought one down hither for Mr. Deane to shew my Lord D——th; but he tells me, there remains nothing of that *gross* absurdity which I saw in your brother's at Mickleton.

The painter[3] whom I just mentioned to have taken some portraits through my recommendation, and to have painted a ruin for my greenroom, offers to give me my picture if I chuse to sit.—Were you here to lend me your assistance, I should certainly comply.—Mean while, tell me what you think of some of the attitudes that I inclose. What I myself prefer at present is, to *lessen* my *dimensions* (which of itself gives a kind of beauty), and to appear in a kind of night-gown agreeable to the attitude marked AA. The man evidently hits off likenesses, and is esteemed to *shine* among the painters of Birmingham. I shall be forced to have your picture copied by him, which, by means of dampness, flies off the canvas; so that, on the whole, I shall re-pay his compliment.—This last article puts me in mind that I owe you my picture, whenever you demand it; but I would chuse to defer it till the spring, for some certain reasons regarding oeconomy. Remember me *always* to good Mrs. [Graves]; and believe me yours, with all possible affection,

W. Shenstone

235. To JOHN SCOTT HYLTON[1]

[November 30, 1759]

My service to Mr Hylton; who I presume by this time begins to think himself not much oblig'd to Mr Alcock — But what better can he expect from a Painter, that has been employ'd to exhibit ye royal Face, to 5000 Spectators? For no Less appeard in Birmingham-streets, at ye Display of ye Fire-works yester-night. However I would have Mr Hylton write to

---

[3] Edward Alcock painted the portrait of Shenstone now in the National Portrait Gallery (see the frontispiece). Shenstone describes him at the end of his letter to Graves of January 8, 1760 (Letter 239).
[1] B. M. Add. MSS 23239, fol. 52.

demand the Finishment of his Picture (as Capt. Wight will go near to do same) — and Let his Boy set out, pretty early.² I have not been quite so well, since my Expedition at Ridgeacre — and am to-night, rather Low in spirit — How goes on ye Damm, & what New?

This is ye best blue I can obtain from Litmus by any operation, whatsoever. I observe y^t on different Papers (as differently charg'd wth Alum, perhaps) it has a different effect.

It will appear bluer by Day y^n Candle-Light.

W Shenstone

Tis now, I think, November the XXX. MDCCLIX.

236. To JOHN SCOTT HYLTON¹

[Friday 7th December 1759.]

My Comp^ts. I received his Parcell from Mr Percy yesterday, with a *Few Lines* only, importing that he w^d write again soon & give Mr H. some acc^t of Particulars — I don't *yet* see matter of much Importance in them; It is possible Mr Hylton *may* — If Mr H. have done any more to his old Ballad, I shall be glad to revise it — It really appears to me, more y^n an adequate Return. And yet I fancy Mr Percy esteems his Present very respectable. Mr Alcock² is now here, & has begun to dead-color my *Drapery* in y^e *first* place — I have slept ill, & am not perfectly well to-day; wch gives me Little Spirit for him to transfuse into my Portrait —

Mr Hollier here yesterday; & on Friday next Mr H. is, with me, to meet him at Mr Clare's.

Perry also dind here at my Request, & went home ab^t 8.

The Journey thro Italy is entertaining — not however, thro any remarkable degree of Connoisance in ye Writer — His Jests are often as rouzing Puns as ever escap'd Pixell, Hobbs, or even Dr Parker himself — yet were the Book mine, I w^d neatly bind it in 2 vols — I have gott Smolletts Don Quixote³ here, wth new Quarto cutts by Hayman — I do not like them better y^n those of Coypell — Write me a Long Billet & return ye Letters —

W. S.

(Will arriv'd.) The other R. Ruin is at Birm. but Mr Alcock shall send it back — unless Mr H. means his Book of Arches. Let Will go in ye Morn^g if he doesn't hear from me. I rather think the *men* bestow'd some

---

² The unity of this text is somewhat doubtful. The first manuscript stops with "pretty early" and the second begins "I have not, etc." I believe the two fragments belong to the same whole, but join them conjecturally. They occur together.

¹ B. M. Add. MSS 27548, fol. 32ff. The date is in another hand than Shenstone's.

² See Letter 234, n3.   ³ Smollett's translation of *Don Quixote* was published in 1755.

superfluous Pains *before* (for their own reasons) yⁿ that they proceed too fast now — Mr Hylton *must* be safe in *this* Request, because ye standing of ye Damn is warranted, for a time y^t must imply it's Durability.

I saw no Letter for M^r H.

The Telescope is, doubtless, a very good One —

What if Mr H. attempts a K. Fisher taken off the *blue* on good Paper.

237. To JOHN SCOTT HYLTON[1]

Decr 9, 1759

My Service —

Will was here about half a Hour, not more, before I wak'd, when I immediately dispatchd him. The Knives will be return'd — Mr Hylton had better not disparage Mr Percy's Present (to *Him*) before he hears what he has to say for it; wch I expect to do in a Day or two — Mr Alcock is engag'd to Capt. Wight, to-morrow-morning — but if my own Picture dries, I believe I shall cause him to break thro y^t engagem^t in order to get it finishd. — He says, he shall finish Mr Hylton's at ye next time he comes to Lapell. I desire Mr H. w^d send me ab^t half a dozen Papers of Bark. Mr Hodgetts[2] is just arriv'd; & I cannot possibly stir out to-day —

There is a rumour of extreme *good* news by Sea — & of *as* bad or worse, in Germany — but no assurance of Either — I dont know justly *when* I shall send any one to Birm^m but Mr Hodgetts will go near to return to morrow, & will carry any small Parcell —

I do not find y^t Mr Hylton's pool goes on so very fast —

Does Mr H. chuse to Look at a Pair of those Pistols I mention'd? Capt. Wight bought a Pair of ye same yesterday, by my recommendation — but I think red Ebony, w^d make them elegant *indeed* — Wight has also bespoke Furniture; but I heard not, of what kind. I shall endeavour to keep Alcock to-morrow; for he has scarce done one stroke at my Face — Tuesday Cap. Wight goes to Kidderminst'r Bewdley &c, dines at ye Adm^{es} on Wednesday so y^t one of those Days Mr Alcock may come to Lapell — He finishes highly in Miniature — & I am apt to think y^t the *Appendages* at least of my Picture will be very pleasing — Has Mr H. heard from Ridgeacre — If I ask them this week, I shall hope y^t some of them will sit For their Picture — I shoud rather *wish* Miss Fanny — tho It be more *requisite* y^t no time shou'd be lost by her Mama. Desire Mr H. w^d write me a Long Answer — Good night —

W. S.

---

[1] Bodleian Montague MSS 25427, fol. 190ff.

[2] John Hodgetts, Shenstone's cousin, and with Graves and Dodsley an executor of Shenstone's will. It was he who published Lady Luxborough's letters to Shenstone. He lived in Birmingham, upon Snow Hill.

238. To THOMAS PERCY[1]

Jan. 7th 1760

My best Compliments to Mr and Mrs Percy, with many thanks for yr last packet — I will not fail to write soon — Is it ye *Tune* which makes me Like this little French trifle, or has it any merit yt can induce Mr Percy to give it us in English? I suppose him as *quick,* as he is *happy* in productions of this Nature.

Mr P.'s acct of ye Farm[2] here must be a Little adjusted — mean time I can not but smile to see what an important Figure my Little Hut makes in His representation —

I've this minute, receiv'd two Folio pages of blank verse[2] from my Friend Dodsley; upon ye same magnificent subject. However, ye Lines are musical, & spirited.

CHANSON[3]

Assis sur l'Herbete,
Tyrsis, l'autre Jour,
Dessus sa musette,
Chantoit son amour;
"Cruelle Bergere,
"Qui sçais tous charmer!
"Pourquoi sçais tu plaire,
"Sans sçavoir aimer?"

2

"Dessus cette Herbete,
"Y a t'il un Berger
"Qui soit moins volage?
"Qui soit moins leger?
"Cruelle &c:

3

"Depuis que tes charmes
"Ont ravis mon coeur,
"Je vis en allarmes;
"Je tombe en Langueur.
"Cruelle &c:

---

[1] B. M. Add. MSS 28221, fol. 31ff.

[2] A description of the Leasowes, wch I had drawn up hastily in 1753 [Percy]. The verses of Dodsley are doubtless those found in Shenstone's *Works,* II (1764), 380–82 [Hecht]. A long prose description of the Leasowes by Dodsley appears in Shenstone's *Works,* II (1773), 285–320. See also the map on page 267 above.

[3] The little chanson, of unknown authorship, the first stanza of which Hecht gives, is here printed in its entirety.

4

"Cesse lesse, cher Sylvandre,
"Le douce entretient:
"Ton Coeur est trop tendre;
"Je crains pour le mien.

"A force d'entendre,
"Que Je puis charmer,
"Je pourrois apprendre,
"Que Je puis aimer."

5

"Au bord du Rivage
"Nous jouons tous deux;
"Je t'offre pour gage
"Mes plus tendres Feux.

"Aimable Bergere,
"Qui puis tous charmer!
"Tu sçais *plus* que plaire;
"Car tu sçais aimer."

239. To RICHARD GRAVES [1]

The Leasowes, Jan. 8, 1760

DEAR MR. GRAVES,

Were I to regulate my compliments by the arrival of *times* and seasons, I should congratulate you upon a *correspondence* which now enters upon its three and twentieth year. — Our *friendship* is of something older date; and is not this an *achievement* that deserves the honour of a *triumph* both for you and me too? — More, I am sure, than the regular destruction of fifteen or twenty thousand wretches in the field; considering how *uncommon* we find friendships of so long a duration, and how *cheap* we find such victories, not only on the Prussian, but on the Austrian side.

Mr. Cambridge (Scriblerus), who called here this autumn, was considering this massacre rather in a philosophical than political view; and, indeed, it does not appear to me that plague, earthquake, or famine, are more pernicious to the human race, than what the world calls Heroes; but enough of this.

Your want of leisure gives me pain; surely, if I may guess by one or two of your last letters, you have enlarged the number of your scholars,

---

[1] Dodsley, *Letters to Particular Friends,* No. C.

and extended your domestic cares, beyond what your circumstances *require*.

You must not judge of my painter's abilities by the small sketch I inclose. — I desired him to give me a *slight* one; and have, perhaps, ruined even *that* by endeavouring to bring it nearer to what the picture now is, *myself*. It will give you a tolerable idea in most points, except the Pan, which has his face turned towards the front; and is not near so considerable. — I chose to have this *term* introduced, not only as he carries my favourite reeds, but as he is the principal *sylvan* deity. — The water-nymph below has the word "Stour" on the mouth of her urn; which, in some sort, rises at The Leasowes. On the scroll is, "Flumina amem sylvasque inglorius," alluding to them *both*. — The Pan, you will perhaps observe, hurts the *simplicity* of the picture — not much, as we have managed him; and the intention here is, I think, a balance.

The dog on the other side is my faithful Lucy, which you perhaps remember; and who *must* be *nearer* the *body* than she perhaps would if we had more room. However, I believe, I shall cause her head to cut off that little cluster of angles, where the balustrade joins the base of the arch. The balustrade is an improvement we made the other day: it is, I think, a great one; not only as it gives a symmetry or balance to the curtain of which you complained, but as it extends the *area* on which I stand, and shortens the *length* of this *half-arch*. The painter objected to a tree; I know not why; unless that we could introduce no *stem* without encroaching too much upon the landscape: but the reason he gave was, it would be an injury to the face. The console is an Appollo's head. The impost does not go further than the pilaster, which ends the corner; and here the drawing is erroneous. We are, I think, to have a carpet, though we know not well how to manage it.

And now, I must tell you the dimensions. The figure itself is three feet three inches and a half the whole picture four feet eleven inches, by three feet two inches and three quarters. — The colour of the gown, a sea-green; waistcoat and breeches, buff-colour; stockings white, or rather pearl-colour; curtain a terra-sienna, or very rich reddish brown. — I think the whole will have a good effect; but beseech you to send me your opinion *directly*. There are some things we can alter; but there are others we must not.

You shall have one of the size you desire in the spring; but will you not calculate for some one place in your room? The painter takes very strong likenesses; is young; rather daring than delicate in his manner, though he paints well in enamel; good-natured; slovenly; would improve much by application. Adieu! W. S.

388

240. To THOMAS PERCY[1]

[Feb. 5, 1760]

My best Compliments to M^r and Mrs Percy — I observed in his Letter to Mr Hylton y^t he desired a Copy of these Verses — what else, I do not remember; for I fancy Mr Hylton has taken ye Letter Home.

Dodsley's Lines want some Correction — and indeed are not equal to a Little sketch of a Complim^t in short verse & Rhime, y^t he shew'd me at the Leasowes.

Could not Mr P. procure M^r [Hylton] one of those Locks of Amazonian Hair, by which the Amazons are reported to have suckled Children behind their Shoulders?[2]

I think entirely with M^r P: with regard to Baskerville's bible — & mention'd ye same to Him long ago.

Mr Percy, I conceive, held ye Little *Chanson* rather too cheap — The translation will not do, either in point of metre, or expression — But, perhaps, to give it as good an English Dress as it has a French one, might cost more Pains that it deserves at best.

I will not fail to answer Mr Percy's Letter, ye First moment I can find Leisure and a Frame of mind; which, verily, are not my Lot at present — He will therefore give me Credit for a Letter, yet continue himself to *write* or to *enclose;* as well knowing y^t I am his very faithfull & affectionate

h: Servt W. S.

Feb. 5. 1760

241. To RICHARD GRAVES[1]

The Leasowes, Feb. 9, 1760

DEAR MR. GRAVES,

I could not understand, by Mr. Dodsley's last letter to me, that he had any *sort* of intention to publish his Fables this winter. Presuming upon this delay, and having neither had the *leisure* nor the *frame* of mind fit to take his preface into consideration, I have hitherto deferred to do so; and can only say in *general,* that I could wish you had happened to be more copious in your observations. La Motte's Discourse on Fables[2] is

---

[1] B. M. Add. MSS 28221, fol. 33.
[2] The reference is to the elaborate hoax perpetrated upon Hylton by Shenstone and Percy. See the Index for other allusions.
[1] Dodsley, *Letters to Particular Friends,* No. CI.
[2] La Motte's *Fables nouvelles* were published in 1719. His *Reflexions sur la critique,* published in 1715, included his discourse on tragedy, eclogues, odes, fables, etc.

a most excellent performance; containing, as appears to *me,* all that need be said upon the subject, and this expressed with all imaginable elegance and perspicuity. I believe I shall advise our friend D[odsley] to make more ample use of this dissertation. There is a translation of La Motte into *prose,* which is altogether *below contempt;* and yet, for aught I know, the *only* one. The word *naive* is very probably *that* for which he has substituted the word *lively;* though by no means of similar import. *Natural* approaches nearer it; but according to La Motte is not precise: and, as the words *naif* and *naiveté* seem of late to become more in vogue, I will here give you an abstract of what he says upon the subject: "Je ne souhaiterois plus rien à l'auteur de Fables, si ce n'est d'être fidele au sentiment, & de le peindre toujours avec la *naïveté* qui le caractérise; car j'ose encore distinguer le *naturel* & le *naïf.* Le *naturel* renferme une idée plus vague, & il est opposé en général au *necherché,* au *forcé;* au lieu, que le *naif* l'est particulierement au *refléchi,* & n'appartient qu'au *sentiment.*

"Le *sublime,* selon cette idée, peut être *naif.* La reponse du vieil Horace à la question qu'on lui fait sur la conduite de son fils; que vouliez-vous qu'il fit contre trois? *Qu'il mourut.* Cette reponse est *naïve;* parce que c'est l'expression toute nuë du *sentiment* de ce Romain; qui préfére la mort de son fils à sa honte. Il ne *répond* pas précisément à ce qu'on lui demande: il dit seulement ce qu'il *sent.* Ce n'est que dans la vers suivant que la *reflexion* succéde à la *naiveté:*

      Ou qu'un beau désespoir alors le secourut.

Il *raisonne* dans ce vers; il n'a fait que *sentir* dans le premier.

"Les occasions du naïf sont, peut-être, plus fréquentes dans la Fable; & l'éloge de La Fountaine est de n'en avoir gueres manquées; dans la Fable du Pot au Lait, le discours qu'il prête à sa Latiere est un chef-d'oeuvre de *naïvété,* d'autant plus singulier, que sous *l'apparence du raisonnement* le plus suivi, le *sentiment* se montre dans toute sa force; ou pour mieux dire, dans toute son *yvresse.*"

And now, let me know what English word you would employ to interpret *naif. Sentimental* has some pretensions; but it is not wholly to one's mind.

I bought the quarto edition of La Motte's Fables, to which this essay is prefixed; though the vaunted cuts which tempted me to this extravagance did not answer my expectation. The author, with much address, begs the Duke of Orleans to be at the expence of them; which, to the best of my remembrance was "deux mille ecus."

Mr. Hurd, you see, is one of Dr. Warburton's Chaplains. I bought his

"Dialogues Moral and Political,"[3] almost as soon as they were published. Sir Edward Lyttelton told me, the introductory one would be omitted in the next edition. The three following are very ingenious; but the two former are a little ambiguous in regard to his intended moral: the two last are wholly political, and I have not perused them, though esteemed the *best*.

Have you seen Dr. Smith's "Theory of Moral Sentiments,"[3] which is prodigiously commended, and which I have bought, but not read? — You will see an account of this in the Monthly Review.

I have lately been reading one or two volumes of "The Rambler;" who, excepting against some few hardnesses in his manner,[4] and the want of more examples to enliven, is one of the most *nervous*, most *perspicuous*, most concise, and most harmonious prose-writers I know. A learned diction improves by time.

I am sorry to find no mention of your ———[5] in all the letters which I have received of late. Do not think of *dropping* or even *delaying* the publication of it; only, if you please, before it goes to the press, let me peruse it once deliberately. — What think you, if Dodsley approve it, of admitting cuts into your scheme?

And now, from *cuts* I proceed to *pictures*. Alcock's portrait of me is in a manner finished; and has been hung up for these nine days past, in its carved frame opposite to the fire-place in my library. *They say* it is a likeness, allowing for the diminution of size. Indeed, if I can conclude any thing from the strong resemblance which he has produced of *others* here, I may form some *conjecture* that he has not failed in mine. — Be this as it will, the picture is, upon the whole, a tolerably pleasing one; and this is the most I must dare to say, considering my own person makes so large a part of it.

What think you of a tawney or reddish brown for the robe or night gown, with black for the waist-coat and breeches, reserving green for the curtain? though green is, with me at least, no very gay colour, nor has it that effect which you apprehended in the drapery. Terra-sienna is a delightful colour; so, I think, is Roman ocre burnt. Let me know, then, what objections you have to the drapery just now proposed. Let me know also any design that you think most pleasing for a back-ground; or any story of two or three figures, that would be suitable for a relievo.

From *pictures* I proceed to *painters*. I believe, Alcock would go and

---

[3] See above, Letter 233, n7.
[4] He too often makes use of the abstract for the concrete. [Sherstone]
[5] Graves's *Spiritual Quixote*, not published until 1773. See C. J. Hill, "The Literary Career of Richard Graves," *Smith College Studies in Modern Languages*, 16:19.

settle at Bath, if Amos Green could be induced to join him. Amos Green is the name of the painter whom I recommended to you *before my fever*. He is esteemed inferior to no one in England for fruit. He also paints flowers, insects, and dead-game, *very* well. To this he would adjoin the business of water-painting. Alcock would paint portraits in oil; and to this he would add enamel painting: both of them the best-natured young fellows in the world Now suppose them also *ingenious,* and tell me whether they would have a chance to *thrive*.

You ought to have very considerable *amends,* if you are to be plagued with writing and with music-masters. — I believe I rate your time and trouble at a much higher price than you do yourself.

Dr. Blackstone[6] has raised himself to a very eminent figure indeed in the world of letters. I rejoice at it, without one particle of envy, both as he is your friend, and a person of merit. I believe no one besides yourself would have dreamt of your odd analogy betwixt him and me. — I know not *how* they came to insert that insipid Song of mine in the Chronicle. — What sensation it caused in me, was that of disapprobation; as it looked like laying stress on what one knows to be of no importance.

The chief points where n my picture varies from your drawing is in the corner below the base of the pedestal; where an antique vase is introduced with a flower and two or three leaves of the scarlet Geranium. The gilt vase agrees well enough with the gold fringe on the edge of the curtain; but the whole is so *subdued,* as not to catch the eye too strongly. It was chiefly meant to obviate the disagreeableness of the *parallel* lines and angles occasioned by the step in that corner; but it crowds that side a little, if one look from top to bottom; and, though a pleasing object, it is hard to say whether it do more good or harm.

It is time now to take my leave, with my hearty respects to Mrs. Graves, and with the usual assurance, that I remain your most affectionate and faithful friend,

W. Shenstone

Do write soon.

[6] Sir William Blackstone (1723–80), the famous jurist, a graduate of Shenstone's college (Pembroke), had published his *Considerations on Copyholders* in 1758 and his edition of the Great Charter in 1759. The *Commentaries,* his greatest work, appeared between 1765 and 1769.

242. To THOMAS PERCY[1]

The Leasowes, Feb: 15. 1760

DEAR SIR,

I forget what fine Lady recommends it to her Husband, always to quarrel *en Abregé*. Sure I am, that want of Leisure, & the manifold Articles to which I've not reply'd, make it expedient for Me at present to *correspond* in the *same Manner*.

The Old Ballads I pretended to adjust, cannot possibly *appear* with my consent, had I ever so much Leisure to transcribe them. They are corrected indeed, but that in a manner so very contrary to my present Sentiments, yt I cannot endure to transcribe them as they *are;* nor have I opportunity, or a State of mind, proper for making Alterations.

I never see ye *Critical* Review, — so yt I know not upon what Paragraph there, you ground ye apprehensions from Dr Smollett.[2] He advertises, I see, a *Licence* for his original Papers in the Brit: Magaz: Is not this stooping pretty *Low,* for one that writes ye History of England? But you'll perhaps deny it to be a *Condescension.* I have no knowledge yet, of ye Nature of your Chinese Publication:[3] Pardon me, however, if I propose One Question to you. Are you never prejudic'd by ye *Air of Learning,* ye *obscurity,* ye *rarity,* and, perhaps, the *Difficulty,* of your work, to imagine something in it more extraordinary, yn the Publick will perhaps discover? One is many times led by ye foresaid circumstances, to incurr ye blunder of a Mole, & to fancy one's self *deep,* when one is extremely *near ye surface.* This is, Tibi *Soli,* as ye Jesuits say: and I can guess but Little of your undertaking: But I have known a Person of ye truest genius take great Pains to translate a Poem, when with one tenth Part of ye Labour he could have compos'd a Poem ten times better. For Instance, Merrick & his Tryphiodorus.[4] See Dr Young on origl Composition; & yr Friend Dr Goldsmith's book.[5]

For my Part, I am much pleasd with many parts of that Volume; particularly the station He assigns to *Taste,* of reconciling Literature & the Sciences to Common-Sense. It has ever been my own notion; and I was glad to find it so well authoriz'd. My Maxim, almost invariably, is,

---

[1] B. M. Add. MSS 28221, fol. 34ff.
[2] The *Gentleman's Magazine* for February, 1759, lists in its Register of Books "A Letter to Tobias Smollett, M. D. occasioned by his criticism upon a late translation of Tibullus, by Dr. Grainger." Smollett's adverse criticism had appeared in the December, 1758, *Critical Review.*
[3] The novel *Hau Kiou Choaan.* See Hecht's note, p. 109 of his work.
[4] James Merrick (1720–69), *The Destruction of Troy. Being the Sequel of the Iliad. Translated from the Greek of Tryphiodorus* (Oxford, 1739). See Hecht's note, p. 110.
[5] Review of Polite Literature in Europe. 12º. [Percy]

to take no Notice of undeserv'd Censure. If a Person's object be reputation, Let him press forward toward the Goal: Not even stop, unless *quite* necessary, to *l*ash a Dog that attacks his Horse.

The Orientals afforded a new, & very fertile subject for eclogues. Poor Collins[6] did not wholly satisfy me; having by no means sufficiently avail'd himself of their many local peculiarities.

I cannot positively say whether I sent those Notes to John de Reeve, *without a Cover,* or not. I suppose you would have me always use a Cover.

Maupertuis's Letter on possible Discoveries, I had before observ'd. It put me in mind of an Improvement that I've long thought might be made in our Magazines; were ye proprietors to give encouragement for persons to point Defects in all arts & sciences; for others to propose improvements in em; and to allot a Page or two, for these Purposes, only.

I have now, I think, taken *some* notice, of all yt was pass'd over in yr former Letters. I have now to add about a Page de novo, & so conclude.

Mr [Hylton] is making a Pool, which will add much *Lustre* to his situation. 'Tis really a well-judg'd Piece of work; if he finds no occasion to regret ye *Expence* of it. It answers many important Purposes — It repairs his Road for an 100 yards where it would least admit of reparation: It supplies him with as many Fish, as he can possibly want, from year to year: It gives his House some Figure as you approach it, & is a beautifull object from his Windows. These are important works, & — wt you please. As for me who was, last year, a *Book-binder,* I am become, this year, a *Painter*. I mean my *Amusement* has been, to sit beside a Painter, who has taken mine and about half a dozen other Portraits of persons in the neighborhood, at my House: [Hylton]'s for One, with a noble *Conch* in his left hand; & his Pool &c: in ye back-ground. Motto (for Conchyology I regard not) is propos'd to be:

   J—— S—— of H—— heare stand I,
   Who built a new shit-house, & made ye Pool bye.

As to reading, I have, for the first time, perus'd a vol: or two of ye rambler, & think for *Judgment* & *perspicuity* he equals any writer I ever read — & for ye musick of well-turn'd Periods I do not *know* his equal. For I am hardly *satisfy'd* with any one in ye eng: Language, beside Him.

Have you read ye "Theory of moral Sentiments" by Dr Smith, a Scotchman? or ye "Dial: moral and political," by Mr Hurd?[7] Both which I purchas'd.

---

[6] William Collins (1721–59) published his *Persian Eclogues* in 1742, and republished them as *Oriental Eclogues* in 1757.

[7] See above, Letter 233, n7.

My Ode to Venus is not yet, to my Mind — so that I shall *probably* make *Alterations* — I think, if a proper Reference c^d be made from y^e *beauty* we *admire* in this Venus, to *what* we require in a modern Garden, it might furnish out a madrigal, not wholly inelegant — But I have, however, sent you my *present* Edition of it.

What think you of ye Valentine, receiv'd yesterday by my Under-servant Hannah? With some Difficulty, I obtain'd a sight of it; and have given you ye best Idea of it, I was able.

Such employ^mts, you will naturally say, do not suppose a want of Leisure: and indeed they do not — but they suppose a *mind* wishing to amuse you, & which for ye sake of y^t event, will trespass a Little upon ye time wch is really requir'd for other purposes. Believe me with Comp^ts to Mrs Percy, y^r most affect^ate

W. Shenstone

243. To RICHARD GRAVES [1]

The Leasowes, July 7, 1760

DEAR MR. GRAVES,

I must confess that I do not altogether find your argument conclusive. — And hurry of business *may* be necessary, and somewhat inconsistent with frequent correspondence; but a state of *leisure,* which I wished you, does not imply a course of *dissipation;* which makes your present apology for not writing to me before. And so, betwixt business at one time and dissipation at another, I am to be defrauded of a correspondence that is quite essential to my well-being. Pardon me, if, on such occasion, you find me extremely clear-sighted in the foibles of my friends; and do not say with the man in Horace, "Cur in amicorum vitiis, &c." The *matter* is too *important* for me to connive at any sort of sophism. — However, to make you easy on this head, I am convinced the letter was owing to *you;* for which I will draw my apology neither from *business* nor dissipation: and yet how justly might I palliate my long silence upon *either* footing! Since I wrote to you, I have been *busied* in bringing about a conclusion with D[olman]. The letters, journies, &c. *previous* and *posterior* to the execution of articles, would afford me noble matter for excuse. — The constant attendance upon workmen (of which I have fourteen or fifteen this very day), making a piece of water below my Priory, would produce more on the score of *dissipation* — you remember the place. This, at present, is my chief employment, although Alcock is drawing on the side of my table. — I wonder you do not get some little

---

[1] Dodsley, *Letters to Particular Friends,* No. CII.

urns turned, in any sort of wood, about fourteen or fifteen inches high, and painted on the side with figures, in the manner of some antique basso-relievo. He has done something of this sort for me. You may, if you so please, have the ground a dark *bronze,* and the figures a *light* one. I am of late grown fond of bronze (which you yourself may easily execute), and I think it always was your taste. — Dodsley comes hither in about a fortnight, and prints *one* edition of his Fables by means of Baskerville's press and paper. *Mean time,* he is to *give* me his picture done by Reynolds; and to *send* me two bronzed plaster urns, of about twelve inches, with basso-relievo; and two figures (ditto) of Homer and Virgil (of about twenty-one inches) for two niches in my library. The parcel is to be pieced out with Ogilby's Virgil, which I want for the sake of the landscapes. — And now to the particulars of your letter.

I can readily conceive how much greater pleasure you must receive from the *retinue* of your journey, than an Archbishop can from all his equipage; and I can truly assure you, I find a pleasure in every pleasure you enjoy.

Your room indeed, will be a noble one; but be sure remember the "Imploravit opes hominis, fraenumque recepit," and guard against it — to speak my sentiments, I think you will. I think with you in regard to Tristram Shandy;[2] so does the author of the Monthly Review, you will see. I bought Webb[3] instantly; but have not read it. Lord Lyttelton is *allowedly* the author of those Dialogues;[4] whose the very last, I do not know. There is a noble specimen of Scotch poetry translated from the Erse language — I have had two copies sent me from Scotland; and, had I two franks, would send you one. "Chrysal, or The Adventures of a Guinea" (real characters intended,) will amuse you. Something *ever* occurs that obstructs my travelling at all — and though I long *ardently* to visit you, the Lord knows when it will be; yet *be* it certainly will, when I accompany Mr. Knight to Mr. Bamfylde's: where I am pressingly invited by that gentleman and his neighbours, Lady Egmont, Sir Charles Tynte, &c. — I have about an hundred things more to say; which I must defer till I have heard from you. — God bless you and yours!

W. Shenstone

[2] The first two volumes of *Tristram Shandy* appeared in 1760, and the later ones from 1761 to 1767, when the whole work was published in nine volumes.
[3] Daniel Webb (1719?–98) published his *Inquiry into the Beauties of Painting* in 1760.
[4] Sir George Lyttelton's *Dialogues of the Dead* were first published in 1760. *Four New Dialogues* appeared in 1765.

244. To THOMAS PERCY[1]

The Leasowes, August 11, 1760

DEAR SIR,

I should be extremely glad if the *slow arrival* of any Letters you expect from Me, might in no sort interfere with any *good Intention* of your *own*. I can at best claim to be no other yn a very *desultory* correspondent, who may at *one* time make Amends, for what he is deficient at *Another*. However, I ought *now* more *particularly* to apologize for my Delay, being ye result of a little too much Inattention to your Desire of an Answer by *return* of the *Post*—Indeed I do indulge myself in ye Hope of seeing you some time in Northamptonshire; as I do, likewise in *that* of seeing many *other* pleasing sights, perhaps infinitely less affecting yn the sight of an Ingenious Friend. The Hope affords me present Pleasure—But when! or where!—I'm weary of Conjectures!—having too often been mistaken in my visionary schemes of Happiness—Were I to say all yt occurs, in regard to Master [Hylton]; it would engross my whole sheet of Paper, which I do not intend it *shall*. He has indeed, for some *time,* held but a Low place in my Esteem: altho' what Quarrel we have at *present,* is altogether of his *own* Contrivance; For I by no means wish'd to *break* with Him; on account of yt *amusement* which our Connection afforded *each* of us, & of which he will hardly say that he had *Less* yn an equal share. The Discovery regarding Moody & the Mulberry-tree,[2] was posterior to our Fray; and employ'd by Him as an *After-Thought* to account for much *preceding* Impertinence. The Advice you gave Him was obviously right; but *thrown away* on One, who cannot distinguish, between solid Censure & harmless Raillery. On the whole, he has of Late display'd so much of the *froward Child* & the *officious Gossip,* yt we shall scarce be again upon civil terms, till he have made Concessions which he may not approve—I ought to have told you of our Fray before; yt ye Letters he wrote might not surprize you. I have never *yet* sent Him your *Catalogue* of Rarities; nor a parcell of curiosities from yr Friend Miss Hickman. But a Friend of Mine has, thro' my Hands, presented Him with upwards of 300 Medals; which, as I'm just beginning to make a Collection, I almost wish I had secur'd for *Myself*.

I thank you heartily for your Letter to Johnson. I do very unfeignedly respect both the *Writer* & the *Man;* and should be sorry to forfeit, by a neglect on my side, any degree of esteem he discovers for Me. I am also truly glad to hear of your Friend Grainger's success. I hope however he

---
[1] B. M. Add. MSS 28221, fol. 46ff.
[2] Another reference to the hoax perpetrated upon Hylton by Percy and Shenstone. See the Index.

will not sacrifice too *much* of his Life, *abroad*. When he can once qualify himself to make a little *external* Figure Here, his *intrinsick* merit will ensure success at *Home:* And *then,* I should expect that Home would be more *agreeable* to Him — if I am not blinded by ye Pleasure I propose to myself from his farther acquaintance. I am oblig'd to you for y^e *Incidents* you offer relating to my ludicrous essay on false Taste.[3] Pray fail not to communicate, aught you observe of ye same stamp. I fear y^e *whitewash'd* tree will appear somewt incredible — however, I'll see what may be done, whenever I have *Leisure* and *good spirits*. My good Friend Mr Spence intends a whole *Pamphlett* of this *kind;* which he calls ye History of false Taste: but I do not expect any great matter, from a subject of *Humour* in my Friend's Hands. *Dodsley* gave me this Intimation; who resides here for near two months, to correct ye edition of Fables begun by Baskerville. He has given me a Portrait of his head by Reynolds, ye Price of which I am asham'd to mention. He seems to entertain no doubt y^t your Chinese novel will excite Curiosity — You will perhaps be desirous to know what I have of late been doing about my Farm. One Piece of water below my Priory has *confin'd* me, *employ'd* my servants, and *enslav'd* my Horses all this year — I hope to finish it, the next week; but have often been *deluded* by such expectations. I have had a large conflux of visitants; and expect *more,* when Ld Lyttelton brings all ye world to his new Palace. Pray how do you like his Dialogues? or who is ye Author of ye Remarks, that is so partial as to mention *me* with honour? As to *other* Books, you *must instantly* procure y^e "antient Fragments"[4] of Scotch Poetry — I would wish you to read "Webb's treatise on Painting"[5] "Elegies descriptive & moral"[6] and, if you love *mischief,* the two Odes[7] y^t ridicule Grays & Mason's manner. Have you ever yet seen the "*Prolusions*"[8] containing Overbury's wife, the Notbrowne Mayde, Sackville's Induction, ye tragedy of Edwd III. (as suppos'd by Shakespear) & a Poem of Sir John Davies? Tis indeed a specimen of *type* & *paper* y^t is meant to *alarm* my neighbour Baskerville; & had not ye Editor admitted so many *affectations*, I should hardly know where to assign y^e

[3] The history of false taste was never written, but in his essay on taste, in *Works,* II (1764), 311–30, Shenstone deals with false taste incidentally and refers in illustration to the mulberry tree episode.
[4] Macpherson presented the *Fragments of Ancient Poetry* (the first publication of Ossian) in 1760; in 1762 came *Fingal and Other Poems by Ossian;* and in 1763, *Temora, with Other Poems by 'Ossian.'*
[5] See Letter 271, n3.
[6] *Four Elegies: Descriptive and Moral* (London, 1760) by John Scott (1730–83) of Amwell, Hertfordshire. [Hecht]
[7] The *Odes to Obscurity and Oblivion,* printed anonymously in London in 1760, were by Robert Lloyd (1733–64) and George Colman the elder (1732–94). See Hecht, p. 116.
[8] The *Prolusions* (1760) were compiled by Edward Capell (1713–81).

Palm. However Tonson having sent it to Baskerville, is to find it *surpass'd* in Dodsley's Fables. I presume ye enclos'd to be ye Papers you *mean*, I wish I had happend to take a copy of them. I will attend to Ovid ye first Leisure moment, if you will believe me to be, on all occasions, yours & Mrs Percy's most true & faithfull Servant,

W. Shenstone

245. To THOMAS PERCY [1]

The Leasowes, Octr 1. 1760

DEAR SIR,

I am truly glad that you deriv'd any Pleasure from your visit, which afforded Me a very considerable One: And I shall esteem myself yet *more* fortunate, if any Pleasure it gave you, may induce you to repeat it, when you find a proper Conveniency. There will indeed be no *end* of *writing* all we have to say on the present occasion: A week's Conference on the Subject, when things are in somewhat greater Forwardness, will be more effectual than fifty Packets, as much distended as your last — Besides, I'm a little suspicious that my *winter-Spirits* may render me Less punctual yⁿ you will expect me to be. I will, however, *try* to return your Parcells within a Post or two; together with my Judgment of *acceptance* or *reprobation*. After this, I would have you transcribe what you think proper, in a Large Paper-book, & let me reconsider them *all together*, before they are sent away to Press. Many of those in *Print* need not be transcribd *at all;* only their *Titles* regularly inserted in those *Places* that you shall allott them.[2]

As to *Placing* them, I would not have y^e *Long* ones *ever* follow one Another; unless there happen to be some very *particular* reason for their so doing. My Motive is, that Any that think them dull, should esteem *doubly* so, on account of their *Length;* and then — you know ye Consequence.

I believe I shall *never* make any objection to such *Improvements* as *you* bestow upon them; unless you were plainly to *contradict* Antiquity, which I am pretty sure will never be the Case.

As to alterations of a *word or two,* I do not esteem it a point of *Conscience* to *particularize them* on *this* occasion. Perhaps, where a whole *Line* or *More* is alter'd, it may be proper enough to give some Intimation of it. The Italick type may answer this purpose, if you do not employ it on other occasions. It will have ye appearance of a modern *Toe* or *Finger,*

---

[1] B. M. Add. MSS 28221, fol. 50ff.
[2] viz. The proposed Collection of Reliques of ancient Poetry, &c. [Percy]

which is *allowably* added to the best old Statues: And I think I should always let the Publick imagine, that these were owing to *Gaps,* rather yⁿ to *faulty Passages.*

I have *us'd* myself to these three marks of approbation, + for the least, ++ for the next, and # for the highest. I shall therefore employ them in the present Case; but I would not have you *insert* any Pieces that sink *below* the *second* Mark.

I could indeed wish you not to place your Thoughts on extending the *size* of your Publication. However, I shall not object to 3 such vols as Mallet's, if you can by any means fill them *properly,* even with yᵉ addition of *Scotch* Ballads. You did well in ordering me that Collection of old Ballads:³ I doubt, however, I shall not be able here, to borrow "Dryden's Miscellanies."⁴

I am more fearfull of your *admitting* what may not suit the Class that will be your principal Readers; than I am of your omitting a few good pieces, which may, at worst, be added in some future Volume.

With Regard to the Celtic Poem, I think there is something *good* in it — The absolute *Necessity* of Notes, will be the Rock that you may chance to split upon. I hope they will be as short as possible, & either at the end of every Piece; or thrown into yᵉ Form of Glossary at the end of the *Collection.* Perhaps some small Preface at the Beginning also, may supersede the Use of *Many* — I would rather chuse to have yᵉ translation be a kind of *flowing* yet *pompous Prose;* & printed in *Paragraphs* accordingly — The Original, I should think, had much better be omitted; partly for yᵉ Reasons you give yourself; and partly, lest this, *together with* the Notes, may *load* the Text more yⁿ is agreeable. I should be glad enough to revise, *with you,* this whole Collection when tis put together; In the mean time, I would not trouble you to send each particular Piece; as it is very probable I shall not have means to afford you much assistance.

A Question of yours remains with regard to yᵉ *smaller* Fragments of yᵉ Celtick Poetry — There should be *certainly* nothing of this kind inserted, yᵗ is *Less* considerable yⁿ what you send me; And as to these, and a *Few* of the Kind, they, perhaps may not be much exceptionable. However, if it be yᵉ least necessary to add *notes* by way of *explanation,* One may readily enough conclude yᵗ they had better all be totally *omitted.*

Thus I think I have shewn my Obedience to your Injunctions, for the Present; & if I ever happen to do *otherwise,* I hope it will not be imputed

---

³ That in 3 Volˢ 12 mo. 1727 [Percy]. This was, however, the third edition. The first two volumes originally appeared in 1723 and the third in 1725. Ambrose Philips was perhaps the editor.

⁴ Dryden's *Miscellany Poems,* by various writers, were first published in 1684 by Jacob Tonson, who brought them to completion in six parts in 1709.

to want of *Inclination*. Dodsley is gone to spurr *Baskerville;* returns on Friday to spurr *me;* when I will deliver him your Compliments, & make *this very Letter* my *Excuse.* Mr Melmoth[5] is not yet come, but is expected every Day — I am also made to expect a very clever woman, one Mrs Gataker, with a party of ingenious Persons from London, in a fortnights time. I shall be truly glad to see Mr. Thornton; but I hope he will by no means scruple to make himself known to me on his arrival. I believe Dodsley's original Fables will be printed off in about a Fortnight; when I shall find myself more at *Leisure.*

The printed Ballads you sent, are, I think, by no means worth preserving.

I will here conclude myself very affectionately both yours & Mrs Percy's; if I think of any thing more I will not fail to add it by way of Postscript.

W. Shenstone

Eight o'Clock; Tis now time y^t my Packet should be *made up,* ready for to-morrow morning. I have nothing more to add, except that I have been attending on a Sir J. Mostyn with a Party of Ladies & Militia-Gentlemen,[6] y^t have been long quartered at Bridgnorth. They seemd very good sort of People, without any great Depth of *Taste.*

W. S.

246. To THOMAS PERCY[1]

The Leasowes, Novr 10th 1760

DEAR SIR

I send these few Lines, merely to acquaint you, that I have not yet received the Collection of Ballads from London; &, of consequence, am not enabled to write such an answer as you may expect from me — I am going with Mr Dodsley this afternoon, as far as Birmingham; who goes from thence to town on Wednesday-Morning, & will order those volumes down with all convenient expedition — I will have regard to ye improvements you mention, while the Pieces you allude to, are under my examination — There is no room that I can see, to question ye reception y^t your Work is like to meet with — If I have any talent at Conjecture, All People of Taste, thro'out the Kingdom, will rejoice to see a judicious, a correct & elegant collection of such Pieces — For after all, 'tis such Pieces, that contain ye true *Chemical* Spirit or Essence of *Poetry;* a Little of which properly mingled is sufficient to strengthen & *keep alive* very considerable Quantities of the kind. — Tis y^e *voice* of *Sentiment,* rather

---

[5] William Melmoth the younger (1710–99).
[6] Among these was my Relation Mr Price of Bringpeice, Flintshire. [Percy]
[1] B. M. Add. MSS 28221, fol. 52ff.

yⁿ the *Language* of *Reflexion;* adapted peculiarly to *strike yᵉ Passions,* which is the only Merit of Poetry that has obtained my regard of late.

I have been mentioning yᵉ Quere to Mʳ Dodsley, about yᵉ *argument* or *Introduction* to each ballad — I will say *more* in my *next* Letter — At present, I shall only intimate, that I would wish you to consult for *Simplicity* as much as *possible. Some* old words, I presume (which it will be perhaps necessary to preserve) must be explained by modern ones — For these alone, I would reserve the *bottom* of each Page — The remaining Quere will be, whether yᵉ little Anecdotes yᵗ you insert by way of illustration, should be placed at yᵉ *beginning,* or the *end* of yᵉ ballad — If they are short, perhaps, they may not be amiss in Italicks, at yᵉ beginning. However should you begin each Ballad at yᵉ head of a Page, you will often have *room* for notes of a *larger extent* at the Close of yᵉ Foregoing — and perhaps you may want here to introduce a *particular* note, as well as a *general* Argument. In this Case (yᵉ bottom, as I said, being reserved for mere *verbal* explanations) I would throw both yᵉ general argument & particular notes together at the *Close;* for otherwise your text will be almost smotherd by these incumbrances in every part — However I do not yet decide; & should be glad to hear farther what you have to say — According to this Plan, I fear yᵉ notes would often encroach upon yᵉ top of a Page, if you do not guard against it, while you are printing — I *doubt,* whether you ought to *sort* yʳ pieces; or to *vary* them as much as possible — I will return yᵉ old Ballad next Letter, having at present not a moments Leisure. Mʳ Dodsley's Fables are not quite printed off here, thro' some Mistakes yᵗ have occasioned yᵉ Loss of three or four reams of Paper — However wⁿ fresh Paper arrives, they will be finished in 3 Day's time — Mʳ Dodsley desires his Compliments, as I do mine to Mʳˢ Percy — Pray write soon, & believe me ever yours

Will: Shenstone

247. To THOMAS HULL[1]

The *Leasowes, Jan.* 7, 1761

DEAR SIR,

I am with you aware, that the Story of the *Spanish Lady*[2] is rather too simple, too destitute of Matter for the Generality of People who frequent the Galleries of a *London* Theatre; but might not some Incidents of Humour be extracted from the Group of Sailors, which must necessarily

---

[1] Hull, *Select Letters,* Vol. I, No. LXX. This is the first of five letters to Thomas Hull (1728–1808), actor and dramatist, who played at Covent Garden for forty-eight years, produced a number of mediocre dramas, and edited the *Select Letters* (see the Bibliography).

[2] *The Spanish Lady's Love,* in Percy's *Reliques.*

be introduced in the Piece? There are in real Life various, and very striking Characters among our *English* Tars. Indeed, much Use has been made of them already, and to very pleasing Purposes.

Observe, I propose (or rather merely *allow*) this Violation of the Simplicity of the Story, as a Means to make it answer the Purposes of Emolument to you, if you choose to undertake it; for, as far as relates to my own Taste, I think, even in Representation, it could not be preserved too simple.

The Consideration that an Author is compelled to forego, in many Instances, his favourite Intention, renounce a Compliance with his own Judgment, and even sometimes abolish the very Excellences of his Genius, to gratify the vitiated Taste of a few noisy Auditors, who otherwise would condemn the Work, is rather melancholy; and could not by any Species of Reason be supported, except that which you advanced, namely, that your Theatres in *London* are maintained in these Days at a very great Expence, and that Expence must be repaid; consequently, if Shakespeare cannot elicit a full House, Harlequin must extort it; but woe the while for the State of Letters and Genius! — Such was not the genuine End and Intention of a Theatre. I, for my own Part, look upon it as a Temple raised to *Moral Virtue;* the Design of it is to instruct through the Medium of Delight; to shew Virtue and Vice in their respective Colours: and the Business of the Audience is, to judge, compare, define, to distinguish between what is given for example, and what for Precaution: so conducted and preserved, a Theatre truly merits the Denomination I have given it; but if *Moral* is to submit to *Matter,* if *fine Sentiment* is to give Way to *fine Scenery,* it falls from the Purposes for which it was originally instituted, and becomes a Place of *Shew* indeed, but not of *Science*.

All these Absurdities and Misfortunes are owing to the Audience; and it is much to be lamented, that the Conductor of an useful Place of Amusement cannot oppose and rectify them; but I clearly see he cannot. Your Anecdote of Mr. Garrick's laudable Attempt, some Years ago, to remove from public View an annual Object of Indecorum and Immorality, and substitute a Piece, which (however antique) furnished Matter for the moral Hogarth to display his Genius on, diverts me much, and would (were I of any Country beside *England*) most probably astonish me. As an Englishman it does not. The Attempt was as much to the Credit of Mr. Garrick, as the Defeat of it was disreputable to the Audience.[3]

[3] It had been a Custom at both the Royal Theatres, for many Years, to perform the *London Cuckolds* on the Lord-Mayor's Day; Mr. Garrick, from Motives of Propriety, endeavoured to substitute the old Play of *Eastward Hoe;* but the Audience exploded it. [Hull]

This Subject might, I think, by itself furnish Matter for a tolerably-sized Essay; and I marvel that some Writer, who has rather more Affection for the Use of a Pen than myself, does not adopt it. A Reflection on the very severe Trial a dramatic Writer undergoes, when he offers his Work to the Public, has frequently called forth my Compassion; the Means to procure general Approbation are so vague and precarious, that I almost wonder when I hear of any one hardy enough to stand a Candidate for it.

My Zeal in these Particulars has made me deviate from the principal Object of this Letter, which was to request you to make a little Sketch of my favourite Story upon dramatic Principles, during the Course of this Winter; and let us (Deo favente) when next we meet at the Leasowes, see how the Design appears. It may be an agreeable Amusement, if it answers no other Purpose.

Whether I may ever execute the Elegy which Mr. Dodsley has recommended is very uncertain, though I much approve his Plan. Suppose you were to attempt it — I have some Reasons for thinking that Elegy would suit your Disposition and Abilities. The Mention of Dodsley's Application[4] to me has procured me *twelve* Lines, for which I hold myself indebted. You do not tell me who they were written by, so I suppose I am to ask no Questions.

When you get any more such original Morsels, your communicating them will be a Kindness. While I am thus a Winter Solitudinarian, while

    Scarce one Friend my Grass-grown Threshold finds,

You can hardly conceive how much Value such Trifles bear.

                  I am, dear Mr. Hull,
                  your very faithful and affectionate,
                          W. Shenstone

248. To ROBERT DODSLEY[1]

Feb. 11, 1761

DEAR MR. DODSLEY,

I have spoken to Mr. L—— upon the Subject of his Dedication;[2] and he agrees with me, that there can be no properer Person to procure the Leave we want than Mr. D——. Suppress, therefore, if you please, my

---

[4] In a letter dated December 1, 1759, Dodsley suggested to Shenstone that he write an elegy on the death of General Wolfe. See Hull, *Select Letters,* Vol. I, pp. 270ff.

[1] Hull, *Select Letters,* Vol. I, No. LXXIV.

[2] I believe this paragraph alludes to the Baskerville Horace, edited by John Livie, dedicated to Lord Bute, and published in May, 1762. Mr. L—— is thus John Livie; Mr. D——, Mr. Dalton (see below, Letter 272); and Lord B——, Lord Bute.

Letter to Mr. L——, and engage Mr. D—— as soon as ever you can, to do his best Offices in this Affair. They wait only for the Plates, and my Lord's Answer, before they can order his Arms to be engraved. I blundered, in regard to L——'s University; a Blunder so much the more unlucky, as they have no Masters of Arts at *Edinburgh;* he was of *Aberdeen.* As to the rest, you will give Mr. D—— any proper Information my Letter affords you. L—— does not expect a Present; he will be perfectly satisfied if the Work entitle him to any Degree of Lord B——'s Esteem: and this Mr. D—— may *say* should his Lordship give him an Opportunity. Perhaps it need not be mentioned, that L—— is a *Scotchman,* unless my Lord should make particular Enquiry. Betwixt Friends, I believe, that having no Establishment, he means hereafter to ask some little Matter, by Means of a *Scotch* Lady, who is my Lord's Relation.

The smaller Drawing you enclosed is really a perfect Beauty, and must be executed at all Events when I return it, which I mean to do on *Saturday;* I shall give the Engraver one or two Directions.

I wish I could think as highly of the Frontispiece. In Truth, it does not please me; and what to do, I cannot tell. The Designer does not seem to enter into the Spirit of the Story; and the Circumstance of the Shield hung upon the Pillar, (a single Pillar of the Temple had been sufficient) with the Motto being wholly omitted, throws the whole Stress upon the Merit of the two Figures in the Foreground. I am sorry to say, these do not answer, Maecenas appears with no Dignity, and Horace's Attitude I can't explain. If the Floor had been raised one Step where the Patron sits, and his Person tall, or his Chair embellished a little, &c. and if Horace were shorter, (as his Nature was) his Attitude no Way violent, and his Head down-cast, it would, perhaps, have removed some of my Objections. But if there were no Possibility of hanging a Shield, &c. on a Piece of a Temple, and so making the Back-Ground important, (as the Designer surely might have done) yet there evidently were Means of rendering it more beautiful than it appears here. Hayman[3] certainly should have been the Man! But more of this when I write on *Saturday.*

When shall I see *Baptista Porta?* As also the Frontispiece only to the Ornaments, &c. of Temples and Churches? The Verses in the *London Magazine* are tolerably well printed, though my Punctuation is not observed. Your Brother was to send me also the *Annual Registers;* all, except that for the Year 1759. I believe W—— has or will desire your Brother to supply him with the few Magazines he distributes here. This Letter is written amid much Hurry and Confusion of Brain, when I can

---

[3] Francis Hayman (1708–76) designed the illustrations for Hanmer's Shakespeare (1744–46) and for Smollett's *Don Quixote* (1755).

really express nothing to my Mind, much less the Esteem and Affection with which I am,

> Dear Sir, your most obedient,
> W. Shenstone

249. To RICHARD GRAVES [1]

> The Leasowes, Mar. 1, 1761

Dear Mr. Graves,

Although this interval in our correspondence must be placed, I fear to *my* account, you will hardly think it mends the matter to *fill* my present letter even with the best-grounded apologies — I will only mention a bad state of health, which has been my lot this winter, as a general excuse for two or three months silence; and then declare, as with truth I may, that the esteem and affection which you have so well deserved of me have never undergone the least diminution or abatement. It is with me a melancholy task, to *write* letters when I am not well; although it be the time, of all others, when it is most necessary for me to *receive* them. — Our friend Dodsley, I presume, has sent you a book of his Fables before this time. What merit I have there, is in the *Essay;* in the *original Fables,* although I can hardly claim a single Fable as my own; and in the *Index,* which I caused to be thrown into the form of *Morals,* and which are almost wholly mine. I wish to God it may sell; for he has been at great expence about it. The two rivals which he has to dread are, the editions of Richardson and of Croxall.[2] — The Fables in Croxall are tolerably written: his *reflections,* little to the purpose, either for boys or grown people. — Richardson's *Improvement of L'Estrange*[2] would be a better collection, both for the Fables and the *moral Reflections,* had he not admitted, through an extravagant and mistaken love of drollery, that vulgarity of phrase which in many places is not *common-English.* — This I think a true state of the case: say the best you can in behalf of Dodsley. — As to his cuts, though to *him* expensive, they will hardly, I fear, meet with much of your approbation — the scale is much too small — and the emblematic prints which are larger will scarce, I fear, be understood. — I procured a copy from Basserville *before* the plates were *inserted,* and have caused my painter (Alcock) to supply the vacancies with some devices of my own — some account of which I send you, as it may amuse you for a minute. I want one or two to compleat my scheme, and should be glad if you would propose some in your next letter. — I return you my

[1] Dodsley, *Letters to Particular Friends,* No. CIII.
[2] Samuel Richardson published his edition of *Aesop's Fables,* based on L'Estrange's, in 1740. Samuel Croxall's *Fables* were published in 1722.

hearty thanks for the hints you gave for the Cambridge verses; but when I received them it was too late, and I myself too much indisposed, either to throw them into proper form, or even to answer that gentleman's letter, which I thought a very genteel one — I know not what he did on that occasion, having seen neither Cambridge nor Oxford verses. — Mr. Dodsley gave me "The Environs of London."[3] — Between friends, I wish he may find five thousand readers, whom the management of that work pleases more than *me*. — I will try to get you some of the *cuts,* if you desire me to do so, though it will reflect a kind of tacit dislike of the *whole* performance. — His brother publishes this winter "The Works of Soame Jenyns,"[4] in three pocket-volumes; and a Chinese novel from a MS. translation,[5] revised, &c. by a friend of mine. You have perhaps heard me speak of Mr. Percy — he *was* in treaty with Mr. James Dodsley, for the publication of our best old ballads in three volumes. — He has a large folio MS. of ballads, which he shewed me, and which, with his own natural and acquired talents, will qualify him for the purpose as well as any man in England. I proposed the scheme for him *myself,* wishing to see an elegant *edition* and good collection of this kind. — I was also to have assisted him in selecting and rejecting; and in fixing upon the best readings: but my illness broke off our correspondence, the beginning of winter; and I know not what he has done since. — There is a New Peerage going to be published;[6] with, I believe, the draughts of the Peers houses — Lightholer called here, and said he had taken Lord Lyttelton's, and Lord Stamford's, for that purpose; the latter of which he shewed me. — Thus I have told you what I hear of new *publications*. As to what passes in the busy world, I know no more than the Chronicle informs me — unless when *your* letters happen to be *rounded* with little anecdotes from Bath. — Have you seen Baskerville's new Prayer-Books? My Lord Dartmouth has undertaken to present two to the King and Princess. — Do, for *charity's* sake, make me some amends for this long chasm in our correspondence, by a very early and long letter. — I am sick to hear from you; being, with ardent and sincere affection, your ever faithful friend and servant, W. Shenstone

[3] *London and Its Environs* (6 vols). Possibly edited by Robert Dodsley, and published by him December 6, 1760.
[4] The collected poems of Soame Jenyns (1704–87) were published in 1752; his *Free Enquiry into the Nature and Origin of Evil* was published in 1757; they were both republished in 1761. His *Miscellaneous Pieces in Verse and Prose* were published in 1770.
[5] Percy's *Hau Kiou Choaan.*
[6] Evidently William Guthrie's *Complete History of English Peerage . . . Illustrated with Elegant Copper-Plates of the Arms of the Nobility, etc.* (2 vols., 1763). The *Gentleman's Magazine* for September, 1762, announces "Guthrie's Peerage, No. I. To be published quarterly."

250. To THOMAS PERCY [1]

[1761]

I procured a copy of the Fables from Mr Baskerville, *before* the Cuts *were inserted,* & have by help of Mr Alcock (a Painter) supplied the places of the *emblematick* prints with some devices of my own. I send you some account of them y^t you may be induced to favour me with Hints for two or three more — which will be wanting to compleat my scheme, & which you can very readily *supply* — but which I *can not.*

A Drawing of Mr Dodsley from Richardson. Frontispiece — One of the Graces taking away the Shield & Helmet from Minerva; while another crowns her with a wreath of Roses & the third brings her a silken robe.

Truth leading a Child along ye Margin of a precipice to ye temple of virtue. An agreeable & striking sketch, & ye Landskip very pleasing.

A Statue of Esop — not a handsome Esop.

Two Boys busyd in reading a Book of Fables, that half covers them — makes a pretty ornament.

Boys hanging Flowers round a large Shield of Minerva.

A Sphinx &c.

A Mask, with ye Syrinx, tibia & Laurel.

Three Boys admiring a double-headed Busto — Two staring at ye beautifull Face of a *young Lady* (ye Fable) the third, on ye other side, pointing to a Philosopher's head (the moral) a pleasing ornam^t enough —

The young Hercules strangling serpents; from the Antique — alluding to children being taught early to triumph over vice.

Mercury teaching Cupid to read, his Mother standing by — from a Picture of Hannibal Carracci.

Aurora, with winged steeds, & ye morning star by way of Pompon, driving away y: Night — alluding to ye effect of Instruction upon youth — (taken from Tooke's Pantheon.)

Children dancing round a Statue of Truth, as it were gladdened by the rays reflected on them by her Glass. The prettiest picture amongst 'em, and used as a tail-piece at ye Conclusion.

I can procure you ye names of the *writers* on Dodsley's Fables, if you chuse to have them — some of them certainly are such, as ought to credit the Performance.

---

[1] B. M. Add. MSS 28221, fol. 59ff. Percy has entered the year (1761) in the upper margin. As Hecht observes, this letter probably precedes in order of time the letter dated "Saturday, April, 1761." Some of the phrasing is practically identical to that of Shenstone's letter to Graves of March 1, 1761.

251. To THOMAS PERCY[1]

[April, 1761]

I desire my best Respects to Mr and Mrs Percy, & will not be long before I return a fuller Answer to his obliging Letter — I cast my eye upon it this morning, & observed, to my utter Confusion, that the advertisement[2] should have been returned immediately — I wish it may not come too Late — chiefly that Mr Percy may be less disposed to censure my Inattention to his Request — For, in reality, I have discovered nothing that it is very material to alter — Dodsley has sold 2000 of his Fables, & begins to talk of second & third editions. I would have him permit Baskerville to print one more edition for the Curious, with no other decoration than a Frontispiece with new emblematical Top & Tail-pieces — I want much to see the Chinese Novel; & will lend what assistance I can in regard to the old Ballads. I hope however that the prodigious pains Mr Percy proposes to take in this affair, will be employed rather to fill a moderate Collection with the *best readings* of good Ballads, than to swell such Collection to any very great extent.

Adieu, for a Few days.

Will: Shenstone

Saturday, April, 1761

252. To THOMAS PERCY[1]

The Leasowes, April 24, 1761

DEAR SIR,

You must accept a sort of *Piece-meal* performance of my Promise — I could indeed easily send you an account what Ballads & Songs I have marked in *those* Collections; but before I can properly recommend Any for your Insertion, it is altogether expedient that I should be well acquainted with your *Plan* — The Adjustment of This, will be a matter of Importance, & pretty intricate determination. For Instance, do you make any Distinction betwixt a Ballad, & a Song; and so confine yourself to the *Former?* With the common people, I believe, a Song becomes a ballad as it grows in years; as they think an old serpent becomes a Dragon, or an old Justice, a Justice of Quorum. For my own part, I who love by means of different words to bundle up distinct Ideas, am apt to consider a Ballad as containing some little story, either real or invented.

---

[1] B. M. Add. MSS 28221, fol. 58.
[2] The Advertisement prefix'd to ye Fragments of Chinese Poetry, 4th vol. of Chin. Hist. [Percy]
[1] B. M. Add. MSS 28221, fol. 61.

Perhaps my notion may be too *contracted* — Yet, be this as it will, it may not be of much Importance to consult Etymology on this occasion, as it will be necessary herein to follow the ordinary opinion of the world, at Last.²

Again, if you admit what *I* call *Songs,* you must previously acquaint me, within what *Date* you think it best to circumscribe yourself. And this will lay you under difficulties when I come to teize you with Horace's argument — demo unum, demo etiam unum, Dum cadat elusus &c: For what will become of the new "William & Margarett", "Leinster fam'd for Maidens fair" & many more of a good stamp, which it will touch you nearly, to omit? Again, what will you determine as to old renowned songs, that perhaps have little or no Merit; & would not have existed to this day, but for the tunes with which they are connected? And again, how will you manage the Scotch? Will you allow them a separate volume, & a Glossary? which many of them will too much require? These Points & Many others cannot be so well adjusted as by a Conference betwixt us at the Leasowes; where I hope you will have Leisure to pass a Day or two, when you have dispatched your other publications.

253. To RICHARD GRAVES¹

The Leasowes, May 2, 1761

DEAR MR. GRAVES,

I will, upon your last assurance, take it *ever* for granted, that you do not omit writing upon any score of ceremony. This will render your silence, at least in some *degree,* less irksome to me; when I do not think it the effect of my own procrastination. — Mr. Dodsley had sold two thousand of his Fables long ago; but complained that he should *lose* thirty pounds by my neighbour Baskerville's impression; and that he should not be more than ten pounds gainer, upon the *whole*. I told him it was enough, in books of *this sort,* if the first edition paved the way for their future establishment in schools. And surely so it is: for a book of this kind, once established, becomes an absolute estate for many years; and brings in at least as certain and as regular returns. I would *wish* him to give the polite world one more edition from Baskerville's press; admitting only a *new* sett of emblematical top and tail-pieces; and confin-

---

² In a later letter (264) Shenstone makes this same useful and interesting distinction (perhaps the first so explicitly stated) between a ballad and a song. Hustvedt quotes Shenstone's definitions from the letter to Hull *Select Letters,* Vol. II, No. XXXIX), the date of which (Christmas Eve, 1761) he apparently overlooked. See S. B. Hustvedt, *Ballad Criticism in Scandinavia and Great Britain* (Oxford, 1916), p. 161.

¹ Dodsley, *Letters to Particular Friends,* No. CIV.

ing those empty cuts relating to each Fable to the cheap edition which he prints at London. A second edition of this latter sort will appear in a little time; and if you have any improvements to propose, he will very thankfully receive them. Mr. Spence offers him to write the *life* afresh; and Spence, Burke, Lowth, and Melmoth, advise him to discard *Italicks*. I confess he has used them to a very great *excess,* but yet I do not think they should be utterly discarded.

I did not intend that Mr. Davenport should ever hear of those verses; and how he came to do so, is past my comprehension. He seemed to me to have deserted Worfield, without any intention to return again. I therefore meant to inscribe them under my own Venus, in order to afford some novelty, at an *easy rate,* to those who are curious enough to *repeat* their visits here. Pray, if you see Mr. and Mrs. Davenport, present my best respects to them; and as to the verses, I will send you a copy for them, if you *desire* or *advise* me to do so. — Mr. S—— is agreeable, not void of learning, has some smartness, but little taste. Mrs. S—— has *much* of the latter; and perhaps imagination, which makes a part of taste, may have had no small share in converting her to Popery. Mr. Powys I have almost forgot. — You are ingenious and very inventive in regard to the means of giving yourself mortification. I dare to say, your new building suggests no such idea as you conceive; and I think it sufficient in a parsonage-house, if one sees detached specimens of taste or elegance, without uniformity, or even without consistency.

I do not find but that you *figure* among the gentry near Bath. Dr. Charleton, who was here yesterday with Sir Francis and Mr. Knight, gave me an account that the B—— of G—— had been to pay his respects to you. I will not enter into particulars, but would wish you to cultivate his acquaintance. I shewed Sir Francis the dead colouring of the picture which I intend to send to you; but you must know that Alcock is the most volatile of all creatures that have not wings: by way of improving the picture I meant for Dodsley, he has made it infinitely less like; and yet it must go to London as *it is,* for God knows when he can be brought to alter it.

I asked the Doctor, how Mr. Blackstone came to obtain a seat in Parliament; and his answer was, "The King insisted on it, as he was a man of learning and ingenuity." — The enmity betwixt Lord L[yttelto]n and Mr. P[itt], I find, continues in its full force: insomuch that my Lord is to have no place while Mr. P[itt] continues in the ministry. — My Lord B[ute]'s promotion was, it seems, demanded by the D. of N[ewcastle] and Mr. P[itt], as they would not be exposed to bear the blame, while he was the chief mover behind the curtain. These little particles of intelligence have, I believe, Sir —— for their author. — I was told by another politician, the same day, that we were not to expect a peace; that the French, who might give up the Colonies, would not resign the Fishery.

Mr. Knight, his mother and sister, go through Bath to Mr. Bamfylde's in about three weeks, if nothing intervene. I am teazed greatly to accompany them — by my own *inclination,* I can assure you, as well as their *importunity.* I do not say I will *not,* nor must I ever promise you *beforehand* that I *will.* I have good reasons to the contrary. They have some thoughts of bringing Dr. Charleton into the party.

Believe me ever yours and Mrs. Graves's
W. Shenstone

254. To THOMAS PERCY [1]

Wednesday, June 11th 1761

My best Compliments to Mr Percy, who already owes me a Letter; yet would I give him credit for another, if I had *Leisure* at this time to write again — Mr Baskerville has sent me a specimen of Horace,[2] about twice as large as ye small Elzevirs; He proposes to copy Elzevir, but y^e *Punctuation* has been objected to — It seems Elzevir omits ye semi-colon universally, & is not accurate in ye application of y: 3 remaining stops — Quere, what is to be done: & whether he had not better substitute some other edition in regard to *text* as well as punctuation? As to ye Former, I was thinking of Francis — Pray tell me your Opinion — I did *not* send y^r Letter to Mr Hylton, for reasons I will give, when I have more Leisure to explain myself — I will however send the Biography, & mention y^r request, in a Day or two's time — I took ye Liberty of asking Mr Dodsley for your Chinese Novel, as I knew you were so good to intend me a copy. —

W.S.

255. To THOMAS PERCY [1]

The Leasowes, July ye 5th, 1761

DEAR SIR,

I am truly glad to find that all things conspire so happily to favor your undertaking, & to further an event I have wished so long, as that of a

---

[1] B. M. Add. MSS 28221, fol. 64. Hecht does not print this letter in full.
[2] Baskerville's Horace was published in May, 1762. John Livie, the editor, dedicated it to Lord Bute.
[1] B. M. Add. MSS 28221, fol. 67ff.

good edition of old Ballads—I know not how that Ballad of "Rosamond" came to be totally omitted in my List: I found it distinguished in the Book wth a mark of second-rate approbation. *More* than this, I cannot allow it; notwithstanding any merit I could discover, on a reperusal. It seems to me a melancholy Fact, smoothely & decently related, without any great indication of *poetical Spirit* in the Composer. Compare it with "the Spanish Lady", either in point of *Sentiment* or poetical embellishment, & I should imagine, you wou'd find a difference, much in Favour of the Latter. I will only add that you should by all means *insert* it, as it will [be] proper to have a Ballad on the Subject.

I have read "the Hive"[2] in 4 vols, & the vocal miscellany in 2, since I rec^d your last Letter; marking ye songs with a different number of crosses, according to ye different quantity or proportion of *poetical Spirit* I observed in them. You shall have a List, when I can find Leisure to transcribe one; or rather, I will find the Leisure for that purpose, when you let me know that you require it. I must confess, the Task has been a little irksome to me; as the number of frothy & affected Pieces I found there written on ye subject of Love, has almost habituated me to read, without any sort of Attention. I rather chose, however, to admit many, for you to reject; y^n to reject one, for you to admit. I will depend upon seeing you & your collection (at least a *List* of your collection) before you send it to the Press. I told Dodsley in my last Letter y^t I was sure the work w^d be a noble One; if I might guess from y^r activity, y^r Learning, y^r Diligence, & your connexions. I wished it might be an elegant edition; & very greatly shall I be deceived, if there be not large numbers in the Kingdom y^t will be as much pleased with such a work, as *our* Friend Mr Johnson, Mr Garrick, or myself. I have a very good Friend in Scotland,[3] who has a taste for Vertu & for Antiquity. He has made me a Present of many books from Scotland; and, I am sure, so soon as I can write to him, will gladly be of service to your undertaking—I am glad you wrote, y^r *self,* to Mr Warton, for (tho' I *would* have done it in y^e *end*) yet, to my shame be it spoken, I never wrote to thank him for the Present he made me of his Critique upon Spenser.[4] The Preface to y^r Letter was very pertinent; & must engage him to serve you, to the utmost

---

[2] *The Hive* (4 vols., London, 1724) and *The Vocal Miscellany* (2 vols., London, 1734) were collections of popular songs.

[3] John MacGowan, Writer to the Signet. A letter from him to Shenstone, dated June 21, 1760, is printed in Hull's *Select Letters,* Vol. II, No. XLII. See also Shenstone's letter to him, No. 259 below.

[4] Thomas Warton's (1728–90) *Observations on the Faerie Queen* first appeared in 1754. His *Life and Literary Remains of Ralph Bathurst* (1620–1704) was published by Dodsley in 1761.

of his Power — I have only seen *extracts* from his Life of Bathurst — I suppose he rather *means* it as a pious tribute to the memory of a benefactor, than a work which will much interest or entertain the Publick. I will assist you, what I can, in *Designs* for this Collection; but should chuse to enter on ye task, when you are here.

I have recd your Chinese-Novel,⁵ but have not yet had time to read it. Tis a neat edition, I see; & I wish you all success. Do you not suppose "ye *House* of Sussex," a little too pompous in yr Dedication; or do you *mean* it *should* be pompous, in Lieu of much *other* Panegyrick? — The six last words in yr Dedictn had surely better be omitted — I have hitherto read no farther, & I shew a Confidence in yr good-nature, by making thus free— Mrs Lyttelton (ye Governor's⁶ very agreeable Lady) presented me with Almoran & Hamet;⁷ as a ballance for wch I gave her Dodsley's Fables, in Morocco. In truth, I cannot think Dr. H. by any means a first-rate writer. His *taste* in writing seems defective. See his poor Taste in regard to Fables, in ye 18th Adventurer vol. the First. Mr Johnson's Rasselas deserves applause, on account of ye many *refined Sentiments* he has expressed with all possible *elegance* & *Perspicuity* — As to Almoran, I subscribe to yr Sentiments; & have some others of my own, wch are by no means in it's Favor — I cannot however esteem his Love-story a very pleasing one. The King's Notice may establish ye Author; but will hardly be able to establish the Book — I think Baskerville should hardly *venture* to follow *Bentley* in his Edition of a small Horace; but I am sure there are 4 or 5, at least he ought to follow, in preference to Elzevir — He is now at London.

I shall probably write to you again in a Post or two; but do not suffer any expectation of this Sort to deprive me of a Letter, when you have Leisure to write one. I am very affectionately both

yours & Mrs Percy's
Will: Shenstone

⁵ *Hau Kiou Choaan* is inscribed "To the Right Honourable The Countess of Sussex." As Hecht observes, Shenstone's timely warning was heeded.

⁶ William Lyttelton, Governor of South Carolina [Percy]. William Henry Lyttelton was the younger brother of the poet-statesman. In June, 1761, he married Mary Macartney of Longford in Ireland.

⁷ *Almoran & Hamet,* an oriental novel somewhat comparable to Johnson's *Rasselas,* was published in 1761. The author was John Hawkesworth (1715?–73), one of the founders of *The Adventurer* (1753–54), and an editor of Swift (1755).

256. To THOMAS HULL[1]

[Birmingham, Aug. 29, 1761]

I desire my Compliments to Mr. Hull and Miss Morrison,[2] with many Thanks for the Pleasure I received from last Night's Play.[3] It was, indeed, acted with great Spirit, and as far as I could judge, afforded the Audience no small Satisfaction — not, perhaps, equal to what they derived from the Appearance of the Dun Cow, &c.[4] for that is hardly to be expected.

I think the Play has now so much *good* in it, that it may be worth Mr. Hull's while to give it a few more finishing Touches. Suppose a Confessor or Friar, either out of Hatred to the Queen, view to his own Advancement, or any *selfish* Motive (which he might explain in a short Soliloquy) persuaded Rosamond to aspire to the Throne, and to urge the King to a Divorce; that Rosamond should avow her Abhorrence of such Injustice to the Queen, intimating, that her Love had no other Object than the King's Person and heroic Virtues; that this Refusal should affront the Friar, who in Revenge should inform the Queen, that Rosamond actually *had* those very Intentions with which he had been endeavouring to inspire her, &c. This would throw more Plot into the Play, (which it wants) would more sufficiently account for the Queen's sudden Change from a mild Character to a revengeful one, and, as Mr. Hull thinks the Play too short, would add two new Scenes. Some further Improvements I would recommend in the Close, and a few more Places; but Mr. Hull's further *Attention* to the Play, will render it needless to point them out to him.

If you should ever complete this Undertaking to your Liking, and produce the Piece on a *London*-Stage, I would recommend, that you should by all Means give it a double Title in the printed Bills; namely, *Henry the Second, or the Fall of Rosamond.*

I should esteem it as a Favour, if Mr. Hull would send me down a Copy of the Prologue and Epilogue as they were spoken; which I will not communicate without his Permission. Either his or Miss Morrison's Muse seems to favour them at a Minute's Warning.

Mr. Hodgetts, with whom I am at present, would be glad that Mr.

---

[1] Hull, *Select Letters,* Vol. II, No. XXXVI.

[2] Miss Morrison was one of Hull's principal actresses. He married her in 1760.

[3] A hasty and imperfect Compilation of some scenes, on the subject of Rosamond, which, however, laid the Ground-Work of the present tragedy, acted at Covent-Garden Theatre. The Public may easily discern how fully the Author has availed himself of the kind and judicious Hints contained in the Letter before us [Hull]. Hull's tragedy, *Henry II,* was played in 1773 and published in 1774.

[4] Introduced in a Pantomime performed the same Evening. [Hull]

Hull would dine here, about two; and so should I, if it be no way inconvenient to him.

I had almost forgot to thank you for the Stanzas[5] you left at the *Leasowes,* when I was on a Visit to *Hagley.* They are well constructed for the Occasion, and the Idea seems to arise from a humane Sensibility, warmed with honest Indignation.

I am very affectionately yours,
W. Shenstone

Snow-Hill, Birmingham, Aug. 29, 1761

257. To RICHARD GRAVES [1]

The Leasowes, Sept. 14, 1761

DEAR MR. GRAVES,

I ought to have thanked you many weeks ago, for a very *long* and *entertaining* letter; the *length* of which, as well as the *entertainment,* was increased by a postscript a few days after. — But as the Winter is with me a dull and uniform season, so the Summer is a time of universal dissipation; and very happy do I think myself, when, after a continual succession of company, visits paid, and excursions taken, I can sit down in peace and quietness, to attend to the business of correspondence and friendship. Either reason, habit, or complexion tells me, that I am never *otherwise* so properly employed.

The last digression I made was to the concert at Worcester, to hear "The Messiah" well performed; to meet a number of faces one knows; but first, and principally, to visit your brother, *without* which motive I had not gone. In the two *former* respects, the journey answered my expectation: — but, alas! your brother was gone into Herefordshire. I, however, alighted out of the chaise; and the house-keeper very civilly shewed me his delightful parlour, that looks into the meadows, the Prebends' gardens, and down the Severn to Malvern-hills. A more agreeable town-house cannot possibly be found anywhere. But I regretted, when I reached the inn, that I had not asked to see his children; for I either heard them upstairs, had a glimpse of them at the window, or fancied, to a degree of conviction, that they were most of them within the house. I now return to remark upon some particulars in your letter. — I believe it is that indifference you complain of, which is the *grand* detriment to genius in an advanced part of life. In all *poetical* affairs, we

---

[5] See Hull, II, 118–20.
[1] Dodsley, *Letters to Particular Friends,* No. CV.

Richard Graves
From an engraving in the National Portrait Gallery, London

are too apt to cry out with Pallas, "Non est mihi tibia tanti;" and this renders all our efforts tame, prosaic, and judicious. But this propensity, as well as many others, we should guard against, upon the approach of age; change the object of our amusement; cherish hopes, well or ill-grounded, of finding that pleasure in the novelty of objects, which we have not found in any individual. These are the means of *preserving our vivacity* a somewhat longer time than it naturally lasts; but how far it is *prudent* to attach ourselves to the world that we must leave, is a point which *you* better can determine. Refined taste, as it implies a *love* of physical beauty, has this tendency.

There is nothing can be more rational than what you say about the expediency of *losing no time,* if I mean to collect and publish what I have written. You are indeed very partial to my abilities; but, allowing for *that,* what you mention *coincides* with what I have thought myself, and this for some years past. A more agreeable kind of *distraction* in summer, and an indifferent state of health and spirits in winter, have hitherto prevented any progress in the correction of my pieces. To these I might add a *suspence* about the compositions, and the manner proper for publication. I am now most inclined to make a collection of the whole; I mean, the best of what are already printed or in MS; to publish them by subscription in a large *quarto* size for the sake of profit; and to apologize for this method, by mentioning the expence of top and tail-pieces, with which I mean they shall be embellished. Some of *these* (by the bye) may be taken from my farm, the rest emblematical, in an easy and careless, but, at the same time, elegant manner. I should think the instance of Mr. Pope might render this method not disreputable; and it might be advertised (as was done by Mr. Spence), that, unless a certain number were subscribed for, the whole affair should be no farther prosecuted. This would put it in the way of many friends to serve me, who (I flatter myself), *with inclination,* esteem themselves void of *opportunity*. Let me beg you to think seriously of this, as well as of a general title-page, before you write again.

Thank you kindly for all the little diverting anecdotes that are contained in your letter. I am glad to hear your *place* brings you company; partly, as it tends to amuse you; and yet more, as it tends to make your merit more conspicuous. You and I have led a life of total disinteressment. Let me advise you to seek some *advantage* from your commerce with *great men*.—The boy, who was here with you and Mrs. Graves, was here last Friday evening with a Mr. Jolliffe and his son; the latter of whom observed your name upon the bench, and seemed proud to declare that he was once your school-fellow. Mr. Stratford (to whom I had written about gold-fishes) says in his answer, "I had the pleasure from Bath of waiting upon Mr. G[raves], and was as much satisfied with the miniature beauties of his place, as with the polite reception I met with from the owner." If you have an opportunity, you will oblige me by presenting my compliments to that gentleman. — I met Dr. Charleton[2] at Worcester, who stands high in my esteem. — The account of Gothic architecture, &c. is curious; but I have found it in Dr. Warburton's edition of Pope. — I inclose the verses on the Venus de Medicis — I told you before my intentions, &c. concerning them; and since, I hear that they have appeared in some one of the Magazines — through Dodsley's or Percy's means, for I surely gave a copy to nobody besides; and those copies must be much imperfect. — My picture shall be sent you as soon as I can possibly get Alcock over, who has promised to come every week for these three months past. I believe he *will* come soon. — I did not know of Mr. Warton's compliment; but he is very obliging to me on all occasions, and sends me all that he publishes. — I have not yet read Dr. Robertson's History, to my shame be it spoken, though I have the honour to know the author. — I hope the King *will* oblige the Irish Peers with a place in the procession, as that people seems greatly out of temper; and, I fear, not without some reason.

I see my friend Dodsley has *let off* his little *squib* upon the marriage, in the Chronicle. "The King sought a partner," &c. And last night was brought me, from Baskerville's press, on the same occasion, very *pompously* printed, the most despicable Grubstreet I ever saw.

I have made some little improvements about my place; have taken away the wall in front, and made a handsome ring; have extended my path, in one piece of ground, greatly for the better — but the grand water in the valley will make no figure till next spring.

I have also assisted my friend Hull the comedian in altering the Tragedy of "Rosamond;" had it brought upon the stage to a full house at Birmingham, where it was very well received; put Hull into a way of making an indirect compliment to the present King in the ten last lines of his Epilogue, which was followed by "God save great George," &c. in a full chorus of the audience and actors drawn out abreast upon the stage.

Since this, there has been deposited in my hands a large collection of

[2] Dr. Rice Charleton (1710–89) for many years practiced medicine at Bath, and from 1757 to 1781 was physician to the Bath General Hospital. He published tracts on the Bath waters between 1750 and 1774.

Poetry, by a Miss Wheatly of Walsall:[3] many of the pieces written in an excellent and truly classical style; simple, sentimental, harmonious, and more correct than I almost ever saw written by a lady. They will be published, I believe, by subscription, under the patronage of Lord Dartmouth.

But nothing in the poetical way has pleased me better than a compliment which I received about nine days ago by the post, under the feigned name *Cotswouldia*.[4] — She must be some Gloucestershire lady that has seen the place; as she raises up a Fairy in my grove, into whose mouth she puts the compliment. It seems written by somebody of fashion by the style. — Can you form any conjecture?

There was a Mr. Freeman of Betstow (or some such name) with two or three ladies in a coach and six that were here not long before; a very genteel and polite young man.

I really know not how to stop, when I begin a letter to *you;* and it is one reason why I look upon the task as too considerable to be undertaken at all times. Pray write soon, and believe me wholly yours and Mrs. Graves's.

W. Shenstone

258. To THOMAS PERCY [1]

The Leasowes, Sept^r — 1761. Saturday

DEAR MR. PERCY,

Accept a few hasty Lines, after a long series of dissipation, which must account for my Late silence & my present Incoherency. The Mind takes some time to settle, after having been distracted by Concerts & Horse-races; and were I to see the Coronation, which I do not mean to do, it would be stuffed with nothing but Lace, ermin, Feathers, Coronets & velvet, for this half-year.

I hardly know how to re-unite the thread of our Correspondence; But this I know, that having read Hau Kiou Choaan,[2] I ought to have returned you earlier thanks for the Pleasure it afforded me. Let me tell *you* my *truest* sentiments, at the time I tell others my most *favorable*

---

[3] Miss Mary Whateley's *Original Poems on Several Occasions* were published by Dodsley in 1764; a second edition appeared the same year; an enlarged edition in two volumes was published in 1794 in Walsall. The poems show the influence of Shenstone. Hecht, pp. 122–23.

[4] Shenstone's *Works*, II (1764), 376–78. Hecht (p. 123) identifies her by a note (Graves's) in his copy as Mrs. Thomas, a sister of Lord Amherst, and the wife of the Rev. John Thomas, rector of Nutgrove and Welford in Gloucestershire; a lady "celebrated for her poetical talents," according to Collins (*Peerage of England*, VIII, 169).

[1] B. M. Add. MSS 28221, fol. 73ff.

[2] Lady Gough borrowed it, kept it a Fortnight, & read nothing but ye dedication. [Percy]

ones; for this I think is the business of Friendship, in all circumstances of this kind. The Novel, tho' in some parts not void of Merit, must certainly draw its chief support from its value as *a Curiosity;* or perhaps as an agreeable means of conveying to the generality all they *wish* or *want* to know, of the Chinese manners and constitution. I think the Publick must esteem itself as much obliged to the *Editor,* as the editor has grounds to be offended at the *Printer.* Very numerous indeed are the errors that remain, over & above what appear in the tables of errata: & very sollicitous *indeed* does ye Editor appear, least, by ye omission of any *possible* Improvement, he should disoblige the Publick. This, perhaps, to an excess, of ye *better kind.* Your Annotations have great merit; yet, on ye whole, I can form no *Conjecture,* what vogue it will obtain. I can only say I wish it all that you co, or even Mr J. Dodsley.

I long much to hear how you proceed in regard to your Ballads. Tis undoubtedly a popular scheme; and, with all deference to my Friend Mr Dodsley, deserves to be rendered to the Editor more advantageous yn he has yet made it. You must not intimate yt I *say* this; but I certainly *think* it. The names of the Ballads I selected, shall be sent you whenever you want them; & when this is, you must let me know. There was a Little good-natured, welch-man called upon me t'other Day; I think he said his Name was Rice;[3] &, as far as I could make out, he is Chaplain to the Earl of Bradford. He told me yt, by his means you had settled a Correspondence in Wales, & left with me a Little welch Ode, wth a Literal translation of it in Latin — You must send me a word how far you've gone, and whether there be any Hopes, that we may see the Collection next winter.

There is a Miss Wheatly, about six miles from hence, who has written a pretty Large Collection of Poetry[4] — I have been attending to it for this week; & really think yt many Pieces are written with a truly classic elegance. If she can obtain my Lord or Lady Dartmouth's Leave they may possibly appear this next winter, under one or other of their Names.

Company intervenes, & I must take my Leave; having many things to *say,* but Little or nothing to *write* — Is not ye natural *Inference,* that you must call upon me as soon as may be?

You will find Dodsley's verses on the Leasowes,[5] in the Gent's Magazine for *last* month, ill-printed; & probably, printed better, in ye London-Magazine, for *This.* But I have last week received a Copy of verses from

---

[3] Rice Williams, Rector of Weston near Shifnal and Newport, Shropshire. [Percy]

[4] See note 3 to preceding letter.

[5] *Gentleman's Magazine,* 1761, pp. 374–75; *London Magazine,* 1761, p. 499. Reprinted in Shenstone's *Works,* II (1764), 380–82.

some fair Lady of Glostershire,⁶ which I like much better. They are sign'd Cotswouldia, & came by the Post. You shall see them soon, one way or other. My best respects to Mrs Percy & my best affections wait on you.

W. Shenstone

P. S.

Dodsley's Verses were sent both to the London-Magazine, & the Gentleman's; that I might preserve my Impartiality betwixt those two original Magazines. The Proprietors of y^e *Latter* printed them very incorrectly; and, of the *Former,* not at All. Dodsley himself, being now in Town; means to reprint them in one or other of ye periodical papers: probably in the L. Chronicle, or London Magazine, in each of which he has some Property.

Pray was it You or He, that caused a Copy of my Verses on the Venus de Medicis, to be printed in some one of the Papers?⁷ For so Mr Jago tells me, he saw them. I rather impute it to Mr Dodsley, who served me so, once or twice before. They are called, it seems, "Directions for Taste, taken from &c." This is quite contrary to my Maxim of never saying any thing at ye Head of an Ode which may give Intimation what you are to expect. I am vexed at Baskerville for acting otherwise, in ye Little Pocket Horace y^t he has almost printed; Any *short* argument must be imperfect & any *Long* one, utterly absurd. The scotch editor judged better, & his edition *looks* ye better for this Omission; tho I know B. lays no small stress upon ye beauty of his *Italick* Type. But to return from this digression — These said Verses of mine are printed without a Name, or any other Circumstance relating to 'em; by which means they answer no other purpose y^n that of expletives to a Magazine. Besides this they were printed prematurely, & are since improved by an additional stanza — Clear yourself of this affair.

Let ye Liberties taken by the Translator of the Erse-Fragments be a Precedent for *You*. Many old Pieces, *without* some alteration, will do nothing; &, *with your* amendments, will be striking.

W. S.

17 Septr 1761
Pray what do you hear of the Queen?

⁶ See above, Letter 257, n4.
⁷ They were printed by Dodsley. [Percy]

259. To JOHN MacGOWAN[1]

The Leasowes, Sept. 24, 1761

DEAR SIR,

I have indeed been guilty of the most absurd hypocrisy that ever was, having suffered an appearance of neglect to rob me of the pleasure of your correspondence, when no one living could have been more sensible of the obligation it laid me under. Sure I am that I must be greatly indebted to Mr. Roebuck's[2] representation for the place I still retain in your esteem, and which I should utterly have given up for lost, had not your goodness, by many ouvert acts lately convinced me of the contrary.

'Twas indeed the view of accompanying my letter with something worthy of your acceptance, that has kept me silent so long, in spite of all your friendly provocations. I wanted to transcribe one or two pieces of greater length than the trifles I inclose. Alas, that I have not, even now, an opportunity of so doing! Dr. Roebuck goes tomorrow, and you must accept of an irregular disjointed letter, in which I find it my duty to acknowledge so many different favours.

The Scotch press,[3] of which you sent me so many agreeable specimens, has, I think, not a rival in the world, unless it be that of my neighbour Baskerville. Here I find myself unable or unwilling to decide the preference. Amongst friends, however, I would whisper, that Baskerville's impressions are more striking to the eye, either on account of his ink, his paper, or his type; yet, at the same time, it may be much doubted whether the Scotch editions will not be deemed the best for use. Martial has expressed what *may* prove the case at the close of one of his epigrams:

Laudant illa, sed ista legunt.

As to correctness, the Scotch seems to have hitherto the advantage; but if Baskerville find encouragement to print many Latin books, he purposes, I believe, to employ a Latin editor. There will shortly appear an Elzevir Horace from the press, revised by Mr. Levy,[4] which you will probably like to see.

---

[1] This letter was published in the *Edinburgh Annual Register for 1809*, pp. 549ff. There is an extract from it in Nichols' *Illustrations of the Literary History of the Eighteenth Century*, VII, 220–22.

[2] Dr. John Roebuck (1718–94), the famous chemist and physician, founder of the Carron Iron Works, and patron of Boulton and Watt.

[3] That of the Foulis' of Glasgow, and Murray and Cochrane of Edinburgh. The former house is now extinct; the latter still subsists, and is still honourably characterized by attention and accuracy. [*Edinburgh Annual Register for 1809*, editor's note]

[4] John Livie, tutor in the household of Dr. Roebuck, was employed by Baskerville in connection with the Horace. For other references to him, see the Index.

As to the Erse fragments,[5] you judged very rightly, that amidst the applause they were sure of receiving from the world, they would not fail to afford me a very peculiar satisfaction. I am indeed unfeignedly thankful for the early copy you sent me, and for the ingenious letter which accompanied them. It seems, indeed, from a former version of them by the same translator, (which Mr. Gray, the poet, received from him, and shewed my friend Percy,) that he has taken pretty considerable freedoms in adapting them to the present reader. I do not in the least disapprove of this; knowing by experience, that trivial amendments in these old compositions often render them highly striking, which would be otherwise quite neglected. And surely, under all the infirmities of age, they may be said to have an absolute claim to some indulgencies of this kind. I presume the editor follows the same model of translation in what he is now going to publish. I would wish him particularly attentive to the melody of his cadences, when it may be done without impeachment of his fidelity. The melody of our verse has been perhaps carried to its utmost perfection; that of prose seems to have been more neglected, and to be capable of greater than it has yet attained. It seems to be a very favourable era for the appearance of such irregular poetry. The taste of the age, so far as it regards plan and style, seems to have been carried to its utmost height, as may appear in the works of Akenside, Gray's Odes and Church-yard Verses, and Mason's Monody and Elfrida. The public has seen all that art can do, and they want the more striking effects of wild, original, enthusiastic genius. It seems to exclaim aloud with the chorus in Julius Caesar,

Oh rather than be slaves to these deep learned men,
Give us our wildness and our woods, our huts and caves again!

I know not how far you will allow the distinction or the principle on which I build my remark, namely, that the taste of the present age is somewhat higher than its genius. This turn, you see, favours the work the translator has to publish, or has published already. Here is indeed pure original genius! The very quintessence of poetry; a few drops of which, properly managed, are enough to give a flavour to quart-bottles. And yet one or two of the pieces (the first, for instance, together with the second) are undoubtedly as well planned as any ode we find in Horace.

I have perused the Gentle Shepherd with all imaginable pleasure; and

---

[5] The first publication of Macpherson, entitled, "Fragments of Ancient Poetry collected in the Highlands of Scotland, and translated from the Gaelic or Erse language." 1760. [*Edinburgh Annual Register for 1809*, editor's note]

here again am indebted to you, sir, for the assistance of your glossary. 'Tis rare to find a poem of this length, where simplicity of sentiment and of language are so very well sustained. The metre is generally musical; and the old Scottish words form an admirable kind of Doric. Good sense expressed naturally, in a phrase easy, perspicuous, and not wholly void of ornament, seems the talent of Ramsay, whose taste in composition was perhaps more remarkable than his genius; and in whom greater fire and invention would certainly have deprived his readers of the Gentle Shepherd.

And now, having thanked you for the Scotch snuff, (better than any I ever tasted before,) I come to ask, whether you have any old Scotch ballads, which you would wish preserved in a neat edition. I have occasioned a friend of mine to publish a fair collection of the best old English and Scotch ballads; a work I have long had much at heart. Mr. Percy, the collector and publisher, is a man of learning, taste, and indefatigable industry; is chaplain to the Earl of Sussex. It so happens, that he has himself a folio collection of this kind of MSS; which has many things truly curious, and from which he selects the best. I am only afraid that his fondness for antiquity should tempt him to admit pieces that have no other sort of merit. However, he has offered me a rejecting power, of which I mean to make considerable use. He is encouraged in his undertaking by Sam. Johnson, Garrick, and many persons of note, who lend him such assistance as is within their power. He has brought Mr. Jo. Warton (the poetry professor) to ransack the Oxford libraries; and has resided and employed six amanuenses to transcribe from Pepys's Collection at Cambridge, consisting of five volumes of old ballads in folio. He says justly, that it is in the remote parts of the kingdom that he has most reason to expect the curiosities he wants — that in the southern parts fashion and novelty cause such things to be neglected. Accordingly he has settled a correspondence in Wales, in the wilds of Staffordshire and Derbyshire, in the West Indies, in Ireland, and, if he can obtain your assistance in Scotland, hopes to draw materials from the whole British empire. He tells me there is, in the collection of Mag. Coll. Libr. a very curious collection of antient Scottish songs and poems, he thinks not published or known: many of Dumbar, Maitland of Lethington, and one allegorical poem of Gawain Douglas, too obsolete for his collection; and one yet more obsolete, called "Peebles in the Play," mentioned in Christ's Kirk on the Green. He met Mr. Gray in the university library, who is going to write the Hist. of English Poetry. But, to put an end to this long article! his collection will be printed in two or three small octavos, with suitable decorations; and if you find an opportunity of sending aught that may be proper for his insertion, I think I can safely answer for his thankfulness as well as my own.

He shewed me an old ballad in his folio MS, under the name of Adam Carr: three parts in four coincide so much with your Edom of Gordon, that the former name seems to me an odd corruption of the latter. His MS will, however, tend to enrich Edom of Gordon with two of the prettiest stanzas I ever saw, besides many other improvements. He also has a MS of Gill Morrice, called in his copy Childe Morice. Of this more another time. I must at present take my leave. Should you see Mr. (Douglas) Hume,[6] Mr. Alexander, or Dr. Robertson, I desire my best respects to them. And should you see my good Lord Alemoor and Mr. Professor Smith, I beg you would please to assert how unfeignedly I am their servant. I hope to muster up sufficient assurance, even now, to acknowledge by letter their acceptable presents of books; however the fire of gratitude was not less intense for having lain concealed and produced no blaze. I have many more Scotch friends whom I wish to particularize; but these, if I am not mistaken, live in the neighbourhood of Edinburgh. I am, dear sir,

your most obliged humble servant,

Will. Shenstone

I will endeavour to procure and send you a copy of Percy's translation of a genuine Chinese novel, in four small vols., printed months ago, but not to be published before winter.

260. To THOMAS PERCY [1]

[Oct.: 1761]

DEAR SIR,

To *reward,* or rather to *distinguish,* your Fidelity, I enclose what I think a better Copy of those verses upon the Venus, than any that has *yet* appeared. Some Places remain yet, y^t require correction, or would admit of Improvement: and it convinces me, what *Pains* are requisite to give a degree of accuracy to the merest Trifle. Well enough may one conceive how Horace bestowed years upon the correction of an Ode, that was to endure the test of Ages. Nothing, I believe, can have duration *without* this; and, *with* it, Nothing that is not written in a dead Language.

---

[6] Evidently John Home (1722–1808), author of *Douglas* (1757), who called on Shenstone as early as May, 1758.

[1] B. M. Add. MSS 28221, fol. 77ff. The date is added in red by Percy.

I will teize you no more with my Hints about the Necessity of an *exclusion*-bill. It is very true, y^t, in a larger Collection, you may have a greater chance to find pieces of Merit; but it is also true, that, from a Larger Heap, one is apt to help one's self more liberally, than from a small one: and my only Fear has been, that mere Antiquity should sometimes impose upon you, in the Garb of merit. But I have *said enough* on this Head, & I believe you are upon *your guard*. As to your First Quere, it would have a very odd appearance, were you to leave such *large* Intervals, as you necessarily must *sometimes,* were you to assign a fresh Page to the beginning of every Ballad. The Notes (which, I think, you place at the Close of each), would *sometimes happen* to fill this vacancy; but, at *others,* to make a fresh One. Well-judged & elegant wooden tail-pieces (an ornam. much wanting to every Press in Europe) would leave you at Liberty to pursue this scheme; but unless *your* Press affords you some that are *tolerable,* I would have you think no more about it. II. I should greatly approve your method of beginning with the *oldest* (and this, for the reasons you yourself lay down) *but* on account of the Danger you would incurr of throwing too many ballads *together,* that were irregular in point of Metre, or subobscure in point of Language; And this, at the *beginning* of *your work,* might perhaps be liable to give disgust — If you can surmount this Objection, Suppose you were to class them according to aeras of 20, 40, or 50 years. III. your third quere puzzles me. However, I should think it *safer* to defer the publication of such old Pieces as have rather more merit in the Light of *Curiosity* than *Poetry* (such as the tragick one of "the Fight at Otterburne" and the Comick one of "John the Reeve") 'till you have experienced the Publick's reception of the two First Vols: Which reception will be rule sufficient in regard to all that are to follow.

The *Lists* I will send you so soon as you can inform me what you have received already; for I declare I have forgott.

It were impossible for *my* Arrangement of *those ballads here,* to be of Service to you; because I take it for granted y^t many of them will require to be intermix'd with your other Pieces. However, were *you here,* much of this work might be done in a day or two.

I am truly glad to hear what you tell me of the King and Queen. I hope she will rather *promote* than *discourage* any Favor he may shew to the Arts and Sciences. The prettiest verses I have seen *yet* on occasion of their Nuptials, are an ode of one Pullein's[2] in the London Magazine.

I believe I have marked most of the typographical errata in Hau Kiou

[2] Samuel Pullein, *On the King's Marriage* appeared in the *London Magazine,* 1761, pp. 499–500.

Choaan; but would by no means advise you to affix any thing *more* of *this nature* to the volume. I have some thoughts of sending a Sett in boards to John M'Gouan Esq.; writer to the Signet, in Edinburgh. This you must know is the Gentleman wth whom I mean to bring you acquainted. I wrote him a long acc^t of your present scheme,[3] about a Fortnight ago; but Dr. Roebuck who was to convey the Letter, post-poned his Journey till this week. I will send you the first Letter I receive from him; which will be in No long time. He is a generous spirited Man, a Person of taste, & a Scholar, with a considerable tincture of the antiquarian.

Perhaps I can make you smile by giving you a specimen of the comical Humours of Lady G[ough]. She was here wth L^dy Sanderson; &, *before* I could come to receive them in the Parlour, L^dy G[ough] had peep'd into a Letter of Dodsley's, that lay upon ye marble Slabb. This passed — but upon her return, she desired Pixell would counsell me to break off all correspondence wth that *Dodwell;*[4] for that she had heard he was an Infidel — You will easily unriddle the mystery: Peeping into a folded Letter (wch by the way she *ought not* to have done) as the De'll would have it, she mistook the name of our Friend *Dodsley* for *Dodwell* — She has since accused our Friend Dodsley of no Less than *Blasphemy;* by reason y^t he in his verses makes so free w^th *silvan Gods* & *rural deities,* & even compliments me with being such a genius, as to have no occasion for their Assistance. Would you have thought she could have been so ignorant? but she is also subject to *Envy,* and her Chaplain P. (under the Rose) now & then diverts himself in finding it employment.

The printed Copy of Dodsley's verses, in wch I caused ye Birm^m Press to make some alterations, I have sent; but beg you to return it with the other MS. Copy of Lady Cotswouldia's Encomiasticon. Who she is, the Lord knows; but there is something ingenious in her Design, & Execution.[5]

Ld Lyttelton was here last Thursday, wth Lord & L^dy For'scue, & his Children; but I happened to be at Birmingham.

Baskerville's Horace[6] will be *printed* about ye End of this month; but be not *published* before Xt^mas. It is really a beauty — and upon ye whole as good a *Text* as any we have *yet* — but, excuse my vanity; who think I could have rendered it *better,* if they had suffered me to have the *final* determination of *it.* You know B. imagines y^t his *Letter* is *every thing,* on wch ye merit of a book depends; he was nevertheless *induc'd* to employ

---

[3] See Letter 259.
[4] The deist, Henry Dodwell the younger (d. 1784), author of *Christianity Not Founded on Argument* (1741), a particularly malicious satire on revealed Christianity.
[5] She is identified above, Letter 257, n4.
[6] See the Index.

a Mr Levy,⁷ residing as a private Tutor at Dr. Roebuck's; no bad Grammarian or Classick, and, now & then, they suffered me to have a Finger in the Pye. Samby's is but an indifferent Text, it seems; the Scotch Editⁿ but so so; A little Edition of mine printed at Hamburgh much superior to either,⁸ that I did not cause them to print it *precisely* according to Bentley — Pray my Comp^s to Mrs Percy — Write soon, & believe me yours most affectionately,

W. Shenstone

Is there any small edition of Bentley?

I hope that you yourself allow some consideration for the space of *time taken up by the Post* which you recommend so much to mine — Pray how prospers Hau Kiou Choaan?

How happens it, I beseech you, that you have suppressed the *Runick Fragments* &c., 'till M^r M'Pherson has published *His* Poem? Why will you suffer the Publick to be quite *cloyed* with this kind of writing, ere you avail y^rself of their *Appetite?* I cannot say whether you should *now* defer the publication, or publish directly.

I asked Dr Roebuck to subscribe my Name for Fingal,⁹ in Scotland; if I did not commission him too late: at the same time I abominate *Quartos;* and think most writers in a Conspiracy to plague me. What reason is there that a Quarto-shape shou'd please more in a *Book* yⁿ in an *human Figure?* — I found indeed M'Pherson's account of the Fragments, & some extracts from his Poem, in ye Chronicle¹⁰ of yesterday. I think a translator of a finer *Ear,* might cause these things to strike infinitely *more,* & yet be faithfull to the Sense.

I fancy Dodsley thinks of causing Baskerville very soon to print a new Edition of his Fables; & to have the Designs I shewed you, engraved for it. 'Twould be attended with Labour, expence, & Hazard — *otherwise,* it would, in my Opinion, make his Scheme more perfect, to assign one entire volume to *old* Fables; & another to *modern* & *new-invented* ones. There are many *Old,* & many *modern* Fables, of singular merit, left out of his Collection. After all, if he means it principally for ye use of Schools, perhaps it *ought,* or *need,* not be more voluminous; and yet

---

⁷ John Livie, for whom see the Index.

⁸ The editions here mentioned are the following: Quinti Horatii Flacci *Opera.* Londini: apud Gul. Sandby. 2 vol. 1749; Quintus Horatius Flaccus etc. Glasguae: Robertus et Andreas Foulies. 1756; Q. Horatii Flacci *Poemata, Es castigationibus observationibusque Bentleii, Cuningamii & Sanadonis emendata.* Hamburgi; Typis A. Vandenhoeck. 1733 [Hecht]. R. Bentley's Horace first appeared in 1711.

⁹ *Fingal, an Ancient Epic Poem &c. Translated from the Galic Language,* by James Macpherson, appeared at the beginning of December, 1761; the title page bore the year 1762.

¹⁰ *London Chronicle,* December, 1761, pp. 531-33.

Rousseau, with a sly sarcasm, intimates y^t *Children* are not his *proper Readers*.

The Little Echantillon[11] I have enclosed will make you wonder — However send me y^r Opinion, if you please, without saying a tittle of ye affair to any one, 'till you hear from me y^t I am *quite determined* — I have just mentioned it in a Letter to Mr Graves & to Mr Dodsley, *only* — I should like to collect my trifles in some such manner, y^t a Friend may buy them together, at a Bookseller's. To print them *elegantly, without assistance,* implies a risque I do not chuse to run; nor would it be consistent with *Prudence* for me so to do. On the other Hand if ye Publication in this manner, could be made *advantageous,* without being *disreputable,* I see no reason why I should decline it — Let me see what can be said *for* it, in *my* particular Case — and with such regulations &c. as I would lay it under — First, I will not suppose ye Book so *very* worthless as to make *no kind* of recompence for ye subscriber's money — Next, I fancy the Degree of Acquaintance wch my Ferme ornee has occasioned me wth numbers of Gentry, will preclude any Necessity for *overurgent* applications — At least I do not mean to use them — "Come wth a good will, or come not at all" as the Children say at Play; & further, to avoid ye air of a mendicant, I can plead the expence of Printing & offer, in failure of a decent number, to return ye money y^t shall be received. Next, does not the Subscription-method save One from the *gross* mortification of seeing one's books remain unsold? Lastly, Is there not something agreeable in collecting together ye Names of Numbers, which one must imagine to have a good Opinion either of one's Genius or one's disposition? After all, *the Method* has been so vilely prostituted, y^t the Name of it, at first, will sound disreputably. And yet this method was in no much better Name, when Pope, & Spence condescended to make use of it — you will say "w^t a Difference of Cases!" — but however — Some temptation I must have, to go thro' ye trouble of revising my pieces: & What temptation were ye View of Fame (even supposing there were ye least *chance*) to so *domestick* a wretch as I? To see a neat edition of one's Poems, wth elegant decorations; & to acquire *some* Money, which I value only for ye sake of employing it — These might be some temptations — Consider then of these matters, and w^t are ye best methods of evading y^e *Discredit* of a Subscription — Some will say it renders a man Dependent — but has not the Subscriber an elegant & amusive *toy* for his money? — I should, no doubt, think ye better of my Friends for subscribing, but none ye worse of myself for accepting ye subscription.

[11] Proposals for a Edit^n of his Poems by Subscription [Percy]. This projected publication, of which frequent mention is made (see the Index), never materialized.

261. To THOMAS HULL[1]

The Leasowes, Oct. 18, 1761

DEAR MR. HULL,

If I recollect aright, both you and Ned Alcock were here this last Autumn, on the Evening when my Fish-Ponds had been robbed, and the Fish destroyed. You were an Eye-Witness of the Circumstances, therefore cannot but retain them in your Memory. I find I have been arraigned of *Lenity,* by several conscientiously-upright Neighbours. *"I have screened a Robber from Justice;"—"I have given Encouragement to future Thefts,"* &c. Such are the Aspersions wherewith I have been loaded. I make a material Distinction between a *Robber* and a *Pilferer;* nor can I assign the former Appellation to a poor Wretch, who, in his Hunger, has taken two or three *Fishes,* or as many *Loaves.* It is true, I would rather have given more than the Value of them, to have prevented my *finny Friends* being disturbed in, or taken away from, their elemental Habitation; it is also as true, that, in my first Warmth, on the Report that the Fellow had bruised the poor Creatures to Death against the Stumps and Roots of Trees, I could not only have delivered him over to Justice, but have been almost induced to become myself his Punisher; but when that Warmth submitted to cool Reflection, *I felt it impossible* to resist his Argument, of having a Wife with five Children at Home, and not a Doit to procure them a Meal. I verily believe too he spoke the Truth. Poverty and Affliction seemed to work and plead within him, and his Words were the Words of Nature.

I cannot be so severe against these petty Misdemeanours as many are; nor can I, though I revere the Call of Justice, be a rigorous Supporter of its Claims, except in atrocious Cases. Beside, what had it availed me, to have consigned the Offender to the Power of a Magistrate? Rather say, what Pain and Inconvenience should I not have entailed on myself? I should have had the Trouble of attending the Examination; have had the Fellow imprisoned many Days; and the additional Mortification of travelling, perhaps to *Warwick,* or *Worcester,* in order to convict him. And after all, no Restitution is made for my Loss, though it were ten Times more valuable than a whole *Draught of Fishes.* There is surely something deficient in our Laws, concerning the Meum & Tuum; the Person robbed not only abides the Loss without Amends, but is even put to Expence, as well as Inconvenience, to get the Robber punished.

Then again, the Wife and five Children!—The poor Fellow subsists, chief Part of the Year, only by carrying News-Papers round the Country.

[1] Hull, *Select Letters,* Vol. II, No. XXXVII.

Had He been shut up, what was to have supported the ragged Family meanwhile? I am beside inclined to think, that half a Crown, and a little wholesome Admonition, that is, if he be not a practised and stubborn Offender, might go as far towards amending his Morals, as an Acquaintance with the Inside of a Prison, and the Conversation of such Associates as he might find there.

I have suffered myself sometimes to doubt the Excellence of our Laws, relative to Life and Death, notwithstanding I know it has been asserted by many People, that they are wiser than those of any other Nation. What then? Is the Man who takes a few Guineas from you on the Highway, on a Level with him who commits a deliberate Murder? And is there no Punishment to be found more adequate to the first Transgression, than taking away the Life? Surely, one Example made by a visible Brand, a Mark of Disgrace, which could never be washed away, would more avail towards the Prevention of future Crimes, than half the Executions in the Kingdom, which have now, from too great frequency, lost the chief Part of their Purpose and Terror. The Punishment which was inflicted by a Regent in some Part of the East, (I think the Circumstance is related in the *Arabian Nights Entertainments*) on a Judge who had been induced, by Gold, to give an unjust Decision, is admirable. The Brand, placed on his Habitation, in legible Characters, *"Here lives a corrupt Judge"*, was, in the highest Degree, consonant to Justice, inasmuch as it made the Crime its own Punishment.

I have been led into these Reflections by finding how severely I have been arraigned, only for having been *an innocent Defrauder of the Law:* so have troubled you with them; but here I come to a conclusion. You are at Liberty to draw what Inferences you please from, or make what Objections you like to, my Opinion.

I am now to thank you for the Anecdotes you have given me, as well as for the Perusal of the enclosed Ballad.[2] I am particularly pleased with the Image,

> Appear they not as drizling Dews
> Fresh'ning some faded Flower?

I am, dear Sir, very faithfully,
Your Friend and Servant,
W. Shenstone

[2] The ballad alluded to appeared in Hull's *Select Letters*, II, 125–31.

262. To THOMAS HULL[1]

The Leasowes, Nov. 26, 1761

DEAR MR. HULL,

I esteem myself beholden to you, for having made me acquainted with the Reality of the two Writers, Dr. Lancaster[2] and Henry. I have admired them both in their Pages, but knew only their Names. In fact, when I first read the *Essay on Delicacy,* I imagined the Name of Lancaster to be fictitious, and that the Work might be the Production of the Author of *Sir Thomas Fitz-Osborne's Letters.*[3] There is great Spirit, fine Sentiment, and true Elegance of Style throughout; and my Friend Dodsley's preserving it in his *Fugitive Pieces* is truly meritorious. It well deserves to be rescued from Oblivion. But what a Pity that your Uncle does not make a more frequent Use of his Pen! the World does not abound too much in such Writers. How much likewise is it to be lamented, that a Man of such Abilities should lie concealed in an obscure Part of *Essex!* He should have remained in the World—that is, I mean, for the Sake of the World; to his own Happiness, probably, Retirement was most conducive. It is most certain, that no Men are fit for Solitude, but those who find the Source of Amusement and Employment in themselves. Fancy, Reflection, and a Love of Reading, are indispensably necessary for such a Situation. It is downright Lunacy for a Man who has passed his Life in a Compting-House, or a Shop; who possesses, possibly, but a moderate Share of natural Understanding, that Understanding too not cultivated by Education, and who has never known what it is to look into a Book—It is, I repeat, downright Lunacy, for such a Man to think of *retiring.* He knows not, the Fatigue he is going to encounter; he will want Employment for his Hours; most probably, may shorten his Existence; and while he retains it, it will be one continued State of Apathy, if not disorder.

Henry, you say, is a Mr. Griffith, of the County of *Kilkenny* in *Ireland.* A Friend brought me over the Letters of Henry and Frances,[4] when they were first published in *Dublin;* they are most admirably clever and comprehensive; I have enjoyed and re-enjoyed them; and while I have admired the Writings, have loved the Writers. In the private Character you have given me of this amiable *Pair,* I feel as if I were acquainted

---

[1] Hull, *Select Letters,* Vol. II, No. XXXVIII.
[2] Dr. Nathaniel Lancaster, Hull's uncle, was, as Hull explains (I, 70), for many years rector of Stanford Rivers, in Essex. His *Essay on Delicacy* was first printed in 1748 and was preserved by Dodsley in his *Fugitive Pieces* (1761).
[3] William Melmoth the younger (1710–99).
[4] *Letters between Henry and Frances* (2 vols.), listed in the Register of Books of the *Gentleman's Magazine,* April, 1757.

with them. Before the Information received from you, I have sometimes suffered myself to think, and even communicated to an intimate Friend or two, that there was a Similitude of Disposition between Henry and myself; but when I look on your Description of him, I entertain much Doubt. In the active Parts of his Philosophy, his Perseverance, and Resolution, I fear I am far behind him. He is a Man qualified for any State or Situation; Business or Amusement, Solitude or a Crowd. — And you have spent Months with him at *Kilkenny!* — I give you Joy of such an Happiness.

Again I thank you for the Enclosures you are ever and anon sending, and am,

Dear Mr. Hull, yours very affectionately,
W. Shenstone

263. To MISS M——[1]

The *Leasowes, Dec.* 8, 1761

Dear Miss M——,

I ought to have returned Thanks for your agreeable Account of the Excursion to *Chepstow,* some Time ago; but these are Duties which I do not always perform so soon as I ought — you know I don't — Neither will I waste my Time and Paper in apologizing for a Failing which you are so ready to forgive, convinced that I am not less grateful on that Account.

I have great Joy in reading these little pleasurable Travels, in a private Letter, related, as yours are, without Formality, describing, with Ease and Simplicity, every little Occurrence as it falls out. I can journey with you in Imagination, and partake every trivial Difficulty and every Delight. *You* are fond of these little *Parties of Pleasure,* as they are called, and in you it is, by no means, reprovable; but in general, they are very dangerous to young Folks. *You* have Means and Time, at your own Disposal; your Party is small and select, both in Point of Reputation and Understanding; you likewise turn your Excursion to some Advantage; you make Observations on all you see, form nice Distinctions between different Places, Points, and Characters, and draw just Conclusions from them — But, as I said before, these Parties too often are hazardous; the Mind once indulged in them, is apt to covet them too often; they are sometimes the Means of drawing a Female into improper Company; they encroach on Means and Time, neither of which, probably, can with Propriety be bestowed; they have their Source in Dissipation, are con-

---

[1] Hull, *Select Letters,* Vol. II, No. XL. This seems to be an answer to a letter to Shenstone dated July 21, 1760, and signed J—— M——, in Hull, Vol. I, No. LXXI.

tinually attended with Hazard, and too often end in the Worst of Mischiefs. In short, I would wish all young Folks, who have neither Leisure nor Money at Command, to shut their Ears against the very Name of *a Party of Pleasure.*

More than once in my Life, I have been solicited by Friends to visit foreign Climes. I had an Invitation of this Kind lately; but it is now too late; at least, I think so — Besides, why should a Man go so far for Objects of Curiosity, who has seen too little of his own Country? Many Parts of *England, Wales,* and *Scotland* equally (I should think) deserve our Admiration, and we need not risque Winds and Waves, to which I feel *some* Objection. Numbers of our travelling Gentry peregrinate too early in Life, before the Mind is sufficiently formed to make proper Observations on what they see and hear.

A Friend once related an Anecdote, which is apposite to my Subject. A very young Man, of good natural Understanding, and Heir to an affluent Fortune, would needs be one of these inconsiderate Travellers. In the Course of his Adventure, he fell into Company, in *Naples,* with some well-travelled, and well-informed Foreigners. They were conversing on what they had seen in *England;* and some little Difference of Opinion arising about the Architecture of *Windsor*-Castle, they naturally referred themselves to the young *Englishman* for Decision. With much Confusion and Hesitation he was compelled to confess, he had never seen the Building in Question. The Company, with true foreign Politeness, only testified their Admiration in a silent Smile — but the Reflection instantly struck, and pained the young Gentleman. The Result was, that he returned for *England* within two Days, rationally determined to instruct himself in the Knowledge of his own Country, before he pryed into those afar off. His Reflection and Determination did equal Credit to his Understanding.

Our Friend Hull has, as usual, been amusing us with as good a Drama, as our neighbouring Town can give Encouragement to; but says, he returns no more. I know many who will be sorry on this Account. He has not departed, however, without having excited Curiosity in a very peculiar Way; on a small Plan, indeed, but to a very commendable Purpose. He enticed with him his two principal Actresses, Miss Morrison and Miss Ibbot, (both possessed of great Merit in their Profession) some few of his Band, two Voices, and gave an Evening's Entertainment of *Singing* and *Reading,* at the little Town of *Stourbridge,* some few miles off; the Profits devoted to the Assistance of a Tradesman, who had suffered under repeated Misfortunes. The Success, I hear, more than answered his Expectations; the little Assembly-Room was crouded, and with much good Company. A slight Cold made me fearful of being out late, but the Particulars were given me by a neighbouring Clergyman who was present. The Pieces selected for Reading were well-chosen. I do not remember the whole Number, but I recollect that Miss Carter's *Ode to Wisdom,* Prior's *Henry and Emma,* and Gray's *Elegy in a Country Church-Yard* were amongst them. The latter gave particular Satisfaction, my Friend told me, to the Gentlemen of the Pulpit, of whom he counted seven. The whole was received with great Approbation. You are to observe that Hull and his Party, so far from proposing any Emolument to themselves, declined even to be re-imbursed the Expences they were at in going, and the Master of the Assembly-Room *gave* the Use of it. From this confined Instance of such a Scheme, I am apt to think an Union of Poetry and Music, executed on a larger Plan, would be an admirable Two-Hours-Entertainment, either in a public Room or private Family.

I enclose a Piece of Writing,[2] which a Friend of mine sent me in a Frank last Week. I think the Subject calculated for your Liking. It was planned, and partly written, in Mr. Hoare's lovely Grounds, at *Stourton* in *Wiltshire;* and the Thought suggested by surveying, from an Eminence there, a woody Vale, wherein Alfred is reported to have once concealed himself from the *Danes.* Send it back, when you have done with it.
       Adieu, dear Miss M——.
          Yours very faithfully,
            W. Shenstone

264. To THOMAS HULL[1]

[December 24, 1761]

SIR,

I am greatly obliged both to you and Miss Morrison, for the Ballads[2] you were so good as to enclose to me. The Speed you have used in sending them, testifies the Reality of that Delight you seemed to express at the *Leasowes,* when I first communicated my Friend Dr. Percy's Design. I sent them directly to him; he has begun to print off his venerable Collection with an Eye to the Publication of it sometime next Winter. One of your Ballads is truly beautily and extremely proper for his Purpose. It has that *Naivete,* which is so very essential in Ballads of all Kind; and which requires no more than, that *sublime,* or *elegant,* or *tender*

---
[2] *Cadwal,* a legendary tale in two parts, printed in Hull, II, 149–66.
[1] Hull, *Select Letters,* Vol. II, No. XXXIX.
[2] For the ballads referred to see Hull, II, 139ff.

Sentiments be expressed in a simple and unaffected Manner — *Sentimental* Language would be no ill Term for it; or, perhaps, the Essay before Dodsley's *Fables* does not improperly stile it, the *Voice* of Sentiment, in Opposition to the *Language* of Reflection.

As to the *other,* Miss M[orrison] well distinguishes, that the Merit of it is almost wholly confined to the Sentiment at last. This is both *natural* and *tender;* and would *she* take the Pains to new-write the *whole* on this Account, (for even this Sentiment is not *expressed* so very simply as one could wish it) I dare say it is in her Power to render it very pleasing. I know not how far I am *singular;* but as I love to avail myself of different Words, to bundle up Ideas in different Parcels, it is become habitual to me, to call *that a Ballad* which describes or implies some *Action;* on the other Hand, I term that a *Song,* which contains only an Expression of *Sentiment.* According to this Account, I believe one of your Pieces would appear a *Ballad,* and the other a *Song.*³

The *Play-House* Coronations answer the Purpose of all those who chuse to compound the Matter betwixt *Indolence* and *Curiosity.* Mr. Garrick has given a very genteel Turn to this Taste among the Citizens, in his Epilogue to the new Play.⁴ I have not *yet* seen this Performance; and should be glad if you would give me some Account of its Appearance on the Stage. Why does not *your* Dr. Lancaster⁵ compleat his *Essay upon Delicacy?* I read it, since I wrote last, in Dodsley's *Fugitive Pieces,* and think it mighty well deserves the Labour necessary to its Continuation.

'Tis true, that Specimens of Wit or Humour have been dispensed this Winter but sparingly from the Press; and even there in *political* Pamphlets, where I am least inclined to seek them. But we must swim with the Tide, if we would collect the Shells and Corals that it leaves behind; accordingly I have read two or three of these Pamphlets which have answered my Expectations. Should any other appear that strikes you, be so good as to enclose it to me in a Frank. As to *Lavinia,* or other dramatic Schemes, I must defer them till I see you again at the *Leasowes,* which whenever it happens, will afford me Pleasure, being very faithfully and affectionately

your most obedient Servant,
W. Shenstone

Christmas-Eve, 1761

³ See above, Letter 252, n2.
⁴ Epilogue to the Tragedy of Hecuba, produced that year at Drury-Lane Theatre [Hull]. This was evidently John Delap's adaptation of Euripides' play, produced at Drury Lane December, 1761.
⁵ See above, Letter 262, n2.

265. To MATTHEW BOULTON[1]

Decr 25. 1761

My Christmas-Compliments to M^r and Mrs Bolton. I hope Mr Bolton's engagements at the Sohoe[2] will turn out much more advantageous to *Him*, than they have done to *me;* if it be to *them* that I am to attribute his Long absence from the Leasowes. Mr Perrott, his neighbour, dines here on Sunday: & as *this*, at least, must be a Day when he will be disengaged from his attendance upon Workmen; if he have no *other* Avocation, I shall be truly glad of his Company.

Will: Shenstone

266. To THOMAS PERCY[1]

Jany 1761/2

Dear Sir,

I sincerely thank you for the *delicacy*, with which you express your sentiments on my Publication:[2] very judicious in all respects; except the too great Partiality therein shewn to y^r *Friends* abilities.

Should the affair *proceed*, and would the Publick excuse the mere *Act* of asking a Subscription, they shall be *sure* to find nothing illiberal or disingenuous in ye conduct of it. I think I may promise *this*, Let the *Loss* or *Gain* be what it will.

The Mistake I observe in my Date (1762 instead of 1763) may *possibly* have led you to suppose that my Collection was to appear *this* Spring — Alas, it will be as much as I can possibly do (even *presuming upon* ye enjoyment of tolerable health & Freedom of Spirits) to prepare Matters, against Spring following — I find y^r Advice extremely rational, "to be very carefull how I restrain myself by naming too early a Day" — I also approve what you say, wth regard to stipulating for a *number* of subscribers. I did it chiefly in order to give myself some Air of *Indifference,* as to the Publication — Consider this *motive* if you please — I did *not* use ye term *Essays* for ye sake of introducing a red Letter &c. I thought *essays* (or "*Attempts*") a more *modest* Intimation of what the Publick was to expect — namely a sort of *tryals of ones hand* in different *kinds* of Poetry — made chiefly in ye younger part of Life — & in order to convince *myself,* w^t *Kind* suited with my Cast of Genius. —

I hoped also for somewhat more indulgence, on acc^t of the variety, or

---

[1] Reproduced from a manuscript in the Assay Office Library, Birmingham, England.
[2] It will be recalled that Boulton moved from his smaller factory on Snow Hill to his great one in Soho in 1762.
[1] B. M. Add. MSS 28221, fol. 85ff.
[2] This much discussed project for publication never materialized.

different *Kinds,* of Poetry. — There will be time enough to consider this before Febry; wch Mr Dodsley says, is allowedly the properest time for these Advertisements — you should have considered what I sent rather as a Model for *Proposals,* yn a Title-page to the *Book itself;* in which Light, at least, it might not be improper to let ye Publick in to some Particulars — For Instance, that my *Elegies* are to be in the Collection &c:

I am not partial to a Full title-page — being a Passionate Lover of *Simplicity* — You need not fear therefore, but I shall take care that Mine shall not offend you by it's number of Parts — To say a Piece looks *busy* (crowded) is, wth *Baskerville,* one of the highest terms of Approbation — as it is with *Me,* a term of Reproach.

I am, *myself,* dissatisfy'd with my new Orthographies of ye word "Leasowes". The Chief Point was to banish ye Preposition wch however I find impracticable.

You will hardly convince me yt any Pains of mine, in point of revisal or correction, have a tendency to *hurt* the *little* Pieces I produce. This I believe is very *seldom* the Case, when a Person's taste is not notoriously *perverted* — My chief endeavour, on these occasions, has been to produce *ease,* & Simplicity; if not melody of expression, so far as this cd be effected without *impoverishing* the Sentiment: And were I *not* to employ this Labour, Many of my *Trifles* wd appear ye most affected, & the most *laboured* things that ever were. Pastoral Poetry, in my opinion, should exhibit almost *naked sentiment.* Tis possible yt some parts, in yr Copy of my ballad, may appear preferable to those yt were finally inserted — But this was not owing to *over-correction:* but to the decision of Friends; who on my shewing them a number of stanzas (upon whose merit I could not determine) occasioned me to reject some, & admit others, as their Tastes were more or less fond of *Art.* In short I believe many of ye *rejected,* and the *inserted* stanzas, were written almost simultaneously — There *is* however a time when this Labour does mischief — Tis when writers (of wm you may recollect some) think they can not too much *stiffen,* or *raise,* or alienate their Language from ye common Idiom. By this they procure a Kind of Homage, parallel to wt is acquired by *reserved behaviour* — the dignity of Distance — the awe pertaining to Eastern monarchs — but never once ye more valuable effects of genuine affection or sincere *applause.* But too much of this —

Adieu

267. To THOMAS PERCY [1]

[Feb. 3, 1762]

My Compliments — I am afraid that my Awards[2] hitherto have resembled the Umpirage of Chaos "who by Decision more embroils the Fray" — However, I would have you allow yourself *time* for the *thorough* examination, of this dilemma that occurs at *First*. For my own part, I ever considered y^r old MSS. as the noblest treasure in a *Poet's hands;* even as pure gold in dust or Ingots, which the Owner might either mint himself, or dispose of in the shape he found it, for the Benefit of other *Artists*. Remember I use ye word *Artists* — for if you publish these old pieces *un-improved only,* I consider them as not every one's money, but as a prize merely for either *virtuosoes;* or else the *manufacturers* in this kind of ware. The Poets namely. The purchasers however of this sort, will lie under a disadvantage not incident to ye present owner; who possesses his treasure in secret, & not in common wth all mankind. Quere then, whether you yourself chuse to wave both the trouble & the Credit that would accrue from such improvements as you are well able to bestow — I am really not sufficiently sanguine to *dictate,* on this Head, yet hope the Hints I throw out at times, & the different Lights in which I place things, may be of some little use to you in y^r determination at Last.

Quere. What if you proceed from old to newer ballads *in every distinct vol^{me}* supposing y^r improved Copies to appear towards the Close, & there be just refer'd to the *original* Copies? This would at least prevent ye first volume from being too much loaded with obsolete pieces, which were not agreeable to the *general* Taste — And So, make First, second, & third series, in *every distinct* volume. Consider well wth y^rself, the *advantages* this would give you. I think I begin to like it.

If you consider *improved* Copies as the *standard or principal* ones, & give *them* a first place, I do not see y^t you need hereby violate y^r purpose of arranging according to the date. — They may still rank as old Barons, let the robes they wear be ever so modern.

From all this you will conclude, that I hardly know not [*sic*] what to say —

Chaos

From Mr Shenstone's Brain
    Feb: 3^d 1762

P. S. Dr. Roebuck comes home to-day, by whom I depend upon hearing from M^r M'Gouan in Scotland.

[1] B. M. Add. MSS 28221, fol. 87ff.
[2] On the subject of the Ancient Reliques of Poetry. [Percy]

Lend ye Assistance in ye following whim — I am making a sett of *boxes* y^t are to appear on ye outside like books, & each to be Lettered — The titles used in Lettering might have some wit or humour, in lieu of w^t *these books* may want *within;* and such may be drawn either from titles that are Puritannical, — such as "a new round to Jacob's Ladder" — "A spiritual Shove" — "Volley of holy shot" &c &c &c:

Quaint & antiquated — such as "a tragedie of pleasaunt thinges" &c such as Skelton &c of old time may easily furnish. Witty & Satyrical — on such subjects as make a good Figure in Ld Rochester.

Nothing — "Dutch Wit" — "French Probity or Ridicule upon false science — or grave and frivolous Disquisitions upon unimportant subjects — the virtuoso — taster — Coins — mosses — Butterflies — Roman Fibulas &c &c &c. But you will find y^r field *too* large, without these hints of mine — only remember the titles must be expressible in a *few short words* — I *have* some Few. What say you to Fingal —? I've only seen extracts, waiting for an 8vo Edit. They are, however, fine indeed! What a treasure *these* for a modern Poet, before they were published.

268. To THOMAS PERCY [1]

[3^d March 1762]

* * * I think with *you*, in regard to what I've yet read of Fingal, or rather of the Pieces annexed to that Poem; for my head has been so bad of Late, y^t I durst not undertake to read, w^t is *called* an *Epick-poem* — I admire many detached Sentiments &c in Ossian; but have *many* Objections to his Translator's management, wherin I think wth you.

Thank you for y^r humourous titles — you did not observe, y^t they consist in general of more *words* than can be inserted — Beside this, my scheme is *changed* — As these books are *really* boxes to contain ye Letters of some choice Correspondents, I shall Letter ye Backs with my Friend's Names. I've been plagu'd much of Late wth Designs for ye Ornam^ts to Baskerville's Horace — Ld Bute accepts the Dedication — & the Ornam^ts I *hope* will be somew^t agreeable.

I've also been busy'd in contributing my joint Endeavours to procure a new turn-pike road to Stourbridge. Have you seen Miss Carter's Poems?[2]

I am y^r most affectionate & faithfull Friend

W. S.

[1] B. M. Add. MSS 28221, fol. 91. The date is in Percy's hand.
[2] Elizabeth Carter (1717–1806), a bluestocking and the daughter of a Kent clergyman, was a friend of Richardson and of Johnson. She contributed two numbers to *The Rambler*, and in 1758 published a translation of Epictetus. Her *Poems on Several Occasions* appeared in 1762.

—— —— has caused our toll-gate petition to be postponed, till ye merits of ye cause can be farther examined. — We cannot *now obtain an act,* before ye latter end of next year — Nor perhaps get our road mended, sooner y^n ye end of 2 years, after that. I hate the affectedly-wise Face of unnecessary *deliberation;* 'tis ye mien of *wisdom,* but ye masque of *Folly.*

269. To JOHN LIVIE[1]

March ye Last, 1762

Mr Shenstone's Compliments to Mr Livie, and to the Doctor & Mrs Roebuck.

Mr Livie will please to let me know (either by the Bearer, or from London) *where* a Letter will find Him in our great Metropolis.

At all Events he will give me a Line, within a few Days after he arrives in town. Should he see Mr Warton (on his Road thro Oxford) I desire my Compliments to that Gentleman; & that He may be acquainted wth the Pleasure it gives me, to find that He assists my Friend Mr Percy — He will readily know y^t I allude to the *antient Ballads* Mr Percy is collecting; a Scheme I've long wished, & am now likely, to see executed with Success.

Mr Livie mentioned, I think, that either Dr Ash or Mr Peeke had purchased "Mr Walpole's Lives of the Painters" — Would it not be possible to procure a sight of it, for a Few Days, from One or other of those Gentlemen?

If I should like it, I shall certainly purchase it — Mr Livie will I hope lend me his good offices on this occasion. I have not ye Pleasure of being so well acquainted wth Mr *Peake,* as I could *wish.* The Bearer may wait for Mr Livies Answer, if he should order him to do so —

270. To THOMAS PERCY[1]

I really have not heard *yet* from Scotland wch amazes me — but I do believe M'Gouan is endeavouring to procure something y^t he may enclose for you — He sent me word (a month ago) y^t he w^d then write in a weeks time.

I desired Mr Livie[2] (who is gone up to town about ye publication of Basks Horace, of wch he is ye Editor) as he had Letters for Mr Warton, to make him also my Comp^ts & tell him what pleasure it gave me to find

---

[1] B. M. Add. MSS 22548, fol. 108.
[1] B. M. Add. MSS 28221, fol. 93. The letter is not dated but evidently belongs chronologically in its present position.
[2] See the preceding letter.

y^t he countenanced y^r Uncertaking. The said Horace will be extremely beautifull; & tho it have not every *reading* I could wish, is on the whole more to my mind, y^n any other that is extant—Sandby's is bad, it seems—& the best Livie c^d find was a small one I lent him of Merveillius printed at Hamburgh comprehencg w^t is good in Bentley, Cuningham & Sanadon[3]—I will send you a Copy; if you'll tell me, after what manner it is practicable.

Have you seen Horace Walpole's book on Painters[4]—I was quite divided, *after* I had read it, whether I should purchase it or no—The Cuts turned ye scale; & I bespoke it. His *own* remarks are sprightly & judicious—but these are thinly interspersed—& a very great part of the 30.^s vols.[5] consists of ye most trifling anecdotes of inconsiderable Artists—I never knew so much Genius as Walpole's in such a Bigot to Antiquity—For, tho I call *you* an Antiquarian, yet you are not near so great a Bigot—He is extremely inaccurate in his Language, tho he says it was corrected by Gray—I've also purchased Lord Kaims[6] on Criticism; from wch I hope some Entertainment on acc^t of his *Subjects*—tho I scarce expect to find him, any ways equal to my Fr^d Burke.[7] I have for these 3 weeks been much out of order, but am sorry to hear ye same of you. I am now rather better; and when *you* are so, pray let me reap ye benefit.

W. S.

271. To THOMAS PERCY [1]

The Lessowes, May 16th 1762

Dear Mr. Percy,

I am really sorry that my last Remarks did not arrive in due time; as I am not concious that I *delayed* to send them, & as I thought myself perfectly *clear* in most things that I proposed—In regard to the present Packet, I have less to say. You will think it proper to insert something that comprizes the actions of this great Champion *Guy,* as well as those of King *Arthur;* and yet there is evidently not a single particle of poetical Merit in *either* of the Ballads. Once for all, it is extremely certain that an *Over*-proportion of *this Kind* of *Ballast,* will sink your vessel to the Bottom of the Sea. Therefore be upon your guard, in *time:* Neither have you

---

[3] See above, Letter 260, n8.
[4] Horace Walpole (1717–97) published the first three volumes of his *Anecdotes of Painting in England* in 1762; the fourth appeared in 1780.
[5] Three volumes; the manuscript reads 30.^s, apparently indicating the price.
[6] Henry Home, Lord Kames (1696–1782), published his *Elements of Criticism* (3 vols.) in 1762.
[7] Burke's *Philosophical Inquiry into the Origin of Our Ideas of the Sublime and Beautiful* (1756).
[1] B. M. Add. MSS 28221, fol. 94ff.

Any reason to be apprehensive that your vols should be deficient in point of *Bulk*. You are not to accost the Publick, as Jerry Hopkinson did his Customer: "Sir, you must consider that these volumes have all together a *deal of Stuff* in them." But I've perhaps harped upon this string too Long, & will leave these matters to your own decision. It is not *necessary* that your 3 vols should be any thicker than *"the Hive."*[2] — I am sorry to find that the mention of *Coventry* in my Superscription does not make my Letters arrive a Jott the sooner. — I will take Care to leave an Horace for you, so soon as I can receive the Few y^t are allotted me, & can get one bound. I believe y^t you will not find it disappoint your expectations. Why it was not published near a Month ago or what the Gravers &c: are doing, is much beyond my comprehension — I have read Webb,[3] who has something clever in his Essay upon Poetry; but he is too Laconic, & does not say enough for what his title implies. Besides, there are some of his Illustrations from Shakespear, y^t seem not greatly to *his purpose.*— On the whole you must needs read it; but I think will not esteem it equal to His treatise upon Painting. His account of the Distinction betwixt *Wit, Taste,* & *Genius,* is very clear & satisfactory; and of these three accomplishments that of *Taste* seems to be the *Author's* Portion — I begun to read Ld Kaims; but found the introductory part too abstracted for the *then* state of my Brain. I hope, erewhile, to make a fresh Essay — The *Indies* themselves should hardly bribe me to read over Cambridge's *Indian-War*.[4] I saw ye Book at a Friend's House, where I *read* his preface, & *dipt* into other parts. The Author once did me the Honour to dine here; & is a Person of multifarious Knowledge; wit, humour, & Imagination. His Hobby-horse (or Foible) is the Construction of *Boats,* calculated to swim in different waters, & according to the models of different Countries. But how he came to write a Book of *this Stamp,* can be explained only by the God of *Whim*. Let me, however, do a piece of Justice to his Character. He is a truly worthy & good-natured Man, & much esteemed by all his Acquaintance — The best thing in Mallet's Poems[5] (2^s) is, his verses upon Mr Charles Stanhope, which are truly characteristick. His Emma has not y^t simplicity or Beauty, which one would expect from so tender a subject.

She, shivering, sigh'd, & *died!*

[2] See the Index.
[3] Daniel Webb's *Remarks on the Beauties of Poetry* was first published in 1762, by Dodsley. His *Inquiries into the Beauties of Painting* had appeared two years before.
[4] Richard Owen Cambridge's *Account of the War in India, between the English and French, on the Coast of Coromandel, from 1750 to 1760, etc.* (London, 1761).
[5] David Mallet, *Poems on Several Occasions* (London, 1762). *The Reward, or Apollo's Acknowledgement to Charles Stanhope,* written in 1757, is found on pages 19–24; *Edwin and Emma* on pages 57–69.

A notable Line this, for a Conclusion! Have you seen ye pompous Edition of Thomson's works?[6] And does not his Monument put you in Mind of what the Publick owes to Mr *Richardson?*[7] For my own part, I never Look into his Works, but with greater Admiration of his Genius — and then, if we regard ye extensive good they were *so well* calculated to promote, there are Few Characters to whom the Nation may be said to *owe* greater Honours — Baskerville has of late been seized with a violent Inclination to publ sh Hudibras, his favorite Poem, in a pompous Quarto; with an entire new sett of Cutts — Dr Warburton has, I hear, also engaged Him to publish a Quarto-Edition of Mr Pope — Pity but Guthrie had employed him to print his account of the British Peerage;[8] wch is to be so highly decorated with the Arms, seats, Robes, &c. &c. &c. to come out in 5^s Quarto-Numbers & to amount perhaps to 12 or 14 Pounds. Hume (Douglas) is writing a tragedy upon some Subject in Fingal; wch abounds with Hints enough of that Kind, for any person of *true* Genius — A Friend of Mine wants an Edition of Plutarch's Lives in English: Can you inform me what Editions there are? I saw a neat sett in 8 vols, bought the other Day at a Sale, with Medals of the chief persons, but not above half as big as a common *12mo:* than wch no Edition should be *smaller.* — I shall probably buy Dr. Goldsmith's Book,[9] *directly* — This Letter is already a perfect Hotch-potch; and so I proceed to tell you that there is a place near me that is called "the Ganno-green" and also an inclosure, that is called 'the Bewspers". Tell me ye Etymology of y^e *former;* & whether I am right in deriving the *Latter* from "Beau Esperance."[10]

I have of Late been meditating a Place for inserting a Seat to you in my Shrubbery; by which I class you with two Prime Friends, of whose Fidelity I have had experience ever since I was at School, with One; & University, with t'other. Mr Graves & Mr Jago; Both Men of Literature, Taste & Genius; with some distinction however of Character.

The *Renovation* of Spring has given me a pleasure in my Walks, which I always despair in *Winter* of their ever more affording me. But the *truest* Pleasure such things give, is of the *social* & *only-lasting* Sort; I mean the Pleasure *reflected* upon the Proprietor from y^e Pleasure they *give a Friend.* Should you come over & be delighted here, the Pleasure

---

[6] Thomson's *Works* (Patrick Murdoch, ed., 2 vols., London, 1762).
[7] I want an elegant 8vo Edition of Richardson, with fine cuts. [Shenstone]
[8] William Guthrie's *Complet= History of English Peerage . . . Illustrated with Elegant Copper-Plates of the Arms of the Nobility, etc.* (London, 1763) was printed in two quarto volumes by Dryden Leach.
[9] His *Letters from a Citizen of the World to His Friends in the East* (2 vols., 1762).
[10] Beau & Belle have been used indiscriminately — Beau desert & Bel-desert &c. [Shenstone]

w^d be encreased an hundred-fold. For *New* Objects are always found necessary to *Self-amusem^t;* but the *same* Objects, if they give pleasure to a Friend, will never be indifferent to ye well-disposed Owner.

W. S.

272. To RICHARD GRAVES [1]

The Leasowes, May 20, 1762

DEAR MR. GRAVES,

I find you will *not* write, unless I give a regular answer to your letters; and yet, God knows, I have a better excuse for my delay, than I wish my friend to have for his punctilio; I mean, indisposition. — Whence it has happened, I cannot say, unless I may blame these continual east winds; but I have suffered more from the smiles of Spring, than I have really done from the frowns of Winter.

Having premised thus much, I lay your letter before me. The expence of printing a sheet of those commendatory verses at a common press is eighteen shillings; and at Baskerville's about three pounds ten shillings: nor do I mean any decorations, unless perhaps "The King-fisher," or "View of my Grove," which, you know, I *have* engraven ready to *my* hands. So you see that *this* offering to vanity is not likely to be the most expensive.

I wish you had bestowed somewhat more attention upon *the title;* in which case, I really believe the job had been executed long ago. Pray be so kind as to re-consider it. — Is not "The Garland of Friendship" a little too quaint? for that, as I remember, was what I proposed. — The *motto* which you proposed was a very good one; and I think also, that the addition of the next line would be an improvement to it; "Et isti errori nomen virtus posuisset honestum." But I do not love *double* mottoes; so if I admit this, I must exclude what I proposed; which, to speak the truth, was of my own invention.

The custom of prefixing commendatory verses to collections of poetry is now seemingly grown obsolete. Besides, in my case, they would only shew that I had *taken* up more fame than my funds would answer. I return you many thanks for *your* poetical benevolence; but why do you mention it under the name of *Epigram?* I do not even chuse that it should have the air of *simile* from the *beginning:*

> Lo the tall youth, by partial fate's decree,
> To affluence born, and from restraint set free;
> How pleas'd he, &c.

---

[1] Dodsley, *Letters to Particular Friends,* No. CVI.

I have taken *this* and some *other* liberties with it, and shall insert it among the rest; unless you chuse to *redeem* it, with something more to your satisfaction: for, to speak with frankness, I think it better calculated to do *me* honour than *yourself;* though I could esteem it *good,* if it came from a person whose abilities I respected less than yours. There is a subject here, which I would recommend to you, if by so doing I should lay you under no *restraint.* It is my principal cascade. Its appearance well resembles the playfulness of infancy; skipping from side to side, with a thousand antic motions, that answer no other purpose than the mere amusement of the proprietor.—Other similitudes, &c. would here occur;

      Cui enim nascenti faciles arriserunt Musae, &c.

It then proceeds a few hundred yards, where it *rolls* and slits iron for manufactures of all kinds; resembling the graver toils of manhood, either in acquiring money, or furnishing the conveniences comforts or ornaments of life; and in this manner it proceeds, under the name of the The Stour, supplying works for casting, forging and sharping iron, for every civil or military purpose. Perhaps you may not know that my rills are the principal sources of this river; or that this river supplies *more* ironworks than almost any single river in the kingdom: for so my friend Mr. Knight told me.

The Mr. D—— you enquire after, and who wrote the *best* address Sir Robert Walpole ever *received,* is Mr. Dodington.—Did I never send you a list of all the concealed names in that Miscellany?—I began to transcribe one from my own set; but find one part of my list is lost; I however send it, and will piece it out when I find an opportunity: as I purpose also to give you some account of our several merits in Dodsley's Fables. By the way, do not the verses to Dr. Cornwallis (now Bishop) affect you sensibly, vol. VI. p. 138?—They do *me,* whenever I read them; and I cannot help applying them to myself. I feel somewhat of the same sensation when I read "The Letters of Henry and Frances;"[2] in which (from self-partiality, no doubt) I find myself extremely like Henry.

Pray let me hear, if you please, of Mr. Davenport.—I wish I had learnt to *draw* well in early life; it would have given me some very great advantages.—Let me hear also much of Mr. Melmoth, who, I presume, has left you long before this time. I did once design to have sent you down my proposals for a subscription, and requested the favour of you two to settle them finally without any further reference to myself; but my head and spirits have been too bad to undertake even a common

[2] See above, Letter 262, n4.

letter. — What think you of Dr. Lowth's Grammar?³ — Livie met him at Mr. Dodsley's; and says, he is well pleased with *our* frontispiece, &c. to Horace. Livie could not present his book to Lord Bute,⁴ *himself,* on account of my Lord's indisposition. Mr. Dalton (Dr. Dalton's brother), who teaches the King to draw, presented it. It seems, this Mr. Dalton (who gave the drawing of Lord Bute's arms) has lodgings in the palace, and sees the King every day. *While* Livie was *with* him, word came that the King was coming into his room; upon which, Livie was sent out another way. — The King asked Dalton, whom he had with him? — and was answered, an editor of Horace, who had inscribed it to Lord Bute. — Dalton is to present a copy to the King.

I inclose to you a specimen of the decorated parts of Horace, with the frontispiece. — The book will be published in a month's time, when I mean you a copy from those that are allotted to me.

My Lord Bute's arms are unexceptionably well-finished. — The other plates, either through negligence, or the wilfulness of the designer and engraver, have given me infinite trouble and vexation. However, with about *two-thirds* of my directions observed, they will, I hope, afford you some pleasure; and discover somewhat more *beauty* and *spirit* than one commonly finds in such designs. — Send me your remarks very particularly, I beseech you.

W. S.

273. To JOHN LIVIE ¹

[June 15, 1762]

Mr Shenstone desires his Compts to Mr Livie — I have, for this Fortnight past, lost my Faculty of Speech; as well as been otherwise indisposed — I hope, however that I shall be able, in a couple of days, to bid Mr Livie welcome here, somewhat more plainly than in *Whispers;* as I conceive Hopes yt my Voice is beginning to return.

I have procured a Book from London, bound I *presume* precisely Like the Horace given to Ld Bute. If it be seasonable, I should be glad to get my remaining Copies of Horace delivered to Mr Hodgetts, to whom I've given Instructions about the Binding.

Dodsley comes hither the 29th.

The Leasowes, Jun: 15. 1762

³ Dr. Robert Lowth published his *Introduction to English Grammar* in 1762.
⁴ See above, Letter 248 to Dodsley.
¹ B. M. Add. MSS 22548, fol. 111.

274. To JOHN LIVIE[1]

[July 7, 1762]

Mr Shenstone's, with Mr Dodsley's, best respects to Mr Livie; who will present ye same to Mr Baskerville & his Family — I believe we shall both dine at a Friends in Birmⁿ on Friday & ye Hay-harvest will not be quite compleeted this week, so y^t I cannot help wishing ye Favour intended me by Mr Stuart's Family may be defer'd 'till ye week after — If Mr Livie chuses to ride over, *before* he will find us at home, & glad to receive him, upon any other day yⁿ Friday.

S

July 7th 1762
Any purple leather yet arrived?

275. To THOMAS PERCY[1]

The Leasowes, Augst 10, 1762

DEAR SIR,

I was upon the Point of sending the inclosed, & giving you an account of my late silence, when I received y^r Letter which informs me that you would spend a day or two here next week.[2] I will apologize therefore when I see you; & only mention at present that I shall be at Home, & very *glad* to see you, at the time proposed — I build much on Dr Grainger's Poem.[3] both on account of his *Subject* & His *Abilities;* which I think extremely happy — He has taken Possession of a Field of Poetry, which is both *large* & *fertile,* & yet *un-occupied;* And the Cultivation of which must be a *popular* measure to Many Amongst us — But I say no more, till I see you & the Poem; only, if you write to Him directly, please to present my best respects.

I have been under a strange mistake with regard to what you call *Revises,* which I understood to mean *Sheets that were finally printed off.* I therefore kept them y^t I might see ye appearance of y^r ballads as they succeeded one another — whereas I now find that I have been expected to send these Revises directly to you — Pardon the Mistake — It was indeed a Foolish one.

I have been tolerably well this last month, or six weeks — since the time I got rid of my Cold.

[1] B. M. Add. MSS 12113, fol. 14.
[1] B. M. Add. MSS 28221, fol. 98.
[2] The visit was afterw^{ds} deferred till the end of September & I took Mrs. Percy. [Percy]
[3] Dr. James Grainger's *The Sugar Cane, a Poem in Four Books,* with notes, was published in 1764.

I have an Horace at y^r Service, either in scarlet or in Purple — Baskerville has begun to print a Virgil[4] of y^e *size* of the Spectator; which I think a better, y^n that of his Horace. *I* have also *some* things to say; but may as well reserve them 'till I see you — So wishing you a good Journey, I remain y^r ever affectionate

Will: Shenstone

276. To THOMAS SMITH[1]

[Aug. 27, 1762]

To Mr. Smith at Birchy-Close

Mr. Shenstone's service to Mr. and Mrs. Smith. I expect the Harborne tenant to come about my Farm to day, but cannot well tell at what time. If Mr. Smith shall be at Home I will let him know so soon as the man comes; and shall be glad to have him step over and assist me in the Letting it.

Saturday, Aug. 27, 1762

277. To THOMAS PERCY[1]

[Nov. 14, 1762]

* * * My friend Whistler of whom you have heard me speak, was never above half pleased with my Pastoral-ballad;[2] which used to give me some mortification. Let us however be of good courage — We have I think a more distinguished party on the other side [of] ye Question. Mr Dryden, a Man of *Fire,* was not less favorable to our Cause, y^n Mr Addison, a man of *Delicacy;* and amongst *my* Acquaintance y^u will have a Mr Graves to ballance a Mr Jago. — The Novelty, & romantic Air of ye Plan, in ye gentle heardsman,[3] gives an additional value to its other beauties — Quocirca vivite fortes! &c. As to y^r being known to ye world in ye Light *merely* of a Ballad-monger, you may be told, once for all, y^t I never mention you as such, without throwing in other matters, to prevent *this* passing for y^r *chef-d'oeuvre.* Depend upon't, y^r Character shall not suffer by any discovery I make on this head; & that I am well

---

[4] Baskerville's new Virgil was published in 1766. The editor was John Livie, who had edited the Horace.

[1] Reproduced from James Kenward's *Harborne and Its Surroundings* (2d ed., Birmingham, 1885), p. 40. Smith was an attorney of Halesowen. To him Letters 46 and 47, from the same source, also are addressed.

[1] B. M. Add. MSS 28221, fol. 101ff. The date is in Percy's hand.

[2] Shenstone has written between the lines, "Pardon my quoting my own performance; it was ye same, with regard to *other* Ballads — and he was passionately fond of Smith's Phaedra & Hippolytus, where ye Language is lifted so much more y^n ye Sentiment."

[3] See the Index.

aware a *general* & *indiscriminate* explanation of this sort would not only hurt you wth some Folks, but Would lay you under improper restraint in ye execution of y^r Plan.

You must dun me once more for "The Boy & the Mantle," & then it shall be ready — As to the Head-pieces, it doesn't appear to me y^t you can *want* them, before the whole be printed off. I would always have them relate to the *whole* book y^t follows, whether they be allegorical or not — Some of y^rs seem to *promise* well — but I have not yet had Leisure to consider them so attentively as I could wish; & should be better able to do so, were I to see ye whole volume together.

Alas no more has yet been done in regard to the *Description*[4] you mention. My Head has not of Late been fit for it — *Indeed* it has not — and yet I have had ye boldness to offer myself as a companion to great Folks; having made a weeks excursion, & passed a few Days at Ld Foley's[5] — He is a very lively agreeable Man (almost ye reverse of w^t I expected). His table ye most luxurious of any nobleman's in this Country — and his Chapel, where I attended him &c last Sunday, at once so comfortable as well as superb, y^t it is perfect Luxury to say one's Prayers in it —

I have about 4 or 5 more of these visits to make, soon; after which I shall resign myself to Winter solitude & to literary matters, *if my Health allows me.* — I wrote yesterday to Mr Rice Williams; availing myself of y^r remarks on ye Welsh-Ode he sent me; altho it stands much higher in y^r opinion y^n it really does in *mine*. The solemnity of ye writers invocation & transition thence to his Subject is well; but it abounds with infinite tautology; &, what is worse, deals so much in *general* terms y^t it has with me Little poetical merit.

I sent y^r Book of old Poems to Mr Sketchley, & believe I *did* mark some few Pieces with a Pencil — Perhaps you may admit some of those y^t have first-rate marks; but I question whether you should go so low as second-rate, unless you have particular reasons for so doing. — Do no[t] let y^r volumes be too thick, nor y^r notes too verbose — & take great care what you admit.

Be so good as Let me hear from you as soon as you well can; and believe me to be, with constant affection;

      Y^r most faithfull hum: Servt.
         W. Shenstone

My best respects to Mrs Percy.

[4] Description of the Leasowes. [Percy]
[5] See Letter 278, to Dodsley, and Letter 279, to Graves.

Sheridans Pamphlet[6] has some just remarks, which were new to me; but he is not always right in ye application of his Rules: & it is a cursed quarto of half a guinea.

"Ogilvies Poems"[7] ye same — but also ornamented with Cuts from ye authors own designs. The Specimens y^t appear in ye monthly review, give me no Pleasure.

I believe I shall purchase ye 2 additional volumes[8] of Dean Swift.

What think you of ye Reviewer's remarks upon ye New Liturgy, in y: Review for Nov^r[9] last?

Could you any way contrive for me to see ye Poems by Scotch Gentlemen?[10]

There is I believe a mighty neat Edition of (John) Philips's Poems[11] just published with Cuts. — Adieu — you see I've nothing to say — No Facts to communicate, & no Imagination to supply ye Place — wch is perhaps ye same Case with that of a Kingdom wch abounds neither in Cash, nor Paper-credit.

278. To ROBERT DODSLEY[1]

The *Leasowes, Nov.* 20, 1762

MY DEAREST FRIEND,

It is a very *surprising* and a *cruel* thing, that you will not suppose me to have been *out of Order,* after such a Neglect of writing, as can hardly be *excused* on any *other* Score. I cannot, indeed, lay Claim to what the Doctors call an *acute Disease:* but *Dizziness of Head,* and *Depression of Spirits* are at best no *trivial* Maladies, and great *Discouragements* to writing. There is a lethargic State of *Mind* that deserves your Pity, not your Anger; though it may require the *Hellebore* of sharp Reproof. Why then did you not apply this pungent Remedy, before the disease was

---

[6] *A Course of Lectures on Elocution: Together with Two Dissertations on Language; and Some Other Tracts Relative to Those Subjects* (London, 1762), by Thomas Sheridan (1719–88), father of Richard Brinsley Sheridan.

[7] John Ogilvie (1733–1813), *Poems on Several Subjects. To Which Is Prefix'd, An Essay on the Lyric Poetry of the Ancients; In Two Letters Inscribed to the Right Honourable James Lord Deskford* (London, 1762).

[8] Volumes 13 and 14 of the edition of Swift's *Collected Works* that began to appear in 1755.

[9] This should be October last. [Hecht]

[10] *A Collection of Original Poems,* "by the Rev. Mr. Blacklock, and other Scotch Gentlemen" (2 vols., Edinburgh, 1760–62). Thomas Blacklock was the patron of Burns.

[11] *Poems Attempted in the Style of Milton* "with a new account of his life and writings" (London, 1762).

[1] Hull, *Select Letters,* Vol. II, No. I. The date is confirmed by the reference to the visit to Lord Foley (see Letter 277, of authentic date). Hull does not identify the addressee, who, however, is obviously Robert Dodsley.

gone so far? But seriously, I pass too much of that Sort of Time, wherein I am neither *well* nor *ill;* and being unable to express myself at large, am averse to do so by Halves. From the strange Laconicism of your Letter, I am really in Doubt, whether you are not angry at me; and yet had rather this were owing to *Anger* that *may* subside, than to any persevering *Fondness* you may have for such unusual Brevity. Should the latter become habitual, I shall see the Letters of a Genius dwindle to "per first will advise the Needful." God forbid such a Transformation!

Your *former* Letter, to my great Confusion, was dated *Sept.* 18. Let me speak first to some few Parts of it — The Lampreys[2] arrived safe, and were as good as I ever tasted; but every Time I tasted them, I wanted *you;* and you are mistaken if you imagine, I can half relish such Cates *alone:* however, I return you Thanks.

You gave me no Account how far the *Bath* Waters, &c. were judged expedient for you. A *charitable* Action called you up to Town; and you, in the Benevolence of your Heart, presume, that this *accounts* for the Neglect of every Advantage that concerned *yourself*. Pray let me know whether the Bath was proper for you [and] at the same Time inform me, whether you were able to serve Mrs. H——. I shall be sorry for *you,* as well as *her,* if you should miss the Gratification you would derive from the Success of such an Endeavour.

Were I rich, I would erect a Temple to *Simplicity* and *Grace;* or, as the latter Word would be equivocal, to *Simplicity* and *Elegance*. I am glad to hear that Mr. W[ren] has undertaken to deify the *former;* as he will produce better *Grounds* for such a *Consecration* than was ever done by Pagans, or by Papists, on any *such* Occasion. By the Way, I take that Goddess to be a remarkable Friend to Ease and Indolence. There is another well-deserving Personage, *Delicacy,* whose Cause has been strangely deserted, by either Mr. Melmoth or Dr. Lancaster.

Will it make better for me, or worse, to say, I've not yet written to Mr. Graves? But I will positively write, within this Week, if it cost me a Dose of Salts to clear my Brain. As to what he says about my printing immediately, he *may* be *right,* and I am *sure* he is *friendly:* but more of this in a little Time.

Since the Receipt of your last Letter, Mr. Percy and his Wife came and spent a good Part of the Week here; and *he,* also, would needs write a Description of the *Leasowes*. During the latter Part of his Circuit, my Friend Jago and I accompanied him; and what was produced on that Occasion, you will go near to know in a little Time. Mean while I am

[2] Dodsley's letter to Shenstone, dated September 18, 1761, mentioning the lampreys, is in Hull, *Select Letters,* Vol. I, No. LXXVII.

more and more convinced, that no Description of this Place can make any Figure in Print, unless some *Strictures* upon *Gardening,* and *other* Embellishments be superadded.

Mr. Jago has been with me twice, having written a Poem in blank Verse, which he leaves here for my Revisal. 'Tis a descriptive Poem, called *Edge-Hill,*[3] and admits an Account of the Battle fought there, together with many legendary Tales and Episodes.

About a Week ago, I paid a Visit of two or three Days, which I had long promised, To Lord Foley. His Table, for a Constancy, is the most magnificent of any I ever saw: eighteen or twenty elegant Dishes; a continual Succession of Company; his Behaviour, perfectly hospitable, and his Conversation really entertaining. I most readily own myself to have been under a Mistake, with Regard to his *companionable* Character. My Reception was as agreeable as it could possibly be. As to the rest, he has a most admirable House and Furniture; but without any Room or Utensil that would stand the Test of *modern* Criticism. The Views around him, wild and great; and the Park capable of being rendered *fine; twice* as striking as it is at present, if he would fell some Oaks, under the Value of a Crown, and some Hawthorns, under the Value of a Half-penny: but 'tis possible, at his Time of Life, &c. nothing of this Sort will be undertaken. The two Things at present remarkable are, his *Lodge* and his *Chapel.* The Portico of the former, (designed by Fleetcroft) affords three different and striking Prospects. The Chapel is so very superb and elegant, that Mrs. Gataker has nothing to do but send you and me *thither,* to say our Prayers in it. In reality, it is perfect Luxury; as I truly thought it, last *Sunday* Se'en-night; *his Pew* is a *Room* with an handsome Fireplace; the Ceiling carved, painted in Compartments, and the Remainder enriched with gilt Stucco-Ornaments; the Walls enriched in the same Manner; the best painted Windows I ever saw; the Monument to his Father, Mother, and Brothers, cost, he said, 2000*l.* the middle Aisle rendered comfortable by Iron Stoves, in the Shape of Urns; the Organ perfectly neat, and good, in Proportion to its Size: and to this Chapel you are led through a Gallery of Paintings seventy Feet long — And what would you more? You'll say, a good Sermon — I really think his Parson is able to preach one.

And now I come, lastly, to speak of your Letter I received on Monday. What an uncommon Man you are! to take so much Thought for *those,* who never took *any* for themselves! — I have enquired after Mr. Wedderburne, and it seems he is a very clever and a very rising Lawyer; to whom

---

[3] Published in 1767.

I am the more obliged for mentioning me, as I fear I have not the Honour of being the least known to him.

Pray write to me as soon as possible, and I will make you Amends (if *Writing* will make Amends) for the scandalous *Omissions* of which I have been guilty. I have somewhat to tell you of Lord L——'s usual *great Kindness,* when the Lords D—— and W—— were last at *Hagley;* but I have not Time, and must conclude, my dearest, worthiest Friend!

your ever obliged
W. Shenstone

279. To RICHARD GRAVES [1]

The Leasowes, Nov. 20, 1762

DEAR MR. GRAVES,

Do I really owe you an apology? you who are embarrassed with such a number of momentous concerns, as hardly allow a fair trial to letters of mere amusement? Alas! I cannot shelter my long silence under a supposition of this kind. I believe, I even *hope,* that you have disapproved my long neglect; as I can very faithfully assure you I have repeatedly done *myself.* There are certain times and seasons when I have not either the *power* or the *will* to write: as Hannibal said about attacking Rome, "Quandoque mentem non dari, quandoque potestatem." This being an intellectual kind of *lethargy,* it would have been at least a friendly office, if you had *rouzed* me, as you *might* have done, by a supernumerary letter. I never receive a line from you, but I feel an almost irresistible propensity to answer it that very instant. Impediments sometimes occur; and, that instant being neglected, matter is accumulated for a longer letter than I am always resolute enough to undertake: at the same time, I can never content myself with uttering one half of what I have to say. — Pray is not that *good sort of man,* to whom you allude, a Mr. K——? Let him be ever so good a sort of man in the common estimation, I dare aver him to be neither an ingenious person nor a candid critic. There may be fifty or more preferable readings to what are received in this new Horace; [2] yet he will find a better *text* there, *upon the whole,* than in any one edition before extant. As to the *beauty* of *type* and *press-work,* it is too obvious to need vindication. The accuracy of the *latter* almost exceeds what was ever found in any other book. Then as to the *frontispiece,* it is, I think, much superior to such as *ordinarily* occur; the *subject* animated, and well-chosen; and the *execution* very commendable: At least, if we allow for the *nice* touches which it required, and the

---
[1] Dodsley, *Letters to Particular Friends,* No. CVII.
[2] The Baskerville Horace. See the Index.

uncommon difficulty of getting any thing of this kind done to one's direction.

Mr. Walpole is a lively and ingenious writer; not always accurate in his determinations, and much less so in his language; too often led away by a desire of routing prejudices and destroying giants: and yet there is no province wherein he appears to more advantage, in *general,* than in throwing new light upon Characters in British History. I wish he would compose a regular work, making this his principal point. He has, with great labour, in his Book of Painters, recorded matters of little importance, relative to people that were of less. I have a right to be severe, for his volumes cost me above thirty shillings; yet, where he drops the *antiquarian* in them, his remarks are striking, and worth perusal. — I have sent for "Gesner's Rural Poems," and intend to see "The Death of Abel;"[3] though I expect to find small pleasure in this *poetical prose,* unless exquisitely well-tuned. — Thank you for the anecdote of Lord Courteney: a thousand such sort of things, that engage the public attention, are never capable of penetrating the depth of my retirement.

Mr. Melmoth you will probably see often, as he intends to make Bath his place of residence. The *Omphale* you sent me is a most excellent figure, and I shall wish much to get a good cast of it; at least, when I am able to afford it. — When I write again, I will give you the best account I can of *my share* in Dodsley's new Fables; though it will be no easy matter to speak *separately* of it with any precision.

And now, I think, I have spoke to most of the articles in your last letter. — Mr. Dodsley, who says he invited you, would acquaint you how we divided our time whilst he was here, into two *principal* parts, "l'un à dormir, l'autre a ne rien faire." Yet we paid our devoirs to a good deal of genteel company; of which this season has afforded me at *least* an equal share with any that went before. I will particularize a few; opening the list with no less personages than the Duke and Duchess of Richmond — Mr. Walsh, Member for Worcester — Earl of Bath, with Dr. Monson, Mrs. Montague[4] (who wrote the three last Dialogues printed with Lord Lyttelton's), and other company, from Hagley — Sir Richard Ashley — Mr. Mordaunt — Dr. Charleton with Mr. Knight — Earl and Countess of

---

[3] The Swiss poet Salomon Gessner (1730–88) published his *Idyllen,* upon which his fame largely rests, in 1756. They were widely read and translated, and are probably the "Rural Poems" to which Shenstone refers. His *Abels Tod,* published in 1758, was very popular. In 1761 a translation by Michael Huber appeared in Paris; the poem was also translated into other Romance languages and into English (see W. Creizenach in *Allgemeine deutsche Biographie,* 9:122–26). The Register of Books of the *Gentleman's Magazine* for January, 1762, announces "The Death of Abel; in five books."

[4] Mrs. Elizabeth Robinson Montagu (1720–1800), a leading bluestocking; she was also the author of an *Essay on the Writings and Genius of Shakespeare* (1769), in which she defends the poet against the strictures of Voltaire.

Northampton — Mr. Amyand — Lord Plymouth and Sir Harry Parker — Mr. and Mrs. Morrice of Fercefield — Lord Mansfield with Mr. Baron Smythe, Lord Dartmouth and Mr. Talbot — Marquis of Tavistock and Earl of Ossory — your nephew Mr. Graves, with Mr. Hopton and one of the senior Proctors of Oxford — Lord and Lady Dacre — Baron Plessen, Gentleman of the Bed-chamber to the King of Denmark, with a Mr. Wendt his Tutor — Lord and Lady Vernon of Sudbury with his children, Sir Charles and Lady Tynte, and Mr. Garrick's brother — Mr. Melmoth and Mrs. Melmoth — Colonel James — Lady Ward and Lady Uill, with Miss Wrottesley, Miss Pigott, &c. — Lord Lyttelton, Mr. Lyttelton, and Mr. Rust — Lord and Lady Dartmouth with Lord and Lady Willoughby de Broke — Mr. Anson of Shuckburgh with Mr. Stuart the painter and publisher of 'Athenian Ruins" — Mr. Pepys and Sir W. Wheeler's son, Mr. Pitt's nephew, &c. — Colonel Bamfylde, with Mr. Knight's Family, &c. &c. — I did not imagine my list would have engrossed so much of my paper, and leave so little room to speak about the individuals. — Lord M[ansfield] appeared to me rather a *man of wit* than a *man of taste;* Baron Smythe, the reverse. — Mr. and Mrs. Morrice, extremely polite and agreeable people, invited me pressingly to their habitation; I could not help reflecting on the singular happiness of Mr. Morrice to be possessed at once of a large fortune, one of the finest situations in England, and a wife whose taste for rural improvements appears even superior to his own; at least, if the *beauty* of her *person* did not impose upon my judgment. There are many others whom I would distinguish, if my time or paper would permit. — I suppose that you and Mr. Dodsley would be mighty unanimous with regard to the propriety of setting my subscription on foot.[5] I do not dispute any of your arguments — they tally exactly with my own opinion: at least, allowing for the higher idea you have of my pieces than they deserve — the truth is, that I have deferred the publication too long *already* — till many of the compositions will not appear to the same advantage as before, and till I have not half the power that I had formerly to improve them. When I am low-spirited, I almost shudder at this tremendous contract with the publick; when my spirits are elevated, I see the necessity that you do, of not losing a moment's time — were you here a week, you would put the matter upon a footing that was unalterable — would to God you *were* here, or any one *like* you! however, it is probable you will *soon* hear from me again upon this very subject — I *know* this, that, *if* I print at *all,* the subscription is by no means to be neglected this present winter. — I have seen our friend Dr. Charleton many times this season; at The Leasowes; at Mr. Knight's;

[5] This much discussed project for publication never materialized.

at his own house; and at my Lord Foley's. This visit to my Lord Foley's was performed about three weeks ago. I went with young Knight; and the company of the Doctor and Sir Francis Charleton took off all restraint, and made the visit perfectly agreeable. My Lord's behavior was entirely free and hospitable; and his conversation lively and entertaining — I must confess, far beyond the idea which I have been taught to conceive of him. His table the most magnificent, I believe, of any Nobleman's for thirty miles round. His park, and Woobery-hill adjacent, afford views that are either extensive, wild, beautiful, or grand. The portico before his lodge deserves particular notice. His house large, and commodious, and well furnished; but scarce any of the rooms *high* enough to stand the test of modern criticism. But what strikes more than all the rest, is the magnificence of his chapel — which however I cannot stay to describe; for I this very *moment* receive your letter. — After having written so much before, I can only touch upon some few particulars. — I believe, my scheme of publication will proceed in a little time, and that you will soon hear from me again. — If you can possibly excuse me to Mr. Davenport, and keep me well with him for a week or fortnight, I will not fail to write him a respectful letter. — I am truly ashamed of my neglect; but have written more letters within this week, than I have done for a quarter of a year before. — That there is a faction forming against Lord B[ute], I readily believe. The war may suit the *mercantile* world; and the City of London has generally the art to represent the *landed* and *trading* interest as *precisely* the same thing: but I think there is a very material difference; which it would be no way difficult to demonstrate — at least I am one that cry out,

> Nulla salus bello; pacem te poscimus omnes!

I am quite unacquainted with the affair relating to Colonel Wilkes and Lord Bute's son. — And now (though I mean to write again soon) I will release you from this unpleasing scrawl. I beg however that you would not fail to write to me *directly*, if you can find leisure; being quite impatient to converse with you, after such a chasm in our correspondence; and being, with unvariable affection, my dear friend, for ever yours. — Pray my best respects to Mrs. Graves.

W. Shenstone

My friend Dr. Grainger has written a Poem, in blank verse, which he calls "The Sugar-Cane."[6] — It is divided into four books, and is capable of being *rendered* a good Poem. My friend Jago has written another Poem, in blank verse also, which he calls "Edge-hill."[7] It is descriptive

[6] Published in 1764.   [7] Published in 1767.

chiefly of the prospect—but admits an account of *the fight* there, and many little *tales* and *episodes;* with compliments also to the gentry of Warwickshire.—It lies now upon my table.

280. To RICHARD JAGO [1]

[Dec. 18,] 1762

My dear friend,

    A thousand thanks to you for the very obliging and humorous Poem[2] which you are so kind to send me. I really think it very ingenious, and, upon the whole, extremely correct; although I have taken the liberty of proposing one or two hints for farther improvement. The relation that it bears to me and my place *may* tend to prejudice my *judgment;* but I cannot conceive that it requires aught beside *impartiality,* to relish the beauties of this Poem. I beg I may receive a fair copy in your own hand, as soon as possible; and I will consider, in the mean time, how to shew it to the publick in the most advantageous manner. It certainly does me *honour:* as things are at present circumstanced, it may *tend* to do me *good;* which I am very sure you would be glad to see. I am a little ashamed to be so much behind-hand with you, in favours of *this* and *other* kinds: but I live in hopes there may come a day, when I shall find occasion to express my gratitude. The pictures you sent arrived safe on Thursday: and have been since cleaned, and put up in their places. I cannot enter upon this subject now; finding it almost six o'clock at night, and having just received a letter from Mr. Dodsley which he requires me to answer by return of post. It relates to the *scheme* mentioned in his last, which is intended for my emolument; but which I must not expect to succeed, without considerable mortification. This *inter nos.*—You must by no means lay aside the thoughts of perfecting *Edge-hill,* at your leisure. It is possible that, in order to keep clear of flattery, I have said less in its favour than I relly *ought*—but I never considered it otherwise than as a Poem which it was very adviseable for you to compleat and *finish.* I am now to desire my best respects to Mrs. Jago, and to bid you an affectionate adieu!

        Tu comes antiquus! tu primis junctus ab annis!

    I am, my dear friend! ever yours, with the truest esteem,

                                          W. Shenstone

Dec. 18, 1762

[1] Dodsley, *Letters to Particular Friends,* No. CVIII.
[2] The reference is apparently to *Edge Hill,* mentioned later in the letter.

281. To SHERRINGTON DAVENPORT[1]

The Leasowes, Jan. 4, 1763

DEAR SIR,

Mr. G[raves] tells me, that you have done me the honour to lay some stress upon receiving a letter from me. Alas! it must be owing purely to your benevolence, which makes you wish to hear of an absent friend, and not to any expectations you can reasonably form of entertainment from his pen. The long letter with which you favoured me was so very lively as well as ingenious, that I despaired of drawing from my fountains the vivacity you do from the Bath waters. But, be this as it will, the vein of friendship that runs through your letter demands my amplest acknowledgments; and if you will accept of *such* returns, I promise they will be as *hearty* as they are *insipid*.

I agree with you, that the first sallies of imagination will generally prove the most sprightly, and that they will often comprehend the principal features of a subject. They are of the nature of dead-colouring in a portrait; which one sometimes thinks more spirited than the same performance when finished. And yet a *good* painter will not *hurt* a portrait by the subsequent labour he bestows upon it, nor will a *good* writer injure his piece by the pains he takes to round and perfect it. It must be some defect in the taste of either that makes his diligence detrimental, or gives occasion for a stander-by to cry out, "Manum de tabula." I believe it will appear upon examination, that works which cost most labour have generally been thought the *easiest* and pleased the *longest*. One cannot, however, deny that there is a sort of persons formed by nature for *shooting-flying* (which, by the way, I could never *do*), and that their sallies of imagination are what they can hardly improve by any future pains. These may be called men of wit and fire, but it is the union of taste with these that constitutes fine writing. True taste will never stiffen or over-charge any performance: it will rather be employed to smoothe, simplify, and give that ease on which *grace* depends. One can as little, deny that there are *kinds* of writing which have a better chance than others to succeed without much labour, which start forth mature at *first*, as Pallas did from the brain of Jupiter. Works of *humour* are often of this sort; and there are many instances in Butler's Hudibras. Yet I think the humour of *Swift* was greatly owing to a judicious *revisal*. — Pardon me, my dear friend, for this tedious discussion, which you little thought of bringing upon yourself by the obliging hint you gave concerning those verses upon Venus. I do acknowledge that an additional stanza there,

[1] Dodsley, *Letters to Particular Friends*, No. CIX.

containing a reflection on Chinese architecture, were better laid aside. It seemed to me one of the "splendida peccata" that might be a little *popular* at this *time;* and has, therefore, for this season, appeared on a board by the side of the Venus. We, who cannot erect fresh temples, or even add a new garden-seat every spring, are obliged to make the most we can of a new and tolerable copy of verses, that cost us *thought* instead of *money;* and even at a pinch to piece out a dull scene with duller poetry: how else could I keep my place in countenance, so near the pompous piles of Hagley? And yet there are few *fashionable* visitants that do not shew an *affection* for the little Amoret, as much as they admire the stately Sacharissa—"plerumque gratae *divitibus vices.*" I have often considered why those possessed of palaces yet esteem a root-house or a cottage as a desirable object in their gardens.—Is it not from having experienced the imperfection of happiness in higher life, that they are led to *conceive* it more compleat beneath a roof of straw; where, perhaps, it may really be as defective as in the apartments of a King or a Minister?—A thousand thanks to you and Mrs. Davenport for the accommodations you so kindly offer me. Experience will no more suffer me to question the *cordiality* than the politeness of your reception. What an amusing picture have you given of Bath! pleasures carried to the utmost height, and opiates ready when one is cloyed with pleasures! And yet let me confess a truth, you have *lightly* touched upon those *very* articles which would prove to me the most *specifically* pleasing. For can any temptation be stronger, than to say that *you* reside there! and does not my friend G[raves] reside at Claverton, of whose genius and friendship I have had proofs these twenty years past? and have you not Mr. Webb, and now Mr. Melmoth, to make Bath *enviable* for the residence of literature? What a joy would it afford me to go on a party with you to Percefield, whither Mr. and Mrs. Morrice gave me the most pressing invitations!—These surely are pleasures of which—I *hope* one day to partake.

My health, generally bad in winter and spring, has hitherto been tolerable. The *influenza* of last spring continued to depress me half the summer. Would you think the verses I inclosed were written on that occasion by a young journeyman shoe-maker;[2] and one that lives at the village of Rowley, near me! He considered my disorder in somewhat too *grave* a light, as I did not think my life endangered by it; but allowing for this, and the *partiality* he shews *me,* you will think the lines pretty

---

[2] James Woodhouse (1735–1820), the cobbler-poet whom Shenstone befriended and in a measure patronized, published his *Poems on Sundry Occasions* the year after Shenstone died (1764); they were republished as *Poems on Several Occasions* in 1766. Woodhouse addressed an elegy to Shenstone in 1759. The verses referred to, *To William Shenstone, Esq; in his Sickness,* appear at the end of Volume II of Shenstone's *Works.*

extraordinary for one of *his occupation*. They are not, however, the *only* or, perhaps, the *chief* specimens of his genius; and yet, before he came to me, his principal knowledge was drawn from *Magazines*. For these two or three years past, I have lent him Classics, and other books in English. You see, to *him*, I am a great Maecenas; although you and my friend expect me to become an author by subscription. On this head I will say no more at *present*, than that I am infinitely obliged by your extreme friendly offers. My friend G[raves], who knows my sentiments, has sometimes the honour of waiting upon you; I ought not, therefore, after this tedious epistle, to begin to trouble you with a written explanation of them. Believe me, dear Sir, with my most respectful compliments to Mrs. Davenport,

Your ever obliged and most obedient servant,

W. Shenstone

I will send you some other of Woodhouse's verses, when I can get him to transcribe them.

282. To RICHARD JAGO[1]

The Leasowes, Jan. 4, 1763

DEAR MR. JAGO,

My last letter must have been confused, and the arrival of it, I fear, uncertain.

The hare and birds, in one of the pictures which you sent me, I think, are well; the other parts of it indifferent; the greyhound worst of all. The portrait is by no means equal to its companion, either in beauty of the person, or skill of the painter; yet it matches so well with the other, that I find my parlour very much embellished by it. Pardon the freedom with which I criticise your present; and accept once more my very thankful acknowledgements.

I am truly glad to find so worthy a Nobleman, and so warm a friend of yours, as my Lord Willoughby[2] is, made a Lord of the Bed-chamber.

I have heard nothing since I wrote last in regard to *my* affair;[3] though I expect to do so every day. I have such a tribe of humours and peculiarities, that it is easier to make me rich than to make me happy; and ten to one that the favour will not be conferred without disgusting some of these said humours, &c. However, one must make the best of it; and

---

[1] Dodsley, *Letters to Particular Friends,* No. CX.

[2] It was through the good offices of Lord Willoughby that Jago got, in 1746, the livings of Harbury and Chesterton.

[3] Lord Loughborough had applied to Lord Bute for a pension for Shenstone, but he did not live long enough to enjoy it.

reflect, that mortifications in one place may preclude mortifications in another.

I go tomorrow, by appointment, to Enville; where I may probably stay till Saturday. I have wished most heartily for a copy of your Fable to take with me; but Dodsley has not yet returned that I sent him. Pray consider my proposed alterations rather as hints than real improvements, and let me have a copy as soon as you can. I wrote my criticism over twice, and know not whether I sent the best or the worst copy; so I send the other, though perhaps much the same. I forgot to particularize many shining parts in your little Fable, that are either elegant or humourous: of the former sort, nothing could be happier than what you say about H[agley]; as it touches in the *gentlest* manner, on a possible truth, which, if expressed rather than implied, might not be altogether inoffensive. This beauty is produced by substituting H[agley] instead of L[yttelton], the place instead of the proprietor.

I have lately read "The Death of Abel."⁴ It is not void of merit; but might have been made much more pathetic by a more simple and prosaic style.

I desire my best respects to Mrs. Jago and your family. — May not I see you here this Christmas? as I wish to do, because it is the season present; and not that I am not at all times and at all seasons most unfeignedly glad to wait upon you, and most affectionately your ever faithful servant:

> Tecum etenim longos memini consumere soles,
> Et tecum primas epulas decerpere noctes.
> Unum opus, & requiem pariter disponimus ambo, &c.

Your kind remembrance of me in your Edge-hill has brought these quotations into my head. Adieu!

W. Shenstone

283. To RICHARD JAGO¹

Jan. 11, 1763

MY GOOD FRIEND,

I am suspicious that my letters (of which I have sent two) do not reach you by the way of Warwick. This is meant as an experiment whether they will arrive by way of Southam. It is meant withall to remind you of perfecting your little Fable, and dispatching it to me as soon as may be. I would fain transmit a copy to Lord S[tamford]'s before the family separates, or leaves Enville; by whom, I am sure, it would be admired.

⁴ See above, Letter 279, n3.   ¹ Dodsley, *Letters to Particular Friends*, No. CXI.

I am just returned from a visit which I made there, of four or five days, passed very happily. At coming away, I shewed my Lord two or three of Mr. D——'s last letters, which laid open to him the scheme that was carrying on for me. I requested also, if there should be occasion (which there possibly might *not*) that he would allow me the honour of being known to him. He said, "he was glad to find what was going forward; and had long wished to see something of that sort begun before: that he should be in town, I think, in February; and would do me any service in his power. He desired me also to acquaint Mr. D—— (in allusion to the latter's uncertainty about my Lord's political connexions) that he thought it the duty of every honest man to support the present Government; and that he should continue his regard for the Minister, so long as he saw nothing in his measures that was prejudicial to his Country."

I know that you will take a friendly part in any good that may befall me. Pray write, be it ever so carelessly; and believe me ever yours and Mrs. Jago's most affectionate and faithful

W. S.[2]

284. To THOMAS PERCY [1]

Jan: 16, 1763

Mr Shenstone's[2] comp^{ts} to M^r & Mrs Percy — I received your Packet at Enville; and, if I pay my respects to Ld Ward before he go to London, it must be the Beginning of this week — So that I cannot possibly return an answer to y^r Letter, just at present — When I can, I will — Meantime y^r Books are arrived at Sketchley's; & I have just *dipt* into every *one* of them. The Frost is too severe for me to use Exercise, & I am quite pampered with Snipes & Field-fare — At ye same time, my Mind Starves, & I hunger more for a six-penny Pamphlet, yⁿ I do for ye freshest Barrel of Oysters. The wit of ye times is to be found in Partybooks; & I profess *no* Party, but *moderation*. This I take to be both Ld Bute's & the King's; and for this reason, if I am *warm* on any side, it is on Their's.

---

[2] The writer survived the date of this letter but a short time, his death happening on the eleventh of the following month, to the inexpressible grief of his more intimate friends, and the generous concern of those, who, too late acquainted with his merit, were indulging themselves in the pleasing thought of having provided for his future ease, and tranquil enjoyment of life [Dodsley]. It will be recalled that efforts were being made at this time to provide Shenstone with a pension. Lord Loughborough had made application to Lord Bute, but final action had not been taken.

[1] B. M. Add. MSS 28221, fol. 106.

[2] The excellent Writer of this letter died February 11th following universally lamented. [Percy]

Index

Items of mere documentation, such as purely bibliographical references and the identification of letters, have not been indexed; neither have Shenstone's most casual allusions to persons and places of no importance. Fictitious characters are entered within single quotation marks. Approximate titles of literary works are indicated by double quotation marks.

Abels Tod, see *Death of Abel*
Account of the War in India (Cambridge), 443n
'Adams, Abraham' (Parson Adams), 44, 138
Addington, Dr. Anthony, 179
Addison, Joseph, 192n, 258, 377, 449
Adventurer, The, 414n
Aeneas, 209
Aesop, see *Fables*
Agriculture, first book of *Public Virtue* (R. Dodsley), 285, 286
Akenside, Mark, 71, 373, 381, 423
Alcock, Edward (painter), 379, 383, 384, 385, 388, 391, 395, 406, 408, 411, 418, 430
Alemoor, Lord, see Pringle, Andrew
Alfred, King, 435
Allen, Mr., 130, 134, 139, 142, 176, 180, 193, 198, 203, 242
Alley, The (Pope), 42, 107
All's Well That Ends Well, 33
Almoran and Hamet (Hawkesworth), 414
Amyntor and Theodora (Mallet), 82n
Analysis of Beauty (Hogarth), 290n, 293
Anecdotes of Painting in England (Walpole), 442n
Anglesey (Anglesea), Earl of, 43n
Annesley, James, 43n
Anson, Lord and Lady, 273, 274
Arabian Nights' Entertainment, 431
Archer, Lord, 144, 162, 166, 186
Architecture, see Gothicism; Landscape architecture
Argyle, Duke of, 34
Aris, Thomas A., 147, 194, 245n, 246, 327, 364
Aristotle, 165
Armstrong, John, 21n
Arne, Thomas, 56n, 59n, 327
Arnold, Mrs. (Shenstone's housekeeper), 12, 24, 50, 53, 54, 58, 139, 160, 210, 222
"Arno's Vale," 65, 70
"Asteria" (Mrs. Knight), 70
Astley, Sir John, 55
Aubrey, Mr., 61n
Aubrey, Mrs., 62, 63. LETTER TO, 61
Aylesbury, Lady, 213, 217, 297

'Mr. B——' (*Pamela*), 24
Bacchus, 96
Ballad, distinguished from song, 409; defined, 436; opinion of, 345. See also *Reliques;* individual ballads
Balmerino, Lord (Arthur Elphinstone, sixth Baron), 80n, 81
Bamfylde, Mr., 349, 357, 396, 412
Banks, Miss Peggy, 272, 274, 275
Barbarini, 40
'Barnwell, George,' 56
Barrels (home of Lady Luxborough), 8n and *passim*
Bartholomew, Lucy, see Graves, Mrs. Richard
Baskerville, John, 300, 321, 332, 354, 362, 396, 398, 399, 401, 408, 410, 418, 428, 445, 448; editions of: Horace, 404n, 412, 414, 421, 422, 427, 440, 441, 442, 443, 447, 449, 454; *Hudibras,* 444; Milton, 360; prayer-books, 407; Virgil, 339n, 449n
Bath, Lord, 43
Bath, 20, 21, 23, 28, 55, 60, 64, 73, 74, 78, 79, 80, 135, 216, 231, 236, 241, 242, 257, 261, 268, 296, 297, 303, 304, 325, 326, 332, 348, 349, 367, 372, 373, 375, 376, 392, 407, 411, 412, 418, 452, 459, 460
Bathurst, Lord, *Life and Literary Remains of* (T. Warton, Jr.), 413n, 414
Battle of Otterbourne (in *Reliques*), 426
Beauchamp, Lord, 92, 107, 114, 133n, 135
Belchier, Mr., 301n, 302, 306, 308, 310
Bellamy, Mrs. (actress), 357, 362
Beltishazzar, 36
Bentley, Richard, 414, 428n, 442
Bergen, 84n, 85
Berkeley, Mr., 273, 274, 318, 321
Bewdley, 310, 385
Binnel, Robert, xvii, 76, 330n, 369, 372, 381
Birmingham Gazette, 245n, 246
Blackbirds, The (Jago), 50, 94, 96n, 121, 293, 294, 311, 312n
Blacklock, Thomas, 451n
Blackstone, Sir William, 392, 411
'Bluff' (in Congreve's *Old Bachelor*), 33
Boileau, 153

Bolingbroke, Henry St. John, Lord, xxi, 71, 149, 152, 187, 211, 227, 232n, 233, 235, 237; tracts, 100; essay on patriotism, 150; memoirs, 255, 259
Bond, Mr. (painter), 276, 366
Boughton, Sir Edward, 292
Boulton, Matthew, 351n. LETTERS TO, 351, 353 (3), 354 (2), 355 (2), 437
Boy and the Mantle, The (in *Reliques*), 380, 450
Bradford, Earl of, 420
Bridgenorth, xvii, 401
Bridgewater, Duchess of, 213, 229n, 274
Bristol, 66, 80, 334
British Orpheus, 56, 64
Brobdingnag, 178
Broom, xvii, 74, 76, 115, 118, 119, 121, 161, 191, 266
Broughton, John, 36
Brown, Lyttelton, 57n, 59, 60, 61, 63, 64
Brutus, 70, 105
Builder's Jewell (Langley), 176
Bulfinch in Town, The (Lady Luxborough), 307, 308n
Bunyan, John, 214
Burke, Edmund, 376, 377, 378, 441, 442
Bute, Lord, 404n, 405, 411, 412n, 440, 447, 457, 461n, 463
Butler, Samuel *(Hudibras)*, 30, 377, 444, 459
Byng, Admiral, 339

Cabinet, The, or Verses on Roman Medals (Graves), 221, 277, 314
Cadwal, 435n
Caesar, Julius, 235, 322. See also *Julius Caesar*
Cambray, Bishop of, 200, 201
Cambridge, Richard Owen, 215n, 221, 345, 373, 375, 387, 443
Campaign, The (Addison), 192n
Capell, Edward, 398n
'Capulet,' 211
Caractacus (Mason), 370, 372
Card playing, opinion of, 216
Carey, Henry, 38n
Carr, Adam, 425
Carrington, Miss, 55
Carte, Thomas, 94
Carter, Miss (of Cheltenham), xviii, 58n, 60, 62. LETTER TO, 62
Carter, Elizabeth, 435, 440
Carteret, Lord, 58, 71
Cassius, 70
Casteels, Peter, 207n
Castle of Indolence, The (Thomson), 107, 125, 126, 128, 129, 131, 219
Catholicism, Roman, 19, 411
Catilina ou Rome Sauvée (Voltaire), 255n, 260
Cato, 81

Cave, Edward, 18
Celtic poetry, 400
Chace, The (Somervile), 13, 174, 193, 196, 198, 199
Charles II, 181
Charleton, Sir Francis, 411, 457
Charleton, Dr. Rice, 358, 378, 411, 412, 418n, 455, 456
Cheltenham, xviii, 55, 57, 59, 61, 62, 63, 230
Chesterfield, Philip Stanhope, fourth Earl of, 52n, 357
Chesterton (Jago's living), 297, 461n
Chevy Chase, 145, 155
Child, Hon. Josiah, 256n
Chinese novel, see *Hau Kiou Choaan*
Choice of Hercules (Lowth), 93n
Choice, The, To Sir Robert Walpole, 33
Christianity Not Founded on Argument (Dodwell), 427n
Christ's Kirk on the Green (Ramsay), 424
Chrononhotonthologos (Carey), 38
Chrysal, or The Adventures of a Guinea, 396
Cibber, Colley, 14, 15, 33, 44, 57, 174
Cinna, 70
Citizen of the World (Goldsmith), 444n
Clare, Mr., 200, 204, 205, 280, 329, 384
Clarendon, Lord, 377
Clarissa Harlowe, 195, 199, 202, 288, 290
Claverton, 216, 217, 232, 236, 260, 348, 349, 357, 367, 373, 460
Cleone (Dodsley), xxiii, 316n, 332n, 338, 357, 360n, 362n, 367, 368n, 369, 371, 372
Clive, Kitty, 15, 29, 40
Clogher, Bishop of, 379
Cobham, Lord, 143
Collection of Old Ballads (A. Philips), 400, 401, 413
Collection of Original Poems (Blacklock), 451n
Collection of Poems (Dodsley), xix, 107, 277, 280, 288, 297, 303, 304, 307, 308n, 309, 312, 313, 314n, 315, 316, 318n, 319n, 320, 321n, 323, 324, 325, 327n, 336, 339, 340n, 341, 343n, 350, 352
Collier, Jeremy, 14
Collins, William, 394
Colman, George, the elder, 398n
Complaint, The, or Night Thoughts (Young), 44, 66, 107
Complete History of English Peerage (Guthrie), 407n, 444
"Compliment, 1743," 343
Comus, 16
Congreve, William, 33
Conjectures on Original Composition (Young), 370, 393
Cooper, John Gilbert, 195n, 345n
Coriolanus (Thomson), 138

"Cotswouldia" (Mrs. Thomas), 419, 421, 427
Cotterel, Thomas, 252
Cotton, Charles, 30
Courteney, Lord, 455
Coventry, Lady, 356
Coventry, Lord, 78n, 294
Coventry, Francis, 225n, 318n
Coventry, 295, 322, 379
Cowley, Abraham, 181, 208
Coypell, 384
Crispinus, 381
Critical Review, 393
Cromertie, 81
Croxall, Samuel (*Fables*), 374, 406
Culloden, 81
Cumberland, Duke of, 326
Cyder (J. Philips), 46

Dalton, Mr., 227n
Danger of Writing Verse, The (Whitehead), 16
Dartmouth, Lady, 420
Dartmouth, Lord, 407, 419, 420
Dashwood, Sir Francis, 357
Davenport, Sherrington, xxii, 268, 297, 304, 329, 342, 373, 380n, 411, 446, 457, 461. LETTERS TO, 3, 304, 459
Davies, Sir John, 398
Death of a Favourite Cat, On the (Gray), 231n
Death of Abel, The (Gessner), 455, 462
Deerhurst, Lord, 9
Delap, John, 436n
Delicacy, Essay upon (Lancaster), 107, 432, 436
Delmany, Lord, 297, 298
Dennis, John, 105
Derbyshire, 51, 56, 64, 424
Dettingen, 53n, 58
Dialogues of the Dead (G. Lyttelton), 396n, 398
Dido, 46
Discourse on Fables (La Motte), 383, 389
Doddridge, Philip, 114n
Dodington, Bubb, 142, 321n, 326, 446
Dodsley, James, 304n, 405, 407, 420
Dodsley, Robert, xv, xvii, xix, xxii, xxiii, 21n, 44, 97, 99, 107, 128, 131, 134, 277, 280, 281, 283, 286, 288, 293, 295, 297, 303, 308, 311, 313, 314, 315, 316, 318, 319n, 321, 322, 323, 324, 325, 326, 327, 329, 332, 333, 336, 337, 338, 339, 340, 341, 342, 343, 345, 346, 347, 350, 352, 356, 357, 360, 361, 362, 363, 364, 365n, 366, 367, 368, 369, 370, 371, 372, 373, 374, 375, 376, 377, 378, 381, 382, 383, 386, 389, 390, 391, 396, 398, 399, 401, 402, 404, 406, 407, 408, 409, 410, 411, 412, 413, 414, 418, 420, 421, 427, 428, 429, 432, 436, 438, 446, 447, 448, 455, 456, 458, 462. LETTERS TO, 316, 320, 343, 364, 404, 451
Dodwell, Henry, 427n
Dolman, young (brother of Maria), 82, 296, 315, 328, 331, 349, 352, 373, 379, 395
Dolman, Jack, 60, 64
Dolman, Maria, xix, 76, 82, 108, 109, 113, 114, 115, 122, 123, 125, 135, 154, 156, 157, 162, 165, 191, 226, 289, 290, 375
Dolman, Thomas, xvii, 74, 76, 86n, 93, 95, 107, 116, 118, 119, 122, 133, 135, 140, 146, 154, 156, 157, 158, 160, 161, 191, 228, 266, 289
Don Quixote (Smollett's translation), 384, 405n
Donnegal, Lord, 350, 358
Douglas, Gawain, 424
Dragon of Wantley, The (in *Reliques*), 36
Dryden, John, 44, 124, 400, 449
Dubos, Abbé, 375, 377
Dudley, Lord (Ferdinando Dudley Lea), 16n, 17, 19, 51, 84, 87, 95, 96, 122, 123, 125, 127, 130, 134, 141, 156, 157, 160, 164, 168, 174, 210, 211, 233, 237, 243, 244, 246, 247, 249, 250, 252, 262, 264, 266, 270, 272, 274, 275, 276, 279, 281, 282, 284, 287n, 293, 294, 298, 300, 301, 306, 308, 317, 328, 337, 341. See also Grange
Dunciad, The, 36
Duncombe, John, 336, 381n
Duncombe, William, 336, 381, 382

Earl of Essex, The (Jones), 258, 259
Eastward Hoe, 403n
Economy, see *Oeconomy*
Edgehill, scene of the battle of, 187, 188n, 189, 293
Edge Hill (Jago), 7, 453, 457, 458n, 462
Edom o' Gordon (in *Reliques*), 369, 372, 380, 425
Edward III, tragedy of, 398
Edwin and Emma (Mallet), 443n
Egmont, Lady, 396
Electricity, interest in, 90, 351, 353, 362
Elegies (Shenstone), 47, 84, 106, 125, 129, 135, 136, 356, 367
Elegies: with an Ode to the Tiber (Whitehead), 339n
Elegy in a Country Churchyard (Gray), 221, 225, 423, 435
Elegy on Lord Sussex (Percy), 359
Elegy to an Old Beauty (Parnell), 214
Elements of Criticism (Lord Kames), 442n
Elizabeth, Princess, Shenstone's ballad on, 285, 309
Elocution, Course of Lectures on (Thomas Sheridan), 451n
Elzevir Horace, 412, 414, 422
Emblems (Quarles), 109

Emme (post-woman), see Scudamore, Emme
Environs of London (Dodsley), 407
Epictetus, 440n
Epigoniad (Wilkie), 372
Epilogue to *Cleone,* 338, 357, 362, 367
Erasmus, 181
Erse fragments, see *Fragments of Ancient Poetry*
Essay on Delicacy (Lancaster), 107, 432, 436
"Essay on Electricity" (Jago), 362
"Essay on Oeconomy," see *Oeconomy*
"Essay on Reserve," 47
Essay on Spirit (Bishop of Clogher), 379
Essay on the Present State of Learning (Goldsmith), 370
Essay on the Writings and Genius of Shakespeare (Mrs. Montagu), 455n
Essay upon Taste (Gerard), 378n, 381n
Essays on Men and Manners, xv, xxiv, 32n, 107n, 365
Etymologicum (Lye), 372
"Eugenio" (William Somervile), 70
Euripides, 436n
'Evans, Parson Hugh,' 7, 178
Evening Post, London, 33, 77
Exeter, Dean of, *see* Lyttelton, Charles

Fables, Croxall's, 374n, 406; Dodsley's, xxiii, 342, 365n, 370, 374, 377, 382, 396, 398, 399, 401, 402, 406, 408, 409, 410, 411, 414, 428, 436, 446, 455; La Motte's, 389n, 390; L'Estrange's, 374n; Ogilby's, 365; Richardson's, 406
Fables for the Female Sex (Moore), 254
Faerie Queene, 30, 42
'Falstaff,' 16, 23, 55, 56, 67, 124, 166, 176, 202
Fancourt, Dorothea, *see* Jago, the first Mrs. Richard
Fancourt, John, 94n, 96, 153, 195, 221, 222
Fane, Lady, 72
Father Francis's Prayer, 318, 321
Fawn, The (Marvell), 124
Field Sports (Somervile), 30
Fielding, Henry, 44, 138, 140, 131n. See also *Pamela; Tom Jones; Tom Thumb*
"Fight at Otterburne," see *Battle of Otterbourne*
Fingal (Macpherson), 398n, 428, 440
Fitzosborne's Letters (Melmoth), 100, 432
"Flattery, or the Fatal Exotick," 47
Fletcher, Winney, 74. LETTER TO, 75
'Fluellin,' 234
Foley, Lord, 358, 378, 450, 453, 457
Fontenoy, battle of, 76
Fortescue, Lord and Lady, 427
Foulis, Andreas, 422n, 428n
Foundling, The (Moore), 181n

Four Elegies: Descriptive and Moral (Scott), 398
Fox, Henry, 326
Fragments of Ancient Poetry (Macpherson), 398n, 421, 423
Franklin, Benjamin, 351, 353
Frederick, Prince of Wales, 221
Freeman, Ralph, 17
Freke, John, 90
Fugitive Pieces (Dodsley), 432, 436

Gainsborough, Lady, 37
Gainsborough, Lord, 197
Gamester, The (Moore), 258, 259
Gardener's and Florist's Dictionary (Miller), 146
Gardening, see Landscape architecture
Gardiner, Colonel, Life of (Doddridge), 114
Garrick, David, 33, 40, 138n, 338, 357, 403, 413, 424, 436
Gataker, Mrs., 401
Gaunt, John of, 74
Gay, John, 105
General History of England (Carte), 94
Gentle Herdsman (in *Reliques*), 369, 372, 380
"Gentle Jessy," 64
Gentle Shepherd (Ramsay), 423, 424
Gentleman's Magazine, 257, 420n, 421
George II, 34, 54, 57, 58, 227
George III, 407, 411, 418, 426, 447
Gerard, Alexander, 378n, 381
Gessner, Salomon, 455n
Gibbs, James, 164, 169
Gill Morrice (in *Reliques*), 345, 346, 347, 425
Goldfinches, The (Jago), 50n, 124, 125, 311, 312
Goldsmith, Oliver, 370, 393, 444
Gothicism, 149, 153, 154, 159, 160, 174, 178, 187, 188, 190, 195, 209, 234, 350, 357, 358, 418
Gough, Lady, 272, 419n, 427
Gough, Sir Harry, 186
Gower, Lord, 127
Graham, Lord George, 43n
Grainger, James, 318n, 321n, 346n, 359, 362, 364, 370, 393n, 397, 448, 457
Grange, The Halesowen (home of Lord Dudley), 83, 160, 245, 246, 247, 264, 268, 270, 274, 275, 277, 289, 301, 306, 341, 342
Graves, Miss, xviii, 41, 62n, 117n, 121, 246. LETTER TO, 4
Graves, Morgan, xviii, 45, 68, 266, 383, 416
Graves, Richard, xvi, xvii, xviii, xxi, xxii, 9, 12n, 28n, 37, 50, 59, 98, 101, 105, 131n, 220, 221, 251, 260, 261, 281, 285, 288, 294, 314, 319, 329, 380, 418, 429,

468

444, 449, 452, 459, 460, 461. LETTERS
TO, 18, 21, 26, 29, 31, 33, 38, 41, 44, 45,
47, 52, 55, 64, 65, 67, 72, 73, 77, 79, 80,
84, 110, 111, 116, 215, 230, 238, 245,
248, 257, 265, 276, 289, 291, 296, 302,
317, 325, 332, 338, 340, 347, 349, 352,
355, 361, 366, 373, 376, 382, 387, 389,
395, 406, 410, 416, 445, 454
Graves, Mrs. Richard (Lucy Bartholomew), 101n, 105, 216, 217, 230, 232,
249, 250, 257, 258, 259, 261, 269, 277,
291, 292, 297, 326, 329, 333, 339, 341,
348, 351, 352, 356, 358, 361, 368, 376,
379, 383, 392, 412, 417, 419, 457
Gray, Thomas, 221, 225, 231n, 423, 424, 435
Green, Amos, 334, 337, 348n, 353, 354, 368, 392
Gresset's *Le Mechant,* 108n
Grey, Lord, 323, 356, 360
Grey's edition of *Hudibras,* 179
Grimston, Lord, 197
Guernsey, Lord, 294
Guilford, Lord, 253
Guthrie, William, 407n, 444

Hagley (Lyttelton estate), xxiii, 52, 55, 83,
109, 111, 115, 117, 118, 119, 120, 121,
125, 126, 127, 129, 141, 149, 150, 169,
171, 172, 175, 177, 183, 184, 189, 190,
194, 205, 209, 225, 229, 233, 243, 248,
255, 256, 259, 263, 272, 273, 274, 277,
280, 285, 323, 336, 342, 368, 416, 454,
460, 462
Halesowen, xvi, 240n, 246, 256, 259, 263
Halifax, Lord, 227
Hall, Mr., 87, 91, 94, 121, 122, 123, 125,
127, 128, 139, 141, 145, 146, 147, 156,
159, 165, 168, 174, 176, 180, 190, 193,
197, 203, 208, 209, 223, 225, 227
Hall, Thomas, 120, 292
Hamlet, 69, 73, 180
Hammond, James, 52
Handel, 356, 416
Hands, Mr., 169, 170, 175
Hanmer, Sir Thomas, 36, 405n
Hannibal, 454
Harborne, 449
Harborough, xvi, xxiv, 5, 6, 111, 296; suit over, 296, 328, 329, 331, 349, 352, 373, 376, 395
Harbury, 250, 252, 253, 282, 287, 292, 293, 297, 314, 324, 335, 362, 461n
Hardy, Mr., 94n, 96, 108, 120, 125, 131, 194, 202, 204, 206n
"Hark to the blackbird's, etc.," see *Bulfinch in Town*
Harris (the Jew), 212, 214
Hau Kiou Choaan (Percy), 380n, 393n, 407n, 409, 412, 414n, 419, 420, 425, 426, 428

Hawkesworth, John, 381, 382, 414n
Hayman, Francis, 384, 405
Head, Sir Thomas, 71n, 246
Hecuba, tragedy of, 436n
Helen of Troy, 105
Henley, 99, 127, 140, 378
Henry II, or the Fall of Rosamond (Hull), 415, 418
Henry IV (Part 2), 74
Henry V, 234n
Henry VIII, 57
Henry and Emma (Prior), 435
Hentzner, Paul, 344n
Hercules, see *Choice of Hercules* (Lowth); *Judgment of Hercules*
"Here in cool grot," 148, 150
Heroines, The, or Modern Memoirs (Graves), 312n
Hertford, Lady, see Somerset, Duchess of
Hervey, James, 106, 114
Hervey, Thomas, 36
Hewell Grange (home of Lord Plymouth), 281, 282, 287
Hill, Aaron, 150n
Hippisley (Hippelsley), John, 29
History of England (J. Lindsay), 179
History of English poetry, projected by Gray, 424
History of Scotland (Robertson), 365, 418
Hive, The, 413, 443
Hoadley, Benjamin, 181
Hodgetts, John, 385, 415, 447
Hogarth, William, 290, 293, 403
Hollier, Mr., 334, 337, 343, 384
Holyoake, Master Franky, 99
Holyoake, William, xxii, 98, 100, 273, 282, 301, 310, 328, 331. LETTER TO, 331
Home, Henry, see Kames, Lord
Home, John, 350, 425n, 444
Homer, 105, 165, 396; "the Edinburgh" (Ramsay), 358; Pope's, 372
Horace, 44, 198, 204, 270, 276, 390, 395,
405, 410, 425; editions by: Baskerville,
404n, 412, 414, 421, 422n, 427, 440,
441, 442, 443, 447, 449, 454; Bentley,
414, 428n, 442; Cunningham, 428n,
442; the Duncombes, 336, 381, 382;
the Elzevirs, 412, 414, 422; Merveillius,
442; Pine, 138; Sanadon, 428n, 442;
Sandby, 179, 428n, 442
"Horace and Lydia" (Whistler's translation), 314
Hudibras, 30, 179, 444, 459
Hull, Thomas, xxii, 418, 434, 435. LETTERS TO, 402, 415, 430, 432, 435
Hurd, Richard, 381, 390, 394
Hylton, John Scott, xvi, xxii, 243, 260, 262,
264, 266, 270, 272, 274, 280, 282, 284,
288, 292, 293, 295, 301, 302, 306, 308,
310, 318, 322, 324, 327, 329, 337, 346,
351, 353, 364, 372, 379, 394, 412; hoax,

370–71, 372, 381, 389, 397. LETTERS TO, 277, 289, 323, 328, 336, 337, 341, 342 (2), 343, 358, 363 (2), 368, 379, 383, 384, 385

"I told my nymph," 343
Idyllen (Gessner), 455n
Il Penseroso, 318
Ilay, Lord, 45
Iliad, 105
Impartial Review; or, Literary Journal, 379, 380n
Induction (Sackville), 398
Introduction to English Grammar (Lowth), 447n
Irene (Johnson), 138
Irish peers, 418

Jago, John, 194, 213n
Jago, Richard, xvii, xxi, xxii, 13, 24, 25, 55, 56, 110, 213, 290, 297, 363, 369, 421, 444, 449, 453, 457, 461n. LETTERS TO, 7, 15, 16, 19, 22, 24, 25, 29, 35, 36, 42, 50, 53, 57, 69, 71, 83, 88, 92, 95, 119, 124, 131, 149, 152, 194, 205, 220, 250, 253, 254, 286, 292, 310, 313, 324, 335, 361, 458, 461, 462
Jago, the first Mrs. Richard (Dorothea Fancourt), 26, 58, 70, 72, 94n, 95, 97, 120, 124, 125, 149, 196, 222, 36 n
Jago, the second Mrs. Richard (Margaret Underwood), 361n, 369, 458, 462, 463
Jemmy Dawson, 341n
Jenyns, Soame, 321n, 407
'Jewkes, Mrs.' *(Pamela)*, 24
"John the Reeve," 426
Johnson, Samuel, xvi, xx, 138n, 345, 370, 378, 394, 397, 413, 414, 424, 440n
Jones, Henry, 258n
Jones, Inigo, 92, 98n, 102
Jones, Mary, 343
Joseph (Lady Luxborough's servant), 226, 227, 237, 242, 248, 275
Joseph Andrews, 44n, 138
Journey into England in the Year 1599 (Hentzner), 344n
"Journey through Italy," 384
Judgment of Hercules, The, xix, 17, 19, 44, 55, 93
Julius Caesar, 423

Kames, Lord, 442n, 443
Kidderminster, 329, 385
Kilmarnock, Lord (William Boyd, fourth Earl), 81
"King sought a partner, The" (Dodsley), 418
Kneller, Sir Godfrey, 207, 300
Knight, Edward, 342, 343, 349, 354, 355, 357, 368, 396, 411, 412, 446, 455, 456, 457

Knight, Mrs. Henrietta, *see* Luxborough, Lady

La Bruyère, 352
La Fontaine, 374
La Motte, 370, 383, 389, 390
Lancaster, Nathaniel, 107n, 432, 436, 452
Landscape architecture, xv, xxiii, 102, 117, 139ff, 149, 154, 157, 160ff, 170ff, 182ff, 186ff, 193ff, 199ff, 206, 210, 215, 281, 288, 293, 298, 299, 305, 350, 453
Lane, Mrs., 248, 263, 271, 272
Langley, Batty, 142n, 143, 145, 176
Lansdown's poems, 362
Lappal (home of Hylton), 279, 293, 323, 351, 385
"Lark, The," 89
Latin grammar (Lily), 380
Lawyers, opinion of, 359
Lea, Miss (of Halesowen Grange), 125, 243, 245, 266, 270, 306, 368
Lawyer's Fortune, The: or Love in a Hollow Tree (Grimston), 197n
Leasowes, The (Shenstone's *ferme ornée*), *passim*; map, 267; Dodsley's verses on, 386n, 420
"Leinster fam'd for maidens fair," 410
Lely, Sir Peter, 207
L'Estrange, Sir Roger *(Fables)*, 374, 406
Letter on Possible Discoveries (Maupertuis), 394
Letters, opinion of, 296, 303
Letters between Henry and Frances, 432, 433, 446
Letters Wrote by a Peruvian Lady, 134n
Levities, 125
Lichfield, Lady, 233
Lichfield, Lord (George Henry Lee, third Earl of Lichfield), 357
Ligonier, John (field marshal), 76
Lillo, George, 56n
Lily, William, 380
Lindsey, Mr. (chaplain to the Duchess of Somerset), 190n, 192
Linnets, The (Jago), 121
Litchfield, Lord and Lady, *see* Lichfield
Litchfield, 74, 76, 127, 135, 160, 161
Little Cur, The (Graves), 12
Lives of the Painters (Walpole), 441
Livie, John, 404n, 405, 412n, 422, 428n, 441, 442, 447, 449n. LETTERS TO, 441, 447, 448
Lloyd, Sarah (the "school-mistress"), xvii, 37
Lloyd, Robert, 398n
London and Its Environs (Dodsley), 407n
London Chronicle, 421, 428n
London Cuckolds, 403n
London Magazine, 405, 421, 426
Loretto, Our Lady of, 128, 184
Loughborough, Lord, 461n, 463n

470

Lovat, Lord (Simon Fraser, twelfth Baron), 199
Love in a Hollow Tree (Grimston), 197
Lowe, Miss, letter to, 6
Lowe, Thomas, 14
Lowth, Bishop Robert, 93, 411, 447
Lucretius, 48
Luxborough, Lady (Mrs. Henrietta Knight), xvii, xviii, xix, xxi, xxii, xxiii, 9, 39, 50, 70, 81, 84, 94, 120, 123, 125, 131, 152, 221, 249, 256, 265, 266, 282, 283, 285, 298, 299, 307, 314, 316, 318n, 325, 331n, 385n. LETTERS TO, 39, 49, 82, 86, 87, 90, 98, 100, 102, 106, 108, 113, 115, 118, 121, 122, 126, 128, 132, 135, 138, 139, 142, 143, 145, 147, 154, 155, 157, 158, 159, 161 (2), 162, 165, 167, 169, 171, 176, 180, 183, 185, 187, 189, 191, 196, 198, 200, 203, 208, 210, 218, 222, 224, 226, 229, 232, 234, 236, 241, 242, 247, 259, 261, 263, 269, 271, 273, 275, 279, 284, 298, 300, 301, 305, 307, 309, 315, 321, 327, 328
Lycidas, 97
Lye, Edward, 372
Lyttelton, Miss, 228, 233, 275, 297
Lyttelton, Charles, 20, 55, 83, 209, 232, 252, 272, 277, 278, 279, 280, 334
Lyttelton, Lady Christian (wife of Sir Thomas), 102n, 115
Lyttelton, Sir Edward, 381, 391
Lyttelton, George, 9, 12, 13, 20, 29, 31, 52, 55, 66, 83, 85, 109, 114, 119, 125, 126, 127, 142, 149, 162, 188, 213, 217, 231, 232, 233, 243, 248, 255, 260, 263, 273, 274, 277, 278, 279, 280, 287, 297, 298, 314, 329, 334, 348, 377, 378, 396, 398, 407, 411, 454, 455
Lyttelton, the first Mrs. George (Lucy Fortescue), 55
Lyttelton, the second Mrs. George (Elizabeth Rich), 158n, 162, 233, 275, 293
Lyttelton, Sir Richard, 54, 213, 229, 255, 263, 266, 272, 274, 277, 283
Lyttelton, Sir Thomas, 17, 157, 162, 163, 232, 233, 334
Lyttelton, William, 127n, 153, 239n, 272, 277n, 278, 279, 280, 283, 285, 297, 310, 329, 334n, 414. LETTER TO, 334
Lyttelton, Mrs. William (Mary Macartney), 414
Lyttelton family, xxiii, 83, 129, 153, 154, 233

MacGowan, John, 413n, 427, 439, 441. LETTER TO, 422
Mackenzie, Dr. James, 13, 40
Macpherson, James (Ossian), 398n, 421, 423n, 428, 440
Maecenas, 405, 461
Magdalene College Library, 424

Mahomet (Voltaire), 71
Maintenon, Madame de, 255, 259
Maittaire, 266
Mallet, David, 21, 82, 237n, 366, 400, 443
Malvern Spa (Perry's verses to Dr. Wall), 340n
Maratt, Carlo, 96
Marlborough, John Churchill, first Duke of, 43, 192n
Martial, 422
"Martin's Magazine," 340
Marvell, Andrew, 124
Mason, William, 370n, 372n, 423
Maupertuis, 394
Medals, Graves's verses on, see *Cabinet, The;* Shenstone's interest in, 351
Meditations and Contemplations (J. Hervey), 106, 114
Melancholy, statements concerning, xv, xxi, 23, 25, 28, 52, 106, 113, 129, 166, 168, 173, 217, 232, 236, 238, 239, 291, 296, 299, 318, 340, 406
Melmoth, William, 100, 257, 357, 401, 411, 432n, 446, 452, 455, 460
Melpomene (Dodsley), 316n, 338n, 340, 367
Memmius, 64
Memory, Ode to, 285, 304
Meredith, Sir William, 262, 306, 310, 325
Meredyth, Mr., 36, 155, 186, 190, 192, 197, 198
Meredyth, Miss Patty and Mrs., 164, 167, 168, 170, 172, 173, 174, 180
Merope (Hill's adaptation of Voltaire), 150
Merrick, James, 393
Merry Wives of Windsor, 7, 15
Merveillius's Horace, 442
Messiah, The (Handel), 356, 416
Methodists, 53, 56, 145
'Mezentius,' 100
Mickleton (home of Morgan Graves), xviii, 3, 4, 5, 45, 57, 110, 357, 361, 383
Miller, James, 71
Miller, Philip, 146
Miller, Sanderson (of Radway), 83, 119, 149, 152, 160, 161, 162, 182, 186, 187, 189, 195, 213, 243, 252, 253, 255, 280, 287, 293, 294, 324, 336
Miller of Mansfield, The (Dodsley), 316n
Milton, 16, 25, 26, 45, 56, 97, 231, 239, 255, 318, 360, 366
Milward, Mr., 337
Miscellanies (Dodsley's), see *Collection of Poems*
Miscellanies in Verse and Prose (Mary Jones), 343n
Miscellany (Ramsay), 358n, 360
Monody (Mason), 423
Monody to the Memory of a Lady (G. Lyttelton), 231n

471

Monson, Dr., 455
Montagu, Mrs. Elizabeth Robinson, 455
Montesquieu, 378n
Montezuma, 342
Monthly Review, 352, 396
Moore, Edward, 181n, 254n, 258n, 259
"Mopsy" (Graves), 339, 341
Moral and Political Dialogues (Hurd), 381n, 391, 394
Moral Essays (Pope), 148n
"Moral Index" to Dodsley's *Fables* (Shenstone), 365n
More, Sir Thomas, 81, 181
Morrison, Miss, 415, 434, 435, 436
Mostyn, Sir J., 401
Much Ado about Nothing, 20
Mynde, James, 37

Neale, Mr. (actor), 15
Newcastle, Duke of, 181, 326, 348 411
Night Thoughts (Young), see *Complaint, The*
Northampton, Earl and Countess of, 455, 456
Not-browne Mayd, The (in *Reliques*), 398

Observations on the Faerie Queene (T. Warton, Jr.), 413n
Ode, 1739, 343, 344
Ode on Solitude (Grainger), 318
Ode on the King's Marriage (Samuel Pullein, 426
Ode to Fancy (Marriott), 318
Ode to Health (John Duncombe), 336, 343
"Ode to Lady Luxborough," 350
Ode to Lucio, 308
Ode to Memory, 285, 304
Ode to the Nymph of Bristol Spring (Whitehead), 221, 225
Ode to Wisdom (Elizabeth Carter), 435
Odes (Gray), 423
Odes on Several Subjects (Akenside), 373, 381
Odes to Obscurity and Oblivion (Robert Lloyd and G. Colman the elder), 398
Oeconomists, The, 101
Oeconomy, 47–48
Oeconomy of Life (Dodsley), 31€n
Oeconomy of Love (John Armstrong), 21
Ogilby, John 37, 365, 396
Ogilvie, John, 451
Oldbarrow, 273, 274, 275, 300
Omphale, figure of, 455
On the Death of a Favourite Cat (Gray), 231n
'Ophelia' (*Hamlet*), 69, 73, 180
Ophelia's Urn, 6n
Orford, Lord, *see* Walpole, Robert
Oriental Eclogues, see *Persian Eclogues*
Original Poems on Several Occasions (Mary Whateley or Wheatly), 49n, 420

Orleans, Duke of, 390
"Orpheus and Eurydice" (Somers), 15
Orrery, Lord (John Boyle, fifth Earl), 237n
Ossian, *see* Macpherson
Othello, 101, 244
Outing, Captain, 29, 34, 35, 40, 51, 71, 88, 102, 103, 104, 114, 115, 119, 121, 122, 125, 127, 128, 134, 142, 149, 162, 163, 174, 184, 185, 190, 192, 211, 233, 244, 248, 249, 260, 262, 264, 279, 282, 307, 308, 309, 322, 331
Ovid, 48, 89, 314, 369, 370, 381, 399
Oxford, xvii, 22, 30, 38, 46, 180, 295, 320, 348

Packington, Sir John, 275
Pain and pleasure, ideas concerning, xx, xxi, 31, 91, 101, 113, 118, 119, 129, 168, 185, 196, 235, 239, 241, 279, 299, 340
Pamela, 24, 68, 202
Panacea, or the Grand Restorative (Graves), 314n
Paradise Lost, 26, 45n, 56, 239n, 255
"Parallel betwixt Malliabecqui and his Taylor" (Spence), 363
Parliament, 319, 321, 325, 411
Parnell, Thomas, 93, 214
'Parolles' *(All's Well That Ends Well),* 33
Parrat, Mr., 318n, 321n
Parties of pleasure, 433, 434
Parting, The (Graves), 314n
Pastoral Ballad, xv, xix, 59n, 62n, 229n, 309n, 327n, 449
Pastoral Ode (to Sir Richard Lyttelton), 255, 263, 272, 277n, 283
Patchen, Mr., 357
Patriotism, On the Spirit of (Bolingbroke), 150
Pearsall, Mr., 190, 225, 279, 287
"Pedley, Old," 174, 178, 179, 182, 183
Pen Lez, or Penter, Bosavern, 181
Penn family, xvi, 296
"Pepper-box, The" (Graves), 341, 352
Pepys collection of ballads, 424
Percy, Thomas, xxii, xxiii, 319n, 359, 379, 384, 385, 407, 418, 424, 435, 441, 452. See also *Hau Kiou Choaan; Reliques.*
LETTERS TO, 345, 359, 368, 371, 380, 386, 389, 393, 397, 399, 401, 408, 409 (2), 412 (2), 419, 425, 437, 439, 440, 441, 442, 448, 449, 463
Percy Lodge, 106, 134, 282n
Peregrine Pickle, 231
Persian Eclogues (Collins), 394n
"Peruvian Letters," 134n
Phaedrus, 374
Philips, Ambrose, 38, 400
Philips, John, 30, 46, 48, 362, 451

Philosophical Inquiry into the Origin of Our Ideas of the Sublime and Beautiful (Edmund Burke), 376, 378n, 442n
Pilkington, Mrs. Laetitia, memoirs of, 114, 221
Pine's Horace, 138
Pitt, Humphrey (of Shifnal), 27, 83, 85, 119, 121, 149, 160, 162, 280, 310, 360, 369
Pitt, William, 18, 411
Pixell, John, 150, 207, 226, 228, 247, 252, 261, 264, 294, 341, 363, 372, 394, 427
Pleasure and pain, *see* Pain and pleasure
Pleasures of Imagination, The (Akenside), 71
Pleasures of Melancholy (T. Warton, Jr.), 318
Pliny, 20, 251
Plutarch's *Lives*, 444
Plymouth, Lady, 272, 275, 281
Plymouth, Lord, 275, 280, 281, 282, 288, 378. *See also* Hewell Grange
Poems Attempted in the Style of Milton (J. Philips), 451n
Poems on Several Occasions (Elizabeth Carter), 440n
Poems on Several Occasions (Mallet), 443n
Poems on Several (Sundry) Occasions (Woodhouse), 460n
Poems on Several Subjects (Ogilvie), 451n
Poems upon Various Occasions (Shenstone), xix
Polite Literature in Europe, Review of (Goldsmith), 393n
Politics, xxiii, 77, 78, 79, 273, 274, 275, 325, 326, 327, 411, 412, 457, 463; essay on, 81n
Polymetis (Spence), 93
Pomfret's poems, 362
Pompey the Little, The History of (F. Coventry), 225
Pond, Arthur, 327
Pope, Alexander, 4, 12, 21, 36, 42, 44, 71, 72, 107, 133, 148, 152, 153, 211, 237, 372, 376, 417, 418, 429, 444
Portrait of Shenstone (Alcock), described, 388
Post-woman, *see* Scudamore, Emme
Poussin, 375
Praise of Folly (Erasmus), 181
Prayer-books (Baskerville's), 407
Pretender, The ("James III"), 81, 94
Primrose, Lord, 298
Pringle, Andrew (later Lord Alemoor), 358n, 425
Prior, Matthew, 258, 435
Progress of Taste, The, 219
Prolusions (Edward Capell), 398
Proposals for publication of his own poems by subscription, 417, 429, 437n, 438, 456

Public Virtue, see Agriculture
Pullein, Samuel, 426

Quarles's *Emblems*, 109
Quin, James, 16, 176

Radway (home of Sanderson Miller), 188, 189, 287, 293, 294, 324
Rambler, The (Johnson), 391, 394, 440n
Ramsay, Allan, 358n, 360, 424
Raphael, 249
Rasselas, 377, 414
"Raven and the Magpie, The," 377
"Receipt to Make Fame," 132
Reflexions critiques sur la poesie et la peinture (Abbé Dubos), 377n
Reflexions sur la critique (La Motte), 389n
Rehearsal, The (Buckingham), 38
Reliques (Percy), xxiii, 345n, 399n, 400, 401, 402, 407, 409, 410, 412, 413, 420, 424, 425, 426, 435, 439, 441, 442, 450. *See also* individual ballads
Remarks on the Life and Writings of Dr. Swift (Orrery), 237n
Reserve, essay on, 47
Reward, The, or Apollo's Acknowledgement to Charles Stanhope (Mallet), 443n
Reynolds (Reynalds), "Jackie," xxii, 121, 134, 135, 203, 256, 261, 274, 275, 279. Letters to, 8, 13, 14, 34
Reynolds, Sir Joshua, 396, 398
Richardson, Samuel, 24, 68, 195, 199, 202, 285, 288, 290, 350, 406, 408, 440n, 444
Richmond, Duke and Duchess of, 455
Rival Brothers, The (Young), 258, 260
Robertson, William, 365, 377, 418, 425
Rochester, Lord, 247, 440
Rock, Mrs. Sally, 270, 272, 302, 337
Roebuck, Dr. John, 422, 427, 428, 439, 441
Romeo and Juliet, 183n
Rosa, Salvator, 96
Rosamond, ballad, 413; Hull's play, 415, 418
Rousseau, 429
Runick Fragments (Percy), 428
Rural Elegance (to the Duchess of Somerset), 48n, 91, 199, 219n, 255n, 257n, 263n, 264, 265, 272, 276n, 280n, 282n, 283, 286, 288, 319n, 321, 325
Rural elegance, Shenstone's blank verse on, 48
"Rural Poems" (Gessner), 455

Sackville, Thomas, *Induction*, 398
Sandby's Horace, 179, 428, 442
Sanderson, Lady, 427
Sandys, Lord, 300
Saunders, Tom, 364. Letter to, 333
Scholar's Relapse, The, 55n

473

School-Mistress, The, xv, xix, 30, 37, 38, 39, 44, 75, 80, 93, 97, 98, 99, 107, 110, 370
Scotland, 298, 350, 352, 356, 360, 424, 434
Scott, John, 398
Scribleriad, The (Cambridge), 218, 221, 373, 387
Scudamore, Emme (post-woman), 98, 99, 127, 165, 167, 171, 185, 191, 295, 337
Seasons, The (Thomson), 81
"Select Beauties," *see* Smith, Thomas
Sévigné, Madame de, letters of, 273, 376
Shaftesbury, Anthony Ashley Cooper, third Earl of, xxi, 109
Shakespeare, 7, 15, 16, 20, 23, 33, 69, 73, 74, 76, 101, 103, 124, 166, 176, 177, 183, 211, 212, 234, 346, 371, 393, 405n, 443. *See also* individual plays and characters
'Shallow,' 74
Shenstone, Joseph, xvii, xix, 68, 69, 108, 114, 115, 119, 123, 135, 140, 156, 157, 220, 223, 224, 225, 226, 228, 235n, 238, 240n, 241, 251, 290n
Shenstone, Mrs. Mary, 58n
Shenstone, Thomas, 58n
Shenstone family, xviff
Sheridan, Thomas, 451n
Shilling, The Splendid (J. Philips), 30
Shuckburgh, Mr. (bookseller), 35, 44
Shuttlecock, The (Whistler), 99n, 130
Sickness, a Poem (Thompson), 107, 114
Sidney, Sir Philip, 145
Sir Charles Grandison, 285, 288, 290
Smith, Admiral, 204, 242, 273, 275, 280, 298, 310, 329, 333n, 350, 364, 379
Smith, Adam, 381, 391, 394
Smith, Harry, 343
Smith, Thomas, of Derby (landscape painter), 109, 110, 116, 118, 130, 131, 134, 137, 194, 196, 197, 225, 234, 382
Smith, Thomas, of Halesowen, 68n LETTERS TO, 68, 69, 449
Smith, Utrecia, xviii, 6, 8n, 57n
Smollett, Tobias, 231, 346n, 363, 364n, 370, 380, 384, 393, 405n
Snitterfield, 294, 297n
"Snuff-box, The," 219
Soame(s), Sir Peter, 193, 211, 271, 298
Socrates, Life of (Cooper), 176, 195
Somers, Henry, 15n
Somerset, Duchess of (Frances Thynne, Countess of Hertford), 91, 94, 106, 114, 129, 133n, 135, 137, 166, 190n, 191, 192, 219n, 255n, 257, 263, 264, 265, 272, 276, 280, 282, 286, 288, 298. LETTERS TO, 264, 282
Somerset, Duke of, 153, 179, 191
Somervile, Captain, 260, 275, 279
Somervile, Lord, 35n, 298

Somervile, William, xvii, 9, 12, 13, 14, 18, 29n, 30, 34, 42, 43, 70n, 169, 173, 174, 175, 176, 177, 184, 191, 193, 196, 198, 201, 204, 226, 228, 273, 286, 318
Song, Written in Winter (Lady Luxborough), 307n, 308n
Spanish Lady's Love, The (in *Reliques*), 402n, 413
Spectator, The, 449
Spence, Joseph, 93, 104, 350, 352, 356, 360, 362, 363, 366, 373, 375, 376, 398, 411, 417, 429
Spencer, John, 43
Spenser, Edmund, 30, 32, 42, 75, 80, 107, 110, 126, 413
Spiritual Quixote, The (Graves), 357n, 361n, 367n, 378n, 391n
Stamford, Earl of, 190, 192, 195, 209, 229, 329, 352, 358, 407, 462, 463
Stamford, Lady, 192
Stanhope, Charles, *see Reward, The*
"Stella and Flavia," 64
Sterne, Lawrence, 396
Stoics, 103
Stonehenge, 46
Stonehouse, Dr. James, 381n
Stourbridge, 192, 280, 434, 440
Stowe, 57, 88, 233, 272
Strawberry Hill, 344n
Sublime and Beautiful, On the (Burke), 376, 378n, 442n
Subscription, Shenstone's project for publication by, *see* Proposals, etc.
Sugar Cane, The (Grainger), 448n, 457
"Sun-flower and the Tuberose, The," 377
Sussex, Countess of, 414n
Sussex, Lord, 372, 424
Swift, Jonathan, 28, 30, 44, 204, 237n, 414n, 451, 459
"Sylvia, wilt thou waste thy prime?" 64

Taste, opinions concerning, 215, 233, 393, 401–02, 423, 459; essay on, 398n
Taylor, John, 342, 364
Temora (Macpherson), 398n
Temple, Lord, 272, 274
Theocritus, 231
Theory of Moral Sentiments (Adam Smith), 381, 391, 394
Thomas, Mrs., *see* "Cotswouldia"
Thompson, William, 107n
Thomson, James, 81, 83, 85, 92, 94, 107, 112, 121, 125, 126, 128, 129, 130, 131, 138n, 283, 444
Thucydides, 48
Thynne, Frances, *see* Somerset, Duchess of
Tibullus, 52; controversy over Grainger's translation of, 346, 362, 364n, 370, 393n
Tissington, 45, 65, 67

474

To a Lady of Quality, Fitting up Her Library, 1738, xxin, 308, 340
Tom (Shenstone's servant), 86, 95, 120, 155, 159, 162, 204, 207, 220, 226, 228, 269, 274, 284, 286, 308, 328
Tom Jones (Fielding), 138, 139n, 140
Tom Thumb (Fielding), 38
Tonson, Jacob, 399, 400n
"Topographical Letters" (Patchen), 357
Tories, 78, 79, 127, 326
Toy-shop, The (Dodsley), 316n
Trajan, 113
Trentham, Lord, 180
Tristram Shandy (Sterne), 396
True State of the Case of Bosavern Pen Lez (Fielding), 181n
Tryphiodorus (Merrick), 393
" 'Twas not by beauty's aid alone," see *Ode, 1739*
Tylney, Earl, 256n
Tynte, Sir Charles, 396
Tyrconnel, Lord, 109, 194, 197, 382

Vane, Lady, 221
Venus de Medicis, verses on, 395, 418, 421, 425, 459
Verses Written towards the Close of the Year 1748, To William Lyttelton, 127n, 239n, 277n
Vespasian, coin of, 113
Vida, 151
"Villa, The" (Graves), 65
Virgil, 41, 48, 112, 318, 375, 396; Baskerville's, 321n, 339, 449; Ogilby's, 396
Virgil's Grove, the Leasowes, 83, 109, 111, 112, 121, 123, 148, 150, 174, 179, 190
"Vista, The," 266
Vocal Miscellany, The, 413
Voltaire, 71, 150, 255, 260, 378n

Wales, 57, 59, 63, 420, 424, 434
Walker, Charles, 221, 260
Walker, Thomas, 291
Wall, Dr. John, 109, 223, 337, 340n, 341
Wallingford, Lord, 209
Walpole, Horace, xx, 306, 344, 441, 442, 455
Walpole, Robert (Lord Orford), 18, 33, 34, 36, 43, 137, 446
Walsh, Mr., M. P. for Worcester, 455
Warburton, William, 74, 237, 390, 418, 444
Ward, Lord, 141, 192, 210, 211, 273, 294, 356, 378, 463
Warton, Joseph, 350, 424
Warton, Thomas, Jr., 318, 321n, 350, 358, 413, 418, 441
Watkyn, Sir, 181
Watson, Sir William, 90
Watteau, 168, 174
Webb, Daniel, 396, 398, 443, 460

West, Commodore, 153, 154, 233; Captain, 228
West, Miss, 153, 154, 228, 233, 275
'Western, Squire' (*Tom Jones*), 140
Westminster School, 260
Westmorland, Lord, 321
Weymondesold (Wymondesold), Mr. and Mrs., 152n, 154, 166, 210, 227, 243, 256n
Whateley (Wheatly), Mary, 419, 420
Whigs, 78, 79, 273
Whistler, Anthony, xvii, xix, xxii, 5, 29, 30, 32, 36, 46, 47, 51, 64, 66, 72, 73, 77, 79, 80, 98, 99n, 101, 111, 112, 115, 118, 130n, 131, 166, 168, 215, 231, 246, 249, 257, 258, 261, 268, 276, 281, 288, 290, 291, 294, 296, 297, 303, 314, 318, 449. LETTER TO, 59
Whistler, John, xxii, 291n, 292, 296, 297, 303
Whitchurch, 30, 77, 98, 111, 168, 215, 216, 231, 249
Whitefield, George, xvii, 383
"Whitefield's Journal," 383
Whitehead, William, 82, 221, 225, 339, 373
Whood, Captain, 242, 273, 275, 280
Wilkie, William, 372n
"William and Margaret" (*Fair Margaret and Sweet William,* in *Reliques*), 410
Williams, Mr. (postmaster, Birmingham), 86, 154, 161, 165, 167, 168, 170, 171, 220, 226, 271
Williams, Rice, 420, 450
Willoughby, Lord, 358, 461
Wilmot, Pynson, 37, 163, 168, 182n, 211n, 212, 368
Wintle, Mr. (perfumer, London), 179
Wissing, Willem (painter), 204
Woffington, Peg, 40
"Wolf and the Crane, The," 377
Wolfe, General James, 404n
"Woman in Miniature," 36
Woodhouse, James, xxiii, 460n, 461
Worcester, xviii, 13, 74, 273, 294, 356, 376, 416, 418, 430
Worfield, xxii, 304, 342, 411
Wren, Master, 240, 245, 295
Wren, Christopher, xvii, xxii, 93, 94n, 149, 194, 324, 362, 452. LETTERS TO, 212, 213, 240, 244, 295
Written at Ferme Ornée, near Birmingham, August 7, 1749 (Lady Luxborough), 308n
Written to a Near Neighbour in a Tempestuous Night, 1748 (Lady Luxborough), 308n
Wroxall, 194, 195, 207, 324

Young, Edward, 44, 66, 106, 107, 258, 260, 370, 393

475

OHIO UNIVERSITY LIBRARY